Germany's rise to industrial might has traditionally been attributed to the development of "organized" capitalism, which is said to encompass large, bureaucratic corporations, a unique system of universal banking, centralized peak associations, and an accommodating state. Gary Herrigel argues that this conceptualization of the sources of German industrial power is highly misleading because it ignores the achievement of a very robust alternative form of capitalism within the boundaries of the German political economy and overestimates the coherence of the national system of industrial governance. Herrigel shows that alongside the organized capitalism system, the development of the German political economy, from the 18th century to the present, was also driven by highly specialized and flexible small- and medium-sized firms, deeply embedded in a larger system of relations with labor, communal organizations, educational institutions, and local and regional governments. These two distinct forms of capitalism were able to coexist within the same national political economy, Herrigel shows, through the construction of a composite of distinct governance mechanisms at the national level. The upshot of Herrigel's argument is not only that there were several processes of industrialization that occurred simultaneously in German history, but that there has never been a single boundary between industry and the rest of society and politics in Germany; there have always been several. Theoretically, the book rejects the fundamentally unitary conceptions of industrialization and political economy underlying the Gerschenkronian, Schumpetarian, and Chandlerian principles that shape the traditional organized capitalism research program in the study of the German industrial economy and argues for a more open social constructivist approach.

Structural analysis in the social sciences 9

Industrial constructions:
The sources of German industrial power

Structual analysis in the social sciences
Mark Granovetter, editor

Other books in the series:

Ronald L. Breiger, editor, *Social mobility and social structure*
John L. Campbell, J. Rogers Hollingsworth, and Leon N. Lindberg, editors, *Governance of American economy*
David Knoke, *Political networks: The structural perspective*
Kyriakos Kontopoulos, *The logics of social structure*
Mark S. Mizruchi and Michael Schwartz, editors, *Intercorporate relations: The structural analysis of business*
Philippa Pattison, *Algebraic models for social networks*
Barry Wellman and S. D. Berkowitz, editors, *Social structures: A network approach*
Stanley Wasserman and Katherine Faust, *Social network analysis: Methods and applications*

The series *Structural Analysis in the Social Sciences* presents approaches that explain social behavior and institutions by reference to *relations* among such concrete entities as persons and organizations. This contrasts with at least four other popular strategies: (a) reductionist attempts to explain by a focus on individuals alone; (b) explanations stressing the causal primacy of such abstract concepts as ideas, values, mental harmonies, and cognitive maps (thus, European "structuralism" should be distinguished from structural analysis in the present sense); (c) technological and material determinism; (d) explanations using "variables" as the main analytic concepts (as in the "structural equation" models that dominated much of the sociology of the 1970s), where structure connects variables rather than actual social entities.

The social network approach is an important example of the strategy of structural analysis; the series also draws on social science theory and research that is not framed explicitly in network terms, but stresses the importance of relations rather than the atomization of reductionism or the determinism of ideas, technology, or material conditions. Though the structural perspective has become extremely popular and influential in all the social sciences, it does not have a coherent identity, and not series yet pulls together such work under a single rubric. By bringing the achievements of structurally oriented scholars to a wider public, the *Structural Analysis* series hopes to encourage the use of this very fruitful approach.

Mark Granovetter

Industrial constructions: The sources of German industrial power

Gary Herrigel
University of Chicago

CAMBRIDGE
UNIVERSITY PRESS

University Printing House, Cambridge CB2 8BS, United Kingdom

One Liberty Plaza, 20th Floor, New York, NY 10006, USA

477 Williamstown Road, Port Melbourne, VIC 3207, Australia

314-321, 3rd Floor, Plot 3, Splendor Forum, Jasola District Centre, New Delhi-110025, India

79 Anson Road, #06-04/06, Singapore 079906

Cambridge University Press is part of the University of Cambridge.

It furthers the University's mission by disseminating knowledge in the pursuit of education, learning and research at the highest international levels of excellence.

www.cambridge.org
Information on this title: www.cambridge.org/9780521462730

© Cambridge University Press 1996

This publication is in copyright. Subject to statutory exception
and to the provisions of relevant collective licensing agreements,
no reproduction of any part may take place without the written
permission of Cambridge University Press.

First published 1996
First paperback edition 2000
Reprinted (with corrections) 2000

A catalogue record for this publication is available from the British Library

Library of Congress Cataloging in Publication data
Herrigel, Gary.
    p. cm.
  Industrial constructions : the sources of German industrial power
/ Gary Herrigel.
  Includes bibliographical references and index.
  1. Industrialization—Germany—History. 2. Small business—
Germany—History. 3. Capitalism—Germany—History. 4. Germany—
Economic policy. 5. Autarchy. I. Title.
HD2329.H47 1996
338.943—dc20
                                                95-17437
                                                 CIP

ISBN 978-0-521-46273-0 Hardback
ISBN 978-0-521-77859-6 Paperback

Cambridge University Press has no responsibility for the persistence or accuracy of URLs for external or third-party internet websites referred to in this publication, and does not guarantee that any content on such websites is, or will remain, accurate or appropriate. Information regarding prices, travel timetables, and other factual information given in this work is correct at the time of first printing but Cambridge University Press does not guarantee the accuracy of such information thereafter.

This book is dedicated to my father
Bruce D. Herrigel
and to the loving memory of my mother
Joy McGill

Contents

CHAPTER ONE
Introduction: Problems with the German model ... 1

    The traditinal conception of German Political economy and its problems ... 3

    Reconceptualizing the sources of German industrial power ... 19

    Organizatin of the argument ... 31

CHAPTER TWO
Blending in: Decentralized industrializations in Germany ... 33

    The origins of decentralized industrial order ... 34

    Decentralized adaptation: industrilization 1800–1918 ... 41

    Recomposition and stabilization, 1900–1945 ... 58

    Conlusion: Alternative industrialization ... 71

CHAPTER THREE
Repositioning organized capitalism into regions: Autarkic industrial order in Germany ... 72

    Regional preconditions for autarkic industrial order ... 73

    Case studies of autarkic industrialization: Volume and batch producers ... 75

    Conclusion: Sutarkic industrialization ... 110

CHAPTER FOUR
The national context: 1871–1945 ... 111

    Constructing natinal institutional frameworks to accommodate different regional capitalisms ... 112

The Imperial Reich	115
The Weimar Republic	123
Nazi accommodation	139
Conclusion: Composite architecture of national governance mechanisms	142

CHAPTER FIVE
Return to regions: The development of the decentralized industrial order since 1945 — 143

Abandoning the decentralized industrial order	146
Continuity in decentralization: Capital goods producers and the reconstitution of decentralized industrial order	163
The rise and decline of the decentralized form of industrial order since the 1980s	177

CHAPTER SIX
Autarkic industrial order: 1945–1994 — 205

The reconstitution of autarkic industrial order in western Germany	206
Crisis and transformation: Autarky since the mid 1970s	235
Conclusion: Crisis in the autarkic industrial order	253

CHAPTER SEVEN
The national context: 1945–1994 — 255

The accommodation of autarkic and decentralized industrial order during the economic miracle	257
The period of centralization, 1956–1980	262
A new period of decentralization	275
Conclusion: Constructing governance	286

NOTES	289
BIBLIOGRAPHY	405
LIST OF INTERVIEWEES	459
APPENDIX: MAPS	467
INDEX	473

Preface

This book has taken a long time to write. Along the way, I received enormous amounts of help, advice, suggestions, criticisms, encouragement, and support from people and institutions who are so numerous I am sure that my effort to name them here will be incomplete. I offer my apologies to those that I overlook.

First, I would like to thank those people who commented on all or part of the manuscript in some form or in some way: Gerry Berk, Rudolf Boch, Neil Brenner, Edward Castleton III, Geoff Eley, Tom Ertman, Jim Fearon, Michael Geyer, Gernot Grabher, Hal Hansen, Vicky Hattam, Franz Henne, Carol Horton, Peter Katzenstein, Horst Kern, Bruce Kogut, Dieter Läpple, David Laitin, Tony Levitas, Richard Locke, John McCormick, Alan Milward, Hans Medick, John Padgett, Bob Pepperman Taylor, Mike Reay, Woody Powell, David Sabean, Charles Sabel, Anno Saxenian, Jeff Seitzer, George Steinmetz, Daniel Verdier, Uli Voskamp, Volker Wittke, Nick Ziegler, Jonathan Zeitlin, and a number of anonymous reviewers at the Cambridge, Princeton, and Cornell University Presses. I would like to give extra thanks to Mark Granovetter for thinking enough of this book to include it in the *Structural analysis in the social sciences* series and for providing me with extremely helpful suggestions for revision.

I would also like to thank the participants and organizers of the Organizations and State-Building Workshop and the Historical Sociology and Comparative Politics Workshop at the University of Chicago, the Workshop for the Study of Business in Europe at the Center for European Studies, Harvard University, and The Conference on Labor in Industrial Society at the University of Notre Dame for the opportunity to present versions of chapters to them.

Edward Castleton III, Cora Goldstein, Maureen Healy, Matthew Hill, Michelle Mayer, Mike Reay, Jeff Seitzer, and Brad Thayer provided invaluable research assistance over the course of the project. Michael Schumann and the SOFI Institute in Göttingen and Hans-Joachim Braczyk and the Akademie für Technologiefolgenabschätzung in Stuttgart provided office space and stimulating intellectual support during various stays in Germany. John Mearsheimer of the Political Science Department at the University of Chicago and Abbey Collins at the Center for European Studies at Harvard also provided invaluable advice and intellectual and administrative support to me at crucial junctures in the composition of this work, for which I am extremely thankful. I would also like to thank Elizabeth Neal of Cambridge University Press and Paul Schwartz of Ampersand Graphics for helping this book along to publication with patience, skill, and a spirit of cooperation.

I received valuable financial support from the following institutions and grant-giving bodies during the research and writing of this book: The German Marshall Fund of the United States, The Social Science Research Council, The Fulbright–Hays Committee, The Center For European Studies and the Center for International Affairs at Harvard University, The International Motor Vehicle Project at MIT, and The Division of Social Sciences at the University of Chicago.

Every author, I suppose, has an inner circle of friends and friendly critics who are always willing to talk one more time about problems and chapters that even those friends have already nearly memorized. In my particular case, this inner circle performed yeoman-like service well above and beyond the boundaries of the reasonable. These people are: Chuck Sabel, Jonathan Zeitlin, Tony Levitas, Richard Locke, Anno Saxenian, and Nick Ziegler. At the very last minute, Bob Taylor read the entire manuscript with lightening speed and provided the author with helpful advice and much needed reassurance. No words can really express my thanks for the unfailing support of these friends throughout this entire process. Carol Horton, my wife, gets her own sentence in this particular line of thanks. She not only agreed to read things at particularly difficult junctures and provide advice, but she also learned over time to distinguish between what was truly a problem and what was merely neurosis. I'm not so sure how happy she is to have been able to learn this latter skill, but it was very helpful to me that she did. In a very different vein, I would like to extend my gratitude to our dog, Cleo Horton, who, though she had no idea of what my project was about or of the substance involved in the stresses in my life, provided me with constant and unqualified love and support as I struggled along.

Finally, I would like to dedicate this book to my parents, who encouraged me in my endeavors even when the substance and direction of the latter seemed to them to be utterly obscure and foreign to their own experiences. I deeply appreciate them for that.

1

Introduction: Problems with the German model

Most historical and contemporary accounts of the political economy of industry in Germany written since the end World War II depict a highly centralized, large-firm-dominated, ultimately neocorporatist industrial system whose characteristic institutional features all can be traced back to Germany's "late" industrialization. Interest in this national industrial system, which has been variously described as "organized capitalism," "coordinated managerial capitalism," or a "coordinated market economy"[1] has been widespread both because of its consistent historical success in world markets, and because this success often has been taken to demonstrate how countries can achieve economic development by actively shaping market forces rather than being shaped by them. The argument of this book agrees with much of the latter lesson drawn from the German case, but claims, nonetheless, that the received post World War II model of the German industrial economy and its history is highly misleading, partial, and rooted in a problematic understanding of industrialization.

The alternative picture of the German political economy presented in this book is one in which the traditional model of the German industrial system is repositioned into a larger, regionally differentiated, national framework. My argument is that two distinct, parallel, and internationally competitive systems of industrial organization and practice, located in different regions, have characterized the German experience at all levels of the economy and society since the very onset of industrialization. These different systems continue to shape adjustment in Germany today.

One of the regional systems, which I will call the *decentralized industrial order*, will be, as a system, unfamiliar even to many readers knowledgeable of the German case. This alternative form of industrialization is composed of multitudes of highly specialized small- and medium-sized producers and a host of extra firm-supporting institutions. Together, these actors have created (and in part were created by) a system of governance mechanisms that stimulate innovation, socialize risk, and foster adjustment, at both local and national levels, in ways that do not resemble the governing principles of either markets or hierarchies. Finally, the decentralized industrial order is not at all the outcome of late industrialization. Its origins can be traced back into the seventeenth and eighteenth centuries to regions that had property relations and political structures that favored the small property holder and supported simultaneous engagement in agricultural and petty industrial pursuits.

The second regional system, which I will call the *autarkic industrial order*, resembles in many respects the model that shapes the attention of traditional accounts: It is dominated by very large scale, vertically integrated enterprises with close ties to universal banks and it came into existence relatively late in the 19th century. The autarkic industrial order differs from the traditional organized capitalism system, however, in that it is understood to be a regional system whose primary organizational and strategic characteristics in production and governance are shaped at least as much by the desire to cope with environmental uncertainty than by the imperatives of efficiency. Indeed, for much of the history of industrialization in Germany, producers in the autarkic industrial order were similar to producers in the decentralized industrial order, in that both types of producer attempted to maximize flexibility in production and favored the production of relatively specialized products. The two forms of organization differed in that the autarkic form of industrial order relied upon the firm and the large-scale enterprise to govern this strategy, whereas the producers in the decentralized industrial order did not.

An important consequence of conceptually repositioning the organized capitalism model of the German political economy into a larger framework of multiple regional industrial systems is that the problem of the governance of the national political economy as a whole has to be reconceptualized as well: How have two different systems of industrial practice in Germany been governed within a single national political economy? As a solution to this problem, this book suggests that the heterogeneity of governance that exists at regional and industrial levels in Germany also exists at the national level in the form of a nonintegrated, composite architecture of national industrial-governance structures.

The logic behind this claim is straightforward. Since the process of industrialization in Germany was not a unitary social transformation, but a variety of regionally distinct ones, it also was true that the process of creating national-level rules, policies, and institutions for the governance of economic processes (e.g., national financial institutions, taxation schemes, tariff structures, railroads, legal rules about contract, industrial agencies, and policies, etc.) did not involve the construction of a single, uniform system of governance, nor even a single or uniform boundary between the national institutions of economic governance and society. Rather, unique and discreet institutional solutions were sought and, in most cases, provided for the national-level governance problems posed by the regionally distinct systems of industrial order. The national political economy of Germany has always been a complicated composite of industrial-governance structures – even when at particular historical moments there appeared to be considerable integration between the different industrial orders – and continues to be so today.

The vehicle for this reconceptualization of the industrial order of the German

Introduction: Problems with the German model 3

political economy is an insistently constructivist orientation to economic and industrial processes: All organizational and governance forms that shape production, including the institution of the firm itself, are viewed as outcomes, not the starting points, of historically specific social, economic, and political conflicts about the structure of the social division of labor. Moreover, where traditional narratives assume that industrialization was a single unitary process and that firms and markets were the primary mechanisms shaping the development of production, the analysis here emphasizes the organizationally and governmentally heterogeneous character of industrialization. Each of the regional industrial systems to be presented in this book involve very different ways of organizing and governing industrial production, are shaped by different logics of competition, and involve different relationships between industry, society and politics, at all levels of social life. In order to emphasize the embedded and constructed character of these regional industrial systems, I use the term industrial *order* rather than the more standard, yet more narrowly economic terms such as industrial structure or industrial organization to characterize their organization.

It is the task of this introduction to explain, elaborate and justify these claims. The chapter will thus have three parts. The first section presents and critiques the traditional "late development," organized capitalism conception of the German political economy and the underlying vision of industrialization that it contains. The second section then presents the empirical outlines and theoretical underpinnings of the alternative account that subsequent chapters in the book will develop. A final section outlines the overall organization of the book.

The traditional conception of German political economy and its problems

The advantages of the latecomer and organized capitalism

Much of what today can be considered to be the standard understanding of the contemporary German industrial system and its historical development can be traced back to the early post World War II writings of Alexander Gerschenkron.[2] His work both sketched out the main institutional pillars that make up what came to be the received post War view of the German industrial political economy and helped to create a paradigm for understanding the relationship between the economy and politics more generally in the process of industrialization. His influence has been pervasive in post 1945 comparative politics and political economy as well as in much of the scholarship on the history of business and industrialization. This is true, moreover, not only of the post World War II literature on Germany, but also of the broader literature on the political economy of industry and industrial development throughout the developed and developing worlds.[3]

Gerschenkron's most influential general claim was that nations could improve their position in the international division of labor through political and institutional adaptation. The German case, he argued, illustrated this extremely well. Before industrialization, Gerschenkron's Germany was a backward country. It had no industrial infrastructure – no skills, poorly developed markets, little capital, and few entrepreneurs. The essential pieces required for economic progress, in other words, were all absent. There were no firms to organize production, no factories with mechanized production, and no free labor markets. The basic starting point for Gerschenkron was his rejection of the idea that market forces alone could produce the pieces needed for economic progress.[4]

The Germans circumvented the market in three ways. First, with the help of the state they acquired the most advanced technologies then available on the world market. Second, they utilized the advantages of their own backwardness to construct large efficient plants. Latecomers such as Germany, Gerschenkron suggested, could produce with very large scale production economies because they were not beset by the problems of competition among numerous smaller firms, which often slowed the pace at which earlier industrializers achieved efficient scale economies. The Germans could create firms that started out at the largest and most efficient scale of production as dictated by the reigning international standard of efficiency. Finally, Gerschenkron pointed out that to finance all of this development, the Germans developed a unique form of bank that combined the strengths of both the British commercial banks and the French investment banks. German universal banks collected short-term deposits and pooled local capital in order to subsidize long-term investments to industry. Taken together, these three achievements created the core characteristics of the traditional conception of the German industrial system.

This combination of technological and institutional innovation, in his view, ultimately affected both the structure and organization of industry. Bankers directed their industrial clients into the fastest-growing industries – especially the heavy industries, such as electrical engineering, iron and steel, heavy machinery, and chemicals – and gave them the capital they needed to continue purchasing the best technology and implement it at the most efficient scale. Finally, as financial capital became more concentrated toward the end of the 19th century, this resulted in the concentration of industry as well. Centralized control of large swaths of an industry prompted the banks to encourage their holdings to take advantage of scale economies through amalgamation and cartelization.

In the post World War II period, this story of overcoming backwardness and the model of the core characteristics of German industrialization – advanced technologies, large plants, concentrated markets, universal banks with close linkages to large industrial enterprises, and a helping state – was generally accepted as a seminal portrait of the most characteristic and distinctive features of German capitalism and its experience of industrialization. Since the publication of Gerschenkron's original essay in the early 1950s, there have been a number of important extensions, elaborations, and modifications of particular pieces of Gerschenkron's argument with specific regard to the German case, and many of his general causal claims have been solidly refuted.[5] Yet, as with most robust research programs, the criticisms and refinements have affirmed the value

Introduction: Problems with the German model

of the initial insights about the central institutional characteristics in the German industrial experience.[6]

Jürgen Kocka and many of his students, for example, deepened the Gerschenkronian view by linking it to the pioneering work of Alfred Chandler on the development of the modern industrial enterprise.[7] This link was forged by showing how the development of the corporation in Germany was shaped by the timing of industrialization. Sharing Gerschenkron's assumption about the lack of industrial talent and institutions in agrarian 19th century Germany, Kocka argued that German corporations were forced to grow very large very rapidly. The lack of any industrial infrastructure in the face of exogenously generated technological opportunity and competition forced the firms to incorporate most of the operations of production in-house.[8] Moreover, given the highly fragmented structure of the consumer markets that German producers served, it was difficult for producers to achieve the kinds of production economies that were typical of large producers in the United States. The distinctive character of large German enterprises was their broad diversity and their capacity to produce specialized products in relatively small, single-lot sizes. Now, following Kocka, Chandler himself has recently emphasized that large German enterprises grew large by optimizing economies of scope rather than economies of scale.[9]

In the view of this school of German business historians, these artifacts of the lateness of German industrialization were further enhanced by another dimension of the lateness of German development: bureaucratization. Kocka pointed out that although the Germans industrialized late relative to Britain and other western European powers, in the political sphere German states had been quite advanced in their construction of modern bureaucratic organization. Indeed, because these bureaucracies had emerged before the process of industrialization began, the new industrial firms constructed their own large organizations by self-consciously borrowing organizational principles from the states.[10] This isomorphism had two consequences. First, it explained how large German enterprises tended very early on to develop many of the kinds of managerial hierarchies and internal functional specializations that Chandler had shown to be the outcome of large-enterprise development in the United States – in many cases even before such innovations occurred there.[11] Second, the central importance of vertical integration combined with the availability of bureaucracy in general created a strong tendency among German industrial firms to circumvent the market and rely on the bureaucratic governance of their industry through the use of cartels, close linkages to banks, and other forms of interfirm cooperation. Modern capitalism in Germany, according to Kocka and his colleagues, was "organized capitalism," or in the more recent words of Alfred Chandler, "Cooperative Managerial Capitalism."[12]

A second current of modifications of Gerschenkron's original theses came from technological historians such as David Landes and a host of other more specialized writers. Landes, in particular, traced in great detail the slow pace by which "advanced" British technologies, such as the steam engine, the self-acting mule, and the puddling process in steel making were transferred to Germany.

Their sudden adoption near the middle of the 19th century came at a scale that catapulted Germany into rapid industrialization.[13] Once industrialization had come on line, Landes showed, the development of German technologies in chemicals, steel, and electrical engineering benefitted from the timing of the industrialization process as well. Their original lateness had encouraged the German state to develop institutes to pay attention to the new industrial technologies and educate people to produce them. This created a continuously self-replenishing pool of engineering talent, and just as importantly, an extensive infrastructure of public support for industry that enabled Germany to move into "science-based" industries such as chemicals and into the most advanced forms of steel making. This, moreover, at the same time as (and in the case of chemicals, even ahead of) the British.[14]

A third critical modification of the Gerschenkron model came from Richard Tilly's work on the development of German banking, which shows clearly how commercial banks were able to pool scarce capital to subsidize the growth of massive firms, although he claims that the intensely close bank–industrial firm ties described by Gerschenkron were not especially important in the early period prior to 1871.[15] After 1871, however, Tilly showed how extremely close relations between joint stock companies (which represented, in his view, the most "modern" sectors of the economy) and the banks played a crucial role in sustaining German industrial growth up to the first World War. The contribution of large banks was to foster the continued growth of the largest and most technologically and organizationally advanced enterprises, and the growth of these enterprises made overwhelmingly significant contributions to growth.[16]

Finally, the very important work of Sidney Pollard, Hubert Kiesewetter, Rainer Fremdling, Richard Tilly, Klaus Megerle, and others took Gerschenkron's insight that the timing of industrialization creates the possibility for variety in the speed and character of industrialization and turned it on Gerschenkron himself. They called into question Gerschenkron's taken-for-granted emphasis on the nation–state as the appropriate unit of analysis for understanding the process of European industrialization.[17] In place of the nation–state these authors emphasized the crucial importance of the region as a differentiating factor in the process of industrialization. In their view, industrialization in Germany was simultaneously a part of a larger European process and a regional phenomenon: It occurred only in certain specific regions and among those regions it began earlier and later, faster or slower, depending upon (a) the social, political, technological, and resource endowments that existed there and (b) the extent and character of trade and supply linkages with industrializing regions elsewhere in Germany and Europe.

The key aspect of this literature is that its explanatory focus is less on the development of institutional, organizational, and especially governance forms and practices than it is on relatively more macro- and narrowly economic variables (such as growth, income, consumption, productivity, industrial output, exports, etc.). Consequently, these authors have never disputed the basic organizational teleology in the above, modified, Gerschenkron view (i.e., that large

Introduction: Problems with the German model

firms, vertical integration, universal banks, and advanced technologies were what industrialization in Germany developed toward, when it occurred). They simply have pointed out that regions embarked on this process in different ways, at different times, due to different economic and political causes, and with different sectoral and technological emphases and peculiarities. The work of this school has done much to encourage more differentiated research, both regionally and sectorally, into the industrialization process and to shift attention from national macro-aggregates to regional ones.

This historical work on the industrialization process in the 19th century, all of which took its cue, in one way or another, from the initial framework Gerschenkron provided, has formed the conceptual groundwork for interpretations of the experience of the German political economy in the 20th century. Post World War II analysts of the Weimar industrial economy, and students of West German industry and political economy since 1945 accepted the historical argument about lateness and the increasingly nuanced picture of large-scale organized capitalism that the Gerschenkronian research program produced. Even when the evolution of industrial practice and organization as such was not the primary focus of attention, historians and political economists framed their analyses in ways that highlighted and privileged the core Gerschenkronian structure of universal banks, large firms, and important supporting institutions attached to the state as the most advanced and most important sections of the German industrial economy.

In the Weimar discussion, for example, much of the literature on the industrial economy informed by the organized capitalism framework focuses on the initially cooperative but then increasingly desperate and bitter struggles among large-firm actors, unions, banks, and the government to establish an institutional framework of governance for the stabilization of the economy.[18] Another important stream of research takes up where the previous one leaves off and focuses on determining the precise role played by big business in the Nazi rise to power.[19] In both literatures, the primary actors within the picture of the modern economy developed by the above Gerschenkronian research program – large industrial enterprises in an array of (by the 1920s, more and less) advanced sectors, universal banks, and the central state –are also presented as the dominant and/or advanced core of German industrial capitalism.[20] By studying the politics of these groups within the German political economy and not that of other industrial actors, the authors freely imply that the former are the most important ones for understanding the German experience.

In the case of the post World War II political economy literature, the focus has generally been on the way in which the system of large firms, universal banks, supportive state institutions, and neocorporatist arrangements have contributed to the stability and growth of the West German economy.[21] What was most impressive about these arrangements, particularly in the period between the onset of international economic turbulence in the 1970s and the deep industrial crisis in the mid-1990s, was the way that this system apparently allowed for a uniquely successful negotiated form of continuous industrial adaptation and adjustment. Many, for example, pointed to the success of large firms in rapidly growing export sectors such as automobiles, chemicals, electro-technical products, and machinery and showed how they benefitted from close ties to universal banks and from continuous communication with state ministries and other supporting parapublic institutions (such as all kinds of educational institutions) for the stable transfer of technology and supply of skilled labor.[22]

Others, such as, Wolfgang Streeck and his school, supplemented this work on large industry with close analyses of the way in which the system of industrial relations in Germany functioned in relationship to large firms. They found that the flexible dual system of plant-level works councils and centralized collective bargaining on the part of national unions had two major advantages for German competitiveness. It benefitted large enterprises by fostering cooperation and internal monitoring within them, making it possible to reorganize work and technology without significant disruption. And it benefitted German workers and the rest of German society by presenting a strong and responsible organized presence of industrial workers in national-level wage and work time negotiations. Organized German capitalism in the Streeckian view was full of hard formal institutions that supported and disciplined large industrial producers.[23]

Small firms in organized capitalism

In developing this portrait of the standard post World War II image of the German political economy and its history, I naturally do not intend to imply that any of the above, very large, literatures utterly overlooked the existence of and role played in the political economy by small- and medium-sized firms in any of the four modern German regimes. Many writers, though not all, did take the existence of such producers into account. It is simply that the Gerschenkronian/organized capitalism framing of the industrial economy that the above groupings of otherwise often quite disparate writers shared led them to characterize the development and significance of these other industrial actors in a very particular way.

Small- and medium-sized industry generally was viewed as different from large industry primarily in size and in degree of reliance on market forces (smaller firms participated in more competitive markets). Within these broad boundaries, however, authors differed widely on how they judged smaller producers and their role and place in the economy. In some cases they were termed archaic, inefficient, and backward. In other cases, authors recognized that smaller producers could be prosperous within a special and nongeneralizable niche in relationship to the large enterprises, despite the latter's larger scale and more advanced technologies. In still other cases, particular subsets of smaller producers were singled out – such as the artisanate, in particular – and shown to be functionally useful to the large-firm economy through their capacity to provide manpower and training.

In accounts of the 19th and early 20th centuries up to 1945, for example, these ways of understanding small- and medium-sized business led scholars to interpret crises or adjustment difficulties among these producers as having a particular historical weight: The unitary forces of industrialization were understood to be pushing these producers to a subsidiary, dependent, and more fragile position on the historical stage.[24] Bigness and scale were associated with modernity and small- and medium-sized producer efforts to address their problems in the market and in politics were filtered through this historical understanding. Their efforts to stabilize themselves therefore frequently were called antimodern.[25]

Among observers of the period after 1945, small- and medium-sized producers were not characterized as antimodern,[26] but they were still considered to be marginal and embattled by the forces of bigness and the pressures of concentration. The survival of small- and medium-sized producers, at least in the period prior to the 1980s, was typically explained in one of two ways: Either they participated as suppliers to large mass-producing firms during periods when demand for the latter's products overstretched its internal capacity to supply (e.g. automobile parts suppliers) or they lodged themselves into small and specialized niche markets in which large-scale production had no intrinsic competitive advantage (e.g. machine tool producers). In both cases, the existence of a space for small- and medium-sized producers was seen to be derivative of either production or technological characteristics of large firms.[27]

During the 1980s, the framing of small- and medium-sized firms changed slightly, largely in response to their relatively better performance in world markets than large firms.[28] In some cases, the view that small firms flourished by occupying niches was simply modified by the claim that the size and/or number of specialized niches was growing larger.[29] Other writers recognized that the phenomenon of small- and medium-sized firm growth was larger than the niche argument allowed and modified the framing of such producers even further. A very important strand of argument pointed out that the survival and general health of the artisinate was linked to the survival of large German firms. The former supplied the latter with training and labor and the latter allowed for the juridical protection of the former because they knew they benefitted from this as well. In this view, small-firm success and large-firm success traveled in unison.[30] This view essentially dissolved all small- and medium-size enterprises not producing for niches into the artisanate.

As the above paragraphs indicate, in neither the postwar period, nor in the discussion of the period prior to 1945, was the claim made that small- and medium-sized *industrial* producers were constituted within a distinct system of industrial practice and governance. Nor was the claim advanced that the systems in which small- and medium-sized producers were embedded continuously succeeded, through the active strategic behavior of the actors within those systems, in adapting to new historical circumstances in German, European, and world markets. Rather, the view was a unitary one: Small- and medium-sized producers were industrial firms like any other and were governed by the same principles that governed large ones; they were simply more specialized, less competitive, and/or more dependent than their larger cousins.[31] Their survival was attributed to quirks of the modern industrial structure, which was dominated by the institutional structures of organized capitalism, rather than to any active strategic behavior on the part of small- and medium-sized enterprises themselves.

This traditional set of institutional images and arguments about the German system and its development was constructed by scholars (historians and political economists) writing after 1945 in Europe and the United States. It builds on the work of earlier writers, both German and non-German,[32] but the particular understanding presented above, which is the current one, is a relatively modern view: The postwar authors were responding to and attempting to make sense of the developments of their own time. In this sense their emphases on large firms and large scale in production and their particular way of framing the experience and position of small- and medium-sized firms in society made them part of a much larger international discussion that viewed these things as constitutive features of "modern" capitalism.[33]

Moreover, this model of the German system, *as a conceptual system*, proved to be more robust than many other country models during the turbulent 1980s. During that decade, the international discussion shifted to the general problems generated by the fragmentation of mass markets, the shortening of product cycles, and the acceleration of technological change. As countries struggled to adjust to these new conditions, scholars were forced to revise their conceptual understanding of how such countries worked.[34] Since German industry performed relatively well in this decade, it appeared to observers that the central institutions of the German model played a decisive role in this: The Germans were in a better position to react flexibly in this kind of environment, many argued, because their traditional industrial system had a kind of native flexibility that many of the other Western nations lacked and which was rivaled only by the Japanese. Indeed, as we saw above, the relative absence of mass production in the economy was one of the features of the system that distinguished it in international comparisons.[35]

The theoretical underpinnings of the traditional account

An important feature of this Gerschenkronian/organized capitalism conceptualization of the German industrial economy is that its theoretical genealogy can be traced back through a very robust tradition of economic reasoning that, in contrast to neoclassical economics, seeks to highlight the essential role of institutions and institution building in economic process. The classical economists and Joseph Schumpeter were the theoretical influences on the research program, not the marginalists or postwar neoclassicals like Walt Whitman Rostow and Robert Solow.[36] Indeed, the model of the German industrial economy often has been presented by its developers as evidence for the limitations of the neoclassical view and of the significance of the role of institutions and power in the process of industrial development.[37]

As a positive view however, and not simply as a critique of neoclassical economics, three things in particular are important about the broad theoretical structure of the Gerschenkronian/organized capitalism literature: a unitary conception of industrial development, the assumption that the firm is the natural organizational form for the governance of industrial production, and the view that there exists a strict division of labor between firms and governments in the governance of economic practice.

Unitary industrialization

The claim that the postwar constructors of the model of the German industrial system held a unitary conception of industrial development is not intended to imply that they held views about the necessity or inevitability of development. Nor should it suggest that they believed in Marx's famous dictum that the more-industrialized land shows the less-developed land a picture of its own future. Rather, it suggests that they believed that industrialization, if and when it occurred, and regardless of the various institutional innovations that were required to bring it into being, was a particular kind of social process with a specific logic and with identifiable rules at the level of production and the social division of labor. The activation of this logic and diffusion of these rules involved a general transformation of society. The postwar unitary understanding of industrialization also involved clear directionality and progress (although, again, without inevitability): Industries and economies become "modern," "mature," or "advanced" as a result of the unfolding of the logic of the industrialization process.

Charles Sabel and Jonathan Zeitlin have pointed out that this kind of unitary conception of the development of production is deeply rooted in the logic of classical economic argument.[38] Adam Smith and Karl Marx both developed similar conceptions of the general trajectory of capitalist progress in the division of labor: Productivity could be increased when complex jobs were divided into specialized tasks; hand work, skilled labor, and customization gave way, with increasing returns to scale, to increasing mechanization, deskilling, and standardized mass production.[39] Within this scenario, variation in the division of labor was induced by variation in the extent of individual markets and by the technological peculiarities of mechanized production: Niches in the labor process, for skilled workers, and in industrial markets, for lower volume flexible producers, were understood as artifacts of the constraints imposed by technology or special by-products of the development of the process of specialization itself.[40] At the level of the economy as a whole, the classical vision of the trajectory of capitalism driven by the increasingly specialized use of resources in production was as follows: Individual industries moved historically from craft production in guilds or rural production through the putting-out system to rational mechanization and centralized, vertically integrated factory production. The traditional feudal forms of organization in production and its governance were cast aside and increasingly replaced with the modern institutions of the firm and the market.

Clearly, the narrative recounted above about Germany overcoming the disadvantages of agrarian backwardness, adopting advanced technologies, realizing economies of scale and scope in production and management is a version of this

12   *Industrial constructions*

classic argument. Agrarian Germany gives way to German industrial society or capitalism. The divide between the two is clear and the outcome is singular. Even deviations from the expected outcome are explained as comprehensible side effects of the logic itself (e.g., the relative lack of mass production in general and the concentration on niches among small enterprises in particular). In the dominant postwar narrative of industrialization in Germany there are not several versions of industrial society or of capitalism that come into being – only one. This is important, because it allows for the assumption that, despite the documented variation in the timing and character of the process of industrialization by region, all of the regions were pursuing the same developmental end of mature industrial society. In this way it was possible to think that all of industry could be accommodated within a single, coherent national architecture of governance mechanisms.

Schumpeter and the large enterprise

Although the classical logic worked well at the level of the division of labor in direct production and at the level of the social division of labor within the national political economy as a whole, it had great theoretical limitations for efforts to come to grips with the structures and organizations within the vast realm of social and economic life between those two levels. Indeed, by the time Gerschenkron was beginning to think about the industrialization process, it was well known that the consequences of the classical trajectory in the division of labor for the organization of the production unit or firm were less rigorously worked out in either one of the classical traditions. Even by the beginning of the 20th century, liberal economists had found themselves in the frustrating position of simultaneously praising strategies that resulted in increases in productivity and efficiency and criticizing the organizations created by those who pursued those strategies because they undermined the sovereignty of the market.[41] Marxist economists were less surprised at the emergence of such organizations, but they were nonplussed by their remarkable dynamism and resilience.[42]

Joseph Schumpeter's great innovation (which deeply influenced not only Gerschenkron, but Chandler and Kocka as well) was to provide an answer to these paradoxes in a way that provided both a clear mechanism for change (the innovative or "creative" entrepreneur) and a central institution (the enterprise) by and through which classical economic progress could be realized. The core of Schumpeter's achievement was the famous distinction between adaptive and creative behavior in the economy: The former accepted given constraints as binding, while the latter did not.[43] In Schumpeter's view, the trajectory of development in the economy was an evolutionary one that occurred in waves of "creative" destruction in which "creative" entrepreneurs broke from their short-term optimizing strategies of adaptive behavior and instead engaged in organizational and technological innovation to create new advantage.[44] For Schumpeter, this kind of successful innovation always brought efficiency gains: The new organizations and technologies displaced less efficient ones.

Clearly, Schumpeter did not reject the classical idea of a logical trajectory in production; he simply made it possible to understand organizational innovations such as the large-scale enterprise as compatible with – indeed vehicles for the realization of – the classical logic of development. This characterization of the large scale enterprise opened a very important analytical space in postwar discussions of economic development between neoliberal and Marxist critics of the large enterprise and industrial concentration. Where the other two traditions doubted the large-scale enterprise's stability, dynamism, and contribution to growth, Schumpeter viewed it as the quintessential modern capitalist organization and the logical outcome of the process of economic growth. It is not hard to see how both Gerschenkron's view of organizational innovation to overcome the disadvantages of backwardness and Chandler and Kocka's view that entrepreneurs create managerial structures in the face of technological and market opportunities follow a line of thinking about the enterprise that has its roots in Schumpeter.

The possibilities and limits of politics

The final significant feature of the structure of the theoretical discourse that produced the postwar conception of the German industrial system was the way the boundary between government and production was viewed. In the eyes of classical economists, of course, government was viewed, at best, as an obstructive force. It is well known that Adam Smith argued strongly that too many rules and political institutions impinging on the conduct of productive activity by autonomous entrepreneurs would act primarily as obstacles to the extension of the market and ultimately to the process of growth and development in the economy. Similarly, for Marx, growth and development came about through constant progress in the development of the productive forces (technology), driven by individual competing capitalist firms, and this form of technological progress always ultimately came into conflict with social and political structures. Such structures accommodated the progress of technology within units of production, not the other way around.[45] Thus, though the argument is different than Smith's, the analytic separation between production and the institutions of government (and the implicit privileging of the institution of the firm in production) was the same.

During the post World War II period, Gerschenkron, and then after him Schonfield, Kocka, Tilly, Landes, Katzenstein, Streeck and many others argued against the classical tradition, pointing out that political intervention in the economy need not always play such an obstructive role in economic processes. Indeed, the powerful and widely observed lesson often drawn from the way that the postwar literature has constructed the German experience is that political and institutional innovations make it unnecessary for all industrializing countries to follow the exact same path to sustained industrial growth.[46] For those studying already developed societies in Western Europe and the United States, this same view of the relationship between the economy and the polity has been taken to explain how the economic and industrial successes in many advanced industrial states often hinge on the capacity of the state to develop appropriate institutions and policies for intervention and guidance.[47]

The interesting theoretical feature of this political–economic movement in the postwar literature, however, is that despite its clear break with the classical tradition regarding the role of politics in affecting the rate of economic growth and industrial adjustment, this new view continued to share with the earlier tradition the belief that the public institutions of government were separate from the actual dynamics shaping the governance and direction of progress in production itself. In this particular sense, the economy and the polity continued to be conceived of as distinct institutional and behavioral realms of social life with their own characteristic actors (bureaucrats and interest groups on the one side, firms, managers, workers, and associations on the other) and mechanisms of governance (power and authority versus markets and hierarchies).[48]

To be sure, many writers on the German political economy recognized that political actors, or in some cases social (i.e., corporatist) organizations, could encourage or discourage firms to deploy their resources in ways that affected the rate at which a firm grew or that enhanced its competitiveness in the international economy.[49] They also pointed out that coalitions of firms and industries could lobby for the diversion of resources in their direction or for the creation of an institutional framework that would enhance their competitiveness.[50] But, wherever this "politics" ultimately established the boundaries between the economy and government, within the former sphere it was never considered to be the case that social or political organizations that were not firms engaged in the actual governance or organization of the production process itself.[51] Writers simply took it for granted, much as Schumpeter had, that in a modern capitalist economy production was the exclusive province of the industrial firm.

These theoretical categories have contributed to the construction of a very powerful case against strictly neoclassical, institutionless accounts of German economic development on the one hand, and overly deterministic class-structural accounts characteristic of much writing in the Marxist tradition on the other. By emphasizing the role of institutions, human agency, and innovation in structuring economic practice, writers in this broad tradition have gone far toward the construction of a nondeterministic institutionalist understanding of the German industrial economy. Indeed, I will have frequent occasion to argue throughout this book that the arguments that grow out of these categories do an excellent job of explaining the development and growth of the industrial system of large firms in Germany.

The problem with this theoretical tradition, which the section that follows will now address, is that it has not taken its own nondeterminist argumentation far enough. As a result, it has badly mischaracterized the role and position of small- and medium-sized firms throughout the entire history of German industrialization and rendered invisible an array of very fundamental forms of industrial practice and governance in the economy.

Introduction: Problems with the German model

Critique: Anomalies and the weakness of theoretical categories

Even as this composite understanding of the structure and character of the German industrial system was reaching its most fully worked-out state during the 1970s and 1980s through the accumulation of specialized monographs and better syntheses – indeed, as part of this process itself – anomalies and signs of weakness began to accumulate within the research program. Information about the process of industrialization in Germany and elsewhere was consistently unearthed that did not correspond to the unitary, large-firm-centered model envisioned in the received accounts. In most cases, upon initially encountering this material writers simply attempted to assimilate the anomalies into the traditional picture. Yet, the more that emerged, the more it became clear that the traditional postwar understanding of the German industrial political economy outlined above either excluded or greatly mischaracterized a broad range of perfectly viable forms of industrial activity.

The dilemma is revealed in the way in which scholars have dealt with the continued persistence of regional systems of small- and medium-sized firms in the industrial economy. It appears not only that scholars have significantly mischaracterized the experience of small- and medium-sized firms, but also that in doing so they have misunderstood the development dynamics within the German large-firm system as well. First to the reading given to small- and medium-sized firms.

Recent historical research, some of it conducted by scholars involved in the turn to regional studies of industrialization mentioned above, but also by social and labor historians, has uncovered the existence of entire industrial regions nearly completely dominated by highly specialized, in many cases quite dynamic, small- and medium-sized producers.[52] The best documented examples to date are the metalware and cutlery producers of Remscheid and Solingen in the Berg Land;[53] the specialty textile, machine, fine-mechanical, and optical-equipment producers in Württemberg;[54] the specialty lace, hat, and textile producers of Elberfeld and Barmen;[55] the toy, fine-mechanical, specialty textile, and weapons manufacturers of Thüringen;[56] the specialty silk, cotton textiles, and special machinery producers of the left bank of the Rhine (Mönchengladbach, Krefeld, etc.);[57] and the special machinery and textiles producers in the Kingdom of Saxony.[58]

Two facts are striking about all of these regions: First, contrary to the unitary expectations of the classical trajectory of specialization, there was no clear division within these regions between industry and agriculture and they were by and large dominated by craft and specialized production. Second, it was also true that for all of the nineteenth century and a large part of the beginning of the twentieth century, large enterprises had very little presence in these economies. Indeed, traditional technologies and even entire industries were not immediately or ever entirely shifted into factory production. In these cases, progress was not achieved through increasing specialization and the product-specific use of resources, but through broad cooperation among producers, all of whom typically used general-purpose tools to produce a wide variety of products. Often in such cases, forms of production and its governance developed that completely blurred the boundaries between firm and market, workshop and the surrounding institutions and practices of the local society. For example, producers depended upon trade associations and local and regional governmental authorities to perform crucial administrative and governing functions, such as the coordination of their choices of specialization so that unnecessary competition could be avoided.

None of these forms of industrial practice match the standards of efficiency, or utilized the industrial, financial, or political institutions that structure the understanding of industrial practice in the postwar model of the German industrial system. On the whole, there have been two kinds of reaction in the scholarly literature to the emergence of this anomalous evidence. The first has been to overlook or discount its significance. Largely, this occurred because the people who unearthed the anomalous evidence were not interested in the alternative industrial practices as forms of industrial organization per se. Instead, they were interested either in the quantitative economic data these industrial forms generated or in the social, political, and cultural relations in which the human actors within them were embedded.[59] In neither of those cases is the level at which these alternative forms of industry are anomalous (direct production and its governance) the immediate object of analysis, so the anomalies could be dismissed as noise or particularity without disturbing the dominant narrative.

Nevertheless, there were many who could not overlook these anomalous industrial forms in this way. The second kind of reaction to the anomalous evidence, therefore, was to understand the regional systems of small- and medium-sized firms in the way in which the postwar paradigm always understood them: writers either assumed that the alternative forms of industrial organization would prove ultimately incapable of adaptation and self-reproduction and would recede once real industrialization occurred, or they assumed that the regional clusters of small firms were sustainable but ultimately subordinate or marginal to the advanced large-firm sectors of industry in other regions.

The problem with the first view, as people like Megerle and Kiesewetter have pointed out, is that these anomalous industrial regions were among the most densely industrialized in all of Germany throughout the entire period of industrialization. Indeed, they became more, not less, industrialized as time went on.[60] If one used the percentage of the population engaged in industrial pursuits, Megerle pointed out, regions dominated primarily by vibrant districts of small- and medium-sized enterprises, such as the Kingdoms of Saxony, Baden, and Württemberg, parts of the various dutchies of Hesse, and many parts of the Rhine Province consistently had above-average industrial density throughout the 19th and early 20th centuries (Table 1).

Scholars like Megerle, however, haven't taken the data that they have uncovered and turned it into an argument for a full-scale recalibration of the institutional model of the industrial system. Instead, for the most part, they have tried to assimilate the new facts into the dominant narrative of the large-firm German system with theories of dualism and regional development. Relying on

Table 1 *Number of workers carrying on a trade per 100 inhabitants*[1]

Region	1861	1875	1882	1895	1907	1925	1933	1939
Kingdom of Saxony	18.54	22.91	26.33	30.38	34.25	42.95	28.91	44.76
Württemberg	13.67	15.31	14.72	18.86	22.08	31.00	26.86	38.38
Rhine Province	12.86	19.00	20.57	22.97	26.25	32.85	23.28	35.62
Baden	11.41	15.82	15.51	20.94	25.42	30.22	23.02	34.95
Hesse	11.07	15.20	15.05	19.33	21.56	27.36	21.05	31.24
Westphalia	11.29	18.50	18.37	21.24	24.43	31.66	22.14	33.80
Bavaria	10.90	14.09	13.01	17.25	20.38	25.08	20.89	31.57
Prussia	9.51	19.09	15.43	18.54	21.81	29.11	21.29	32.47
German Reich:	10.96	15.14	16.23	19.64	23.14	30.04	22.35	33.39

[1] The data in this table has been taken and modified slightly from a table in Klaus Megerle, "Regionale Differenzierung des industrialisierungsprozesses: Überlegungen am Beispiel Württumbergs," in Rainer Fremdling and Richard Tilly (eds.), *Industrialisierung und Raum. Studien zur regionalen Differenzierung im Deutschland des 19 Jahrhunderts* (Stuttgart: Klett-Cotta, 1979), p. 113.

the more nuanced accounts of small-firm development in industrialization, such as, in particular, Wolfram Fischer's, these writers suggest that industrialization systematically creates a dual industrial structure with a large-scale, technologically advanced core and a more small-scale, backward, and fragile periphery – both at the level of industries and at the level of regions.[61]

Thus, in Megerle's particular argument, the dominance of a small- and medium-sized-producer-based industrial system in Württemberg during the 19th and early 20th centuries meant that it was a peripheral region. With the emergence of a very favorable set of technology and trade conditions in Europe during the early 20th century, however, he suggests that it became possible for the region to develop into a technologically dynamic core region with large firms and dynamic automobile and electronics industries. In taking advantage of these new conditions, and this is key in the argument, the Württemberg economy modernized and abandoned its backward or less-efficient forms of organization in production and its governance and adopted the large-scale factory system. The regional periphery moved elsewhere, while the small- and medium-sized firms that survived in Württemberg did so by adjusting into secondary supplier markets or niche specialty ones. Growth transforms dualism and also recreates it.[62]

This proposed scenario, however, does not really fit the actual German experience. Much of the literature on the experience of those same anomalous regions in the latter half of the 20th century, including Württemberg, shows that they continued to be dominated by forms of organization in industrial production and its governance that differed significantly from the modernized organized capitalism picture of Germany, well into the 1980s and 1990s – i.e., despite the emergence of large firms there. Indeed, the emergence of large firms in advanced or growth sectors apparently undermined neither the density of smaller industrial producers in these regions nor their peculiar organization and forms of governance.⁶³

Moreover, much of the writing on the West German province of Baden Württemberg in the 1980s made plain that it was not possible to analytically consign these producers to the dependent and protected artisinal sector in these economies. Such producers understand themselves to be distinct from artisans, are organized differently than artisans, and belong to different associations. Indeed, this has been the case for much of the industrialization process.⁶⁴ Given this kind of evidence, it seems just as reasonable to claim that the emergence of large firms during the 20th century represented the emergence of a new system of industrial practice alongside an already existing and still robust system in this region as it does to claim that the older system in the region was transformed or replaced by the newer and larger firms.

Finally, even during the supposed periods of peripheral existence and backwardness in the 19th century, those regions often competed successfully in German, European, and international markets and were widely known for specific industrial specialties (such as Solingen cutlery, Krefeld silks, Tuttlingen surgical instruments, Thüringian toys, etc.). Such producers were not perceived by their peers and competitors, nor do they appear to be when viewed in comparative historical perspective, any more or less backward than their other German and European competitors: Producers in many of these industries were able to remain constantly competitive, absorb new technologies, and bring out new generations of their specialty products, all *within* their traditional "backward" structures.⁶⁵ Again, the fact, then, that many regional groupings of producers continued to do this throughout the 20th century seems less attributable to the technological and market side effects associated with the growth of large firms in their midst than it does to the successful reproduction, evolution, and adjustment of a much older regional strategy.

Such evidence suggests that it is not so much that small- and medium-sized industrial producers are or were in fact backward, peripheral, dependent, or less efficient. It is that analysts are forced to interpret them in that way by the categories of analysis that they use to understand the process of industrialization. In the many cases where such small- and medium-sized producers do not appear at all in the discussions of postwar scholars, it is because the traditional categories of analysis *blend out* the smaller producers and render them literally invisible. Where their existence is noticed and addressed, the traditional categories of analysis *mischaracterize* the experience of these small- and medium-sized producer-dominated industrial districts. Such producers and regions seem to have been developing parallel to large producers for much of their history rather than in a subordinate relation to them.

Indeed, this fact suggests an alternative reading of the experience of German large producers, in particular of the increasingly widely noted fact that German large firms only slowly moved into serious production for economies of scale and mass production. If smaller, specialized producers are understood to be not *inferior* but simply *different* than larger producers, it becomes immediately clear that the way in which the two different kinds of producers differed was *not* along the lines of flexibility and specialization. Instead, they differed in the ways in which they *organized and governed specialized production*. This kind of perspective on the development of large firms is difficult to construct, however, within the traditional research program because the latter assumes that the firm and then ultimately the large-scale enterprise is the natural outcome of the search for efficiency in production. If the above alternative line of argument is true – and this book will show quite extensively that it is – then the large-scale enterprise must be understood less as the natural outcome of struggles to cope with the organization of production and more as a contingent and historically specific one. The difficulty, of course, is how to do this. It is to that problem that we now turn.

Reconceptualizing the sources of German industrial power

Three positions will underlie all of the positive arguments that will be made in this book. The first is the claim that the image of the German industrial economy developed by the postwar Gerschenkronian/organized capitalism research program is empirically incomplete and conceptually flawed because it mischaracterizes and blends out dynamic regional systems of small- and medium-sized firms from the national narrative of industrialization. The second is the argument that the traditional understanding of large firms within the "organized capitalism" framework is conceptually suspect because it neither appreciates the commonality of problems that the large firms shared with smaller producers, nor the contextual specificity of the large-scale enterprise as a solution to those common problems. The third position is the belief that the traditional research program is constrained in its ability to appreciate these alternative readings of the German experience by the theoretical principles that undergird its understanding of the industrialization process. In order to fashion these alternative insights into a new view of the broad character of the German industrial system and its history, those categories must be thoroughly reexamined and in large measure rejected. This section will outline the structure of the empirical and theoretical arguments that will be built from these positions throughout the rest of this book.

The empirical dimension: Two forms of industrial order and a composite of national-level governance systems

The core empirical argument presented in this book is that the regions of highly specialized small- and medium-sized industrial firms that were blended out of or mischaracterized in the postwar research programs actually experienced their own independent form of industrialization. Indeed, my claim is that it is possible to outline two regionally distinct, internationally competitive patterns of industrial development that parallel (and sometimes conflict with) one another throughout all of German industrial history in the 19th and 20th centuries.

20 *Industrial constructions*

One pattern will be referred to as the *decentralized form of industrial order*. Within it, production and its governing institutions grew to be embedded in a dense network of relations among and between producers and public and private institutions in particular regional political economies. In most cases, production within the decentralized industrial order was specialty production: Often (but not always) series sizes of products were very small and the boundaries and identity of particular products were continuously shifting and changing. The regions of small- and medium-sized firms and industries mentioned above – Württemberg, Baden, the Kingdom of Saxony, the Berg Land, the Siegerland, and the left bank of the Rhine – were the primary locations of this pattern of productive organization. (see Map 1 in Appendix).

Industry in these regions developed on top of and out of a preindustrial infrastructure of craft skills and smallholder property. Many areas, such as Württemberg, were dominated by the putting-out system, while other areas had been traditional centers of handicraft metalworking for centuries, such as Remscheid and Solingen. Regardless of the specific roots, the existence of an infrastructure of skill and handicraft, combined with property relations that preserved small property holdings, made it possible for producers to construct mechanisms of governance that made it unnecessary to grow large and vertically integrated. Most producers remained small- and medium-sized. Usually, they were family owned.

Significantly, because producers did not incorporate all phases of the production process under their control, their capital costs were correspondingly lower than in the regions dominated by the other pattern. Indeed, in general, regions dominated by this decentralized form of organization developed quite outside the purview of the universal banks that the Gerschenkronian research program saw as crucial for Germany's economic growth in the 19th century. To a large extent, local governments and producers in these regions created their own savings and cooperative banks; the latter pooling capital from among the many family owned small-scale industrial establishments in the community. These regions of decentralized industrial production have traditionally been the breeding ground of the German *industrielle Mittelstand*.

The other pattern will be referred to as the *autarkic form of industrial order*. In it, all aspects of production and its governance came, over time, to be entirely embedded within the institutional framework of the private firm. As such, it has many characteristics familiar to us from the traditional organized capitalism view of the German industrial system. The main centers of this form of order were the Ruhr Valley, northeastern Westphalia, the old court and trading cities such as Hannover, Kassel, Braunschweig, Nuremberg, Augsburg, and Munich, and the vast central Prussian plain, including the provinces of Brandenburg and Saxony. (see Map 1 in Appendix).

It was in these poor, agricultural regions, relatively free of preindustrial handicraft infrastructure and with a relatively large class of propertyless labor, that the classic large-concern form of German industrialization took place. Regardless of the kind of product they produced or of the size of the series in which they were

Introduction: Problems with the German model

produced, firms in these regions grew very large very rapidly because the lack of surrounding infrastructure forced them to incorporate most of the stages of manufacture under their control. And, because the capital requirements of such a strategy were so high, these large combine firms grew up with very close relationships to major universal banks. Moreover, the timing of industrialization in these areas was quite late relative to Britain and Belgium, so firms often developed on the basis of technologies and organizational forms that they borrowed and adapted from those countries. Most of the famous large German combines are all located in these regions: Krupp, Thyssen, Siemens, AEG, the Gutehoffnungshütte, Demag, Henschel, the M.A.N., and many others.

Conceptually, the important move in this redescription of the development of this form of industrial order is the fact that it moves the key institutions, actors, and arguments of the postwar paradigm away from the central, dominant position they occupy in that ideal typical system and repositions them as a particular, regionally specific form of industrialization. Moreover, throughout the account of the development of this form of industrialization it will be pointed out that because of differences in regional resources and as a consequence of its own past strategies, *not because it was involved in a fundamentally different form or strategy of production*, this form of industrial order reacted very differently to problems of governance and market order than did producers in the small- and medium-size-firm-dominated decentralized industrial order.

The final aspect of the empirical argument in this book concerns the way in which both forms of industrial order were governed within a single national political economy. Making an argument about the significance of autonomous regional forms of industrialization does not entail an argument that the national level was unimportant. On the contrary. The development of the decentralized industrial order, for example, posed a number of problems at the level of the national economy as a whole, including especially:

1 the need to define the relationship between regional cooperative and savings banks and the national capital markets
2 the need to balance regional government needs for revenue to support local decentralized production with the revenue needs of the central imperial government
3 the need to construct a national system of railroads that was sensitive to regional cost and production differences
4 the need to harmonize traditional regional legal codes that established rules and facilitated adjudication within very specifically structured political economic systems with the need to establish a national system of law.

All of these areas (and more) were crucial at different times (sometimes several times) in the history of the last two centuries for the ability of the decentralized industrial order to be able to reproduce itself in the national environment. Much of the national-level energy extended by actors and organizations from the decentralized industrial order in each of the four modern German regimes since

1871 has involved efforts to find adequate solutions to these problems. Naturally, an analogous, but not identical, list demarcating how to define the relationship between the local practices of the autarkic industrial order and national-level institutions can be constructed. The argument that this book will present is that efforts to construct national-level solutions to governance problems that arose within each of the regional forms of industrial order resulted in a composite architecture of national governance. By this I mean a mixture of isolated, parallel, and interpenetrant systems of national-level governance, rather than a unified, coherent single system.

In most cases, parallel systems of national governance were constructed for each of the forms of industrial order: This was most notably the case in the banking sector, where the universal banking system and the cooperative and savings banking systems each have their own internal systems of rules, hierarchies, and capital flows. In other cases, the construction of a set of arrangements between the national and local in one order had little impact upon the governance of the other order: This was the case, for example, within the system of German federalism in the regulation of fiscal relations and functional responsibilities between the central and regional governments. The preservation of considerable regional autonomy was terribly important for the decentralized industrial order, but, within certain limits, it was a matter of indifference for actors in the autarkic industrial order. Finally, there were special kinds of problems for which it was not possible or practical to construct completely parallel and independent solutions. In these cases, such as in the construction of a national legal code, the Germans succeeded in constructing a single system capable of preserving tremendous regional heterogeneity.

The outcome of all of these efforts at the national level was not a unitary or single system for the governance of the political economy. Instead a variety of governance arrangements were established within functional areas (finance, tax, civil law) as well as across them. These arrangements involved the construction of different kinds of national institutions, each with different boundaries between the state and the industrial economy. The German national political economy, therefore, was and still is a composite of different systems of governance, all of which, in different ways, are concerned with stabilizing and facilitating the reproduction of one or the other of the systems of industrial order that exist within the economy.

The theoretical dimension: Constructivist political economy

The reader will certainly have noticed that in outlining the basic features of my empirical claims I refer to the different regional patterns of development as forms of *industrial order*, rather than using more familiar terms, such as "industrial organization" or "industrial structure." I do this because those latter terms carry meanings in neoclassical economic theory that presume a kind of relationship between organization in the economy and the rest of society and politics that is far too rigidly and narrowly drawn to be able to capture the way in which crucial dimensions of industrial practice are organized, especially in the regions in which the alternative, decentralized, development took place. By suggesting that the different patterns of industrial development in Germany be thought of as forms of order, then, I am attempting to flag for the reader the fact that I am using a broader lens to analyze economic practice.

I do not, however, intend for there to be anything causal or determining in the concept of industrial order per se; that is, independent of the sets of relations the lens allows me to identify. My analysis of industrial order in Germany is not intended to be, in itself, a *theory* of industrial organization. Rather, using the term industrial order to describe the two ideal typical regional patterns of industrial practice is an interpretive move that allows me to draw on a variety of different traditions of social theory in order to make what I think are better explanatory claims regarding the way in which the two systems I have identified work than can otherwise be achieved.[66]

But then, how does the analysis I deploy in this book break from the theoretical structure that underlies the postwar Gerschenkronian paradigm or, indeed, from the neoclassical writing on the firm and industrial organization which uses the conventional language I so dislike? Generally, the approach I take in this book will be a constructivist one. By that I mean that I will attempt to view both the social realm of the economy and the organizations and institutions that populate and govern it as the outcome of historically specific struggles among social actors over the constitution of the social division of labor. In this view, even the relations and arrangements immediately involved with direct production itself are not conceived of as occupying a realm of the social world distinct from politics or society. Rather, historically specific social, economic, and political ideas and institutions constitute together what the "economy" and industry are understood to be at any given time and what the identities of the actors within these social spaces are. Change in the economy, so conceived, involves, immediately, reciprocally, and inseparably, corresponding changes in its articulation with society and politics. This view attempts to get away from the distinction in much of social and economic theory between the background conditions, constraints, and structures of an environment and the actors who must strategize and act within them. Throughout this book, thinking, learning, and strategizing agents will repeatedly be depicted as making their environment even as they are being formed by it.[67]

This orientation challenges and departs from the theoretical principles that structured the traditional postwar paradigm by pointing out that at crucial points those principles conceive of relationships and boundaries within the social division of labor as being natural or relatively fixed and transparent, when in fact they are not. The theoretical principles that guided postwar writers tended to underestimate the degree of uncertainty confronting actors in the developing economy as well as the range of possible adjustment strategies available to them as they confronted new challenges. This kind of illusory transparency enabled writers in that tradition to conceive of the clean historical breaks, unambiguously superior organizational forms, and sharp social boundaries between direct production and public institutions that shape their narratives of development.

The alternative approach that will be taken here does not and is not intended to yield a new general logic of industrialization as an alternative to the classical conception of a trajectory of specialization. All it seeks to do is make it possible to see that the organizational forms of production and governance that existed in the process of German industrialization were not natural (or even most efficient) outcomes of the logic of industrialization, but rather were highly contingent and contested outcomes that resulted from conflicts and strategizing under often very turbulent and highly uncertain economic, social, technological, and political conditions. By conceiving of the process in this way, my narrative should make it possible to see that there were several industrial logics unfolding in the history of different German regions.

To make this theoretical strategy clear, it will be helpful to show how the theoretical categories of the old research program made it possible to overestimate the clarity of contexts within which actors strategized, underestimate the degree and impact of the uncertainty they faced, and ultimately made it impossible to appreciate the integrity of alternative processes of industrial development that actors under such conditions constructed. Let us look at each of the three categories mentioned earlier, in turn.

Against unitary industrialization

The central claim of the classical tradition that made its conception of industrialization unitary was that progress occurred through a process of increasingly specializing the way that resources were deployed both in direct production and in society. As Sabel and Zeitlin suggest,[68] the history of development that resulted from this view was one of epochal changes. Operations in production that had been performed by a single skilled artisan were divided into more specialized suboperations and transferred to mechanized machines that were absolutely more productive and eliminated the need for the former artisan's skills. Factories replaced dispersed homework and handicraft workshops and transformed standards of efficiency in the market. Industry replaced agriculture and large-scale, concentrated industry dominated smaller competitive industry. Each new epoch transformed identities and careers, workplaces, markets, and industrial society in its wake, placing pressure on actors to abandon their traditional practices, adapt to the new conditions, or be left behind or crushed (or both).

The anomalous evidence of the regions of the decentralized industrial order suggest that, in fact, the epochs demarcated by the classical view were less epochal and the actors were not confronted with the kind of stark choices assumed in the classical view, or, if they were confronted with them, they refused to make them. These regions both retained and transformed their ties to agriculture and the guild system, their traditional practices at work, and forms of industrial organization. Progress in these regions did not occur through the "creative" emergence of a new system of practice that cleanly supplanted the old. Instead, the old itself progressed by recomposing its practices in production and its organizations and governing institutions in ways that allowed them to adapt to new challenges. The traditional was modernized in these regions; it was not abandoned.

Sabel and Zeitlin claim that the difficulty with the classical view is that it makes a rigid distinction between the background conditions and constraints of action and the actors themselves: Prisoners of their given contexts and resources, classical economic actors respond to market, technological, or organizational challenges either by optimizing what they have (lowering wages, taking lower profits, forgoing investment) until it proves impossible to compete any longer. Or they abandon what they have and adopt the newer and superior form of the challenger.[69] The alternative conceptualization Sabel and Zeitlin suggest, and which will be adapted here, softens the distinction between economic actors and their contexts by emphasizing the strategic as opposed to merely maximizing dimensions of behavior. By this they mean that economic actors are at least as much concerned with constructing institutionally, discursively, and practically the context they are in as they are in pursuing what they take to be their advantage within any context. Actors, in other words, reflect upon and seek alternatives to the constraints that they face, even as they act self interestedly within them.[70]

Conceiving of actors in this way presupposes two things about the character of industrial change. The first is that actors are always aware both of the relative fragility of their own production organization and governing institutions and of the strengths and weaknesses of competing forms they encounter on the market. Industrial actors, especially the German ones that will be observed in this book, are not isolated atoms; they travel across cultures and markets looking at and learning about the industrial systems that compete with them. Actors have the capacity to reflect upon the possibility of and consider alternatives to the practical and institutional situation in which they find themselves.[71] Adjustment thus must be understood as taking place through a kind of conversation among relevant actors about the relative vulnerability and mutability of their world of production. An essential part of this conversation, naturally, involves judgements regarding the vulnerability and mutability of competing systems. One way of summarizing this alternative view is simply to point out that Industrial actors are reflexive, social, and capable of learning.[72]

Second, this process of collective self-reflexion ultimately means that industrial change occurs more frequently through the reconstruction of already existing institutions than it does through the complete replacement of the old by the new. This is typically true not so much (or only) because actors are constrained by the institutional resources they have available to them, but rather, in many cases, because of their uncertainty regarding the permanence of the challenge they face. Industrial actors in the turbulent world markets of the 19th century, just as those in rapidly changing late 20th century ones, could rarely be so certain of what the future had in store that they were willing to completely burn all their bridges behind them. The result, ultimately, is a hedging strategy in which new and foreign forms are syncretically appropriated and interwoven with the old and familiar – some steps forward, other steps back.

Engaging in this kind of activity presupposes self-reflection and, in particular, the capacity to reinterpret the rules, practices and institutional designs that have previously shaped one's behavior in new ways. This, for example, occurred in the metalwares industries of the Berg Land when the decentralized production structure was modified to accommodate the introduction of large and more productive industrial hammering technologies.[73] Or, as Chapter 2 will show, when the French Jacquard loom diffused throughout the home weaving districts of Württemberg and Saxony. The process of unpacking the pieces of a familiar system in the face of possibilities and challenges posed from the outside in order to see what can be changed can itself create new possibilities, simply by casting new light on old relations. "By constantly reinterpreting their own past and others' interpretations of the future" Sabel and Zeitlin write of industrial actors, "they [create] more possibilities for themselves as individuals and communities than our historical accounts and our theoretical traditions have allowed us to perceive."[74]

Understood in this way, it is very difficult to conceive of the industrialization process as a unitary phenomenon, at any level. Different groupings of industrial actors, in different regions, with different histories, institutions, and cultures, will invariably conceptualize, organize, and enact industrial activity in ways that reflect their own peculiar pasts and contextually and discursively engendered conceptions of and strategies for the future. This conceptualization of the development process ensures that the substantive experience of industrialization in substantively different regions will be quite different.

It does not, however, mean that different experiences of industrialization will have nothing in common. Regions anywhere, especially the historical regions in Germany that are the subject of this book, are part of larger markets and cultural spaces in which technologies, political ideas, and organizational and managerial strategies are exchanged and compete with one another. Regions with different substantive histories, such as the autarkic and decentralized forms of industrial order, are confronted alike by challenges emanating from this larger environment. For example, both the autarkic and decentralized industrial orders were confronted with the challenge of mechanization and factory organization in the 19th century and of mass production and Fordism in the 20th century. The development of both of the forms of industrial order will thus inevitably reflect their embeddedness in this larger world. Their capacity to self-reflect, strategize and learn, however, ensures that the development of neither will be completely determined by the context in which they are embedded.

This book's narration of two different, regionally distinct processes of industrialization in Germany will be told in a way that presupposes this understanding of the relationship between industrial actors and their contexts and the syncretic, recombinatory character of economic change. The discussion of each form of industrial order will first clearly embed industrial organization and

Introduction: Problems with the German model

practice in common sets of regional societies and highlight the distinctive dynamics in production and its organization and governance that are engendered within each system of industrial practice. Then, however, the discussion of the development of each form of industrial order will focus on the way in which each reacted to often quite similar challenges, in particular, the emergence of factory organization and mechanization in the early 19th century; the diffusion of mass production principles and forms of managerial organization in the early and mid-20th century, and the emergence of highly flexible and open systems of production in Japan, North America, and elsewhere in the late 20th century. Inevitably, the story that this book tells involves tremendous continuity and remarkable change and transformation in both forms of industrial order.

Markets, hierarchies, and decentralized industrial order

The second structuring theoretical principle in the post World War II research program's conception of the German industrial system concerned the key organizing role played by firms and large enterprises in production. For Gerschenkron, Kocka, and Chandler, as for Schumpeter before them, the incorporation of all aspects of the production process within the boundaries of the firm appeared not only to be a natural or logical outcome of the process of specialization in the division of labor, it was virtually the culminating development of 20th century capitalism.

The key theoretical dilemma posed by the alternative production forms in the decentralized industrial order is that production was never systematically collected within the boundaries of firms and, indeed, it is not clear that the firm as such is the appropriate unit of analysis for understanding the development of that form of industrial order. Producers within the decentralized industrial order developed great technological sophistication and innovativeness within sets of relations that involved extreme mutual dependence. Most peculiarly, these relations were (and continue to be) sustained for great lengths of time and never have given rise to integration. Today as in the 19th century, producers in the decentralized areas constantly subcontract with one another and share information about markets, technologies, and skills. Rather than combining their activities in a single firm, or having some producers subsume the activities of many others, producers in these regions systematically construct institutions that help to reproduce both their independence from and their dependence upon one another.

The kind of Schumpeterian theory underlying post World War II analyses of the growth of the large-scale enterprise and industrial organization has difficulty accounting for why relations of mutual dependence do not ultimately produce integration. Schumpeterian theory (like neoclassical theory) begins with the assumption that individuals and firms are fundamentally driven by self-interest. It is *natural*, therefore, to conclude that such actors would find it nearly impossible to sustain enduring relations of mutual dependence because the participants in the exchanges would not be able to trust one another. Each would be worried that a close collaborator would use his or her special knowledge of the other to his or her own advantage.⁷⁵ Given the absence of trust, only three outcomes could be considered possible: 1) producers would discontinue further relations; 2) producers would agree to create a hierarchy through the exchange of property rights that allows for the hierarchical coordination of the desired exchanges; or 3) the stronger producer would exercise power over the weaker producer and incorporate the latter into its own operations.⁷⁶

The difficulty within Schumpeterian theory of dealing with these alternative production forms is part of a much larger lacuna in contemporary economic theory. Even more recent nuanced forms of neoclassical analysis, which look to the institutional background conditions for market order or which are attentive to variations in the character of hierarchy, have difficulty with the forms of governance that regulate the mutually dependent practices in the decentralized industrial order. For example, it is conceivable that an argument could be made claiming that the observed relations in the decentralized industrial order are really fully consistent with market relations. The claim would be that after a period of evolution, in which alternative and competing organizational forms were tried and rejected, the institutional structure and multiple and mutually dependent exchanges that characterize the decentralized industrial order emerged as the most efficient expression of the individual value preferences of participating actors. The decentralized industrial order would in this way constitute a spontaneous market order.⁷⁷

The difficulty with this kind of explanation is that the distinctive thing about the relations of mutual dependence in the decentralized industrial order is that the governing institutions that are created to stabilize them are invested with the capacity to realign relations and redraw the jurisdiction of the actors whose affairs they govern. As we shall see in Chapters 2 and 5, this frequently occurs in the decentralized industrial order when the governing committees in trade associations attempt to preserve the conditions for trusting practice (and therefore ultimately for constant innovation) in the industry through the redefinition of minimum standards of quality or even of intraindustrial relations of specialization. The order that exists in these districts in which relations of mutual dependence predominate, in other words, is not spontaneous at all, it is self-consciously and deliberately constructed.

A different alternative explanation, still within the framework of neoclassical theory but guided by the logic of transaction-cost economics, might attempt to get at the problem posed by the decentralized industrial order by taking a fully opposing tack. Rather than accounting for the relations of mutual dependence and their governing institutions as a kind of market order, transaction-cost analysis would contend that the decentralized practices point to the existence of versions of hierarchy called relational contracts.⁷⁸

Here the logic is that even though it is true that mistrust makes it difficult to sustain mutually dependent relations, this only has to result in the fusion of property rights and the creation of hierarchy under conditions of extreme dependence. An example of this would be when the market is extremely volatile and producers engage in repeated and very specialized exchanges that have caused them to invest in technology and knowledge that cannot be used in any other way. In less dramatic cases, as when the exchanges are not so specialized or when the market is not so volatile, producers establish arrangements (write clauses in contracts, designate an arbiter, etc.) in which future disputes between them can be arbitrated in a mutually recognized manner. This is a rational thing for each of the parties to do, the argument goes, and it might plausibly be used to account for the existence of such powerful extrafirm governance institutions as exist in the decentralized industrial order.

The problem with this argument is that it has to explain relations of mutual dependence with an argument that says in actual fact the producers are not so mutually dependent after all. But as we will see, the thing about the producers in the decentralized industrial order is that in most cases they are so specialized that they need to engage in exchanges with other producers in order to be able to produce anything at all: They are *absolutely* dependent upon one another. And because all are similarly constituted, though differently specialized, the result is that they essentially engage in highly asset-specific exchanges every time they engage in an exchange. Producers in the decentralized industrial order are part of a thick network of specialized producers that is much more than the sum of its parts. The institutions that they create to govern their activities are invested with the power to redefine or refine their specialties to ensure order and competitiveness, but they do not act to make producers less specialized or mutually dependent. Nor are they in any conventional sense attached to the producers through exchanges of property rights. Rather, these institutions constitute important fora for producers to engage in negotiation and establish understanding regarding the definition of and relationship between their individual and collective interests.

These practices and institutions characteristic of the decentralized industrial order, I think, represent important problems to neoclassical and Schumpeterian theory. The kind of order that exists within the decentralized industrial order resembles neither a pure market order, a system of relational contracts, nor any other forms of hierarchy. Moreover, though they may have some of the characteristics of those intermediate forms that the logic of economic theory allows (such as mutually recognized dispute-adjudication procedures), it seems to have them under conditions in which economic theory would expect something entirely different. It is no wonder that the kinds of governance structures in place with the regions dominated by the decentralized industrial order have been so seriously misunderstood and miscast. In describing the alternative governance mechanisms in the decentralized industrial order, it is important to remain aware of this kind of blind spot within contemporary economic theory. Doing so facilitates taking the decentralized industrial forms seriously on their own terms and leaves open the question of the trajectory of their development and their competitiveness against other governance mechanisms, such as markets and hierarchies.[79]

It is also important to point out, briefly, that the above deconstruction of the neoclassical theory of the firm not only has consequences for the study of small-

and medium-sized firms, it affects the way in which the development of large firms must be viewed as well. This is particularly true, I suggest, of the large German enterprises, because at the level of production strategy and market orientation, these producers did not differ significantly from the decentralized industrial producers – both were relatively flexible and specialized producers. What made them different was that under similar conditions in the market, the autarkic producers created large firms, whereas those in decentralized areas did not. This alternative outcome in the organization of production, the above analysis suggests, cannot be understood as the logical result of pursuit of efficiency gains, however defined. The different forms of organization in the autarkic and decentralized industrial orders must be explained according to the same principles, and if those principles cannot account, as we saw, for one set of outcomes, it makes it is difficult to know why they should be held as appropriate for the explanation of the others. Consequently, in this book, both forms of industrial order will be analyzed through a different, constructivist analytical lens: As noted in the previous section, the particular regionally distinct governance outcomes will be viewed as the historically specific constructs of strategic agents in substantively different social, political, and economic situations.

The division of labor in production and politics

The final theoretical principle underlying the traditional account of German industrial development that overestimates the clarity of boundaries, underestimates the degree of uncertainty, and blocks from view the mechanisms of governance and processes of reproduction and adaptation within the decentralized form of industrial order has to do with the relationship between industrial practice and politics. We saw that both the classical tradition of political economy and the post World War II Gerschenkronian research program considered the institutions of government to be something external to the motive forces governing economic and industrial organization. But as the analysis of the decentralized and autarkic forms of industrial order will show, this role for politics is better understood as a historical outcome rather than as a given fact about industrial development. The role of politics in industrial organization can often become central to the very way in which production forms work and reproduce themselves on a daily basis. As we shall see, this is especially the case with the decentralized industrial order.

To see this, one has to recall that the organization of production in the decentralized order does not occur exclusively within the boundaries of a firm. Indeed, because the direct production of the various pieces of a given product is often dispersed among mutually dependent groups of producers and subcontractors, the functions of administration (marketing, sales, research, production) are often decentralized as well. Further, institutional solutions to governance problems that arise among such producers can be constructed and carried out collectively or they can be delegated. Under such conditions, governments may and often do take (or are asked to assume) responsibility for the provision of all or part of specific administrative functions directing the organization of regional production. This is the case, as we will see in Chapter 5, in the way in which the government of Baden Württemberg during the 1980s became involved, through its Steinbeis Foundation and *Fachhochschulen*, in the rationalization of production processes and the transfer of technology into and among small firms. In still other cases, a government may become an important superintending monitoring agent participating in the governance of the production forms, as when a set of disputes that arise inside a trade association concerning the rearrangement of specialization relations in an industry can be referred to the outside authority of the Cartel Office.

As we shall see in the chapters that follow, the role of the government in these ways may vary over time; it may be contested and it may be redundant to roles performed by private actors. Yet, nonetheless, in the cases where the government assumes these roles, it becomes literally impossible to conceive of production without the participation of the government. When production is decentralized, many institutions and actors are involved in its organization, and in many cases, some of these organizations and actors are part of the state.

Organization of the argument

The critical theoretical remarks made in this introduction have been meant to highlight the major conceptual considerations underlying my alternative account of the development and national organization of industry in Germany. They make it possible for me to create a theoretical space for the existence of a viable and resilient tradition of small- and medium-sized producer dominated industrial organization in Germany and to reposition the traditional industrial system of organized capitalism as a highly contingent outcome to regionally specific governance problems.

The central claim of this book, as mentioned above, is that there have been parallel patterns of industrial development throughout the history of industrialization in Germany. I refer to each of these patterns of industrial practice and development as forms of *industrial order* to highlight their dependence upon the social and political characteristics of the regions in which they exist. This social and political conditioning, however, is constituted in very different ways in each of the forms of industrial order. In the decentralized industrial order the political institutions and social practices of the regional society are intimately involved in the organization and governance of industrial practice. The distinctive feature of the autarkic industrial order, by contrast, is that production and its administration grew to be completely embedded in the institutional structure of large vertically integrated corporations and a clear boundary was drawn between the industrial institutions shaping production and the rest of the social and political institutions in society.

My argument is that both of these forms of industrial order have proven to be historically and economically resilient from the beginning of industrialization to the present. The overall narrative of the argument in the book divides the history of Germany into two parts. The first part deals with the emergence of both forms of industrial order in the 18th and 19th centuries and then follows their development up through the Third Reich. Chapter 2 describes the experience of the decentralized industrial order over this entire time period. Chapter 3 traces the development of the autarkic form of industrial order for the identical period. Both chapters make explicit efforts to show how the organizational and governance forms that emerge in each case are profoundly shaped by the social and political characteristics of the regions in which they are located. Chapter 4 shifts the discussion to a national level of analysis. It focuses on the political and economic conflicts that were involved in the construction of a composite architecture of national-level governance mechanisms for both regional forms of industrial order.

The second part of the book, Chapters 5–7, focuses first on the West German and then later on the unified German experience and covers the period from the end of World War II, through the reunification of Germany in 1990, into the deep economic crisis of the mid 1990s. Once again the decentralized and autarkic industrial orders receive separate treatment in individual chapters (Chapters 5 and 6). Both chapters trace how the two industrial orders reconstituted themselves after the war and analyse how each form of industrial order was confronted by a similar set of challenges: first, the diffusion of mass production, and Fordist managerial strategies throughout Europe in the 1950s and 1960s, and second, by the emergence of extremely flexible and open systems of production and management in Asia and North America during the 1980s and 1990s. The chapters will show how during the 1950s and 1960s, the common challenge of mass production and Fordist managerialism led to a kind of integration between the two forms of order for the first time and how this particular integration has been unravelling in the 1980s and 1990s. Chapter 7, much in the manner of Chapter 4, shifts the analysis back to the national level and analyses the ways in which the developments at the regional industrial level gave rise to efforts to reconstruct and reform the architecture of national-level governance mechanisms in each form of industrial order.

In the final chapters, the narrative of the book ends with the German industrial economy in extremely deep crisis and with all of the central actors engrossed in debate about the future structures of and relationship between autarkic and decentralized forms of industrial order. Unsurprisingly, I suggest that there will likely be regional variation in the outcomes that emerge from these contested conversations and institutional struggles. I also suggest that each outcome is likely to contain nonintuitive mixtures of radical break and remarkable continuity with the organizations and practices of the past

2

Blending in: Decentralized industrialization in Germany

This chapter begins my alternative portrait of the development of the German industrial system by analyzing the emergence and development of the decentralized industrial order between the 17th and mid-20th centuries. Within the Gerschenkronian/organized capitalism research program, the producers and regions in which this alternative form of industrialization took place were by and large characterized as less efficient than and peripheral to the large-firm-centered development processes that research program highlighted. Against that image of the industrialization process, this chapter will present the development of industrial producers within the regions of decentralized industrial order as extraordinarily dynamic, competitive, and capable of continuous adjustment in the competitive German and European economies over the course of the last two and a half centuries.

Simply stated, the development of the decentralized industrial order constituted an alternative path of industrialization. The major factor that distinguishes the decentralized industrial order from the industrial system portrayed in the organized capitalism accounts is that it is not firm-centered. Instead, the organizational development and growth of the regions and industries highlighted in this chapter are best understood as occurring within inter- and extra-firm *regional* systems of production that constitute and shape the behavior of the various producer units, governance mechanisms, and sectors within them.

The chapter is divided into three sections. The first offers an account of the origins of the decentralized industrial order in the regional concentrations of putting-out industries which were constructed in a variety of German regions during the social and economic changes that followed the end of the Thirty Years War. German economic geographers traditionally refer to these 17th and 18th century regional concentrations of petty industry as *Gewerbelandschaften*, or, roughly, industrial landscapes, to highlight the deeply regional character of organization in production. Because no equivalent term exists in English, the chapter will frequently deploy the German term when discussing these industrial regions.

The second section of the chapter then turns to the construction and development of the main strategic, practical, and institutional contours of regionally decentralized industrial production over the course of the 19th and early 20th centuries. The focus will be on the way that the already well-established *Gewerbelandschaften* adapted to the technological challenge of mechanization, the organizational challenge of the factory, and the competitive challenge of generalized, capitalist industrialization in Europe and North America. The final section of the chapter (which has blurry temporal but distinct conceptual boundaries with the second) then turns to the turbulent years of the first half of the 20th century when the specialized industries within the regions of decentralized industrial order were forced to establish rules and enforcement mechanisms for the stabilization of their own practices and the protection of intraindustrial relations of trust in the face of the economic turbulence, stagnation and crisis.

As emphasized in the previous chapter, the account provided in each of the three sections of this chapter will continually underscore the *constructed* character of the organizations and practices of industrial actors within the evolving form of industrialization. Regional actors within very specific substantive and historical contexts, in both social and political realms, use the resources they have on hand, combined with their own ingenuity, to respond to and take advantage of industrial challenges. In the process, they frequently transform both themselves and the contours of their own action contexts.

Telling a story of this character makes for a demanding narrative: The dramatis personae and the structure of the stage are continually changing. My solution to this problem has been to focus analytic and narrative attention in each of the three sections not on particular actors or institutions (such as particular industrial firms or regional governments) but on three distinguishable, yet mutually dependent, problem contexts that all of the evolving relevant actors participate in, help define, and collectively construct solutions to: a) the nature of the market, technological, and other challenges or opportunities producers faced; b) the social organization of the division of labor in production; and c) the forms of governance that were devised to regulate practice in production. Structuring the narrative in this way makes it possible to highlight the way in which continuity and transformation interpenetrate in the process of historical change in industry.

The origins of decentralized industrial order

Regional *Gewerbelandschaften* before the age of mechanization

The decentralized industrial order has its origins in the regional property systems that existed in early modern Germany in the western and southern portions of what ultimately became the old Prussian Rheinprovinz,[1] portions of western and southern Hesse,[2] Baden and Württemberg in the southwest, the lower Main[3] and upper Franconian regions of northern Bavaria, the Kingdom of Saxony,[4] and the Thüringen States (see Map 1 in Appendix).[5] In all of these regions, as in the rest of Germany west of the Elbe, peasants held extremely strong claims to the land, well before the formal emancipation of the peasantry in the early nineteenth century.[6] Estate farming, or *Gutsherrschaft*, had given way to so-called *Grundherrschaft*, where noble seigniors did not run their estates themselves, but lived instead from rents and taxes.

The regions singled out here, however, differed from other regions in west-Elbian Germany[7] in that each had some combination of characteristics which 1) placed pressure on small property holders to engage in industrial by-employments and 2) limited the emergence of a class of "propertyless" labor that would be vulnerable to collection into factory production. These conditions shaped the way in which rural industry became organized in the region, and more significantly, the way in which those rural industries adapted to the competitive, technological, and organizational challenges of the 19th century.

In the Rhineland, the Southwest, southern Hesse, and the mountainous areas of Thüringen the key factor shaping industrial development and the formation of labor markets was the practice of *Realteilung* or partible inheritance on the land: i.e., where the land holding of a father was distributed among all of his children. Over generations, this practice produced a structure of extremely small and fragmented peasant holdings. Dwarf holdings, in turn, gave rise to both intensive agriculture and extensive engagement in industrial by-employments (separately and together) as compensatory strategies.[8] The parcelling of land due to *Realteilung* created a rural labor force available for – even desperate to get – industrial employment, yet which was not "landless." Peasants held arable land, albeit small plots, and could not only significantly contribute to their subsistence through its cultivation, they could also ally with other small holders, through strategic marriage and other devices, to enlarge the arable property that they had access to.[9]

In the rest of Thüringen and the whole of the Kingdom of Saxony *Anerbrecht* or impartible inheritance was the rule. Here a single child (usually, but not always, the oldest son) received all of the father's land. On the whole, peasants held strong rights to their holdings in these regions, and holding sizes were small- and medium-sized.[10] Poor soil and small holdings, especially in the regions north and south of the Thüringer Forest, made such peasant farmers available for industrial by-employments much as they did small-holder peasants in the *Realteilung* regions of the west.

An additional set of relations, however, made the situation in the Kingdom of Saxony unique among the *Anerbrecht* regions of early modern Germany. Owing to especially strong peasant property rights, an abundance of unpopulated land, and vital village self-governance structures, the population increase of the 17th and 18th centuries which created a class of landless peasants in other *Anerbrecht* dominated German regions, in Saxony gave rise to a significant small-holder class of cottars. Known either as *Gärtner*, because they owned a house and held rights to a small arable plot, or *Häusler*, because they only had their own house but enjoyed access to the commons, these propertied rural dwellers supported themselves by engaging in subsistence agriculture and rural industry.[11] They became so entrenched in the local social structure (by 1750 they accounted for over 30% of the population of Saxony), that the division of the village commons after the peasant liberation in the early 19th century was conducted on terms favorable to them and the 1838 Statute on Rural Communities (*Landgemeindeordnung*) gave them the right to participate as citizens in the self-governing village councils.[12] This growth of an uncommonly large cottar class, the members of which became a kind of propertied rural industrial labor force, arrived by a different route at a labor market structure that resembled that which existed in the highly parcelled western and southwestern *Realteilung* regions.[13]

Early rural industrialization

Rural industrial production in all of these regions began to grow after the Thirty Years War. Most economic historians agree that by this time population had largely recovered from its collapse during the late middle ages, but agriculture had fallen into a long depression that lowered grain prices. To different degrees across Europe, this price deflation liberated income from expenditures on necessities and made it available for expenditure on relative luxuries, such as, among other things, manufactures. At the same time, low prices created interest in the differentiation of production on the land. Urban merchants, confronted with increases in demand for luxuries, found it difficult to meet the new increases in demand by relying on the existing urban industrial capacity, hence they began to give production out to rural producers. This contingent marriage of rural and urban interests gave rise to the proliferation of many regional rural industries or *Gewerbelandschaften* throughout Germany (and western Europe).[14]

In Saxony, the Chemnitz region became a center of cotton textiles in this period, while the Vogtland specialized on a variety of cotton textiles as well as musical instruments (especially violins). The Erzgebirge had traditionally been a center of mining but it developed a wide variety of industries in this period, including ceramic handicrafts, iron wares, textiles (lace making and trimming), and toys. Western and Southwestern Germany also witnessed an explosion of *Gewerbelandschaften*. Both banks of the Rhine south of the Ruhr, the Sauerland and Siegerland regions of southwestern Westphalia, southern Hesse, Northern Württemberg, the Schwäbische Alb in central Württemberg, the Black Forest, and Thüringen all were important regions of protoindustrial production by 1800. Major products were: linen, silk, woolen, and cotton textiles (Aachen–Stolberg–Düren; Krefeld–Gladbach–Rehydt; Southern Schwarzwald, Schwäbische Alb, Elberfeld Barman); metalwares (Remscheid–Solingen; Sauerland, Siegerland, Thüringen); and handicrafts such as clocks, mirrors, musical instruments, and toys (High Schwarzwald, Thüringen).[15] In most cases, the regional industries were export oriented – German spun-flax linens, for example, sold extensively in the Americas and southern Europe during the 17th and 18th centuries; toys from the Erzgebirge were known throughout the world[16] (see Map 2 in Appendix for the location of regions).

The archetypical form of regional industrial organization in a *Gewerbeland-*

schaft was the putting-out or *Verlag* system. Here a merchant from a town supplied a number of outworkers with materials that they would then transform into a more finished product. The industrial outworkers engaged in spinning, weaving, grinding, hammering, polishing, bleaching, etc., and generally owned their own tools.[17] Because both urban and rural locations were involved in production in these systems, both production and its administration were fragmented. It is important to look at the organization of these systems in some detail because they constitute classic examples of purely regional – "firm-less" – industrial production and as such frame the outer boundaries of decentralized industrialization.

Production and governance within premechanized industrial systems

Production within the above-mentioned *Gewerbelandschaften* took place in the homes of peasant families and the workshops of urban and rural artisans – the rural workers being dispersed, often quite widely, across a region. Each producer was responsible for a particular part of the process of making a "protoindustrial" commodity. Work was always handwork, most often aided by simple tools and machines, such as spinning wheels, looms, grinders, polishers, etc. When one family or workshop finished with their part of production, the product would be taken to another producer at another location who would then perform a different set of operations on the good. The production process in *Gewerbelandschaften* was consequently very geographically dispersed.

The governance of such dispersed production processes involved a variety of actors and institutions. The most important of these were merchant capitalists, the outworkers, and regional governments.

The merchant played a central, yet ultimately limited, administrative role in this system. He (virtually all were men) supplied capital and materials to the outworkers. In return for finished wares, he paid very low wages. Finally, he sold the goods he received at a higher market price. The merchant administered the process by distributing different aspects of production between different outworkers or groups of outworkers in different locations in the countryside. Further, he controlled when there was work to do and when there was not: If the business cycle turned downward, the merchant simply did not put out work. Because his costs were all variable costs, the merchant risked his money only when he gave out work. On the other hand, if he did not give work out, he would not make any money. In this sense, the merchant depended on the outworker within the production system.

Outworkers, on the other hand, had no control over investment. But there were two ways in which they were not entirely dependent upon the merchant in the administration of the putting-out production process. First, a merchant could not control the actual pace of work either within the peasant household or in the artisan workshop. Outworkers were simply given raw materials and encouraged to finish them in due course. Moreover, because many outworkers engaged in some form of agriculture, they often could resort to their agricultural work if the demands of the merchant became too onerous or if the business cycle turned downwards, although the leeway here was often quite limited.[18]

The second limitation on the administrative control of the merchant concerned the relative lack of mobility of labor. In the regions mentioned above there was no free labor market. Outworkers in most cases possessed what amounted to de facto ownership rights to the land, or, if they were urban artisans, made their careers within relatively structured corporate worlds. A merchant could in neither case easily draw such workers into central factories. To increase the amount of goods he was able to bring to the market, the merchant was forced simply to increase the amount of peasant families or artisans that worked for him. Achieving a very large output could thus turn into an extremely unwieldy project, with many peasant and artisan producers performing a wide variety of finishing operations all over a region. The larger the operation of the merchant became, then, the more his ability to oversee the production process became attenuated. In many cases this provided outworkers with room to engage in independent selling, or to diversify their production for a number of merchants. The administrative control of the merchant capitalist over the organization of production was ultimately limited by the outworker's administrative power over the conduct of production.

The third important group of institutional actors helping to shape the governance and administration of production in the *Gewerbelandschaften* were regional governments. Three things were important to these governments: stability, revenue, and power. Regional kingdoms and principalities encouraged the development and expansion of *Gewerbelandschaften* because they provided employment to the population and served as important sources of revenue, particularly if the industry sold most of its output in export markets.[19] Success at these things in the 18th century world of petty mercantilist absolutisms in Germany was considered to be both essential to the reproduction of state power and a way of fulfilling the prince's obligation to maintain a prosperous, orderly "Haus." One contemporary reduced the logic of political economic rule into a dictum: "The state made powerful by the populous nourishing community; a populous nourishing community made this by the state's care."[20]

There were, of course, risks associated with the encouragement of industry. By fostering the spread of rural industries, governments also created a potential threat to the power of the state: The merchants that controlled the flow of resources could transform their position into political leverage.[21] In the face of this, governments such as the Württemberg Crown or the Saxon Monarchy did two things, both of which involved them crucially in the administration of production. First, through the selective use of tariffs, monopolies, and subsidies, regional governments sought to exercise final control over the level of economic activity in the region and of the kinds of trade that their subjects engaged in. They kept the products of other regions out of their own if they threatened to damage domestic producers and made trade deals with other principalities for mutual political benefit. The Herzog of Württemberg together with the council of estates (*Landschaft*), for example, repeatedly refused to permit outsiders to enter the territory and engage in new trades that would threaten those already practiced in the region.[22] There was no industrial production or trade without government sanction.[23]

Second, in order to stave off the growing power of the merchant classes, governments tried to prevent the concentration of production into a few hands.[24] The government of Württemberg, for example, simply rejected a proposal from a group of important merchants in a number of trades to establish a Company for General Commerce in Ludwigsburg. This would have brought all trade in and out of Württemberg under the auspices of a single monopoly company, directed by twelve large merchants.[25] More subtly, in its monopoly linen trading house in Urach on the Schwäbische Alb, the same government of Württemberg condoned a limited amount of independent selling by countryside producers even though it was outside its auspices. Government officials knew that if they attempted to stop independent sales completely, smuggling would intensify and revenues from the countryside would go down. The result was that the monopoly remained profitable, while an important class of small entrepreneurs arose in the villages of the countryside. But even though the state implicitly fostered their growth, it also acted to make sure that the class of entrepreneurs never accumulated enough wealth to become a threat. Blatant and consistent violation of the monopoly was punished. So rather than invest in the expansion of their production operations to challenge the dominance of the monopoly – and hence run the risk of political harassment – these petty entrepreneurs typically invested their surplus in land.[26] It was through dynamics such as this one that mercantilism in decentralized regions perpetuated decentralization.

This ideal–typical model of production and administration in the regional economic order of the *Gewerbelandschaften* could be implemented in countless numbers of ways in practice. In terms of production, there was most frequently a more complex division of labor between town and country, where several stages of finishing were done in different locations in the countryside and initial production in the towns or vice versa. There was neither an exclusive location nor organizational unit of production. Spinning could be performed in the countryside and weaving in the city, weaving in the countryside and bleaching in the city, forging in the city and grinding and polishing in the countryside. Whatever the specific form of division, regional production was characterized by organization that linked countryside symbiotically to city and sometimes city to city and region to region in the production of a single product.[27] In many cases, a system of "decentralized manufacture" (*dezentralisierte Manufaktur*) evolved in which certain parts of the production process became centralized in large workshops or factories, most often in the cities, while the rest of production was dispersed throughout the countryside.[28]

With respect to administration, the variation could be almost as broad. When the regional economy was growing, the relationship between outworker, merchant capitalist, and state was reasonably stable as each enjoyed the benefits of increasing revenue. On the other hand, when the business cycle turned downward, all generally suffered. If a downturn in the business cycle was combined with overpopulation on the land or with a bad harvest, then the outworkers generally found it more difficult to quibble with the terms that the merchants demanded.[29]

Regarding the role of the state, there was also considerable variation. In the Prussian Rhineland (the Duchies of Kleve, Geldern, and Mark), the geographic separation between the locus of power in Berlin and the site of economic activity had a very special consequence. On the one hand, the Prussian state was not strong enough to regulate all of the activities of the emergent merchant–capitalist classes. On the other hand, however, the apparatus that it had established did undermine the legitimate authority of the towns and guilds. Consequently, merchants were free to ignore the guilds and put work out into the countryside, but were not subject to the kind of state restriction imposed by other German governments, including the Prussian government in Brandenburg.[30] In other areas, such as Württemberg and Saxony, however, the regional government was quite active in shaping the development of "its" industries.[31]

The central point to be made here, however, is that even with all of this variation in the urban–rural systems, industrial production in *Gewerbelandschaften* was in all cases an undertaking that involved entire regions. It blurred the line between countryside and city and was embedded in the social practices and property structures of regions. The system was administered and regulated by a historically shifting set of power relationships between three major actors: merchant-capitalists who provided money and direct coordination, outworkers (rural and urban) who were engaged in direct production, and regional governments that regulated the industry and tempered the power of merchants and independent producers alike.

As systems of industrial organization, these *Gewerbelandschaft* political economies were not very dynamic. There was growth, but it was extensive rather than intensive: Productivity gains came as a result of adding more labor, rather than making the labor performed more productive. Nevertheless, the production of industrial products in these regions in the 17th and 18th centuries grew to be extremely important features of regional economies. Population in many areas increased as industrial production spread.[32] Agricultural production became increasingly specialized and intensified.[33] Regions that were engaged in industrial production began to import grains and other agricultural products. This was not only sold to the rural producers, but also to the growing numbers of rural artisans who emerged to provide services to the rural workers. The regions I have discussed had the densest concentration of rural artisans of all German territories.[34] By 1800, regional *Gewerbelandschaften* had grown to exhibit many characteristics associated with modern industrial economies, yet without the central features that have traditionally defined industrial society – mechanization, factory production, and a free landless labor force.

Decentralized adaptation: Industrialization 1800–1918

The growth of mechanized factory production in Britain and the appearance of machinery-produced British wares in their traditional markets transformed the competitive situation confronting these decentralized industrial *Gewerbelandschaften*. Mechanization in Britain produced three different kinds of effects in continental markets: it sent lower priced, standardized goods into traditional markets; it sent valuable and lower cost inputs into traditional industries; and it made possible the creation of many entirely new markets.

The *Gewerbelandschaften* adapted to these challenges in ways that completely recombined the components of production and its administration in the old premechanization regional systems. There was at once tremendous change and considerable continuity. Mechanization, factories, and market mechanisms were integrated into the organization of production and its administration. Yet, far from being threatened by such changes, the decentralized regional character of production was intensified and made more wide ranging.

Strategic behavior in the market

For the most part, German producers met the challenge of British competition by seeking to avoid it, exploit it, or both. The array of responses among textile producers in the Rhineland, Saxony, and Württemberg is in many ways typical. Regional industries avoided direct competition with the British by specializing in products the British did not produce, or by moving into new kinds of product markets in which British competition was not strong. Among cotton textile producers in Saxony, for example, David Landes found that "most small firms rested their survival on the development of a specialty not produced abroad."[35] Chemnitz became a center of hosiery, lace, and embroidery and drew its thread from mills in small cities and villages in the surrounding region. Plauen producers specialized in high-quality lace making.[36] Other peasant producers and their merchant suppliers in Saxony moved out of spun and woven cotton products into woolens, especially worsteds, and into knit goods that were complicated to make but which had considerable export potential.[37]

Germany, never an important center of woolens production, began to become one as important enclaves emerged not only in Saxony but in the Rhineland as well. Paradigmatically, such production was largely based upon imports of cheap British factory spun yarn. German exports of woven woolen cloth tripled from 1836 to 1864.[38] Producers in Württemberg moved more gradually out of linens – which were becoming increasingly displaced by cotton substitutes – into cotton knit goods, such as stockings and underwear. In the Rhineland, producers in Aachen specialized in carded wool products, while in Mönchengladbach, where producers continued to produce cotton goods, they specialized on higher-quality items, in particular mens coats and suits. Specialization was also the dominant strategy in Elberfeld and Barmen (now Wuppertal) in the Berg Land. There producers made fashion articles, such as silk hats, fine cotton prints, and quality woolens.[39]

The evolution of iron and steel producers in these *Gewerbelandschaft* regions conformed to this pattern as well. Initially, iron and steel producers in the traditional regions around the Siegerland, Sauerland, Thüringen, and parts of Württemberg initially competed head-on with the British. The quality of their products produced with traditional charcoal-based methods was in most cases equal to that of British iron and steel wares produced with a new coke-based production technology.[40] But after the locus of growth shifted to the large-scale cast products of the Ruhr at mid-century, the traditional regions continued to compete effectively in a wide range of specialized iron and steel products (nails, pins, hooks, wire, etc.) well into the 20th century.[41] Chemical producers, less affected by foreign competitors, nevertheless also focused on specialization because they had to produce many different kinds of specialty aniline dyes for the (highly fragmented and specialized) German textile industry.

It is important to emphasize that the strategy of avoiding the British and of exploiting the cost advantages and market-creating potential that British (and ultimately continental) mechanization created stimulated producers to focus on the relationship between the possibilities of technology and the desires of the market. A hallmark of this orientation was that firms were constantly focused on product change and customizing. Silk hat producers in Barmen, for example, by continually trying to stay ahead of changes in fashion, constantly accelerated the process of product change. The same was true of Solingen cutlery producers and even of the producers of specialty iron products. The Solingen industry focused on high-quality cutlery tailored to local tastes all over the world, and they explicitly sought to keep the quality of their goods well ahead of their international competitors in Britain (Sheffield), France, and the United States.[42] In order to stay in the market and remain competitive against lower-cost bulk producers, smaller producers of specialty standard metal products such as screws, nails, pins, and tacks devised ways to continually shift production from one sort of product to the next, constantly searching for some optimal combination of scale economies and scope economies.[43]

These strategies of specialization and customizing had become so characteristic of whole regions of German industry by the beginning of the 20th century that they provoked the British economist Alfred Marshall to remark on the Germans in *Industry and Trade*:

> The Germans excel in the sedulous adaptation of their manufactures to local needs, high and low. They are quick to take account of differences in climate, of taste and custom, and even superstition. They make cheap things for people of compulsive temperament; who prefer a brilliant gala dress, to one made of durable solid material. And with equal patience they get to know enough of the business affairs of individual traders to be able to sell with relatively small risk on long credit, where Englishmen sometimes demand prompt payment:

In all this they are much aided by their industry in acquiring languages of Eastern Europe, Asia, and South America. Even in markets in which English is spoken they push their way by taking trouble in small things to which the Englishman will not always bend.[44]

Mechanization, factories, and decentralization

Even though the producers in these regional industrial systems sought to avoid a head-on confrontation with machine-made British products in the market, they did not turn away entirely from British technologies and principles of organization in production. Here it is necessary to distinguish between different discrete phases in the regional production process. In most, but not all, cases, mechanization occurred simultaneously with the creation of factories. But it was often the case that such mechanization and centralization occurred in only one aspect of a larger production process, the rest of which remained embedded in the decentralized regional structure of outworkers in households and small shops. Ultimately, over the slow course of more than a century and a half, mechanized factory production triumphed over the domestic industry in these districts. But the slow transition and the character of the triumph itself shows the enduring importance of decentralized production: The factory system replaced homework, but not the decentralized, production-fragmenting, subcontracting networks upon which it was based.

The diffusion of mechanization in the textile industries in these regional systems provides a good example of the development process that took place in the organization of production. Nearly everywhere the first process to be mechanized was spinning and the introduction of spinning machines invariably involved the centralization of spinning into spinning mills. In most of the *Gewerbelandschaft* regions dealt with here, the capacity of weavers to turn spun yarn into cloth far exceeded the capacity of hand spinners to supply them. With the invention of the power-driven spinning machine by the Englishman Arkwright, it became possible to produce a wide variety of consistently spun threads in considerable quantities far more rapidly than individual hand spinners could. Many merchant putters-out or independent entrepreneurs thus set up centralized spinning mills, often in the already existing *Manufakture* in the towns (such as those surrounding Chemnitz – Zschopau, Flöha, Falkenau, and Mittweida), to supply the weavers in the countryside with yarn. In Saxony, cotton spinning mills began to appear as early as the 1760s; in Elberfeld and Barmen the first cotton spinning machines were introduced in the 1770s; in Württemberg spinning machinery was not introduced until the early 19th century.[45]

But while spinning centralized, decentralization in weaving continued to flourish. Weaving in all branches of textile fabrication in these regions (primarily cotton, wool, and silk) resisted the factory for nearly a century after the introduction of spinning mills. As late as the 1850s, virtually none of the woven cloth in the Wupper Valley was performed on mechanized factory-based looms. The cotton textile industry in Saxony followed a similar pattern, with decentralized hand weaving persisting until well into the late 19th century. Weaving was, moreover, not a trivial part of the industry: in 1846, still more than 75% of the estimated total capital in the German textile industry was in the weaving and finishing sector.[46] In most cases, the gap in the mechanization of different processes can be explained by the fact that the mechanization of one step in a process helped handicraft production elsewhere in the region remain competitive by cheapening the cost of inputs or of finishing.[47] Moreover, on the whole, producers in the regional economies mechanized and centralized when doing so facilitated and improved their strategy of specialization. In many weaving specialties, the extant English organizational and technological innovations were simply inappropriate for the needs of producers: the Cartwright loom was too rigid and expensive, and grouping individual weavers producing broad ranges of constantly changing specialties together under a factory roof seemed unnecessarily costly.

It is important not to interpret the absence of British technology and organization in these sectors as indicative of a lack of interest in or resistance to new industrial technology. Though weaving proved unreceptive to British techniques, it was not otherwise resistant to new technologies. Indeed, the French Jacquard loom, which was extremely flexible and could be run by hand in a household or a small craft shop, was adopted in large numbers throughout the German textile districts.[48] In many of the *Gewerbelandschaften* in which mechanization was adopted toward the end of the 19th century, it involved machinery that could be operated by skilled laborers and craftsmen employed by (or working as) independent small- and medium-sized producers. For example, a *Spitzenklöppenmaschine* (lace making machine) developed in 1877 for use in the Barmen high-fashion hat industry made it possible for home workers to mechanically produce lace of almost the same quality as hand made, but at a much cheaper price. Also in the 1870s in Elberfeld/Barmen, a small power loom that could produce large series staples, such as single-color hat and blanket ribbons, in wide, ever-changing variety was specifically developed for use by traditional artisan producers. In this case, the technological innovation gave rise to a kind of hybrid form of factory organization: in order to gain economies of scale in the use of steam engine power, master weavers used the new machines in what were known as *Mietfabriken* (rented factories). These were large workshops in which space on the power source could be rented by a number of master weavers.[49]

The effect of the lack of simultaneity in processes of mechanization and centralization on the actual spatial location of different aspects of production was further complicated by the fact that individual producers in a single phase of production often combined mechanization and nonmechanization, centralization and decentralization. Many firms implemented mechanization only gradually, often producing some portion of their output with machinery inside a factory and another outside in peasant households or in artisan shops. In Württemberg, such systems were described as *geteilte Betriebe* (divided workshops). Megerle documents numerous such establishments in the 1830s and 1840s:

> One can find a combination of centralized factory work and homework in all branches: for example, the spinning and weaving estab-

lishment Gebrüder Zöppritz in Mergelstetten bei Heidenheim employed 112 workers inside the factory and 105 people outside of it; the same was true among establishments in Metalworking, the production of leather gloves, or in the chemical branch. For the Firm owner, this strategy permitted the dispersion of capital investment costs onto a broader basis of producers. It also allowed him to recruit labor more flexibly and respond with greater elasticity to swings in the business cycle. The government welcomed this form of establishment out of social welfare and socio-political concern.[50]

Approximately 40% of all those counted as "factory workers" in Württemberg during the 1840s were actually employed outside of the factory; the figure was over 50% in textiles, leather, and wood working.[51] In the Wupper Valley in 1861, only 59% of all employed in manufacturing worked in centralized production units in Elberfeld; 60.7% in Barmen.[52] According to Gustav Schmoller, Elberfeld/Barmen had the greatest concentration of factory workers of all German cities in that year.[53] Even as late as 1907, when Elberfeld/Barmen was the German city with the highest concentration of manufacturing employment as a percent of the population (27.3%), it still counted 8.4% of that manufacturing employment in household industry.[54] In 1861, the city of Zwickau had the largest concentration of factory workers as a percent of total employment (9.2%) in the Kingdom of Saxony (itself the most densely industrialized *region* in Germany at the time), but homeworkers in Zwickau as a percentage of total employment in the same year accounted for 34.8%.[55] The situation was even more extreme in less urban industrial areas such as the Black Forest and in Thüringen, where domestic production and factory production continued to interact, with the former always having a slight edge, well into the 20th century.[56]

All of this makes clear that industrialization of production in these regions occurred in a distinctly decentralized way. Production was located, organized, and technologically outfitted in different ways in different phases in the production of a single product, and, in the case of the *geteilte Betriebe*, it even occurred in different ways and locales within the same phase of production. As in the *Verlag* system, so in the new industrial, mechanized system, production remained divided among various producers in town and countryside. Each process in the chain of producing a product was handled by an independent, often uniquely skilled, producer. And because each producer relied on the flexibility with which they could respond to changes in the demands of customers, they emphasized closeness and cooperation with their customers up and down the chain of production. Hoth's description of specialty textile industries in Elberfeld and Barmen, Bormann's description of textile and metalworking trades in Mönchengladbach, Lloyd's description of the Solingen cutlery industry, Flik's comparison of textile producers in Heidenheim and Calw in Württemberg, Kreidte's description of the Krefeld specialty silk industry, and Sax's descriptions of the various rural craft industries in Thüringen all emphasize the significance of these intricate relationships between independent producers active in various unit forms of organization.[57] Ultimately, as these regional economies industrialized, the agglomeration of producers in them related to one another and to customers in neighboring regions as participants in a larger regional production process in which each played a specific and indispensable part.

Organizational growth and evolution

Growth in these decentralized systems of production over the course of the 19th century generally produced three developments: 1) the slow decline of industrial employment in homework, 2) the proliferation of small- and medium-sized establishments, and 3) the diversification of the industrial base of the region. As craftsmen and households took on more work, they found that they could expand by purchasing new machines and hiring additional helpers. Peasant homeworkers and cottars slowly and in nonsimultaneous ways shifted from a life in which they concentrated on agriculture and engaged in industry as a by-employment to a life in which exactly the reverse was true. According to Erich Benndorf, in 1907, 57% (100,517) of all "farms" in Saxony were "dwarf" holdings, under two hectares.[58] According to Heinrich Gebauer, "the overwhelming majority of these farmers have some other activity as their main job (*Hauptberuf*): e.g., as wage worker in industry or as independent operator in industry, trade or transport."[59]

And, indeed, in very significant numbers, this shift into full-time industrial work occurred not by moving into factory work, but by individuals setting up their own small production facility or working in that of a neighbor. If one follows the statistical path of development of firm size within Württemberg, or Mönchengladbach, Remscheid, Elberfeld/Barmen, Thüringen, or Saxony, it is difficult to know precisely how to understand developments because household workers and factory workers are both counted as industrial workers, while artisans are counted separately, and all of the contemporary and ethnographic accounts emphasize that all three categories tended to blend together in practice.[60] What at least does seem clear is that the decline in household and artisinal industrial production in these districts was, over the long duration of the 19th century, compensated for by the proliferation of small- and medium-sized industrial establishments.[61] Over time, outworkers or groups of outworkers performing craft work for industry were transformed into small manufacturers doing the same. The industrialists Robert Bosch and Gottlieb Daimler, both from Württemberg, are only two of the most famous examples of countless other specialized artisans who followed similar trajectories.[62] Agglomerations of decentralized, interconnected outworkers over time evolved into agglomerations of decentralized, interconnected small- and medium-sized firms.[63]

The case of Saxony is very interesting in this regard. Industrialization clearly led to the rise of factory production and to the growth of cities. According to one measure, between 1882 and 1895 the number of homeworkers declined from 121,000 to 79,000.[64] Moreover, by the turn of the century, Saxony was the most "urban" region in Imperial Germany, with over 779 persons per square mile. It had thirty cities with over 10,000 inhabitants, including Leipzig and Dresden, which both had over 500,000 inhabitants and supported extremely robust and varied manufacturing and service activities. In addition, Erich Benndorf's statistics show that in 1915, in most sectors, the percentage of Saxon firms employing over 50 employees (officially a "large" firm) exceeded the average for the Reich.[65]

But it is not clear how much one can conclude from such statistical information. Over half of the densely packed population continued to live in towns of under 5,000. Benndorf's statistics also note that even though Saxony had an above-average amount of large firms, these firms were much smaller than the average large firm in the Reich (by number of employees): Saxon firms over 50 employees accounted for 13.2% of all such German firms, but those firms employed only 11.7% of all German employees who worked in such firms. Moreover, middle sized firms (employing between 6–50 employees), were present in percentages much above the Reich average. Megerle's statistics reveal that large firms clustered in the 50–200 employee category.[66] As early as 1861, Kiesewetter's research shows that Saxony had the largest number of spindles in spinning mills in all of the area of the Reich (31.6%), but ranked eighth among the ten leading German regions in number of spindles per establishment.[67] Family or single individual owned businesses dominated Saxon industry: the Kingdom accounted for only 8.9% of all German *Aktiengesellschaften* (joint stock companies) in 1907, and even more interestingly, the area employed only 6.7% of all German employees who worked in such enterprises. Saxony even had relatively few limited liability companies (so-called GmbH's) – only 6.7% of the total number in the Reich, accounting for just 4.9% of total capital.[68]

The picture that slowly emerges is that of small and moderately sized, closely held specialized businesses surrounded by vast numbers of extremely small enterprises providing a broad range of equally specialized inputs. Ninety-nine percent of all Saxon textile firms employed less than 50 workers, accounting as a group for 44.2% of all employed in the industry. In metalworking, 48.3% of workers were employed in firms with fewer than 50 employees. This kind of structure is more or less replicated in virtually every important Saxon industrial sector.[69] Historians and contemporaries attempting to describe the Saxon economy at the turn of the century were struck by the abundance of small-scale, specialized firms. Writes one:

> Small isolated mills and mines employed skilled craftsmen as well as cheap labor and required little venture capital.... There was little large scale but much household or home industry.... Thousands of family owned firms turned out hundreds of different kinds of consumer goods like brushes, saxophones or watches for home and foreign markets. Industries such as textile or Garment making or softcoal mining could and did thrive with a large number of small firms competing against but not absorbing one another.[70]

The point that these examples are intended to make is that industrialization in the industrial districts of Württemberg, the Rhineland, Thüringen, and Saxony started out extremely diffuse and decentralized and remained so, even as independent producers adopted machinery and the organizational techniques of the factory. Two factors made the abiding significance of decentralization possible: the specialist orientation of the producers and a broad distribution of small property holders. Specialization demanded flexibility and flexibility made the extension of fixed costs in production always a risk. Consequently, expansion and growth in individual firms tended always to be accompanied by decentralization (i.e., subcontracting, use of outworkers, etc.). In effect, firms grew by spreading their risks onto one another. The growth of a firm was inseparable from the growth of an industry; the growth of an industry inseparable from the growth of a region.

At the same time, the process of decentralized regional expansion was also shaped by ownership patterns on the land and in rural communities. Because many domestic and craft workers held property (often with arable land), they had a degree of independence that those without property or access to arable land did not have. Moreover, property holders enjoyed a particular status in their communities and held political rights to participate in local government councils that the propertyless did not have. Thus, such small-propertied industrial workers had incentives, and within certain limits, the capacity to pursue a career as an independent producer in industry that gave them extremely little remuneration, rather than go into factory work. Certainly, the premium the specialized regional industries placed on rapid change and craft skill subsidized this inclination for small-scale production. But, the subjective dimension of status associated with property should not be underestimated. It seems to have been associated with a deeper cultural attachment to autonomy. Regularly, small firms were founded, expanded, and then spun off new shops because the dependent craft workers desired to make themselves independent.[71]

Movement and change among the small- and medium-sized craft producers was the foundation for stability within the regional system. Countless success stories match just as many failures. Alfred Marshall described the growth of systems of this kind as resembling a forest with new saplings continually emerging within and out of the old and dying trunks of trees. Craftsmen strove always to be employers, yet spent much of their lives also as employees: either by subcontracting with another craftsman in the town or by actually moving into a nearby workshop when times were tough, only to leave again when things looked better.[72]

This process not only increased the number of independent firms that existed in a region, it also often led to the broad diversification of the industrial base. Specialists within one industry, such as hammer works in the cutlery industry, used their knowledge of their subspecialty to produce related products, in this case machine tools, in entirely new industrial sectors. Regions, such as that around Aue in the Erzgebirge, which had been relatively dominated by one industrial specialty (in this case *Tuch* or cotton cloth), became during the nineteenth century centers for a variety of manufacturing industries: bedsheets, textile machinery, machine tools, lead-production machinery, smoking-pipe-head manufacture, and a variety of woven cotton specialties.[73] Similar stories of regional industrial diversification can be told about Württemberg, Baden, Thüringen, and other regions in the Rhineland, such as Mönchengladbach–Viersen–Rehydt and the Wupper Valley.

The trend over the course of the 19th century was for development within these regions to concentrate increasingly in cities and rural towns. In many cases, clusters of towns, such as Stuttgart, Cannstatt, and Vaihingen in Württemberg or Elberfeld–Barmen in the Rhineland, by the first quarter of the 20th century had grown to be so densely interconnected by networks of producers that they effectively constituted single urban agglomerations. The development of industrial towns in rural regions in Württemberg occurred, according to Megerle, because industrial producers could not lure workers off the land to the city, so they took their establishments to the towns in the countryside. But it is just as plausible to argue that the growth of rural towns in Württemberg resulted from the indigenous growth of already existing artisinal and homework workshops.[74] This is broadly consistent with Schmoller's observation that German industrialization had not focused primarily on large cities, but on small- and medium-sized ones, due to the importance of small- and medium-sized artisinal specialists in regional industrial production.[75]

New forms of administration and governance

These changes in the technology, organization, location, and composition of production were combined with parallel changes in the way in which production was governed. The roles played by each of the key actors in the previous *Gewerbelandschaft* economy – merchant–capitalists, outworkers, and regional governments – were completely transformed and relations among the new roles were recalibrated. New actors in the administration process emerged: the independent "undertaker" or entrepreneur and the wage laborer.[76] Markets began to play an important role in the coordination of relationships between regional producers. As part of the emergence and diffusion of markets, a number of new institutions were created to organize the way in which the key inputs of technological know-how, skilled labor and investment capital were generated and distributed within the specialized industrial districts. Throughout these processes of change, regional governments acted as important advocates and regulators and were responsible for the institutionalization of decentralized industrialization.

The greatest changes in the direct administration of production resulted from self-blocking tendencies within the governance structure of the putting-out system. In the most general sense, the radically dispersed structure of control in the system undermined itself because it separated risk so dramatically from production. If British factory-produced wares proved to be more competitive than those produced under the putting out system, the merchant–capitalist (holder of the capital), simply had to find an alternative form of investment. He was in no way committed to industrial production. Only the outworkers had that responsibility, and they did not have the capital to adopt the new mechanized machinery needed to compete with British products. Those who had capital did not have to invest it. Those who needed to invest, had no capital. Such a system could not survive the important challenges posed by the emergence of British competition.

In the regions under discussion, the adjustment process involved bringing risk and production more closely together. Either a merchant capitalist would decide to invest in a new technology, such as spinning machinery, and become himself an industrialist, or an outworker or group of outworkers would gain access to capital, perhaps from a speculating merchant-cum-banker or by pooling assets, and use that money to purchase technology. In either case, with the growth of mechanization, responsibility for production became increasingly tied to the figure responsible for investment.[77]

Bound up with this process, of course, was the emergence of wage labor. Owners of production facilities employed nonowners to work in them. In the case of factories, such as the spinning mills, this led to the creation of classic capitalist power relations in which the power of the property owner was pitted against the relative value of the skills of an individual laborer. In urban areas, where the factory workers were recruited from dispossessed parts of the rural population or from the equivalent urban population, this structural inequality was compounded by a social one in which the propertyless and propertied occupied very different social positions and had different political rights. In smaller specialized workshop operations, however, this basic structural relation was tempered by the relative social equality of the employer and employee, and by the high degree of circulation of owners in and out of wage labor.[78] Thus, in the urban factories the principle of hierarchy emerged as a governance principle in production, whereas in more specialized workshops the governance of production was more collaborative and guided by mutual dependence and respect.

Nevertheless, in both cases the fact that firms pursued strategies in the market that involved rapid product change and produced products that required considerable skilled input provided workers with considerable direct power over the production process inside of firms. If the owner of capital was not also a fellow worker, he was often completely dependent upon skilled production workers' knowledge of the machinery in the production process to accomplish rapid product changes. If the owner of capital was a fellow worker, the process of production likely presupposed cooperation among skilled colleagues. In this way, wage workers, particularly the skilled, played an important role in the management and governance of flexibly specialized production.

These developments away from the governing practices of the putting-out system were associated with additional ones. The market, for example, emerged as an important coordinating mechanism in production. With the merchant–capitalist (functionally) gone, outworkers (or subcontracting workshops) did not receive materials delivered to them as they had in the Verlag system; instead they had to purchase their own material inputs. Even in those cases where there was no mechanization in the artisan shops within these regional systems, the orientation and direct sensitivity of producers to the market was increased dramatically.

There was an important paradox in these developments. The control of individual producers over the production of their particular product was increased, but centralized coordination of regional production was dissipated. Rather than rely on the merchant–capitalist to coordinate their output in the production, say, of a lace and silk hat, a piece of furniture, or a musical instrument, producers gradually came to deal with one another as independent specialists, each capable of performing a crucial operation in the production of a regional product. The new relations were contractual, that is to say, they were market relations. Yet because the regional product was often of high quality and always highly changeable, relations between producers were not established simply by the pure calculation of ideal typical market actors. Instead, business relationships were most often established through negotiation that produced a mutual understanding of common ends. Frequently, once established these shared understandings were maintained and monitored by ties of honor and loyalty. The administration of production in the new system was thus both without a clear directing center and embedded in a fabric of relations in which market rationality, shared understanding, honor, and, monitoring were inextricably intertwined.

These changes were accompanied by the creation of a number of new institutions designed to help decentralized producers acquire the capital, labor, and technical knowledge they needed to carry out their flexibly specialized market and production strategies. Two sets of new institutions in particular were important: vocational and technical training institutes and cooperative regional banks.

All of the important districts of industrial production – Württemberg, Saxony, the individual districts within the Rhineland (Krefeld, Mönchengladbach, The Wupper Valley, Remscheid, etc.) – witnessed the creation of institutes dedicated to expanding the technological capacities of the regional industrial producers. Such institutes conducted research, experimented with new products and materials, and trained technicians and engineers for local firms. The impetus for the creation of these institutes, in the first instance, came from the local producers. Producers in Reutlingen in Württemberg, for example, established an institute devoted to the development of new textile products (new materials, weaves, dyes, etc.) and production techniques in the 1850s. Silk producers in Krefeld and textile producers in Mönchengladbach also established similar institutes.[79] The edge-tool producers in Remscheid established an institute for specialty steel research.[80] Small metal-products producers formed an institute in Siegen to attend to metallurgical problems (Fachschule für Kleineisenindustrie).

To understand how groups of independent producers could act together to create institutions for their collective benefit, one has to appreciate the decentralized, interconnected and fundamentally regional character of production in these districts. It was simply not the case that each individual producer looked upon its business as a neoclassical economist would, i.e., as an island in a sea of sovereign firms in which each completely assumed all of the costs of production and development in their business. On the contrary, each producer understood itself as a specialist among specialists, all of whom together were engaged in the production of the output of an industry. What mattered was that the industry remain competitive, that it had the capacity to continuously acquire new technologies, product ideas, and engineering skills. For individual producers, this was a collective, industrial, regional problem, not an individual one.

This orientation was at work in the formation of an institutional framework for the training of skilled labor as well. Skilled labor was an indispensable input in region-based specialty production. Individual producers depended upon it, and because there was so much mobility among and between firms, regions depended upon the generality of training standards. Traditionally, these problems of supply and standardization were solved by the master–journeyman system in the artisan guilds and through the generational devolution of craft knowledge within the families of outworkers in traditional craft districts (e.g., in the Black Forest, families making cuckoo clocks). As early as the 1830s, it became clear that these traditional mechanisms needed to upgrade themselves in the rapidly developing technological environment. Master craftsmen in many districts began to establish "continuation schools" which required journeymen apprentices to attend school after hours or on the weekend to receive additional technical training. Many industrial employers, who often themselves were not easily distinguished from the artisans, cities, and regional governments welcomed and in some cases participated in and subsidized the continuation schools.

But by the late 19th century, it became clear that such informal arrangements were faltering and that the strain on the artisans was too great for them to provide such services without systematic public support. In the end, the dual system of training and continuing schooling was legally institutionalized in 1897, because the Imperial government became persuaded that preserving a place for the artisans and the specialized industrial producers its training efforts supplied would provide a bulwark in society both against creeping proletarianization and socialism and against monopolization in industry. No one could become a skilled worker in Germany without certification by a master artisan and his Chamber, and all businesses were legally compelled to release their workers during normal hours for school attendance. In the Weimar Republic, it became clear that despite this subsidization the demand for skilled workers in industry could not be filled by the artisans alone and the jurisdictional certification capacity within the dual system was extended to Chambers of Industry and Commerce as well. The significance of this system of vocational training for decentralized, small firm based production cannot be overemphasized. It distributed the costs of training among artisans, industrial firms, and the state, and thus effectively socialized the cost of a crucial input for specialized regional economies.[81]

As with the supply of technological know-how and vocational training, the specialized producers in the industrial districts also found that in order to ensure an adequate supply of investment capital into their regions, they had to create organizations, in this case cooperative banks (*Genossenschaftsbanken*), that would shape the way in which the regional capital market functioned.[82] With the extension of the railroads and the progressive lifting of trade restrictions throughout Germany between the 1830s and the 1860s, intraregional trade increased significantly, leading to increases in regional demands for credit.[83] But small- and medium-sized specialist producers could not easily find credit because their rates of profitability and growth tended to be lower than those in rapidly growing industries, such as steel, coal, and railroads, or into types of businesses that enjoyed high rates of profitability, such as mechanized factories.[84]

Ultimately, smaller industrial and craft producers concluded that if they wished to survive in the new competitive environment, they would have to create institutions that would solve the problem of their access to capital. The most famous, though not the only, proponent of cooperative banks as such a solution was the liberal lawyer Hermann Schulze-Delitzsche.[85] He conceived of the small producer, artisan, and skilled wage worker all as having common interests and argued that they could collectively embrace industrialization and adapt its principles to their advantage. His view comes out clearly in a speech to a meeting of German artisans and workers in 1853:

> Rather than complain about the invasion [*Eingriffe*] of the factory and trade, of the superiority of capital, one should take control of the advantageous aspects of factory production and commercial organization and make capital work to ones own advantage.[86]

Schulze-Delitzsche believed that this kind of adaptation should be organized through the principles of self-help and mutual aid.[87] The credit unions that were eventually created – there were 80 Volksbanken by 1859 with 18,000 members – pooled the resources of producers in a given area, and then circulated funds among banks in the region, usually through the creation of a regional "central" clearing bank (*Verbandskasse*). This structure created a kind of closed money system that made it possible to make credit available at rates beneath those that could be obtained from commercial banks.[88] Cooperative banking spread quite rapidly. By the 1880s, cooperative banks had established themselves as foundational institutions in the emerging decentralized industrial regions. The first cooperative banks in Württemberg were established during the 1850s, but the movement really started to gain intensity during the 1860s, after the regional government lifted all remaining restrictions on trade. By 1900, there were 112 cooperatives of this kind in the Kingdom of Württemberg alone. In 1895, the Prussian state government helped create a Central Bank for Cooperative Societies (Centralgenossenschaftskasse) in Berlin. This central bank pooled the capital from the local cooperative banks to provide the economic and social interests served by those banks even more clout in the credit markets. By World War I, cooperative banks were beginning to be able to perform all of the banking functions that the great commercial banks in Germany provided, and yet they never abandoned their commitment to the economic health of the industrial *Mittelstand*.[89]

Finally, in all of these processes of change and institutionalization, regional governments played an important role in the newly emerging regional industrial economies. But to understand the administrative role of regional states in these areas, it is important to see that as a result of the profound political developments in late 18th and early 19th century Germany and Europe, as well as the changes brought on by the challenge of British industrial competition, the various regional governments became involved in their economies for very different reasons than those that had guided their involvement in the old *Gewerbelandschaften*. Three things in particular changed the terrain and even the identity of regional governments: 1) changed political boundaries, 2) peasant emancipation, and 3) considerations of a united Germany.

First, the victory of Napoleon over the combined German states of the Holy Roman Empire resulted in a radical political restructuring of German regions. After the Peace of Westphalia in 1648, there were nearly 1,800 more and less politically autonomous units governing German territory. After 1815, this number had been reduced to 36. Most of the *Gewerbelandschaften* of concern to us here were grouped into larger political units: Württemberg was enlarged to cover the industrial districts of south Württemberg, Schwäbische Alb, and the Stuttgart area. Baden, prior to 1806 a small duchy, was even more radically enlarged to incorporate both the Black Forest and the area around Heidelberg Mannheim. The Duchies of Berg and Jülich and the Archbishopric of Cologne were incorporated into Brandenburg Prussia. The Kingdom of Saxony, on the other hand, lost a large chunk of its fertile northern flatland to Prussia (i.e., the area that came to be known as the Saxon Province).[90]

The most significant change bound up with these changes in political geography was the separation of political power from property ownership. Previously, political boundaries were identical with those of feudal obligation: princes were also principal landowners. Outworkers in the *Gewerbelandschaften* took political regulation seriously because it came from the authority that also regulated their rents. After 1806, the indirect dependence of rural producers on political authority was severed. Political power in Württemberg, Baden, and Saxony came to be based on a constitutional authority, which represented a set of compromises between the various estates of the realm: nobility, townspeople, peasants, and small holders. Legitimacy of power had increasingly to be created and recreated; it was no longer attributed.[91]

This task was complicated by the emancipation of the peasantry. Promulgated by or after the example of the Napoleonic victors, peasant emancipation created a large class of independent "free" producers, very often half engaged in agriculture, half in industry, with ambiguous obligations toward authority. The states needed to retain the allegiance of these producers in order to maintain their power.[92]

Finally, a third pressure confronting the regional German governments during the 19th century was the specter of German unification and the relationship of the regional political economy to a national or federal one. The dilemma here was a simple one: if the regional government did not seek to ally itself with the German nation, it would be swallowed up by the rest of Europe; if it did ally itself with the German nation, it stood to be swallowed up by the nation itself. Hence, all regional governments were concerned with protecting their autonomy and enhancing their position within the emerging national entity.[93]

Given these three political changes in the first half of the 19th century, the performance of the regional economy became extremely crucial for the regional authorities. On the one hand, the government needed to make sure that its economy remained competitive in the inter-German and World economies. If it did not, it would lose revenue, its people would suffer unemployment and hardship, and, significantly, it would lose leverage in inter-German political battles over how the German polity and economy should be defined. Bad in themselves, all of these outcomes carried the additional disadvantage of making the emergent society more difficult to govern. On the other hand, if the regional governments indiscriminately imported or allowed for the importation of the new technologies and principles of organization from Britain, it faced two possible problems. One, industrial competition and the emergence of centralized factories created the possibility that important private concentrations of power could emerge that could challenge the autonomy of central political authority. And, second, the experience of Britain demonstrated to the governments that the effects of centralized factory production on the living conditions of working people could be devastating.[94] Thus, governments wanted both to promote industrialization in the interest of prosperity and welfare, and yet they wanted to ensure that technology and capital diffused widely in the regional economy so that the decentralized small- and medium-sized actor character of production would be preserved.

Practically, these sets of concerns resulted in the creation of communal savings banks (*Sparkassen*) focused on the provision of capital and infrastructure to small- and medium-sized industry and crafts, and in the development of quite extensive industrial and technology policies for regional industries. Savings bank legislation was first passed in Prussia after 1816 and then soon in other German states. The legislation gave cities the right to establish simple savings banks to provide security to depositors and to pool capital for the locality. Funds were initially used for relief for the poor and for infrastructure improvements. With the coming of industrialization, regional governments attempted to direct the lending policies of these banks in ways that would block the proletarianization of industry (for fear of fanning the growth of socialism) and the concentration of industry (to avoid the emergence of strong private actors that would challenge their authority). During the 1840s, the banks were permitted to make personal loans for the first time. But at the same time, states placed limits on savings deposits in order to ensure that the banks would be oriented toward smaller producers. Such banks and their infrastructure and middle class lending orientations grew steadily throughout the 19th century, though, as the parallel growth of the cooperative banks outlined above indicates, savings bank lending alone was not sufficient to cover small-scale industry and craft credit demand. By the 1920s, savings banks were able to perform nearly all of the functions of commercial banks and were connected throughout Germany by central check clearing houses.[95]

In addition to Savings banks, many regional governments attempted to use industrial policies to further the development of their regional industries. In many cases, the original impetus to encourage industrialization was not competition from outside manufactures but the weakness of agriculture. As Kiesewetter has recently shown, the Kingdom of Saxony could not feed its population with its domestic agricultural output alone and hence viewed its regional industry literally as a way to feed the population. The primary vehicles of support for industry from the Saxon government were measures aimed at the diffusion of know-how and the provision of public goods: the government aggressively subsidized technology transfer of all kinds into the region (e.g., by sponsoring exhibitions), sponsored technology competitions by offering prizes, subsidized expeditions to view technology in other countries, and targeted the improvement of infrastructure in the region.[96] Such policies, much as in the case of the research institutes and vocational training system described earlier, socialized much of the costs of acquiring knowledge of new technologies for small- and medium-sized producer-dominated industries and consequently had the effect of preserving the decentralized industrial structure.

The government in Württemberg also sought to encourage decentralized industrialization. Indeed, the entire early debate on industrialization in Württemberg centered on how to introduce mechanization into industry in ways that would take advantage of the uniquely decentralized structure of production that the *Realteilung* had made possible. Some of the writings are quite amazing, given the traditional view of German industrial development. Take the following statement from an 1823 report on the condition of Württemberg industry by the finance minister of the Kingdom, Ferdinand Wecherlin. After pointing out that it has become generally true throughout Germany that regional populations cannot support themselves solely on agriculture, Wecherlin argued that the special advantage of Württemberg was:

> the unconditionally permissible division of landed property. On property of paltry size, the industriousness, thrift and ingenuity of the owner blossoms. He nourishes himself in the character of a businessman [*Gewerbsmann*], indeed, he becomes ... a businessman. ... Württemberg is not distinguished by the existence of individual large factories. But all of Württemberg is a factory, a Manufactory. No matter where one looks, one finds everywhere industrious artisans, highly skilled manufacturers and thoughtful merchants. That is the character of industry in this land.

Wecherlin was proud that no one in the region was dependent upon a great factory boss, rather:

> Supported by their small farms ... they are at least able to salvage a meager existence until luck or genius brings to them better times. Our manufacturers [i.e., workers] will be neither beggars nor rabble rousers.[97]

By the 1840s the government began to become seriously involved in sponsoring technology transfer and expeditions abroad to view foreign technology and organization, and interestingly, one of the earliest government-sponsored expeditions was a research trip taken by the bureaucrat Moritz Mohl to view developments in small-producer-dominated industrial districts in France.[98] Then, through the efforts Ferdinand Steinbeis, a separate ministry was founded, the Centralstelle für Gewerbe und Industrie, which developed industrial policies, much like those already being pursued in Saxony, that emphasized constant technology transfer into the small-producer industrial structure of the region.[99] By encouraging local producers to be exposed to outside technology and organizational innovation, governments such as the Saxon and Württemberger did not want to change the decentralized regional character of production. On the contrary, they wanted to preserve and strengthen it by helping local producers adapt to the new kinds of technological possibilities emerging in the world economy.

Finally, an additional, crucial, means by which the governments were able to direct the character of industrialization was through tariffs. Drawing on the writings of List, among many others, governments in these regions carefully followed a strategy of protecting their industries as they attempted to adjust to the important competition of British producers. Much of the famous Zollverein, established in 1834, worked in this way. By constructing tariffs against important non-German producers, while at the same time allowing significant, though limitable competition among German producers, the member states in the Zollverein were able to shape the environment in which their regional producers developed.[100]

These technology policies and tariffs encouraged the traditional production forms to change, yet did not undermine the aspects of the structure that were considered to be favorable to economic and political stability. Often, as we have seen, the state would take its cue from local producers' own efforts to construct institutions that would help them collectively compete and stave off processes of concentration. Many of their initiatives were quickly and enthusiastically supported by the regional governments. The Government of Württemberg, for example, helped to subsidize the development of cooperative banks as well as technical institutes, including the one in Reutlingen.[101] Municipalities in the Western Rhineland, such as Krefeld and Mönchengladbach, also contributed considerably to the development of an educational infrastructure and to the creation of cooperatives.[102]

For the most part, this kind of communication between developing industry and the government was institutionalized through the unique institution of the Chamber of Commerce and Industry (Industrie und Handelskammer, IHK). These chambers were public bodies run by private interests in which membership was compulsory. They were mandated by the various governments (in different ways) to collect information and statistics on local industry. In some cases they even collected taxes and served as key points of exchange between industry and the state. The Chambers ensured that the state was constantly informed about the health and needs of industry while they acted as conduits to industry of information about the state's policies and interest with respect to the regional economy.[103]

As this listing of institutional developments shows, the development of decentralized industry in many ways ultimately led to the emergence of an entirely new and more complicated form of industrial order than the relatively simple order of the protoindustrial putting-out system. But, nevertheless, the important point about the transformation of the regions of decentralized production is that attempts to adapt to the challenges of new technology and organization in the international economy were not seen as inherently incompatible with the preservation of the traditional, decentralized, forms of economic order in a region. Such regions embraced both mechanization and the factory, but in ways that sought to avoid centralization in production and concentration in industry. Industrial producers and government actors together constructed institutions and policies that socialized costs and broadly distributed market and technological information.

Recomposition and stabilization, 1900–1945

The production practices and governing institutions described above were all developed during the period of industrialization and characterized order in decentralized industry up to the beginning of the 20th century. In the decade or so leading up to World War I, however, and then with great intensity during the war and the turbulent interwar period, important additional changes in the way in which decentralized production was governed began to be implemented. The key reason for this was that for producers in all industries in the decentralized regions – textiles, machinery, electro-technical, specialty steels, chemicals, toys, optical and fine mechanical equipment, etc. – the competitive environment during the first several decades of the twentieth century, and especially after World War I, began to change. Traditional markets in Germany and Europe became much more difficult to enter than they previously had been. More and more European regions were industrializing, bringing increasing numbers of producers into markets. During the early 1920s, a radical inflation led to the further proliferation of many small producers in many areas of specialty production, leading to significant overcapacity in many sectors. Then, as a result of the inflation, the banking sector was seriously weakend and domestic credit became difficult to obtain.[104] These changes in the economic environment created extremely difficult problems in the regional organization of production which, ultimately, gave rise to efforts to construct new forms of governance.

The problem in production: The character of competition among specialists and the fragility of honor-based self-restraint

By and large, production in the decentralized regions was specialty production. In the 19th century system, such production was coordinated by an inseparable mixture of market and nonmarket relations: exchanges of information, know-how, and actual products and services occurred within a market framework, but

Blending in: Decentralized industrialization in Germany 59

among producers who were at the same time embedded in negotiated relations of common understanding and interest in exchange.[105] When, for example, a producer of specialty silk in Krefeld required a particular finishing operation from a finishing subcontractor in order to make the specialty product desired, he or she had to sit down with the finisher and determine exactly what was needed and what was technically possible. The finisher learned about the changing fashions in silk product markets and the silk producers learned about the changing boundaries of the possible in silk finishing and, hence, in their own possibilities for the creation of specialized products in the future. The actual contracted exchange may have been only for the finishing work performed on the silk contractor's silk, but the exchange was much more than that, and the producers knew it. The surplus exchange was not paid for in money, but in a mutual and explicitly negotiated understanding that the realization of individual interest entailed cooperation with and obligation to one's interlocuter in production.

Interwoven social and market relations of this kind existed not only vertically, that is between producers and their subcontractors, but also horizontally in the decentralized regions. Because all in a given industry and a given region were specialists, none actually competed directly against one another. The "market" that they competed in was actually a myriad of different markets. Each firm had to continuously provide a product that no one else made, be it a silk tie with a special pattern, a special machine, a particular shape of glass, etc. In the best of times, other successful firms were not competitors, but neighbors in the market. Producers exchanged information about changes in technology and in regional taste and the character of demand among themselves and with people in the various supporting institutions, such as local research institutes, chambers of commerce, regional governments, and local banks. In many areas, if a producer was unsuccessful in developing a product for a particular season – if it did not sell or if it received few orders – the producer could become a subcontractor for another regional producer who had met with success. In such an environment, producers had an interest in sharing information. No single firm could conceive of monopolizing information, much less the market for all products within a specific industry. Self restraint in such systems was honorable. No producer wanted to breach the understandings that led to cooperation for fear of being excluded from common prosperity by the community of producers.

Vulnerability in crisis

Systems of this kind were stable only as long as there was continuous growth. Downturns in the business cycle – or worse, the conditions of domestic stagnation and international turbulence that existed throughout the interwar period – led to acute disorder among producers. Whereas in a healthy and growing market, many specialists were able to win orders for their particular specialty and spread their success through subcontracting with others, in a declining market this was not possible. Not only were producers not always able to spread their success through subcontracting, in many cases they were unable to win orders at all.

This characteristic of market relations among decentralized producers created extremely serious problems of industrial order. Rather than cooperating with each other to take advantage of an expanding pie, the highly flexible producers competed against one another in a contracting one. Firms in industries that were by nature supplier industries, such as the silk finishers, found that their customers played them off against other finishers in an effort to get the lowest possible price. Desperately in need of business, individual producers would feel compelled not only to simply play along, but to aggressively undercut their neighbor's price or delivery conditions. When there was tremendous overcapacity and no growth, producers had no incentive to do otherwise.

The result was far more damaging than a simple breakdown in market order. The degeneration of competition undermined the relations of cooperation, negotiated understanding and honor-based self-restraint that made the decentralized system work. Producers became cut off from the risk-spreading characteristics of the system. This problem of ruinous competition emerged in virtually all the decentralized regions and in all the industries in these regions. It had been a traditional characteristic of cyclical downturns during the period of industrialization, but in the first third of the 20th century the conditions that produced market chaos among specialized producers were chronic. These problems in production posed important challenges for the governance of the decentralized regional economies.

Governance solutions

In the eyes of the decentralized producers, the problem of ruinous competition stemmed from a defect in the way in which the market controlled and co-ordinated relations among producers. In the trough of economic stagnation, market regulation permitted and even encouraged firms to withdraw from the processes of negotiation that produced shared understanding, cooperation and a mutual sense of obligation. Moreover, the dynamic that market degeneration unleashed was not self-correcting. As long as the level of demand was lower than the capacity of producers in the industry to supply, the market encouraged opportunistic forms of behavior.

During the crisis of the interwar period, there were many attempts to create alternative mechanisms for coordinating producer relations and exchange which would guard against the degeneration of market order. In most cases, the problems with market organization were resolved by the construction of institutional arrangements that fostered communication while preserving the regionally embedded character of production and its governance. Lack of integration in production and a decentralized form of governance continued to characterize the new arrangements within the regions dominated by the decentralized industrial order. In an important minority of cases, however, this was not possible to achieve. In order to resolve the problems created by the dynamics of the market, producers in certain industries, in particular the chemical branch, opted to abandon the decentralized system and centralize administrative control within the institutional framework of a large corporate trust.

The many different strategies undertaken in this period may be condensed to four basic types: price cartels, term-fixing cartels, finishing associations or specialization cartels, and communities of interest/trusts.

Price cartels

A price cartel was established between producers by replacing market price setting with negotiated price setting. Crucial to these kinds of cartels was a common intraindustry standard for cost calculation. By establishing what the minimum efficient cost level in an industry was, the members of the cartelized industry could agree on a price level that brought all participants an adequate return.[106] With the level of prices set by a central organization (i.e., the cartel), a crucial dimension of competition between individual producers in the industry was eliminated.

This kind of cartel was rarely constructed among decentralized producers. In most cases it was simply impossible to arrive at a legitimate intraindustry cost standard. In industrial sectors where most of the producers were engaged in high volume, standard product production, such as the coal and steel industries in the autarkic form of order, it was generally possible to do this. But in specialist industries, firms often engaged in the construction of products so specialized that they were not only unlike others produced within its industry, but they were often unlike others previously produced within their own firm. Without a common cost standard, it was not possible to get all producers in the industry to agree on a standard for prices in the industry. The literature on cartelization in the textile and machinery industries continuously points this out in explaining the limited price cartelization in their industries.[107]

The exception to this rule were those specialist producers who, due to peculiarities in the character of their relation to the end market and their raw material and labor inputs, could calculate their costs, at least in a general way. Examples are the subcontracting industries in cotton textile finishing and cutlery.

Cotton textile finishers performed finishing operations on woven cotton products. Producers were highly specialized (in printing or coloring, by piece or in bulk, etc.). They acted almost entirely as subcontractors and were composed overwhelmingly of small- and medium-sized firms.[108] The main component of their production costs was accounted for by wages and salaries (in some cases more than 40% of the total in the late 1920s), and these levels had been set by collective bargaining since the 19th century. The price of their primary raw material inputs (dyes and other chemicals) fluctuated relatively little and contributed in any case negligibly to the final price of their product.

Even with broad specialization among cotton textile finishers, these conditions were relatively uniform and hence even in the prewar period the producers were able to stabilize their relations by establishing a system of minimum selling prices.[109] The cartels in this industry were located in specific regional markets (e.g., Mönchengladbach, Wuppertal, Saxony, Thüringen) and were comprised of all regional producers in a given specialty. The first cartel, founded in 1892 in Mönchengladbach among all materials printing and piece coloring establishments was both a cartel and a trade association: Verband Westdeutscher Stoff-Druckereien und Stück-Färbereien. During the war, the activities of all cartels in the textile finishing trades were coordinated by a central association that in 1919 converted itself into a trade association representing the interests of the cartels in legal and political matters: Gesamtverband Textilveredlungsindustrie.

An analogous form of cartelization occurred among the metalworking homeworkers and small- and medium-sized artisanal producers in the Solingen cutlery trades. Here however, instead of small- and medium-sized subcontracting shops engaged in chemical treatment, the industry was composed of artisinal outworkers making specialty knives, mostly on a subcontract basis for larger contractors. Their production costs also were composed primarily of wages. Very early in the 19th century (in the 1840s), outworkers banded together to establish a system of minimum prices to protect themselves from possible sweating from the larger contractors. Unlike the textile finishers, however, who by-and-large were composed of small- and medium-sized companies, the Solingen outworkers did not form a trade association in the process of creating a cartel – they formed a trade union.[110]

Despite the different forms of organization in the silk and cutlery trades, each aimed at achieving the same result: controlling competition and lifting the setting of prices out of the marketplace.

Term-fixing cartels

This kind of cartel set standard guidelines for payment and delivery schedules in an industry. In so doing, it prevented such factors from becoming objects of competition. It was the classic cartel for specialists because it controlled competition in the market without having to regulate the way that costs were calculated or the way that prices were constructed. It simply prevented selling firms from destroying one another by attempting to gain orders by offering to perform services on increasingly unreasonable terms. They also prevented customers from playing their suppliers off one another for better and better payment terms for themselves.[111]

These arrangements were very frequent among the specialized producers in the decentralized areas, particularly in the many fashion-sensitive branches of the textile industry and among specialist machinery producers. Term-fixing cartels first emerged in the early part of the 20th century on a broad scale after several rather rapid and severe downturns occurred that unleashed extremely harmful cases of market degeneration.[112] In both cases, the terms and conditions of payment were drawn up by trade associations and firms were entreated to accept them. The organizational changes in associations and industrial structure in both industries during the war and afterwards led to a broader proliferation of term-fixing cartels during the 1920s.

Blending in: Decentralized industrialization in Germany

The more important and broadly accepted such term- fixing arrangements became, the more deeply integrated the trade associations became in the maintenance of order in industries located in decentralized regions.[113] This was true from very early on in the textile trades. Regionally based term-fixing cartels and trade associations developed together around the turn of the century. In most cases the trade associations organized the cartels, but there were cases where the cartels in an industry organized a trade association to take care of their affairs, such as in the silk weaving industry.[114]

In the machinery industry, on the other hand, the establishment of term-fixing cartels did not occur in any significant way until the 1920s. These cartels were encouraged by the trade association, the Verein deutscher Maschinenbauanstalten (VDMA). The role of this trade association in the industry in the 1920s was a fairly significant departure from past practice. Before the war, the VDMA represented primarily the interest of the large autarkic machinery producers. During the war, however, the association was entrusted with the responsibility of organizing the procurement of government wartime machinery needs. A dense internal network of cartels and associations was created within the VDMA itself to organize the machinery industry. This extended the influence of the VDMA into areas of the German economy that it had previously stood outside of. During the twenties, this war time structure turned to the problems of overcapacity and instability that plagued the industry. The maintenance of term-fixing cartels was one of its primary activities.[115] This shift in the activities and responsibilities of the association was also reflected in its national-level lobbying activities. As the 1920s progressed, the VDMA's former identification with the large autarkic producers gave way to a distinctive small- and medium-sized producer orientation.[116]

Finishing associations (specialization cartels)

This form of organizational alternative to the market was in the interwar period widely accepted in many branches of the machinery industry and other similar highly specialized, mostly capital goods producing industries, such as the electrotechnical industry, fine mechanical, and optical industries. Finishing associations implemented stronger forms of control over competition in the industry. In many cases they were responses to the incapacity of term-fixing cartels to eliminate competitive poaching of orders in a market environment characterized by overcapacity and stagnant growth.

In pure form, finishing associations were specialization cartels.[117] Member firms agreed to specialize in one or several lines of a product (e.g., particular machine tool types, such as lathes) while ceding other lines to other members of the association. The bottom line of these agreements was that all parties would agree not to produce other members technologies, even in bad periods of the business cycle.

Although there are important examples of such specialization cartels strictly conceived, such as the machine tool cartel known as VDF (Vereinigte Drehbankfabriken), which coordinated the product offerings of three producers of lathes, such arrangements were more the exception than the rule.[118] In most cases the specialization agreements were not codified in law because the evolution and change in technology was typically so completely fluid that the construction of a legal arrangement would have only substituted rigidity for instability. Instead, firms simply agreed to commit themselves to continual negotiations over the definition and demarcation of markets between themselves.[119]

The benefits of these arrangements were great. They eliminated competitive poaching. Highly flexible firms with talented skilled workers were forced to channel their flexibility and concentrate their energies on a particular market segment. In addition to moderating competition among decentralized producers in general, finishing-association arrangements also reduced the level of production capacity for each type of product. Before the specialization arrangements, highly flexible industries such as the machinery industry had many producers who could potentially enter almost any machinery market. Hence, the potential capacity in any given line of machinery technology was quite high. The worse the market environment, the more this potential overcapacity became an actual problem as firms desperately sought to win orders. Specialization agreements put a stop to these practices, and hence prevented the potential capacity in any given sector from becoming the actual capacity.

Even though participation in a specialized confederation brought stability to a given branch of industry, it also increased the individual risk a firm confronted. By participating in a finishing association, a firm was forced to remain innovative or leave the industry. The structure of this arrangement gave participating firms an incentive to cooperate (isolation from others in a specialization arrangement would be no better than the conditions the firm confronted in ruinous competition). The key problem in the establishment of finishing associations, then, was to devise stable nonmarket mechanisms that would take account of, foster, and protect this interest in cooperation.

As in the case of term-fixing cartels, much of this burden fell on the trade associations.[120] First, they provided an essential forum for member firms to meet and negotiate the terms of their mutual specialization. In the machinery industry this took place in what is still today referred to as the Norm Committee (*Normenausschuss*).[121] Second, the trade association played a supportive role in a wide range of service areas that could not be covered by individual firms alone. For example, they provided market information to firms, especially for exports, and made legal information available on German and foreign laws regulating industry and competition. Third, the trade association helped coordinate the relationship between individual member firms and other institutions in the decentralized industrial order. For example, joint research projects between machinery makers and textile producers were organized in research institutes, such as those in Mönchengladbach, Krefeld, and Reutlingen.[122] Gradually, the trade association began to perceive its role as an information broker in a decentralized system. By identifying holes or weaknesses in the know-how base of its members, it dedicated itself to constructing linkages between the firms and needed sources of information.

It was not only the trade associations, however, that carried the full burden of

Blending in: Decentralized industrialization in Germany

cultivating cooperation and tempering the character of competition. Once agreement on the lines of specialization within a given branch were achieved, cooperation could be cemented in a variety of ways. In many industries, producers often banded together to jointly market their wares in export markets by setting up legally independent sales companies.[123] A well-known example of this was the Unionmatex trading company which sold the products of a group of specialized textile machinery producers in Mönchengladbach and Wuppertal. Each of the participants in the trading company produced a special product that did not compete with any of the others, and the Unionmatex enabled the producers as a group to bid on the construction of entire textile mill complexes in developing-country markets overseas and in eastern Europe.[124] Similar arrangements emerged in many industries for purchases of raw materials. This was especially true of the textile trades.

The cases dealt with thus far are all examples of how producers within the decentralized industrial order were able to amend the institutional character of order in their region-based systems to successfully resolve problems that a change in the environment had revealed. In each case, producers discovered solutions that perpetuated the centerless character of administration and dis-integrated nature of production typical of the decentralized form of order. Indeed, by transforming the role of the trade association, it is possible to say that governance in industry became even more decentralized.

Communities of interest

But the examples given above do not exhaust the possible ways that producers within the decentralized order found to resolve the problem of competitive instability and market breakdown. Other solutions were implemented, but they differed from the ones just named in that they involved not a preservation of the principles of decentralized industrial order, but an abandonment of them. This was the case with the formation of communities of interest and trusts.

In certain branches of industry, especially in the chemical trades, producers essentially opted for institutional solutions in which all matters relating to production and its governance were shifted inside the framework of a giant firm. The new institutional structure systematically removed itself from the relationships of decentralized administration and dis-integrated production that were the hallmark of the regionally embedded decentralized industrial order.

The dye producers in the chemical industry within decentralized areas provide a good example of this phenomenon.[125] Manufacturers of coal tar based dyes for the textile industry, from a variety of different decentralized regions (the Rhineland, Hessen, and Baden), had formed special arrangements with one another (known as *Interessengemeinschaften*, or IGs) before World War I to coordinate the production of dyes and other chemically related products, especially fertilizers. The two major IGs were between Bayer (of Elberfeld and Leverkusen), BASF (of Ludwigshafen), and Agfa (of Berlin), and between Hoechst (of Hoechst/Frankfurt), Cassella (of Frankfurt), and Kalle (Wiesbaden).[126]

Each firm within the community of interest specialized in a particular regional market. The product range of each firm had distinct strengths, but there was considerable overlap in production. The firms retained full legal independence, but all profits were pooled together and distributed among the members according to a specific formula. Aside from this last factor, the structure of a community of interest did not differ significantly from that of a finishing association, except that the participants were legally obligated to participate in the arrangement.

Two factors encouraged producers to adopt such methods of coordination. Specialized producers in chemicals, as in other specialized industries, benefitted from the exchange of know-how with other firms. Such exchange in the chemical industry literally acted as a process of cross-fertilization and led to the creation of new products. A unique feature of specialist exchange in the chemical industry was that know how both about products and the processes that manufactured them were patented. This meant that know-how exchanges, which in other specialist industries were simply governed by relations of trust and mutual interest and obligation, were in the chemical industry governed by law and proprietary interest. When one combines this latter factor with the need of specialists to exchange know-how about their markets and products to foster innovation, it becomes clear why the legal community of interest structure would be the form of cooperation chemical producers would adopt.[127]

But, additionally, the capital-intensive character of the process also encouraged producers to make these explicit cooperative arrangements on a very large scale. Because chemical processes, even in specialty areas, and even before World War I, involved continuous process flow production, firms needed to have a stable market. This was not possible if firms were fighting over their right to use patented products and processes in their own operations because, as in other areas, firms would undercut their competitors in order to keep their expensive production processes running. To avoid these problems, chemical producers struck agreements with major competitors that both moderated and controlled competition. But the formal legal character of these arrangements meant that the only way for a firm to enhance its possibilities for new products and specialties was to include as many producers in the formal agreement as possible. This explains why most chemical communities of interest were so large and diversified.

By 1913, the German coal tar dye industry was the largest in the world: it controlled approximately 88% of the world's chemical dye production.[128] The war gave considerable stimulation to foreign chemical producers and thus encouraged the German firms to continue to improve their scale economies and seek ways to stabilize their domestic relations even further. During the war (1916), the two IGs, along with two other major independent firms[129] were fused into one very large IG known as the Interessengemeinschaft der deutschen Teerfarbenfabriken. Again, this community of interest brought the firms together into a profit- (and loss-) sharing consortium, but it did not strip the participating firms of their independent legal status.

German chemical producers' fears for their relative position in world markets during the war turned out to be vindicated. By 1924, the German share of world dye-stuff production had fallen to 46%, while the United States' share grew to 20%, the United Kingdom's grew to 12%, and France's increased to 9%. The German share still exceeded that of the three victors of the war, but it was a significant relative shift in their position in the market. It soon became apparent to the leading managers in the participating firms of the IG that the capacity of their production facilities needed to be rationalized and brought into line with the relative German share of the world market.[130]

The problem was that they could not achieve that kind of consolidation in the form of an IG. Dr. Carl Bosch, Chief Executive of the new company that emerged out of this set of difficulties, I.G. Farbenindustrie AG, explains quite clearly the dilemma the community of interest confronted:

> When one is in a situation where 50% of sales has been lost and no prospect for recovery exists, then one has to very energetically attempt to retrench, that is, close half of one's operations. At the same time, in the face of very high tariff barriers, it becomes necessary to lower production costs as much as possible. In such a situation, moreover, it becomes imperative that one proceed in a consistent and businesslike manner. All of these factors gave us an opportunity to reflect upon ourselves as a company. This brought us very rapidly to the conclusion that our traditional form of *Interessengemeinschaft* would be incapable of implementing the organizational changes necessary for our restructuring. After overcoming tremendous resistance and objections, we decided on a structure of total fusion.[131]

The fusion that created the IG Farbenindustrie AG (IG Farben) in 1925 consolidated the assets of all of the prior members of the community of interest into one of them, BASF (Bosch's firm). The old firms were dissolved and their various operating units grouped into regionally organized production divisions.[132] Each plant within an individual production division was allowed to produce only one kind of dye: e.g., the plant in Ludwigshafen produced only indanthren dye; the works at Hoechst, outside of Frankfurt, produced dyes for wool and silk fabrics, etc. Even though the rationalization plans in IG Farben suffered from some of the same difficulties that characterized rationalization efforts among the large autarkic concerns it resembled, there was still a net reduction in capacity within the industry.[133]

The case of IG Farben is important for a number of reasons. Most importantly, it shows how the structures of decentralized industrial order are capable of being reproduced among producers in an industry only when they allow those producers to resolve the particular problems encountered in production and its administration. If producers cannot resolve their problems in a decentralized way – or if they have both the incentive and possibility to resolve those problems in a centralized way – they will abandon the principles of organization that constitute the decentralized industrial order. There is nothing given or historically inevitable about decentralized industrial order.

Much like their regional compatriots in the decentralized industrial order, the operations of the IG Farben were largely specialist operations. The organization of the company was designed to facilitate stable transfers of knowledge and patents among members of the same industry. In this sense its logic of operation was no different than the logic driving the formation of term-fixing cartels and finishing associations. The idea was to provide a kind of institutional discipline that would permit players to continue to trust one another enough to engage in constant noncontractual exchanges. The difference was that with the later forms of organization, the crucial social relations of trust and mutual interest that market competition threatened, could be restored through institutional reform in the decentralized order. In the chemical industry, because the specialist relations of trust and mutual interest were channeled into legal relationships (through patents), it became more practicable to organize the system of specialization within the institutional structure of a single firm.

Other adjustments in governance institutions during the first half of the 20th century

The formation of institutional mechanisms for controlling or replacing the operation of the market among producers in the decentralized industrial order was not the only dimension along which reform in the institutions of centerless administration took place in the first part of the 20th century. A whole set of problems combined to throw two crucial institutional actors in the system of decentralized governance into crisis: the local banking system and the municipal and regional governments.

The changes that occurred in these crucial institutional components of the decentralized industrial order all followed from a change in the constitutional structure of German politics that took place with the formation of the Weimar Republic. In an effort to increase the revenue-raising capacity of the federal government, made necessary by the heavy external reparations burden placed on Germany by the victorious powers at Versailles, the framers of the Weimar constitution reversed the lines of taxation competence that had existed in the Wilhelmine Reich. The federal government was given the legal right to issue direct taxes, while that same right was taken away from municipal and regional governments. Cities and regional governments in decentralized areas were thus no longer in the position to recycle the resources generated in their economies back into the region. Instead, tax revenues were siphoned off by the federal government and used to pay for external obligations.[134]

This problem was compounded by the fact that the weight of constitutional responsibilities distributed between the federal and local governments in the Weimar constitution were not changed. Cities and regional authorities continued to be responsible for the provision of education, police, and social welfare. Without their previous base of revenue, moreover, regional governments found it difficult to finance discretionary, but for the regional economy crucial, programs in technology transfer and development. Even in a period when the economic situation was favorable, such as the years between 1925 and 1929, this burden was difficult for the regional governments to handle. In periods of high unemployment and industrial reorganization, the system came under tremendous stress.

Throughout the Weimar period, an intense battle raged over the proper distribution of financing burdens, to no avail to the communes and the regional governments.[135] Lack of funds compelled local authorities to adopt alternative financing strategies. Most invented new kinds of taxes, which often pressed precisely those local producers their policies were often intended to help. This was particularly true after the onset of economic crisis after 1929. Revenue from land and building taxes in all regional governments (*Länder*) increased by 16.7% from 1929/30 to 1930/31 and commercial tax (*Gewerbesteuer*) was held at about the same level despite a continual fall in business activity. The regional governments of Baden, Württemberg, and Bavaria, seeking new sources of revenue, invented a slaughter tax that was subsequently adopted by all regional governments in late 1932.[136]

The two main other strategies were to expand the tax base or to borrow. Most of the major cities in Germany, particularly, though not exclusively in the decentralized areas, incorporated surrounding suburbs into their political and financial administration. Cologne incorporated the suburb of Worringen in 1922. In 1929, Krefeld was fused with Wertingen, Remscheid with Lennep and Lüttringhausen, Rehydt with Mönchengladbach, and Barmen with Elberfeld (to form the city of Wuppertal). Frankfurt increased its area by over 40% by incorporating the suburbs of Griesheim, Sossenheim, Schwanheim, and Hoechst. Stuttgart also expanded its borders throughout the Weimar period: in 1922 it incorporated Obertürkheim, Hedelfingen, Botnag, and Kaltental; in 1929 Hofen; in 1931 Rotenberg and Münster; and in 1932 Zuffenhausen.[137]

Borrowing was the other alternative open to the regional governments. During the middle, more stable years of the Republic (1925–1929) most of the borrowing that went on seems to have been to finance large projects: e.g., a large hydroelectric plant, large transport systems, etc. These were necessary projects that could not be funded out of normal revenues without imposing difficult austerity.[138] The magnitudes involved were impressive. Communes were barred from taking on foreign debt in 1927 by the central government and they still accounted for 11.9% of all German long-term debt owed to US banks between 1924 and 1929.[139]

Once the international crisis hit and rates of unemployment increased dramatically, cities, especially, began to borrow extensively from local municipally owned savings and loans (*Sparkassen*). In 1929, a law was passed that permitted savings and loans to commit up to 50% of their deposits to consolidate consumer debt, but Harold James claims that in many cities the level of borrowing exceeded that.[140]

This fiscal squeeze on the local banking system disrupted the main markets for capital for the small- and medium-sized producers in the decentralized industrial order. The *Sparkassen*, along with the cooperative banks, had developed as major sources of funds for small- and medium-sized industry before World War I. But during the Weimar Republic they were never able to regain their former position. Because they depended upon small depositors for their capital, the *Sparkassen* were hurt by the inflation. According to James, "after 1924 the small depositors, frightened by the experience of the German inflation and having lost almost everything, were reluctant to loan again."[141] Prussian *Sparkassen* had only a little more than half (61%) the deposit volume in 1929 that they had in 1913. When one couples this with the desperation of the communes in the local financial markets, it becomes clear that the local banks had little surplus capital to make available to specialized small- and medium-sized producers seeking to expand.

Given these difficulties, disenchantment with the Weimar regime among producers within the decentralized industrial order began to grow. It is likely that this disenchantment contributed to the broad appeal that the Nazi party held in many decentralized areas. Nazi ideology attacked the Weimar democracy and its constitution. Moreover, the early victories and main organizing commitment of the Nazi party in the late 1920s and early 1930s focused on winning representation at the level of city government. And many of their earliest victories were in decentralized areas, such as Thüringen and Saxony. The city governments in Remscheid and Solingen both became politically polarized: Solingen was governed in the late 1920s by a communist mayor who was later overwhelmed by the Nazi political victory. Württemberg and Baden showed moderately strong support for the Nazis (Baden was a bit more solidly Nazi than Württemberg).[142]

The Nazis' appeal in the decentralized areas was straightforward. They cultivated a sense of dissatisfaction among the decentralized producers and blamed their economic difficulties on the large banks and the central state. Their popularity was not based on a promise to return the constitutional structure of the Reich to the status quo ante. Rather, it was based upon an appeal to transform the political structure of the Reich so that it represented the interest of small- and medium-sized producers.[143]

But disenchantment with the existing regime is only a necessary, not a sufficient, factor in explaining support for the Nazis. In the strongly Catholic areas in the decentralized industrial order, i.e., Cologne, Mönchengladbach, and Aachen, for example, producers proved remarkably resistant to Nazi appeals.[144] Significantly, their anti-Nazism was not necessarily driven by love of the Weimar system. These areas were centers of Rhenish separatism and Catholic socialism. Both of these ideological tendencies placed a central emphasis on the importance of local self-government, which the Weimar constitution had taken away.[145]

Though the evidence linking disenchantment with the Weimar regime among the decentralized producers with the support of those producers for the Nazis is mixed, it is clear that once the Nazis had achieved power, the new regime did do many things to support the producers within the decentralized industrial order. The Nazi regime converted all trade associations in the German economy into agents of the Nazi state. Each was given responsibility for the organization of cartelization in its industry and, relatedly, with the distribution and allocation of raw materials. The converted trade associations, known as *Wirtschaftsgruppen* (economic groups), were thus capable of arranging strict specialization cartels in those industrial sectors and branches where previously they had been slow to take root.[146]

Blending in: Decentralized industrialization in Germany

The *Wirtschaftsgruppen,* in conjunction with Nazi war planners, also rewarded decentralized producers with extensive defense-related contracts.[147] In at least one case – the machine tool industry – the Nazi planners fostered the development of advanced mechanical automation technologies by the small- and medium-sized machine tool producers in Württemberg, rather than among the larger autarkic machine tool producers in Bielefeld and Berlin.[148]

It is important to emphasize that in restructuring and reproducing the decentralized industrial order, the Nazi regime also transformed it. Capital and other resources were made available to decentralized producers at a local and regional level, but the old institutions that had allowed producers to govern the allocation of these resources themselves – city and regional governments, local banks, and voluntary trade associations – were dismantled or allowed to atrophy. In order to preserve decentralization within the industrial order, political decentralization was abandoned. The "decentralized" system that emerged thus had a distinctly Nazi character, which in a practical, political realm differed considerably from the participatory, locally autonomous systems of the past.

Conclusion: Alternative industrialization

The main aim of this chapter has been to document the existence and describe the development of a coherent form of regional, small- and medium-sized-firm-dominated industrialization that emerged in a specific set of German regions in the 18th century and developed and evolved throughout the 19th and early 20th centuries. The distinctive feature of this form of industrialization is the importance of extrafirm forms of governance in the way in which decentralized production was organized.

The decentralized form of industrial order confronted head-on all of the main technological and organizational challenges of the classical era of European industrialization. Some of the pieces of that challenge were assimilated into the decentralized framework of industrialization (especially particular technologies), while in other cases, producers within that framework were able to devise ways to avoid direct confrontation with the challengers. This form of decentralized industrialization was so successful and robust that by the beginning of the 20th century, the biggest challenges facing actors within the order did not come from abroad, or from larger producers elsewhere in Germany. Rather, the major challenges stemmed from the need to find governance solutions to competitive dynamics generated by the structures and strategies of decentralized producers themselves. The solutions arrived at involved profound experiments with and struggles over the boundaries between industry, society, and politics. The next chapter will now turn to an analysis of how actors within substantively different regional contexts in Germany, when confronted with broadly similar challenges and opportunities over the same period of time, constructed a radically different form of industrialization.

3

Repositioning organized capitalism into regions: Autarkic industrial order in Germany

This chapter will cover the same historical time period as the previous one, only here the subject of analysis will be the development of what I call the autarkic industrial order. The aim of the chapter is to show that the familiar pattern of large firm based industrialization in Germany, as represented in the organized capitalism research program, was actually a *regional*, not a general national, process as that research program suggests. The chapter will also make clear that producers in the autarkic industrial order, both volume and batch producers, confronted problems of the market and in production that resembled those that confronted decentralized industrial producers, and yet, because of the different substantive situation in autarkic regions, autarkic producers handled these challenges in dramatically different ways.

The autarkic industrial order had its origins in regions in which by the beginning of the 19th century there was very little, or extremely fragile, protoindustrial activity and in which large numbers of propertyless peasants existed. Both the location and the organizational development of industry in these regions were shaped by this initial distribution of resources. As the narrative of the chapter will make clear, however, the very existence of industrialization at all in these regions was also the result of the fact that actors aggressively intervened to construct the context for industrialization. Indeed, in many, but not all, cases, early entrepreneurs explicitly set up the production of new technologies and organizational forms, such as the factory, in these regions because traditional decentralized industries were not there to obstruct them. Once set up, the growth of these new industries took place in an extremely vertically integrated way because there was very little local industrial and handicraft skill to draw on. The key feature of this regional form of industrial order is that, in contrast to the decentralized industrial order, all immediate aspects of production and its governance were centralized within the boundaries of large, vertically integrated enterprises.

The narrative challenge of this chapter is to make the reader understand a familiar story in a new way without having to provide a detailed account of the history of all the producers, sectors, and regions that the traditional story covers.[1] My solution has been to strategically contrast case studies of the origins

Autarkic industrial order in Germany

and evolution of producers in three very important industries in the regions dominated by what I call the autarkic industrial order: the iron and steel industry, light manufacturing industries, and the nonelectrical heavy machinery industry. The account of the steel industry will focus primarily on producers in the Ruhr industrial region,[2] while the machinery industry case will focus on the development of producers throughout the regions I designate as autarkic. The light manufacturing case will focus on the unique production arrangements that developed in regions that were formerly impartible-inheritance-based *Gewerbelandschaften*. The virtue in the machinery and steel cases is that they portray very large portions of what are conventionally recognized as dominant "great" industries in Germany. They are by now almost reflexively offered up as examples in discussions of the general characteristics of the German model of industrialization.[3] The light manufacturing case is inserted between the above two cases to discuss an important development that the steel industry case does not make it possible to bring out: The growth of modern dualist subcontracting relations in the context of larger series production.

The value of matching the steel and light manufacturing cases with the machinery case is that they are also conventionally understood to constitute polar types: Two are volume producers and one is a batch producer. The cases thus allow me to show that the contours of the autarkic industrial order were shaped by particular regional characteristics by addressing sectors that in the traditional understanding demarcate the outer boundaries at or between which the organizational strategies of most producers varied. If my regional argument matters in these industries, in other words, it must then matter in the others that I do not cover.[4]

The narrative of the chapter will first lay out the particular regionally distinct systems of agrarian property relations that formed the basic preconditions for the emergence of the autarkic industrial order at the beginning of the 19th century. The following three sections will then follow the evolution first of the Ruhr steel producers, then of the light manufacturing industries, and finally of the machinery producers. Each section will trace the development of each industry from their origins in the 19th century up through World War II. In a way that parallels the story told in the previous chapter, in each case an original founding period of industrial order in the 19th century will be followed by a period of important institutional adjustment in the mechanisms of governance in the early 20th century.

Regional preconditions for autarkic industrial order

The regional context was extremely different in the regions in which what I call the autarkic industrial order developed than it was in the regions dominated by the decentralized industrial order. As we saw in the previous chapter, the key feature in the regions in which the decentralized industrial order emerged was the existence of a thick network of small property holders in possession of industrial and handicraft skill and experience. This crucial base of skilled small property holders was lacking in the classical industrial regions of Germany, such as the Ruhr Valley and northern and eastern Westphalia, the Prussian province of Saxony, Berlin, Silesia, and many of the old medieval court and trading cities, such as Hannover, Kassel, Nuremberg, Augsburg, and Munich (see Maps 1 and 2 in Appendix). In these regions, property relations in agriculture by the 18th century produced large and relatively productive holdings and a growing landless class. East of the river Elbe, the landless were dependent serfs working directly on large manorial farms; west of that traditional dividing line between *Guts-* and *Grundherrschaft*, such landless peasants toiled as day laborers on the farms of wealthier peasants and cottars. In all of these latter regions, *Anerbrecht* or impartible inheritance, was practiced on the land. But unlike the decentralized industry-dominated Kingdom of Saxony, where impartible inheritance was also the dominant practice, a substantial independent cottar class did not develop in these regions.[5]

The existence of a large surplus population with little direct attachment to the land and even less political and social status in their communities blocked these regions from being able to pursue the decentralized path of industrialization. This was true even when superficially it might appear that this could have been possible. For example, decentralized *Gewerbelandschaften* developed in a number of the areas mentioned above after the Peace of Westphalia in 1648, such as the linen industries in the areas around Bielefeld, Minden-Ravensburg, and Paderborn in Westphalia, the linen industry in Silesia, and the textile and handicraft industries in Nuremberg and Augsburg in Bavaria. But because these protoindustrial landscapes were organized on the basis of an impoverished rural propertyless class of laborers rather than rural property holders, they proved to be very fragile and incapable of adapting to the new mechanized competition of the 19th century. In the face of new competition and technologies, these traditional industries declined and the landless workers, those without feudal rights, little status in their communities, and absolutely dependent upon industrial production for their livelihood, fell into notorious misery (e.g., the Silesian weavers).[6] Thus, whereas industrial outworkers in the decentralized regions retained their ties to the land and transformed their skills in a way that perpetuated decentralized industrial practice, in the autarkic regions the landless watched their traditional skills become useless and increasingly found that they could not stay in the countryside and survive.[7]

As it turned out, these conditions were extremely favorable for the different, but more familiar, centralized factory-based industrialization that actually did occur in these regions. Large numbers of landless people formed a reservoir of potential industrial laborers that enterprising entrepreneurs in possession of new and often foreign technology and access to speculative capital could draw into new workshops and factories with the promise of work and wages.[8] The broad outlines of industrialization in these German regions have become crucial parts of the narrative repertoire of studies of political economic development in comparative politics, historical sociology, and development economics. This development occurred relatively late in the century (1830s–1870s), usually in great spurts, and often in industrial technologies borrowed from abroad that had no traditional connection to the indigenous economy. Tremendous up-front capital costs gave rise to innovative banking institutions and the whole young phoenix-like industrial system had an ambivalent yet intimate relationship to the traditional-elite-dominated state.

In contrast to the producers in the decentralized industrial order, and regardless of their sector or production strategy, the new industrial producers that emerged in these regions organized nearly all tasks directly involved with production and its governance within the boundaries of firms – hence my characterization of the industrial order as "autarkic." In using this term, however, I do not mean to imply that the autarkic firms had no extrafirm ties. On the contrary, these firms, like the decentralized producers, were embedded in a larger system of order that included, in particular, ties to universal credit banks and a variety of relations with the state, which were often very ambivalent. The point is not that these vertically integrated industrial producers had no relationship to society or politics. It is rather that because they relied so exclusively both on the factory as a cite of production and on the firm (rather than a regional system) as the organizer of numerous related production processes, marketing, and sales venues that their relationship differed systematically from that in the decentralized order. Industrialization in Germany was defined, conceptualized, and institutionalized in different ways in different regions. Let us turn now to the way in which the regional characteristics noted above resulted in this particular pattern of development in both volume production and batch/specialty production based industries.

Case studies of autarkic industrialization: Volume and batch producers

The Ruhr iron and steel industry

The emergence of the Ruhr

Prior to the 19th century, the Ruhr region[9] was traditionally free of *Gewerbelandschaften* and was primarily agricultural. The little nonagricultural activity that did exist in the region was insignificant. There were a few state-owned mining corporations that employed small numbers of people, and there was a small amount of outwork in the portions of the region that belonged to the Duchy of Mark, primarily in textiles.[10] The iron and steel industry was introduced to the region from outside. The first iron works were created at the end of the 18th century to provide for a local demand for metal parts in state workshops experimenting with the production of British-designed steam engines for use in the state mines. These early iron works were extremely small and financially unsuccessful.[11] Some were saved in the early 19th century by entrepreneurs who came from merchant families, such as the Haniels, who traditionally had little to do with industry, but who thought they could make money producing British-style machinery for the German market and thus wanted to use the iron works to supply their venture.[12] But for all that, such operations were isolated and small. As late as 1820, pig iron production in the Ruhr accounted for only about 5% of total production in the area of what would eventually become the German Reich.[13]

By the 1860s, however, the Ruhr had emerged as the dominant region of iron and steel production in Germany. Moreover, the overwhelming majority of this production was organized by joint stock enterprises financed and operated on the whole by people from outside the region employing the most advanced British iron and steel making technologies. The key to understanding why these entrepreneurs were lured out of their traditional pursuits and/or locations and into iron and steel making in the Ruhr valley is the happy coincidence of two factors: first, the growing importance of coal, with which the Ruhr region was richly endowed, in the making of iron and steel and, second, the fact that there was no traditional steel making industry in the Ruhr region.

In the very early 19th century, the smelting of pig iron could be conducted in one of two ways: either it was produced in blast furnaces fueled by charcoal or it was produced in blast furnaces fueled by coke. The conversion of that pig iron to wrought or bar iron and steel, further, was either conducted in traditional-charcoal fueled hearths or in coal fueled puddling furnaces.[14] Both of the coal-based technologies were developed in 18th century Britain and quickly replaced the charcoal-burning methods of smelting and refining iron in that country. But in Germany, the new coal-based technologies were adopted very slowly, especially in the case of the coke-fueled blast furnace. In large part, this had to do with the continued competitiveness in the early 19th century of the traditional production methods as they were practiced in the decentralized iron districts of the Siegerland, the Sauerland, the Lahn Dill region of northern Hesse, the Eifel and Huensruck regions of the western Rhineland, and parts of Württemberg, Thüringen, and Saxony. These regions produced what was considered to be a higher quality iron than the British. In the absence of significant demand for iron and steel, the drawbacks of the system vis-à-vis the new techniques – legally mandated restrictions in refinery output to regulate and conserve fuel usage in smelting and a traditionally fragmented and legally protected division of labor between forest management (for charcoal fuel supplies), ore mining, smelting, and various small hammer and rolling works meant that the districts were much better at producing specialty goods than high volume standard ones – were offset by the higher price the quality product could command on the market.[15]

Despite the competitiveness of the traditional regions, the new British technologies were revolutionary, even in Germany, because they made it possible to separate the business of producing steel from the regional way of life it had become in the ecology and political economic structures of the decentralized regions. This fact, along with the slow growth in demand for iron and steel in the early 19th century, led people outside of the traditional areas of ironmaking to speculate on the technology and, implicitly, on the money making potential of British production methods. Early Ruhr entrepreneurs, such as Friedrich Harkort, Hermann Piepenstock, and Franz Haniel, profiled themselves as experts in British technologies, at first because it gave them a market niche, but surely too they had a hope that such techniques would have considerable growth potential in Germany.[16] Though only Haniel was born in the Ruhr area (Ruhrort), the locational benefits of the Ruhr for these early pioneers was clear. The region was abundant in coal, which they needed to fuel the puddling furnaces, and it was near important and navigable waterways, which allowed them to purchase pig iron from the traditional German districts and from Belgium and Britain. Also, there was no conflict with local authorities, cooperatives, or guilds with a vested interest in making steel in a particular way, as there was in the traditional regions.[17]

These advantages became overwhelmingly attractive with the growth of the railroads during the 1840s and 1850s, which created tremendous demand for rails, ties, fastenings, wheels, and other materials. The specialized and fragmented traditional regions of production simply proved unable to keep up with the tremendous demand. Indeed, there was such a shortfall that much of the early railroads in Germany were laid with track produced either in Britain or Belgium.[18] It did not take long for it to become clear to many in Germany involved with railroad construction, such as the independent steel producers and refiners, bankers, and locomotive producers, that there were tremendous opportunities for domestic iron and steel producers if they could shift to the higher volume British methods of coke-based pig iron production and coal-fired puddling.[19]

Thus, during the 1850s many establishments employing both of these technologies were founded and in no place as dramatically as in the Ruhr. The region's total output of pig iron accounted for only 8.7% of total production in the German customs area in 1852 and then jumped to 25.7% by 1860. The number of coke fueled blast furnaces jumped from 15 in 1851 to 55 in 1870. Production of pig iron in the Ruhr grew at a yearly rate of 30.6% between 1851 and 1860.[20] Steel production in the Ruhr area also increased dramatically during this period, jumping from 37.8% of all German customs union production in 1852 to 44.9% in 1860 and then 54.5% in 1870. Revealingly, the ratio of charcoal-fueled to coal-fired puddled iron furnaces catapulted from 1:9 in 1851 to 1:99 in 1860. Twenty-one new puddling works were established in Dortmund alone between 1853 and 1857 and the total number of puddling furnaces in the Ruhr increased from 80 in 1852 to 246 in 1860.[21]

The region's older enterprises expanded tremendously in this period. Piepenstock, for example, converted his company into a joint stock enterprise (called the Hoerder Verein) and built six coke-fueled blast furnaces over the course of the decade 1851–1860 to feed his 44 puddling furnaces.[22] But the remarkable growth of the Ruhr was also driven by the founding of new enterprises. Perhaps the most important was the Phoenix Works, created in 1852 with the participation of French and Belgian capital. After some initial difficulties it became the largest producer of pig iron in the Ruhr in the 1860s.[23] The most interesting feature of the new enterprises was much like that of the old. They were primarily founded and funded by people from outside the Ruhr, who invested there in particular technologies and production organization to take advantage of a very specific kind of demand.[24]

This initial phase (*Gründungsphase*) of entrepreneurial start-ups in the Ruhr was followed by a second in the early 1870s. Like the first, the second phase was stimulated by a boom in railroad construction and the possibility of implementing a new technology, but this time the technology was the larger capacity Bessemer converter, which widely and rapidly replaced the puddling process in the Ruhr. Most of the by then already quite large and important producers in the Ruhr, such as GHH, Krupp, Phoenix, Hoerder, and the Bochumer Verein, shifted massively to the new technology and greatly expanded their production operations. The most important new companies to be founded were the Dortmunder Union, the Rheinische Stahlwerke, the Hoesch Iron and Steel Works, and the Gewerkschaft Deutsche Kaiser (later to become the August Thyssen AG). Like the earlier firms, these companies were funded by outside capital and were headed by entrepreneurs with their roots outside the region.[25]

The evolution of production in the Ruhr

This transformation of the Ruhr was driven by the desire to produce iron and steel in large quantities, and this desire drove the development of all subsequent production. The scale of production throughout the rest of the century was continually increased by the introduction of newer and more efficient steel making technologies. After the Bessemer converter was introduced in the late 1860s, it was followed by its cousin the basic Thomas converter in 1879, which enabled the Germans to produce much larger volumes with their relatively low-grade ores. By the end of the century, the Siemens–Martin "open hearth" was beginning to be adopted by producers, many of whom were already capable of producing on a scale that was unparalleled anywhere else in Europe, including Great Britain.[26] Within 50 years, the Ruhr grew from a largely agrarian region with unimportant concentrations of industry, even in relationship to the rest of Germany, into one of the largest concentrations of heavy industrial power in the world.[27]

The early speculative character and rapid pace of industrialization in the context of the local regional environment of the Ruhr led producers to organize production along lines that had no relationship either to traditional steel making in Germany or to anything that had previously existed in the Ruhr area. Producers produced, even initially, on what was a comparatively tremendous scale. They centralized and integrated many operations that in the traditional areas had been organized in a decentralized way. The major concerns, so called "*gemischten Werke*" (Krupp, GHH, Phoenix, Bochumer Union, Hoerder) all operated blast furnaces for the production of pig iron, Thomas and later open hearth furnaces for the conversion of pig iron to steel, and then a wide variety of rolling operations for the production of final products, such as steel rails. Even the less-integrated works, such as Rheinische Stahlwerk, Thyssen, and Hoesch in steel making, were more integrated than producers in the decentralized regions: Steel works all had rolling mills and hammer works for the production of finished products directly attached to them.[28]

This initial centralization did not simply come from a desire to imitate British methods. In fact, the integration of steel works with rolling mills had still not become the rule in Britain even by the beginning of the 20th century.[29] A large part of the greater centralization and integration in the early Ruhr iron and steel mills has to be explained by the lack of a regional infrastructure of experienced steel making handicraft. Investment in one technology often simply required investment in many of the attendant ones in order to be in the business at all, much less satisfy demand. In this way, regional political economy shaped not only why the technology was located in the region, they effectively ensured that it would be implemented in a centralized way.[30]

This pressure to centralize coming from the regional political economy was then reinforced by pressures to mechanize production coming from producers' desires to produce in volume and achieve economies of scale. Within each of the different branches of the steel industry, mechanization in one aspect of the production process often created bottlenecks in other parts of the process, which, in turn, stimulated further efforts to integrate, innovate, and mechanize.[31] David Landes described the way that this chain of integration and mechanization ran through a German steel producer quite nicely:

> A furnace turning out 3000 tons of pig iron a week consumed 6000–9000 tons of ore, perhaps 1000 tons of limestone and some 4000 tons of coke. It took some six hundred freight trucks, averaging 20 tons capacity, just to bring the materials to the mill.... And once there, these materials had to be fed somehow to the flames. The traditional winch and counterweight systems for hauling small tilt wagons to the lip of the furnace – supplemented on occasion by human brawn and hand shovels – were hopelessly inadequate. In their place appeared continuous conveyors, traveling cranes and suspended railways powered by electricity.[32]

The classic effect of mechanization is to transfer the operations performed by the hand of a skilled tradesman, or by a single machine operator to a machine.[33] Production in autarkic German steel mills generally followed this classic logic. The highly skilled craft of puddling was eventually replaced by the more automated Bessemer, Thomas, and Siemens–Martin processes for converting iron to steel. The skills required by the newer machines were not as high or complex. By the turn of the century, some of the achievements of the German steel producers in this area were quite impressive. For example, moving raw iron from a furnace and transferring it into a refinery so that it could be turned into wrought iron or steel was an extremely labor-intensive process, especially in the early years of using the Siemens–Martin process. As Landes shows, the iron had to be tapped, poured into molds, lifted, and broken for resmelting. To shorten the time it took to perform this procedure, Ruhr firms tried to eliminate these steps. They built huge (100–300-ton) tiltable furnaces, equipped with hydraulically or electrically powered charging apparatuses. The effect of these improvements in productivity was to cut the number of workers required per hearth by more than half and, according to Landes, cut labor costs by 58%.[34]

Many of the less-skilled jobs created ultimately were filled by migrants and immigrants, largely from agricultural regions. The industrialization of the Ruhr (as well as other autarkic regions such as Berlin, Bielefeld, or Nuremberg) was inseparable from waves of migration.[35] The first workers came from the immediately surrounding regions, where impartible inheritance had created a population of landless day laboring peasants. But once this supply was exhausted, firms drew their unskilled help from farther afield. New industrial workers came from all over eastern Germany and eastern and southern Europe. The importance of Polish workers in the industrialization of the Ruhr Valley is well known. The town of Hamborn north of Duisburg, nicely portrayed by Lucas, had the largest percentage of foreign workers in its labor force of any industrial town in the Ruhr. In 1910, over a third of the city's population (36.6%) was not German.[36]

The final characteristic of production in the autarkic order of the steel industry concerned the impact that this form of industrial development had on the relationship between autarkic firms and the regions in which they were located. Because production occurred in such a highly vertically integrated fashion, a significant population of small- and medium-sized firms (an *industrielle Mittelstand*) never developed that could provide specialty materials or subcontract work as was the case in the decentralized regions. And because producers (or the speculative capitalists they allied with) had entered the regions in an effort to flee traditional systems of industrial production, there was no blurry boundary between the industrial and agrarian sectors, as existed in the decentralized regions. The new cities in the Ruhr emerged as autonomous industrial metropolises whose economic integrity had extremely little relationship to the agrarian countryside that surrounded them.[37]

Moreover, in contrast to the decentralized regions where the regional system of production was far more than the sum of producers within it, the autarkic evolution in the Ruhr increasingly reduced the region as an economic category to that remainder which was outside the systems of production inside the imposing boundaries of the large corporate firms.[38] Location increasingly came to be understood simply as "place" and as disembodied factor costs. By the end of the 19th century, Ruhr producers were selling their products all over Germany and the world and the inputs to production that they did not supply themselves, such as iron ore and in many cases pig iron, were just as likely to be drawn from international markets as local ones. The Minette region of the Lorraine was an important source of pig iron and ore, for example, and Sweden became the Ruhr's main supplier of iron ore. The paradox contained in this process of deregionalization in production should be noted because it is at the root of my argument about autarkic industrial order. The very particular regional conditions in the Ruhr shaped the development and growth of the organization of production in a way that ultimately made its rootedness in regional peculiarities invisible and seemingly irrelevant. In many Ruhr cities, it is only a slight exaggeration to say that the autarkic steel producers were not simply part of the local economy; the local economy had become them.

This fact about the extreme integration that existed in the organization of production was also an orientation. It is what the new industrialists believed that modern industrial practice was meant to be. It shaped their strategies regarding new location. When August Thyssen wanted to expand his operations in the 1890s, for example, he selected the small village of Hamborn near Duisburg (near where the Ruhr enters the Rhein) because the land was cheap and because there was very little preindustrial trade and handicraft. Thyssen wanted to create a greenfield plant with the most modern production methods and did not wish to contend with the possible obstructionist tactics of organized artisans or experienced industrial workers that a more established center of trade would have invariably presented. He erected a set of integrated mines and factories that in the space of ten years employed over 20,000 people. The local economy was identical to the Thyssen works.[39]

Governance in the Ruhr

The framework of institutions that governed these centralized and vertically integrated production operations not surprisingly differed significantly from those that governed production in the decentralized industrial order. In the latter industrial order, many individual producers together with a host of actors in supporting regional institutions combined and coordinated their actions to conceive, produce, distribute, and sell a given product. In the autarkic regions, the vast majority of operations involved in combining and coordinating all aspects of the production and sale of a good were conducted by the individual corporate enterprise itself.

By now a considerable literature has built up on the development of the modern industrial enterprise in Germany.[40] Although this literature is largely oblivious to regional differences or even location, overwhelmingly such firms were located in autarkic regions.[41] Feldenkirchen notes that before 1914, half of the 50 largest companies in Imperial Germany were in the "heavy" industries of iron, steel, and coal.[42] Producers in the autarkic regions were world leaders in the development of the modern corporation. Many organizational innovations, such as what Kocka calls the combination of both integration and diversification (scale and scope), were developed in some cases even before the more widely known developments in counterpart institutions in the United States.[43]

With the exception of the very oldest enterprises (Krupp, Haniel, Piepenstock), most of the large autarkic iron and steel companies that emerged in the two *Gründungsphasen* were created from the start as joint stock companies. Particularly from the 1880s onwards, these enterprises developed functional departments with extensive, professionally staffed managerial hierarchies to administer production, sales, marketing, finance, research, and development.[44]

The logic behind the integration of marketing and sales was the same as that driving the integration of production. Because the new producers were fleeing the traditional systems of production, they could not rely on, and frequently became direct competitors of, the merchants who organized traditional production and sold its output. As a result, the new producers sold their own products and constructed organizations of their own that enabled them to do so.[45] Starting from this regionally induced integration, the larger the scale of production and the greater the diversification of products or the geographic reach of the markets served, the larger and more extensive the management systems, or in Chandler's language, the "organizational capabilities," of the firms became.[46]

Initially, the administrative reach of autarkic corporations also extended to areas outside the immediate problems of production and distribution, such as vocational training but, again, for similar reasons. Unlike the regions where the decentralized industrial order developed, there was a weakly developed artisanate in the Ruhr region. Perhaps even more importantly, there were clearer boundaries in this region than in the decentralized ones between the large, unambiguously industrial producers and the smaller artisan ones. So even in those autarkic cities and regions where a traditional artisanate existed, it tended to lack the capacity to train workers with the new industrial skills that the autarkic producers demanded. Thus, for much of the 19th century, large autarkic steel concerns trained many of their skilled workers "in-house."[47] Krupp even established an entire school, with 16 different classes, to make up for the fact that the local government could not even supply basic schooling to adequate numbers of workers.[48]

In itself, this was both expensive and logistically demanding and thus further contributed to the expansion of managerial organization within the enterprises. But in-house training was not without its advantages for the firms. It allowed companies to cultivate loyalty to themselves and insured that there would be a steady supply of capable employees trained in ways that were advantageous to the firms.[49] Firms such as Krupp, GHH, the Bochumer Verein, or even Thyssen's works were very paternalistic. They provided not only training but also housing and other social benefits to their workers, all to maintain their loyalty and inhibit disobedience.[50]

The authority and administrative reach of Ruhr enterprises was also sometimes crassly exaggerated by the income-based three-class voting system that organized urban self-government in the Prussian cities of the Ruhr. For example, between 1886 and 1894 in the city of Essen, Alfred Krupp's income was so much greater than all other residents in the city that he was the only voter in the first (and most powerful) voting class and thus had the power to appoint directly one-third of the administrative appointees in the city of nearly 100,000 people. The second class was composed largely of leading Krupp executives and owners and executives of other autarkic firms in the city. Managing the city, in other words, was just one more dimension in the administrative framework of Krupps' business. And as Krupp was to Essen, the Bochumer Verein was to Bochum. Large works in smaller Westphalian towns, where corporations were counted as citizens and could vote, could by the same principle completely shape the government of their communities.[51] In light of these kinds of factors, it is only with slight exaggeration that some German commentators looked upon the great autarkic enterprises as miniature "states within the state."[52]

The extent of this kind of autarky was very remarkable in the Ruhr and stands in striking contrast to the highly disintegrated forms of production and governance that existed in the decentralized regions. Nevertheless, the organizational and administrative reach of the autarkic corporations was not limitless. There were dimensions of economic process in these regions that these firms yielded to other organizations. In particular, autarkic enterprises relied on outside bankers for capital and on the regional government in Prussia for the provision of many infrastructural and educational public goods. But even here, where it might appear that relations between individual producers and extrafirm institutions resembled similar ties in the decentralized industrial order, the differences far outweighed the similarities.

Autarkic enterprise and universal credit banks. Unlike the decentralized producers, who had access to investment capital from state-supported savings banks or from collectively initiated and self-governed cooperative banks, autarkic steel producers relied on private credit banks (*Kreditbanken*). These banks were initially started by speculating merchants, such as David Hansemann and Gustav Mevissen, who in many ways engaged with the autarkic firm in the manner of present-day venture capitalists. The banks these merchants ultimately formed collected capital from a broad base of short-term commercial depositors and then distributed that capital in the form of long-term loans to industrial enterprises. These investors and their banks provided the initial capital to most of the original founding entrepreneurs in the steel industry during the successive railroad booms in the 1850s and 1870s. The large banks also financed the move into Bessemer and Thomas steel making technologies in the 1870s and 1880s. By the 1890s, however, when the next great investment boom occurred with the shift into Siemens–Martin open hearth technologies and the broad diversification into new finishing markets, the influence of the *Kreditbanken* seems to have waned. Much of that investment was financed through earnings that the producers had accumulated over the decade of the 1880s.[53]

Thus, as important as the banks were to the autarkic producers, it would go too far to claim, as many have, that the banks in any way caused the trends toward increasing bigness and concentration that took place in the steel industry.[54] Rather, it seems more reasonable to argue, as Kocka does, that "the banks acted like large flywheels; they did not initiate most changes, but, rather, reflected and strengthened existing trends."[55] The long-term stake that banks held in firms, in other words, made them servants, not shapers, of the autarkic enterprise. In any case, the growth in size of banks and concentration in the banking sector paralleled the growth in size of firms and concentration in autarkic industry. *Kreditbanken* were initially regional actors (such as the Cologne based Schaffhausen'scher Bankverein) speculating upon the success of a partic-

84   *Industrial constructions*

ular type of industrialization. As the scale and capital needs of the firms they participated in increased, it no longer became possible to provide for them with primarily regional resources. Hence, *Kreditbanken* began to link and fuse across regions in order to be able to pool their resources and provide for the needs of increasingly large-scale autarkic industry. In this way, the autarkic German universal banks gradually became just as detached from their original regional bases as the firms to whom they provided credit.[56]

The state and the autarkic industrial order. Finally, large autarkic steel producers in the Ruhr drew clear boundaries between themselves and the Prussian state with respect to their business affairs. Unlike the decentralized producers, they believed that government should not be involved in the organization of production. The decentralized producers viewed the many levels of government as coactors in the organization of the industrial system that they both made up. Both participated in the continuous exchange of information and experiences about markets, technology, and business conditions that was constitutive of the dynamic flexibility in the decentralized industrial districts.[57] But, as we saw, the autarkic producers often set up their operations in relatively unindustrialized areas, seeking to escape precisely that kind of dense network of mutual obligation between state and society in traditional decentralized industry. To them, the traditional system was a barrier to change, progress, and fortune.

It is no surprise, then, that the early steel entrepreneurs (as well as their fellow financiers) tended to be ardently individualistic and suspicious of outsiders, particularly those with authority, seeking to engage with them in matters close to the strategy or inner workings of the firm. The state was not viewed as a colleague in a regional system, but as a hostile body covetous of the industrialist's rights to property and continuously seeking to arbitrarily intrude in the private realm of manufacturing and money making.[58] Autarkic producers were ardent advocates of private control over the market (if not market freedom), and limited (though not necessarily democratic) government. In addition, these producers, who assumed great risk in building Germany's railways and transforming whole regions according to their own designs in production, eventually began to believe that their activities and their achievements were the expression of the virtues of the modern bourgeois class and a self-governing society. To them, their creative achievements, not the authority or reputation of German princes, were the foundation of German national greatness.[59] Many of the wealthiest and most powerful of Ruhr industrialists, such as Emil Kirdorf, August Thyssen, Hugo Stinnes, F. A. Krupp, and Carl Funke, were so proud of their bourgeois identity that they even turned down patents of nobility offered to them by Kaiser Wilhelm II during the Second Empire.[60]

But this autarkic arrogance concerning their right to freedom did not translate into an absolute divide between their businesses and the activities of the Prussian state. There were many complex interpenetrations and points of exchange. Many, for example, have pointed to the influence of Prussian bureaucratic traditions on the construction of the early German autarkic corporations.⁶¹ The organizational mechanisms of authority and command developed in the Prussian army were also very influential in shaping the way in which autarkic producers constructed their own organizations.⁶²

Such influences had less to do with direct interventions by the state into the affairs of firms than they did with appropriations by entrepreneurs of important local models for their own ends.⁶³ But there were also ways in which the state actively sought to influence and aid the development of industry as well. The Prussian Crown was ambivalent about the emergence of the newer autarkic producers.⁶⁴ On the one hand, it opposed the growth of a new centralized industry operated by an aggressive bourgeoisie and understood its potential social and political power to be a threat to its own traditional authority. On the other hand, the Prussian state, wounded by defeat and occupation in the Napoleonic wars, clearly believed that its future as a power in Europe lay in its capacity to industrialize. The Prussian Kaiser thus pursued a policy of blocking the political aspirations of the emergent producers while at the same time sponsoring the acquisition, development, and diffusion of foreign manufacturing technologies.⁶⁵ The Prussian state itself operated a number of industrial workshops and corporations, particularly in mining, engine building, and weapons manufacture, which it used to raise revenue and experiment with foreign technologies. It operated several mining corporations in the Ruhr until the 1860s.⁶⁶

But it was educational institutions that were the most interesting to the autarkic steel producers. The Hohenzollern government created the Berliner Gewerbe-Institute in 1821 (later to become the Technische Hochschule Berlin–Charlottenburg in 1879), the first of a number of institutions created to introduce new technologies and skills into the Prussian economy. As the size of their operations and their need for engineers expanded over the latter part of the 19th century, large iron and steel firms drew their young engineers and managers from the universities. The steel engineering academy at the Technische Hochschule Berlin, the coal mining academy in Aachen, and the Rheinwestfälische Hüttenschule in Bochum were major institutes serving the steel industry. Firms worked closely with university research teams on problems of particular long-term interest to them. These universities were by the end of the 19th century world leaders in nearly all areas of technical science and engineering.

Relations between autarkic producers and the state were also shaped by important business exchanges. Autarkic steel producers, for example, conducted significant business with different governments in Germany, particularly the Imperial government, which purchased a great deal of munitions and other weaponry that provided firms with extremely lucrative contracts. Krupp, the Bochumer Verein, Hoerder Verein, GHH, and the Phoenix Works were the main suppliers in the famous German Navy buildup in the years leading up to World War I, for example.⁶⁷ Krupp was the main supplier of war materials among the German producers. The Bochumer Verein had a very large export business in munitions, but played a minor role to Krupp on the domestic market.

86 *Industrial constructions*

Krupp's contractual relations with the German Reich intensified over time. The company exported about 80% of its munitions-related output in the 1880s, but exports then declined to only 30% by the beginning of World War I.[68]

The list of business relations with government could be easily extended, though the significance of autarkic business with the state, in any area, should not be exaggerated. The point is that the autarkic producers had an ambivalent relationship to the state. They wished to keep it out of the immediate realms of production and distribution, and yet were willing to accept infrastructural support as a public good or to do business with the state when it was clear that they would make money. Whereas for the decentralized producer the regional government was a collaborator, advisor, and agent as well as the provider of public goods, in the autarkic industrial order the government was more a kind of night watchman and a customer.

Adjustment in autarkic industrial order: Redefining the relationship between autarkic firms and autarkic industry

The autarkic industrial order in the steel industry was embedded in industrializing German society in the 19th century in almost every respect differently than the decentralized industrial order. Production and its governance was concentrated and centralized in the one and diffuse and decentralized in the other. Industry related differently to the artisans, agriculture, the regions in which they were located, and the regional government. The two different forms of industrial order even utilized different kinds of banks. The various components of the autarkic order that I have outlined here began to be fully in place in the steel industry by the 1880s.

Much like the producers in the decentralized industrial order, autarkic steel producers gradually found that this initial form of order generated dynamics of competition and development that led to problems of instability and even market breakdown. The initial problems the iron and steel producers encountered were at the level of individual, already established product markets. But later, as the industry grew and began to diversify, it became apparent that problems of order existed at the level of the industry as a whole. In the first case, producers created price cartels to stabilize production. In the latter case, particularly after the war and the transformation of the overall economic environment in the interwar period, less cooperative and even more autarkic solutions took center stage and ultimately transformed the industry. In both cases, the spectrum of possible solutions was constrained by the regional and organizational characteristics of order that have been outlined.

Problems of order in individual product markets. In the early decades of the development of the autarkic steel industry, when demand for steel was concentrated in a few product markets (primary products, primarily for the railroads), producers were confronted with problems precisely the reverse of those the decentralized specialists encountered: that is, rather than excessive flexibility, autarkic producers' problems stemmed from excessive rigidity in production. The logic of the dilemma they confronted is that many producers with exceedingly high fixed costs producing standardized products are confronted with considerable risks both in periods of downturn and in periods of renewed growth. When the demand for a high-volume standard product declines, it is natural for producers to attempt to maintain their level of sales by lowering prices because they do not want to run the risk of not being able to produce at capacity and hence of losing money on idle production equipment. The relative rigidity of that equipment in such product lines, moreover, forecloses the flexible option of turning it to the production of other products. The problem, however, is that if producers do adjust by cutting prices, and all of their competitors do as well, then a downward pricing cycle ensues which causes all competitors in the market to lose any hope of being able to sustain a profitable business. In a rising market, the risks are the reverse: each producer desires to take advantage of rising demand by increasing prices, but fears that if he or she does so, one's competitors will not follow and the market will be lost.[69]

Ruhr steel producers attempted to control such risks by cooperating over the setting of prices, i.e., by establishing price cartels[70]. The rails and other high volume standard items (such as other railroad materials, pig iron, or semifinished goods that had to be melted again for finishing) proved amenable to this because it was possible to establish an intraindustry standard for the calculation of costs. Such cartels were constantly established in numerous, usually regional product markets in the iron and steel industry during the late 19th century. Many producers belonged to numerous cartels simultaneously. Most of the cartels lasted for short periods of time, usually only as long as the period that created the above risks lasted. Some, however, lasted much longer, such as the rail cartel, perhaps the most important cartelized commodity in the Ruhr steel industry. The first rail cartel (the *Stahlschienengemeinschaft*) was established in 1876 and at that time, due to the central importance of railroad demand to the industry, the cartel effectively organized pricing on three quarters of the steel industry's total output.[71] This rail cartel lasted until 1892, when it was replaced by another one after renegotiation of its boundaries.[72]

Problems at the level of the industry as a whole. By the turn of the century, the situation in the steel industry began to change in a profound way, giving rise to a new set of problems that could not be solved as easily through the traditional mechanism of price cartels. The key development was the stabilization of demand in traditional high-volume primary steel markets, such as railroad materials (rails, ties, etc.) and semifinished as well as structural steels.[73] This led steel firms to shift the trajectory of their expansion by diversifying into a wide range of rapidly growing secondary or finished steel markets, such as merchant bars, rolled wire, steel plate, pipes, and cast and forged pieces. The shift in this direction was very significant. Sales of primary products in 1911/12 were

32.24% above 1904/5 levels, while finished steel sales in 1911/12 were 106% above the earlier year.[74] According to Feldman, by 1912 these finished goods accounted for over two-thirds of the steel industry's total production.[75]

Unlike the semifinished goods, rails, and structural steels that they had previously produced, many of these new goods had a broader variety of potential users and were difficult to standardize. With diversification, steel producers began to try to enter the multitude of specialty markets and industries that dominated the German economy, both in decentralized and autarkic regions. This meant that steel quality and mix were varied far more than had previously been the case, as were rolling programs.[76] Individual firms and works developed close relations with customers and tailored orders to their special needs. Value added from the quality and complexity of the end product often compensated for lower volumes.[77] The movement into secondary product areas thus not only created many additional lines of business for the steel producers, each one of those additional lines could itself be infinitely fragmented, at least potentially.

The problems that the breakneck expansion into these finished goods markets created were on the surface very easy for the steel producers to identify. Rapid expansion lead to uncoordinated, sometimes predatory pricing and overcapacity. But finding a way to manage these problems proved to be much more difficult for producers than the earlier, relatively straightforward problems that led to the creation of price cartels. In that case, firms had already committed themselves to high-volume production strategies, and all producers, consequently, were calculating with a logic that emphasized continuous standardization and the search for economies of scale. But this was not the case during the period of rapid diversification in the decade or so before World War I. Instead, there was tremendous ambiguity concerning the kind of production strategy producers seemed to be pursuing, even within individual firms. Two broadly different possibilities, each with very different implications for the way in which industry-wide problems should be framed, much less resolved, can be discerned, though retrospectively and with artificial distinctness: one involved the continuation and expansion of the producer's capacity to offer specialty goods, while the other involved a desire to shift into a more standard product-based mass production trajectory.[78] Any solution chosen to solve the surface problems of market order depended in no small part upon what kind of an industry producers believed that the new, more diversified industry would become.[79]

If the industry were to be specialty production based, it would have to deal with problems of pricing and capacity in ways that resembled those that confronted the specialized producers in the decentralized regions. Recall from the last chapter that the problem for the decentralized producers was that unregulated, highly flexible, specialized production self-destructed during economic downturns. Producers poached on each others markets, underbid, and offered better delivery conditions, for example. Decentralized producers minimized this problem of market order by institutionalizing industry-wide forms of coordination in production. The classic example is the finishing association or specialization cartel in which producers agreed to specialize on particular products and not poach on each others specialties. If, however, the autarkic steel industry were to be oriented around high-volume mass production strategies, then the problems of pricing and capacity would have to be taken as signs of a need to restructure the industry by reducing the number of producers, consolidating capacity and constructing more efficient, larger-scale production facilities. In the one scenario, the result would be greater coordination and flexibility among a broad array of steel producers, while in the other there would be greater rigidity and fewer producers.

The first impulse of the steel producers during the initial period of diversification and expansion was to address these problems through the traditional mechanism of the cartel. This proved to be a dismal failure. The famous Steel Works Association, or *Stahlwerkbund*, a giant syndicate created in 1904, included 29 companies controlling 74.5% of production in the industry. The syndicate was explicitly created to manage the diversification process and was invested with the authority to regulate prices and allocate capacity among its members in both primary, what it called "A" products, and secondary or "B" products. It succeeded only in the slowly growing and standardized "A" product areas, but it could never get producers to agree on how to deal with the expansion of capacity in the finished-product markets. By 1907, efforts to create a marketing syndicate for secondary products were dropped, and by 1912 the syndicate no longer set price and output schedules on finished goods.[80]

The problem with the cartel was that it could not resolve the very particular kinds of problems that either possible solution to the autarkic industry's problems required. There were voices within the industry advocating a rationalization of the industry through merger and trust formation along American lines. But this position was distinctly in the minority.[81] Unlike the autarkic producers in the electro-mechanical industry, where two clearly dominant producers restructured the industry through merger, no single or even small group of producers in the steel industry was in a position to take on all of the others.[82] But without a clear leader for restructuring, the only alternative left to achieve the necessary industrial consolidation was negotiation. And this was asking the impossible. Even if everyone in the industry had agreed on the necessary outcome, successful consolidation at best would have had to involve the complicated negotiation of property rights among participants in a physically consolidated and technically integrated process and at worst required firms to agree to eliminate themselves as producers. Staunchly independent members of the same industry, each governing a nearly self-enclosed world of production (sometimes in their family name), were simply not capable of negotiating this kind of outcome.[83]

But if market rationalization for mass production could not be negotiated by means of the cartel, neither could cartel negotiations rationalize the industry for stable specialty production. This may at first seem paradoxical because it was precisely through cartelization that the specialized producers in the decentralized areas were able to institutionalize stable, coordinated specialized production.[84] But the precondition for the success of such governance forms in decentralized areas was the existence there of an extensive risk-spreading infrastructure of

Table 2 *Concentration of coal, iron and steel production in the German Reich, 1913*

	Percentage of national output produced by the five largest Ruhr enterprises* (according to balance sheet sums)	percentage of national output produced by the five largest producers according to production area
Coal	16.1	21.0
Pig iron	31.2	34.8
Raw steel	30.5	30.7

*The five largest were: Krupp, GBAG, Deutsch–Luxemburg, GDK, and Phoenix.
Table taken from Wilfried Feldenkirchen, *Die Eisen- und Stahlindustrie des Ruhrgebeits 1879–1914*, p. 268.

suppliers and service providers who gave producers constant access to specialist knowledge and production expertise, which enhanced the capacity of producers to stay competitive within their specialty. Without an infrastructure capable of socializing risk and knowledge in this way, a program of coordinated specialization would actually increase the vulnerability of firms in the market. In the autarkic industrial order of the Ruhr steel industry, of course, there was no infrastructure beyond the boundaries of the firm capable of socializing the risks associated with specialization. Hence, firms had no incentive to in any way limit or coordinate their diversification strategies. Indeed, precisely the reverse was the case – they aggressively diversified and expanded their production capacity.

In the years after 1907, it became increasingly clear to many in the industry that no solution to the industry's problems could be arrived at by means of cartel negotiation. But at the time, this failure to find an industry-wide restructuring strategy did not lead to a crisis because, despite the unease that the diversification process created among producers, cartelization still worked in "A" products and the steel market was basically a prosperous and expanding one right up to the beginning of World War I. Producers simply put off embracing one or the other of the above horizontal restructuring strategies. Instead, they made sure that their expansion strategies were well-hedged across a number of different market segments inside and outside of the steel industry by engaging in numerous vertical mergers. Horizontal blockage gave rise to vertical concentration.[85]

Large firms, such as Krupp, GHH, and Thyssen, bought into new industries – the machinery industry for example – which could absorb some of their excess capacity. At the same time, these and other producers merged backward and forward within the various input and product markets of the steel industry itself in order to avoid high cartel prices on key inputs. Many companies purchased coal mines for this reason. By the outbreak of war, the industry had a very peculiar structure in which no single branch market of the steel production complex (coal, pig iron, crude steel, and finishing) was particularly concentrated, and yet the largest Ruhr combines numbered among the leading producers in every branch. Concentration in the industry grew, in other words, but it was deep, not wide[86] (see Table 2).

From short-term adaptation to transformation: Specialist konzerne and a mass production trust in the interwar period. This practice of vertical merger, pursued relatively unsystematically and piecemeal because the industry could not find any other way to stabilize its expansion, ultimately provided the industry with the strategy it needed to transform itself in the interwar period. Paradoxically, the transforation basically allowed for the institutionalization of both of the contending prewar conceptions of the industry. In the changed economic conditions in the aftermath of World War I, some large enterprises discovered that they could overcome the obstacles to the pursuit of a stable specialization strategy, most particularly the absence of an external infrastructure for the socialization of risk, by creating a kind of autarkic risk-spreading structure *inside* the enterprise itself. Firms created holding companies or *Konzerne* in which their production operations were spread across a broad array of coherently related market and industrial segments. Redundancy among operating units was eliminated and interoperating-unit communication was facilitated by a superintending central holding office. The technical and market knowledge diffusing capacity of the external infrastructure and subcontracting practices in the decentralized districts were in this way recast *within* the framework of these vast *Konzerne*.

The success of these developments, which moreover occurred in the early postwar years of inflation, completely changed the strategic possibilities for the other enterprises in the industry that were less diversified, less interested in specialization, or whose efforts to create *Konzerne* had failed. That is, the more extensively that the leading firms in the industry succeeded in creating *Konzerne*, the easier it became for the few producers who remained to consolidate their resources and undertake a horizontal rationalization of the remaining steel markets to allow for efficient mass production. In the former case, the autarkic producers institutionalized the flexibility and specialization of the decentralized industrial districts in an autarkic way. In the latter case, the remaining Ruhr producers ultimately resolved the tension that had existed between the individual autarkic firm and an industry of such firms by dissolving the industry into the firm.

The cost of this restructuring was a much more concentrated industry. Whereas in 1922/23 the top six producers in the steel industry accounted for approximately 55.4% of total industry output, by 1930 they accounted for over 80%. By 1938 the percentage increased to over 95%.[87] The industry was completely divided between six highly diversified *Konzerne* producing primarily specialty steels and finished products on the one hand and a vast multidivisional enterprise, the *Vereinigte Stahlwerke* (Vestag), covering nearly half of the industry's output and oriented primarily to the production of mass and bulk steel products, on the other.[88] The following two sections will look in turn at the emergence of *Konzerne* and the formation of the Vestag.

Konzerne: *Autarkic governance of specialty production.* The rise of the *Konzerne* must be understood in the context of the catalyzing changes that occurred in the immediate aftermath of the World War I that both disrupted the industry and provided individual actors with temporary liquidity that allowed them to engage in mergers. Disruption in the industry had many sources. During the war, the steel producers lost most of their overseas markets to foreign competitors. Then, the reorganization of German borders in the Versailles Treaty, which sent the steel making districts of Lorraine, the Saarland, and Silesia to other countries, deprived Germany of 72% of her iron-ore reserves and hived off large chunks of domestic capacity in pig iron and crude steel making. This completely disrupted the integrated operations of producers such as Thyssen, Deutsche-Lux, Gelsenkirchener Bergwerksgesellschaft, and the Klöckner Group. At the same time, with the growth of new states and the expansion of industries in western Europe, European steel capacity increased significantly.[89] These disruptions were, however, balanced out by a unique postwar political and economic climate in Germany that paradoxically provided producers with considerable cash and incentives to merge. Fear of socialization in the coal industry and new and extensive sales taxes provided incentives for vertical integration, while the increasingly inflationary economy made it possible to raise capital without incurring significant debt. Moreover, all of the concerns that lost their facilities in the Lorraine and the Saar were handsomely compensated for the loss by the new Weimar state.[90]

The construction of *Konzerne* was driven by the idea that the best way to survive in the new more competitive and fragmented market conditions was to develop the capacity to compete in as broad an array of specialty markets as possible. The major steel *Konzerne* created after World War I were Hoesch, Klöckner, GHH, Krupp, and Mannesmann.[91] Several others were also constructed, in particular the Siemens Rhein Elbe Schuckert Union (SRSU)[92] and the Stumm Works, but these were not financially sound enough to survive the great inflation of 1923–24.[93] These steel companies systematically acquired holdings in a variety of related technologies and markets, especially in finishing areas and other downstream manufacturing industries, especially machinery producers. Such acquisitions significantly reduced the overall involvement of the firms in steel production. Moreover, for the most part, none of the acquired firms were volume producers. Instead, the companies either produced small-volume specialized products or they specialized on their ability to marshal large amounts of capital for highly specialized and continuously varying production projects. An example of the former would be large, powerful diesel engines, while one for the latter would be large, technologically multidimensional ships or engineering projects such as dockyards. Developments at GHH and Krupp will be used here to illustrate the wider trend.

GHH purchased a whole host of smaller and larger companies in the years after the war: J. Tafel Eisenwerk of Nuremberg (iron castings) (1919), Maschinenfabrik Esslingen (machinery) (1920), Maschinenfabrik Fritz Neuemeyer A.G. (machinery), Zahnradfabrik Renk A.G. (gears and gear units) in Augsburg

(1920), and the largest acquisition of them all, MAN (machinery) of Augsburg and Nuremberg. GHH also shared control with the AEG and the Hapag company of Deutsche Werft (shipyards) in Hamburg. By the end of this set of purchases, the original GHH company accounted for only 24.5% of the capital stock of the total holdings of the *Konzerne*. And since the original company itself already had extensive nonsteel-related divisions (machinery, bridge building, barges, turbines, materials handling equipment), integrated steel production accounted for even less than that.[94]

Krupp also was already extensively involved in nonsteel manufacturing activities before the war, especially in machinery and weapons building. It also owned Germania shipyards in Kiel, Westfälische Drahtindustrie (wireworks) in Hamm, Grusenwerk, Magdeburg–Buckau (machinery), and Blechwalzwerk Capito and Klein (plate-rolling mills) in Duesseldorf. After the war the company shifted the emphasis of its diversification into nondefense areas. The capacity of old weapons works was shifted over to the production of locomotives and agricultural machinery. To supplement this production and alleviate a number of patent conflicts resulting from the diversification, Krupp engaged in a number of IGs with large producers in those industries, such as Bavarian Maschinenfabrik Fahr, a producer of agricultural equipment, and the locomotive producer Rheinmetall.[95] With the establishment of these IGs, which amounted to tightly coordinated technology and profit-pooling arrangements, all of which were completed in the first two years after the war, Krupp, too, had reduced its steel operations to a much smaller percentage of its total operations.

The *Konzerne* were constructed from what one concern builder called "the vertical point of view." And for Hugo Stinnes, the most visionary of *Konzern* builders, a vertical point of view meant "that all forms of production were ultimately connected [and that] the possibilities of vertical combination were almost boundless."[96] According to the grandiose ambitions of one of Stinnes' allies, the giant coordinated holding company should "be able to take advantage of technical improvements . . . and . . . create an economic body which ought not to go unnoted and unasked for any project that comes up in this world."[97] In the SRSU, Stinnes wanted to create virtually an autarkic internal industrial economy ranging from coal to personal telephones. But his gargantuan vision proved to be impossible to realize. He could not supplement the marriage he had brought about between the Siemens electro-technical holding and his own Rhein–Elbe Union with the important intermediate technological steps of steel finishing and machinery production. Consequently the *Konzern* was vertically polarized, overleveraged, overly bureaucratic, and, ultimately, could not survive the inflation.[98]

All of the successful *Konzerne* accepted Stinnes' strategic vision in principle, but made sure that their holdings were closely related to one another either technologically or economically. By bringing related but distinctly new and technologically more complicated businesses into orbit with one another, the steel industry *Konzerne* sought to create a giant pool of know-how that each of the individual businesses could both draw on and contribute to. This had the dual advantage of spreading the risk that the enterprise as a whole incurred across a very broad array of specialized product markets and businesses while at the same time embedding each of the member businesses within a network of related companies with whom they could cooperate and exchange information. By using this synergy between the parts of the *Konzern* it would be possible to continuously move into new and developing technologies and markets.[99]

The logic of risk spreading across related industries and product markets within the *Konzerne* was then supplemented by a logic of rationalization among and within each of the individual units of the holding. Specialized production units were aligned so that there was very little overlap in what they were able to produce, and yet, at the same time, so that there were very few holes in the range of products the *Konzerne* could offer. This kind of autarkic coordinated specialization eliminated the risk of unproductive competition within the *Konzern* for orders or capital. Indeed, by forcing the operating unit to specialize, it provided an incentive for it to turn to other related and similarly specialized units for information or technical assistance. Much like the finishing associations in the decentralized industrial order, but in an autarkic way, the *Konzerne* forced specialization on operating units while simultaneously embedding the operating units in an infrastructure of relations that diffused the risk that specialization created.

Konzerne were organized as holding companies to simultaneously enhance the flexibility of the member companies and facilitate the provision of trans-*Konzern* services that embedded them in a risk-spreading infrastructure. Gutehoffnungshütte, Hoesch, and Klöckner created independent central holding offices that controlled, through stock participation, the assets of their original companies and their new downstream enterprises.[100] Responsibility for the day-to-day business of production operations, as well as the profits and losses that resulted from them, were transferred to the local operating units and their managers. The main concern of the central holding office was to maximize the return that the group as a whole could receive from its mix of products and companies. To do this it provided a variety of general services to the operating units, such as statistics, research, access to trade networks, and lobbying. More practically, the central office encouraged and facilitated continuous contact among member firms, either in the form of regular meetings about general business conditions or in the form of direct exchanges of market and technological information.[101] The superintending offices of the holding adjudicated disputes that arose among *Konzerne* operating units. And, finally, the central office controlled the long-range investment strategy of the *Konzern*. It could thus discipline units that were not performing well and direct investment toward the development of new and promising areas of technology and growth that utilized the strengths of the concern members. In some cases, *Konzerne* even established independent banks for its subsidiaries.[102]

It is important to see that these *Konzerne* were not efforts to create giant, self-contained, vertically integrated production systems. Steel producers did not purchase machinery producers because the latter would be able to absorb their entire steel output. They did so because through contact with the machinery producers, the firms' finishing businesses could have continuous contact with users of special varieties of finished steels. The integration was one of knowledge, experience, and information, not of production. Of GHH, Feldman writes: "It was expected that the member firms would purchase from one another when price and quality equaled what was being offered by outsiders, but it was a general rule that firms were to purchase where they were best served."[103] Hoesch, for example, which began purchasing finishing operations and machinery producers before the war and then radically diversified in the early postwar years, sold on average only 20% of its rolling mill output to its own downstream operations in 1927.[104]

The paradox of the *Konzerne* is that they were designed to accomplish a kind of institutional stabilization of specialty production that resembled the logic of solutions that existed in decentralized areas. Yet because the crucial extrafirm infrastructure that allowed decentralized producers to socialize the risks of specialization did not exist in the autarkic regions, the autarkic producers were compelled to recreate them within the boundaries of an enterprise. Moreover, this was not a development confined to the steel industry. Producers in other industries where production was always oriented toward specialty production also exhibited similar institutional developments. We will see this below in the discussion of the machinery industry. But the extent of the development of *Konzerne* in German industry during the 1920s was much broader. Siegrist notes that in comparison to the 1907 list of companies, the top one hundred corporations in 1927 were practically all *Konzerne* and the holding form, whether pure or functional holding in character, had become generalized.[105] Maisel claims that over 65% of all stock issued in Germany in 1926 came from concerns of this type.[106]

Horizontal merger: Vereinigte Stahlwerke. The success of the specialization strategy in the steel industry through the formation of *Konzerne* had the paradoxical effect of facilitating the capacity of the remaining steel producers to consolidate and rationalize assets in the industry to allow for efficient and large-scale mass production. The *Konzerne* were less dependent upon steel production than they had been before the war, and their internal rationalization strategies had led them to concentrate their steel making activities increasingly in more specialized areas. Consequently, they were both less interested in large-scale steel production and less threatened by efforts on the part of other producers to consolidate the industry in ways that would make that kind of mass production possible.

The four original founders of the Vereinigte Stahlwerke, or Vestag, were all either large steel producers who had only modestly diversified outside of steel production (Phoenix, Rheinstahl, Thyssen) or who had tried to establish a *Konzerne* and failed (the Rhein–Elbe Union). In addition, the new company, which was formed in 1926, also purchased much of the plant and equipment from other steel companies that went bankrupt during the hyperinflation and its aftermath: the Stumm Concern, Charlottenhütte A.G., Rombacher Hüttenwerke, and several other smaller companies. By the beginning of the 1930s, the company's share of the German steel market was nearly 50%.[107] The logic behind the merger was clear enough. By absorbing competitors and coordinating the productive plant of the merged firms, the company could control a very large percentage of the entire German market for standardized types of basic steel.[108] Once the contours of the market were stabilized, the thinking went, productive capacity and plant could be rationalized to match it.[109]

Over the course of the latter half of the 1920s, the firm pursued a systematic strategy of integrating its capacity technologically and consolidating it geographically. Albert Voegler, formerly of the Deutsch Lux AG and president of the concern, wanted to create a "completely integrated work" (*eine absolute Betriebseinheit*) out of the Vestag. Those plants that were not technically first rate or which did not fit geographically into the combination were to be closed. The sprawling operations of the four major member concerns were divided nto specialized groups, each with a particular type of market and with an appropriate supporting infrastructure of coal mines.[110] The concern divested itself (or committed itself to do so) of all downstream nonsteel manufacturing interests.[111]

A tremendous amount of capacity within the concern was eliminated in the process of internal rationalization. In testimony before the Enquette Commission in 1928, Voegler said that of the seven open hearth plants in the concern, which had together a total of 19 open hearth furnaces, six of the works, and 11 of the furnaces were or were in the process of being dismantled. Of the eight steel mills in the concern, which in total had 30 Siemens–Martin furnaces, four plants and 15 furnaces were being dismantled.[112]

This internal rationalization did, indeed, affect the productivity of the concern, though the exact impact is still disputed among historians. In his testimony, which he gave only two years after the creation of the Vestag, but right in the middle of the late 1926–1929 boom, Voegler maintained that the gains were quite large. Before the rationalization, he claimed, the August Thyssen Works produced 75,000 tons of steel with 10,000 workers; after the rationalization, it produced 170,000 tons of steel with only 9,900 workers. The Hoerder-Union works made 40,000 tons of steel before the rationalization and 85–90,000 tons after. Its employment numbers increased slightly from 4,500 to 5,700. Rheinstahl and Phoenix increased their production from 110,000 tons to 150,000 tons while reducing their worker total from 11,000 to 9,600. With everything figured in together, according to Voegler, the total sales in the concern increased 70%.[113]

Governance at Vestag. These changes in the organization of production were matched by corresponding changes in the structure of corporate governance. When it was originally formed, the lines of ownership and control within the Vestag were very complicated. Rather than merging the interests of three of the original companies into the fourth, an entirely new company was formed. This was because some of the firms interested in amalgamation were not willing to throw all their property into the merger, and because the plan was for the new company to be established without taking over the existing debts of the old companies. The new concern, Vestag, owned most of the steel making plant and equipment of the old companies, while those companies continued to exist as the principal shareholders in Vestag.[114] Control over the financial aspects of the concern were thus decentralized throughout a series of interlocking relations involving holding companies representing the old concerns, while control over production was centralized in the new Vestag.

At the time, the important point was that the new centralization of control over production allowed the firm to move toward implementing the rationalization schemes, particularly in the area of plant integration, described above. But by the early 1930s, the complicated structure of the company needed to be reorganized. On the one hand, the decentralized financial structure made it difficult for the concern to raise capital,[115] while, on the other hand, the centralized lines of authority over production proved too rigid in the face of continued uncertainty in the development of the European steel markets.

The reorganization, which took place in 1933, reversed the lines of centralization and decentralization. All the companies having ownership in Vestag transferred their total properties and assets to Vestag by exchange and permutation of shares. But all the various operating units of Vestag were given greater operating autonomy. Each was made to specialize on a different special type of standard steel product.[116] Specialization among the operating units was to be coordinated by the newly established Vestag holding company (Dachgesellschaft), but the operating units themselves were to attend to the day-to-day competitive problems of the vast array of steel operations that they collectively encompassed. The holding company's responsibilities were shifted to general areas of concern to all members of Vestag: research and development, finance, cost accounting, statistics, and scientific comparisons of the production processes of the different works.[117] The adoption of the holding company form in this case is slightly unusual, although as Chandler points out, it resembled in many respects the integrated multidivisional enterprises that had been created in the United States.[118] The key to understanding the governance structure of Vestag was that it was designed to afford the maximum amount of flexibility possible to the operating subsidiaries [12 joint stock companies (AGs) and 14 limited liability companies (GmbH's)].

Unlike the *Konzerne*, the aim of Vestag was not to create an internal system for the distribution of risk and the transfer of technological and market information. The primary purpose of Vestag was to achieve a rationalization and consolidation of the steel industry capacity that the independent autarkic steel enterprises had not been able to achieve through negotiation. If the *Konzerne* reacted to the absence of extrafirm infrastructure in the autarkic regions by creating an autarkic industrial district, Vestag reacted to the existence of decentralized property rights among autarkic standard goods producers by organizing an autarkic standard goods steel industry within itself. In both cases, the developments in the 1920s were profoundly shaped by the autarkic regional pattern of industrialization that had preceded them in the 19th century.

98 *Industrial constructions*

Cartels. Once the structure of the steel industry was stabilized through the formation of *Konzerne* and Vestag, firms began to resort once again to the use of price cartels to stabilize production. Indeed, now that the boundaries between various producers' markets had been clarified and the number of remaining producers radically reduced, it was much easier to get firms to agree on pricing and output growth in a broad array of even highly finished products. Between 1925 and 1930, the number of cartels in all of the different markets of the steel industry increased from 73 to 108. In 1925, firms in the industry created the German Steel Community, the A-Product Association, the Tube Association, the Rolled Wire Association, the Raw Tin Association, the Wrought Iron Association, and the Band Steel Association. These associations controlled as syndicates both the quantity and price of steel products sold. When formed, they accounted for 89% of the total production of rolled steel products.[119]

Variation on a theme: Autarkic volume producers outside the steel industry and the phenomenon of economic dualism

Before turning to the craft production case of the autarkic machinery industry, it is important to briefly deal with an important phenomenon that emerged in autarkic regions that was not brought out by the steel industry case: economic dualism. Outside of the autarkic steel industry, volume production was not widespread in Germany prior to the 1950s. But there were some sectors in autarkic regions in which efforts to mass produce had been undertaken, particularly in textiles and in many light machinery markets, and especially during the interwar years. Unlike the steel producers, the turbulent economic conditions of the interwar period often blocked the efforts of producers in these sectors to effectively rationalize production in the industry as completely as had Vestag and the *Konzerne*. In most cases the rigidity that came with the rationalization of volume production created spaces in the market into which less efficient, though more flexible, independent firms could enter. In contrast to the rationalized volume producers, the survivors were capable of providing standard products at a lower total cost, even though their absolute per-unit costs may have been higher than the more efficient producers in the industry. Always unstable, this secondary ring of firms performed a variety of roles: sometimes as end-product producers, sometimes as subcontractors for a larger, more advanced firm, or both.[120]

Industrial structures of this kind emerged in many industries in all autarkic regions, but it was particularly obvious in those autarkic regions that had previously been *Gewerbelandschaften* under regimes of impartible inheritance, such as the region around Bielefeld[121] (see Map 1 in Appendix). Mechanized industrialization came to these areas in the last third of the 19th century after their premechanization systems of industry had fallen into serious decay and the entire base of handicraft skill had been slowly destroyed. The mechanized industrial growth that eventually did occur was based on industrial products and processes

Autarkic industrial order in Germany 99

that required comparatively less skill. In Bielefeld, this meant, ultimately, specialization in "American" technologies, such as sewing machines, and American style labor-saving machine tools. Both standard, volume products could themselves be produced on machinery that was labor saving. It was the kind of technology that could be easily produced in regions that had never had or had lost a base of skilled handicraft labor.

By the 1920s, the region of Bielefeld was a major center for the production, not simply of sewing machines and American style labor-saving machine tools, but also of automobiles, calculating machinery, and bicycles, as well as factory-produced standardized textile products. Few other regions of the German Reich had specialized so extensively on volume production. Each of the sectors represented in Bielefeld had a handful of very sophisticated producers that numbered among the major producers in their specialty in Germany as a whole, such as Dürrkopp in sewing machines and automobiles and Gildemeister in machine tools. But none of these companies were capable of completely dominating their market segment. Unsteady demand, rapid upswings, and precipitous downswings made it possible for smaller, less efficient companies to continue to compete in their markets.[122]

In Bielefeld, there were two ways in which this was true. Core firms left a portion of the market for less efficient producers because they feared the consequences of overcapacity. Small firms competed for that percentage of demand not taken by the more efficient producers. A second way in which smaller, less efficient producers continued to survive in the volume production environment was as subcontractors. Volume producers often sought to cover a portion of peak demand through outsourcing of production rather than increasing capacity internally.

Importantly, during the 1920s, this so-called *verlängerte Werkbank* subcontracting extended not only to clusters of smaller shops in the region, but into households as well. Homework exploded during this time in most regions that had previously been impartible-inheritance-based *Gewerbelandschaften*.[123] Sustained high unemployment forced the unemployed unskilled workers who had previously left the region for more dynamic industrial districts to return to their family holdings in the countryside. There the unemployed, unskilled, landless population could be exploited for cheap labor during upswings in the business cycle by hiring them to perform certain operations in their homes. When demand subsided, one simply did not hire them any more.[124]

In this way, low wages and exploitation became integral features of the autarkic system of volume production during this period. It followed from the logic of a situation in which rationalization efforts were tempered by instability. Where firms succeeded in rationalizing, the rigidity it created encouraged them to purchase their flexibility from the outside as cheaply as they could. Where they were not successful in fully implementing rationalization measures, they left room for less efficient producers.

This confluence of strategic actions and reactions created an extremely paradoxical set of developments in the labor force within autarkic areas. On the one hand, successful rationalization reduced the dependence of firms upon skilled workers and caused the demand for white collar employment to increase. On the other hand, the same rationalization measures caused the number of those employed in traditional homework to increase as well. The growth of the new middle classes and the perpetuation of very traditional household structures in the countryside were thus linked in the way that production in autarkic systems developed during the Weimar Republic.[125]

Autarkic batch producers: The machinery industry

Origins

Machine building is an important industry in all of the regions I have designated as autarkic: the Ruhr Valley; northeast Westfalen; the Province of Saxony; Berlin; old court and trading cities, such as Hannover, Kassel, Nuremberg, Augsburg, and Munich; and the harbor cities on the northern seacoasts, such as Hamburg, Bremen, Kiel, Rostock, Stettin, Danzig, and Königsberg. These areas either had no previous handicraft or protoindustrial infrastructure, or that which they did have was small, such as in Berlin, and/or it was in severe decay by the first half of the 19th century, as in Augsburg and Nuremberg.[126] Unlike the machinery industry in the decentralized regions, which largely developed by supplying the local specialized industries with their production equipment, machinery production was imported into autarkic regions from the outside. The importers were either regional governments or entrepreneurs and private bankers or other monied speculators interested in promoting the development of a particular technology. In these cases, machinery production was from its very inception factory based.

The earliest example of this is the case of steam engine production. This technology was invented in Britain in the 18th century. Despite efforts to keep the principles of the technology secret on the part of its inventors, many countries on the European continent were able to obtain the know-how to produce the machines. In Germany, the initial impetus for this came from the Prussian state, which wanted to use the new technology to pump water out of its mines. First they sponsored a number of trips by public officials, including the great reformer Freiherr von Stein, a director of state mines in Westphalia, to Britain to look at (and steal) the technology.[127] Then they established factories in and around Berlin, and eventually a school of engineering as well, to make the engines. Gradually, state production facilities gave way to private workshops that were started by engineers trained in the state's schools. Production was primarily for the state's mines.[128] These private workshops, such as that of F.A.J. Egells in Berlin, eventually became what Kocka refers to as "nursery" firms, training and generating new generations of machinery entrepreneurs.[129]

Another major example of state-fostered machinery production was locomotive building.[130] As in the case of steam engines, this technology was invented in Britain and had to be imported into Germany in ways that were both legal and illegal. All of the original German producers of locomotives received state guarantees to begin the undertaking. Many of the founders were educated in state engineering schools and traveled to Britain to learn about the technology. Others were simply farsighted merchants or bankers who placed their capital and entrepreneurial ken behind a British engineer to get a state contract. The Munich locomotive builder Josef Anton von Maffei, who Redlich described as "a farseeing banker, merchant, and tobacco manufacturer," followed this latter model.[131] Most of the original German locomotive producers were already important producers of steam engines, such as Egells and Borsig in Berlin. But in some cases, the line of connection went the other way around. Firms that received state guarantees for the production of locomotives often were then able to diversify into steam engine production. This was the case of the Maffei Machinery Company in Munich.

In addition to the state, bankers and other monied interests played a role in helping locate a machinery industry in the autarkic regions. In fact, as we saw earlier in the steel example, early steel producers in the Ruhr were also pioneers in machine production. The first Ruhr machinery producers made steam engines for the mining corporations in the surrounding regions. Their businesses were either supported by the coal mines themselves, or by bankers hoping to profit from the implementation of the new British technologies in German markets. Most were established by merchants or patrician speculators with an interest in the British technologies.[132] Most stable were the companies backed by bankers, such as Harkort & Kamp in Wetter, or those that were started as subsidiaries of larger companies, such as GHH's steam engine workshop at Sterkrade.[133]

As in the case of steel, the early machinery firms and other newly created ones grew very large very rapidly after the railroad booms of the 1850s and 1870s.[134] From their initial concentration on steam engines and locomotives, firms quickly diversified into a wide array of related technologies and markets. Led by firms such as MAN in Augsburg and Nuremberg, DEMAG of Duisburg, Borsig, Schwartzkopf, Orenstein & Koppel, and Ludwig Loewe of Berlin, Henschel in Kassel, Maschinenbau Buckau R. Wolf in Magdeburg, Hanoversiche Maschinenbau AG (Hanomag) in Hannover, Vulkan Werke of Hamburg and Stettin, and many others, large autarkic German machinery producers became by the beginning of the 20th century world leaders, not only in the production of locomotives and steam engines, but in the production of rolling mill equipment, blast furnaces, giant carousel lathes, diesel engines, boilers, pumps, valves, central heating systems, cranes, bridges and dams, huge steam shovels and other construction equipment, diesel motors, gas engines, textile machines, chemical apparatus, printing presses, and much more. By 1913, the Germans were the world's largest machinery exporters, ahead of both Great Britain and the United States. German producers supplied 68% of world import demand for nonsteam engines, 45% of world locomotive imports, 42% of railroad rolling stock imports, and 56% of machine tool imports in 1913.[135]

These firms shared many of the characteristics of the rapidly growing steel producers. They grew close to banks and created complex and functionally differentiated management systems, for example, which could coordinate production, marketing and sales distribution of machinery products world-wide.[136] Like the steel producers by the time of the founding of the Reich, the machinery producers were also embedded in extensive national and increasingly international markets. They comported themselves with strong bourgeois pride and believed deeply in the national significance of their technical prowess.[137] They understood themselves to be part of the same class as the emergent large steel and electro-technical enterprises in Germany and defended with them the principles of industrial self-government, by which, of course, they meant that the organization and administration of production should be the exclusive affair of firms. Finally, like the steel producers, large autarkic machinery producers drew their engineers from state-run engineering schools and conducted considerable business with the government, building its bridges, dams, and locomotives for example.

Differences in product market structure and production organization

The development of autarkic machinery producers differed from the development of the steel producers in that they confronted a qualitatively different kind of market, hence they were forced to organize production and its governance in different ways. In this they resembled other capital-goods producers, such as the electrical machinery and apparatus producers. The key difference in market character between the capital goods producers and their heavy-industrial counterparts was that tremendous demand for relatively standard products did not exist for the machinery producers, nor could it be created. Markets in Germany and Europe were highly fragmented, regional differences in demand and production style were very great, and as a result machinery producers very frequently had to tailor their wares to the local needs of their customers. Moreover, in those cases, such as in the steel industry, where there was volume production, these customers were not "volume" consumers of machinery. Instead, they often required very particular sorts of machinery that were tremendously expensive and required very specific production characteristics and materials. With such fragmented and specialized product markets, the series size of products for machinery producers remained very small – often one of kind – and the amount of change in the product and product market of the machinery firm was very high. Firms had to react flexibly to the market.[138]

This product market structure, naturally, had an important impact on the organization of production. Because their was so little standardization, many of the principles that organized production in the other heavy industrial firms did not apply. For example, the drive for economies of scale and progressive mechanization of production was not present in the machinery industry to the degree that it was in the steel industry. There was machinery in production, but it was used in extensive rather than in sequential or intensive ways. Rather than single-purpose machines, firms deployed more general-purpose varieties to facilitate continuous changes. Significantly, this created a much larger demand for skilled labor than existed in the steel industry. Producers had to rely on skilled workers to get their production machinery to shift from making one relatively unique type of product to another.[139]

For all of this, autarkic machinery firms were still more like the autarkic steel producers than they were like decentralized machinery producers in that all aspects of their sprawling production processes were contained within the boundaries of the firm itself. Because the firms were located in areas without extensive traditions in metal working and because many of the technologies that the firms produced were huge or themselves destined for factory production, firms could not draw on a base of skilled outworkers in the artisanate or elsewhere as the machinery producers in the decentralized regions could. Even those firms in regions where a tradition of artisinal metalworking existed, such as the Cramer Klett Company in Nuremberg, were only able to draw artisans into the factory and did not subcontract work to the technologically comparatively primitive artisan shops.[140] Vertical integration was so extensive that most companies operated their own foundries and forges for the transformation of crude steel into the cast shapes they needed.[141] Machinery firms were not, however, able to go further than that because their volume of production could rarely justify large-scale backward investment in steel companies or coal mines.

Inside the firm, the various phases of the production process were related to one another very differently in the machinery industry than they were in the iron and steel industry. The goal in the steel industry was to sequentially coordinate and streamline blast furnaces, converters, and rolling operations in order to optimize their individual output, increase throughput rates and reduce the amount of time and energy lost in transferring product between stages. For the machinery producers, however, the production process was organized to enhance overall flexibility. Firms were congeries of workshops. Sequence in production was less important, though complete modularity was rarely achieved. More often, general-purpose machines of a particular type were grouped in single workshops, such as the turning room (*dreherei*), so that all the turning work could be performed in a single workshop for the entire plant. As the volume of demand increased and the product palette became more diversified, groups of workshops were created in which the production of a variety of related products would take place. An example of this is the rolling parts in steel making equipment.[142]

Differences in governance

Given this orientation to production, it is not surprising that there were also a number of differences between the way that machinery producers and steel producers governed production. A major difference had to do with industrial training. Whereas the steel producers engaged to a large degree in their own internal vocational training programs, machinery producers drew heavily on the traditional metalworking artisanate of locksmiths, mechanics, and blacksmiths.

This initial training was frequently supplemented by training programs within the firms themselves, but there was great value in the artisanal familiarity with metal. Customizing often involved important hand work that artisans were expert at performing. Large machinery firms drew on large regional and even national pools of itinerant "wandering" craftsmen. Even as the century wore on and the industry's needs for skilled help began to outstrip the capacity of the artisanate to supply, the machinery industry's strong demand for skilled labor and its traditional reliance on outsiders to supply it led the industry to become strong advocates and backers of the national systems of vocational training that eventually emerged in 20th century Germany.[143]

Another difference from the steel producers had to do with the management of production strategies. Large machinery firms tended to be far more diversified than pre-World War I steel companies.[144] Some were active in literally hundreds of product markets and had customers in a broad array of industries. Berthold details the evolution of one company located near the Ruhr that typifies the product palette evolution of many autarkic machinery producers: established as a mechanical workshop in the 1820s, the company began by making printing presses, components for grain mills, and transmissions. It then shifted into the production of steam engines and boilers with the growth of the local iron industry in the 1850s and 1860s. By 1915, the firm produced steam engines for all purposes, machines for mining and steel making, compressors, diesel motors, as well as a wide array of special machines related to these product areas. A separate division for iron and sheet-metal structures produced and constructed entire blast furnace works, materials handling systems, converters, and gas tanks.[145] To take another example, MAN in Augsburg and Nuremberg by the beginning of the World War I produced many different varieties of machines for the mining, metal, metal processing, metal fabricating, chemical, food, textile, lumber, and printing industries, as well as for utilities.[146]

The aim in such broad diversification was both to spread risk and to create a dynamic of cross-fertilization across technologies and markets that enhanced the firms capacity to customize. On the one hand, the more products a firm could produce, the less likely a downturn in any one market would hurt the firm. Machinery companies not only had expensive production equipment that cost considerable money when forced to be idle, much like specialist producers in decentralized areas, they were threatened with the loss of their valuable skilled workers during downturns. Diversification helped them avoid that by allowing the firm to keep their workers occupied through intrafirm subcontracting. But diversification also helped the firms ensure their competitiveness by creating a broad pool of intrafirm technological and market knowledge. By fostering manager and worker circulation through the workshops of the plant, firms sought to create the possibility for cross-fertilization and thereby enhance their ability to offer special solutions in a broad array of markets. In this way, much like the *Konzerne* and the finishing associations of the decentralized industrial order, machinery firms developed their capacity to offer special products by embedding increasingly specialized production workshops in their plants in an infrastructure that spread risk, disseminated information, and ultimately enhanced the ability of those workshops to remain continuously innovative.

Finally, the desire to facilitate information flow and cross-fertilization within the works also involved a unique kind of balance between management control and workplace autonomy within the machinery firms. Customizing and specialty production oriented machinery firms attempted always to balance two mutually incompatible attitudes toward their workforce. First, they wanted to have full control over the production process because they were routing a complex and large variety of orders through the plant. Moreover, they changed products quickly. Production managers needed to be able to direct skilled workers to new jobs and pull them, sometimes abruptly, from old ones. Control was essential for flexibility. On the other hand, producers also relied heavily on the skill and flexibility of their workers. But in order to enjoy the benefits of the skilled workers' flexible capacity, the managers had to cede control over the conduct of work to the workers. It was not possible to tell a skilled worker all that he or she needed to do. There were simply things about the production of their products that only the workers and not the managers were aware of. Autonomy in the workplace for the workers was the key to flexibility.[147]

The prerequisite for achieving a balance between these two kinds of pressures was a mutual recognition on the part of management and labor of the rights and integrity of the other. In early machinery firms, this often took the form of a willingness of the owner and top managers of the firm to deal directly with skilled workers, that is, hear their grievances and even seek out their input. This personal orientation was then also supplemented by paternalistic practices designed to cultivate worker trust and loyalty. The MAN companies, for example, had a number of *Sozialeinrichtungen*, such as medical insurance, pension and emergency funds, a savings bank, and company housing.[148] But as firms grew larger and the number or workers and processes expanded, it became increasingly difficult to satisfactorily achieve the kind of cooperation and trust that was required through personal interaction and charisma alone. Toward the end of the century, and in association with the evolving ideas of socialist mutualism and social, liberal, ethical, and Catholic thought in Germany at the time, firms began to establish works councils that established an institutional vehicle that facilitated constant negotiation between labor and management.[149] The Maschinenfabrik Nuremberg recognized its first works council in 1891 and the Augsburg works had its first in 1905. The importance of these institutions as vehicles for the reproduction of workplace cooperation in the context of specialty production cannot be overestimated.[150]

On the eve of World War I, large German machinery firms were truly unique industrial forms. Many, such as MAN or Demag, were so large and diverse that they were in effect autarkic industrial districts. Moreover, unlike the steel industry at the same time, the machinery industry was not riven by contending strategies to define itself as a volume or specialty industry. On the contrary,

106 *Industrial constructions*

autarkic machinery producers were at the top of their form, peerless in world markets as large-scale craft producers of industrial machinery.

Adjustment and change in the interwar years: The autarkic rationalization of a specialist industry

The turmoil of the interwar period accelerated the trends that were already in evidence before the war in production and its governance. Workshops became increasingly specialized, but now efforts were also made to limit the product range through the creation of standard types of machinery and to cut costs through the introduction of norms. This process of rationalization inside the firms was echoed by efforts among firms in particular product markets to coordinate specialization and capacity. Like the finishing associations in the decentralized regions and the *Konzerne* in the steel industry, autarkic machinery producers stabilized specialty production through coordinated specialization.

Market change. During the interwar period, there were two very profound changes in the character of machinery markets. First, the imperative to export was much greater than it had been before the war. Even though the prewar German machinery industry was, by 1913, the world's largest machinery exporter, it accomplished this from a base of steadily growing industrial production in the domestic market. In the interwar years, the domestic market was fairly stagnant, and the level of investment demand for capital equipment excruciatingly low. Firms were forced to turn to the export market more systematically. They were also encouraged in this by the government, which desperately needed to accumulate foreign reserves to be able to import raw material and food and to make good on Germany's tremendous reparations obligations.[151]

The world market, however, had changed considerably since before the war. There were a number of factors that shaped the development of German machinery firm strategies in the world market. The first was the new financial power of the United States. The ability of the United States' government and banks to aid its manufacturing firms in foreign markets, especially newly industrializing ones in Latin America and Asia, effectively shut out the financially much weaker German producers.[152] German machinery exports to Latin America, which had been steadily increasing in the decade leading up to the World War I, especially to Argentina, Brazil, and Chile, fell off precipitously. This affected the large heavy engineering houses the hardest. Lucrative contracts for the construction of bridges, steel mills, locomotives, and rolling stock were all lost to U.S. producers with better financial backing. Similar conditions prevailed within the European market, though there the market was more differentiated.[153]

Another major market challenge had to do with the industrialization strategies of newly industrializing states. Before World War I, the United States, Germany, and Britain produced over 90% of the world's machinery, and the export share of those three countries also exceeded 90% of all world trade.[154] After World War I, countries such as Hungary, Czechoslovakia, Italy, Brazil, Sweden, Poland,

and the Soviet Union all attempted to foster the development of their own machinery industries. In an effort to protect their nascent industries from the large foreign producers, these countries raised tariff levels very high.[155]

The combination of low domestic investment demand and the unwelcoming character of the world market cast the German machinery producers into a prolonged process of adjustment. The producers really had three choices. They could seek out capital-rich partners who could provide them with the capital they needed to remain competitive in international markets, despite the dramatic shift in the global balance of power in capital. Or they could move up-market and attempt to win potential customers in export markets by offering products that were more technologically sophisticated than those of their competitors. Or, finally, they could go in the opposite direction and attempt to produce machinery products that were priced low enough to remain competitive despite tariff barriers. All three strategies were pursued in the industry. The first strategy was a *Konzern*-joining strategy. The third, strategy, sweating, was common in the parts of the machinery industry that had emerged late in the 19th century, producing American style tools and located in areas that had previously been impartible-inheritance-based *Gewerbelandschaften*, such as Bielefeld, Osnabrück, and some of the producers in Berlin. Neither of these strategies involved a large segment of the machinery industry, although in the case of the *Konzern*-joining strategy it involved some very significant firms, such as MAN. Both of these strategies have already been dealt with in this chapter. The up-market strategy, however, has not, and this strategy seems to have prevailed in the bulk of the autarkic machinery industry.

Consequences in production. One of the main reasons that the large machinery producing firms opted for the up-market strategy was that the historical strength of the labor force in their plants blocked any attempts to push wages down to exploitative levels. But just as importantly, large heavy machinery producers were really not in a position to radically change their orientation to the market. They had tremendously large organizations and expensive plants that could not be easily reoriented to the production of cheaper, more large-series machine products. The only realistic hope for these machinery producers was for them to improve the quality of their products and control costs, especially nonlabor costs, within production. The logic behind the hope was that the sophistication and custom character of the products and quality of manufacturing would warrant slightly higher prices.

One has to imagine the kind of problem these large autarkic machinery firms confronted. Giant firms composed of a multitude of workshops, often in several locations, each with general and particular capabilities, producing hundreds of products, which, because they were almost always custom built, could be made in effect in infinite variation, generated many inefficiencies. Orders could get lost or delayed, capacities could be duplicated several times in different workshops, parts such as screws, bolts, and gauges could be designed in infinite variety. Controlling costs in this context meant trying to introduce standardization and coordination, create norms and eliminate redundancies. Most importantly, this had to be achieved without upsetting the dynamic cross-fertilization of ideas and techniques that stemmed from the combined strategies of diversification and specialty production.

The invention of cost-cutting techniques within these parameters was called "rationalization."[156] The first step involved improving the firm's ability to coordinate the flow of work through workshops. This meant further refining the grouping of workers and production machinery, placing common skills and technological capacities together, and making a greater effort to be more precise about the particular operations that given workshops should perform.[157] At the same time, firms tried to create norms and standards within the factory. By becoming more clear about the procedure to be followed in the movement of a given project and its multitude of parts through the plant, about systems of wage payment, and about the kinds of products that were used repeatedly in the production of a firm's diversified product palette, such as nuts, bolts, and screws, a firm could achieve tremendous cost savings. The less variety of products a firm produced, of course, the more standardized the procedures could become. But the effort to create norms and standards alone could lead to considerable cost savings.[158]

Perhaps the most profound change brought on by rationalization was the seemingly innocuous effort to introduce standard types of machinery into the product palette. Making standard types of machinery was no small matter in a firm active in hundreds of different machinery markets. It made a world of difference, for example, if a firm self-consciously specialized its production on specific machinery types – say, crushing machinery for coal mining – rather than focusing broadly on an area of end use in which a wide variety of technological and engineering principles relating to the crushing of rock applied. "Typification" meant that firms transformed themselves from large craft production houses into industrial producers of machines.[159] Even if the company continued to engage in customizing, the mere fact that it did so around a particular type of machine introduced elements of routine into the production process and thus made possible savings from standardization and the creation of norms.

All of these reforms within the firms involved the creation of more internal specialization within the firm among its workshops and its product lines. In the end, this proved not to be a threat to the process of dynamic cross-fertilization that the diversified firms depended on; indeed, it actually improved it by focusing the amount of interworkshop and interdepartment communication that had to take place. Specialization, standardization, typification, and the creation of norms all were ways of optimizing specialty production. Firms limited their involvement in any given product technology and simultaneously hedged the risk they incurred from specialization by the continued existence of broad specialization in the product palette. The aim was the same as it was before the war: to ensure that the interrelationships between the various specialties within the firm complemented one another and fostered technological learning within the firm. But the process involved was less chaotic, redundant, and inefficient.

Autarkic industrial order in Germany

Rationalizing markets. These reforms in the way in which firms organized production were matched in many product lines, especially in the latter half of the 1920s after the great inflation, by efforts among competing enterprises to cooperate with one another to organize their markets. This was especially the case in product markets in which there was overcapacity, such as locomotive, boiler, and other forms of heavy machine construction. But it also occurred in other growing markets, such as power unit, prime-mover production, and diesel engines, where firms wanted to avoid constant competitive bidding in continuously cyclical markets. There were a number of different ways in which the organization of the market could take place. One strategy was to purchase smaller producers and consolidate existing capacity with that of the new firm, eliminating duplication. Between 1927 and 1930, there were many mergers or majority participations in the industry: 24 in 1927, 28 in 1928 and 25 in 1930.[160] In other cases, two independent firms entered into specialization arrangements to reduce capacity in the industry. Two or three producers making the same range of machines, say agricultural machinery, printing presses, or refrigeration equipment, would agree to align their production palettes in such a way as to split the range of machines among the two or three producers in a way that eliminated competition between them. The absolute production capacity in the industry would not change, but its distribution became, with the exchange, more efficient.[161] In still other cases, firms would agree on a strategy of specialization. Thus, two locomotive producers also engaged in a variety of other lines of machinery production would strike an arrangement whereby the total locomotive production capacity of both companies was allocated to one of the firms, while a second specialty would be allocated to the other firm.[162]

By paying attention both to the state of competition and capacity in particular branches outside the firm and to potential beneficial interrelationships between different products in the product palette within the firm itself, large corporate machinery producers began to systematically divest themselves of some activities and invest in others, all to maximize the total performance and flexibility of the firm. The right combination of products, which at the most microlevel involved the right mix of specialized workshops, became the strategic goal of the enterprise. The task of the top management of such enterprises was to provide the infrastructure for the diffusion of knowledge and risk across the firm's diversified holdings: engineers and workers had to be circulated through the firm; sales, design, development and production people had to be regularly brought into contact; information about future technologies and markets needed to be disseminated among the workshops; and poorly performing markets and cross-firm rationalization possibilities had to be identified.

Here we see autarky at work. Operations that were performed by a broad array of actors in the decentralized industries were all performed within a single enterprise in the autarkic machinery industry. Autarkic machinery producers looked very much like the autarkic *Konzerne*, though they were much smaller and were involved only in the production of machinery. They differed from Vestag in that they continued to be specialty producers.

Conclusion: Autarkic industrialization

The purpose of this chapter was to reposition the narrative of the development of large-scale industry in Germany into a story of regional industrialization. All three case studies reveal that organizations and governance structures in industry within the autarkic regions were profoundly shaped by the agrarian circumstances out of which industrial experiments grew. Indeed, these initial circumstances to a certain extent shaped the kind of experiments that were attempted. The distinctive feature of the kind of industrialization that emerged out of these initial starting conditions, of course, was that most aspects of production and its governance were organized within the boundaries of very large enterprises.

A second feature of the narrative of large-firm development presented in this chapter is that, like the decentralized producers, the development of the industrial order involved constant efforts to reshape production, the institutions of governance, and even the context in which action took place. These strategic and transformative efforts occurred in response to challenges and opportunities that emanated both from abroad, in the form of technological and organizational challenges, and from within the developing form of order itself, as growth and strategic behavior created ambiguity regarding the relationship between industrial production and its broader context.

Now that both the initial industrialization experience within both forms of industrial order within the German economy have been described, the next chapter will turn to the way in which each of the regional systems of industrial order were accommodated at the national level within the entire German political economy.

4

The national context: 1871–1945

The aim of this chapter is mainly to explore the implications that the remapping of the industrialization process in the previous two chapters have for the way in which governance problems cast at the level of the German political economy as a whole can be understood. As such, what follows shifts the discussion to a higher level of analysis. Whereas the previous chapters focused on each of the patterns of regional economic order in isolation, this one will consider the ways in which the two different kinds of industrialization were accommodated within the various regimes that governed the German political economy between 1871 and 1945. The chapter will show that where accommodation was achieved it came through the construction of a composite structure of national-level governance mechanisms, in which multiple boundaries between the central state and the economy were institutionalized.

The main point the alternative perspective developed here makes versus traditional narratives of the development of the German political economy is the following: If the process of industrialization is understood not as a unitary social transformation but as a variety of regionally distinct social transformations, then the process of creating national-level rules, policies, and institutions for the governance of economic process (e.g., national financial institutions, taxation schemes, tariff structures, railroads, legal rules about contracts, industrial agencies and policies, etc.) cannot be understood as involving the establishment of a single, uniform system of governance nor even a single or uniform boundary between the national institutions of economic governance and society. Rather, the discussion below will make clear that development of each of the regionally distinct systems of industrial order posed very different kinds of national governance problems for which unique and discreet institutional solutions were (or were not) provided.

To avoid confusion at the start, the argument here is decidedly not that the relationship between the autarkic and decentralized industrial orders in the industrializing German political economy constituted a systematic political cleavage. Indeed, the problem under analysis here is only indirectly related to classic problems of state building: The focus instead is on the construction of national-level institutions and mechanisms of industrial governance. The state, at

112 *Industrial constructions*

a variety of levels, can be and was involved in the construction of these mechanisms, but governance as a general problem does not *require* state involvement at any level.[1] Furthermore, as an abstract matter, there is no reason to think that different national-level governance problems should necessarily be incompatible with one another, although it is conceivable that they could be. Nor is it necessary that the provision of a solution to national-level problems for one form of industrial order should mean that the solution to national-level problems posed by the other order cannot be found. Indeed, the historical argument that follows shows clearly that, most of the time, the two forms of industrial order did not conflict with one another at a national level of governance and that their strategic interaction seldom resulted in a zero-sum game either politically or economically.

Nevertheless, the coexistence of two different processes of industrialization within the boundaries of a single national political economy had to be managed and different mechanisms were constructed to insure the stable reproduction of each form of order within each of the unified German regimes that existed between 1871 and 1945. The construction of such mechanisms often involved both political debate and conflict. My argument is that the outcome of these struggles was ultimately that there was never one uniform national-level system of governance in the German political economy before 1945; there were always several. The notion of *accommodation* as it will be used throughout this chapter (and again in chapter seven) refers to the successful provision by a particular historical regime of the mechanisms necessary for the stable reproduction of an industrial order. Lack of accommodation refers to failed efforts to define an array of governance mechanisms that provide for stable reproduction. *Coexistence* refers to the stable reproduction of both forms of industrial order within the political and economic boundaries defined by a given historical German regime (i.e., the Wilhelmine Reich, the Weimar Republic, and the Third Reich).

Constructing national institutional frameworks to accommodate different regional capitalisms

The basic questions that this chapter attempts to answer are: How were the two different patterns of regional industrial order, as they have been described in the previous two chapters, accommodated within the boundaries of a single national political economy and what kinds of (if any) political conflicts were involved in the creation of a national institutional architecture of governance mechanisms that made such accommodation possible? Most accounts of the development of industrial capitalism in Germany do not address the problem of accommodation as it is posed here because they work within an interpretive frame that understands the process of industrialization to be largely unitary: The forces of industrialization and modernization (bourgeois and working classes, liberalism and socialism, large firms and mass production) are pitted against the forces of traditionalism and reaction (Junker agriculturalists, backward and embattled

The national context: 1871–1945

artisans, aristocratic conservatives and nationalist soldiers) in one large national arena. To the extent that a problem of accommodation is posed at all within this kind of framing, it is usually cast at the level of major national-level institutions: That is, how does the process of unitary industrialization interact with and impinge upon the development of, for example, liberal parliamentary government, the institutions of the welfare state, or the central associations for the representation of business and labor interests.[2]

Within these larger dramas, the more narrow problem of the governance of industry has been posed in terms of the relationship between large-scale producers in fast-growing industries (e.g., steel, coal mining, chemicals, and electromechanical producers during the second half of the 19th century), universal banks, and the emerging central state. As is well known, this has primarily involved attention to the character of universal bank–large industry relations, the emergence and political activities of significant business associations, and the orientation of the state itself around such macropolitical economic problems as the structure and availability of capital, the level of tariffs and, more fundamentally, the character of law (e.g., the protection of contracts).[3]

The obvious problem with all of these traditional framings is that they focus too exclusively on what I have described in Chapter 3 as the autarkic industrial order. The small- and medium-sized businesses of the decentralized industrial order described in Chapter 2 are mostly blended out of (or seriously mischaracterized within) these historical narratives of the emergence of the German political economy. At best, these producers and their governing institutions are constructed as a residual category, thought either to be cast outside of or simply subsumed within the core architecture of governing institutions within the modernizing German industrial political economy. Mostly, however, in the historiography of German industry, small decentralized producers are simply considered to have been of relatively little interest. Indeed, in the larger political narratives of German history, such producers wind up being interesting at all only because they overwhelmingly became Nazis.[4]

This judgement of the political and economic significance of the producers within the decentralized industrial order has existed basically for one of two reasons, both of which the previous chapters have proven to be inaccurate. The most traditional reason to relegate decentralized production to the periphery of discussions regarding the construction of a national political economy in Germany is based on the view that industrialization ultimately eliminates that kind of production. The second reason, responding to the patent implausibility of the first, argues that industrialization systematically creates a dual industrial structure with a large-scale, technologically advanced core and a more small-scale, backward, fragile periphery.[5]

The preceding chapters make this latter view implausible on at least two grounds. First, the producers in the decentralized industrial order were not technologically backward. On the contrary, the evidence adduced in Chapter 2 showed that these producers were highly competitive exporters in world manufacturing markets. Machinery and textiles made by decentralized producers in

Saxony, Württemberg, and the Rhineland, cutlery from Solingen, Krefeld lace, musical instruments from Thüringen, specialty steel and iron products from the Sauer- and Siegerlands all had extremely strong positions in world markets by the outbreak of the World War I and were extremely respected producers both within Germany and throughout Europe.[6] Second, the decentralized areas were not full of subcontractors for larger producers in autarkic regions. Beyond the purchase of raw materials, there was little real exchange between the two different kinds of regions – autarkic producers were autarkic and did not subcontract very much. Decentralized producers made finished products in a broad variety of industries, many of which overlapped with and competed directly with products made in autarkic areas. The decentralized industrial order was not peripheral or dependent; it was a different, viable, self-reproducing system of industrial production within the German economy.[7]

If the primary lens through which the decentralized producers were interpreted turns out to be based upon untenable assumptions about the nature of industrial process, what consequence does that have for the national-level narrative of governance and industrial politics that bases itself in those assumptions? Placing the larger questions of the development of liberal parliamentarism and the welfare state to the side, I will argue here that there were two very important consequences. One concerns the institutional character of relations between the industrial economy and the state, and the other involves the interpretation of the politics of the decentralized producers (the *industrielle Mittelstand*) as reactionary and backward.

Basically, the first point is that the process of industrialization and state-building in Germany continuously involved struggles over the construction of architectures of national-level governance structures for the economy that could accommodate the existence of both forms of industrial order. The most successful constellation of frameworks in the pre-1945 period, I will argue here, was constructed within the Imperial Reich. There a national institutional framework was created that accommodated the decentralized industrial order by allowing for considerable regional political, legal, financial, and infrastructural governing autonomy. A largely separate and parallel framework was also constructed to accommodate the autarkic industrial order. This framework included the development of an extensive set of policies (such as protective tariffs) that protected and facilitated the stable reproduction of the autarkic producers. Finally, the Wilhelmine regime provided to both forms of industrial order legal protections for the inviolability of contracts. It also established a single currency and a single authority issuing it, which benefitted producers within both forms of industrial order.

The most problematic national framework of accommodation was the Weimar Republic, which severely curtailed local autonomy and continuously attempted to interfere in the internal affairs of autarkic firms, thus effectively alienating producers within both forms of industrial order. The National Socialist regime that followed attempted to address the concerns of both the decentralized and autarkic industrial orders, but without guaranteeing either local autonomy or freedom from intervention. My claim is that the regime collapsed before it was possible to determine how successful the framework the Nazis constructed actually was.

Regarding the political strategies and attitudes of small- and medium-sized producers in Germany, generally, the argument will be that they were motivated not by a fear of being blown away or marginalized by the process of industrialization, but by a desire to establish, protect or defend the contours of public authority that allowed them to stably govern and reproduce their particular conception of industrial society. This was true in the Imperial Reich, under the Weimar Republic, and under National Socialist dictatorship.

The Imperial Reich

Composite structures of accommodation

The formation of a unified Germany was achieved in 1871 (see Map 3 in Appendix). The remarkable thing about this unification from the point of view of political economy is that there was very little direct and overt struggle between the two different forms of industrial order that were developing within the various German regions. Theoretically, there are two ways in which one could imagine that the coexistence of the two different kinds of industrial order could be threatened by being placed within the boundaries of a single political unit. The first way places considerable emphasis on the homogenizing capacity of market competition. For example, if it were the case that the differently organized regional economies had developed independently of one another in relatively protected market environments, and then suddenly found that with political unification the competitive environment had been adversely transformed because markets were unified, the argument would be that homogenization of industrial forms would be likely to occur. Market unification would quickly establish a standard of efficiency and the more efficient form of industrial order would triumph over the less efficient one. The less efficient forms of organization would, gradually, decay.

The other way in which one could imagine that the possible coexistence of both forms of industrial order within the boundaries of a single political economy could be threatened would place emphasis on the homogenizing power of politics. That is, if one or the other form of industrial order was larger numerically or financially more powerful than the other, it could potentially command greater attention and resources from the new central state. The smaller and less powerful form of industrial order could then potentially suffer from a diversion of resources or interest by the central state away from its concerns to those of the larger and more powerful order. Over time, this could lead to the decay of the neglected order.

Neither of these scenarios occurred in Imperial Germany because an architecture of governance structures within the new regime was constructed which

116 *Industrial constructions*

prevented both from happening. Some of the most important structures were features within the Constitution of the new Reich, while others involved the construction of important public and infrastructural institutions in ways that enabled both forms of industrial order to stably reproduce themselves.

The key to the achievement of successful accommodation within the Imperial Reich lay in the fact that the local governance arrangements in the preunification states of the German confederation were preserved within the structure of the new Reich. Prior to the unification of Germany in 1871, the different regional forms of industrial order were contained within separate political units. The main regions of the decentralized-based industrial order – the Kingdom of Saxony, Hessen-Nassau, and the various Thüringen states – were independent countries until 1866, while Württemberg and Baden remained independent until 1871. Autarky was located in Prussia, Hannover, and Bavaria. These were also independent countries: Prussia and Hannover until 1866, and Bavaria until 1871. Even though these states had all participated in the same unified market within the *Zollverein* since the 1830s, each retained full political control over its external relations with other states. More importantly, within each of these small political economies, state resources and mechanisms (e.g., monies for technological experimentation, technical training, export marketing, etc.) could be devoted undistractedly to the reproduction of the economies within them in the manner outlined in previous chapters.

Thus, within the confederal structure of the preunification *Zollverein*, competition from larger autarkic producers was countered in decentralized regions through the construction of compensating institutions, such as cooperative banks, research institutes, and educational facilities at the regional level. Such institutions helped to socialize many of the basic costs of production and enabled smaller producers to remain competitive in increasingly interconnected markets. As a result, by the time of the unification of the Reich in 1871, most purely market-based threats to coexistence were largely nonstarters. A unified German market was achieved before political unification and, as discussed in Chapter 2, was in many ways an important factor in shaping the particular institutional development of the decentralized order.[8]

The political unification of Germany in 1871 was able to preserve the multiplicity of industrial practices that the confederal structure had made possible through the construction of a constitutional framework that balanced decentralized political and industrial autonomy with greater national standardization. One can see this, first of all, in the structure of the state itself. The state that was created through the defeat of the Danes in 1864, the Austrians at Königgratz in 1866, and the French in 1871 was not a unitary, centralized political structure. On the contrary, it was a federal structure in which various independent, largely self-governing, constitutional monarchies participated in the government and direction of their common affairs through a supraordinate government structure. Local authority in this structure was not replaced by national authority, but rather was supplemented and complemented by it.[9]

The heart of the federal structure was the upper chamber of government, the

The national context: 1871–1945

Federal Council or Bundesrat. All of the 25 individual states that composed the Reich sent delegates to this council, which held the power to alter the structure of the Constitution.[10] The individual political territories were not represented equally in the Bundesrat; rather, they received a quantity of votes based upon size and population. Of the 58 votes cast in the body, seventeen belonged to Prussia alone.[11] This allowed Prussia to block any constitutional changes it did not approve of, and indeed, to determine a broad array of policies in the Reich. But it was also an amount insufficient to allow it unilaterally to dictate dramatic constitutional changes affecting the rights and boundaries of the other states.

The Federal Council was the expression of a compromise between Prussia and the member states that had been brokered at the time of the unification of Germany. Max Weber cynically referred to it as the "representative solidarity of the princely courts and ministries" and viewed it – in its Imperial incarnation at least – as an obstacle to effective parliamentarization.[12] For our purposes, however, it is important to note that the Bundesrat was designed to have the power to defend the relative autonomy of the member states of the Reich. Indeed, for the smaller states, this was an important condition of entry if they were to join a Reich headed by Prussia, as opposed to aligning themselves with another power, such as Austria, or, more remotely, France.[13]

The Constitution of the Reich accorded the individual states considerable responsibility. Essentially, the Federal Government was ceded all powers in foreign policy and commanded the military in time of war. The Federal Government also had legislative authority in the field of commercial and tariff policy, matters of transportation and communication, control of the banking system, coinage and international exchange, weights and measures, etc. But here the capacity of the central state to structure these common features in ways that would be beneficial to some and detrimental to others in different localities was constrained by the fact that all guidelines and policies had to meet the approval of the Bundesrat and the Reichstag. The examples of the Imperial Railroad system and the Uniform Civil Code provide good examples of how the consolidating and standardizing efforts of the central state were consistently constructed in ways that helped to ensure continued regional political and economic autonomy.

Take first the example of the Imperial railroad system. Prior to the unification, railways in Germany, though extensive, were a complicated mixture of publicly and privately operated enterprises whose relations were largely coordinated within an Association of Railway Administrations, which coordinated the transfer of property and the construction of lines. Regional Traffic Associations set rates and negotiated relations between different market areas, which was an important mechanism for the calibration of interregional markets. Initially, immediately after the unification of Germany, Bismarck attempted to consolidate all German railways within a central authority, which would have not only established standards and coordinated building, but would have set freight rates as well. Viewed as a threat to their regional autonomy, the Bundesrat vetoed Bismarck's bill three times.

Ultimately, the system that evolved was extremely sensitive to the need to calibrate traffic and rate structures in ways that respected regional economic interests. By the beginning of World War I, most railways in Germany had been nationalized, but instead of there being one single German railway, there were eight separate regional railway systems run by different regional governments (including Prussia). A central Railway Traffic Association was given authority to establish national rate structures, but it was mandated to do so in conjunction with regional government appointed Regional Railway Councils made up of representatives of trade, industry, and agriculture. Relations between decentralized and autarkic regions were thus subject to continuous negotiation through this highly decentralized national system.[14]

A further example of the manner in which the autonomy of regional interests were retained despite the creation of a national system involved the formation of a uniform civil code. The establishment of a uniform civil code of law was an extremely important goal of the liberal groups that had supported Bismarck in his efforts to unify Germany. A uniform code of law was held to be not only crucial for the establishment of a proper *Rechtsstaat*, but also to provide the foundation for a united German nation. A committee of prominent legal scholars – most of whom were the proponents of the distinctive German legal positivism of the day – was assembled to conduct the tedious task of creating a single code out of the many different regional systems that had developed within the various states in Germany. The politics surrounding the creation and composition of the committee were intense because many of the regional governments feared that the creation of a national code would not only undermine their regional authority, but would also jeopardize the stability and existence of traditional regional relations and practices which the local law had protected. Ultimately, these kinds of fears worked to structure the mandate of the committee. Rather than constructing a completely new system of liberal law out of whole cloth, the mandate of the committee, according to Michael John, was to "aim to be a systematic compilation of the existing legal systems of the German states."[15] Regional particularity, in other words, was to be preserved within the national code, not supplanted by it.

These examples are important because they show how the local institutions that were constitutive of the different regional industrial orders could have been preserved despite the existence of significant powers in the hands of the central state. There were many dimensions of the infrastructure of governance within the Imperial Reich that had this kind of unified yet decentralized character. The most relevant further examples that can be pointed to have already been extensively discussed in Chapters 2 and 3 and therefore need not be given a great deal of attention here: the structure of the banking system and of vocational training. In each of these latter cases, much as in the cases of the railroads and the civil code, national-level institutions were created that facilitated the reproduction of local diversity. There were, for example, three distinct kinds of banking systems in the Imperial Reich: commercial banks, savings banks, and cooperatives. In the latter two cases, as Chapter 2 made clear, the construction of national-level organizations transpired with the explicit purpose of strengthening the lending capacity of local members. The construction of the Imperial Reich in part helped to facilitate and in part accommodated these diverse institutional efforts: One important achievement, very much in line with the theme of uniformity in the interest of diversity and decentralization, was to eliminate competition between similarly structured banks in different regions through the imposition of a single currency and a single currency-issuing authority. Banks had been using their capacity to issue currency as a competitive tool to enter markets of competitors in neighboring regions. Centralizing this capacity introduced a form of competitive order and stability into banking markets and actually helped stabilize the emerging three-pillared, regionally rooted banking system in Germany.[16]

But the power of regional interests within the Imperial Reich was even greater than these examples allow. The examples focus on the powers that the central state had and on how those powers were limited or accommodating, not intrusive or homogenizing. Yet, within the constitutional order of the Imperial Reich there were obvious and enormously important powers that the Federal Government *did not have*, such as, in particular, the power to collect direct taxes.[17] Though the central state could collect revenue from customs duties, consumer taxes on beer, salt, and other staples, and transportation tolls, an important percentage of the revenues accruing to the new state created by Bismarck came from yearly payments by the member states to the Reich as a "matriculation fee." Member states also retained considerable other rights and responsibilities: All matters that affected the citizen's daily life and the safety and well-being of his or her family fell under the jurisdiction of the independent federal states, including education, health services, and the police. Württemberg and Bavaria, moreover, actually retained their own armed forces, which they recruited and trained, even though they were ultimately subject to the command of the Federal Government during wartime.

All of this was the expression of the political compromise that Prussia had entered into in order to establish a unified Germany under its hegemony.[18] But as such, it was a structure that allowed the various regions to retain a considerable amount of local autonomy and self-government. From our point of view, the key aspect of the structure was that it allowed the member states to protect their economies from all of the potential homogenizing threats noted above.[19] Relatively autonomous administration and the power to collect their own taxes fragmented the structures of the central state and ensured that resources would not be diverted by a central government to other regions. Significantly, local control over education also meant that resources could be continually made available for the manpower and technological needs of local producers.

On the whole, regions dominated by the decentralized form of industrial order were integrated into the Reich as independent states, such as Saxony, Württemberg, and Baden. The major exception to this was the Rhineland. This was not only a province in Prussia, where regions of autarky and decentralization could be found, it was also itself divided into areas of autarkic organization and those of decentralized organization. The Rhineland was able to manage the coexistence of the different industrial orders through a different kind of local political autonomy. In the Rhineland, the level of the city was crucial rather than that of the member state. Cities in Prussia – and to varying degrees, throughout the rest of Germany – were accorded significant self-governing powers. They had their own administration, collected direct taxes (both income and real estate), and administered all social welfare services.[20] Moreover, they had governments that were popularly elected, though, in Prussia, this meant that the highly skewed three-class voting system was operative. Cities in the Rhineland such as Remscheid, Solingen, Elberfeld, Barmen, Krefeld, Mönchengladbach, Aachen, Düren, and others governed systems of decentralized industrial order in a relatively autonomous way. The structure of Prussian law provided the cities with a fiscal and administrative autonomy that ensured that resources could not be diverted away from their local economies.[21]

These institutional features of the Imperial Reich all accorded subsidiary regional governments and regional economic actors with administrative, fiscal, and legal autonomy, even in those areas in which the central state held nominal authority. As such, they were necessary for the coexistence of two different patterns of industrialization within the same national political economy during the 19th century. The institutions of local autonomy were extremely important to the decentralized producers because much of their system of order was completely embedded in a regional political context. For producers in autarkic regions, however, the existence of local autonomy was of less importance. Autarkic producers did not rely on local authorities to provide inputs and services that were crucial for the operation of the autarkic order. In the autarkic order, all aspects of production and its governance were performed within the boundaries of the firm. Problems that autarkic firms did not or could not manage to control through their own individual or collective efforts tended to be located at the level of the national economy and demanded the attention of the central, rather than the local, state. This was true, for example, of basic background institutional matters such as the protection of the sanctity and independence of contracts and property, the maintenance of a trustworthy and stable currency of exchange and, after the 1870s, the protection of price levels in particularly sensitive sectors from the challenges of competitors from outside Germany. And, on the whole, as Chapter 3 outlined, the central state was very accommodating to the autarkic producers.

In this manner, the structure of political economic governance in the Imperial Reich succeeded quite well in accommodating the demands and governance problems of both forms of industrial order that were developing in different regions within its national political economy. Crucially, the national architecture of governance was in no way uniform: The institutional arrangements that accommodated the problems of decentralized industrial order were quite distinct from those that accommodated the autarkic industrial producers. The stable reproduction of industrial practice within the Imperial Reich thus occurred within a framework that was constituted through multiple boundaries between the state and society. Economic governance at the national level was not one system; it was a composite of several.

Industrial politics

These differences in the way in which decentralized and autarkic producers related to the state and were incorporated within the governing framework of the national political economy shaped the way in which modes of industrial interest representation and political activity developed among industrial producers within each of the industrial orders. Predictably, the importance of national-level policies for the autarkic industrial producers led to the formation of organizations for the representation of industrial interest at the national level. In 1876, during the struggle over the question of the tariff, producers in the Rhineland and Westphalia (according to Gerschenkron, mostly iron and steel producers and spinning mills) formed the Centralverband für Deutsche Industrie (CVDI).[22] This group represented the interests of those industrial producers that had attempted to compete head-on with foreign factory-produced goods. To protect their investments and limit competition, German factory producers sought to shut foreign producers out of the domestic market. The central business association was built upon a base of participating sectoral organizations that had been organized to represent the interests of individual industries. Many of the member associations were actually fronts for operating cartels. As an interest group, the organization continued to be active on the political stage until World War I. It was identified with heavy industry, large-scale factory production, protectionism, and cartels.[23]

As noted in Chapter 3, autarkic producers had a very ambivalent relationship to the state. This was expressed quite clearly in the orientation of their interest organizations. On the one hand, they engaged wholeheartedly in politics and sought to involve the state in the configuration of their market environment. This was especially true of the tariff policies and cartel law, but it also ranged to questions about the structure of popular suffrage and the voting system. Large industrialists consistently supported the government in its efforts to stave off political movements trying to reform the unequal voting system and increase the powers of parliament. They feared the potential power of the social democratic movement and sought to uphold the constitutional features of the polity that would prevent the socialists from growing more powerful.[24]

On the other hand, the autarkic industrialists zealously defended their own sphere of autonomy against incursions by the state. Production and its administration was their province, and the state, in their view, had no right to intervene in those processes that fell within the boundaries of firm and market. This, in particular, was their view with respect to cartelization and to growth by merger.[25] When the Prussian government attempted to nationalize part of the coal industry in the early 1900s to check the growth of concentration among dominant firms, the industrialists of the Ruhr fought bitterly against it. As their firms grew larger and more powerful, autarkic producers and their associations grew increasingly confident, even arrogant, about the central importance of their role as producers in German society. Not only should the state stay out their affairs, they believed, it should honor and support the contribution to national greatness that industry made.[26] Sources of conflict between the state and the large firms of autarkic industry revolved around differing conceptions of the proper boundary between the responsibilities of firms and those of the state.

In contrast to the development of interest representation in the autarkic areas, for most of the 19th century decentralized producers, on the whole, did not seek to have their interests represented at the national level of politics. Instead, their focus was on the level of local and regional government.[27] Moreover, in place of the sectoral identity typical of autarkic region producers, manufacturers in the decentralized regions tended to identify themselves generally as industrialists without respect to a particular industrial sector. This can be clearly seen in the character and identity of their associations. Unlike the autarkic CVDI, for example, the peak association for autarkic producers, the *Bund der Industriellen* (BDI) was not based upon numerous sectoral organizations representing different industries. Rather, the national organization was based upon subassociations representing the interest of all industrial producers in particular regions: e.g., the Association of Saxon Industrialists (Verein Sachsische Industriellen) and the Association of Württemberg Industrialists (Verein Württembergische Industriellen). For these producers, the particular line of business that they were in mattered less than the fact that they shared with one another a common regional economic system and supporting institutions. The term that was eventually adopted to describe the position of these small- and medium-sized, regionally embedded industrialists in Wilhelmine society was *"industrielle Mittelstand,"* or industrial middle class.

By the end of the nineteenth century, the rapid growth of the autarkic industries had sufficiently transformed the dynamic within the German political economy so that it was no longer possible for the decentralized producers to stay out of national-level politics. In 1895, producers within the *industrielle Mittelstand* throughout the Reich formed the BDI to help them gain influence in national-level political debate. Two factors formed the impetus for the formation of the BDI: The growth of cartels in the iron, steel, and coal industries, and the continuing problem of high German tariffs. Cartels increased the prices of the raw materials that decentralized manufacturers used in production and made their products more expensive in the world market. At the same time, high German tariffs encouraged foreign countries to discriminate against German products. Both of these factors worked to the disadvantage of the decentralized producers, precisely at a time when they were increasingly looking to produce for export markets. The BDI was conceived as a counterweight to the CVDI that could lobby the Imperial state directly. Though the association representing the autarkic producers was more concentrated and richer than the BDI, the new organization had some very predictable advantages over the CVDI: Because of its regional internal structure, the BDI was able to indirectly influence policy on the national-level by lobbying local governments who then participated in national level legislation in the Bundesrat.[28]

The BDI acted in politics with a conception of the state that was consistent with the way its members experienced it in the conduct of their local business affairs. On the one hand, the BDI, like the *industrielle Mittelstand* itself, was covetous of the ability of independent producers to guide and direct their own affairs. On the other hand, however, the BDI also recognized that the state could be a partner to industry in the acquisiton and development of new technologies and also play an important role in creating and supporting institutions that enabled independent producers in a decentralized system of governance to reproduce themselves.

In the early 1900s, the national-level expression of this was the BDI's efforts to get the state to intervene in the way that the iron and steel industry allocated steel. Rather than raise simple materialist arguments based upon the direct interests of the manufacturing sector of the economy – which, for example, the sectorally organized steel-using manufacturing associations in the autarkic order tended to do – the BDI argued for state regulation of the policies of the steel industry on the basis of the industrial middle classes' legitimate claim for a place in German society. The state, in their view, should structure the national market in a way that allowed all important social and economic interests in German society to reproduce themselves.[29]

Conflicts among business interests in the Imperial Reich were catalyzed by factors relating to particular economic problems: tariffs, steel prices, coal prices, etc. As such, the lines of alliance within industry did not always correspond to the lines of division between the different forms of industrial order. For example, the BDI often received the support of autarkic producers in manufacturing industries that were also affected by tariffs and high raw materials prices. The giant electro-technical firms Siemens and AEG and the chemical and machinery producers were the most notable autarkic allies of the decentralized producers. These latter firms could not and did not, however, commit themselves to the particular vision of the relationship between the state and the economy that was developed by the BDI and its supporters in the final decade before World War I. In the end, the decentralized producers held a different conception of the proper boundary between market, firm, and state in the political economy.

The Weimar Republic

In the wake of military defeat, revolution, and the collapse of the Imperial Reich in 1918, concurrent and parallel efforts emerged to stabilize each of the different industrial systems within the newly emerging Weimar Republic. Many of the important institutional features of the old Reich that had played key roles in the stabilization of one or the other of the industrial orders were transferred with little formal alteration into the new Reich. This was particularly true of the multiple banking systems and the basic tenents of civil law.[30] Other institutions such as the railroads were reformed, yet in ways that were compatible with the system that existed under the Imperial Reich. Despite these important lines of continuity in the architecture of national-governance mechanisms with the national political economy of the Second Reich, however, the new Weimar Republic proved unable to construct a set of arrangements that could foster the stable reproduction of each of the industrial orders. In the end, this failure contributed to the willingness of the part of producers in both industrial orders to support moves to abandon the Republic at the beginning of the 1930s.

Partially, the inability of the parliamentary Republic to find an adequate form of accommodation was caused by the inhospitable international economic climate in which the Weimar experience was embedded. Instability and relative stagnation placed a great deal of stress on producers and political actors everywhere in Germany. A stable governing coalition that could have facilitated the construction of institutional mechanisms to accommodate the needs of both forms of industrial order proved impossible to form either inside or outside of parliament. Given the external environment and Germany's position in it, it is possible that no political structure could have helped the Weimar economy overcome the obstacles that it confronted.[31]

But it was also true that the failure to create an appropriate national framework for the governance of the different forms of German industry had to do with specific characteristics of the Weimar Constitution, the politics that surrounded its construction, and the manner in which it shaped relations between the two forms of industrial order. There were two dimensions of the Weimar Constitution in particular that affected the Republic's capacity to accommodate the governance challenges posed by reproduction processes in both forms of industrial order.

The first concerned the division of powers and responsibilities between federal, regional, and municipal-level authorities. The political and ideological forces that emerged from the upheaval of war and revolution, many of which cannot be mapped onto the interests of industry, created a very complicated federalist compromise during the construction of the Weimar constitution that completely undermined the fruitful balance between local and regional autonomy and central authority that had existed in the Imperial Reich. Over time, the terms of the compromise gave rise to political resentment against the central state within decentralized regions.

The second aspect of the Constitution involved the relationship between the balance of parliamentary forces that it made possible and the principles of organization governing the autarkic form of industrial order. Social democratic and Catholic-influenced governments continuously devised policies, particularly in the areas of social welfare and collective bargaining, which annoyed the autarkic producers by infringing upon what they took to be the sovereign governance structures of the autarkic firm. Such intrusions engendered skepticism about democracy and parliamentary government within the autarkic business community. When the world economy collapsed at the same time that it was becoming clear that the Republic was doing a bad job at finding a stable regime for the governance of decentralized and autarkic business, this skepticism turned into outright hostility.

The argument that follows will discuss the relationship between the decentralized industrial order and the Weimar constitution first, the relationship between autarkic order and the Weimar state second, and then the difficulties that emerged among and between the two orders and the state as it became clear that the Republic was doing a bad job at governing its industry.

Federalism, the decentralized industrial order, and Weimar politics

The collapse of the Imperial regime in 1918 gave rise to a strong movement for political centralization and the creation of a unitary state.[32] Regional governments had to fight to protect their identities as political bodies within the newly emerging political structure.

On the extreme left, radically democratic soldier and worker councils advocated the creation of a unitary state based upon council democracy. Against this, Social Democrats, such as the reigning chancellor of the Reich Friedrich Ebert and the influential liberal thinker Hugo Preuss, advocated the formation of a parliamentary republic with a unitary, democratic character.[33] Other, less democratic advocates of centralization envisioned a strong state that could control strong, centralized producer associations.

Many of the voices calling for centralization were fixated on the autarkic industrial order. Typically, these people sympathized with the most radical strands of the council movement or with technocratic corporatist thinkers, such as Wickart Moellendorf and Walter Rathenau. Here, the focus was on the large autarkic firms in the economy, and the interest was in preserving and expanding the corporatistic forms of state control developed during the war economy.[34] Ultimately, the ideal of the radical socialists, corporatists, and technocrats was to direct the future evolution of the industrial economy by rational centralized planning.[35]

Yet it was far from the case that all advocates of centralization were concerned exclusively with autarkic industrial organization. Preuss, who actually composed the initial drafts of the Weimar Constitution, believed deeply in the importance of democratic self-government at a local level (a traditional feature of the decentralized industrial order), yet he did not believe that the intermediate level of regional "land" governments, as they were constituted in Germany, could be made consistent with a nationwide democratic polity.[36] They were defined upon the basis of dynastic rights, with little reference to the interests or will of the populations in them. This, Preuss believed, complicated the problem of sovereignty and unnecessarily fractured the formation of a coherent democratic will in the society at large.[37]

Nor was it the case that all defenders of federalism came from regions dominated by the decentralized form of industrial order. Traditional regional identities played a strong role. For example, the most radical advocate of state rights in the new German state was Bavaria, a primarily agrarian region with pockets of autarkic industry in and around the cities of Munich, Augsburg, and Nuremberg. In the space of a year, Bavaria was both a revolutionary republic and the main seat of anti-republican conservative reaction. In both cases, however, the Bavarian government adopted a radically federalist position that sought to protect the autonomy of Bavarian regional interests and culture from possible intrusions from the traditionally alien, Protestant, north German political forces. Similarly strong regional identity was important in Prussia, especially in eastern agrarian and military circles.[38]

Another major voice in the national debate favoring the reintroduction of federalist structures was Max Weber. Weber was more of a skeptic about the possibilities for dramatic political change than an advocate of decentralization. He took the persistence of regional political identity seriously and was convinced that parliamentary government in Germany would only be possible if the federalist structures were retained. Regional, especially non-Prussian, interests, he argued, would never condone a simple unitary parliament, particularly if it had its capital in Berlin. The events of the revolution, which had transformed previous federal states into independent revolutionary republics, only underscored the practical political impossibility of creating a unitary state.[39]

Even though they were not the only voices favoring the recreation of federalist structures in the new republic, all of the regional governments that had been traditionally deeply engaged in the process of decentralized industrialization during the 19th century – Saxony, Württemberg, Baden, and Hesse – strenuously defended states rights and the principles of regional self-government during the period in which the Weimar Constitution was being composed. This was particularly, though not exclusively, true in the case of financial reform. As noted in Chapter 2, this reform shifted the capacity and power to levy direct taxes away from regional and local governments to the central state.[40]

Peter-Christian Witt, one of the main authorities on early 20th century German public finance, refers to a "bitter" contest (*erbitterter Streit*) between the National Assembly and the Reich finance ministry, on the one side, and the regional governments and their parliaments, on the other.[41] The governments in the decentralized regions of Saxony, Württemberg, Baden, and Hesse, as well as autarkic Bavaria, all publicly opposed the reforms. Four governments[42] issued a joint statement, known as the Stuttgarter Programm, to the National Assembly and the existing government in early April, 1919, which, among other things, protested encroaching centralization and defended states rights to levy direct taxes.[43] A similar document was composed in Heidelberg in July, but proved too late to influence the direction of constitutional reform.[44] Predictably, a main concern of the governments from decentralized regions was that by centralizing the capacity of the national government to raise revenue, the industrial producers in the non-Prussian outlying states would be inevitably disadvantaged.[45]

Compromise

Ultimately, the regional governments proved powerful enough to undermine the efforts of centralizers to eliminate them completely. But they were not strong enough to block efforts to centralize taxation, nor were they able to make the new Reichsrat nearly as powerful as the old Bundesrat had been under the old Regime. The major weakness of the regional governments was that they did not constitute a united front politically.

Prussia, for example, once its place in the Weimar system was established, supported many centralization reforms. Prussia was governed by a coalition government with parties identical to the social democratically dominated national governing coalition (the so-called "Weimar Coalition" of Social Democrats, Catholics, and Democratic Liberals) in the Reichstag. The regional government simply voted in solidarity with the national-level parties, partly on the (wrong) assumption that such a coalition would prevail at the national level for a long time. The Prussian government was able to exercise its influence over a majority of the other, small, more agrarian north German states so that the southern, primarily decentralized region-based governments were outnumbered.[46]

Even if Prussia had not defected, however, fragmentation would have inhibited the formation of a united front. Governments from the decentralized regions of Baden and Württemberg had little in common with the political forces in Bavaria.[47] The latter government was a constant critic of the republican government, while Baden, Württemberg, and Hesse favored states rights, but never quibbled much about their own sovereignty or opposed the formation of a parliamentary republic in Germany.[48] By further contrast, Saxony and many of the Thüringian states were dominated by radical coalitions of independent (left) Social Democrats and Communists.[49] Finally, all of the member states were financially weakened by the war, although not as desperately as the Reich itself. Pressing financial obligations probably limited their ability to push strongly for fiscal autonomy.[50]

Taking advantage of the political disarray of the regional governments, the centralizers went as far as they could to turn the regional governments into administrative instances of the Federal Government.[51] The strength of traditional regional political attachments, however, consistently prevented them from pushing their plans through to completion. In the end, no one was particularly satisfied with the institutional arrangements that emerged from the political battles surrounding the construction of the Weimar Constitution.

Consequences

It is worthwhile to contrast the state of affairs that emerged in Weimar with the one that existed during the late 19th century. Under the old regime, the lines of authority and spheres of political and economic autonomy had been clearly drawn. The considerable political and economic autonomy of regional governments within the second Reich had enabled regions in which the decentralized form of industrial order was located to avoid domination by the central state or by the financial and economic forces of the autarkic industrial order. The new structure in the Weimar Republic, in contrast, made this difficult to do. Financial autonomy had been removed from both the regional and local level governments, while the central state, frustrated by its failure to eliminate the governments altogether, was continuously seeking to extend its power. Industrial, financial, and social priorities and pressures emanating from the center consistently intruded into regional affairs.

The capacity of the center to do this was strengthened by additional new powers. Whereas the 1871 Constitution had forced the Federal Government to rely on regional government field offices to implement its policy legislation, the 1919 Constitution permitted it to establish its own field offices.[52] Finally, the capacity of regional governments to insulate themselves from the center was significantly reduced by the clear elevation of the powers of the Reichstag above those of the Reichsrat. Any legislative proposals, or emendations to existing legislation coming from the new Reichsrat (Federal Council) could be vetoed with a two-thirds majority in the Reichstag (Parliament).[53]

The ultimate consequences on the decentralized industrial order of this compromise over the form of the Constitution have already been noted in Chapter 2: in the midst of the dire economic conditions of the early 1930s, producers became alienated from and resentful toward the state and felt compelled to support groups that wanted to abandon the Weimar Constitution completely.[54] Long before such dramatic forms of unrest appeared in the decentralized areas, however, governments and interest associations located there chafed at the Federal Government's attempts to intervene in their spheres of competence.[55] This was not only because such intervention tended to create extreme bureaucratic redundancy and confusion in the carrying out of policy. It was also because the intrusiveness of the center was an affront to traditional ideas and practices of regional and local self government, which were crucial for the stable reproduction of the decentralized industrial order.[56]

Throughout the Weimar period, for example, the Württemberg government strenuously defended its political rights and administrative responsibilities from federal encroachments. A common refrain was that the traditional practice of creating central standards that preserved local autonomy had given way to efforts to create central standards that supplanted local authority. In 1927, the regional governement composed this official protest to the Federal Chancellory that makes clear its disillusionment with the center's changed orientation:

> The development has now reached the stage . . . that the autonomy of the *Länder* in general has been called into question by broad circles within the public sphere. With deep apprehension especially we south Germans must become aware of the way in which considerations for a standardization of the [governmental structure] of the Reich are misleadingly represented to the public in the sloganeering language of "rationalization" and how this, in turn, awakens false hopes for a speedy return to better times. To say right from the beginning: we want to give to the Reich what it should have. We must also demand, however, that the Reich leaves responsibilities and tasks to the *Länder* that can be performed more expediently and better by the

Länder. It is urgently necessary that the Reich and *Länder* find an appropriate division of labor of public responsibilities.⁵⁷

Regional industrial associations in decentralized areas, such as the Association of Central German Industry (*Verband der Mitteldeutschen Industrie*), also opposed centralization in economic and industrial policy. Again, the worry was that concentration of political, social, and financial decision making with respect to industry at the highest national levels would lead to the neglect of the particular needs of regionally embedded industries.⁵⁸

Such fears were fueled by developments within industrial associational life. The interventionist ambitions of the central state and the concentration of power within the Reichstag, rather than the Reichsrat, made lobbying at a national level a necessity for decentralized business. The old Bund der Industriellen had been merged with the Centralverband für deutsche Industrie in 1919 to form the Reichsverband Deutscher Industrie (RDI) to represent the general interests of German business. Yet although regional interests were taken into account within the structure of the RDI (which included regional as well as industrial associations as its members), such interests tended to be overshadowed by more sectoral conflicts between different groupings of large autarkic firms in the heavy industries, on the one side, and the finishing industries, on the other.⁵⁹ The Weimar Republic forced decentralized producers to engage in national level politics, but made it more difficult for their interests to be heard. Regional associations such as the one mentioned above thus groped for ways to have their concerns addressed.

Political sentiments opposed to the increasing absence of regional political autonomy were also observable at the level of the commune and municipality. Here, however, the sense of who was the intrusive higher authority was more complicated. The federal finance reforms had completely inverted the old system so that regional governments controlled the flow of resources from the Reich to the communes.⁶⁰ Many of the communes, especially the larger cities in the Prussian Rhineland, resented their subordination to the regional governments and often became vociferous critics of federalism and advocates of a unitary state (in many cases, in ways that resonated with the original ideas of Hugo Preuss).⁶¹ But it was the Reich, not the regional governments, that had the ultimate power to compel the communes to follow federal guidelines and constrain the way in which they implemented social welfare and other programs.

The continual interventionist presence of the regional and especially central state engendered political resentment within the communes, who felt that their autonomy as self-governing bodies was being undermined. Though written in the early 1930s, Arnold Köttgen's claims that the growing constraint of the central state on the capacity of cities to act autonomously caused a "crisis in self-government" can be taken as an expression of feelings that had been fermenting throughout the latter half of the Weimar Republic:

> I want to speak of a crisis in communal administration not as the consequence of any exogenous or contingent aspect of the current

historical situation but rather as something that must be explained from within the essence of municipalities themselves. Only then will it be possible to show that the problems of modern communities are not only those of financial and social policy. Because the crisis in the communities stem from within, organizational improvements – no matter how important they may be in themselves – will not be able to bring about the kind of decisive changes currently needed. The administrative structures that we are today in the habit of calling municipalities, in spite of the seemingly unchanged character of their material content, barely correspond to self-governing bodies in the original sense.[62]

The intimate relationship between the forms of organization within the decentralized industrial order and the institutions of local government, which for more than a century were structured through the traditions of self-government, had been disturbed by the centralizing tendencies within the constitutional structure of the Weimar Republic. This created institutional and organizational difficulties at a practical level as the Reich duplicated and encroached upon the services performed by the regional authorities.

The resentment such conflicts gave rise to was clearly political. With regional and local governments as well as associations and interest groups continually fighting to protect the political integrity of regional political life from encroachments from the center, informal regional blocs gradually began to emerge within the formal political structure of the Weimar Republic. Ultimately even parliamentary politics was affected. By the middle of the 1920s, for example, Besson notes that Reichstag delegates from Württemberg gradually began to shift to representing the interest of the Württemberg coalition within the Reichstag, rather than that of the views of the national parties to which they also belonged.[63]

The existence of such informal blocs gave rise, in turn, to a broad dynamic of informal lobbying and bargaining between and among groups of regional interest over the direction of national policy. Governments competed with governments, state agencies with federal ones, and regional party factions with national ones. In this way, politics became exceedingly baroque within the Weimar polity. Ultimately, the emergence of such subsidiary political dynamics, which in the end presupposed political opposition to the central state, contributed to the chronic instability of governments within the Weimar system. Policies were difficult to implement and control; party coalitions were continually unstable and fraught with internecine conflict.[64]

By the end of the 1920s, these problems became so acute that a formal constitutional reform conference (the so-called *Länderkonferenz*) was convened to deal with problems of internal relationships between the various levels of government in the Weimar state.[65] During the ensuing debate, political differences emerged between Prussian and non-Prussian decentralized regions. The differences stemmed from the very different role played by regional-level governments. Outside of Prussia, regional authorities had come to play an essential role in the decentralized form of administration characteristic of the decentralized

The national context: 1871–1945

industrial order. In Prussia, by contrast, where the government was unusually large and subject to pressures from autarkic, agrarian, and decentralized regions, the evolution of decentralized governance structures incorporated communal institutions far more exclusively than elsewhere. Moreover, traditions of self-government had long engendered sentiments of political right and sovereignty vis-à-vis the Prussian state among Prussian cities in general.

Thus, when the issue of reforming the structure of the Reich was placed on the agenda at the end of the 1920s, the decentralized Prussian cities, such as Cologne, campaigned actively for the elimination of regional-level governments (by which they most explicitly meant Prussia) and the creation of a unitary state.[66] The non-Prussian decentralized areas, just as logically, argued for the protection of federalism and a reform in the federal structure that would permit the regional governments better to govern themselves.[67]

One of the key factors shaping the direction of debate on this issue was the strong stand taken by autarkic industry in favor of a unitary state structure. Indeed, the debates surrounding the *Länderkonferenz* throw the basic difficulty in constructing a stable architecture of governance mechanisms capable of accommodating both forms of industrial order in the Weimar Republic into especially stark relief. In order to see how this is true, however, it is necessary to first turn to the relationship between the autarkic form of industrial order and the Weimar Constitution. Once this relationship has been described, we will return to the debate on the reform of the constitutional structure of the Reich.

Autarkic industrial order and the Weimar Constitution

Producers within the autarkic form of industrial order never embraced the parliamentary republic created at the constitutional congress in Weimar with much enthusiasm. Politically, their views seemed to have been essentially agnostic. That is, they had no predisposition for any sort of political ideology or state form whatsoever. Their position at the fall of the old regime was neither zealously monarchist nor aggressively republican. Their main concern was that the political structure that did emerge would be stable and not impose itself on what they perceived to be their legitimate sphere of activity.[68]

The lack of enthusiasm in autarkic business circles for the new government had less an ideological than a practical grounding. The new parliamentary structure gave political forces who represented social interests opposed to the firm based industrial order in autarkic regions access to national political power. The first government in the new parliamentary system was headed by a socialist-led coalition that directly threatened the autarkic tradition of firm-based self-government with talk of central planing, nationalization, and other forms of intrusive state regulation of production.[69] Moreover, the complicated relationship between social democracy and the council democracy movement was viewed by business with great distrust.[70]

Antipathy for the regime was further whetted by subsequent state actions. Autarkic producers were subjected by the state to a series of measures that interfered directly with traditional managerial practices regarding control of the production process, arbitration, unemployment, work time, and social welfare.

The legacy of the revolutionary worker and soldier council democracy movement in Germany was the incorporation of Article 165 into the Weimar Constitution, which consisted of broad-ranging calls for the establishment of factory councils. Such councils, it was hoped, would integrate workers into production planning decisions at all levels of production and its administration.[71] The only concrete result of Article 165, however, was the comparatively modest Works Constitutions Act (Betriebsverfassungsgesetz) of February 4, 1920. While the left criticized this new law as being too limited to social and economic issues within plants, industrial producers perceived it as an affront to their sovereignty in the factory. From their perspective, the "threat" of greater democratization of production and its administration within industrial firms was ever present (if often latent) during the Weimar period.[72]

Additional intrusions of the state into the sovereign realm of production and its governance within industrial firms came in the area of arbitration in collective bargaining. A decree was issued in October, 1923 that established arbitration committees under the direction and supervision of the Reich Labor Ministry. It was further decreed in December of that year that if the representatives of labor and employers could not agree, the labor ministry could impose an award itself. Finally, the labor ministry could also declare the awards to be legally binding, which made subsequent strikes or lockouts illegal.[73] Employers complained about the decrees, and charged the labor ministry with bias when its decisions began to go against them.[74]

Social welfare policy was another realm in which the Weimar state was considered to be distressingly intrusive by large autarkic firms. In many ways, their animosity had to do with taxes. Matthias Erzberger, the Center Party minister who had masterminded the centralizing tax reform in 1919, argued that a major justification for centralization was that it gave the state the capacity to tax the rich more effectively.[75] Such sentiments, generally supported by the rest of the Social Catholic wing of the Center Party to which Erzberger belonged, as well as the coalition partner Social Democrats, were viewed with great hostility by industry.[76] Though Erzberger and the Social Democrats had trouble actually implementing taxes as high as they liked, the general tax burden quota (*Steuerlastquote*) in Germany increased from 9% in 1913 to 17% in 1925.[77] Industrialists tended to blame this high tax burden on excessive state expenditures, especially for social welfare. State expenditures took 14.7% of the social product in 1913, but never fell below 25% during the 1920s.[78]

The list of grievances and perceived threats on the part of large industrial firms within the autarkic form of industrial order could be extended. But the point should be clear that business did not consider the environment provided by the Weimar state and the Weimar Constitution to be optimal. The autarkic principle for organizing all aspects of production and its governance within the boundaries of a firm were constantly challenged in the new Reich, and the autarkic producers resented it. Henry Ashby Turner, who has an unusual ability to step into the world view of the people that he studies, writes that the large autarkic Ruhr firms believed that many of their economic troubles "arose from misguided laws enacted by politicians seeking the favor of the uninformed masses without any regard to the dictates of economic rationality."[79]

Response: Corporatist insulation from the state

In a way analogous to the regional governments within the decentralized industrial order, the autarkic producers responded to the inhospitality of the formal political structure in the Weimar Republic by seeking to construct alternative informal mechanisms that would protect their interest and the integrity of their industrial order. In many cases, especially in the early phases of the Weimar Republic, this involved the formation of some form of corporatist structure. In the later phases of the Republic, autarkic business became increasingly interested in reforming the structure of the Reich itself so that it conflicted less with their conception of a just social order.

Corporatist arrangements constructed by autarkic producers were of two kinds during the Weimar Republic: between organized labor and autarkic producers, and between different sectors of industry.[80] In both cases, the intent was to construct mechanisms for regulating important national-level issues that would at the same time insulate the participants from the politically unpredictable intervention of the state.

The main labor–capital corporatist accord was known as the Zentralarbeitsgemeinschaft der industriellen und gewerblichen Arbeitgeber und Arbeitnehmer Deutschlands, or ZAG. Through this pact, negotiated in late 1918 by the trade union leader Carl Liegen and the Ruhr industrialist Hugo Stinnes, large-scale autarkic industrialists took the unprecedented step of agreeing to recognize the free trade unions as the sole bargaining agents of workers in their plants. In return, they received the cooperation of the trade unions in the initial years of the Weimar Republic on a whole range of political and economic issues. The explicit goal of the ZAG when it was established was to entrench the control of both actors over the organization of their activities and thereby block any potential attempts to intervene in these affairs on the part of revolutionary works councils or the new parliament.[81]

The ZAG was troubled throughout the entire time that it existed and finally was disbanded in 1924. Much of the problem was that autarkic producers resented the presence of trade unions in their affairs. Prior to World War I, trade unions were virtually absent from the plants of the autarkic firms in the Ruhr. It was only the special product and labor market conditions of wartime production that caused the firms to reluctantly accept the need for formal organizations capable of organizing the labor market. In the postwar period, autarkic industry was willing to continue its engagement with the trade unions when, in the midst of a revolutionary situation, it looked as if the choice was between collaboration and expropriation. But as it became clear that the Weimar Republic, for all its faults, would not eliminate private property, the autarkic firms became progressively less interested in collaboration with labor.

Interindustrial corporatism was best exemplified by the 1926 agreement between heavy industrial steel producers and the metal finishing industry producers known as the AVI agreement.[82] This agreement created a system of rebates for consumers of steel selling their products in export markets. The rebate was paid by the steel industry and was intended to compensate manufacturers for the difference between the domestic market price for steel and the world market price. In exchange for the rebate, the finishing industry supported the steel industry's efforts to maintain high domestic tariffs on steel. The agreement recreated a system that had previously existed during the war, only this time it was regulated exclusively by the participating private organizations without any participation of the state.[83]

Both sets of corporatist arrangements were formed not only out of purely economic calculation, but also with a clear political sense of how extrafirm governance of production should relate to the rest of society, and particularly to the state. Autarkic producers preferred to seek solutions to their problems through the creation of institutional arrangements that excluded the state. This point is underscored by the fact that the same producers actively opposed all efforts on the part of the state to create corporatist arrangements during the Weimar period. Autarkic producers, for example, generally opposed the corporatist *Gemeinwirtschaft* ideas of Rathenau and Moellendorf.[84] During the "coal crisis" in 1920, when the government attempted to create a corporatist arrangement to manage the industry, autarkic industrialists consistently undermined their efforts. Revealingly, at one point Rathenau became so exasperated with the suggested solutions offered by the autarkic producers that he charged them with wanting to establish "industrial duchies."[85]

It is worth recalling that the political behavior of autarkic business described here is very consistent with its behavior during the 19th century. Then, when the organizational principles of autarkic order first emerged, producers were willing to engage with the state commercially in numerous ways, yet they energetically resisted any direct interference on the part of the state in production or its governance. This they considered to be their own affair, as a matter of right.[86] In the Weimar Republic, the autarkic producers' conception of the proper boundary between the state and the economy did not change, but their confidence in the security of their rights was weakened. Antipathy toward the state was compounded by mistrust.

Shift from corporatist insulation to constitutional reform

This general attitude prevailed throughout the Weimar period, interrupted only by a brief interlude in the middle years of the Republic. By the middle of the 1920s, the balance of parliamentary power had shifted in favor of the autarkic business community. The Social Democratic Party entered the opposition for the first time and a center–right government, composed of Catholic, liberal and nationalist parties, among whom autarkic producers wielded considerable influence, took their place.[87] The government permitted firms to institute longer working hours, tax laws were altered favorably to corporations, and income taxes on the wealthy were limited. Moreover, the economy moved into an upswing that lasted until 1928. In such an environment, the autarkic business community seemed to have made peace with the institutions of parliamentary democracy. Perhaps the peak of this satisfaction with the Republic was reached in 1926, when the coal industrialist Paul Silverberg, speaking at a meeting of the peak association for German business, the Reichsverband Deutscher Industrie (RDI), called for business to accept the institutions of the Weimar Republic.[88]

Even here, however, Silverberg could not claim to be speaking for the whole of autarkic industry. Autarkic producers of finished goods, such as electrotechnical, chemical and machinery producers (as well as many decentralized producers in these industries from Saxony, Württemberg, and Baden), tended to back Silverberg more solidly than did his colleagues in the heavy Ruhr industries.[89] The latter producers continued to resent what they perceived to be heavy social costs levied by the state on their activities. The state mediated arbitration councils were particularly loathed. Ruhr industrialists, whose firms often dominated local labor markets and who thus traditionally enjoyed rather complete control over the setting of wages, continued to argue with increasing alarm that a biased labor ministry was unjustly imposing "political wages" upon them. Perhaps worst of all, continued social spending by the government was causing Germany's chronic capital shortage to persist even through the upswing. Unable to blame the socialists for these problems (even the labor ministers belonged to the Center Party), autarkic producers in the Ruhr gradually began to place the blame on the structure of the Weimar state itself.[90]

Pressure from abroad soon encouraged the rest of autarkic industry to join the Ruhr in calls for a reform of the Reich's structure. A memorandum to the German government in November, 1927 was sent by the Agent-General for Reparations Payments, Parker Gilbert, an American banker, warning of the growing levels of external indebtedness among German public authorities, especially by regional and local governments.[91] Gilbert's argument was that the reparations creditors and foreign bankers were willing to condone growing foreign indebtedness of private German companies, but not on the part of public authorities. The former were capable of turning debt into productive capital, whereas the regional authorities were not. Since all foreign debt was not covered by the special transfer mechanism in the Dawes plan designed to protect the German balance of payments, the growth of public-sector foreign debt was potentially destabilizing and therefore threatened all future foreign capital investment in Germany, even to private companies. Restraint and an effort to demonstrate future German creditworthiness was, in his view and in the view of American banks, becoming imperative. Gilbert called for the German government to make urgently needed reforms in the structure of state administration and, in particular, to rationalize its financial structure so that restraint could be imposed on the regional and local governments.[92]

136   *Industrial constructions*

Such a warning about the possible withdrawal of foreign credit resonated throughout the autarkic business community. Autarkic producers who, despite the weakness of domestic banks and a general capital shortage in Germany, constructed large holding company conglomerates during the early part of the 1920s had become quite reliant on foreign capital. The RDI immediately issued a statement calling for "a decisive (*einschneidende*) change in the constitutional structure of the Reich."⁹³ Immediately thereafter, a very influential circle of autarkic industrialists called upon the Reichs Chancellor to strengthen the power of the central cabinet over economic affairs and curtail the powers of the Reichstag and the regional governments.⁹⁴

By the beginning of 1928, autarkic industry had formed a special lobbying association, the Bund zur Erneuerung des Reiches (League for the Renewal of the Reich), which dedicated itself to the cause of changing the constitutional structure of the Reich, and in particular the relationship between central, regional, and local governments.⁹⁵ According to Schulz, the League generated enormous propaganda in favor of reform of the Reich during the election campaign in 1928.⁹⁶ It also became intimately involved in the above-mentioned *Länderkonferenz* for constitutional reform that had been convened in that same year.

Autarkic business wanted two things from a reform of the Constitution. First, it wanted to rationalize the structure of public administration so that the "polycratic" cross-cutting, overlapping, redundant bureaucratic responsibilities existing between the Reich, regional governments, and communes would be eliminated.⁹⁷ Such bureaucratic bulkiness inflated the costs of government and led to higher taxes, unnecessary spending, and indebtedness. Rationalization could best be achieved through the creation of a unitary state. Second, business blamed problems of overindebtedness and excessive social spending on the existence of parliaments, and advocated reforms in the mechanisms for the setting of policy that avoided them.⁹⁸ The most extreme autarkic views, which grew in strength after the Social Democrats recaptured power in the 1928 elections and the economy slid into recession soon afterwards, argued for the complete elimination of parliamentary democracy and the establishment of a strong central executive who could take decisive action without parliamentary controls.⁹⁹ The consensus view, at least until the early 1930s, however, was to focus on the elimination of parliaments at the regional and local levels, while at the same time eliminating or transforming regional and local bureaucracies so that they were integrated (and controlled) by the federal-level bureaucracy.¹⁰⁰

Political conflict between the autarkic and decentralized forms of industrial order over the place of each within the German political economy

The position on constitutional reform taken by the autarkic producers and their representative organizations placed them in direct conflict with the political position of the regional governments in the decentralized industrial order. While the former wanted to shift responsibility and representation away from the regional and local levels, the later desired to enhance the political integrity and self-governing capacity of the lower levels. Most importantly, the autarkic interests favoring greater centralization were convinced that a continuation of the existing system – or, even worse, a shift to greater decentralization and self-government – would cause great economic difficulties for big business. Regional governments believed that a shift toward greater centralization would lead to the neglect of local industrial interests and make the reproduction of the decentralized regional economic life that they governed extremely difficult. This conflict constituted the central obstacle to an institutional accommodation of either form of industrial order within the Weimar Republic.

The proposals for regional and administrative reform offered at the *Länderkonferenz* reflected the positions outlined above. Initially, the various regional governments, including Prussia, called for the preservation of states rights and the elimination of cross-cutting "polykratic" administration by devolving and consolidating administrative responsibilities and legal competence in policy formulation downwards.[101] The German Diet of Cities (Städtetag), by contrast, proposed the enhancement of municipal representation at the national level of politics. They demanded the construction of a municipal-policy committee in the Reichstag, the construction of municipal-policy division within the Reichs Ministry of the Interior, and, most dramatically, the representation of cities in the Reichsrat, alongside the regional governments.[102]

The proposal advanced by the League for the Renewal of the Reich was equally as dramatic. It cited the powerful position of Prussia within the Reich as an obstructive "state within a state" and called for its complete dissolution along with that of the other, much smaller north German regional governments. A new territory, or *Reichsland*, would be created and then governed by the federal government – without its own parliament, but with a number of smaller administrative districts that would carry out the policies of the Reich. The other regional governments would be "provisionally" allowed to remain as they were.[103] Such reserve vis-à-vis the medium-sized southern governments of Saxony, Bavaria, Württemberg, and Baden was considered to be politically prudent: Demands for immediate nationwide centralization would never overcome the opposition of these governments. Moreover, Prussia was considered to be the most pressing problem because it was so large, and it was governed by a Social Democratic led coalition which systematically and continuously opposed the policies of the more conservative (and probusiness) Reich governments.

After nearly two years of debate and negotiation, the conference agreed on a compromise reform plan known as the "*differenzierte Gesamtlosung*" (differential total solution). Basically, the plan bought off the southern states by making their continued existence guaranteed in the Constitution, while it followed the League's proposal to break up Prussia into smaller "new states," which shared many of the same kind of administrative responsibilities of the "old states" but with far more limited representative functions. The responsibilities of regional governments generally were made clearer in relationship to those of the Reich. Most significantly, the committee was not able to come to a decision on the problem of taxation and the distribution of taxes between the central and regional governments. Instead, the proposal called for a future reform of the system.[104]

Whether or not such a proposal could have produced the needed institutional environment that would have permitted both forms of industrial order to reproduce themselves within the Weimar Republic is open to debate. Besson remarks that the Württemberg representative, Bolz, became disillusioned with the overly centralist tendencies in the proposal soon after he had given his vote in favor of it.[105] The notorious centralizer Johannes Popitz, an official in the federal ministry of finance, felt that the special status given to the southern states, combined with the breakup of Prussia, would shift the balance of power within the Reich in a disruptive way. "If it is not possible to have a German Reich perched upon the throne of a properly organized unitary state" he wrote, " then at least one should have a German Reich that is supported by the stable stool of Prussia"[106]

Regardless of what the concrete effects of the proposed reform of the Reich might have been, they never became anything more than proposals. The objections of Bavaria and Prussia blocked any efforts to actually implement the reforms. Bavaria objected to the proposals because they did not accord Bavaria the kind of special state status that she desired. For her part, Social Democratic Prussia objected to being dismembered, viewing the reform as an attempt by enemies of parliamentary democracy and the welfare state to eliminate a major source of political irritation.[107] This position was then supported by Popitz and the Reich bureaucracy for reasons noted above. After it became clear that the entire proposal was not going to be accepted, all of the south German regional governments made it plain that they refused to support attempts to implement the reforms piecemeal.[108]

Thus, there was no reform in the structure of the Reich and no establishment of a framework of accommodation that might have enabled both forms of industrial order to coexist in the same polity. And, tragically, with all sides – autarkic business, decentralized business, and central, regional, and local governments – feeling ambivalent toward the existing structure, the international economy fell into crisis and the domestic economy collapsed. The dynamic of deterioration that ensued transformed that ambivalence into resentment and a desire for a clear change.

During the later half of the 1920s, despite the economic stabilization, the Reich had accumulated considerable budget deficits that it was forced to pay for through international borrowing. The deterioration of the economy led to further budget deficits and higher debt. International borrowers placed pressure on the Reich to temper its domestic spending, so it began to allocate less money to the regional and local governments. These governments, already deeply indebted, were viewed unfavorably in international credit markets. Confronted with dramatically increasing social welfare costs due to rising levels of unemployment, they were consequently forced to raise existing taxes and invent new ones, thereby enraging local business and industry, which was already paying considerable federal tax. One by one, regional governments began to lose majorities in their parliaments and found themselves incapable of constructing new ones. Politically and financially crippled, the regional governments enthusiastically ceded responsibility for their local affairs to the federal government.

With the creation of the Bruening government in the early 1930s, the central state tried to impose political control over Germany by utilizing its right to invoke Article 48 of the Constitution. This allowed it (or, more precisely, allowed the Reich's President) to govern by decree and thus create a government that acted by circumventing the procedural and democratic constraints imposed on it by the parliamentary and federalist structures of the Constitution. Even this, however, failed to achieve stability. Resentment and a sense of alienation from the government grew among industrialists within both the autarkic and decentralized industrial orders as it proved incapable of resolving the contradictory economic pressures that each faced.

Ultimately, dissatisfaction with the existing regime led many producers in both forms of industrial order to back the Nazi Party. The autarkic producers believed that they could work with and possibly even control Hitler to achieve stability; the decentralized producers believed Nazi promises to restructure the German nation in a way that would make it more attentive to their needs.[109] The failure to achieve constitutional reform in the *Länderkonferenz* did not necessarily cause this outcome, but it may have been able to prevent it.

Nazi accommodation

The Nazi regime attempted to accommodate both forms of industrial order by means of centralization. It succeeded through this means in improving the economic condition of producers in both forms of order during the 1930s. But its intrusive policies also provoked resentments and conflicts, especially among autarkic producers, which, due to the collapse of the regime, never played themselves out. By the beginning of World War II, however, the resistance of autarkic business to the Nazi's attempt to direct their internal affairs had become so great (and exasperating) that the regime began to build its own production capacity to make it independent of the larger autarkic producers. At the same time, it also began to intensify its alliance with the decentralized producers.

Initially, the new Nazi regime was a friend of the large autarkic producers. The Nazis destroyed the trade unions and allowed autarkic firms to recreate an environment inside the factory and in the labor market that they could control.[110] The destruction of the bargaining mechanism that had been constructed during the Weimar Republic, moreover, led to a wage cost situation that was more favorable to the employers: wage rates barely moved after 1932. And, as the economy recovered during the 1930s, wages fell as a proportion of national income, leaving the surplus for their employers to invest.[111] Moreover, spending by the state on the construction of roads, subsidies to the automobile industry, and increases in military spending created an environment of growth for the

140 *Industrial constructions*

large firms. The creation of aggregate demand by the state made it possible for industry to finance expansion out of its own earnings.[112] As under the Kaiser, during the initial period of Nazi rule autarkic firms gladly did business with the state and thanked it for otherwise staying out of its affairs.

Also sympathetic to the autarkic producers, the Nazis abolished the parliaments in the regional governments and subordinated existing governmental structures there to those of the central Reich.[113] The Reich then restricted the regional and communal governments from financing their expenditures through loans. "For most of the Nazi period" James notes, "the debt levels of the Länder and communes actually decreased."[114] The problem of the sensitivity of the economy to foreign lenders was in any case reduced by the suspension of reparations payments, on the one hand, and by the general crisis in the United States, which made the prospect of getting foreign capital rather bleak, on the other.[115]

The Nazi regime was also accommodating to the actual producers within the decentralized industrial order. But, as the destruction of local institutions indicates, it was so in ways that ultimately changed the character of the decentralized industrial order. Nazi reforms slowly tempered the effects of the crisis in decentralized areas by easing decentralized producers' problems with the financing of investment and the potential breakdown of market order in production. Like the autarkic producers, small- and medium-sized producers in decentralized areas also generally benefitted from the freeze on wages and the elimination of arbitration instituted by the Nazis. This shifted a greater percentage of the benefits of expansion to the firm owner for investment.

More importantly, the passage of a number of laws on cartels in 1933 enabled trade associations (now called *Wirtschaftsgruppen*, or economic groups) to compel all producers in given branches of industry to enter into cartel arrangements that helped to stabilize harmful competition.[116] Finishing associations could compel previously reluctant outsiders to conform to their specialization arrangements. This parcelled out capacity in the industry and allowed decentralized branches to expand steadily during the upturn in the 1930s.[117] Finally, many branches of industry in the decentralized industrial order benefitted from the remilitarization campaign that the Nazi state pursued throughout the 1930s. Industries that either produced weapons directly, or those that produced the investment goods needed for the production of weapons enjoyed a boom during the 1930s (e.g., machinery producers, fine mechanical and optical producers, and electro-technical producers). Overy notes that a significant amount of the early military expenditures had been given to smaller enterprises.[118] Similarly, Geyer's study shows that the Nazis systematically targeted small- and medium-sized producers, especially in the decentralized regions surrounding the Ruhr, to scatter weapons production and make it more easily concealable.[119]

The flip side of the Nazi experience for the decentralized industrial order, of course, was that the local and regional-level institutions were completely relieved of their autonomy. For the most part they were subsumed into the state, as were the trade associations and the Chambers of Commerce. Taxation was completely centralized.[120] The central state also took a greater interest in education and

The national context: 1871-1945   141

began to direct policy from the center. All of these changes meant that the degree to which the decentralized regions remained self-governing under the Nazi regime was sharply reduced. The dispersal of expertise and information throughout an overlapping series of institutions, such as had existed in pre-Nazi times, was replaced by a dirigant apparatus of trade associations that organized industries, allocated raw materials, and channeled contracts, capital, and technological expertise to producers. This was a very different political structure for the decentralized order; but, at least for the 12 years that the Nazi regime existed, it proved capable of reproducing decentralized industrial production.

Whether or not the Nazi system of accommodation would have been, over the long term, a stable one is a moot question. Conflicts between the autarkic producers and the Nazi regime began to emerge in the late 1930s when Nazi desires to commit the economy to total war led them to intervene in the affairs of the large firms more than the large firms desired.[121] Many decentralized producers in industries that were not given priority in the war effort, such as the textile industry, were officially prevented from expanding and hence stagnated during the thirties. It strains the limits of counterfactuality to ask whether or not the system would have had less strain within a peacetime environment, given that the aim of Nazi regime was to make war for a long time.

What does seem clear, however, is that the framework of accommodation which the Nazis devised was not particularly good at preparing for war. By accommodating the desires of autarkic business to operate free of state intervention, the regime was not able to direct the efforts of large producers toward war production in a satisfactory way. Large German autarkic firms were still hoping that they could expand the nonmilitary aspects of their business in export markets in 1939. Many, such as MAN, attempted to clandestinely maintain contacts with customers abroad against express prohibitions by the Nazi regime.[122] Reliance on decentralized producers for its military buildup was not an adequate alternative to the large producers because the small- and medium-sized firms were not capable of producing in needed volumes. Indeed, the incapacity (or unwillingness) of decentralized or autarkic producers to adopt real volume-production methods was a major problem in the German weapons industry. Overy's characterization seems apt: "If German armaments had been less well made and more efficiently produced and paid for, the number of weapons available in 1940 would have been considerably greater."[123]

It is unlikely that the Nazi regime could have done things differently without completely disrupting the frameworks of accommodation that it had created. Its attempt to compensate for the aloofness of the large firms by moving into production on its own (e.g., the creation of the massive Herman Goering conglomerate), exacerbated autarkic producers resentment and caused major disruption in the allocation of raw materials.[124] The regime did pass a law on corporations in 1937 that forced companies with a capital stock of less than 100,000 RM to dissolve, merge with larger companies, or change to an unlimited liability form in an effort to create larger, more efficient production units. But, as Woolston shows, although the law probably resulted in the elimination of

20% of German corporations, this constituted just 0.3% of corporate capital.[125] More dramatic attempts to dismantle the elaborate specialization relationships between small- and medium-sized firms in the decentralized areas in order to create larger, more efficient production units would have constituted an attack on one of the broadest bases of Nazi support.[126] In this context, it is perhaps not surprising that some of the closest allies of the Nazi regime as well as the largest beneficiaries of the defense buildup were firms seeking to break out of the decentralized industrial order, such as IG Farben, Daimler-Benz, and Robert Bosch.[127]

Conclusion: Composite architecture of national governance mechanisms

The aim of this chapter has been to survey the efforts to accommodate the governance needs of each of the forms of regional industrial order at the national level of the economy. On the whole, we found that a stable regime of coexistence was created only during the Imperial Reich. Both the Weimar Republic and the Third Reich created only temporary or no stable set of national-level governance structures. The central point of this chapter is that institutional structures governing processes within one form of industrial order were often distinct from and independent of those governing the other form of industrial order. In those cases where a single system governed both forms of industrial order, it was generally because the system was capable of accommodating variation internally, such as in the case of the civil law or the railroads. The composite character of national-level governance in these three modern German regimes makes it clear that there was never a single boundary between industry and the rest of society and politics in 19th and early 20th century Germany; there were always several.

5

Return to regions: The development of the decentralized industrial order since 1945

This chapter turns from the higher, national level of analysis of the previous chapter and returns to the focus on regional forms of industrial order that was the focus of Chapters 2 and 3. In particular, it picks up the narrative where Chapter 2 left off: The focus in what follows will be on the transformation of the decentralized industrial order in the German Federal Republic since the end of World War II. The chapter that follows this one will resume the narrative of the development of the autarkic industrial order during the post World War II period. Chapter 7 will then return to the national level of analysis that was the focus of Chapter 4 in order to show how both forms of industrialization were governed at the national level in the postwar period.

Two broad macrohistorical developments in the remarkably robust period between 1945 and 1994 affected the institutional framework and routine practices of the decentralized industrial order. The first was the emergence for the first time in Germany and Western Europe of political and economic conditions making possible the broad diffusion of strategies of large-scale mass production. The second development, which we are still experiencing, follows from the emergence of political and economic conditions that have made it impossible to follow old-style large-scale mass production strategies any longer. Within the regions dominated by the decentralized industrial order, the first development made it possible for large firms to gain a foothold for the first time and gave rise to a unique form of coexistence between autarkic and decentralized actors. The second development has produced pressures that are pushing toward the transformation of these postwar arrangements.

Once again, this period, like the previous one, is difficult to write about because it involves throughout a complicated mixture of radical breaks from and remarkable continuities with the traditions of industrial organization and practice that had gone before. Moreover, any effort to reconstruct what happened in this period is hampered by the fact that neither the contemporary actors themselves nor much of the scholarly literature proved to be very good at presenting differentiated portraits of the flow of postwar change as it was occurring. A simple comparison of the experience of the first part of the period with that of the second makes the narrative difficulty clear. In the first several decades of the postwar period it appeared to many that the emergence of large autarkically organized mass producers after the war so dramatically transformed the old decentralized economies that the old small- and medium-sized firm dominated system of order, as described in Chapter 2, either had already disappeared or was destined to with the further diffusion of mass-production principles in the economy. Such "traditional" forms of organization, it was argued, were simply victims of the inevitability of economic progress and modernization.

This understanding, of course, was shattered by the experience of the 1980s when the mass-production system began to fall into crisis everywhere. In that period, these same regions, particularly Baden Württemberg, became centers of a renaissance of high-tech craft production in which small- and medium-sized firms played a central role. Once again, many participants and onlookers in this period, taken up by the drama of significant social change, portrayed the successful decentralized system as being everything from a vindication of a historical legacy of petite bourgeois hard work to a paradigm for the way in which all industrial production in Europe was headed. Yet, if in the first period small firms tended to disappear in the self-understanding of the age, in this second period the large firms did.

In both periods, the degree of change was truly dramatic; yet in neither case were the enthusiastic narratives quite in line with reality. Large mass-producing firms utilizing many of the governance techniques of the autarkic industrial order did indeed become a permanent feature of industrial life in the regions formerly dominated by the decentralized industrial order during the middle decades of this century. But far from disappearing during the 1980s, such firms sought to move away from mass production and autarky by utilizing the local reservoir of skilled labor and flexibly specialized small suppliers to maintain their competitiveness. Similarly, small- and medium-sized producers within the decentralized industrial order did not disappear during the 1950s and 1960s only to emerge like a phoenix from the ashes in the 1980s. Instead, decentralized small- and medium-sized producers were able to accommodate the emergence of large autarkic producers engaged in mass production by finding niches in which it was unprofitable for the emerging large mass producers to compete. Their success in the 1980s was due to the fact that they were able to capitalize on their greater flexibility in the market.

For most of the postwar period, then, the remarkable story and real break with the 19th and early 20th century experience is that large, mass producing, autarkically organized firms emerged for the first time within decentralized regions and that, despite this, small and large autarkic and decentralized producers found a way to coexist. By the middle of the 1990s, however, this situation appeared to be changing once again, and in a highly paradoxical way. Strong competition from highly flexible Asian and American producers has intensified pressure on both large and small firms to accelerate product changes while radically reducing their production costs. Both types of producer appear to be having tremendous difficulty achieving this. Indeed, in the current period, the question of large versus small firms seems to be entirely beside the point: The existence of dif-

The development of the decentralized industrial order since 1945

ferent forms of industrial order within regions formerly dominated by one of them seems less important than the fact that all the forms of order have great difficulty competing. It is conceivable that a break on the order of that which occurred at mid-century is in the process of occurring now as the century comes to a close.

Organization of the chapter

The burden of this chapter is to draw a line of narrative that makes the experience of radical break consistent with the reality of remarkable continuity. The key is to focus on the initial way that large firms established themselves within regions traditionally dominated by decentralized industrial order. The emergence of such firms disrupted, but did not destroy, the framework and practice of that regionally embedded form of order. Once the fact of coexistence is established in the narrative, it will be possible simply to follow its evolution into crisis in the 1990s.

Thus, the first section of this chapter outlines the conditions that gave rise to and the processes involved with the emergence of large mass-producing firms within regions traditionally dominated by the decentralized industrial order. The section does this by characterizing the unique context of the mid-century international political economy and then, through a case study of the development of the firm Daimler-Benz, showing how this context presented opportunities for firms to break out of the framework of decentralized industrial order and engage in mass production.

The second section of the chapter then lays out how the decentralized industrial order was reconstituted after the war even as it was being affected by the emergence of these mass-producing large firms. The crucial formative development that saved the decentralized order was that the same conditions that fostered the development of large firms made it possible for small- and medium-sized specialist producers in capital-goods sectors (in which demand for customized and batch-produced products never abated) to survive. Small and medium sized producers in noncapital-goods sectors in these regions, by the same logic, were disadvantaged by the shift to mass production.

The third section of this chapter then shows how the transformation of the political and economic context in industrial Europe during the 1970s and 1980s up-ended the hegemony of the mass-production organizational logic in the economy. This fostered, initially, a renaissance of small- and medium-sized firm specialty production as well as large-firm experiments with both specialization and decentralization in production. But the section will conclude by showing how by the middle of the 1990s, as the tempo of change in world markets continued to accelerate, it began to look like the flexibility implicit in German decentralized craft production was not flexible enough. Both large and small producers were having difficulty competing with the dynamic challenges from competitors in Asia and North America who were deploying a wholly different form of flexible organization.

Abandoning the decentralized industrial order

Unprecedented market opportunities and mass production

At mid-century, a variety of producers broke out of the framework of relations that governed production in the decentralized industrial order because a set of market conditions emerged in West Germany and Western Europe at that time that made it possible for the first time to pursue large-scale mass-production strategies on the market and in production. As we saw in previous chapters, international and domestic market conditions during most of the early 20th century in Germany and Europe had never been favorable to the adoption of large-scale mass-production techniques, certainly not to any extent approaching the way such methods were employed in the United States.[1] Domestic market conditions in Germany were too unstable and turbulent, while international trade and financial relations in Europe were fraught by rivalry and bilateral trade wars.[2]

After World War II, the political and economic context in Europe changed dramatically, making what once had been impracticable much less so. There were four main reasons for this: the creation of a stable and open intra-European trading area, the diffusion of the Keynesian welfare state throughout Europe, the experience of unprecedentedly strong postwar economic growth throughout Western Europe and the aggressive presence of directly invested American mass producers in European markets.

The movement toward greater intra-European trade in the 1950s and 1960s, facilitated initially by the Marshall Plan, the European Coal and Steel Community, and, finally, by the formation of the six-member European Economic Community and the seven-member European Free Trade Area, allowed individual producers to calculate production strategies with the certainty that they would have relatively free access to consumers beyond the borders of their domestic markets.[3] Increases in scale and capacity could be undertaken with an eye to the larger European market.[4] The creation in most European countries of elaborate welfare states and the movement toward Keynesian demand-management policies stimulated producers by ensuring the existence of stable consumer demand.[5] Though the West Germans did not engage in Keynesian demand management to any important extent during the 1950s, they certainly benefitted from its practice elsewhere in Europe: in the 1950s and 1960s, over 60% of German exports went to Western European countries. Moreover, German good fortune does not appear to have been coincidental. By all accounts, the West Germans self-consciously focused their macroeconomic policy machinery on the maintenance of domestic price stability and the encouragement of exports – free riding, in effect, on the demand-stabilizing effects of Keynesian macropolicies in West European export markets.[6]

The third factor, growth, was important because it created a climate in which producers were willing to undertake the kind of paradigm-shifting investments that mass production required. To understand this, one has to appreciate the

Table 3 *Twelve highest growth rates among Western nations, 1950–1960*

Country	Annual Rate of Growth of Total Output, 1950–1960 (%)
West Germany	7.6
Italy	5.9
Switzerland	5.1
Netherlands	4.9
France	4.4
Canada	3.9
Norway	3.5
Denmark	3.3
Sweden	3.3
United States	3.2
Belgium	2.9
United Kingdom	2.6

Taken from Angus Maddison, *Economic Growth in the West*, p. 28

magnitude of the postwar European miracle. In the first 10 years of the postwar period, up to the time that the Common Market was actually formed, West Germany grew at rates faster than any others in Europe and those countries were growing as fast as they ever had[7] (see Table 3). This growth, moreover, was extremely stable. Growth rates in West Germany, for example, increased every year after the 1948 currency reform until the first postwar recession in 1966–1967 (though the extremely high rates of growth in the 1950s were not sustained in the 1960s) (see Table 4).

Stable growth engendered confident evaluations of investment risk and encouraged commitments to new large-scale forms of mechanization. The sacrifice of flexibility that such investments ultimately were to entail seemed a cheap and relatively low-risk way to gain greater profits in the context of what, by the beginning of the 1960s, seemed to be an almost permanent economic upswing. According to Angus Maddison, total gross domestic investment as a proportion of total GNP at current prices in Germany averaged 14.3% between 1925–1937, but increased to 24.0% between 1950–1960.[8]

Finally, if these three factors were not enough to get German and European producers to commit themselves to mass production strategies, they were for producers from the United States. There has often been much made of the influence of American manufacturing methods in Europe during the first part of the 20th century (Fordism, rationalization, etc.) and, indeed, at the level of rhetoric and ideology American manufacturing ideas did enjoy broad currency at that time.[9] But, in fact, direct American competition in most continental manufacturing markets prior to the World War II was never more than marginal[10], and, moreover, the trend was for the direction of American trade to shift away

Table 4 *Real growth of the West German economy, 1951–1980 (%)*

Year	%	Year	%
1951	10.4	1966	2.9
1952	8.9	1967	−0.2
1953	8.2	1968	7.3
1954	7.4	1969	8.2
1955	12.0	1970	5.8
1956	7.3	1971	3.0
1957	5.7	1972	3.4
1958	3.7	1973	5.1
1959	7.3	1974	0.4
1960	9.0	1975	−2.7
1961	5.4	1976	5.8
1962	4.0	1977	2.7
1963	3.4	1978	3.3
1964	6.7	1979	4.5
1965	5.6	1980	1.8

Source: *Die Zeit*, August 29, 1975, vol. 69.
Taken from V. R. Berghahn, *Modern Germany*, p. 262

from Europe (for example, German imports from the United States, as a percentage of total imports, decreased during the 1920s).[11] European markets were notoriously too fragmented for American producers and, during the 1920s, too cash poor. But after the war, in the context of the above changes and American political commitment to European recovery, American business interest in Europe began to change. American multinationals moved into the European market in a relatively continuous stream – slowly but surely in the years before the formation of the EEC, and then quite rapidly once the Common Market (with its common external tariff) was officially in place.[12]

These American firms enjoyed a tremendous comparative advantage over the Europeans. They knew much better than the Europeans how to use standardization and economies of scale to compete in a large market area. Large-scale mass production had been the dominant form of production in the United States at least since the turn of the century. The "American Challenge," as the Frenchman Servan-Schreiber called it, placed European producers under tremendous pressure to adopt mass-production strategies to remain competitive in their own markets.[13]

Ultimately, these changes in the environment and in the nature of competition did give rise to tremendous changes in the organization of production and its governance among producers within the autarkic and the decentralized forms of industrial order in West Germany. The changes in the autarkic order will be dealt with in the next chapter. In the regions dominated by the decentralized industrial order, producers that adopted mass-production strategies did so by breaking out of the institutional and practical framework that governed decentralized production and administration. I will use the case of Daimler-Benz, the largest and most important firm to break out of the structures of decentralized industrial order, to illustrate the dynamic of recomposition and invention at work in this period. Its story can be taken as representative of a whole host of others, such as Robert Bosch, Standard Elektrik Lorenz (SEL), Liebherr, and Klöckner-Humboldt-Deutz.[14]

Daimler-Benz AG: Abandoning decentralization for Fordism

The Daimler-Benz AG was formed in 1926 as a fusion of the Daimler Motoren Gesellschaft of Stuttgart (Untertürkheim) and the Benz and Cie., Rheinische Automobil- und Motoren-Fabrik, Mannheim.[15] Before that both companies had been leading producers of luxury cars, engines, and trucks. Daimler and Benz were two of the oldest automobile producers in the world: both produced their first automobiles in the mid 1880s.[16]

Production

Production of automobiles at Daimler-Benz before World War II had consistently developed toward the adoption of mass-production principles, without ever actually making it that far. The closer it came to actual mass production within the boundaries of the firm, the more the company severed its direct production links with the surrounding regional industrial order.

Before the World War I, both Daimler and Benz looked very much like specialized machinery producers: they produced a variety of complicated products with an emphasis on quality of workmanship, at relatively low volumes.[17] At both companies the production of automobiles was initially an insignificant complement to their main businesses of industrial- and ship-motor production. Only during the decade before World War I did motor vehicle production become the central line of business for the companies.[18] Moreover, both companies self-consciously pursued higher quality and customizing strategies against what they considered to be the slipshod mass-production methods being developed in the United States at the time. Director Ernst Berge of the Daimler Motorenwerke explained that his company did not adopt American production methods because they hurt the quality of the product:

> We, the Mercedes-Works, have not adopted these American principles of doing business. It is only possible to achieve dramatic reductions in production costs by sacrificing the quality of materials and craftsmanship in the product. In the production of a Mercedes car, however, we operate under the principle: Only the best can be good enough for production. We are a long way from the conditions that prevail in America, where every sales clerk can own an automobile. For the most part, in Germany the automobile is a mode of transportation for the better situated classes.[19]

The first steps toward volume production came during World War I as the companies turned massively toward military goods production.[20] These initial changes had little impact on the way that work and production were organized in the firms. Primarily, they affected the design of models and parts, i.e., the creation of norms and standards. The need for easily serviceable vehicles led the War Ministry to create a bureau, the Kraftfahrtechnischen Prüfungskommission, which established uniform standards for parts and models in the industry. The goal was to create a body of parts that could be used interchangeably on a variety of models from a given firm. Daimler reduced the number of models that it produced from 15 in 1914 to four in 1915 and produced over 6000 trucks, transporters, tractors, and ambulances between 1915 and 1918, as well as over 20,000 aircraft engines.[21]

But wartime increases in output at Daimler and Benz came as much through higher levels of employment as they did through organizational advances. For a short time during 1918, for example, Daimler employed over 15,000 employees at its Untertürkheim factory alone, more than twice as much as the entire company employed in 1915.[22] Production continued to be organized according to the old workshop system in which all like machines were grouped together in particular workshops. All parts that required turning and milling, for example, were transported from the turning room to the milling room, rather than sequentially moved from machine to machine in the assembly line fashion of a mass-production process. And since all parts for all models went through the same rooms, the machines in use were primarily general-purpose tools that required skilled labor to operate. In a sense, one could say that the war time production strategies of Daimler and Benz pushed the principles of organization in the old, specialist craft-production model of organization to their limit, without actually reorganizing them into something else.[23]

The second set of changes in the direction of mass production came during the interwar years and followed from the merger of the two companies.[24] The fusion lead to three kinds of changes in production inside the boundaries of the new firm.

First, it allowed the two companies to eliminate overlapping product lines and consolidate the number of car models they collectively produced – ultimately seven.[25] Truck and omnibus operations were consolidated in a similar way. Second, consolidation of models allowed for greater standardization of parts within the broader production palette and a far-reaching reorganization of production. Parts that could be used for more than one model could be produced with greater scale economies. For example, because the drive shafts, rear axles, and undercarriage of the 2 liter and 2.5 liter "Stuttgart" models were identical, they could be produced on the same line.[26]

More important, reorganization of production to achieve greater scale economies also lead to the creation of a new system of organization that reduced inventory bottlenecks. In the place of parallel workshops (milling room, turning room, foundry, etc.), Daimler instituted a system of "group production" (*Grup-*

penfertigung). Here workshops were organized not by mechanical function, but by parts of the car (radiators, water pumps, transmissions, etc.). Machines were sequentially arranged and these arrangements were more or less dedicated to the production of specific pieces or parts of the car. This, in turn, permitted the utilization of more dedicated types of machinery that could be operated by less-skilled workers.[27]

Third, greater standardization and the desire for efficiency led to the specialization of plants. Between the time of the fusion in 1926 and the beginning of the 1930s, Daimler-Benz rearranged production so that 2 liter cars (motors and undercarriage) were produced in Mannheim, 4 and 6 liter ones (motors and undercarriage) in Untertürkheim, trucks under 4 tons in Gaggenau, those over 4 tons in Berlin-Marienfeld, and car body assembly, wheel, and steering wheel production in Sindelfingen.[28]

For all of this, actual increases in volume and productivity at Daimler-Benz during the interwar years were fairly modest. The company never produced more than 8,000 cars per year during the 1920s. Its best year during the entire period, including the war, was 1937, when it produced 27,955 automobiles and 12,367 trucks. It did this, however, with 30,523 workers, or 1.32 motor vehicles per worker.[29] The Ford Motor Company, by contrast, was producing over 5,500 vehicles per week in the 1928.[30]

If one measures Daimler-Benz's achievements against the paradigmatic mass producer, it was no mass producer. But it is not clear that it wanted to be. Throughout the period, much as it had before World War I, the company emphasized the importance of quality in its products and targeted primarily luxury car consumers. The changes in production during the interwar period did not constitute a shift away from that strategy. Rather, they allowed the company to pursue a strategy of high-quality production more efficiently. Instead of comparing Daimler-Benz with a mass-production firm such as the Ford Motor Company, it is more appropriate to make the comparison to contemporary specialist metalworking producers in the decentralized regions in Germany. As we saw in Chapter 2, these firms were organizing their product palettes and defining more narrowly their areas of specialization in an effort to coordinate and thereby stabilize the system of decentralized industrial order.

Nevertheless, it is clear from the way in which production was reorganized along group production lines, that Daimler-Benz possessed many of the necessary technological and organizational preconditions for a move into higher-volume production. During the late 1920s, the shift to group production was always discussed in terms of a movement toward "American" methods.[31] All that the firm lacked was a suitable level of demand. Once this demand began to appear in the 1950s, the firm's shift into mass production happened very rapidly. In 1950 the company produced 33,906 automobiles. That number increased to 63,683 in 1955 and 174,007 by 1965.[32] Employment in 1950 stood at 30,846 for all motor vehicle production (cars and trucks). This increased to 46,226 in 1955 and 81,845 in 1965. Sales grew at a tremendous rate: from 502 million

DM in 1950, sales increased almost 200% to 1.437 billion DM in 1955. This rate of expansion was then surpassed again in the following decade. By 1965, annual sales were 4.939 billion DM.[33]

Production at this level of volume and at such a rapid pace led yet again to some modification in the internal organization of production. The skill level of the workforce in particular was gradually flattened and the degree of mechanical automation increased substantially. By the end of the 1950s, the tremendous growth in employment at Daimler-Benz as well as in the rest of the West German economy ultimately led to labor shortages.[34] Daimler-Benz began to employ its first migrant workers in the late 1950s.[35] Further expansion on a base of unskilled immigrant workers during the 1960s meant that the firm needed to redefine the production process in a way that reduced the amount of hand afterwork performed on parts and optimized the internal production flow of parts through the plant.[36] The group production methods developed in the 1920s were streamlined and rationalized during the 1950s and 1960s.[37]

Connected to this logic of rapid growth with a shortage of labor was the implementation of various forms of mechanical automation, e.g., transfer lines for the production of engine blocks, etc. There was a way in which these forms of mechanical production were absolutely more productive than the old group production methods. By standardizing a part (such as an engine block) so that there was no variation between cars in the same model line, a mechanical transfer line could produce high volumes of identical parts in a highly efficient way. With the tremendous growth in demand for Daimler-Benz products throughout the postwar years, the company implemented several different varieties of mechanical automation for the production of specific parts, simply to be able to keep up with the expansion of demand. One of the first transfer lines the company implemented came online in 1951. The new line consisted of 12 linked machine tools that performed 196 different operations in the machining of six-cylinder heads.

As the 1950s boom continued and the labor market began to tighten, however, mechanical automation began to become attractive to production planners at Daimler-Benz not only for their great productivity, but for their labor-saving characteristics. Transfer lines could increase the rate of output for given parts without making it necessary to make corresponding increases in employment. Thus, by as early as 1956, Daimler-Benz was running transfer lines for the production of engine blocks, front axle shanks (*schenkel*) and the rear-axle cross bar and housings, in addition to cylinder heads and other standard parts. By the beginning of the 1960s, the company was known to have some of the most advanced automation technology on the European continent.[38] A further advantage of this kind of automation was that because the type of laborer working on such equipment tended to have skills that he or she learned on the job, it was possible to man such equipment with lower-paid immigrants and un- and semi-skilled workers.[39]

All of these developments show that during the 1950s and 1960s, Daimler-Benz began to adopt the kind of strategic changes in production that were occurring generally throughout the European economy. But there were some interesting characteristics in the trajectory of production at Daimler-Benz that reveal that the new developments were as much a redefinition of the firm's old specialist strategy as they were a shift into American-style mass production. Daimler attempted to combine specialization with volume production.[40] Ultimately, the strategy of the post World War II company was to target its mass-produced cars at the high end of the mass-consumer market.[41] For this reason, unlike many of the other postwar European car makers, Daimler did not move to radically streamline its product palette. In the 1950s, as we shall see in the chapter that follows, while Volkswagen was making spectacular gains in world markets with a single model, Daimler still produced six different models in a number of different variations. The least expensive of its models was targeted to be competitive with the higher-quality models of Daimler's European and American competitors. The coup of this strategy was an internal standardization policy that allowed the company to produce with economies of scale on some parts and work with the methods of group production on others.

Verlängerte werkbank: *Dualist subcontracting*

These developments within production all occurred inside the boundaries of the Daimler-Benz firm. Yet they had consequences for the firm's relationship to the decentralized system of industrial order that surrounded it. As the company increasingly adopted the techniques of mass production, its relationship to other firms and subcontractors in the surrounding decentralized industrial region became less and less cooperative. Basically, the evolution was from a region-based model that contained Daimler and Benz as specialist producers within a thick network of many specialist producers to a firm-based one in which Daimler-Benz held a monopoly position within the region over the production of motor vehicles. In the new system, Daimler could dictate (with some important exceptions) the terms under which it engaged in subcontracting with neighboring smaller supplier firms. It was along this dimension of production that the "break" from the old system was most decisive.

The key to the change was the policy of concentrating production on discrete models. This move, which occurred very early in the 20th century, enabled the firm to gain a modicum of scale economies in production by eliminating the extensive customizing in which the company was engaged. But it also fundamentally altered the way in which the value of the company's product was produced as well as the way that the firm calculated its risks.

In producing customized goods, the value that a firm brings to the product it makes comes from the process of customizing. Its "product" is its special expertise in a particular area and its ability to work with appropriate materials, machinery, or resources to provide a solution for a customer. Degrees of vertical integration among specialist producers, who were all engaged in customizing and located in decentralized regions, were relatively low. Since the value that a firm generated came from the *solution* it offered, it was possible to subcontract out parts of the actual *production*. Relations between subcontractors in such a system were, at the limit, completely horizontal. Each specialist would make its money from customization and rely on the collective know-how and production skills of other independent producers in the decentralized region (its "capital," broadly conceived) to enhance its ability to deliver the customized solution.

A move into the production of discrete models changed this whole set of relationships because it shifted the locus of value creation. Producers of models eliminated the interactive process that characterized customizing and sold a particular "predeveloped" solution, or *model*. Value was thus shifted from the product (or solution) to the way that it was produced. This fact tended to encourage producers to increase their degree of vertical integration: the more they produced that contributed to the value of the product they sold, and the more efficiently they did so, the better off they were. Whereas in the customizing process, a product in the form of a solution was distinct from the way it was produced, product and production were increasingly unified in model-oriented production. In this system, because the entire production process was specialized toward the production of a particular model or group of models, customizing became at best a distraction and at worst a source of inefficiency in production. Typically it was considered to be a burden that was shifted onto the customer.

This value-based calculation to vertically integrate was reenforced by a different set of calculations concerning the risks that the firm faced once it decided to produce discrete models. Since the firm made its money on the competitiveness of its product in the market (and not on its ability to satisfy customer wants through customizing), much more of the firm's market success rested on the quality or unique technological character of the actual product and the way that it was produced. In this context, subcontracting became a high-risk activity. At the very least, a subcontractor could be late in its delivery of a particular part and hence create a bottleneck in production. At the most, the subcontractor could take the particular technology that it developed for its customer and sell it to one of its competitors. By way of contrast, it will be helpful to recall that customizing in the decentralized system depends upon this.[42]

There were three ways in which this logic of vertical integration in the context of model-oriented production could be blocked.

One was that a firm might not attempt to integrate the production of certain products when they involved technological expertise outside the immediate skills of the producer and/or when the supplier firms themselves were very large and powerful. The Robert Bosch company's ability to survive in the automobile industry for nearly a century as a producer only of electronic auto parts can at least in part be explained in this way. The company grew to be much larger much earlier than its customers by supplying a special but standard part (magnetos) that was needed by all producers of internal combustion engines. By the time the auto producers (such as Daimler-Benz) became big enough to rival Bosch in size, Bosch was already too big, too broadly diversified and too closely held to be "integrated" in any practical sense into any single producers' operations.[43]

A second limiting factor had to do with the rate of expansion. If a producer found that its market consistently exceeded its available capacity, then it would try to service the extra demand through subcontracting. Finally, a firm could resort to the use of suppliers to stabilize production flow and employment in its own plants. In this case, the firm would invest in production capacity that would allow it to service the stable component of demand, or the level of demand at the bottom of the business cycle. When demand exceeded this level, the firm would be either likely to subcontract to meet the extra demand or simply cede that portion of the market to other independent producers.[44]

The above-noted principles help to explain why Daimler-Benz steadily removed itself from the horizontal, cooperative networks of independent producers and increasingly concentrated production inside the boundaries of the firm. Anita Kugler has shown that prior to the introduction of model production (with the launching of the "Mercedes" in 1902), Daimler's production was very decentralized: suppliers were used for the production of a broad variety of sub-components, not the least of which was the entire outer carriage of the car.[45] Yet after shifting into model production, the company began to steadily integrate different parts of production. In 1910, for example, Daimler established its own body assembly works to "reduce as far as possible its dependence upon suppliers."[46] Although the firm continued to rely on important specialist suppliers, such as Robert Bosch for magnetos, the narrower the product palette and the more important economies of scale in production became, the more salient the problem of vertical integration became. With the example of the high degree of vertical integration in American factories in mind, Daimler-Benz executives around the time of the merger instituted a long-term strategy to increase the level of vertical integration in the new company so that it approached "American" standards.[47]

During the 1950s and 1960s, rapid growth forced the company to alter its vertical integration strategy. Demand grew much more rapidly than the company could invest in capacity to supply it so the firm turned massively toward subcontracting. Consistently over 64% of the value of production at Daimler-Benz was accounted for by purchases from suppliers in this period.[48] The number of suppliers also increased significantly. In 1950, the firm had 12,643 suppliers, 90% of whom had less than 20,000 DM total sales. By 1958, the firm had 15,388 suppliers, 82% of who had sales under 20,000 DM.[49] That these increases were driven by growth, and not by a desire to reenter the collaborative networks of production in the surrounding decentralized order, is revealed by the fact that throughout the expansion Daimler-Benz always held a monopoly on design and engineering know-how for its parts. In the new hybrid mass-production strategy at Daimler-Benz, suppliers were used not as partners but as external sources of manufacturing capacity.

This new situation was brought out in a public debate between Daimler-Benz and the Arbeitsgemeinschaft Selbständiger Unternehmern (ASU).[50] In 1959, Daimler-Benz published a report on the relationship between large companies and small- and medium-sized suppliers in which it pointed to the figures of subcontractor growth mentioned above as an indication of how the tremendous

156 *Industrial constructions*

growth of Daimler-Benz during the 1950s had been beneficial for small- and medium-sized companies.[51] The ASU responded by pointing out that there was more to the increase in suppliers than met the eye. First, the most rapidly expanding group of suppliers was the largest group (i.e., those with more than one million DM in sales per year). That group that composed only 1.3% of all Daimler suppliers tended to produce very specialized (and therefore indispensable) products and accounted for over 71.7% of total supplier sales to Daimler-Benz in 1957. Second, the ASU noted that in 1957 the amount that Daimler-Benz drew from suppliers declined from 66.63% of the costs of production to 64.41%, while the total sales increased by 9.3% in that year (from 1.6 to 1.8 billion DM).

Daimler-Benz, in other words, had simply drawn a portion of production inside, leaving former suppliers to find alternative outlets for their products or to take a cut in sales. And, as the ASU emphasized, it was highly unlikely that the cutbacks in outside orders came at the expense of the larger subcontractors, such as Bosch (auto electronics), Zeiss (glass), or Continental-Gummi (tires). Rather, it was the small- and medium-sized producers who suffered from the arbitrary, year-to-year purchasing policies of the financially far more powerful Daimler-Benz.[52] Evidence confirming the disadvantaged position of suppliers in the Baden Württemberg economy after major producers had shifted into mass production is quite plentiful and spans the entire postwar period.[53]

Daimler-Benz's changed orientation to its suppliers shows how the shift to the employment of mass-production methods, especially during the 1950s, entailed the removal of the firm from the system of cooperative networks that was characteristic of production within the decentralized form of industrial order. Nevertheless, it is important to see that if product strategy and the organization of production are taken together, it is clear that the mass-production system that the Daimler-Benz company developed over the course of the 20th century bore the markings of its decentralized past. The mass-production system that it developed was a hybrid that combined elements of the system of decentralized production with those of firm-based mass production. We will see that this was also true of the ways in which the system of governance at Daimler-Benz was restructured.

Governance at Daimler-Benz

At the level of governance during this period, the shift toward greater scale and volume production saw Daimler-Benz also attempt to gradually remove itself from dependence upon the extrafirm infrastructural institutions of governance within the decentralized order. Control over production was centralized in ways that were reminiscent – probably imitations – of autarkic forms of organization. The company became very closely tied to the Deutsche Bank. Increasing amounts of functions essential to the competitiveness and reproduction of the firm, such as research and development, were internalized. And, finally, its interests began to extend far beyond the immediate region to the national and international

The development of the decentralized industrial order since 1945 157

issues of macroeconomic and foreign economic policy. Its heavy investments in mass-production techniques encouraged it to pay more attention to the environmental dimensions of managing the relationship between its own capacity and the level of demand.

Centralization. The centralization of administrative control over production at Daimler-Benz occurred in the same kind of piecemeal fashion that the movement toward mass production had. During the early 20th century, before World War I, both the Daimler and the Benz factories were run essentially as a federation of workshops (milling room, turning room, etc.) each supervised independently by a master craftsman. There was no central hiring and no overall direct coordination by management.[54] Masters were aware of the needs of the company and of the market and saw to it that they worked together to get their workshops to supply the needed product. The boundary between these producers and those of independent small firms outside the company was extremely blurry, and, indeed, many a skilled craftsman from these shops would leave the company and establish a small shop in the region after a stint at Daimler or Benz.

The shift to group production in the 1920s and 1930s was accompanied by a change in this system of independent, workshop-level administration. Control over the product and over the flow of production, i.e., the coordination of workshop relations, was now centralized in a single production-planing office, much as it was in large machinery companies in the autarkic regions. A central production office was created to supervise the flow of workpieces through the various workshops. Central cost accounting and finance offices were established to ensure that the level of costs within the company could be monitored and optimized. Control over production was shifted upwards in the organization of the firm, away from the workshops themselves. The culmination of this trend was when the two companies merged in the mid-1920s – all of the separate offices in the companies were merged together into one (i.e., one production planning office, one cost accounting office, etc.).[55]

Increases in the scale of production and the size of the company during the 1950s and 1960s did not force the company away from this centralized structure. The production of all automobile models and all trucks were coordinated from a central-planning office. Within this basically uniform, functionally organized corporate organization, truck production was informally separated from autos. The specialization of plants separated truck and bus assembly from automobile assembly and coordinated production and logistical relations within the Daimler-Benz system so that there was a minimum of redundancy in parts production. Many of the nonassembly plants were kept flexible enough to be able to share capacity between the needs of truck and car products.[56]

Linkages to universal banks from the autarkic form of industrial order: The Deutsche Bank. The removal of the production of automobiles from the surrounding region and its integration securely inside the boundaries of the Daimler-Benz firm had its analog in the changing relationship between the firm and

158   *Industrial constructions*

the capital market. An intimate dimension of the firm's movement toward a more autarkic structure was the establishment of extremely close ties to the large, autarkic Deutsche Bank. The establishment of this linkage to the autarkic form of industrial order, much as the progress toward the adoption of mass-production techniques and autarkic principles of governance, came in a piecemeal and at times even improbable way.

For the entire early period of their operations, Daimler and Benz had very little contact with banks from the autarkic regions. Instead they were engaged with important regional banks: in the case of Daimler, the Württembergische Vereinsbank in Stuttgart, and in Benz's case, the Rheinische Creditbank. For both firms, the role of these regional banks was fairly important. In order to turn themselves into "joint stock" companies, both Daimler and Benz were forced to cede considerable influence to the regional banks. Regional bankers chaired the supervisory boards of the companies before the turn of the century.

Although regional banks played a dominant role at this time, autarkic universal banks were also involved: both with the firms themselves but especially with the regional banks that the firms dealt with. As early as 1906, the Deutsche Bank took a small property stake in the Württembergische Vereinsbank and in that way became the privileged banking partner for Daimler in its dealings throughout the rest of the country. In the years before World War I, as Daimler's involvement in military production increased, direct dealings with the Deutsche Bank became more important. Before World War I, connections between Benz and the Deutsche Bank were similarly indirect yet close: the Württembergische Vereinsbank had a stake in the Rheinsche Creditbank which had been established in 1870. In 1904 the Rheinsche Creditbank, and the Deutsche Bank set up an interlocking relationship of shares and personnel. In 1922, the Deutsche Bank took a majority position in the Rheinische Creditbank and then in 1929 completely assimilated the activities of the regional bank.[57]

These linkages between the regional banks, the Deutsche Bank and the two firms proved to be extremely important in organizing the merger between the two firms between 1924 and 1926. The interests of all three converged on cooperation.

The Deutsche Bank and the regional banks were weakened by the effects of war and inflation. This led to a process of consolidation in the banking industry in which larger universal banks, such as the Deutsche, took over the assets of the smaller regional ones, including the Württemberger Vereinsbank and the Rheinische Bank. Moreover, the effects of war and crisis forced the Deutsche Bank to diversify its lending portfolio into new areas of industrial growth that could replace the business it had lost through its overseas operations and through the creation of more financially autonomous corporate structures in the autarkic regions.[58] Both of these developments made Daimler and Benz attractive potential investments for the Deutsche Bank.[59]

For their part, the initial postwar years cast the two automobile companies into a situation that made them open to, or at least incapable of seeking alternatives to, the resources of the universal banking system. The loss of their military business after the war, coupled with high inflation, significant import competition, and a bad market for cars and trucks caused the financial situation of both companies to severely deteriorate throughout the first years of the 1920s. The idea of a merger between the two companies was attractive because it consolidated the debts owed to their (increasingly interlinked) banks into a single company, while it enabled the firms, as we saw, to consolidate and rationalize their production facilities. The price of this was that the Deutsche Bank, which had replaced the regional banks as the main banker for the companies, would occupy a commanding position in the supervisory board of the new company.[60]

The entry of the Deutsche Bank shifted the financial interests of Daimler-Benz away from the regional capital markets and integrated them more directly into the national capital markets that the universal banks controlled. The union did not grow out of any logic within either the autarkic or decentralized orders, but was a child of the post-World War I turbulence in the German economy. Nevertheless, it represented one of the first significant penetrations of autarkic banking institutions into the decentralized industrial order. In the end, this position of the Deutsche Bank slowly facilitated a deregionalization, not only of the capital market orientation of the company, but in its ownership structure as well. During the 1950s, for example, two important industrialist families from the autarkic regions, the brothers Herbert and Harald Quandt and Friedrich Flick, bought significant interests in Daimler-Benz. For much of the postwar period the company was controlled by three large blocks of interest: Flick (38%), Quandt (14%), and the Deutsche Bank (31%). These interests dominated the supervisory board of the company and were closely involved in the formulation of its major investment policies and strategic evolution.

This close integration of the capital market, ownership control, and management that was not attached in any particular way to the surrounding region gradually led to a regional dispersal of production facilities within the Daimler-Benz concern. Over the course of the period of European integration, the company expanded throughout the Federal Republic, investing in or taking over companies in both autarkic and decentralized regions. By the beginning of the 1970s, the company had production facilities in Düsseldorf, Kassel, Bremen and Hamburg, all cities in autarkic regions, in addition to its core facilities in Baden Württemberg. The firm's strategic investment calculations were increasingly shaped by national and international market factors and not by its embeddedness in a system of extrafirm industrial institutions as had primarily been the case prior to 1924.[61]

The internalization of infrastructure. If the previous two examples show how the transformation of Daimler-Benz resulted in the abandonment of the local institutional structures of decentralized industrial order, the examples of product development (R&D) and vocational training show how the transformation was also a process of institutional recomposition in which the firm's relationship to the institutions of industrial order were redefined. In each of these cases, withdrawal from the decentralized institutions either did not take place at all or was less complete than in the areas of production and finance. This was mostly because the decentralized institutions continued to be useful to the large firm.

In the case of product development and research and development more generally, a process of withdrawal took place, yet it was less complete. The company's commitment to model production gradually lead it to internalize product development and create departments for design and testing of new technologies, i.e., a so-called *Konstruktionsbüro* for engineering and design, and a *Versuchsabteilung* for prototype testing and experimentation.[62] Just as importantly, the firm created a special department committed to the development of racing cars. This allowed Daimler-Benz workshops and engineers to be continuously engaged in attempts to push the boundaries of existing technology.[63]

For all of this, Daimler-Benz continued to maintain research and development ties with local research universities, especially technical universities and *Fachhochschulen*. This was partially because the regional research resources in engine and motor vehicle engineering were very great, and partially because contacts between the more applied educational institutions and the decentralized industrial order provided the firm with continuous access to engineers. In this sense, they were a resource or public good for the firm that it did not need to duplicate internally.

Vocational education was another case in which, despite the transformation that the firm underwent in the course of the middle years of the 20th century, Daimler-Benz found that it was preferable to rely on existing institutional resources in the decentralized industrial order. The existence of the extensive "dual system" of vocational training throughout Germany offered firms such as Daimler-Benz a public good. Just as for smaller companies, large firms such as Daimler-Benz could benefit from the training-cost savings that this system afforded and hence had no need to draw that function completely within the boundaries of the firm.

Matching production capacity to demand. The final set of administrative changes involved efforts to find a match between growing production capacity and the size of demand in the market.[64] The more the company invested in volume-production methods, the more crucial this dimension of administration became. Mass production involved tremendous investment in relatively rigid machinery that was profitable only when it was able to produce in large volumes. To avoid the high costs of idle machinery, the firm had to devise ways to regulate the relationship between the growth of capacity and the growth of demand. At different stages in Daimler-Benz's development toward mass production, different solutions were experimented with. In many ways, the dilemmas that the firm confronted in this area were more an effect of its already having removed itself from the decentralized structures of administration than they were a cause of it.

During the interwar years, for example, when the firm adopted the methods of group production, but was still producing relatively specialized, high-quality automobiles, trucks, and large engines, the measures that it adopted to match production capacity to the level of demand combined elements of solutions adopted by specialist producers in both decentralized and autarkic regions, i.e., coordinated specialization and diversification. Although there was no automobile cartel or even any explicit finishing association, it seems rather clear that Daimler-Benz's strategy during the late 1920s in the automobile part of its business was to target a market niche that was not occupied by many other automobile producers.[65] A modicum of market stability was achieved in this case not so much by controlling competition as much as it was by simply seeking to avoid it. At the same time, the firm also systematically hedged on its commitment to any one of its product specialties by staying diversified in the production of a variety of combustion engine related areas.[66]

During the 1930s, the company supplemented these supply side efforts with an effort to tie itself to a stable source of demand. It did this by systematically seeking to integrate itself into the military procurement strategies of the Nazi state. Daimler-Benz produced significant amounts of military vehicles and aircraft engines and became one of the major military goods contractors for the Nazi Regime. Viewed from the admittedly narrow perspective concerned with administrative strategies to ensure a stable and predictable source of demand, this was a fairly sound (and profitable) policy for the company.[67] In the long run, of course, the strategy did not pay off.

During the period of rapid postwar economic recovery and expansion, the company adopted three different strategies aimed at establishing a stable demand for Daimler-Benz automobiles and trucks (its large-motor and aircraft engine businesses were cut off after the war by the allies). The first, more an aspect of the strategy in cars than in trucks, was to create artificial shortages of Mercedes automobiles. By making sure that production always ran slightly behind the level of orders for cars, Daimler could not only hold its prices higher, it could insulate its investment and capacity growth from short-term shifts in the level of demand. The second strategy was to move into export markets. As early as 1952, 31% of Daimler's total output of cars and trucks went abroad. This proportion slowly increased over the next 20 year period, so that by 1972 the percentage of production going to export markets was 38%. In the next decade, however, as demand in the domestic market began to stagnate, exports increased dramatically. By 1978, 44.9% of the company's car output went abroad and by 1985 51.4% did.[68] The vast majority of Daimler's exports went to Western European industrialized countries.[69]

The final stabilization measure was to consolidate capacity in the broader industrial segment in which it was active through merger. This became a very important strategy in the truck business beginning in the late 1960s and early 1970s. At that time, demand for most sizes of trucks began to flatten, and it became clear that there were too many producers and too much production capacity in the domestic West German market. Daimler-Benz purchased the significant Hanomag-Henschel truck interests of the Rheinstahl corporation in 1969 and then in 1971 entered into several joint-production agreements with the

162 *Industrial constructions*

large autarkic truck producer MAN. Consolidation through merger of this kind was rarer in the automobile division because Daimler had never had significant competitors in its product segment.[70]

The interesting feature of all of these efforts to regulate the relationship between production capacity and the market is that they were strategies undertaken by the firm alone. The horizontal and cooperative relations that had previously characterized such efforts in the decentralized industrial order were abandoned. The sheer size of the company and the global character of its demand encouraged it to think of its own problems of production and its administration independently of those problems among regional producers. In this way, it had grown into a company that no longer thought of itself primarily as a producer within a region, but rather as one of the major corporate pillars of postwar West German prosperity. Its points of reference became other larger West German autarkic corporations, many of which were also intimately tied to the Deutsche Bank, and systematically sought to devise ways to stabilize their exposure to fluctuations in demand by diversifying, exporting and merging with their competitors.

Autarky in decentralization

This case study of Daimler-Benz was designed to show how a certain class of producer within the decentralized industrial order broke out of the institutional structure of the order during the middle years of the 20th century. The extent of this shift out of decentralized production into more autarkic forms of production during the three decades after World War II was very significant, though impossible to determine exactly. Nearly all sectors of industry were affected. The growth of firms such as Robert Bosch in automobile electronics and then later household goods, Standard Elektrik Lorenz in electrical products, firms within the machinery industry such as Liebherr in construction machinery or Klöckner-Humboldt-Deutz in diesel engines, trucks, and agricultural tractors all followed paths of development which, though not identical in every detail to that of Daimler-Benz, certainly were shaped by very similar strategic and organizational considerations.

Quantitative measures of these changes are more difficult to get due to the many changes in the statistics-gathering bodies over the course of the period studied. Nevertheless, if one takes simply a measure of the growth in the relative significance of large firms within the regional economies of Württemberg and then Baden Württemberg over the course of the period under review, one gets the general impression that firms breaking out of the structures of decentralized production was very widespread, especially in manufacturing. The process began with the coming of World War I and the swelling of employment rolls at the manufacturing firms in the region that could produce military products (or supply those who did). In 1907 in Württemberg, only 6.6% of all industrial employees worked in establishments employing over 500 employees. There were

37 establishments employing more than 500 workers. By 1925, the number of establishments employing over 500 workers had increased to 108, and they employed 16.4% of all industrial employees in Württemberg.[71] In 1950, in Baden Württemberg (a larger region), 51% of all industrial workers were employed in establishments with more than 200 workers and 21% were employed in establishments with over 1000 workers. Though the measures are ambiguous due to the change in units measured, the impression of steady growth in the importance of large firms in this former decentralized region is clear.[72]

Continuity in decentralization: Capital-goods producers and the reconstitution of decentralized industrial order

The development of firms such as Daimler-Benz away from the principles of organization that governed production and its administration in the decentralized industrial order was a tremendous blow to many producers within the older industrial order. In particular, those producers in product markets that were conducive to mass-production strategies suffered from direct competition with the large-scale, vertically integrated production forms. Nevertheless, the general historical trend toward mass production in postwar Western Europe by no means meant the end of the decentralized industrial order in Germany. The same environmental factors that led producers to aggressively move in the direction of mass production and abandon their ties to the local order also encouraged producers of capital goods to strengthen their commitment to it.

The logic behind this is very familiar and has been pointed out by many students of industrial organization and technology: the expansion of producers in an economy employing the methods of mass production also entails the expansion of a sector in the economy that does not mass-produce.[73] The more heavily committed to mass production a firm becomes, the more it invests in very specialized, product- and even operation-specific capital equipment that must be customized to the particular specifications of the mass-production process. Mass-producing firms, therefore, employ specialist capital-goods producers to provide them with the customized equipment they need.

The argument of this section is that this characteristic of a mass production dominated economy created a competitive space in which producers of capital goods organized in the decentralized form of industrial order could survive, even flourish. This population of producers was quite sizeable, partly because the weight of capital-goods producers within the decentralized industrial order was already quite large, partly because many producers confronted with competition from standardized consumer products shifted into capital-goods production, and, finally, partly because the structure of opportunities became such that a craftsman interested in establishing his or her own business found the waters more hospitable in capital-goods markets than elsewhere.

164   *Industrial constructions*

Quantitative dimensions of reconstruction in the decentralized industrial order

If the argument were correct that the shift of firms into mass production created a space for small- and medium-sized capital-goods-producing firms that did not mass-produce, then one would expect the capital-goods-producing sectors to have significant numbers of small- and medium-sized firms. Moreover, one would further expect that such firms and such sectors would be plentiful in regions traditionally dominated by the decentralized industrial order. In the traditional macroeconomic treatments of the evolution of West German industry, capital-goods producing industries such as the machinery industry, most parts of the electro-mechanical industry, the fine mechanical and optical industries, and others are generally grouped together into the "investment-goods" producing sector of the economy.[74]

The investment-goods producing sector was the largest and fastest growing sector of West German industry during the so-called *Wirtschaftswunder* or economic miracle.[75] The sector's growth was fueled not only by the growth of mass-production operations in West Germany, but by the spread of mass production throughout the Western European economy. The sector went from accounting for 29% of total West German industrial employment in 1950 to 45.9% in 1970. The next-largest employer was the consumer-goods industries (textiles, consumer electronics, etc.) with 27.3% of all industrial employment in 1950 but with only 23.9% in 1970. Basic production goods (steel and chemicals, but not coal) accounted for 22.4% of industrial employment in 1950 and 21.3% in 1970.[76]

In terms of industrial turnover, investment goods in 1950 accounted for 22.3% of the total for all of industry and in 1970 it accounted for 38.1%. Both the consumer-goods-producing industries (24.8%) and the basic-production-goods industries (27.4%) were larger than the investment-goods sector in 1950, but were considerably smaller in 1970, with production goods taking 30.7% and consumer goods just 16.2 % of total West German industrial sales. Production growth in the investment-goods industries increased over five-fold during the same period.[77]

General figures on the size distribution of firms in the West German investment-goods sector as a whole are difficult to find, but one source has compiled a table comparing the size distribution of firms in all of the major categories of West German industry in 1967 and 1974.[78] This shows that though it declined slightly between 1967 and 1974, the percentage of workers employed in establishments with 500 or fewer workers in the investment-goods sector was greater than a third of all employed in the sector, and those employed in establishments with less than 1000 employees was over half of all employed for the entire period.

The weight of small- and medium-sized enterprises becomes even more apparent when one looks at specific industrial branches within the investment-goods sector. For example, for much of the postwar period, the machinery industry was the largest or among the largest industrial branches in the West German industrial economy, measured by employment and total sales.[79] Small- and medium-sized producers were strongly represented in the branch throughout the postwar period. In 1951, only 34.5% of all employed and 35.7% of sales were accounted for by establishments with over 1000 employees. Firms with 500 employees or less accounted for 50.9% of all employed and 49.3% of sales. By 1965, establishments with over 1000 employees had grown to account for 41.8% of employment and 42.1% of sales. But the equivalent amount of employment (41.8%) and almost the equivalent amount of sales (40.6%) was accounted for by establishments with less than 500 employees.[80]

Other investment-goods branches that were similarly located and structured are the optical and fine mechanical equipment industry and the electro-technical industry. An indication of this is the percentage share of the 10 largest firms in the sector in the total sales of that sector. In the fine mechanical and optical equipment industry, the top 10 firms accounted for 25.3% of the total sector sales in 1954. This share decreased by 0.01% by 1960 to 25.2%. The electro-technical industry, like the machinery industry, located in both autarkic and decentralized regions, was slightly more concentrated: the percentage share of the top 10 firms in the sector in 1954 was 37.8%. This increased by 0.06% in 1960 to 38.4%.[81]

Finally, it is consistently true that branches with a preponderance of small- and medium-sized producers, such as the machinery industry, either remained or grew to be significant industries in the regions dominated by the decentralized industrial order. In North Rhine Westphalia, for example, the machinery industry was the second largest industrial employer (behind coal mining) and the second largest industry in terms of sales (behind the steel industry) in 1965. Fifty-four percent of the firms in the North Rhine Westphalia machinery industry and 46.2% of those employed in the machinery industry in that province were in regions traditionally dominated by the decentralized industrial order.[82]

Baden Württemberg was also a major center of investment-goods industry production. The machinery industry and the electro-technical industry were the two largest sectors in that regional economy for most of the postwar period.[83] Over 60% of all employed in the machinery industry in Baden Württemberg were in establishments employing less than 1000 workers in both 1955 and 1972. Over 40% of all employed in the sector worked in establishments employing fewer than 500 workers in both years.[84]

The emphasis here has been on the postwar performance of the investment-goods industries because they clearly show that small- and medium-sized producers in regions dominated by the decentralized form of industrial order continued to flourish in the postwar period. This was true despite the fact that during the same period many noncapital-goods producing larger firms located in decentralized regions broke out of the decentralized structures of industrial order.[85] The following section outlines the political and institutional adjustments in the character of the decentralized system that accompanied this successful

166 *Industrial constructions*

adjustment of decentralized capital-goods producers into the period of European integration.

Recomposing the institutions of decentralized industrial order

In order for the decentralized industrial order to reconstitute itself along the lines suggested above, a number of important obstacles had to be overcome. Conditions in the early postwar period were not conducive to the spontaneous reconstruction of the prewar systems. Physical and economic disruption created adjustment pressures at a time when the occupation of Germany and the deconstruction of the Nazi state had created a political environment in which none of the old institutional mechanisms at work in German society could presume their legitimacy. Successful adjustment took place through a process of political and economic recomposition.

Reconstitution of coordinated specialization

The first important move toward the reconstitution of the principles of organization in the decentralized industrial order came in the immediate postwar period when the German political economy lay, literally, in ruins. The problem in production at that time was that transition out of the Nazi war economy into a politically fragmented occupied economy created surpluses of capacity in areas where demand no longer existed (or as in the case of armaments production, was no longer permitted) and shortages of goods in areas where production capacity was extremely small. In decentralized areas, where many of the producers across industries were specialists with significant numbers of skilled workers in their plants, the possibility was great that producers in sectors with capacity surpluses would simply abandon their old specialties for those sectors where there were capacity shortfalls. To a certain extent, this was desirable, yet it also created the possibility that competition for entry into the desirable sectors would unleash the kind of unruly competition that had traditionally destabilized decentralized industries: e.g., price-cutting or establishing unrealistic delivery conditions, among others.

In the face of these problems, key institutional actors within the decentralized system of order – trade associations, chambers of commerce, local governments, and banks – intervened (or were enlisted) to ensure that the situation in industry did not degenerate into chaos. In so doing, they reconstructed the structures and principles of organization that had been developed during the interwar period to deal with such problems in production and its governance within the decentralized industrial order, such as term-fixing cartels, finishing associations, and price cartels.

The case of textile machinery producers, who were overwhelmingly located in the decentralized regions of Württemberg, Bergisches Land (especially Wuppertal), and the west bank of the Rhine (Mönchengladbach), provide a good illustration of the way that these traditional mechanisms were put back into place.[86]

The development of the decentralized industrial order since 1945   167

The initial postwar years were quite disruptive for the German textile machinery producers. Only 36% of total prewar textile machinery production capacity existed in the geographic territory that became the Federal Republic of Germany. The main region of textile machinery production before the war had been the Kingdom of Saxony. In some subcategories of textile machinery, knitting and hosiery machinery for example, only 14% of the prewar capacity had existed outside Saxony. For some types of machinery, such as Cotton machinery,[87] production know-how did not exist in West Germany at all.[88]

At the same time, the need for machinery that would increase production capacity in textiles in West Germany was very high. The textile industry was the largest industrial employer in the new country and there was a desperate need for clothing and materials. In itself, this created an interest in the production readiness of the textile machinery producers. But additionally, because textile producers and other industrial consumers in the West German economy were dependent upon imported raw materials and textile machinery was one of the few nonmilitary related machinery export items available to earn foreign exchange, the military government gave textile machinery production considerable attention. Lack of capacity in the industry was perceived as an important problem.[89]

For their part, the machinery producers saw their situation as highly volatile. A constellation of factors threatened to undermine stable and orderly competition in the industry. Capacity bottlenecks in textile machinery production created tremendous windfall possibilities for the person or firm that could produce the machines demanded. West German machine tool companies were forbidden to produce a wide range of their machinery due to a ban on all armaments-related production. Moreover, many former textile machinery engineers from firms located in Saxony in the Soviet Zone of occupation were fleeing to the West carrying with them blueprints from their old textile machinery establishments. In this context, it is easy to see how the production of textile machinery could have turned into a chaotic free-for-all of people and firms literally betting their lives on orders. The *potential* capacity for textile machinery production was at an inflated level.

Chaos was averted because the textile machinery trade association along with local banks acquired the capacity to ensure that the process of adjustment occurred within the traditional system of coordinated specialization in which firms were organized into finishing associations. An opening for the re-creation of these institutions was created because the government authorities, who were willing to provide financial means for firms willing to adopt production of new or desired technologies, had no detailed knowledge of the industry.[90] They turned to the recently reconstituted textile machinery trade association and the local banks for advice and assistance in the carrying out of this policy. Ultimately, the association was given the responsibility of "recommending" firms to the banks, which would then make loans that were federally guaranteed.[91] The association specifically sought to get existing firms to delimit the range of their product palette, and, at the same time, emphasized that all firms taking up the production of bottleneck technologies had to specialize on a limited range of standard machinery types. The system of coordinated specialization that had been developed during the interwar period was in this way gradually reestablished. Producer decisions about market entry and product development were made easier and problems of overcapacity in markets for any given machine type were avoided.[92]

The combined efforts of the state, trade associations and banks were quite successful. By 1952, there were 350 firms producing textile machinery parts and accessories in the Federal Republic of Germany with roughly 33,500 employees. In the same geographic area in 1936, there were less than half as many firms and only 14,000 employees. Moreover, the annual output in 1951 had tripled that of the same West German area in 1936 and was over 90% greater than the entire textile machinery output of the German Reich in 1938.[93]

The experience of the textile machinery industry throws into particularly graphic relief a process that in one form or another occurred throughout the industries within the decentralized areas in the immediate postwar period. Faced with disruption, shortages, dislocation, and political uncertainty, key institutional actors within the decentralized system of order – trade associations, chambers of commerce, regional governments, and local banks – intervened to reconstruct the structures and principles of organization that had traditionally governed production and its administration within the decentralized industrial order.

Political conflicts surrounding the reconstitution of extrafirm institutions of governance

Inseparable from processes of reconstruction of this kind, however, were political conflicts. The efforts of the Allied military powers (and their German allies) to impose a liberal democratic structure on occupied West Germany often came into conflict with the interests of small- and medium-sized industrial producers in the decentralized form of industrial order. Many of the extra-firm institutions of governance that were crucial for their stability and survival contradicted what the Allied occupiers understood to be basic liberal tenets of social order. The decentralized producers had to defend the central political and economic importance of the institutions that governed the decentralized industrial system.

In some cases, such as with the reestablishment of trade associations or banks, the Allied occupiers were anxious to have such organizations reestablished, but they objected to the manner in which these organizations involved themselves in industry. Trade associations were celebrated as pillars of a renewed civil society, but, after the initial reconstruction period, the authorities sought to prevent them from acting as the arena in which member firms could establish finishing associations, specialization cartels, and other extrafirm forms of governance.[94] Savings banks were rapidly reconstituted, but authorities attempted to outlaw the *Girozentrale* that allowed local banks to pool resources and facilitate lending as inappropriate violations of market forces.[95] Similar struggles took place over the reconstitution of regional governments. In all of these cases, the German conception of the role these institutions should play in society prevailed over that of the occupying authorities, but only after extensive political conflict.

On the whole, political differences between the occupying powers and the indigenous decentralized producers emerged, not over the merits of reviving a civil society, but over the role of the market in the organization of social, economic, and political life. The following section will look at two representative conflicts: the reconstitution of the Chambers of Commerce and the passage of a cartel law during the 1950s.[96] The reconstitution of the Chambers of Commerce or *Industrie- und Handelskammern* (IHK), in the postwar period provides a good example of how such political differences were resolved in a way that ultimately reconfirmed an age-old tradition of decentralized industrial governance. The debate and ultimate passage of a law forbidding the formation of cartels shows how the political differences resulted in some compromise in those traditions.

Chambers of Commerce. The Chambers of Commerce, which had been folded into the Nazi state apparatus during the 1930s, reestablished themselves immediately after the war.[97] The Aachen Chamber of Commerce, in fact, was reconstituted as early as March 1945 (two months before the end of the war).[98] Initially the Chambers were used by the occupying powers to perform particular administrative tasks that the military government either preferred not to or could less efficiently perform, such as the preparation of work permits (*Arbeitserlaubnisse*).[99] In this way, the chambers were performing services that were completely consistent with what their traditional role in German society had been. According to the tradition of public law, the chambers had a dual identity in that they were both organizations for the representation of societal interests and administrative servants of the state. Traditionally, membership in regional chambers was mandatory and the administrative leadership of the organizations elected by the membership.

In this traditional form, the Chambers of Commerce played a crucial role in the extrafirm governance structures within the decentralized industrial order by mediating the flow of information and interests between both industry and the state. The Chambers provided firms with information about changing government regulations, markets, technology, and organization at the same time that they provided regional authorities with information on the changing needs of local industry. The Chambers of Commerce also carried on a number of official administrative functions relating to business, such as overseeing and coordinating vocational education programs in a region. Chambers of Commerce concentrated on the background general needs (*die Gesamtinteressen*) of all industries located in a given region. This was distinguished carefully from the realm of particular sectoral-interest representation, which was the province of industrial trade associations.[100] Wülker summarizes the distinction between the two different kinds of organizations nicely: "trade associations must be understood as associations that are in society and outside the state, whereas the Chambers of Commerce are outside of society, more precisely, between society and the state."[101]

170 *Industrial constructions*

Although they initially utilized some of the services of the Chambers of Commerce in the very early days of the occupation, the Allied powers had quite a different long-run conception for the role and legal status that the Chambers of Commerce should have. The Americans, especially, considered the partly public/partly private status of the Chambers of Commerce to be an example of precisely the kind of conflation of state and society that ultimately produced the Nazi dictatorship. In the American view, the way to recast German society to prevent the reemergence of National Socialism was to eliminate institutions that conflated the distinction between state and society.[102] Therefore, the American military government refused to allow the Chambers of Commerce to reconstitute themselves in their zone of occupation. Chambers of Commerce were prevented from performing any "official" activities and were turned into voluntary public service organizations along the lines of those that existed in the United States and Britain.[103]

The Germans argued that the Anglo-American model of voluntary organizations would undermine the Chambers' of Commerce ability to perform their crucial mediating functions. In their view, "Americanized" Chambers of Commerce placed no checks on the growth of particularism. The Americans wanted to encourage any geographic grouping of businessmen to form a Chamber of Commerce, regardless of how small. But this emphasis on voluntary membership, in the German view, would itself only result in the creation of exclusivity in the organization: those that were inside could act against those on the outside. Most importantly, the ban on the Chambers of Commerce performing official functions undermined a crucial institutional link in the flow of information among producers and between producers and the state.[104]

Ultimately, the traditional German conception of the Chambers of Commerce triumphed over the Anglo-American conception. The key to this outcome was the fact that the traditional model was able to root itself in two of the three Western zones of occupation immediately after the war. The French favored the traditional model because it was based upon their own Napoleonic system, whereas the British chose not to insist that the Germans adopt the Anglo-American model.[105] The Americans were the only ones to insist that their model be adopted. In the American occupation zone (parts of Württemberg, Hessen, and Bavaria – see Map 4 in Appendix) the official functions that had been performed by the Chambers of Commerce were assumed by the local and regional authorities. Once the Federal Republic regained sovereignty from the occupying powers in 1955, however, the majority in the rest of West Germany proved to be sufficient to override the American model. In December 1956, the Bundestag passed a law that unified the legal status of all Chambers of Commerce within the Federal Republic along traditional lines.[106] In most cases in Württemberg and Baden, the Chambers of Commerce had anyway never adjusted to the new system and readily returned to the old one.[107]

Conflict over the creation of a cartel law. If the controversy over the identity of the Chambers of Commerce is an example of a struggle that resulted in the reconstruction of an important traditional institution in the decentralized industrial order, the struggle over the cartel law during the 1950s is an example of how producers in the decentralized industrial order were forced to redefine their relationship to the new political regime in order to reconstruct a stable industrial order.

Controversy over cartels in Germany began during the very early years of the military occupation. The various military governments had agreed at Potsdam to decartelize and deconcentrate German industry after the war. The French were the first to outlaw cartels in their zone on October 6, 1947. The British and Americans followed later that year, issuing a joint decree on December 2, 1947.[108]

In an immediate way, Allied antipathy toward cartels in Germany was informed by their understanding of how the Nazi war economy functioned. Cartels had been a key instrument in the Nazi state's ability to allocate resources for the conduct of war. Getting rid of the cartels was thus seen as an integral part of the destruction of German war capacity. But there was a more profound set of considerations animating opposition to cartels among the allies (especially, once again, among the Americans) that was bound up with a conceptual framework for understanding industrial society that linked mass production and a modern middle class to stable liberal democracy.

The logic of the Allied argument was that because cartels work by protecting producers from the pressures of the competitive market, they block the emergence of efficient producers that can mass-produce on a large scale. This allows archaic production forms (e.g., artisanal or small-firm specialist production) and the social beliefs and practices associated with them to survive. Lack of competition, moreover, tends to concentrate wealth and prevent the emergence of a middle class, which is the ultimate source of stability and purchasing power in the economy. Mass production and the middle class were the cornerstones of the American conception of democracy, and if democracy were to be created in West Germany, then the preconditions for the growth of mass production and the emergence of a middle class had to be created. This required elimination of cartels.[109]

The United States had important allies in Germany itself around this question. On a philosophical level, the influential neo-liberal Freiburg or Ordo-liberal school of economists supported the elimination of cartels in the economy because they disrupted the free flow of market forces and thereby created imbalances of power and wealth in society. Such imbalances, according to the Freiburgers, were what lead to the tragic infringements of individual autonomy produced by the Nazi Regime, where an unequal and destablized society overwhelmed the state. They favored decartelization and a strong state that could resist the egoistic desires of particular interests in society and continuously ensure that the laws of the market governed the allocation of resources in society.[110]

On a practical level, the United States had allies on the cartel question in the camp of those producers in the economy that could benefit from a move into mass production: primarily large firms such as Siemens, AEG, Volkswagen, Mannesmann, Daimler-Benz, and the large Chemical producers.[111] Their idea was that, given the increasingly realistic prospect of an open European market, the elimination of interfirm agreements would allow firms to more easily expand, gain control of the evolution of technology in their branch, and produce with the most appropriate and efficient economies of scale.[112] Such firms, as the case study of Daimler-Benz showed, had already during the 1920s and 1930s shifted most of the regulation of production and its governance inside the firm and increasingly abandoned using cartels for anything other than the management of overcapacity. In an expanding market, such as existed in the 1950s, their need even for that kind of cartel was rather low, and the existence of other varieties of cartels only got in the way of their ability to expand. Interfirm and intraindustrial agreements that helped preserve smaller, specialized producers made it difficult to create markets for standardized "mass" products because the specialists fragmented potential markets. By supporting political efforts to ban all forms of interfirm agreements, the large firms made a small sacrifice for considerable gain.[113]

The Minister of Economics, Ludwig Erhard, took a position that mediated between the political views of the United States and the Ordo-liberal school, on the one hand, and the material interests of large-scale industry, on the other. He believed first that the preservation of a market economy was the only way to construct a democratic social order that protected the rights of the individual. But, like the Americans, he also was convinced that the way to achieve this was to create a set of conditions in the economy that would continuously increase productivity and make the spread of mass production possible. As such, he tended to be attentive to the economic interests of large potential mass producers. Most obviously, Erhard restricted his campaign against market behavior that limited competition to cartels, while supporting processes of concentration that lead to an improvement in industrial productivity and efficiency.[114]

This grouping of interests against cartels was directly opposed to the interests of producers within the decentralized industrial order. Most of the arrangements that decentralized producers had erected during the first part of the 20th century to stabilize their industries, such as price- and term-fixing and specialization cartels, came under attack by the American–Erhardian anticartel campaign. The defense of the decentralized industrial order was carried out primarily by the trade associations, including the important national-level associations such as the Federation of German Industry (BDI) and the National Diet of Chambers of Commerce (DIHT), as well as smaller sectoral associations and the local and regional governments.[115]

Arguments against the banning of cartels tended to make two central points. One was that by eliminating the mechanisms that allowed small- and medium-sized industry to stabilize itself, a ban on cartels would lead to a gradual strangulation of that class of producer. Fritz Berg, the head of the BDI and the owner of a firm that manufactured specialty bicycle and motor vehicle parts in the decentralized region of the Sauerland, warned against an "Americanization" of the German economy in which small- and medium-sized producers would be

The development of the decentralized industrial order since 1945   173

wiped out and the economy dominated by giant mass-producing enterprises. In a 1953 speech before the BDI, Berg set out the logic behind his position:

> In the end the natural striving of entrepreneurs is to keep their business going, no matter how much it costs. Consequently, if it is the case that no agreements are possible, a crisis will inevitably cause competition to become ruthless and the system of price setting to fall into chaos. The victims of this are not only the weakest firms, but often even the most efficient producers as well. The experience in the United States demonstrates most emphatically that the consequence of this is a process of concentration which completely destroys industries with a small- and medium-sized firm structure. There is little consolation in the idea that the freedom of these firms is taken away not by force, but in the name of the competitive free market.[116]

Berg stressed the importance of interfirm cooperation in the maintenance of decentralized industrial order. If the capacity to cooperate was taken away, the only alternative left would be to establish order autarkically, that is within the institutions of a firm. In his view, this would lead not only to the concentration of economic and technological control into too few hands, but to the gradual demise of decentralized, small- and medium-sized-firm-based production in a broad range of regions and industrial sectors.

Related to this, a second argument against the cartel law focused on the particular form it took. The United States, Erhard, and the neoliberal economists all favored a general ban on cartels.[117] Both the trade associations and the *Länder*, through the Bundesrat, opposed this by arguing that a ban on cartels invested the central state with too much power over the economy. It was essential, they maintained, to preserve the capacity of society to govern itself (*Selbstverwaltung*). It was precisely this that the National Socialist dictatorship had removed from German public life. Trade associations and regional authorities should have the right to become involved in the governance of the economy in whatever way the actors involved in that economy saw fit. The preservation of such local spheres of autonomy and self-government, they argued, was essential for the construction of a democratic public.[118]

As an alternative to the American–Erhard law, the trade associations argued for the creation of a law modeled after the one that had been passed in 1923 during the Weimar Republic. Rather than giving the federal level government the right to ban cartels, this law gave it the authority to police the economy and ensure that cartel forms of organization did not lead to unfair abuses in industrial practice. This would, in principle, allow producers to engage in forms of cooperative practice that enabled them to create order in their industries, while at the same time ensuring that there would be an authority to police the local systems to prevent abuses.[119]

The debate on the cartel law in West Germany took place throughout the 1950s. Erhard and the United States, which remained the "higher authority" in West Germany until 1955, initially had hoped that they could push the law through in the first legislative session of the Bundestag, which ended in 1953. But opposition to the law was too strong from the trade associations and in the Bundesrat, so a decision was postponed until the second legislative session (1954–1957).[120]

A major factor in the ultimate outcome was that the United States absolutely opposed the counterproposal of a law that would prevent abuses. Those advocating this alternative, therefore, although they were able to block the passage of the law initially, were forced to accept the inevitability of a ban on cartels. During the second legislative round, both the government and the opposition tried to find a way to accommodate the concerns of the decentralized producers and get a law on cartels passed at the same time.[121] After considerable political maneuvering, the final law had a character that was politically acceptable to most parties.[122] The key was that the final law combined an outright ban on cartels with a whole host of important exceptions to the ban which essentially permitted most forms of interfirm agreements that were important to producers within the decentralized industrial order. Moreover, in the most important categories of cartel allowed by the exceptions in the law, the state's role was simply to prevent abuses. Independent producers and the other extrafirm institutions of administration could define and redefine the boundaries of the decentralized industrial order in whatever way they deemed necessary. The new law required only that they inform the cartel authorities of what they had constructed.[123]

The character of the law was congenial to large producers as well. The final version of the law had no provisions that attempted to curb concentration in industry or otherwise constrain the capacity of large producers to adopt mass-production strategies. Basically, the law allowed firms to remain in the structures of decentralized industrial order, without at the same time making it impossible for other firms to break out of them.

The legal framework for market order arrived at in West Germany at the end of the 1950s was thus a compromise that attempted to accommodate the interests of two different forms of industrial strategy and organization: decentralized specialization and large-firm-centered mass production. For the producers within the decentralized form of industrial order the compromise did not so much force them to change the principles of organization that characterized their decentralized character of administration as it did change the relationship between those administrative forms and the federal government. Whereas in the pre-1933 system, firms in the decentralized industrial order coordinated their activities primarily through the institution of the trade association, in the post World War II period the federal government's cartel bureau became more involved in their activities, even if only formally in many cases.

Concentration in mass-production markets, small- and medium-sized suppliers, and the invisibility of the decentralized industrial order

The shift toward mass production in postwar Europe created a niche (albeit quite sizeable) into which producers of capital goods organized within the institutional framework of the decentralized industrial order were able to reproduce themselves in the market. But those producers in the regions of the decentralized industrial order who were not able or did not want to insert themselves into this available niche had considerable difficulty competing in the mass-production context. When firms broke out of the decentralized industrial order in the course of adopting mass-production strategies, it often had negative consequences for other producers in that sector who failed to adopt the new methods of organization. This had to do with the logic behind the withdrawal itself, and helps to explain the high levels of concentration that existed in mass-production based branches.

Typically, a firm began to engage in mass production when it recognized the existence of a large potential demand. Investing in greater capacity, and highly productive, single-purpose capital equipment enabled the firm to realize economies of scale and take advantage of a potential market. But it also exposed the firm to a considerable amount of risk. Mass production equipment was very expensive and rigid. If demand failed to appear, or if it changed very rapidly, the firm that invested heavily in rigid high-volume equipment stood to lose a great deal. Firms with such commitments, therefore, typically tried to reduce their exposure to such risks by gaining a dominant position in the market, often driving their competitors out of the market.[124] With competition at arms length, the successful mass-producing firm, or more accurately oligopoly of firms, could effectively control the evolution of technology in their business and thereby extract the greatest possible value out of its production process.[125]

Now, in general, regardless of the actual conditions that prevail in the market, many individual firms at a given point in time will be convinced that a large potential market for their product exists and thus seek to capture a large part of that market by using all of the resources at their disposal to gain that market for itself and drive other firms out of it. The problem for such producers is that conditions that allow for the success of such a strategy do not always prevail. Indeed, it has often been the case that instead of control, such producers incur tremendous losses either because they acquired capacity that far exceeded an unstable and fragmented market's ability to absorb, or because in attempting to undermine their competition they undermined the stability of market competition and unleashed a process of competitive chaos, or both. Under such inhospitable conditions, successful producers over time become those who recognize the futility of controlling the evolution of technology and see the benefits of stability to be gained from specialization, cooperation, and coordination.

The structures of coordinated specialization and decentralized industrial order are in many ways the fruits of industrial activity under conditions that were not conducive to mass production. Unstable and fragmented demand throughout the history of the European market always undermined the efforts of firms to control the evolution of technology in their sector. Over time, the vast majority of firms realized that the costs incurred by engaging in hostile competition under unstable and fragmented market conditions were too high, while the benefits of order associated with a specialization strategy within the coordinated structures of the decentralized industrial order were too attractive. Collective experience, communication, and learning led to mutual recognition, cooperation, and industrial self-regulation.

Only in the postwar period, when the level of disposable income became subject to regulation and trade barriers throughout Europe were gradually deconstructed did the possibility of gaining a dominant position in a large-size market become a reality. This new environment changed the individual producer's sense of what was possible in its market. The notion that a firm could gain a position of dominance in its branch, confidently invest in expensive high-volume processes, control the evolution of technology, and ultimately impose that technology onto the customer was no longer an impossibility. The effects of such a transition on large firms have already been discussed and will be further elaborated in the following chapter on autarkic industrial order. But the transition into a mass-production-dominated industrial structure had significant consequences for firms in those branches that were unable to gain a dominant position as well. In many cases, such firms were simply wiped out, either through competition and bankruptcy or through acquisition. But in many other cases, firms that had formerly been producers of end products became producers of parts and suppliers to larger firms. Despite the growth of large firms in mass-producing sectors such as automobiles, consumer electronics, and optical equipment, regions such as Baden-Württemberg, the Siegerland, Sauerland, and Bergisches Land did not experience significant reductions of small- and medium-sized firms active in those sectors. Instead, the evidence seems to be that firms in these regions shifted into supplier roles.[126]

By the end of the 1950s, advocates of a strong base of small- and medium-sized producers in the economy, such as Berg at the BDI, were arguing that the forward progress of technological rationalization and automation was unstoppable. Small- and medium-sized producers had to be protected by favorable taxing policies and improved access to capital. Yet even then, Berg maintained, the future lay with the large firm. In an essay entitled the "Age of Automation," he argued that small- and medium-sized producers would have to take advantage of opportunities as suppliers to large industry if they were going to survive.[127]

What at the end of the 1950s was the bitter truth of progress was by the mid-1960s a self-conscious strategy for survival. Countless newspaper articles, books, and dissertations were devoted to the ways in which small- and medium-sized firms could become suppliers to large mass producers.[128] Vulnerability to swings in the business cycle were considered to be one of the major hazards of this strategy, but the tenor of arguments was that such vulnerability was superior to the alternative of impossible competition against a far more efficient and larger rival. The environment had so completely changed that the idea that networks of small- and medium-sized firms could compete with the large producers was considered to be illogical.

The interesting characteristic of these developments is that the logic of the system of mass production that had gradually asserted itself in postwar Europe changed the way that small- and medium-sized firms were perceived. Competition on the basis of economies of scale with standardized products had become the norm in both thought and practice. Small- and medium-sized firms competing in markets through cooperation and on the basis of specialization was incomprehensible in the mass-production dominated markets of Europe in the 1960s. And in the markets for capital goods, where such market order was still conceivable, the success of small- and medium-sized firms was explained as a quirk in technological logic.[129]

Thus, even though the decentralized industrial order managed to reconstitute itself in the postwar period, its existence was by and large invisible. Outside the capital goods branches, the institutional framework of decentralization did not shape economic activity during the 1950s and 1960s. And, inside the capital-goods producing sectors, where those institutions were operative, it gradually came to be thought that those institutions were the consequence of the technology that was being manufactured in these sectors, rather than as the expression of a complex set of historical compromises designed to bring stability and order among industrial producers. Only in the 1980s, when the environmental conditions once again began to change in European and world markets, did the institutional background conditions of decentralized industrial order enter once more into the center of political and industrial debate.

The rise and decline of the decentralized form of industrial order since the 1980s

The logic governing production strategies and making possible the coexistence of mass-producing large firms and small- and medium-sized capital-goods producers and suppliers in the regions traditionally dominated by the decentralized industrial order broke down over the course of the 1970s, 1980s, and 1990s. World market conditions changed in ways that undercut the rigid and hierarchical strategies of the mass producers and favored, at least for a while, the flexible, quality production typical of producers within the decentralized industrial order. Traditionally decentralized regions, particularly Baden-Württemberg, flourished during the 1980s as a result of this apparently happy shift in the character of global competition.

The key to the initial success was that small- and medium-sized firms within the decentralized supporting arrangements proved able to assimilate new technologies, especially in microelectronics, into their traditional production palettes and were able to tailor their products to changing customer desires, always while minimizing (though never eliminating) the cost gap between their more sophisticated products and those of standardized mass-produced ones. Indeed, so striking was the success of small- and medium-sized producers that large firms in these areas, confronted with the reality of the crisis in the principles of production organization that they had committed themselves to a generation earlier, increasingly began to look for ways to integrate themselves back into the framework of decentralized order that existed around them. Whereas in the previous three decades, the coexistence of large and small firms had been based

178   *Industrial constructions*

on the delineation of very clear boundaries between their modes of operation, in this period it appeared that a new form of coexistence would emerge that presupposed the blurring of those boundaries.

As it turned out, the adjustment to the new world market conditions would be more complicated and difficult than the first decade of adjustment made it appear. By the middle of the 1990s, after the German reunification-fueled extended boom of the 1980s ended, two things became clear. First, both the small- and medium-sized producers within the decentralized industrial order as well as the large firms in these regions were having great difficulty keeping up with the continuously accelerating pace of product and technological change that existed in world markets. Increasingly, they were not able to produce high quality new products rapidly enough or at a prices competitive enough to be attractive to consumers. This problem was exacerbated by the fact that more and more producers from the Pacific region and even a rejuvenated U.S. economy were able to do this.

Second, both large and small German producers appeared to be running into similar obstacles in their efforts to adjust to this: Though both had embedded themselves in networks of subcontractors and had widely decentralized production *outside* the boundaries of the firm, both were finding that to increase flexibility further and especially to achieve lower production costs they needed to address problems of hierarchy and jurisdiction *inside* the firm. The continued existence of separate departments for development and production, or the continued salience of skill jurisdictions and skill-based job hierarchies on the shop floor, for example, placed an upper limit on any firm's flexibility. Such internal boundaries were cumbersome and added additional cost to development and production of a product. Breaking these institutional structures down, however, involved challenging central vested interests within the firm who could rightly claim that it had been their expertise and flexibility that was the root of the traditional success of decentralized craft production in world markets in the past. These adjustment problems are profound and will not be easily resolved. If they are resolved, however, the outcome will likely be dramatic redefinition of industrial order on the scale of the redefinition that occurred after World War II.

In presenting this argument, changes in the environment will be presented first, reactions by small- and medium-sized producers second, those by large firms third, and the emergent common areas of competitive weakness last.

Increasing competition and the fragmentation of markets: Shortening of product life cycles, rapid technological change, and increases in development costs

The first step in understanding the transformation of industrial production in the 1980s and 1990s is to see that the international market context within which producers, large and small, now compete differs fundamentally from that which characterized the first several decades of the postwar period. For much of the period of stable and continuous growth in the 1950s and 1960s, a hierarchy of technological sophistication, with the United States at the top and European (and Japanese) producers following behind, was a key mechanism for organizing not only the flow of trade and investment between the United States and Europe, but the character of competition within particular European industrial sectors as well. New products were developed in the most sophisticated market (the United States) and then, as they paid for themselves and knowledge of how to produce them was perfected, production diffused to other markets and ultimately, other producers.[130] Such a hierarchy supported the pursuit of large-scale, but very rigid, mass-production strategies in many different countries by essentially staggering the turns that different national industries had to exploit a particular technology.

During the 1970s, this stable hierarchy of the product cycle broke down. As the European economies developed, they built on the techniques and know-how that came from the United States and used them to be innovative themselves. The richer and more sophisticated the European markets became, the more sophisticated these innovations became. This process of economic growth and technological learning accelerated in snowball fashion until, ultimately, the marginal difference of income and sophistication between the United States and Europe narrowed, to the disadvantage of the United States. By the 1970s, it was no longer clear that the United States was the world's most sophisticated market, nor was it clear that they were the leaders in technological innovation.[131]

This was not only a problem for the United States. The simultaneous maturation of producers in all of the European countries leveled the development and technological hierarchy within Europe. The Italians, Swedes, and French, much less developed than the British and Germans during the 1950s, became their technological equals in a whole array of sectors by the 1970s. This resulted in tremendous levels of overcapacity in many sectors. Coal, textiles, and steel in the 1960s were the first to fall victim to this, but soon even the automobile and consumer-electronics industries were affected.[132] But, just as important, as powerful firms such as FIAT and Olivetti in Italy, or Renault and Thompson in France grew larger, they began to compete more seriously on a European-wide basis, intensifying the character of competition in the sectors in which they were active. And whereas within their own national markets such firms held positions of relatively unassailable market power, it was not as easy to replicate that power in competition with other national champions. Thus, paradoxically, the larger and more expansive European mass producers became, the more fragmented, competitive, and unstable became their markets.

During the 1970s, this intra-European process of market fragmentation was further exacerbated by the entry into the world market of lower-cost industrial producers from other parts of the world. The growth of the Japanese economy made it, by the early 1970s at the latest, a formidable competitor in world markets in a broad array of manufactured products. Their penetration of the European market directly was rather small, but they became active competitors

180 *Industrial constructions*

in third-country export markets.[133] Another challenge came from the developing world. Even though the total penetration of LDC exports into the markets of the developed European economies was small, the rate of growth and the growing sophistication of the exports was viewed with considerable alarm.[134] The comparative advantage of developing country producers was believed to be in markets for standardized, mass-produced items. European producers of textiles, clothing, consumer electronics, ball bearings, valves, auto parts, and many other industrial manufactures, it became increasingly apparent, would lose their comparative advantage vis-à-vis developing countries without significant adjustment.[135]

By the beginning of the 1980s, when these market trends had become clear, there was initially a great deal of debate in the literature concerning the character of industrial responses to this set of developments. What seems clear is that at that time there was not a unified response. Some firms attempted, to the extent that they were not constrained legally and financially at home, to displace production to lower-wage markets overseas.[136] But many others stayed at home and attempted to adjust by shifting their production into higher value-added markets and avoiding direct competition with low-wage producers.[137]

Both of these coping strategies, it now seems, simply made competition in already fragmenting markets even more intense. By the latter half of the 1980s, technology was being transferred more rapidly and the gap between many formerly developing and advanced-country markets was narrowing; technological upgrading and hunting for specialized niches accelerated the process of upgrading itself while dissolving the distinction between a competitive market and a niche.[138] Moreover, in a manner analogous to the oil shocks in the 1970s, the diffusion of microelectronic technologies introduced tremendous incalculability into industrial markets. On the one hand, the new technologies had an unbelievably broad potential for application in traditional areas of manufacturing, the absolute limit of which no one could define precisely. On the other hand, the microelectronic technologies themselves were changing extremely rapidly.[139]

Constant change in technology and continuously fragmenting and mutating markets bred uncertainty: It became impossible for producers to foresee exactly how the product markets they competed in would change in the future. All of this, finally, occurred under conditions of strongly rising product-development costs. The combination of shorter product cycles on the one hand, and the emergence of new and rapidly changing technologies such as, again, microelectronics or in other cases plastics, lasers, photo-voltaics, or composite materials on the other all resulted in enormous increases in development costs for individual firms. Producers not only had to learn how to apply new technologies to their traditional businesses, they also had to do so in a fraction of the time they took to develop traditional products.[140]

This kind of international competitive environment began to emerge in the latter part of the 1970s. It has intensified, deepened, and accelerated ever since, drawing in more and more products and technologies and regions of the world.

A renaissance in decentralized production: Small- and medium-sized firms

Oddly enough, particularly in light of the way the possibilities for industrial competitiveness had been conceived during the mass-production-driven postwar boom, small- and medium-sized producers within the institutional framework of the decentralized industrial order initially proved to be well suited to the new dynamic of competition in world markets.[141] Unlike large producers, they had never committed themselves to the rigid and large-scale technologies of mass production. They competed with relatively flexible technologies and utilized predominantly skilled workers. And, perhaps even more crucially, unlike the large mass producers, small- and medium-sized producers in the regions dominated by the decentralized industrial order enjoyed dense and overlapping ties with a whole array of institutions dedicated to providing them with technological and market information, highly trained people, and contact with other producers with complimentary expertise. Suddenly, at the beginning of the 1980s all of these characteristics of the decentralized industrial order, which had been largely invisible during the period of high mass production, unexpectedly provided small- and medium-sized producers with key resources to negotiate the new market environment: Producers had ready access to a broad local pool of technological and market experience as well as experience with interfirm and extrafirm cooperation – all of which relativized the initial costs of assimilating new technologies and engaging in continuous innovation.

Given that they constituted the largest concentration of producers in the decentralized industrial order during the period of mass production, it was not surprising that capital-goods producers attracted the most attention as examples of successful small- and medium-sized firm adjustment in the 1980s.[142] At the time, it seemed as if these producers had truly created a kind of high-technology craft production. As in the past, their strategy continued to emphasize customizing and specialization. But during the 1980s they began to also focus on continuously incorporating the newest forms of technology into their products, while cutting the cost of customized goods in relation to standard products.

There were many examples of this. Take the Traub Maschinenfabrik of Reichenbach/Fils and the Index-Werke of Esslingen, two former producers of conventional cutting lathes. Both firms responded to a challenge from Japanese machine tool producers, who had entered world markets with inexpensive computer-controlled (CNC) standardized lathes, by producing highly flexible CNC lathes that contained special characteristics that Japanese machines did not have: greater precision and greater durability at higher cutting speeds. Unable to mass produce the higher-quality machines, the companies developed sophisticated modular-design systems that allowed them to efficiently tailor their machines to customer special needs.[143]

Other machinery producers sought to enhance their capacity to respond to very specific, and changing, customer needs for sophisticated microelectronic

182   *Industrial constructions*

technologies and systems. The best examples of this very broad swath of the industry were the two flat-knitting-machine makers, Stoll of Reutlingen and Universal of Westhausen.[144] Both produced a wide variety of CNC flat-knitting machinery for the high-fashion knit-goods industries in Italy, West Germany, Switzerland, and elsewhere. The machines were specially developed to provide small- and medium-sized producers with the flexibility and quickness they needed to respond to fashion changes. A different variant of this strategy was to emphasize the ability to combine engineering prowess with handicraft skill in the production of special purpose machinery. The medium-sized firm PM Putzmeister-Werk, a cement-pump maker in Filderstadt near Stuttgart, was a good example of this. It constructed four special lead-enshrouded cement-pump trucks with a remote-controlled delivery pipe over 100 meters long for use in the Soviet Union at the Chernobyl nuclear power plant disaster site within four months of the disaster.

Although capital-goods producers received the most attention in the renaissance of decentralized areas in West Germany, other sectors, such as textile and apparel producers, which had wallowed in a marginal backwater of inefficiency during the era of mass production, also enjoyed a recovery and rapid rates of growth in the 1980s. Some German fashion-design houses, such as Hugo Boss and Jil Sander, became significant producers on the world market for the first time, while other German producers excelled in the production of specialized industrial fabrics, such as fireproof materials.[145] Small- and medium-sized producers in the furniture, auto parts, fine mechanical and optical equipment, and all branches of the electronics industry also flourished in these areas.[146] Like the capital-goods producers, successful manufacturers in these sectors were those who were able to move up-market into higher-quality products, integrating traditional manufacturing skill with new technologies while at the same time being attentive to consumer desires.

The point about all of these producers, in capital goods, consumer goods, and producer goods sectors, was not that they produced in small volumes. Some of all the above groupings of producers continued, for example, to produce in large volumes. Rather it was that they all possessed, or were able to develop, great production flexibility and were able to use that flexibility to modify old and introduce new products more rapidly than were larger, more autarkically organized mass producers.[147] Although the existing pattern of institutions and practices that constituted the decentralized industrial order provided producers with an advantage in adjusting to the new, more turbulent, market conditions, the adjustment did involve a number of changes in the decentralized industrial order, both in the organization of production and in the way it was governed.

Production: Greater openness and decentralization

The reorganization of production processes in the 1980s involved an extensive shift to subcontracting and collaborative manufacturing.[148] As we saw in Chapter 2, some form of subcontracting was always an important part of industrial practice in the decentralized regions. But the manner in which subcontracting was organized also changed considerably over time. During the 19th century, producers in the decentralized industrial districts subcontracted extensively because they competed in the market primarily as pure customizers. Since they got paid for providing a solution to a customer need, the actual production of the product (or solution) was viewed expediently, not proprietarily, and subcontracting, especially for a small producer, was often the only way it could actually deliver the solution it offered its customers. Here the decentralization of production was nearly absolute.

With the creation, at the beginning of the century, of the arrangements of coordinated specialization in these districts and then the coming of mass production, this extensive decentralization in production was curtailed. Coordinated specialization made firms concentrate on the production of a particular kind of product, albeit often still one that was essentially a customized solution, as with a single-purpose machine tool. Firms voluntarily narrowed down the kinds of solutions that they were able to offer customers, and then sought to compensate for the value lost by capturing more of the production of their own machines. At the same time, they rationalized production inside the firm, allowing specific kinds of skills to become fixed into specific specialties with specific hierarchies of learning and status associated with them. Masters, for example, went from being generalists in broad areas of craft production (e.g., machine making or ironworking) to specialists in particular kinds of vocational expertise, such as lathe operation, tool making, or electrical work. This tendency to vertically integrate and internally rationalize was exacerbated in the postwar period when markets became concentrated and user product cycles were more slowly changing: Relative stability encouraged the proliferation of specialized jurisdictions and of internal value creation.[149]

During the 1980s (and indeed, in the 1990s as well), with progressively rapid product and technological change and great general uncertainty in the market, the tendency within individual small- and medium-sized firms was to attempt to move toward forms of organization that resembled the older, more extreme and open forms of decentralized production that had earlier existed within the industrial districts. This was true for three interrelated reasons.

First, firms attempted to broaden and enhance their access to technological information and manufacturing expertise. Because product and technological changes dramatically expanded the range of possible development trajectories that were possible even within agreed-upon specialty segments, producers increasingly found that their need to offer solutions to customer desires outstripped their in-house technological and production capabilities. In order to compete fully and effectively, producers in a wide variety of specialized industries were forced to break from the older vertical-integration practices and subcontract out significant aspects of production and development expertise, simply to be able to deliver a product that their customers wanted. A machine tool company, for example, may have known that it needed a particular kind of software, but not have known how to develop it itself and thus turned to a software house for the requisite expertise. Or a producer of specialized audio equipment may have found that it needed a particular type and shape of plastic that an injection molding establishment was especially expert at making. Rather than spend the time and money to develop expertise in that area itself, the firm simply engaged the injection molding establishment with its production needs. In order to gain access to a larger pool of know-how and expertise, firms had to redefine their boundaries, become more open, and make production less vertically integrated.

The second reason firms resorted to more external collaboration and subcontracting had to do with the desire to diffuse risk. Since the technological and market environments were so turbulent and uncertain, one did not want to commit one's own resources to in-house development of all the possible technological subspecialties that could be important to one's product market. A wrong choice would involve a lot of expensive idle production capacity. Better to defray such costs and diffuse risks by subcontracting.

The third reason for expanding the character of decentralization had to do with a desire to lower production costs and decrease product-development cycles. Here, moves toward both collaborative subcontracting and internal reorganization came (and continue to come) into play. Collaborative subcontracting enabled firms to rely on the expertise of outsiders, which saved on development costs and time. Internal reorganization increasingly came into play as the pace of technological change made it necessary to develop a new product and design it for production simultaneously. Firms attempted to bring development and production personnel together and carry on their activities in a more collaborative, integrated, and simultaneous way. Success at this would enable a company to save time as well as the added cost of maintaining separate departments within the firm. For similar reasons, internal hierarchies and jurisdictional boundaries within production itself also came under pressure. Consistently throughout the 1980s, firms attempted to broaden craft definitions to create greater latitude for individual skilled workers in the production process and thereby improve the flexibility of the in-house production activities that the firm continued to maintain. As we shall see in the final section of this chapter, however, firms in the decentralized industrial order were far more successful in extending subcontracting and external collaborative ties than they were at redefining internal jurisdictions.

During the 1980s, however, the real key to the success of small- and medium-sized producers was undeniably their ability to shift to more intensive and collaborative subcontracting. Regardless of why it was initiated, the clear benefit of subcontracting was that it dispersed the costs of innovation away from individual producers and onto the collectivity of regional producers and the supporting institutions. Typically, producers cultivated a broad circle of suppliers with which they then worked very intimately, providing manufacturing know-how and collaborating on production engineering of single parts and subassemblies. Many firms even helped their suppliers purchase the equipment they needed to produce a given part, usually by guaranteeing a certain amount of orders so that the supplier firm could get the capital it needed from its local bank. In a way that recalled the practices of their 19th century predecessors, producers began to weaken the boundaries of the firm, spread production more extensively across producers, and bind their existence to the creativity implicit in decentralized networks of suppliers.

At the same time, as intimate as many of these relations became, firms generally refrained from becoming too dependent upon any one supplier. Most cultivated at least two sources for a part and confined their purchases from single suppliers to 10–30% of that supplier's output. Suppliers were thus forced to develop similar relationships with a variety of manufacturers in the regional economy. This arrangement allowed original equipment manufacturer (OEM) firms to reduce orders to any single subcontractor when necessary without endangering the supplier's existence. At the same time, the OEM firm continuously learned from what their suppliers were doing for other customers.[150]

Suppliers themselves placed these kinds of limits on their attachment to particular customers and particular industries. If they were simply job shops or even producers of subassemblies, such as Kern-Liebers of Schramberg/Sulgen in the Black Forest, which served the electronics, automobile, and machinery industries, or Rafi of Ravensburg in Württemberg, which served office equipment, electro-mechanical, machinery, optical equipment, and defence contractors, all firms had an interest in spreading their contacts to a wide variety of firms to ensure continuous work and broad exposure to new techniques.[151]

Significantly, these changes did not result either in the reproduction of old-style dualist relations between customers and suppliers as had existed in the mass-production system, or in more rigidly vertical forms of subcontracting relations typical of Japanese manufacturing arrangements.[152] Instead, the emphasis here became more and more on horizontal specialties and plural ties across them. The key to this new structure of relations lay in the fact that expertise itself was fragmented and decentered: All producers in the production chain increasingly depended upon one another to bring a product to market and none could live exclusively from the expertise or business of anyone else. This is clear if one looks at the subcontracting practices of specialized subcontractors such as Rafi and Kern-Liebers. Both firms cultivated extensive networks of suppliers to whom they transferred know-how and with whom they collaborated on special orders, self consciously pursuing a strategy with their own contractors that their customers were following with them.

Horizontal/plural networks of this kind became so dense in some regions that the dynamic of diversification/devolution was self-reinforcing. For example, the machine tool producer Hermann Kolb in Cologne said that it would actually have preferred to have had fewer suppliers in the mid 1980s, but they could not get any of their suppliers to give more than 10% of their production. The company said that none of the supplier companies it dealt with had more than 200 employees, and many of these were simply job shops. Because the firm could not produce its flexible manufacturing systems without its suppliers, it began to rely on them for important know-how and encouraged them to broaden their contacts to ensure that they would be able to continue to assimilate relevant technologies in the market.[153]

Ultimately, such developments show that in regions such as Baden-Württemberg, the Cologne–Bonn area or the Rhein–Main region, increasing numbers of firms were becoming specialists in particular product areas, rather than in the specific products themselves. Their special know-how consisted in their ability to combine different kinds of technologies and specialties into products that the customer wanted. At the limit, it became impossible to fix the identity of firms as either "subcontractors" or "OEMs" because many firms carried both identities. In the same vein, none of these developments implied in the least that specialist producers could be broken down into "producers" and "assemblers." On the contrary, just as in the 19th century industrial districts, specialist customizers made as well as assembled finished products. But the new development was that as often as not firms regarded production not simply as the bread and butter of being a manufacturer, but as a form of R&D which both enabled them to learn about new technologies and production techniques that were relevant for its business and to better monitor and learn from suppliers.

Machine tool companies like the Index-Werke, for example, could produce better automated manufacturing equipment if they experimented with different kinds of automated equipment in their own production. A producer like Kern-Liebers experimented with injection molding because some of its business involved matching its metal parts to plastic ones, as in the sideburn trimmer on an electric razor. Kern-Liebers still subcontracted out most of its injection molding, but because the character of plastic markets was changing so rapidly it needed first-hand knowledge of the market. Manufacturing, in effect, helped the firm know what it might produce next and where it could possibly look next for collaborators.[154]

The governance of decentralized production

As in the past, the successful decentralized producers in the 1980s depended upon an extensive framework of superordinate institutions for the many aspects of the administration of production. But to say this does not mean that the appropriate resources needed during the 1980s were automatically channeled to producers. Actors within the framework institutions of governance in the industrial order had to adapt the services they provided or invent new services in order to address the current needs of the producers they served. Nevertheless, for all of the newness of the services and programs, it was still the case that, as in the past, financial support, technological information, and expert consulting were provided to decentralized production in a decentralized way. This exoskeleton of support was extremely valuable to producers in the turbulent environment because it meant that crucial dimensions of production, development, and marketing were socialized and thereby made available to firms at much lower cost than they would have been if individual producers had been required to provide them themselves.

Regional banks were quick to respond to the adjustment pressures among their small- and medium-sized clients with capital and consulting advice on business and market strategy. So strong was the initial demand for capital in the industrial *Mittelstand* that by 1982, the savings and cooperative banks in Germany, traditionally focused on small- and medium-sized producers, provided one-half (50.7%) of all loans to industry (up from 37.4% in 1972).[155] Moreover, in addition to lending, savings and cooperative banks expanded the services that they provided to individual customers. Instead of simply reviewing the balance sheets of firms, banks began to routinely become more involved in their client's business, offering advice on business strategy and technology. They described the shift in their business as a change in identity from "advisors" (*Firmenkundenberater*) to "caretakers" (*Firmenkundenbetreuer*).[156] These banks also played a crucial role in facilitating cooperation among small firms by acting as a knowledgeable third party who could provide potential cooperators with reassurance concerning their mutual reliability.[157]

Finally, because the demand for capital within the small- and medium-sized firm sector pushed the threshold of reasonable indebtedness, regional banks, in conjunction with regional governments, established so-called "capital participation corporations" (*Kapital-* or *Unternehmensbeteiligungsgesellschaften*, KBGs) which invested funds in firms that serve as equity. KBGs, which still exist, in effect own a portion of the firm for a number of years and receive a profit-dependent dividend, but, unlike venture capital funds, do not assume any managerial role in the operation of the firm. By 1988 in North Rhine Westphalia, savings banks established 26 such KBGs, making for a combined total investment of 264 million DM and involving 224 firms. Across the Federal Republic by the end of 1989, nearly 60 of these organizations invested a total of 2.7 billion DM in nearly 2000 firms.[158]

Trade associations were also extremely active in helping their members adjust, especially to the new technological challenges presented by the changes on the world market. For example, the machinery producers central trade association, the VDMA, and the electro-technical producers association, the ZVEI, both of which represented legions of small- and medium-sized firms, lobbied intensively and successfully for the creation of a special program to offer indirect financial support to small- and medium-sized firms in the development of microelectronic applications to their products.[159] The modest program, sponsored by the Federal Ministry for Research and Technology from 1982 to 1985, made 450 million DM available over a three year period to producers in all manufacturing industries.[160] The business associations, along with the regional chambers of industry and commerce, also increased their capacity to facilitate linkages between firms in their industry or area and providers of technologies and services that they needed. IHKs in many areas, for example, developed so-called "technology exchanges" in which potential suppliers could be matched with potential clients, and vice versa. Both types of trade association also systematically disseminated knowledge to their member firms of different federal and regional programs available to them.[161]

188 *Industrial constructions*

There was also a dramatic expansion of services provided to industrial firms by both private and public organizations.[162] In Baden-Württemberg, where the regional economy is completely dominated by the decentralized industrial order, the number of private firms engaged in "technical consulting and planning" between 1976 and 1984 rose 40% from 8,662 to 12,130 and their total taxable turnover more than doubled.[163] According to Franz-Josef Bade and Klaus Kunzmann, industrial service employment (those working in R&D and strategic planning), for example, increased by over 50% in the greater Stuttgart region and in the Aachen region, 40% in the Rhein–Main and Karlsruhe regions, and nearly 30% in the region around Bonn and Cologne between 1976 and 1986.[164]

In some regions, particularly in Baden-Württemberg, the expansion of services in the private sector was paralleled by the expansion of services to industry by the public sector.[165] Consulting revenue from the Steinbeis Foundation, an agency created to provide services to small- and medium-sized companies and facilitate consulting relationships between professors in *Fachhochschulen* and small industry, increased from 4.9 million DM in 1983 to 22.2 million DM in 1986.[166] In addition to consulting, the Steinbeis Foundation was involved in a broad array of efforts to institutionalize coordination among small- and medium-sized producers in Baden-Württemberg.[167] In North Rhine Westphalia (NRW), a similar organization was created in 1984 known as ZENIT. This organization provided information to small- and medium-sized firms in NRW concerning technology, venture capital, and potential partners for cooperation. The institution also conducted some technical research, but its role, like that of the Steinbeis Foundation in Baden-Württemberg, was more that of a disseminator of information and a facilitator of contacts. ZENIT was created with the strong backing of the regional VDMA office and ZVEI offices in NRW and came into being after strong lobbying on the part of many small- and medium-sized firms there.[168]

Regional governments with significant areas of decentralized industry also pursued aggressive technology policies aimed at small- and medium-sized producers. Total expenditures for support of small- and medium-sized firms by the government in Baden-Württemberg, including education, technology promotion, applied R&D support, subsidies to reduce interest rates on loans from the regional savings banks, programs fostering interfirm cooperation, and other special programs, increased from 147.4 million DM in 1976 to 298.9 million DM in 1985. Even in NRW, where politics at the *Land* level was traditionally dominated by the autarkic regions of coal, steel, machinery and automobile producers, by the middle of the 1980s the regional government attempted to redirect technology spending toward small- and medium-sized producers. The TPZ program, begun in 1985, provided subsidies for small- and medium-sized producers working in the areas of environmental technology, energy, information technology, biotechnology, materials, and the "humanization" of technology.[169] ZIN, created in 1989, made funds available for private sector cooperation initiatives. One good example was a new regional consulting office in the Berg Land which engaged area firms on matters pertaining to the application of new technologies.[170] In all of these cases in NRW, as in Baden-Württemberg, the emphasis was on the creation of policies that provided resources to and facilitated technological and information flow among small- and medium-sized producers in decentralized production arrangements.[171]

Big firms in the decentralized regions

The tremendous success of small- and medium-sized producers in the decentralized industrial order prompted many, especially in Baden-Württemberg, to celebrate the flexibility and technology driven prosperity of the 1980s as the gratifying triumph of traditional petite bourgeois hard work and diligence.[172] Some even argued that the future belonged to small- and medium-sized firms, and even more were accused of making that claim simply by pointing to the success of smaller producers.[173] But such claims about small- and medium-sized firms were just as exaggerated in the 1980s as were those in the 1960s mentioned above, which viewed them as ultimately marginal players in an industrial economy. The initially successful adjustment in decentralized regions was fostered and enjoyed by the large firms that were located there nearly as much as by the small. But the success of large firms was not based on the traditional technological and organizational practices of old-style mass production that had driven their initial growth in the middle part of the 20th century. Rather, it was due to their capacity to depart from those principles.

Indeed, as with the smaller specialized firms, the competitive environment for large firms was also tremendously altered over the course of the 1980s by new developments in technology, increased international competition, shrinking product cycles, and rising development costs. Large corporations, just as small firms, were driven to change their product palettes more frequently and apply new technologies to their products or in production about which they had little prior knowledge or experience. Invariably, they were compelled to look to outside specialists to help them keep abreast of technology and stay competitive in their markets. Not surprisingly then, throughout the 1980s levels of vertical integration within large firms fell significantly and the number of collaborative subcontracting arrangements increased rapidly.[174]

Though, as we will see in the final section of this chapter, this trend was far from uniform and there was great internal resistance to any decentralization that would entail dramatic reorganization of relations within the hierarchical firm, these efforts created a dynamic within the decentralized regions that departed quite significantly from the one that had existed during the first 30 years of the postwar period. Through their efforts to reduce vertical integration, large firms not only began to interpenetrate with the smaller producers through the establishment of collaborative and subcontracting relationships, they also attempted to adopt principles of organization and practices typical of the small- and medium-sized firm system.[175] Moreover, in contrast to the period of their emergence, when large firms broke out of the decentralized framework of industrial order, in the 1980s many firms in a broad array of industries tried to take advantage of the resources provided by the decentralized form of industrial order that surrounded them. In so doing, they also contributed their own resources to the decentralized pool of knowledge, skill, expertise, and capital that underlay the success of the decentralized industrial order as a whole.

A very good example of this general trend during the 1980s was the giant automobile parts and electronics producer Robert Bosch. This firm is headquartered in Stuttgart and has many additional production facilities located throughout Baden-Württemberg. The firm began to remove itself from the structures of decentralized industrial order even earlier than its neighbor Daimler-Benz. Before World War I, it was mass-producing thousands of spark plugs a day with over 2000 workers in its factory.[176] The firm profited handsomely from the European automobile boom in the years following World War II. But by the early 1970s Bosch began to feel the pressures of mounting European and international competition in their traditional auto parts markets. Moreover, toward the middle of the decade, demands were increasingly made on the firm to integrate microprocessor technologies with its traditional micromechanical products. As the decade wore on, competition became increasingly intense and technology changed more and more rapidly.

Bosch responded to the changes in its markets by engaging in extensive collaborative subcontracting.[177] The firm identified promising subcontractors, then helped them by providing extensive consultation that ranged from general advice regarding new technologies of long-term interest to the supplier to collaboration in the production engineering of single parts.

Bosch's subcontracting practices began to become much like those of other much smaller producers in Baden-Württemberg. The company encouraged long-term relations with particular subcontractors, and, despite its efforts to the contrary, frequently became dependent upon the accumulated expertise that the subcontractor had. At the same time, the company insisted that its subcontractors do no more than 20% of their business with Bosch. This allowed Bosch to reduce orders to its subcontractors without endangering their existence while continuously learning from what its suppliers were doing for their other customers. The gain for Robert Bosch was clear. The bed of specialist subcontractors in Baden-Württemberg became like an external portfolio of technological possibilities for the firm. In a market that was changing so rapidly that it was impossible to tell in the present what would be demanded in the future, this portfolio proved to be extremely valuable. This was not only true of Bosch. During the 1980s, most of the very large producers in Baden-Württemberg, in a broad array of sectors, began to adopt similar subcontracting practices.[178]

Vertical disintegration as an effort to enhance flexibility was paralleled, at least in part, by an internal redefinition of corporate hierarchies, leading to the creation of internal structures inside corporations that mimicked those that existed between firms in the decentralized industrial order. Most successful organization reform came at the level of relations between the corporate central office and its operating units. Reformers at firms such as Bosch, SEL, IBM, and elsewhere succeeded in, haltingly and not without internal opposition, getting the corporation to decouple its vertical operations and provide the new operating units or "profit centers" with greater decision-making autonomy, even in some cases spinning them off into independent (wholly owned) companies. Such organizational change was meant to enhance the autonomy of actors who were previously at a lower level of bureaucracy. At the same time, importantly, it also introduced risk through unmediated exposure to the competitive market that had not previously been associated with the position.[179]

Reformers within the mother organizations also employed the signifiers of roles and organizations from the alternative decentralized order to describe the way in which their own position within their production system was changing. For example, the above-mentioned movements toward organizational decoupling were invariably couched in a discourse that encouraged actors in the new units to experiment with collaboration, engage in outside contacts, and "to become like small companies in the *Mittelstand*." Here the traditional authority of the mother organization, ironically, was deployed to encourage untraditional autonomous behavior in "subordinate" units through the evocation of institutional frames of understanding from the alternative decentralized industrial order. Representatives of the central purchasing department at Robert Bosch, to take another example, readily assented in an interview to the analogy that their strategy of cooperating with their suppliers and providing them with know-how resembled along some dimensions the kind of relationship that such smaller firms already had with local *Fachhochschulen*. They understood the embedded values of openness and collaboration in the other system and forthrightly accepted the implication that their own behavior embodied them as well.[180]

At the regional level, the disintegration of the large firm involved attempts by its various component parts to integrate their operations into the surrounding framework of decentralized industrial order. Representatives from operating units engaged with local municipal authorities, *Fachhochschulen*, and bankers on the general health and preparedness of the infrastructure for the demands of the current market environment. At the same time, representatives of the companies' central, supraoperating unit organization participated at a regional level with regional governmental officials, trade associations, bankers, and other players about the same problems. Operating units also engaged in cooperative relations with regional players, such as formal and informal exchanges of personnel, joint ventures, and collaborative precompetitive research. Semlinger documents a case where a large local auto producer helped Baden-Württemberg producers of turned metal parts, together with representatives of the Steinbeis Foundation, to create a Center for Quality Production, in which the large and small producers cooperated on the establishment of quality standards. The result was significant increases in the amount of business that the auto producer did with the smaller subcontractors.[181]

As large firms entered into exchanges of this and many other kinds with actors within the decentralized industrial order during the 1980s, the benefits for the latter were very great. The massive internal resources and stores of know-how of the large firm, such as research and development laboratories, easy access to high-level university research teams and resources, and contact with technolog-

192 *Industrial constructions*

ical specialists worldwide, entered the decentralized system of exchange as one more redundant input of know-how and institutional capacity in the system of decentralized production.

Coexistence recomposed

These changes in the strategies of large firms and in their relationship to the decentralized industrial order during the 1980s fundamentally altered the balance of power between large firms and regional economies, at least in the clear case of Baden-Württemberg. In the classic age of dependent and vulnerable subcontractors and dominant mass-producing large firms, the economic and industrial health of a region was very dependent upon the continuing willingness of large firms to invest there. If a large firm, such as Bosch or Daimler-Benz, were to decide to shift all of its production of a given product out of the region, the dependent suppliers would have no alternative strategy for production. Lacking in know-how and vulnerable to begin with, smaller supplier firms were faced with the choice of bankruptcy or following the large producer out of the region. Regional governments, unwilling to suffer the consequences of either option, as a result typically went to great lengths to provide large firms with incentives to keep production in the locality.[182]

In the altered environment that emerged in the 1980s, both the capacity of large firms to make credible their threat to leave, and the capacity of small- and medium-sized producers to survive without them changed. And, as a result, the room for autonomous maneuvering for the regional government increased. Large firms began to have trouble making credible threats to shift production entirely out of a region such as Baden-Württemberg because they were uncertain enough about the future evolution of technology and markets that they were unwilling to completely abandon the resources of know-how which the smaller specialist firms made available. The capacity of large producers to remain competitive in a technological environment that they could not control depended on their capacity to cultivate and maintain access to a decentralized network of technological information. This did not preclude efforts on the part of large firms to globalize. Just as they had an interest in cultivating access to information locally, so did they in cultivating access to information in markets in other regions. Their interest, in an environment in which they no longer possessed control over the evolution of technology, was in the acquisition and transfer of information, regardless of its location. Interest elsewhere did not presuppose neglect at home.[183]

For the same reasons, small specialist firms, embedded in dense decentralized networks, did not feel threatened by efforts on the part of large firms to establish global operations. They not only knew that the local large producer relied on them for technological expertise, they also benefitted from investment in the region on the part of foreign multinationals seeking to gain access to the resources located within the region. It has been for this reason not at all surprising, for example, that all opinion polls of small- and medium-sized producers in

Baden-Württemberg, conducted by trade associations, Chambers of Commerce, and by the regional government, have shown universal enthusiasm at every step along the way toward the completion of a single unified market within the European Community.

For its part, the regional government in Baden-Württemberg learned quickly how to take advantage of this situation, both for the benefit of producers in the region and to strengthen its own position. It undertook trade expeditions throughout the world, particularly to market areas where Baden-Württemberg producers were weakly represented, such as the Pacific Rim and Eastern Europe. It subsidized trade shows in these markets, assisted in the arrangement of joint ventures, and instituted formal programs of technology transfer. At the same time, at home in Baden-Württemberg, the regional government reserved large tracts of scarce development space, zoned for industrial use, in the densely populated region exclusively for Far Eastern investors. The local government believed that the more globalization it could encourage on the part of its own producers and the more investment from foreign multinationals it could attract to the region, the greater its own latitude to conduct industrial and technology policies for the benefit of local producers would be.

A surprise crisis: Unexpected rigidity and the challenge of an alternative form of flexible organization in the 1990s

Renewed competitiveness of small- and medium-sized producers, timely decentralization on the part of large producers, and a robust infrastructure for supporting decentralized flexible production all contributed to a very heady atmosphere within the regions traditionally dominated by the decentralized industrial order during the latter half of the 1980s. Baden-Württemberg, in particular, was heralded within Germany as a *Musterländle* (a model or showpiece area) and was widely admired throughout Europe and North America for its dynamic, high-quality producers and its effective industrial policy.[184] Moreover, at a time when it seemed that things could not get much better, the Berlin Wall fell and Germany was unified, giving a new boost to the business cycle and longer life to the already very extended boom. As the 1990s began, it truly appeared that decentralized production in Germany, as practiced increasingly by both large and small producers in the decentralized regions, had hit upon the secret for enduring competitive success in a turbulent, rapidly changing international market environment.[185]

This impression did not last long. By 1992 the German economy had fallen into the deepest recession of the entire postwar period, and the decentralized regions were by no means spared.[186] Indeed, in 1991 GDP growth rate in Baden-Württemberg (2.8%) fell beneath the Federal average of 3.4% for the first time since 1978, placing it behind all other West German provinces except the Rheinland Pfalz. Investment rates, especially in investment-goods branches, fell off dramatically while job growth in those sectors fell off alarmingly: the total number of jobs in the Baden-Württemberg investment-goods industry fell by

194 Industrial constructions

11.4% between 1991 and 1993. Large and small firms in a variety of sectors, especially the machinery and auto and electronics related sectors, announced sometimes dauntingly large losses and layoffs: Daimler-Benz, for example, announced in 1992 that it planned to lay off 29,000 workers and engage in massive internal restructuring, while Berthold Leibinger, a prominent machine tool industry executive, was so alarmed by the dramatic downturn in orders for German machine tools in 1993 that he predicted that nearly half of the industry's jobs would have to be cut by mid-decade.[187] Bankruptcies (both personal and business) in general increased dramatically in the Federal Republic during this period. From a low of 12,437 in 1990 totalling 6.82 billion DM, the number of bankruptcies increased by 1993 to 19,264, totalling some 29.03 billion DM.[188]

Most interesting about this recession is that virtually no one in the decentralized regions believed that it was simply a cyclical downturn. On the contrary, most voices in the industrial order clearly understood the downturn as a structural crisis in which core organizational features of German firms and in the organization of work and production played a central causal role. For example, both an elite, heavily business-dominated *Zukunftskommission*,[189] which was appointed by the Government of Baden-Württemberg to study the economic problems of the region, and a study by the IMU Institute commissioned by IG Metall in Stuttgart concluded that the crisis in the region was due to the incapacity of German producers to keep pace with increasing international competition. Relative to their main competitors in Japan, the rest of the Pacific Rim, and North America, German producers, large and small, were found to bring new products to market more slowly than their foreign rivals; to have more difficulty integrating new technologies into their products in rapid succession; had a tendency to "overengineer" their products; and, finally, were unable to lower their production costs into competitive ranges. Both studies found that producers had become overly rigid and bureaucratic.[190]

Competing with new forms of flexibility: The cases of automobiles and machine tools

The experiences of the machine tool industry and the automobile industry provide paradigmatic examples of what seems to have happened to the decentralized German firms in the 1990s. In both cases, the traditional strategy for success had been, as noted above, to aim for the high-quality segments of markets for particular technologies or products and attempt to narrow (or, as in the case of Mercedes Benz, manage) the price gap between their higher-quality goods and standardized variants. All of the core features of the decentralized industrial order formed the basis for this strategy: high levels of skilled labor in production, craft organization of work, extensive and collaborative subcontracting, and the socialization of cost and risk across a supportive exoskeleton of institutions. The Germans relied on quality and customer satisfaction to compensate for what were traditionally considered to be, given the way they were produced, the *invariably* higher costs of their products.

The development of the decentralized industrial order since 1945 195

The achilles heel of this strategy, of course, was that it depended on the existence of a space in markets for higher-quality and/or customized products that were more expensive than standard variants. This space seems to have disappeared in the 1990s, not because there are no longer consumers interested in high quality and customization, but because a whole host of producers in these industries, particularly in Japan and the United States (though not only there), adopted production methods that enabled them to supply this demand at a much lower price than the Germans can. Moreover, these competitors can do this while driving the pace of innovation to levels even the decentralized Germans are not accustomed to.[191]

The key advantage that successful firms in Japan, the United States and elsewhere have over the Germans is that they have reorganized production in ways that not only break down boundaries *between* firms, as the decentralized Germans have done, but that break down internal divisions *within* their production units as well. Extremely flexible organizational forms have been diffusing, in different ways in different countries, that bring production, purchasing, sales, and development departments together, often along with suppliers, to cooperate in the "simultaneous engineering" of products. These changes have been accompanied by and are integrated with the broad diffusion of group- or teamwork in direct production, modularization of production, the proliferation of U-shaped production lines, and the institution of zero-defect and continuous-improvement policies managed by teams themselves. All of this is organized around and enforced by the maintenance of extremely low inventories throughout the production process.[192]

Such systems attempt to orient the entire process chain in production, from development and design to the assembly of the final product, around the needs and desires of the customer. The key to the system's tremendous flexibility is the fact that it effectively reunites the conceptual development of product and production design with their actual manufacture within production units by removing all fixed roles in the workplace. Product teams design and produce a good and specific tasks are defined and allocated through the process of development and production itself. The key to the system's remarkable innovativeness rests in the close and continuous self-monitoring practices that the new product teams engage in under conditions of extremely low inventory: Because buffers are extremely small, each position in the production process has an incentive to get information about and communicate with the entire set of positions in the process to optimize flow and avoid bottlenecks, thus engendering a continuous discussion in production about its organization and the nature of its product. At its limit, the logic of this alternative system causes the old style "firm" to disintegrate entirely into an infinite recombinable set of roles and relations that the participants themselves reflect upon and structure.[193]

Experience in direct competition has proven the superiority of these alternative methods over the traditional forms of flexible high-quality production that have existed in the decentralized regions of Germany. The significance of the growth of Toyota's luxury Lexus models and Nissan's Infiniti, for example,

Table 5 *Performance and costs of German machine tool enterprises*

Indicator*	Unit	1980	1985	1989	% share of sales 1980	1989
Sales	Million DM	118	134	183	100.0	100.0
Material consumption	Million DM	59	73	102	50.0	55.9
Value added	Million DM	59	61	81	50.0	44.1
Depreciation	Million DM	4	4	7	3.1	3.7
Staff expenditure	Million DM	48	53	67	40.8	36.7
Other costs	Million DM	3	3	4	2.8	2.5
Profit (before taxes)	Million DM	4	1	2	3.3	1.3
Total employees		1081	971	1053		
Data per employee:						
Sales	Thousand DM	109	138	174		
Staff expenditure	Thousand DM	45	55	64		
Value added	Thousand DM	55	63	77		

*Average values for firms with more than 500 employees.
Source: IFO Institut, Statistisches Bundesamt. Table taken from Frank C. Engelman, Christian Heyd, Daniel Köstler, and Peter Paustian, "The German Machine Tool Industry," p. 17.

has been widely appreciated as a threat to German luxury automobile producers, especially Daimler-Benz's Mercedes Benz marques. Without (at least the perception of) any drop in quality, Nissan and especially Toyota, using the alternative production methods, managed to produce luxury cars much more cheaply than Mercedes Benz and quickly garnered a very large section of the American luxury automobile market during the latter half of the 1980s. By the early 1990s, the Japanese were turning toward European markets.

If there was any doubt at Daimler-Benz that the production methods deployed by the Japanese were superior to those in place within its own factories, these doubts were dispelled when it was revealed that their main assembly plant in Sindelfingen was the notorious "anonymous high quality but low productivity European plant" in the MIT Automobile Project's famous study of the world automobile industry, *The Machine that Changed the World*.[194] According to the MIT Report, this plant was "expending more effort to fix problems it had just created than the Japanese plant required to make a perfectly new car the first time."[195] Daimler-Benz itself estimated in 1993 that its production costs were roughly 35% higher than its main competitors in Japan. In that same year, the company announced a record 1.8 billion DM net loss.[196]

The competitive disadvantages of the decentralized German system relative to the more flexible and lower-cost one increasingly being adopted by their major competitors is if anything even more clear in the case of the machine tool industry. Here too, the Germans performed badly relative to the Japanese, and as of the early 1990s, to rejuvenated U.S. producers.[197] As in the automobile case,

Table 6 *Performance and costs of Japanese machine tool enterprises**

Indicator†	Unit	1980	1985	1989	% share of sales 1980	1989
Sales	Million DM	298	458	514	100.0	100.0
Material consumption	Million DM	186	285	323	62.4	62.7
Value added	Million DM	112	173	192	37.6	37.3
Depreciation	Million DM	7	13	16	2.3	3.2
Staff expenditure	Million DM	45	69	77	15.2	165.0
Other costs	Million DM	23	38	34	7.7	6.5
Profit (before taxes)	Million DM	37	53	64	12.4	12.5
Employees	Number	945	1171	1152		
Data per employee:						
Sales	Thousand DM	315.4	390.7	446.6		
Staff expenditure	Thousand DM	48.0	59.0	67.0		
Value added	Thousand DM	118.6	147.3	166.4		

*Converted using 1989 exchange rate.
†Average values for firms with more than 500 employees.
Source: IFO Institut, Japan Development Bank, Ministry of International Trade and Industry (MITI). Table taken from Frank C. Engelman, Christian Heyd, Daniel Köstler, and Peter Paustian, "The German Machine Tool Industry," p. 17

high German production costs and the high quality, greater flexibility, and relentless innovation of competitors have been to blame. Producers of high-quality standardized, computer-guided tools, such as Traub and Index, have been radically outproduced by Asian, especially Japanese, producers. The Japanese have been able to improve their machines to be able to perform the same kinds of procedures the latter two companies' machines can and the Japanese can do this, moreover, at a much better price, and with better service and delivery conditions.[198] At the high end of lower-volume specialty machines, German producers are being squeezed on the one hand by the ever-improving quality and flexibility of Japanese standard machines, which can be used in increasingly broad manufacturing realms, formerly only accessible to specialized machinery. On the other hand, competition in those remaining markets has been intensifying with the resurgence of American producers.[199]

The inefficiency of German production relative to the Japanese can readily be seen in the fact that despite a 74% increase in production between 1983 and 1990, rates of profitability and productivity in the German industry were well below those in the Japanese industry, which grew at an even more spectacular rate (see Tables 5 and 6).

The incursion of Japanese and American producers into markets the Germans once dominated is indicated by the movement of world production and trade figures in the 1990s (see Table 7). Since 1990, both Japanese and German production levels have fallen relative to the United States, Italy, and China, but

Table 7 *World shares of machine tool production 1990–1993 (%)*

Country	1990	1991	1992	1993
Japan	23.3	32.9	25.1	25.3
Germany	18.9	25.0	22.7	18.2
U.S.A.	6.7	9.3	9.2	11.6
Italy	8.5	9.8	8.8	8.4
China	—	—	5.0	6.2
Switzerland	6.8	5.7	4.9	4.8
Taiwan	—	2.7	2.8	3.8
U.K.	3.7	3.6	3.0	3.4
South Korea	—	2.1	1.8	2.2
France	—	2.9	2.9	2.2
Others	—	6.0	13.8	13.9

Source: *American Machinist* and MTTA. Table taken from Philip Cooke, *The Baden-Württemburg Machine Tool Industry*, p. 8.

the German descent has been much more precipitous than the Japanese. More ominously for the Germans, between 1992 and 1993, Germany's total share of world machine tool exports declined by 17%, while the share of the Japanese increased by 25% (despite nearly constant appreciation of the Yen) and that of American industry increased by 20%. The attractiveness of German products in export markets is simply falling off. By 1994, Japanese producers of CNC lathes accounted for 25% of the *German* market for such machines.[200]

Internal reorganization: The end of the decentralized industrial order?

The decisive difference between the highly flexible system of production increasingly being deployed by successful producers throughout Japan, the United States, and elsewhere (each, naturally, to different degrees and in its own way) and the system of flexible production as practiced within the decentralized industrial order in Germany is the far more open and flexible organizational practices inside production units in the former systems. This is extremely paradoxical, because it was thought during the 1980s that, in addition to the capacity to utilize specialized subcontractors, the flexibility of small- and medium-sized German firms (as well as, to a considerable extent even that of large-volume producers) rested on the tremendous resourcefulness and autonomy of broadly skilled workers in production and the close, trusting relations between those skilled shopfloor workers and higher levels of management within the firm. The competitors "lean," "open," or "simple" forms of flexible organization, however, rely on far greater worker autonomy and cross-functional and cross-departmental cooperation within the firm than is currently possible within the traditional internal organization of German craft producers.[201]

The sticking point within German firms are roles, jurisdictions, and hier-

Table 8 *Export share of world machine tools, 1992–1993 (%)*

Country	1992	1993
Japan	21.0	26.5
Germany	27.8	22.9
Italy	8.1	9.6
Switzerland	8.6	8.2
U.S.A.	5.9	7.0
Taiwan	3.8	4.7
U.K.	3.5	3.4
France	3.1	2.1
Belgium	—	2.1
Others	18.1	13.7

Source: *American Machinist*. Table taken from Philip Cooke, *The Baden-Württemburg Machine Tool Industry*, p. 8.

archies that date back to an earlier period of recomposition in the industrial order. We saw above that through the construction and elaboration of an industrial structure of coordinated specialization in the first part of this century, decentralized producers in Germany imposed a degree of stability upon themselves as producers that allowed them to rationalize the organization of work within their factories.[202] Out of this rationalization process emerged two things that have become so pervasive in the organization of industrial order that they are taken for granted as quasi-natural features of the organization of industrial work there and now stand, at least in their current form, as obstacles to effective adjustment to the challenge of alternative forms of flexibility.

The first is an array of specific and circumscribed skill categories in production, for which an entire infrastructure of vocational education exists and within which hierarchical career ladders have emerged. Fixed identities involving the possession of a particular skill, distinct from others, have a kind of corporate dimension in Germany today. Skilled machinists, for example, have been inculcated with an ethic of the value of their own expertise for the firm and of the significance of their skills for the prosperity of the German economy in the postwar period from the very beginning of their apprenticeships. Their identity as a skilled worker provides them with a measure of dignity, and their capacity to exercise their skill and develop it contributes to their élan. Hierarchy in this world is paternalistic: Older master toolmakers, for example, direct less experienced ones and supervise the shop-floor training of apprentices. They organize the labor market and transfer by example and through instruction the values associated with their trade.

The second taken-for-granted feature of the decentralized system that emerged out of the period of rationalization are formal departments for the various functions of management: purchasing, marketing, development, finance, and production. These departments, typically, are staffed by a mixture of managers who have been recruited out of the shop-floor milieu and those with more academic training. They, too, have particular conceptions of the role their department plays in the success of the company and, like the skilled workers, have career hierarchies and status hierarchies based on and cultivated by performance and experience within the milieu of the department itself.

For all of the many strengths and successes of these features over the course of the period since the early 20th century, these characteristics of the German system are proving to be disadvantageous under the current conditions of extremely rapid product and technological change.[203] Each time a new product or a new technology is introduced – as opposed to an old one that is customized for a customer – the various roles that each of the categories of skill will play in the production and development of the new product must be bargained out. Each department, naturally, wants to participate; each has its own ideas and solutions; each defends its turf against encroachments from the others. Electrical masters and technicians, for example, will fight with mechanical ones both on the shop floor and in the design studios over different kinds of technical or manufacturing solutions to problems that have direct consequences as to the amount and character of work they do and how the overall value their position within the firm contributes to the value of the product.

If the new product involves the increasing interpenetration of formerly distinct areas of technology and expertise, such as microelectronics and mechanical engineering, it will take some time to iron out all of the potential areas of conflict. If the market is stable for the product and doesn't change very rapidly, it might be possible to wait until all of these conflicts have been resolved before deciding upon the final design of the product. But, as is the case in the 1990s, if the market is turbulent and unstable and the life span of the current technology is clearly going to be limited, firms are forced to bring their products to the market while the internal conflicts are still being worked out. More often than not, impatient and nervous senior managers under time pressure but with no greater knowledge of the technology or the market than the contending specialists, are forced to broker a compromise between the players in a way that allows the solutions of each – to the extent that they are not contradictory – to be built into the product. It should not be surprising that such products will appear to the customer as inelegant, overpriced, and "overengineered" – they are.

This is what is going on in decentralized German factories today. Jurisdictional disputes driven by the need to accelerate new product introduction at a moment when the boundaries between traditional crafts are being technologically eroded is driving up the cost and driving down the quality of products. Such jurisdictional conflicts don't exist in the alternative flexible system because there are fewer fixed jurisdictions or occupational identities. Because they are able to combine the work of development departments and production (simultaneous engineering) and utilize modular sourcing and U-shaped, team-managed, production lines, Japanese and American producers can bring out new products relatively rapidly that are more simply and elegantly designed, of high quality, produced at very low cost, and meet customer needs.

This is extremely difficult to do in the German system as it is constituted today. To implement more boundary blending forms of cooperation in development and production, the system of discrete skill jurisdictions, career hierarchies and functional pillarization within firms has to be deconstructed and/or its elements recomposed in a new more flexible way. Given the centrality of skill as a form of social organization within the small, medium-sized, and large producers in the decentralized industrial order, however, this has not been easy to do.

Most firms have recognized the need to change, especially since the onset of crisis in the early 1990s and the emergence of the remarkable gaps between German levels of productivity and those of competitors. Yet few producers, large or small, have had success up until now in being able to overcome the opposition of entrenched groupings of skilled workers threatened with the loss of status through incorporation into teams that deny the boundaries of former jurisdictional specializations or of independent departments, reluctant to have their functional areas of power within the firm redefined and diluted through recomposition with other areas. It is difficult, after all, to tell workers and managers who, with considerable legitimacy, understand themselves as having contributed significantly to the traditional success of high-quality manufacturing in the decentralized regions that their roles have become obstacles to adjustment. Many of the flagship firms, large and small, within the regions dominated by the decentralized industrial order, such as Robert Bosch, ABB in Mannheim, the machine tool producer Müller Weingarten, and the medium-sized electronics producer Wandel & Goltermann have all in one way or another been blocked in their efforts to implement new development and production procedures that imitate the successful arrangements of their competitors. In some cases skilled labor is the main obstacle, in other cases it is departmental egoism.

Take the example of an electric turbine producing subsidiary of a large European electrical engineering multinational in northern Baden.[204] As a global concern, this European company has very systematically attempted to implement many of the characteristics of the alternative form of flexible system mentioned above. It has cultivated the development of a new kind of management career in which individual managers move throughout the organization, cross-functionally, accumulating knowledge of the company, its products, its suppliers, and its customers. Promotion within the company is increasingly becoming contingent upon having successfully participated in cooperative product development teams that involve members of different departments as well as key suppliers. To encourage this, the mother company has introduced what it calls a "Customer Focus Program" (CFP) throughout all of its subsidiaries. This program brings managers together across subsidiaries as well as across functional departments on a regular basis to foster dialog on the improvement of company products and the development of new technologies. Not simply a discussion group, however, the CFP, because it constitutes itself regularly, acts as a kind of monitoring forum for projects and subsidiaries throughout the organization. In many of the company's subsidiaries, this collaborative, team- and product-oriented organizational practice has been taken right down to the shop floor in the form of group-work, product-oriented, low-inventory production.

Not so in the German turbine works. Hierarchy flattening has occurred within the departmental structures above the shop floor, where a number of CFP groups exist. But the production process itself remains dominated by the old workshop-based skill system and the old skill hierarchies. The plants in north Baden continued to be organized around specialized machine and/or part production. Typically, any given work station operated with an inventory of up to five days. Operators working on particular machines dedicated to the production of a specific range of parts had little idea where their work object fit into the larger product the plant was constructing; one machinist had no idea where the parts he was making were going to go next in the line of production. Masters and foremen set up machines.

Why this continued existence of the old skill system beneath an increasingly open, flexible, management structure? In part the answer stems from the strategy that the local firm pursued after it original parent company plant was merged with another European multinational in 1988. Prior to the merger, the German plant was capable of making complete electrical turbine generators. After the merger the plant was broken up and parts of the production process were shifted to facilities in other locations. The German plant specialized in large-part production. Thousands of layoffs resulted from these changes in the location of production. Perhaps understandably, given the massive job losses, the works council and trade unions have been reluctant to engage in additional restructuring within the production lines that remain for fear of additional layoffs. The local labor representation was persuaded that additional losses would redound to its disadvantage and therefore defended the traditional structure of jurisdictions and the jobs that were associated with them. Labor resists the new structures and management, which is committed to the European parent, not the German subsidiary, becomes increasingly frustrated and focused on finding other, more profitable locations for production.

In other cases, such as at a large machine tool company in Württemberg, the obstacle to the adoption of the new system is management, not labor.[205] This company manufactures large-scale stamping machines for the automobile industry. It has made tremendous strides toward completely revamping its production process through the introduction of integrated product islands and group work. The traditional workshop system has been modified so that machines are now grouped around the production of particular groups of products rather than around parts for all products. All set-up, production planning, and delivery scheduling tasks, which formerly were performed by the masters and foremen of the individual machine shops or by a level of middle management directly above the shop-floor level, have been integrated into the new product islands. Members of product-development teams, moreover, now continually move between activity in the production teams and the relocated engineering rooms on the shop floor. Technicians, programmers, engineers, and skilled machine operators now

The development of the decentralized industrial order since 1945

work side by side in close cooperation and to some extent interchangeably within the teams. Groups within the islands have begun electing their own representatives to facilitate the coordination of their own internal duties as well as to maintain contact with the operations of the other groups and other product islands.

There are two factors within the firm, however, that significantly disturb the operation of these islands and constrain their ability to produce significant gains in efficiency and cost reduction. First, the changes in production have only been introduced in the areas of direct mechanical production; areas of work preparation, such as tool making, and materials purchasing have neither been organized into teams nor adapted to the needs of teams. As a result, teams have only limited control over their overhead costs. Since the idea of the introduction of teams is to devolve responsibility for holding down costs to the teams themselves, lack of control over overheads engenders frustration on the shop floor and skepticism regarding the effectiveness of the new system. Changing this arrangement, however, involves attacking the privileges of some of the most highly skilled workers in the plant (tool makers), something the management of the firm, at least until now, has been unwilling to do.

Second, changes in production have not been accompanied by corresponding efforts to deconstruct the hierarchical relations between top management departments and the newly emergent product-team structure. Management has retained the right to veto group decisions that it believes will not result in the cost savings it desires. It has also retained control over the budgets of the product islands: Company management, not the teams, make investment decisions and ultimately evaluate the performance of the teams. A spokesman of one of the product islands as well as the head of all manufacturing at the firm claimed that this limitation on local autonomy and the continued existence of hierarchy threatened to undermine the effectiveness of the product islands and teams. When members of the group believe that their success or failure is the direct result of their collective efforts, all have an incentive to make continuous improvements. Without local autonomy, however, such incentives do not exist and the commitment of team members to the success of the team is undermined.

Both examples show that the partial movement away from the principles of craft organization risks making the new organizational principles appear to the participants as a charade. Making a full commitment, however, means taking privilege and authority away from those with little desire to give them up. Clearly, there is no equilibrium with the current arrangement: Doing nothing will lead to the gradual erosion of morale and enthusiasm within the new product islands; returning to the old craft system will price the firm out of the market; moving forward will involve the spilling of blood. Someone is going to lose this battle, and the stakes in the world market at the moment are such that it may be the firm itself.

Both of the above examples show that the stakes in the current adjustment period within the decentralized industrial order are undeniably very high. Adopting the new production arrangements in the decentralized industrial order will involve not only loss of status for central actors in the old system, it will also mean loss of jobs both in production and in management areas. The new arrangements make it possible to produce better products with greater efficiency. Yet, failure to change will perpetuate a set of arrangements that make such firms incapable of competing in the international economy.

The moment at which this book is being written is a very crucial period for the decentralized industrial order. If firms, large and small, succeed in constructing (adopting and adapting) arrangements within themselves that are capable of the same kind of low-inventory, low-cost, high-quality manufacturing as their competitors, it could very well result in the complete transformation of decentralized industrial production in Germany. Already extensive external decentralization (i.e., the existence of collaborative ties beyond the boundaries of the firm) will be matched by the dissolution of the internal architecture of the firm in a way that integrates development and purchasing with the shop floor in the form of self-recombinatory teams. In such a transformed world, there would be no distinction between large firms and small firms, because firms in the traditional sense would no longer exist. Will a production island at a medium-sized firm like the machine tool company discussed above, if it gains the right to control all of its overhead costs and therefore its relations with subcontractors, be significantly different in character from a production island at large firms like Robert Bosch or Daimler-Benz or at a smaller machine tool producer with the same powers?

If, on the other hand, the entrenched interests in the old departments of management and among the various skilled groupings on the shop floor succeed in blocking movements in this direction, it is difficult to imagine, given the dramatic productivity and cost differentials currently separating German producers from their major competitors, how the decentralized industrial order can continue to reproduce itself in the form which it had adopted in the 1980s any longer. This chapter thus ends with the decentralized industrial order in a historical situation not unlike the situation it was in as the chapter opened. An unprecedented and extremely strong challenge from abroad is creating the conditions as well as the incentives for producers to break out of and recompose existing arrangements. Time will tell how plastic the current system actually is and how much of it, if any at all, will be reconstituted in the new environment.

6

Autarkic industrial order: 1945–1994

This chapter covers the same period as the previous one, only with an eye toward the experience of the autarkic industrial order. The macrohistorical context of development is thus in many ways the same: The period was marked first by the emergence and diffusion of mass-production processes throughout the industrial economy, and second by the emergence of a set of competitive conditions in the international economy that made it difficult for producers to follow strategies of old-style mass production any longer.

As with the decentralized industrial order, the reconstitution of the autarkic industrial order during the period of military occupation and the subsequent great postwar economic boom involved considerable reshuffling of relations and practices, even as the order as a whole was reconstituted. Radical breaks with the past were juxtaposed to and intermingled with remarkable continuities. The two most significant changes were the successful imposition of codetermination structures on the internal governance of autarkic firms and the diffusion of mass production as a strategy throughout most branches of German autarkic industry. The most remarkable continuity in this period was the centrality of the firm itself in the organization and governance of industrial production. Indeed, both of the central postwar changes presupposed and reinforced the centrality of the firm as the appropriate social and political location for the organization of production.

In contrast to the experience of the decentralized industrial order, however, where producers experienced a decade of unexpected prosperity and competitiveness in the 1980s before falling into crisis in the 1990s, the reconstituted postwar autarkic industrial order had difficulty right from the start adjusting to the dramatic changes in the competitive context that overtook the international economy beginning in the mid-1970s. Large autarkic firms were plagued repeatedly by an array of self-blocking dynamics that prevented them from adjusting in an effective way.

The problem had the following character. As we saw in the previous chapter, the core dynamics in international industrial product markets that emerged during the late 1970s, and intensified during the 1980s and 1990s, involved rapid and continuous product and technological change coupled with increasing development costs. These environmental changes exerted great pressure on large producers to reintegrate production and product development by breaking down old hierarchies and functional divisions within the firm and shifting responsibility to collaborators outside the firm. But in both cases the institutional and/or regional features of German autarkic industrial order created significant sets of allied interests within the firms that were capable of blocking such moves.

Naturally, circumstances and relations within firms in different locations and different sectors varied considerably. In a minority of cases, very special circumstances enabled some autarkic firms to radically recompose and decentralize production and its governance, thereby pushing the limits of autarkic order beyond anything imaginable among even the most radically diversified *Konzerne* from the interwar period. In a much larger array of cases, however, moves toward internal recomposition and greater decentralization were blocked, either because of internal resistance within firms – often stemming from alliances between departmental and plant managers and works councils – or because of the lack of a local infrastructure of small- and medium-sized firms and extrafirm institutions onto which production and governance could be devolved. Incipient efforts and local political struggles to overcome these obstacles emerged at the end of the 1980s and in many cases the primary actors were emboldened by the example of the success of the decentralized industrial order to attack autarkic tradition. The meager successes that these efforts produced, however, were then all markedly destabilized by the onset of world recession that began in the early 1990s.

This story of the reconstitution, evolution, and self-blockage of the autarkic industrial order over the course of the entire postwar period will be presented in the following way. The first part of the chapter discusses important general changes and continuities within the autarkic industrial order in comparison to the pre-World War II order. This section includes a brief discussion of the significance for the autarkic industrial order of the codetermination laws passed at the beginning of the 1950s, as well as a series of industry case studies that outline the range of consequences that the diffusion of mass production in postwar Europe had among autarkic enterprises. The second part of the chapter addresses the characteristic problems that producers in the autarkic industrial order have had in adjusting to the changed competitive conditions of the 1970s, 1980s, and 1990s. Once again, a series of cases of different producers in different sectors and regions will be presented to show the range of experimentation and organizational change within the firms and regions traditionally associated with the autarkic industrial order.

The reconstitution of autarkic industrial order in Western Germany

Autarky in the sense that I use it in this book involves the centralization of all aspects of production and its governance within the boundaries of a firm. In the industrialization period ending in 1945, autarkic industrial order involved both craft and volume production, extensive vertical integration, close ties with universal banks, and ambivalent relations with public institutions, including the central state. Prior to the collapse of the Nazi regime, autarkic producers consistently resented and resisted state interference in the internal affairs of firms or in the operation of markets, yet they willingly relied upon the provision of certain public goods (in particular education and rail transport). They also energetically engaged in contracts with the state for a broad array of operations, including, but by no means exclusively, the production of military materials and weaponry.

Though, as previous chapters have shown, there were battles over the degree of state involvement in the internal activities of firms during the Weimar and Nazi periods, most of the central contours of the autarkic order were so generically similar to features of large-scale organization becoming dominant in other western industrial economies, in particular the United States, by the middle of the 20th century that they were simply identified with modern industrial production as such; i.e., the large corporation had come to be equated in the self-understanding of the time with the very nature of advanced industrial production. This was true not only among those who owned, operated and worked in the enterprises in autarkic regions, but also among the administrators and politicians who guided the policy making of the military authorities that occupied Germany after the defeat of the Nazi regime. Thus, in contrast to the situation described in the previous chapter on the postwar experience of decentralized regions, no important struggles between the U.S., British, and French powers and German autarkic business interests occurred in the immediate postwar years over the reconstitution of institutions absolutely essential for the reproduction of the autarkic industrial order.[1] If there was to be industrial production in autarkic industrial regions at all, most agreed that firms (as opposed to decentralized networks of public and private industrial actors) would organize it.

There was also, ultimately, agreement (after initial resistance) about the reconstitution of many of the old institutional features of the autarkic industrial order, in particular the unique universal banking system in West Germany and the extensive system of technical universities from which many of the autarkic businesses drew their engineers and managers.[2] Finally, as the cold war grew stronger, the ideological and practical view that the state should protect market order while staying out of the internal affairs of industrial producers asserted itself in the West German Federal Republic.[3]

Despite all of this unanimity regarding the basic organizational contours for the reconstitution of the autarkic industrial order in the immediate postwar period, there was considerable debate and important organizational reconfiguration that took place among many producers and public authorities in a broad array of sectors within the autarkic industrial order. Indeed, two factors make the initial postwar period a watershed in the development of the autarkic industrial order. The first involved the imposition of a fundamental reform on the internal governance of the autarkic enterprise with the codification of plant-level works councils and firm-level codetermination in the initial postwar years. The second factor involved the massive adoption of mass production by German producers during the 1950s.

Codetermination

The introduction of legally mandated codetermination at all levels of enterprise in the first decade after the end of the war was driven by political concerns regarding the relationship between autarkic industry and Nazism. Trade unionists, social Catholics, social democrats and many others held that the unchecked centralized economic power of autarkic industry not only gave rise to investment strategies that contradicted the general interest, it also created the conditions for the unsavory alliances that were forged between elite economic interests and the National Socialist state.[4] Thus, for the advocates of economic democracy, the most important issue in the reform of the German autarkic industrial order was to make it more self-governing and internally democratic and thereby independent of state power.[5] "Codetermination through works councils," argued the Deutsche Gewerkschaftsbund (DGB), "is the guarantee that ensures that industry will provide for the demands of the general population rather than for the preparation for a new war."[6] In addition to the support among the organized groups and political parties already mentioned, there was much popular enthusiasm for codetermination within the rank and file of the German labor force as well.[7]

All of this political support ultimately resulted in the passage of laws. The 1951 Codetermination Law in the Coal and Steel Industry (*Montanmitbestimmungsgesetz*) mandated full-parity codetermination at the highest levels of the enterprises in that industry (with over 1000 employees), including equal representation on the board of directors (*Aufsichtsrat*) of enterprises and an independent labor director on the board of management (*Vorstand*). The 1951 law, however, did not specify the legal parameters of plant-level works council rights, nor did it extend beyond the coal and steel industry. The 1952 Works Constitution Act (*Betriebsverfassungsgesetz*) mandated plant-level codetermination, through works councils, in all West German enterprises, including those in the coal and steel industry, with more than five employees.[8]

It is important to see that the introduction of works council codetermination into German enterprises reinforced the traditional autarkic idea that production occurred within enterprises, not among enterprises and other organizations in a locality as in the decentralized industrial order. The creators of the institutions of codetermination presupposed a particular conceptualization of the economy in which the firm as the basic organizational unit was completely taken for granted. This conception of the economy is, for example, clearly articulated in the concluding statement from the second DGB congress in the British Zone, which took place in August 1946 in Bielefeld:

> The enterprise is the primary [*unterste*] organizational unit within the economic order. If democratization of the economy is to be achieved, it must begin first in the enterprises. It is for this reason desirable in all enterprises large enough to have a supervisory board . . . that the workforce be represented as the carrier of the production factor of labor.[9]

Only within such a world view could the problem of industrial representation be understood to be simply a matter central to the internal governance of enterprises.[10]

Once established both in law and in fact, the legitimacy and accuracy of this way of understanding the basic social organization of the economic order were then solidified by the success of the German economy and of the institutions themselves within the autarkic firm in the postwar period. First, on a symbolic level, the works councils and the other institutional aspects of codetermination were valued by the trade unions and social democrats as foundational pieces of economic and democratic order and of the legitimacy and importance of the working class and its representatives in the German polity. As the economy prospered and stable democracy took root in Germany during the 1950s, these ideas about the underlying organizational nature of the economy received a kind of vindication. They became integral to the way in which trade unions and the Social Democratic Party understood their own contribution to the recovery of the German political economy.[11]

Second, as many have noted, on a practical level, the day-to-day practice of works council governance within autarkic enterprises created a productive culture of reciprocity, conflictual solidarity, and flexibility between labor and management that encouraged both to resolve conflicts resulting from changing competitive conditions through internal negotiation within the firm (as opposed, say, to investment abroad or through subcontracting).[12] It seems further clear that this dimension of works council governance encouraged the creation of centralized management structures within large German enterprises. This was true because the reciprocally open system of works council representation throughout the enterprise forced, as a matter of routine, the systematic generation of detailed information about the internal workings of the company.[13] Such information was useful not only to the workers, but to management as well. Its constant generation allowed higher levels of management to continuously monitor the performance of workshops, plants and even whole segments of their company's business. Opportunistic behavior by lower levels of management or hidden inefficiencies that plagued managers in large enterprises in other countries and encouraged efforts to create decentralized multidivisional structures, particularly in the United States, could be more easily policed and checked in large German firms, making multidivisionalization less necessary.[14]

We will see that all of these characteristics of firm-based economic democracy would prove to be both an asset and a liability in subsequent periods of development.

The diffusion of mass production in the early Federal Republic: Three case studies

The second significant transformation in the autarkic industrial order during the postwar period was the broad diffusion of mass-production practices among a large number of autarkic enterprises. The spread of mass production in the postwar period involved the following: a) the general adoption of the high-volume production of increasingly standardized products; b) the separation of conception from execution in the immediate production process through mechanization, rationalization, and automation; c) increasing separation of product development and design from direct production within the organizational structure of a firm and in relations between producers and suppliers; and d) the emergence of oligopolistic industrial structures as opposed to more fragmented and cartelized structures on the one hand and freely competitive ones on the other.

As we saw in Chapter 3, until the 1930s, autarkic German firms had either resisted the adoption of mass-production strategies and methods in their own operations, or they had found that their capacity to adopt such methods was blocked by market or political conditions (or both). Haltingly during the militarization drives of the late 1930s and early 1940s and then dramatically in the early decades of the postwar period, these obstacles began to fall away. Indeed, as already outlined in the previous chapter's discussion of Daimler-Benz, the postwar environment was extremely conducive to the adoption and spread of mass-production strategies in German industry. The following three case studies – of iron and steel, light manufacturing, and machinery producers – outline the ways in which autarkic industrial producers, from different starting points, negotiated the postwar shift into mass production. Each case involves different degrees of continuity and break with the past. The irony is that the case in which the most radical change took place – the iron and steel industry – was actually one in which volume production had been a staple feature of industrial practice. It is to the details of that case that we now turn.

Case one: The iron and steel industry, 1945–1974

The postwar experience of the autarkic German steel industry is a case in which there was radical discontinuity with the industry of the past. Up to the collapse of the Nazi regime, this industry was a volume-production oriented industry in which, however, the production of specialized and customized products played a very significant role. More importantly, the strategic behavior of firms in the industry and the contours of industrial organization fostered the creation and expansion of vast vertically and horizontally diversified firms aimed at creating an internal environment that would foster continuous innovation.

Deconcentration and decartelization policies imposed by the Allied military governments in Germany broke up this old industry into smaller, more specialized parts. This not only changed the strategic situation confronting individual producers within the industry, it also changed the rules according to which the decimated industry would be able to put itself back together again. The result was the recomposition of the industry along lines that involved very large scale mass production within firms and stable oligopoly structures governing relations among them.

Initial reforms 1945–57: Deconcentration and decartelization. Large-scale German industry, particularly the steel industry, was implicated, both in the German public mind as well as in the opinions of the occupying powers (if more ambiguously, in fact), with the rise to power and outward aggression of the Nazi regime.[15] For this reason, there was initially a great deal of momentum in occupied Germany, certainly ideologically, behind a massive deconcentration of the economy. Deconcentration and decartelization were considered to be politically necessary to prevent the return of German militarism and, at least among western political forces, to establish the conditions necessary for stable democratic political order.[16] Article 12 of the Economic Section (Section B) of the Potsdam Agreement, signed by Stalin, Truman, and Attlee in August 1945, declared the following:

> At the earliest practicable date, the German economy shall be decentralized for the purpose of eliminating the present excessive concentration of economic power as exemplified in particular by cartels, syndicates, trusts and other monopolistic arrangements.[17]

The rather general wording of the decree, however, allowed for a broad array of definitions of "excessive." The real zealots on the issue were German neoliberal economists[18] and American progressive anti-trust lawyers[19] who viewed defeat and occupation as an opportunity to radically reform the German economy by eliminating monopolies and recasting economic practice according to small-scale and competitive free-market principles. But these voices were relatively isolated ones in the debate. Most important players, particularly after the initial year and a half of occupation, had a very different vision of how the German large-firm economy should be restructured. The reformers were not opposed to large-scale firms as such; they wanted to redirect the way that such firms organized production and behaved in the market. Above all, they wanted to rid the economy of the many large horizontally diversified *Konzerne* and *Interessengemeinschaften* and the heavily cartelized market arrangements that they constructed to govern their relations. In their place, the military authorities wanted to establish actors and ground rules that would contribute to the emergence of more specialized, efficient, mass-production oriented firms and oligopolistically structured markets.[20]

At the end of World War II, the iron and steel industry stood out organizationally within Autarkic industry: it was unusually highly concentrated and combined vertically related businesses that crossed sectors.[21] The share of markets in the steel industry not dominated by the sprawling Vestag were dominated by the major *Konzerne*: Most of the producers were broadly diversified across all steel products.[22] The companies all competed in a very broad array of rolled-product markets (the Vestag in virtually all markets), many of which were as a result highly fragmented, with producers making many customized and specialty products. Technical integration among the various processes within steel making, forward integration into manufacturing, and cartelization were all mechanisms deployed to compensate for fluctuations in output in the diverse, specialized rolling mills they operated.

During the early postwar years it was widely believed, particularly by Americans, that the extreme integration and cartelization in the industry had blocked the diffusion of efficient technologies and industrial practices. Outsiders viewed the relatively large numbers of small and flexible rolling mills attached to individual companies as a sign of steel mill monopoly power rather than as an explicit strategy on the part of producers to expand their range of products. The allies agreed that the industry needed to be deconstructed and rearranged in a way that would allow more "modern" and "healthy" – i.e., larger scale and less horizontally diversified – forms of industrial production to take root.[23]

To this end, all of the assets of the iron and steel industry were seized by the military governments in 1946 and early 1947.[24] All six of the major Ruhr steel producers (Vestag, Krupp, Hoesch, Klöckner, GHH, and Mannesmann), which alone during the 1930s had controlled over 78% of German crude steel production, were completely broken up. Bargaining between the allies, the German government and the iron and steel industry throughout the end of the 1940s resulted in a rather constant game of strategic recombination in the industry. Properties and plants were torn apart and repositioned both on paper and in fact.[25] Ultimately, 23 new companies were created, 13 from the old Vestag alone[26] (see Table 9).

The new structure of the industry was organized around steel works: each new company was dominated by one. But, significantly, the degree of diversification in the finished rolling mill product palettes in each of the newly created steel firms was disrupted. Though the Deconcentration Authority for the Steel industry (Stahltreuhändervereinigung) attempted to retain as much integration between existing steel and rolling mills as "was technically necessary," much capacity was deemed unessential and allocated to other steel production units. In this way, parts of the industry's rolling mill capacity was spread across the industry, rather than within firms. This kind of distribution of plant linkages was often extremely awkward: in some cases rolling mills were realigned with steel works that could not supply them with the proper kind of steel and separated from ones that previously had.[27] But this kind of allocation of capacity was desirable from the point of view of the reformers both because it was difficult otherwise to achieve the goal of creating smaller companies and because it raised the costs of diversification and created an incentive for firms to grow by increasing the scale of rolling mills they possessed.[28]

This intentional reallocation of finishing capacity among steel works was most dramatic in the Vestag successor companies, but a narrowing of rolling mill capacity occurred within the steel making operations of the old *Konzerne* as well. Often this was less the result of explicit deconcentration efforts than it was the outcome of war damage or dismantling losses in rolling mill plant that the deconcentration authorities did not attempt to redress. But, whatever the cause, the key outcome of the deconcentration for all firms' steel operations was the need to seriously rethink their strategy in rolled production. The emphasis on

Table 9 *The 23 "new" German steel enterprises created after World War II**

New enterprise	Old
Deutsche Edelstahlwerke AG, Krefeld	Vestag
Rheinisch-Westfälische Eisen- und Stahlwerke AG, Mülheim/Ruhr	Vestag
Bergbau- und Industriewerte GmbH, Düsseldorf	Vestag
Hüttenwerke Phönix AG, Duisburg	Vestag
Dortmund-Hörder Hüttenunion AG, Dortmund	Vestag
Gußtahlwerk Bochumer Verein AG, Bochum	Vestag
August Thyssen-Hütte AG, Duisburg-Hamborn	Vestag
Hüttenwerke Siegerland AG, Siegen	Vestag
Gußtahlwerk Witten AG, Witten	Vestag
Rheinische Röhrenwerke AG, Mülheim	Vestag
Niederrheinische Hütte AG, Duisberg	Vestag
Stahlwerke Südwestfalen AG, Geisweid	Vestag
Ruhrstahl AG, Hattingen	Vestag
Mannesmann AG, Düsseldorf	Mannesmanröhren-Werke
Hansche Werke AG, Duisburg-Großenbaum	Mannesmanröhren-Werke
Stahl- und Walzwerke Rasselstein/Andernach AG, Neuweid	Otto Wolf
Stahlwerke Bochum, AG, Bochum	Otto Wolf
Nordwestdeutscher Hütten- und Bergwerksverien	Klöckner
Hoesch-Werke AG, Dortmund	Hoesch
Hüttenwerk Rheinhausen AG, Rheinhausen	Krupp
Eisenwerk-Gesellschaft Maximilianshütte AG, Sulzbach-Rosenberg-Hütte	Friedrich Flick KG
Luitpoldhütte AG, Amberg	Reichswerke AG für Erzbergbau und Eisenhütten
Hüttenwerk Oberhausen AG, Oberhausen	Gutehoffnungshütte Aktienverein für Bergbau und Hüttenbetrieb

*Ilseder Hütte, the twenty-fourth enterprise, was left unchanged by the rearrangements.
Source: *Die Neuordnung der Eisen- und Stahlindustrie.*

product proliferation and diversification that had characterized the stable prewar structure of steel was now not only seriously undermined, it became only one of a number of alternative strategies available to producers as they set about reconstructing themselves.

In addition to this specialization of core steel production units (blast furnaces, steel mills, rolling mills), deconcentration also aimed at severing all but the most essential nonsteel ties within the old enterprises.[29] The logic here was the same as within steel more narrowly defined. The broad cross-sectoral diversification of the steel producers was viewed both as inefficient and monopolistic. Such enterprise structures were undesirable from an allied point of view in two ways: They allowed steel operations to run inefficiently by providing them with guaranteed markets while at the same time effectively subsidizing the downstream operations that perpetuated inefficiency and market fragmentation there as well. Breaking up cross sectoral linkages, however, undermined the dynamic economies of scope that had sustained the *Konzerne* in the prewar period.

All of Vestag's machinery and manufacturing interests were collected together in the Rheinische Stahlwerke AG, its coal holdings into three independent companies and its trading businesses into the Handelsunion AG.[30] The same vertical deconstruction occurred in most of the *Konzerne*. Mannesmann, Klöckner, and Hoesch, for example were stripped of crucial steel plants, all but their most needed coal mines and most of their down-line engineering interests.[31] The GHH had its networks of coal mines and steel mills expropriated but retained its extensive holdings in manufacturing, primarily in heavy engineering and shipbuilding. Its sizeable former steel operations in Oberhausen were constituted as a fully independent steel company, the Hüttenwerk Oberhausen AG (HOAG).[32] Krupp was forced to sign a commitment to legally separate all of the family's steel making facilities (concentrated primarily in the work at Rheinhausen) and attendant coal mines from the rest of its business, collect them into a holding company, and sell them off. The major nonsteel lines of Krupp's business included some trading companies and a wide variety of specialized heavy engineering workshops located around Essen and in the Ruhr Valley more generally.[33]

Deconcentration thus significantly reorganized and decentralized both the production of steel and rolled products and the broadly diversified companies that produced them. Individual producers were smaller, less integrated (especially with forward nonsteel sectors), and less diversified producers of rolled steel products. These developments totally destroyed the coherence of the companies as they had existed prior to the war and systematically undermined the strategic logic of dynamic diversification that had held them together.

This strategic intent behind all of these deconcentration efforts was reinforced through the simultaneous implementation of very strict decartelization measures in the industry. An outright ban on all cartelization in the German economy was announced by all three Allied governments in the west in 1947.[34] The ban was enforced by the Allied occupying governments until 1955 and continued to be enforced by the Germans thereafter until it was replaced by a new law governing competition in 1957. This ban on cartels was complemented on a European level in the coal and steel industry where the European Coal and Steel Community Treaty and Organization (ECSC) made the rejection of all forms of cartel a condition of membership.[35]

The consequences of this rule change regarding cartels significantly altered the environment in which producers in the steel industry competed. As we saw in Chapter 3, during the first part of the 20th century steel producers experimented with two different ways to restructure their industry as growth in crude steel and standard rolled products began to slow while growth in a broad array of finished steel products exploded. One was to reorganize the capacity of the entire industry, eliminate the number of producers in the market, and make it possible to impose rationalization and standardization in the new product areas. The aim was to make it possible to achieve efficient scale economies in all areas of production. The other option was for individual firms to diversify their production across a broad array of interrelated specialties in the emerging new product markets and in nonsteel manufacturing areas as well. In the latter case, the emphasis was less on the creation of economies of scale than on the creation of dynamic economies of scope, making possible strategies of specialization and customization in many different markets.

As we saw in Chapter 3, the former *oligopoly-creating* strategy emerged out of frustration among certain producers for the ability of cartels to successfully manage the problems that rapid growth in the new rolled steel product markets engendered in the industry. In its very conception, then, this strategy was understood to be an alternative form of industrial governance to the cartel. In the latter, *Konzern-creating* case, producers did not attempt to construct an alternative mechanism to the cartel to govern rolled steel production within the industry. Instead, they abandoned the idea that the entire capacity in the industry could be rationalized into a stable oligopoly and sought to achieve growth through diversification and higher-quality production. As it turned out, as we saw, cartels continued to be important to these latter producers in the interwar period because they stabilized the proportionally smaller, but still significant, parts of their business that continued to be engaged in steel production. Indeed, given the fact that the creation of *Konzerne* in effect perpetuated the continued existence of larger numbers and wide variety of relatively smaller sized rolling mill units in the industry,[36] failure to use cartels would have made producers vulnerable to chronic cyclical losses, given the high fixed costs of even small-sized production units.

The allied and ECSC reform measures created a legal, institutional, and strategic situation in the industry that changed the way in which producers viewed the costs associated with both of the above strategies. The cost of the former oligopolistic strategy was considerably lowered, because the primary barrier to it in the past – a capacity structure embedded in relatively entrenched property relations – no longer existed. The radical fragmentation imposed on the industry by the Allies created the possibility that the pieces could be placed back together, both within firms and across the industry as a whole, in ways that would facilitate larger scale, more efficient, production. Through specialized investment in select markets, greater capacity in each product market segment could be spread across a more limited number of firms than had been possible in the past. The costs of pursuing the latter *Konzern* strategy, on the other hand, were considerably raised as a result of the Allied reforms. The crucial stabilizing mechanism of the cartel was no longer available to producers, so the possibility of making profits in a broad variety of rolled products with only a modest-scale commitment in each was significantly reduced.

These changes in the basic conditions confronting steel producers – narrower product palettes as a result of deconcentration and a ban on cartels – provided a necessary but not sufficient set of reasons for producers to rethink their approach to the industry. The sufficient reasons for opting for one strategy over another would ultimately be provided by the economic environment. That is,

216 *Industrial constructions*

whether or not the expansion of the industry would be greater if one pursued an oligopoly-creating strategy based upon consolidation and large-scale mass production or a *Konzern*-building strategy through diversification across industrial specialties would ultimately depend upon the general rate of growth in demand for steel products. We will see that conditions during the boom years of the first decades of the Federal Republic favored the former strategy.

The steel industry in the economic miracle, 1953–1974

Production. The trajectory of production in the German steel industry in the first 20 postwar years is one of rapid initial growth, followed by slow, stagnating growth, ending in crash and crisis. The deconcentrated and decartelized steel producers of the Ruhr Valley grew very rapidly in the new postwar political and economic conditions of the 1950s. Between 1950 and 1960 when world steel production increased 75% from 200 million tons to 350 million tons, German crude steel production increased by nearly 150%, from 14 to 34 million tons, increasing the German's share of world crude steel production from 7.5 to 10%.[37] All rolled steel products grew even more spectacularly: from 8 million tons in 1950, total rolled steel output in the Federal Republic increased to almost 22.1 million tons in 1960 and reached nearly 24.4 million by 1964.[38] Moreover, within rolled steel products there was a clear redistribution of capacity toward sheet and away from profile steels, reflecting the rapid growth of mass-producing steel users in manufacturing, such as the automobile industry.[39]

During the 1960s, growth continued, but began noticeably to slow. Steel industry growth rates lagged behind the rate of German industry as a whole. And, though world crude steel production doubled from the 350 million ton level of 1960 to 708 million tons in 1974, German production during the same period increased by only 50%, from 34 to 53 million tons, causing its share of world production to drop back down to 7.5%.[40] Rolled steel production grew more substantially during the period, nearly doubling to 43.1 million tons between 1960 and 1974. The shift within rolled steel output continued as sheet steel accounted for 52.2% of production and profile steels 40.5%.[41] But 1974 was a watershed year for the industry. In that year, the industry produced as much crude and rolled steel as it ever has. Crude steel output tonnage levels fell precipitously after 1974 (output was only 40.4 tons in 1975 and 38.9 in 1977) and have never been that high since. The same is true of rolled steel output.[42]

The tremendous growth of the 1950s and 60s inevitably gave rise to efforts by the major producers to modernize, rationalize, and above all increase the scale of their operations. At the limit, the trajectory was toward full integration among the various parts of the steel making process. By the beginning of the 1970s, there were 15 fully integrated steel works (i.e., blast furnaces, steel mill, and rolling mill in one place) in West Germany, with the majority concentrated in the Ruhr.[43] In many cases, however, capacity of each of the three phases of production within individual firms was tightly coordinated among different localities within the region, rather than in the same place. In any case, between 1952 and 1963, German steel producers invested over 14.6 billion Deutsch Marks in the expansion of production technologies. Between 1952 and 1955, well over half of all outlays went to the renewal and expansion of rolling mill facilities – the part of the steel production complex most devastated by wartime bombing and postwar dismantling. For example, 833 million DM of a total of 1297 million DM went for rolling mill expansion in 1955. Then, with rolling mill capacity very advanced, the industry redirected investment toward the expansion of blast furnace and steel making equipment between 1956 and 1960. This then gave rise to imbalances that shifted investment back to rolling mill expansion.[44]

All of this investment and expansion led to increases in the scale of the various steel making operations which were breathtaking. Developments in blast furnace technology for the production of pig iron provide a good indication of the general trend. Before the war, the daily capacity of a blast furnace averaged around 350 tons of raw iron; by the mid-1960s, the daily capacity of a blast furnace averaged around 1,000 tons. The largest furnaces at August Thyssen Hütte had capacities that exceeded two thousand tons per day.[45] The mouth of the bath in prewar German blast furnaces averaged four to five meters in diameter, those in the 1960s averaged between seven to ten meters in diameter. In most cases, firms operated a number of furnaces this size simultaneously. The scale achievements in pig iron production through these developments were remarkable: While output of pig iron tripled between 1956 and 1974 (12.5 million tons to 40.2 million tons) the number of blast furnaces declined in the same period from 123 to 86 units.[46]

Finally, gains in size and girth were complemented by the early implementation of the newest and most advanced technologies. The first nonexperimental basic oxygen furnace was implemented in Germany in 1957 in the Rheinische Stahlwerke's specialty works, the Gussstahlwerk Witten. Others in the industry rapidly followed so that by the middle of the 1960s steel made in traditional Thomas converters, and even in Siemens Martin Open Hearths, was being displaced by basic oxygen steel. In 1954, only 54 thousand tons of steel were produced in basic oxygen furnaces out of a total of 24.5 million tons. By 1969, basic oxygen furnaces produced over 15 million tons of steel, more than either the total output of Siemens-Martins open hearths (14.5 million) or the Thomas converters (7.7 million).[47]

Changes in the character of governance in the industry. Predictably, this experience of very rapid growth and profound technological change followed by stagnation and then crisis gave rise to a host of problems at the level of the individual enterprise and at the level of the steel industry as a whole that producers needed to resolve. It is easier to address the latter problems first, for they provide the context for the changes that occurred in the former. The evolution in the development of industrial organization in the steel industry

218 *Industrial constructions*

during the first two decades of the postwar period can be divided into two phases: consolidation with growing capacity and consolidation with overcapacity and crisis.

Consolidation with growing capacity: 1953–1962. In the first phase, the newly fragmented industry recomposed itself in the process of growth. On a superficial level, the recomposition created an industry structure that resembled the one that the allies had deconstructed. Most of the producers that had been broken up put themselves back together again. In fact, however, what reemerged through the recomposition of the industry was very different from industrial structure of the past. In the context of extremely rapid growth in the demand for (especially rolled) steel, enterprises found that it was not feasible to build capacity across specialties, as had been the common practice within the old *Konzerne*. Expansion of this kind, by neglecting economies of scale, constrained the growth of output in the industry as a whole and threatened to lead consumers to turn to foreign sources to satisfy demand. Thus, just to be able to keep up with the growth of demand and protect their home market, West German enterprises found that it was collectively more prudent to expand by focusing their investment and expansion on a limited range of products that could be produced at tremendous scale.[48]

Capacity, new technology, and product specialties were thus collectively matched with and distributed amongst the existing infrastructure of plants by the major players in the industry. Firms were merged into others, primarily as a way to consolidate capacity, reduce bottlenecks, and facilitate the introduction of new, larger, more productive technologies. Merger and consolidation worked to specialize firms on a limited number of products (in particular, among subgroupings of rolled products) and spread capacity and growth evenly across the industry. The result was that stable oligopoly structures began to emerge within individual market segments in the industry, not just in pig iron and crude steel, but in rolled products as well. In comparison to the prewar industry, individual market segments became more concentrated, but total capacity within the industry as a whole became more evenly distributed.

This process of recomposition in the industry can be clearly seen in the way that the companies of the old Vestag were recombined during the initial period of expansion. Of the 13 steel companies originally created out of the breakup of the Vestag in 1953, only four were left by the beginning of the 1960s: August Thyssen Hütte AG (ATH), Phoenix-Rheinrohr AG, Rheinische Stahlwerk AG (Rheinstahl), and Dortmund-Hörde Hütten Union (DHHU).[49] For the most part, the consolidation and expansion of these companies did not result in direct competition between them. Instead, each expanded and consolidated its capacity in areas that the others ignored. The vast majority of the steel making capacity of the old Vestag was reincorporated within the operations of either ATH or Phoenix-Rheinrohr and their product offerings and specializations in rolled product markets were for the most part not overlapping. ATH specialized in the production of lighter, semi-finished and finished rolled sheet and coils, and wire and specialty steels, whereas the Phoenix-Rheinrohr specialized in the production of steel pipe, heavy plate, semi-finished steels and raw iron.[50] The coordinated growth and reconsolidation between these two companies was facilitated by the fact that both enterprises were controlled by different members of the Thyssen family.

Rheinstahl, which had very broad ownership, was less interested in getting involved in the reintegration of Vestag steelmaking interests. This company received all of the nonsteel manufacturing interests of the old Vestag as a result of deconcentration. It held an interest in only a small number of relatively small and specialized steel works from the old Vestag, and, though it continued to produce steel during the 1950s, it was a very minor player in the industry.[51] The DHHU, for its part, was an important producer of crude steel. But unlike its larger Vestag cousins, the company was not as broadly diversified across steel industry markets. By the beginning of the 1960s, the company was concentrated on two general areas: It was the Federal Republic's largest producer of heavy plate and an important producer of steel bars and structural steel.[52]

Together, these four firms, with their coordinated capacities, accounted for nearly 35% of West German crude steel output in 1960/1961 – ATH and Phoenix-Rheinrohr together accounted for 20.91%. Another 41% of total industry output was taken up by the steel operations of the former *Konzerne* Hoesch, Klöckner, Mannesmann, Hüttenwerk Oberhausen AG (HOAG),[53] and Krupp.[54] On the whole, these producers followed the DHHU pattern of specialization, each attempting to organize its steel and rolled product output in a way that would give the company a strong position in a limited number of markets. Thus, for example, Mannesmann concentrated its production on steel pipe and a variety of high quality fine and zinc treated plate steels, Krupp on specialty steels, structural steels, bar, and semis, Hoesch on sheet steels and fine plate, HOAG on heavy plate, structural steels, and specialty wire, and Klöckner on sheet steels, fine plate, wire, and bar.[55] The producers accounting for the remaining 15% of the industry's output in 1960, who were located both inside and outside of the Ruhr, followed a similar pattern of specialization.

The emergence of oligopolized submarkets and more specialized firms oriented toward mass rather than specialty production ultimately resulted in a distinctly different industry structure than had existed prior to World War II. Before the war, only six companies controlled nearly three quarters of the industry's total output, whereas by 1961 that same share was divided among nine enterprises. More significantly, the share of the successor companies of the old Vestag did not recapture the same dominant share of industry output that had belonged to their ancestor: Vestag accounted for roughly half the industry's total output during the 1930s, whereas the successor companies were only able to achieve 35% by 1961. Decartelization and deconcentration in the 1940s had succeeded in creating a more internally specialized and more competitive German steel industry.

Consolidation in stagnation and crisis: 1964–1974. This new more competitive industrial structure underwent a further process of consolidation during the

Table 10 *Major mergers and acquisitions in the West German steel industry, 1964–1968*

Year	Purchaser	Acquired enterprise
1964	August Thyssen Hütte	Phönix Rheinrohr AG
1965	Friedrich Krupp Hüttenwerke	Bochumer Verein
1966	Hoesch AG (14.5% owned by Hoogovens)	Dormund Hörder Hüttenunion
1967	August Thyssen Hütte	Hüttenwerk Oberhausen AG
1968	August Thyssen Hütte	Stahlwerk Bochum AG (48% stake)
1967	Creation of the rolled steel consortia (Kontoren)	

Table taken from Eckart, K., *Die Eisen- und Stahlindustrie in den Beiden Deutschen Staaten* (1988), p. 254.

1960s and early 1970s as the rate of growth slowed and then crisis struck. But even here the levels of concentration reached did not approach those that had existed in the interwar period. Moreover, the way in which the primary problem confronting the industry – overcapacity in crude and especially in rolled products – was handled shows how far away from the concerns of the prewar industry the postwar industry had developed.

The situation in the 1960s German steel industry was similar in many ways to the one that confronted the industry at the beginning of the 20th century: Growth in crude steel markets was slowing down while rolled markets continued to expand. Unlike the earlier period, however, there was very little thought given to the possibility of individual firm solutions to the industry's problem. On the contrary, producers overwhelmingly believed that diversification and specialization in their individual product palettes was not a realistic alternative to consolidation and rationalization of capacity in the industry as a whole. Specialization on large-volume products, with the huge investments in fixed plant and equipment that they entailed, had made the traditional option of broad diversification too costly for individual producers.

Given this general commitment in the industry to mass production and oligopolistic competition, the best solution to the problem of overcapacity was to rationalize the entire industry: By consolidating operations and assets across the entire industry, firms could both reduce total capacity and make existing capacity more efficient.[56] Between 1964 and 1968 there were five major mergers in the German industry, three of which involved August Thyssen Hütte (see Table 10). Then in 1967, all producers in the German steel industry joined together to create four regional rolled product "*Kontoren*" or sales offices, which controlled all sales of rolled products in the German industry. The stated aim of the *Kontoren* was to save on sales and administration costs.[57] But the informal effect of the *Kontoren* was to rationalize the total rolled product production capacity in the industry and create more efficient and specialized producers.[58]

The arrangement was very successful. Producers in each *Kontor* agreed to coordinate their investments, discard capacity, and mutually limit their production plans to achieve efficient capacity utilization and lower production costs.[59] Between 1967 and 1971, blast furnaces with yearly capacities of up to 4 million tons, steel works with over 10 million tons annual capacity, and rolling mill facilities of over 13 million tons annual capacity were shut down.[60] The most well-known specialization agreement at the time took place between Thyssen and Mannesmann in 1970, when the former gave the latter all of its steel tube operations in exchange for the latter's sheet steel operations.

By the beginning of the 1970s, German steel firms were becoming more specialized, fewer in number, and larger. Nevertheless, despite these gains in efficiency, the industry was still not able to keep up with the continuously deteriorating situation in international steel markets. Even before the onset of what was to become a permanent crisis after 1974, firms could see that the situation in European steel markets was likely to continue to be anemic and uncertain and that growth rates in the industry would continue to trail those of the average of all manufacturing industries. This realization prompted many of the largest firms in the German steel industry to begin to diversify their holdings. Thyssen and Mannesmann, in particular, attempted to supplement their steel operations by purchasing companies in related industries, especially in mechanical engineering. In 1973/1974, Thyssen bought its Vestag cousin, the machinery company Rheinstahl, while Mannesmann purchased the large, diversified, autarkic machinery producer Demag.[61]

The idea behind these purchases had little to do with the old logic that had guided the construction of *Konzerne* in the interwar period. Both companies were seeking alternative sources of income as a hedge against slowing growth and growing cyclicality in the steel business. They were neither looking for synergistic ties to bolster innovation in their steel operations nor were they counting on the newly acquired companies to absorb significant portions of their steel output.[62] Some of these older strategic ideas, we shall see, reappeared in the 1980s, but they were not the ideas guiding the initial purchases. Indeed, by 1974, the German steel industry had grown to be quite unlike the earlier interwar industry. Firms were more specialized and produced on far larger scales. Output within the industry was distributed more evenly across the major firms, rather than being concentrated in one large firm as in the interwar period.

The internal structure of steel enterprises during the economic miracle. These developments at the level of industrial structure were bound up with and helped to shape changes in the internal organization of individual steel enterprises. Indeed, although steel production and its administration continued to be organized primarily within the boundaries of firms, the outer shape of firms and their internal management structures were changed significantly from their interwar incarnations. There were two main developments. The first was that postwar steel enterprises were far more focused on the production of steel than they had been in the interwar period. The second was that in most cases, the managerial structures of the enterprises were highly centralized.

Again, it may strike many as slightly surprising to claim that the postwar steel enterprises were more specialized than their predecessors. After all, by the end of the 1950s, most of the old *Konzerne* had reintegrated the downline and upline manufacturing, coal mining, and trading businesses that the deconcentration authorities had taken from them.[63] The difference, however, was that whereas in the interwar period the trend (and the strategic thinking) was toward an evening out of revenues and output across different businesses within the *Konzern*, during the 1950s and 1960s, the expansion in steel operations was so great that these operations simply overshadowed the other businesses. The movement toward the creation of dynamically diversified *Konzerne* gave way to the development of relatively specialized, high volume steel companies.[64]

Even those firms in the best position to recreate an evenly distributed steel and manufacturing portfolio, such as Rheinstahl and GHH (both of which had extensive machinery operations and historical roots in the steel business), did not do so. Competitiveness in steel required large investments in scale and expensive plant that exceeded the resources and the interest of those players: Rheinstahl became less, not more, involved in the steel industry over time, while GHH never attempted to reincorporate its deconcentrated steel operations.[65]

Specialization on high volume production by autarkic steel producers, in turn, affected the development of the internal management structures. Whereas in the interwar period, the trend was toward the construction of more decentralized structures with a superintending central organization that coordinated relations between operations and adjudicated disputes, the trend during the growth years of the economic miracle was toward greater centralization of control and hierarchy. The sprawling, loosely coupled *Konzerne* structures of the interwar period were replaced by unitary–functional management structures, where all operations were coordinated by a single set of functional departments (production, sales, finance, etc).[66] Such centralization stemmed from the fact that the scale of operations had become so vast and integrated, while the range of product narrowed. The need to coordinate the internal flow of material through the various processes was most easily done from the center. Indeed, the growth of centralization in this manner is another indication of the success of the Allied deconcentration efforts: German steel producers were developing structures that began to resemble those that had been constructed in the United States. As Chandler's accounts of U.S. steel producers in the postwar period makes clear, high volume steel producers in the United States were moving away from managerial decentralization toward more unitary and hierarchical management structures during the growth years of the 1950s.[67]

Thanheiser's 1970 data for the top 100 German industrial firms show that of the largest German steel producers, only Mannesmann had created a multidivisional structure. According to Thanheiser's data, the two largest steel producers, Thyssen and Hoesch, were organized as functional holdings. This meant that the dominant steel operations of the firms were run through a highly centralized functional management structure, while the smaller secondary businesses of the companies were run as entirely separate businesses, with the steel firm as holding company.[68]

Case two: New mass-production industries

The second case concerns the postwar emergence and growth of extensive and large-scale mass production in product lines, firms, and sectors that had previously been relatively underdeveloped within the German economy prior to the 1950s. As the case of Daimler-Benz in the previous chapter demonstrated, the diffusion of this kind of organizational approach to production mostly reinforced the traditional firm-centered character of autarkic production. Among producers within the traditionally autarkic regions, however, the change in production gave rise to some significant modifications in the principles of autarkic production, which were perhaps less striking in the Daimler-Benz case. In particular, as we will see, the more firms mass produced, the more they began to rely on outside suppliers to stabilize their own internal expansion – something that was traditional in decentralized areas but largely unprecedented in autarkic regions.

The two best examples of the kind of general shift into mass production I have in mind are the automobile and the consumer electronics industries, though the shift discussed here occurred in a broad array of light-manufacturing sectors.[69] In both automobiles and consumer electronics, the original steps in the direction of mass production were taken as the result of initiatives on the part of the Nazi regime, but the full flowering of these sectors did not come until the background conditions favoring the diffusion of mass production in Germany and Europe generally were established.[70]

The experience of the Volkswagen AG provides a particularly dramatic example of the kind of transformation that occurred in these sectors. The company was conceived as a greenfield project during the 1930s by the Nazi regime. The idea was to produce a small affordable car, using American techniques of mass production, for broad civil and military distribution. Hitler negotiated personally with the itinerant auto engineer and designer Ferdinand Porsche over the design and development of the "people's automobile" and designated a desolate section of rural easterly Lower Saxony for the location of the factory. All aspects of the production and assembly of the new automobile were to be performed, in archetypical autarkic fashion, entirely on the massive new site. But with the war and the confusion of defense planing within the Nazi regime, the plans to achieve large-scale mass production were never actually made good. Only after the war, with Allied (especially British) assistance did the company move systematically into the mass production of the "Beetle."[71]

The success of this single, standardized, inexpensive volume product in the postwar European and world markets is now legendary. The firm pioneered the use of highly specialized, single-purpose metalworking machinery imported from the United States (as late as 1965, over 40% of the body presses used in the Wolfsburg plant were made in the United States). As we shall see below, their adoption was at first gradual, but nevertheless significant. By 1955, Volkswagen had produced over a million cars – over twice as many autos as the entire German automobile industry could produce in the best of years during the Weimar Republic. As the transformation and integration of the European economy became more entrenched and growth more persistent, Volkswagen's commitment to American production methods and technology became more intense and its capacity to produce, correspondingly, grew enormously. It produced its 5 millionth Beetle in 1961 and then produced five million more in the next three and one half years. By the beginning of the 1960s, the company was producing over 4,000 Volkswagens a day and had over 110 miles of continuous-flow conveyor lines in its Wolfsburg plant alone.[72]

The fact that Volkswagen was explicitly created to engage in mass production makes it a dramatic example. There were a number of other firms that emerged in the early postwar years with similarly single-minded orientations toward mass production, the best example being perhaps the consumer electronics producer Grundig.[73] Many other autarkic producers, however, though they shifted dramatically into mass production during the 1950s, had been engaged previously in different kinds of lower-scale production strategies in the same or related sectors. This was true, for example of the consumer product and electrical motor operations within the giant electro-mechanical producers Siemens and AEG.

Both Siemens and AEG diversified very strongly into the production of light-current electrical goods (especially consumer products) over the course of the 1950s. One estimate for the West German electro-technical branch shows that by 1958 consumer goods production had increased its production value 496% over the 1952 levels, while capital goods production (*Investitionsgüter*) was only three times as high as the 1952 numbers in the same year. In 1952, consumer goods constituted less than 19% of the entire product offering in the industry; by 1958, that number had climbed to 29%.[74]

Such changes at Siemens and AEG were actually quite remarkable given the transition that each company had to endure as a result of war and the division of Germany. Both companies suffered tremendous losses in their Berlin operations from continuous bombing and, later, dismantling. Of the 24,000 machine tools in Siemens' massive Berlin plant, Siemensstadt, in 1945, for example, only 1,300 were left after dismantling, and of those only approximately 400 were immediately usable.[75] The situation was, if anything, even worse at AEG, where over a billion marks worth of assets were lost, including at least six entire plants in Berlin and eastern Germany.[76] Efforts to reestablish operations outside of Berlin in the western part of Germany resulted in a switch in emphases for both companies.

Siemens, which had done a great deal of work in volume production of light-current equipment before the war, did proportionally less, at least at first, after the war. Its main West German operations were based in the heavy-current, capital goods facilities in the Schuckert Works at Nuremberg, and for the short term these products became a larger part of Siemens' product palette. Only gradually did the light-current (to a large extent telecommunications based) technologies regain their place in the company's business. To the extent that it engaged in the mass production of the newer consumer goods technologies, such as radios, televisions, and household appliances, Siemens did so through joint ventures with other major producers, such as Bosch.[77]

For its part, AEG shifted its emphasis dramatically after the war. During the 1920s, AEG's emphasis was on the small series, often highly specialized production of heavy-current capital equipment. It too was forced to shift its production operations to the west, but unlike Siemens, AEG had no major facilities in those regions to fall back on. As a result, the company was forced to literally rebuild itself in the west. In so doing, it moved much more aggressively into the manufacture of mass-produced consumer goods. By 1970, within the consumer-electronics sector, according to Thanheiser, "AEG was said to be Europe's largest manufacturer of certain lines of electrical and electronics equipment, covering about 70% of the potential markets."[78]

Again, these examples are only the most dramatic ones. VW, Siemens, and AEG were part of a general shift in light-manufacturing industries toward mass production. Even some kinds of machinery producers, especially those in branches producing agricultural tractors, sewing machines, office equipment, pumps, armatures, and construction machinery also moved aggressively into volume and mass production over the course of the 1950s and 1960s.[79] All of these producers were alike in that they developed more rigidly standardized products and implemented more productive technologies and production techniques in their plants, such as special-purpose machine tools and transfer lines and other kinds of mechanical automation.[80] The following sections examine the character of this change in these new areas of light manufacturing first in production and then in administration.

The organization of mass production in light manufacturing industry. Regardless of specific sector of light manufacturing, autarkic firms that moved into genuine mass production during the 1950s and 1960s found that they had to reorganize production at three levels: at the level of the plant, the workplace, and the region.

The plant. Specialization was the most significant consequence of mass production on plant organization. In order to take full advantage of the productivity gains afforded by the new large-scale, integrated technology and system of production, firms tried to keep the production process going, uninterruptedly, as long as possible. Changing product characteristics to accommodate customer desires meant down time and shorter runs, which increased the per-unit costs of production. The way to approach the optimum of continuous production was to dedicate a particular production process to the production of a single standard product or to very closely related groups of products. Because of the tremendous scale often associated with dedicated production of this kind, production-process specialization most often resulted in the specialization of an entire plant on a specific, large-volume, standardized product or narrow range of products.[81]

Firms expanded and rationalized by constructing entirely new plants rather than recomposing old ones. All of VW's original plants were highly specialized from their inception. Thus, when the company continued to expand and then diversify during the economic miracle, it had no old facilities to specialize, and was thus forced to construct new "greenfield" plants to efficiently organize its new production. The result was a widely dispersed group of highly specialized plants. The massive Wolfsburg plant was dedicated to the production and assembly of the Beetle. Light trucks and all of VW's engines were produced in a large plant in Hannover that the company opened in 1956. Transmissions, truck front ends, and replacement parts were produced in a complex of production facilities in Kassel. All of the specialty work done on Volkswagen's cars (for example, the conversion of a Beetle into a convertible) was, as early as 1949, subcontracted out to the Wilhelm Karman Company in Osnabrück (also in Lower Saxony). When VW introduced a sports car, Karman did all of the manufacturing for that car as well, known as the Karman Ghia.[82]

Work organization. Two factors were central in the way that work organization was transformed during the transition to mass production in light manufacturing industry: the character of technology and the structure of the labor market.

The key features of technology within a mass-production system are dedication and automation. Dedication is in many ways the foundation stone of technological design in the mass production labor process as such. In order to maximize productivity, the division of labor in production is radically extended: work tasks are continuously broken up and simplified; complicated operations previously performed by hand are transformed into operations performed by machines. The desired outcome of this process of dividing and mechanizing labor, often achieved in the heyday of mass production in the 1960's, is a machine that performs a single operation with extreme efficiency. Special-purpose machine tools are the classic examples of this technology. Mostly custom made for use only in a specific production process, the machines perform the exact same operation, boring for example, on a continuous series of identical workpieces, such as engine castings.

At a basic level, automation in the automobile industry in the 1950s and 1960s was simply a series of dedicated machines linked together. A good example of this is the transfer line in which engine blocks, cam shafts, and other large-series items traverse a line of linked machine tools. They enter as pieces of virgin cast metal and exit as finished pieces. These forms of automation were implemented in a part of the production process, leaving the other parts to manual work (such as tool making or assembly) or to other automated processes.

The implementation of dedicated machinery and the subdivision of tasks tended to direct skilled labor away from the production line. Demand for skills was shifted into areas of indirect work, such as maintenance, electrical work, or tool making. Indeed, as the mass producers within the autarkic industrial order moved increasingly into the use of American "Fordist" methods, the percentage of skilled workers in their plants began to steadily decline, while that of semi- and unskilled workers increased dramatically.[83]

This can be seen, most classically, in the development at VW. In 1940 at Volkswagen, at a time when the implementation of mass production techniques had been only partially successful, skilled workers accounted for 38.7% of its work force. This was a very low percentage when compared to the rest of the then still highly specialized German automobile industry, where skilled labor accounted for 56.26% of the blue collar workforce.[84] But its was considerably *higher* than the 29% of the total workforce that Weltz, Schmidt, and Sass found in their sample of skilled workers in the motor vehicle industry at the beginning of the 1970s.[85]

Though the logic of this transformation of the labor market in West Germany was similar to that in many other advanced industrial nations in the postwar period, the German experience differed from the others in two ways. The most important point about the postwar decline in the proportion of skilled labor in German factories was that it occurred extremely gradually. Indeed, for most of the 1950s, the decline was hardly noticeable. Despite rapid growth and a consensus emphasizing the virtues of productivity and mass production methods, West German producers continued to hedge their commitments to radical rationalization, just as they had in the interwar period. More and more producers moved toward volume production, but they did so using general-purpose machinery and skilled labor.[86] Only as the political–economic situation in Europe and Germany became more certain, while growth and the cessation of the inflow of refugees from the East tightened the labor market, did firms' decisions about technology and the organization of work begin to change in the direction outlined above.[87]

The second peculiar characteristic about German workplaces in the era of mass production and European integration was that even when firms shifted seriously into using the new methods and technologies, the proportion of skilled labor in German factories still remained high relative to proportions in similar plants in other countries.[88] Part of this may be accounted for by the ease with which skilled workers were trained in Germany. The extensive vocational education system socialized the cost of training a skilled worker, and hence, at the margin, made it less costly to employ them.[89] But more importantly, German firms tended to pursue strategies in the market that emphasized higher relative product value. Product series, therefore, tended to be relatively smaller, even in volume production. Skilled workers were often employed more frequently, even if still in indirect areas, to ensure the quality and continuity of production.

The general shift toward automation and the use of semi- and unskilled labor within German light-manufacturing industries transpired in the space of a single decade (1957–1967) and followed a cost–benefit logic similar to the one at work in the specialization of plants. A preponderance of semi- and unskilled workers tending dedicated, often mechanically automated production processes afforded great gains in efficiency and productivity, but at the cost of flexibility.

Regional consequences: The general diffusion of a dual economy. The progressive commitment of autarkic firms to these rather inflexible forms of plant and work organization had important consequences for the development of the economic structure of the regions in which autarkic light-manufacturing plants were located. The increasingly large and rigid production units needed a way to

228 *Industrial constructions*

distribute risk away from themselves and gain some flexibility against swings in the business cycle. Their attempts to do this ultimately resulted in the emergence of a dualist industrial structure of core, technologically sophisticated large firms and a periphery of smaller, less technologically sophisticated firms.

Traditionally, autarkic volume producers achieved flexibility at the plant level through diversification. The employment of high proportions of highly skilled workers and general-purpose machinery allowed firms, such as Siemens, to respond to changes in demand with changes in product. Given such a strategy, moreover, the radical vertical integration that was typical of all autarkic producers made sense because it not only ensured continuous supplies of parts, but it also increased the range of possible combinations of men and machines the firm could group together when it needed to change. The use of subcontractors was unappealing to these old-style volume producers because they introduced undue complication into their planning. More important, independent subcontractors could not be controlled by the firm, so they could only be integrated with great difficulty into the internal process of productive recombination.

The exception to this rule, as you will recall from the discussion in Chapter 3, were the old impartible-inheritance-based *Gewerbelandschaft* regions, such as the one around Bielefeld.[90] There, as a quirk of the timing of 19th century reindustrialization, regional firms specialized in the production of standardized "American" products such as sewing machines, office equipment, and standardized, labor saving American machine tools (the latter mostly through licensing agreements with American firms). Using a less qualified labor force and American machine tools, these firms were more rigid than their larger autarkic cousins in Berlin or the Ruhr Valley. But they also found that they could compensate for their rigidity by subcontracting out work to smaller shops and homeworkers in the region. Out of this so-called *verlängerte Werkbank* (extended workbench) strategy, originally the spontaneous reaction of new industrial producers attempting to cope with unforseen rigidities in a foreign technology, gradually emerged a dual industrial structure. A secondary sector of less sophisticated producers provided relatively rigid core producers with a modicum of flexibility in their ability to respond to swings in the level of demand.

The postwar developments in plant and work organization described above had the effect of turning the old exception into the new rule. The shift to specialized plants and dedicated and automated machinery run by semi- and unskilled operators made postwar autarkic producers of high-volume light-manufacturing products very inflexible. To gain some flexibility, or more precisely, to deflect some of the risk that their rigidity exposed them to in the course of a business cycle, firms turned to subcontracting. The model they followed was that of the *verlängerte Werkbank*. Firms sought to target the growth of their production capacity to service, at most, the level of demand that existed at the bottom of the business cycle. The rest, all that existed during periods of upswing (allowing for a gradual rate of growth), was subcontracted out to small- and medium-sized firms.[91]

There are several interesting features of this "dualist" structure as it developed

Autarkic industrial order: 1945–1994

in the postwar context. One has to do with where the secondary sector firms were located. Another has to do with the technological sophistication of suppliers and a third has to do with the people who worked in these firms.

Autarkic mass producers would seek secondary producers wherever they could find them, but given the generally short-term nature of the relationship, the tendency was for the firm to look close to home.[92] For autarkic producers in regions such as Bielefeld that had once been impartible-inheritance-based *Gewerbelandschaften*, a substructure of small- and medium-sized job shops and industrial parts producers already had been created during the early years of the century. Firms moving into mass production in the postwar period, such as Grundig and AEG's consumer electronics plants in Nuremberg, the Siemens works, and MAN truck plants in Munich, the Audi works in Ingolstadt, and Magirus trucks in Ulm, among many others, found a preexisting base of potential suppliers that they could utilize when they wished.

Those mass producers located in areas that had no tradition of subcontracting whatsoever, such as former agricultural regions like the Ruhr Valley, for example, or the eastern Lower Saxon plain where the Volkswagen works was located, had to look outside of their regions for secondary sector suppliers. Either they turned to producers in regions such as those just described or they looked for suppliers in regions dominated by the decentralized form of industrial order.[93]

For example, regional studies of the relationship between the Ruhr and the regions surrounding it, such as the (decentralized) Berg Land and the (autarkic-agrarian) region of northwestern North Rhine Westphalia, show that economic interdependence between the regions increased substantially after World War II and especially in the 1960s. By 1971, approximately 20% of the output of the iron and steel industry in Remscheid alone went to Ruhr Valley users. In the Westmünsterland region of northwest North Rhine Westphalia, between 25% and 61% of the output of the iron and steel foundry industry, the metalworking industry,[94] the chemical and plastics industry, and the glass, wood, and cardboard industries went to the Ruhr.[95] In its postwar history of the Berg economy, the Chamber of Commerce for the Berg Land emphasizes the extreme cyclical sensitivity of output and employment in the region. It was much greater than that exhibited in the broader national economy. They explicitly attribute the exaggerated economic cycles that their region experiences to its character as a "classic" supplier region for volume producers in the Ruhr valley and elsewhere.[96]

Secondary sector firms within the emergent dualist structure, by and large, tended to be technologically unsophisticated and financially unstable. Most of the contracts that they engaged in with large firms were short-term, lasting only as long as the flow of orders into the large firm exceeded its capacity to produce. Secondary sector firms were always the first to feel the onset of recession and the last to experience a recovery. Not surprisingly, given these unstable conditions, it was difficult for the smaller producers to invest in new plant or equipment. The new technology may have been able to improve the competitiveness of the firm,

230 *Industrial constructions*

but the instability of the firm's market meant that it could never be confident that the machinery could be used efficiently or that the revenues of the company would be steady enough to allow it to service the debt needed to purchase the equipment in the first place. Those job shops and other suppliers that stayed in business usually did so by employing second hand, less efficient machinery.[97]

The irregular purchasing strategy of the large firms was not the only way in which their orientation to subcontractors worked to the latter's disadvantage. In many ways, it suited the larger firms to have technologically less sophisticated suppliers. The less know-how about the large firm's product the supplier had, the less of a threat the supplier posed. Most large firms performed all portions of the product design in-house on those parts they wished to subcontract and simply bid out the actual production. As the practices became more routine, firms began to make sure that they had several subcontractors always vying to win a contract for a given part. This tended to ensure that the cost of subcontracting remained low (competing firms would bid down the price) as well as that the competing supplier firms never made that much money from their work.

The combination of irregular work and low profit margins made secondary sector firms very unstable enterprises. The people who worked in these enterprises, consequently, tended to be those who had little power in the labor market. For example, in one region that had a high concentration of such supplier firms, the Sauerland in southern North Rhine Westphalia, the labor force had above-average numbers of women and migrant or "guest" workers. In 1961, 45.4% of all manufacturing workers in the Chamber of Commerce district of South Westphalia were women. Only other regions surrounding the Ruhr Valley, all from decentralized areas, had higher percentages of women in the manufacturing workforce: Solingen (51.2%), Remscheid (50.1%), Wuppertal (49.6%), and Mönchengladbach (49.5%).[98] Migrant workers (mostly Italians and Greeks) made up approximately 9% of the total Sauerland workforce by 1965. The average percentage in the Federal Republic as a whole that year was only 5.2%. Köllmann notes that over two-thirds of the guest workers in the Sauerland worked in the iron and metal working industries – a sector that was largely dependent upon short-term subcontracts with the automobile industry.[99]

These examples all show that though dualism and *verlängerte Werkbank* subcontracting constituted departures from the strict autarkic traditions of vertical integration, they were in no sense moves toward the creation of the kind of decentralized production systems that existed in the regions of the decentralized industrial order. The fragility and weakness of the secondary sector actors within these mass-production systems underscore the centrality of the core firm unit as the organizer of production. It was within the core firms that planning for production took place and where the bulk of actual production was located.

Governance: Concentration and centralization. Regarding the management of mass production in these rapidly growing light-manufacturing sectors, there were two general developments: one at the level of industries as a whole (industrial organization), and the other at the level of the individual producing firm.

At the level of industrial organization, the shift into mass production in these light-manufacturing markets involved the creation of oligopolistic market structures. In contrast to the previous steel industry case, however, the achievement of oligopoly in these newer markets involved an increase in levels of concentration rather than a decrease. In most cases, prior to the diffusion of mass production as a strategy, product markets in light-industrial sectors such as automobiles, consumer electronics and various machinery products tended on the whole to be relatively fragmented.[100] Indeed, as we saw in the case of Daimler-Benz in the previous chapter, very important parts of these industries were located in decentralized areas and were organized according to the principles of decentralized industrial order.

The diffusion of mass production as a strategy in these sectors militated against the reproduction of market fragmentation for the following reasons.[101] Because heavy investment in dedicated large-scale production equipment made any change in the production process difficult and expensive, firms acted strategically to eliminate potential change in their markets. Most often this meant either driving (mostly smaller) competitors out of business through underpricing, or merging them into one's own business. The ultimate effect of this dynamic was to intensify (or, if the producer was in a decentralized region such as was the case with Daimler-Benz, to create) the autarkic firm-dominated character of production. Producers found that the needed conditions could be best created and maintained by internalizing them, that is, by bringing them under the direct control of the firm itself.

Perhaps the most striking example of the connection between strategies of mass production and concentration is the automobile industry. The first three postwar decades for the West German industry were shaped by a logic that limited domestic competition to a select few major producers. This becomes dramatically clear when one compares the postwar industry with its prewar predecessor. In 1924, there was very little mass production in the German auto industry: 86 producers in the industry produced 126 different types of car. But, by 1949, after Nazi efforts to sponsor a mass-production-oriented automobile industry and Allied-led reconstruction, the top five producers in the industry accounted for over 80% of sales and produced a combined total of just eight different model types.[102] By 1953, the top three firms, VW, Opel, and Daimler-Benz, already accounted for 75% of total output, leaving the rest of the remainder to nine other firms. By the mid 1960s, there were only 5 major firms remaining: VW-Audi, Opel, Daimler-Benz, Ford, and BMW.[103] Mass producers Volkswagen and the two American-owned firms Opel and Ford had managed to eliminate the other domestic German competitors in mass-produced cars, while Daimler-Benz and BMW grew to dominate luxury car production. Similar tendencies toward concentration could be observed during the same period, for similar reasons, in machinery and electro-technical sectors undergoing a transition into mass production.[104]

The second characteristic development associated with the shift into mass production was the centralization of internal management structures within firms. Most commentators in the fifties and early sixties were agreed that the more firms engaged in volume production of standardized products, the more centralized the structure of command and authority had to become. Design and production planning were taken progressively away from the individual workshops and plants and consolidated in the higher level functional departments. Coordination from the top was considered necessary to ensure optimal production flow from design to final product.[105]

Data from Thanheiser's study of the 100 largest industrial corporations tends generally to confirm this centralizing dynamic: The three largest German automobile companies (VW, Daimler-Benz, and BMW) had functional or functional/holding management structures as late as 1970, as did many important postwar electro-technical mass producers, such as Grundig, Bauknecht, Osram, and Miele.[106] Other important producers, such as Siemens and AEG, moved by the mid 1960s toward the creation of multidivisional enterprises.[107] But these companies had very broadly diversified operations in an array of very different businesses (e.g., locomotives and toasters) that involved very different kinds of production (mass, batch, and single series) and substantively different markets (consumer and capital goods), which made a unitary management structure too unwieldy. In these cases the creation of a multidivisional structure allowed the firms to centralize control over their mass-production operations, while continuing to manage their batch and single series product lines in ways that very much resembled the managerial structures of large autarkic machinery companies.[108]

Case three: The post war autarkic machinery industry: Rule-proving exception

If the first case study was an example of radical change in the autarkic industrial order being imposed from outside, and the second was of the emergence of a new type of production among old and new producers, the third case study (on the development of autarkic machinery producers) is one of relative continuity with the practices of the past. As in the 19th century and in the interwar period, the autarkic machinery industry was during the years of the postwar economic miracle primarily a craft-production-oriented industry. The strategic and internal governance problems that preoccupied producers during the interwar period continued to preoccupy them in the 1950s and 60s: Large diversified autarkic machinery producers were continually attempting to achieve rational workshop organization and optimal horizontal strategies among their various product lines and operations. Moreover, as the economic miracle moved into the 1960s, large machinery firms also once again attempted to establish linkages to larger firms as a way to improve access to the capital markets. Two major changes occurred to alter, slightly, the character of this form of development during the boom years of the post-World War II period. One was at the level of production, the other in the area of administration.

Production. The major change in production has actually already been mentioned in the previous case: With the creation of conducive background conditions, many types of machinery producers were able to implement mass-production strategies. Very few machinery producers, however, were able to adopt extreme mass-production methods. Some engine and motor producers and producers of valves and armatures achieved quite large series sizes, while some other branches of the machinery industry were able to increase their series sizes: agricultural equipment and tractor producers (such as Xavier Fendt in the Bavarian Allgäu), construction machinery producers (such as O&K of Dortmund), and certain producers of gears and power drives (such as Friedrich Flender of Bocholt). To the extent that firms in these sectors adopted large-series production strategies, the principles of organization governing production in these firms began to resemble those of mass producers in other sectors: specialization of plants, lowering of general skill levels in direct production, *verlängerte Werkbank*, increasing concentration in the industrial branch, and centralization of management structures so that design and development were increasingly separated from production.[109]

As the previous chapter on the decentralized industrial order pointed out, however, most producers in the machinery industry did not move in this direction. This was true of producers in autarkic regions just as it was of those in decentralized regions.[110] By as late as 1977, a little less than a third of West German machinery producers were engaged in large-series volume production. In many cases, firms were still producing highly customized or extremely small batch items: in 1977 at the very large MAN diesel engine and printing machinery works in the autarkic Bavarian region of Augsburg, for example, the average series size of products was five.[111]

The explanation for the persistence of craft production in capital goods sectors such as the machinery industry is by now very clear: The growth of mass production in an economy structures demand within the machinery industry in a way that discourages larger-series production. Mass producers demand special purpose and single purpose machines that cannot themselves be mass produced. If one follows the growth of productivity rates in the West German economy during the 1950s, the shift to mass production and its affect on the machinery sector can be readily seen. According to Hans Baumann's calculations, productivity in the machinery industry grew at about the average rate of West German industry as a whole, until 1958. After that year, the first full year of the Common Market, productivity growth in the machinery industry fell behind that of industry as a whole, especially consumer goods industries.[112] As the rest of the economy increased its productivity through the implementation of mass-production techniques, the machinery industry's rate of productivity fell way below the average of industry, because they were unable to produce machines in series themselves.[113]

Changes in governance. Because large autarkic machinery producers did not, on the whole, have to radically redefine their production strategies during the postwar period, there were few new problems regarding the governance of production during the first 20 years of the Federal Republic that gave rise to efforts to restructure the internal governance structures of machinery enterprises. Demag, MAN, Henschel, Krupp's engineering works in Essen, and most of the other very large autarkic machinery producers were structured in ways that were virtually identical to their prewar organizational forms.

A major impetus for change in the structure of these companies did not come until the 1960s, when large autarkic machinery enterprises began to become heavily indebted. Much of the indebtedness in the autarkic machinery industry was the result of special problems relating to the production of very expensive, large-scale engineering projects. The time between when an order is taken in by the firm and the delivery of a finished product can be extremely long, often more than two years. This time delay creates a cash flow problem for firms, which they must solve either by negotiating specific, graduated payment schedules with their customers or by incurring debt.[114]

West German machinery producers were able to receive graduated payments on most domestic sales and even in their broader European business. It was overseas work that was extremely expensive. During the years of reconstruction, before the formation of the Common Market, the lack of significant business in the developing world was not a problem because adequate demand existed in Europe. But, as time progressed, the main markets for the kinds of heavy engineering plant and equipment that many large autarkic German machinery producers made, such as steel mills and cement making plants, were increasingly located in the developing world. There buyers often had little capital and could not pay on a graduated schedule. West German firms had to carry increasing amounts of debt to compete in these markets.[115]

To a some extent, the growing indebtedness of the machinery firms was the result of the West German government's reluctance to subsidize their firms' expansion into markets outside of Europe by granting the purchasing country export credits. For much of the 1950s and 1960s, large machinery producers aggressively lobbied the West German government to assist them by subsidizing their export business by granting credits for large plant projects. Until the first oil crisis in 1973, the government consistently refused to get involved in this despite ample precedent of such practices by other governments in the advanced industrial world.[116]

Firms dealt with their growing indebtedness by attempting to create or gain access to more capital. The case of Demag is paradigmatic. In 1964, one report placed the company's debt coefficient, the total external debt capital as a percentage of net worth (*Eigenkapital*), at 158%. Another measure showed that its debt constituted 78% of total sales in 1964.[117] In an effort to improve its ability to generate investment capital internally, the firm converted itself into a multidivisional company with the help of the consulting firm, McKinsey. Far from helping, this move actually created a whole host of new problems for the firm. The divisional structure made it difficult for the firm to manage its strategy of horizontal diversification, which depended upon systematic and continuous interrelations between the various products and workshops.[118] By 1973, the firm, which at the time was one of the largest machinery producers in West Germany, sold itself to

Mannesmann in an effort to improve its ability to raise capital in international markets.[119] At the same time, it began to move away from and modify its multidivisional structure to enhance the process of internal coordination.

Although marriages between steel producers and large autarkic machinery producers received a great deal of attention at the time and are interesting because they evoke memories of the old *Konzerne* structures from the prewar period, the substantive tie between steel and machinery was less important to the large machinery producers than was the financial tie. At least at first, these large mergers were not efforts to recreate *Konzerne*. They were attempts to spread risk (on the part of the steel producers) and attain financial viability (for the machinery producers).

For this reason, it is not surprising that mergers between large-scale machinery producers and steel enterprises were only one of a variety of large-scale combinations that began to take place at this time within the machinery industry. Large machinery producers were bought out by or entered into joint ventures with large autarkic corporations from the electro-technical, automobile, chemical, and other machinery branches as well. Like the Demag-Mannesmann merger, most did not result in the liquidation of the machinery company as an independent enterprise, nor did they, at least immediately, significantly restrict the operating autonomy of the machinery enterprise. This process of constructing interwoven corporate and financial relations in the industry, which began picking up speed in the late 1960s, progressed to the point where, by the middle on the 1980s, of the 58 largest joint stock companies within the German machinery industry, 45 belonged to larger conglomerate enterprises.[120]

We will see below that this movement toward the creation of very large, highly diversified and densely interwoven autarkic enterprises did not remain a simple financial portfolio diversification strategy for long. In the technologically turbulent world market environment of the 1980s and 1990s, these large enterprises attempted to foster collaboration and technology transfer and diffusion among their member operations: Such efforts began to create governance strategies within these enterprises, which strongly recalled the kind of internal governance strategies developed within the interwar *Konzerne*. But, although this became the strategy firms pursued during the 1980s, it was not the logic that gave rise to the initial diversification moves in the early 1970s.

Crisis and transformation: Autarky since the mid-1970s

The previous chapter outlined in some detail the changes that took place beginning in the 1970s in European and international markets that transformed the conditions under which firms in all industries competed. The argument presented there was, in short, that the development of industrial economies in Europe, the Pacific Rim, and Latin America during the postwar economic boom yielded a fundamental recalibration of relations among national economies on a world scale. This gave rise to intensified competition between producers, and accelerated product and technological change in virtually all industrial sectors. World (and European) industrial markets became increasingly fragmented and volatile while the costs of technological development increased enormously. Mass production, according to the principles of organization that developed during the 1950s and 1960s, proved to be no longer possible under the new conditions.[121]

German autarkic producers, generally, had great difficulty adjusting to this transformation of the world market environment.[122] Responses can be divided into two broad categories: absolute decline (e.g., steel, shipbuilding, coal mining, etc.) and halting, partial adjustment plagued by chronic self-blockage. The second category includes many producers and sectors (e.g., most of light manufacturing and machinery) and has been far more typical of the German large autarkic firm experience than the first.

Absolute decline in the new environment

The steel industry serves as a good example of absolute decline and its experience can be outlined very briefly.[123] Growth of sophisticated producers in the rest of Europe and in developing markets (including Japan) during the 1960s and 1970s combined with a gradual shift away from the industry's core product to the use of substitutes (e.g., plastic and aluminum) to produce intense and increasingly fragmented world market competition as well as dramatic levels of world-wide overcapacity. Since the mid 1970s, this industry has been engaged in an industrial politics of strategic shrinkage, often guided by political authorities at national and international levels. In this process, the need to develop more sophisticated products that can be produced more flexibly has been balanced, and sometimes overwhelmed, by the need to absolutely reduce the size and scale of operations in the industry.[124]

Inevitably, as a result of all of this, the number of producers in the steel industry has consistently and unremittingly dwindled, as has the number of workers employed (see Table 11). Whole plants were closed down, some of which had had very long and proud histories, such as the Krupp steel works in Rheinhausen or many of the Hoesch facilities in Dortmund.[125] The decline of this industry and the regions that it dominates was so inexorable and enduring that they came to be synonymous with industrial decay in the public discourse of the Federal Republic during much of the 1980s.[126] After over a century of being at the center of the German collective imagination regarding industrial power in the economy and society, the Ruhr steel industry ironically came to be understood as something it actually always was: a regionally embedded industry.

Halting adjustment plagued by self-blockage

The second type of large autarkic firm adjustment was less devastating than in industries such as steel, though it has been nevertheless still extremely difficult

Table 11 *Steel manufacturing enterprises in West Germany, 1962–1984*

1962	1985	1994
Thyssen-Phoenix	ARBED Saarstahl	Krupp
Krupp	Hoesch	Klöckner
Hüttenunion	Klöckner	Thyssen
Klöckner	Krupp	Preuss AG
Mannesmann	Mannesmann	Mannesmann
Hoesch	Peine Salzgitter	
Gutehoffnungshütte	Thyssen	
Salzgitter		
Rheinstahl		
Röchling		
Otto Wolf		
Flick		
Ilseder Hütte		

Data from 1962 and 1985 taken from Eckart, K., *Die Eisen- und Stahlindustrie in den beiden deutschen Staaten* (1988), pp. 254 and 257; data from 1994 taken from Directory of Corporate Affiliations, Vol. 6 (1994).

for the producers involved and, as the 1980s have given way to the 1990s, the situation seems only to have gotten worse. Rather than the dual problems of overcapacity on the one hand and competition-driven technological change and market fragmentation on the other, producers in a broad array of sectors (virtually all of the light-manufacturing sectors discussed in the previous section as well as the machinery industry) were confronted only by the latter set of conditions. Internationally, as we saw in the chapter on the decentralized industrial order, producers reacted to the onset of these conditions by attempting to recompose the internal structure of firms and to decentralize both production and its administration away from the boundaries of the firm.

Even more than their large-firm cousins in the decentralized industrial order, however, large firms in the traditionally autarkic regions found it extremely difficult to reform their organizations in this way. Whereas producers in the decentralized industrial order were blocked in their efforts to implement *internal* reforms, they at least had some success in decentralizing production away from the boundaries of the firm. Indeed, one could argue that this was an important factor in the success of those regions during the 1980s. Autarkic producers, however, found it difficult even to do this: Their efforts both internally and externally were nearly always halting, partial, and riddled by debilitating compromises. Most of the obstacles to successful adjustment among autarkic firms involved the strongly firm-centered institutional forms of governance in production that had been traditionally definitive of the autarkic industrial order and which the reforms of the postwar period had reinforced.

238 *Industrial constructions*

The logic of internal reform and decentralization

In order to appreciate how it was difficult for autarkic firms to adjust, it is important to recall from the previous chapter the general logic that led firms to embark on projects of internal reform and the decentralization of production in the first place. The key initial catalyst for reform, not just among autarkic German enterprises but among large corporate firms throughout the advanced industrial world, was the realization that the principles of centralization that had been so successful within the framework of a strategy of mass production were simply too rigid and cumbersome to accommodate the constant change that the new environment made necessary. This was particularly true regarding the bureaucratic tendency to separate product development and design from its actual production. In the new environment, products had to be brought to market much more rapidly than had been the case in the 1950s and 1960s and that meant that decisions about what to make could not be easily separated from decisions about how to make it.[127]

Efforts to rectify this problem, as we saw earlier, occurred on two fronts simultaneously: The first involving relations inside the firm, the second involving relations between the firm and outsiders. To foster greater flexibility and communication within operating units and among departments in charge of them, large companies throughout the world attempted to devolve responsibility for the development and production of products downwards within their organizations, closer to the plants and workplaces where the products were actually produced. This involved two sets of changes. First, many production units in this way gradually were converted into autonomous profit centers, and exposed more directly to market pressures. By creating more local freedom and responsibility within the corporation, i.e., *internal decentralization*, the hope was that the overall flexibility of the company would be enhanced and risk taking and innovation stimulated. Second, in an effort to accelerate the time between development and production of new products, functional divisions within operating units (e.g., production, development, purchasing, etc.) were broken down and dissolved into multifunctional teams. Internal decentralization and internal recomposition both aimed at the reintegration of conception and execution throughout the industrial organizations, exactly reversing the trend of development initiated by the diffusion of mass production in the previous period.[128]

As important and disruptive as this kind of internal recomposition could be within large corporations, the truly challenging dimension implicit within the logic of reform proved to be that, once embraced, it was difficult to keep the process contained within the boundaries of the newly autonomous operating units. In a competitive environment where technology and products were changing rapidly and the costs of development increasing, many firms (or newly established profit centers) invariably found that they simply could not afford the level of internal investment in training and technology required to keep pace with new developments, particularly if those developments were taking place on a number of new technological fronts simultaneously (such as in plastics and microelectronics in automobile production). In such a situation, it proved to be more practical to draw on the expertise of outsiders who already had the kinds of skills and knowledge that the firm desired.[129]

Indeed, by engaging in collaboration, rather than attempting to continue to control all production or development in-house, it was possible to lower the level of relatively fixed and rigid investments inside the firm and thereby create a hedge against unforeseeable product or technological changes. Moreover, collaborative subcontracting also made it possible to reduce the size of inventories. This cut costs substantially and encouraged continuous improvement in the production process. Because there were no inventory buffers, production teams had to constantly monitor the flow and organization of the production process itself, yielding a dynamic of self-reflexivity that contributed to continuous learning and improvement. Ultimately, the significance of collaborative subcontracting lay in the fact that through collaboration, the design of the product and the design and location of its production occurred simultaneously and in the context of extremely intimate contact among all the parties. This kind of collaborative, external, decentralization promised to provide producers who were able to achieve it with tremendous flexibility. In conjunction with the recomposition of departmental relations and internal decentralization within the firm, external decentralization increased the quickness with which firms could respond to opportunities or unforseen changes in the market or technology while at the same time spreading the costs of development and adjustment away from the firm.

Adjustment in the autarkic industrial order

This dynamic of recomposition and decentralization, driven by the desire for greater flexibility, has been presented here in ideal typical form as a single interconnected logic. As we saw in the previous chapter, producers within the decentralized industrial order had considerable success with external decentralization but foundered on the problem of internal recomposition through the resistance of defenders of departmental and skill-based jurisdictions. These internal problems also plagued the autarkic producers. But, unlike the decentralized producers, autarkic producers also had difficulty in decentralizing production away from the boundaries of the firm. Thus, in the majority of cases, external pressures to reform the autarkic enterprise to make it more flexible made only a weak impact on the traditional structure of the industrial order. Both internal recomposition and external decentralization were either completely blocked or rendered incomplete and ineffective through compromise. Much of the reason for this stemmed from institutional and political rigidities, inside firms and within the regions in which they were located, which had been produced by the traditional autarkic commitment to extreme vertical integration and firm-based governance.

Such traditional commitments constrained autarkic firms in two fundamental ways. First, the very longstanding historical practice of vertical integration prevented an infrastructure of small- and medium-sized specialist supplier firms from emerging in autarkic regions who could serve as a source of potential collaboration and, more importantly, who could possibly absorb some of the workers and managers released from the home firm in the wake of reform and decentralization. In cases where relations with subcontractors did exist, they tended to be of a very poor and distant character: the *verlängerte Werkbank*, secondary producers who, moreover, in many cases were located outside the immediate region in nearby decentralized regions.[130] Given the underdevelopment of alternative employment opportunities in the regions in which large autarkic firms were located, it was very easy for those employed within firms in such locations, both in labor and in management, to view decentralization as a threat to their livelihood and provide resistance to it.

Second, the idea that the firm was the primary unit for the organization of production in the economy was very entrenched in the self-understandings of both managers and workers within the firm. Plant managers, development engineers and many other managers took for granted the idea that the competitiveness of the firm depended, as it traditionally had, upon their capacity to develop and produce as much of the product as possible.[131] For their part, workers and their representatives could not conceive of their own representative institutions as having a place within a more decentralized, less firm-centered system of production. They therefore viewed decentralization as a potential threat to the viability of the hard-won traditions of codetermination in the Federal Republic.[132]

The existence of such obstacles to institutional reform within large-scale autarkic enterprises goes a long way to explain why these companies enjoyed the upswing of the 1980s much less spectacularly than their cousins in the decentralized industrial order and why they suffered so deeply when the boom turned to bust in the mid-1990s. The rest of this chapter will present three case studies that illustrate the range of outcomes that struggles with these self-generated obstacles produced among large autarkic firms during the 1980s and early 1990s. The first case shows how variation on the above two variables could have significant consequences for the extent of and character of internal reform and decentralization actually achieved. It compares the very extensive recomposition and decentralization strategy implemented by the BMW AG company with a case of blocked reform and decentralization at Volkswagen AG. The other two cases describe distinctly different alternative efforts to compensate for or circumvent the obstacles to effective reform and decentralization outlined above. In all three of these cases, it will be made clear that the institutional legacy of the autarkic industrial order decisively shaped not only the outcomes that one observes, but the process of adjustment and the strategies of actors as well.

Case 1: BMW as decentralized systems integrator versus VW as blocked system integrator. BMW AG is one of the few successful cases of radical internal reform combined with extensive external decentralization among large German autarkic producers – indeed, within the entire German industrial economy. Its success is untypical because of a number of peculiarities surrounding BMW as a company and Munich as a region, which cannot be generalized across other autarkic companies and regions (or decentralized ones). It is useful to look at the case both because it provides an example of successful adjustment by an autarkic German company and because it makes a useful contrast to the more typical, less successful, case of Volkswagen. The comparison will show that BMW is the exception that proves the rule.

BMW produces sports and luxury cars and is located in the autarkic region of Bavaria. Its main production facilities are located in and around Munich, but it also has plants in northern Bavaria (Regensburg) and just across the southern Bavarian border in Austria (Steyr). The company was originally a major producer of aircraft engines and was a major beneficiary of the Nazi effort to build the world's most technologically superior airforce. Although it had produced automobiles in small- and medium-sized volumes as early as the 1920s, the company turned more seriously to automobile production only after the war when its aircraft engine business was dismantled. During the 1950s, the company attempted to compete in both the low-end mass automobile market and in luxury car markets. BMW was moderately successful at this, but it was also much smaller than the larger and aggressively expanding mass producers such as Volkswagen, Opel, Ford and Daimler-Benz. By the 1960s the brutal logic of mass-production competition put the firm on the verge of bankruptcy. It saved itself (with the arms-length aid of the Bavarian government) by shifting into the production of high performance and luxury cars exclusively and positioning itself as a sporty alternative to Daimler-Benz. It performed extremely well during the 1970s and into the early 1980s with this strategy.[133]

By the beginning of the 1980s, however, the company was beginning to feel the effects of competitive pressures that the higher-volume, low-end (mass) producers had been feeling since the middle of the 1970s. Japanese and then South Korean competition in the mass car markets lead mass producers in Europe to move up-market and compete directly with BMW's products. By the end of the 1980s, the Japanese had entered the important luxury car market in the United States and were threatening to enter European luxury car markets directly. Such developments steadily intensified pressure to shorten the firm's product cycle. At the same time, new technologies, in microelectronics, plastics, and ceramics, for example, were forcing the company to spend much more money than it ever had on product development and in technological areas that had very little to do with the traditional strengths of an automobile producer.[134]

BMW's response to these pressures was to radically recompose its internal organization and decentralize production through the establishment of extensive collaborative relations with outside firms. Over the course of the 1980s, the company increasingly redefined the automobile as a system of subsystems (modules) and its role as manufacturer as one of "systems integrator." In so doing, the company began to radically redefine the boundaries of the autarkic firm.[135]

Figures on vertical integration vary considerably, even when the same standard of measure appears to be used. But by the beginning of the 1990s, it was clear that somewhere between 55–75% of the total production costs at BMW came from outsourced parts.[136] People in purchasing at that time claimed that over 80% of the parts purchased involved important collaborative work with a specialist subcontractor that supplied BMW with know-how and design. No single part or module of their automobile was considered to be, in principle, inappropriate for outsourcing. Workshops in BMW's plants were made increasingly autonomous and obligated to prove their production efficiency according to market standards.

Growing emphasis on collaboration turned in-house manufacturing at BMW increasingly into a strategic learning process. Manufacturing was seen less as a source of value added than as a way of exploring the boundaries of new technologies or of maintaining the capacity to evaluate and encourage the efforts of suppliers investigating areas not covered by the assembler's direct expertise. Without this practical know-how across a range of development and production areas, it was believed the firm would be incapable of directing to its own ends the inflows of know-how and information that it was continuously receiving. At the same time, mastery of specific technologies and manufacturing processes allowed the firm to avoid its worst fear: becoming dependent on its suppliers. The idea was to establish a system in which the firm continuously learned from its suppliers without becoming intolerably vulnerable to them.

These shifts in the firm's relation to production were accompanied by corresponding changes in corporate organization. Distinct but overlapping institutions within the firm were erected, in part through the recomposition of old departments, to act as a scanning system capable of continuously identifying and deploying new technologies and appropriate suppliers according to shifts in market tastes and technical possibilities. For example, at the end of the 1980s, a new committee, known as the *Bezugsartenkreis*, was formed that brought representatives of engineering, purchasing and controlling (finance/accounting) departments together to facilitate systematic discussion of issues concerning product development and the location of production inside or outside the firm. In the early 1990s, production was added to this group of interlocutors and the committee was transformed into an integrated department in its own right, under the direct supervision of the top managing board. By incorporating production design into discussions of product development and location, the company hoped to ensure that the development and production of new cars would occur simultaneously.[137]

Additionally, at the end of the 1980s, the company created three subsidiaries that concentrated on specialized or technologically advanced forms of motor vehicle development and production: the BMW Motor Sport Group (ZS Motorsport GmbH), the Advanced Engineering Design Group (ZT Technik GmbH), and the Motorcycle Group (ZX). Each of these subsidiaries, especially the first two, concentrated on pushing the boundaries of motor vehicle engineering and design through extensive exchange, experimentation, and collaboration with outsiders.[138] The idea was to push innovation within the firm by opening the company to the full landscape of auto-related technological developments. Finally, toward the same end, the firm engaged systematically in joint ventures or participated financially in companies with its own venture capital fund. Four areas were regarded with special interest: new production materials, new production technologies (participation with Cecigram in France), electronics (participation in Leowe Opta), and venture capital participations in companies doing mostly basic research in a variety of fields.

The effects of this new more porous and internally and externally collaborative system on the performance and organizational identity of BMW have been remarkable. Output of automobiles increased between 1984 to 1992 from approximately 350,000 cars to nearly 600,000, while sales increased during the same time period from slightly more than DM9 billion to DM31.2 billion – all with steadily increasing profitability.[139] Above all, the new structure made possible radical reductions in development time. The first indication that the reforms were bearing fruit came with the introduction of the Z1 sports car in the late 1980s. Construction of this car was an experimental effort to shorten the eight-year model-development cycle that the company carried throughout the 1980s. The new engineering subsidiary, ZT Technik GmbH, did the engineering for the new car and BMW subcontracted out modules worldwide to firms that did the final design and development of the automobile. Within two years, the company was producing a limited edition of the car at the rate of roughly 17 units per day. The company required another two years before the car could be produced in series. On the whole, the project did much to demonstrate that with the new system BMW could potentially reduce development times to the range – 43 months – previously attained exclusively by world-leading Japanese producers.

The implementation of this strategy within BMW has not occurred without conflict. On the contrary, the new strategy gave rise to a series of conflicts regarding the role of manufacturing in the company among the various departments, divisions, and plants.[140] There was, for example, a long dispute between managers in purchasing and engineering about whether to stop producing cylinder heads for all BMW automobiles in-house. At the end of the 1980s, the decision was to keep production inside because BMW did not want to transfer a crucial proprietary casting technology to a supplier. But all parties at that time agreed that it was unwise to conclude from this that the question of the location of cylinder head production would not be raised again in the future. Conflicts of this nature, between different factions of management and between management and labor, with outcomes favoring both sides, were (and are) legion within BMW.

Nevertheless, up to the beginning of the 1990s, BMW had a great deal of success working through such conflicts when they arose and resolving them in favor of internal reform and decentralization. The reasons for this had much to do with very strong peculiarities in the situation of BMW AG. For one, the conservative Bavarian, predominantly catholic labor force and the company's works councilors traditionally have gone to great lengths to avoid conflict and accommodate the actions of management. Second, the company's Bavarian and Austrian locations, though dominated by the autarkic industrial order, were close to dynamic decentralized industrial districts in Baden Württemberg and northern Switzerland with strong metalworking, electronics, and automobile-component sectors. Moreover, the area around Munich itself had a diversified economy with many other large autarkic firms (e.g., Siemens, MBB, Deckel, and Krauss Maffei). There were, moreover, many newer, smaller firms in a thriving software and high-tech industry, the growth of which was largely stimulated by Government efforts to cultivate a defense industry in the region.[141] These factors not only provided the possibility of employment for workers (and managers) released from BMW, they also provided relatively easy access to sophisticated potential collaborators. All of this made relatively easy the internal politics and raw logistics of shifting production to the outside, locating potential suppliers, and setting up collaborative relations.

Third, BMW was, with the exception of Porsche, smaller than any of the other major auto producers in West Germany. Moreover, it was primarily family owned and therefore fairly immune to the threat of takeover. These latter characteristics, particularly when combined with the first two, in many ways forced the company to pursue the strategy of radical internal reform and decentralization. Unlike larger, more broadly held companies, BMW had few other alternatives open to it through which it could insulate itself from the turbulence on the market and the challenge of highly efficient and flexible international competitors.

Diversified quality production: Blocked decentralization at VW. A more typical case among large autarkic producers was the experience of Volkswagen AG, where the favorable peculiarities of BMW's situation were absent. Confronted with broadly similar – indeed perhaps even more intense – competition, VW consistently found that its efforts to push internal reform and shift toward decentralization were blocked by the institutional and power relations that its traditional autarkic location and practices had brought into being. External decentralization was made virtually impossible, whereas political compromises within the firm yielded distorted and inefficient forms of internal decentralization.

Disadvantageous institutional and political relations at VW can be traced back to the firm's location and its traditional vertically integrated structure. Five of VW's six major production complexes, Wolfsburg, Hannover, Braunschweig, Salzgitter, and Emden, are located in classically autarkic regions in Lower Saxony. The outlier plant is the large VW works in Kassel in autarkic northern Hessen. Emden, Wolfsburg, and Salzgitter are surrounded by agricultural economies, while Hannover, Braunschweig, and Kassel are old court cities in primarily rural regions. Volkswagen began to experience the limits of its own mass-production strategy as early as the middle of the 1970s, but a dramatic move toward decentralization and outsourcing proved to be unworkable in the mono-structural regions in which the company's plants were located. It was plain that such moves by the extremely vertically integrated company inevitably would have resulted in very high levels of unemployment in those regions. And, given the partial ownership of the firm by the government of Lower Saxony as well as a Social Democratic government in power at the national level during the 1970s, the company feared antagonizing its large and powerful works councils.

Logically enough, given their position, the works councils at VW, as well as the metalworkers union IG Metall, exploited the company's contextual disadvantages for short-term gains for their constituents. A number of agreements were struck with IG Metall at Volkswagen in the late 1970s and reinforced throughout the 1980s that exchanged continued employment in the firm (a de facto limit on external decentralization) for a relatively free hand for management to enhance the flexibility of its in-house production facilities.[142] In most cases, these agreements had the explicit support of functional departmental managers other than purchasing and plant-level managers. The latter had a number of reasons for opposing outsourcing and encouraging relatively narrow workplace-level reform in-house: Outsourcing could make their departments, and their jobs, redundant, whereas a relatively narrow focus on the level of the in-house production process diverted reform attention away from rigidities in the structure of management itself.

Most of the attention in the literature on industrial relations in the late 1980s regarding these developments focused on the extensive workplace cooperation between labor and management that these agreements fostered and on the flexibility in shopfloor production that such cooperation made possible.[143] Such arrangements were important in avoiding significant conflict at VW and enabled the company to make important strides in the modernization of its own production technology. Although VW had great difficulty competing directly with the Japanese and was forced to withdraw from the extremely competitive North American market, these changes did help the company maintain its position relative to other continental producers on the European market during much of the 1980s. Impressed by this local success, many commentators, most notably Wolfgang Streeck, described the compromise-driven orientation toward production at VW as an explicit strategy, known as "diversified quality production." In Streeck's view, the success of the company after these compromises showed that more radical decentralization of production or internal reform was not necessary: the rigid mass-production process of the 1950s and 1960s could be modified and made more flexible through greater workplace cooperation and flexibility.[144]

Whether or not this was ever a conscious strategy on the part of VW managers, Streeck's conception of a kind of flexible vertical integration through workplace cooperation was never uncontested.[145] Even as the company was agreeing to the compromises with labor over employment, reform interests within management, in a variety of departments, especially purchasing, were pushing investments in new plant and equipment that would make it possible to implement Japanese production techniques and thereby forced the internal organizational reforms as well as increasing external collaborative decentralization described above onto the operating units. As the decade of the 1980s wore on, it became increasingly clear that, rather than a stable equilibrium of flexible vertical integration, Volkswagen was deploying self-contradictory labor and plant investment and logistical strategies that were resulting not only in conflict but in very cumbersome and increasingly inefficient automobile production.

Take, for example, the experience at the Passat assembly plant in Emden, in the Ostfriesland region of Lower Saxony. The region surrounding the plant has an economic structure similar to the Wolfsburg region. At the Passat plant, the company constructed what at the time (the end of the 1980s) was likely the most flexible and highly automated modular chassis-assembly system in the world. The automated assembly process was designed to be able to receive an almost infinite variety of completed modules from outside suppliers for just-in-time assembly. With the implementation of this technology, the company intended to gradually make the Emden plant more autonomous. Ultimately, the idea was that with greater local decision-making power and responsibility the plant would be able to utilize its closeness to the end-user market and the open generality of the technology to select a palette of suppliers that would make extremely rapid reaction to customer desires possible.

In order to implement the technology, however, VW was forced to modify the larger organizational reform strategy that the technology was part of. First, VW agreed with the works council in Emden that jobs lost through the erection of the new flexible automated assembly machinery in the plant would be replaced by shifting production from other VW plants into Emden. The result was that the Passat chassis was constructed completely out of subsystems or modules, as the company had originally intended, but not from modules produced and delivered by outside suppliers. Instead, the agreement with the works council provided that the modules be constructed in-house in the Emden plant, largely from parts and materials made elsewhere within VW. And, because the company was bound to use its own intracorporate suppliers, it could not implement more efficient organizational reforms, such as low-inventory production and target pricing based parts and subassembly supply. Such reforms would have required suppliers, either inside or outside the corporation, whose production techniques were themselves disciplined by competition from other producers – something the compromise agreement made impossible.

The conflicts that resulted in such compromises not only had the effect of blocking the decentralization of production; they inhibited internal reform and recomposition as well. This was true, moreover, at the level of the entire VW concern as well as the local operating unit. For example, the disputes between the works council and plant managers at the Emden plant over the company's desire to close down its in-house seat production and purchase seat modules from the seat specialist, Keiper Recaro, was so intense at the end of the 1980s that the works council ultimately declared that it was impossible to bargain further with the plant management in good faith. Top VW management in Wolfsburg was forced to withdraw the management at the plant and, as a consequence, sabotage its own efforts to create greater operating unit (plant) autonomy. Instead of creating an operating unit that was closer to the customer and flexible enough to innovate in product design and optimize production flow on its own in collaboration with subcontractors, the Emden plant, despite energetic efforts to the contrary, remained much like a traditional, rigid, VW plant: It was controlled by the central concern and supplied by internal VW suppliers.

Thus unlike BMW, which confronted a more accommodating labor force and was closer to more robust regional labor and supplier markets in decentralized areas, VW during the late 1980s and early 1990s was blocked from pursuing an effective strategy of external decentralization and internal reform. The suboptimality of the vertical integration and centralization-preserving compromise solutions that the company was producing in its plants emerged at first very gradually. For example, Streeck himself noted, in passing, that in the late 1980s, VWs efforts to expand the number of models it produced had made production so complex that the internal cooperative production system was proving unable to maintain manufacturing quality.[146] By the early 1990s, however, it became clear that these (and other) apparent anomalies in the vertically integrated and centralized system of diversified quality production were in fact far from passing; they had thrown the company into crisis.

In each of the initial years of the early 1990s, the company revealed that its production costs were so high and inefficient that despite increases in the volume of sales, it was registering operating losses in the neighborhood of 700 million marks per year.[147] Moreover, it was clear that the internal paralysis over decentralization within the company had caused it to fall alarmingly behind its most advanced competitors. One internal VW estimate showed that it cost VW 5,000 marks more per automobile to produce the Golf in Wolfsburg than it cost Nissan, using very extensive decentralization in its transplants in Sunderland, England, to produce its competing model, the Primera.[148]

VW has responded to this turn of events in a very dramatic way. Its top management has been completely turned over and the new management has been charged with the tasks of radically reducing the level of vertical integration throughout the company, improving ties with suppliers, and reorganizing the internal organization of the departments and operating units of the enterprise – all in order to reduce production costs and accelerate product-development cycles. Estimates of the lay-offs likely to be entailed by these very belated changes have ranged as high as 100,000 for the entire company, worldwide. The numbers, moreover, include both production workers as well as middle management – the two biggest beneficiaries of the rationalization agreements of the previous decade. It remains to be seen, and many believe that the company's future hangs in the balance, whether or not VW will be able to overcome the traditional obstacles to the reorganization of production along decentralized lines. An agreement to radically reduce worktime at the company in order to save employment in December of 1993, struck as this manuscript was being completed, is an indication that the traditional obstacles of autarkic order continue to be extremely salient at the company.[149]

Case 2: Return to *Konzerne* structures. The difficulties in achieving effective internal reform and decentralization in production observable at VW were familiar to many within the community of large-scale autarkic enterprises in Germany during the 1980s and early 1990s. This was especially true of those autarkic enterprises located in traditionally autarkic regions, where the population of potential local collaborators was typically very small, and the traditional prestige and power of local large-scale production management and works councils very great. In the face of such constraints, many very large autarkic firms tried to cope with the intensified competition and rapid technological and product change that they encountered in the market in a way that attempted to circumvent pressures for external decentralization in production at the level of operating units through the erection of compensating internal reforms at the level of corporate structure. They did this in a way that followed an organizational logic strikingly reminiscent of the *Konzerne* strategy from the interwar period: Instead of drawing on experience and spreading risk across producers in a region, large autarkic enterprises attempted to create the diversity, dynamism and risk spreading of external decentralization within the confines of large, internally decentralized holding companies.

For the most part, the firms that embarked upon this kind of project were those that had already traveled down the road of extensive diversification, but for other reasons. The best examples are the large steel companies. As we saw earlier, these firms reacted to the shrinkage of their main business by diversifying into other business areas, especially in the machinery industry. Though, initially, such moves primarily represented efforts to spread financial risk and earnings across a more robust portfolio, the relationship between the mother steel companies and their new subsidiaries soon became more involved than that. At the end of the 1970s, the explosive diffusion of microelectronic applications to traditional machinery, driven above all by aggressive Japanese producers, blindsided large German machinery producers. They needed quick access to the new technology, but had neither the capital nor the internal know-how to develop and apply the technology themselves. Driven largely by the need to save their investments, the holding companies of these firms were forced to come to the aid of their subsidiaries.[150]

Firms such as Mannesmann, Thyssen, and Krupp established (or upgraded) research institutes at the level of the holding company, which they then encouraged to get involved in national and international research projects in new areas of microelectronics technology and software. Such institutes acted as technological resources for all of the many plants and operating units throughout all the businesses of these large holding companies. The management at the level of the holding company also sponsored regular meetings of managers from member firms to foster contact and exchange between their differently specialized businesses. Finally, all three firms, as well as others, such as Klöckner and Hoesch, engaged in additional strategic purchases of new firms with technological expertise in areas of significant interest to the member firms.

The pattern at Mannesmann was paradigmatic of the general trend. During the early 1980s, Mannesmann purchased the precision measuring device and gauge producer Hartmut and Braun in Frankfurt, and the computer and electronic instrument maker Kienzle in Villingen-Schweningen in Baden Württemberg. It also purchased significant stakes in the telecommunications company ANT Nachrichtentechnik GmbH, the computer applications firm PCS Peripherie Computer Systeme GmbH, and the information systems company Alfa System Partner GmbH. Later in the decade, the company made significant moves into the automobile components supply business with the purchase of Fichtel & Sachs and VDO Adolph Schindling AG. In all of these cases, the strategy behind the purchase was to bring important technological expertise into the Mannesmann family of companies as well as to shift the *Konzern*'s portfolio of businesses into areas of growth.[151]

Much like the earlier *Konzerne* of the interwar period, the ambition in the new *Konzerne* was not so much to achieve vertical integration throughout the entire holding as it was to establish an internal flow of information that could foster dynamic adaptation and innovation among the member companies.[152] Also, much as in the earlier *Konzerne*, the central office of the holding company did not attempt to make specific plans or guidelines for production and development among its member companies. Instead, the central office promoted internal decentralization by encouraging local operating unit autonomy, while at the same time attempting to facilitate interoperating unit interaction through the exchange of technological know-how and market information.[153]

Here it is easy to see how by pushing a radical form of internal decentralization through the creation of holding companies while at the same time attempting to foster dense intraholding information flows, these new *Konzerne* were trying to replicate autarkically the dynamic advantages provided by arrangements observable at the time in the decentralized industrial order. During much of the 1980s, this strategy proved to be very successful. Many of the major old German steel companies, most notably Mannesmann, performed impressively in nonsteel markets and began to become known as "*Technologie-Konzerne*" because of their increasingly diverse and sophisticated operations involving high technology.[154]

But the success of this model did not last. One by one, in company after company, the newly acquired businesses proved incapable of maintaining their competitiveness in the international economy. Take again the case of Mannesmann. During the latter part of the 1980s, Mannesmann's investments in electronics (Kienzle, PCS) began to lose money. In 1990, after several years of heavy losses and desperate attempts to restructure, Mannesmann sold its controlling stake in these companies to the Digital Electronics Corporation. Problems in electronics, however, were only followed by problems in automobile-components supply and then, ominously, in the core areas of machinery production in the huge Demag and Rexroth companies.[155] Similarly distressing trajectories occurred at Thyssen and Krupp as well.[156] By the middle of the 1990s, the "*Technologie-Konzerne*" model was clearly in crisis: The companies proved to be unable to maintain the competitiveness of the new companies they acquired, or bolster the innovative capacity of older lines of business.

A key reason for the difficulties these firms encountered had to do with the inability of this form of internal decentralization to keep pace with the continuous pressures to come up with new technological and product innovation in an unremittingly competitive cost environment. Over time, it became clear that even though the internally decentralized structure of the *Konzerne* created opportunities for internal exchange and experimentation, the structure also tended to systematically generate inefficiencies and extra costs that were not incurred in other decentralized production systems unconfined by the boundaries of the firm. These extra costs proved devastating in the competitive marketplace. Two factors, in particular, were most serious.

First, the desire to create as many different inputs internal to the *Konzern* as possible – extending great autonomy to each – while simultaneously focusing attention on the intra-*Konzern* flow of information came into conflict with the local interest of the operating units to insulate themselves from enhanced risk and instability on the market. Invariably, local operating units in the *Konzerne* sought to stabilize production flow and employment through intra-*Konzern* deals and arrangements, in particular, intra-*Konzern* subcontracting arrangements. As late as 1990, for example, the Chairman of Krupp, Gerhard Cromme, complained of the unnecessary expenses the company incurred through intra-*Konzern* subcontracting. Keeping inefficient workshops in operation by supplying them with company business, said Cromme, was a "very old Krupp vice" that stemmed from very extensive internal diversification and local autonomy.[157] Eliminating such practices, however, could only be achieved by curtailing the autonomy of local units and creating more centralized control within the *Konzern* – precisely what Cromme's predecessors had been striving to get away from.

Thus, even though internal decentralization fractured and fragmented development and production costs within the holding company, at an aggregate *Konzern* level, it seems actually not to have reduced them. Indeed, over time it became clear that broad internal decentralization created additional costs. Fixing this problem, moreover, risked undermining the local autonomy that the holdings had striven to create in order to foster risk taking and innovation in the first place.

A second aspect of the autarkic *Konzern* structure was perhaps more inefficient and ultimately more costly than the first. In contrast to the producers in truly decentralized, nonfirm-centered systems of production, which tend to be very specialized in a narrow range of products, the operating units of the *Konzerne* tended to have too many products on offer. This lead to the production of costly inventory and less-efficient production arrangements.[158] Such excessive operating-unit diversification was directly traceable to the location of producers within an autarkic firm and its regional environment. Producers in decentralized production systems, such as those in the decentralized industrial order or in Japanese and American just-in-time systems in the automobile sector, could afford to specialize their product palettes and their production operations because they could rely on the existence of outside collaborators as well as a network of extrafirm institutions to supply them with market and technological knowledge that could be used to foster innovation. Many of the operating units within *Konzerne*, however, because they were located in autarkic regions and had strong traditions of vertical integration, could not rely on such outside providers. The absence of such risk-socializing mechanisms changed the logic of risk calculation: Rather than specialize in a narrow range of products, operating units within *Konzerne* hedged their risks through internal diversification – a more costly, less efficient strategy.

Finally, as in the case of internal subcontracting, the *Konzerne* central offices have difficulty breaking up these arrangements and encouraging streamlinig for many of the same reasons that Volkswagen had difficulty establishing more streamlined and decentralized production and development practices: opposition from functional departments, local plant managers, and works councils; the absence of significant small- and medium-sized local collaborators; and an infrastructure of extrafirm institutions to support them.[159] The institutional arrangements of governing firm-centered production that had long contributed to the competitive success of producers in the autarkic industrial order increasingly constituted obstacles to successful adjustment in the new environment.

Case 3: Autarkic firms attempting to create an industrial district. The third case focuses on the adjustment efforts of a firm, the Nixdorf Computer Company (now Siemens-Nixdorf) in autarkic Paderborn during the 1980s. Nixdorf took the lesson of the above two cases to be that if one wanted to successfully implement internal reforms and decentralize production, one had to break down the boundaries of the firm and break from the autarkic traditions of vertical integration.[160] The Nixdorf case is similar to the BMW example above in that the firm was a medium-sized firm in a highly competitive industry dominated by very many much larger competitors. Much like BMW, the firm's size and its closely held property structure made large-scale diversification along *Konzerne* lines more difficult, while at the same time insulating the company from unwanted takeovers. In other words, during much of the 1980s Nixdorf, like BMW, had little alternative to reform and decentralization.

The distinctiveness of the Nixdorf case, however, is that unlike BMW, the firm did not enjoy close proximity to capable and sophisticated suppliers in its own and neighboring decentralized regions. Instead, the primarily agricultural region of eastern Westphalia around the city of Paderborn was relatively far from the nearest agglomerations of important electronics components suppliers in the south of Germany. Thus, where BMW could engage in collaboration and spread risk with interlocutors in (or very near) its backyard, Nixdorf was forced to attempt to foster the growth of interlocutors in the surrounding region with whom it could then collaborate. In a word, the firm attempted to foster the development of decentralized industrial order in the Paderborn region.

Basically, this involved engagement by the firm along two fronts. First, during the early and mid-1980s, Nixdorf cultivated the development of small- and medium-sized local suppliers, either by providing them with business and helping them become more sophisticated, or by encouraging its own engineers with good ideas to create spin-offs in the region.[161] Hilpert and Sperling were amazed that despite the intimate involvement of Nixdorf with the fortunes of these firms, none of the Nixdorf suppliers that they interviewed were in any significant way dependent for their livelihoods on their business with Nixdorf. On the contrary, the suppliers cultivated a broad array of customers, both among themselves within the region and with important firms outside. Here it is plain that the firm was concerned to foster the capacity of its suppliers to serve as sources of know-how for its own production and development projects.

Second, the company became very involved in the development of the local infrastructure. As we saw in Chapter 3, the involvement of large autarkic companies in the development of local infrastructure has a long tradition in the autarkic industrial order: In many locations, the dominance of a large autarkic firm in a locality was so great – as in the example of Krupp in late 19th century Essen – that the organization and governance of city services were often de facto extensions of the governance of the firm. Nixdorf's efforts to develop local infrastructure followed in that tradition, yet the company's aims were very different. Rather than attempting to integrate public infrastructure into the operations of the firm, Nixdorf tried to create or strengthen extra-firm institutions that would both allow the firm to shift cost and risk away from itself, and support the development of the networks of small- and medium-sized suppliers that Nixdorf was increasingly collaborating with. Hilpert and Sperling note that this engagement involved both threats to the local government that the company would leave the Paderborn region if the local authorities did not undertake the development of services that Nixdorf desired, as well as direct investments by the company in the improvement of the public infrastructure of the region.

The most important contribution to the public infrastructure noted by Hilpert and Sperling was the significant upgrading of the local vocational and continuing education centers to quality levels well above national standards.[162] An example of this was the erection of a new Artisan Training Center (*Handwerkerbildungszentrum*) by the Chamber of Artisans for the training of skilled workers. Even though the center was run by the Chamber of Artisans, over half of the 1700 daily pupils in the center came from and returned to local industrial producers and service providers, including Nixdorf and many of its suppliers. Apprentices in this center received training in all of the most advanced microelectronic production technologies (robotics, CIM, CAD, CAM, CNC, etc). Moreover, Hilpert and Sperling emphasized that the center also served as an informal vehicle for technology transfer. Through collaboration with the center in the education of apprentices, firms were exposed to new technologies and prototypes for organizing production.

As successful as these (and other) efforts on the part of Nixdorf were during the 1980s, they were not enough to save the company from the ferocious competition within the computer industry. By the end of the 1980s at the latest it had become clear that Nixdorf had fallen dangerously behind in the development of technology in its main product markets and that it did not have the capacity to improve its position. Moreover, the charismatic founder of the company, Heinz Nixdorf, died suddenly at the end of the decade and the company lurched into loss. In 1990, the company was sold to Siemens and merged with that company's Data and Information Systems Division to form Siemens-Nixdorf. Although the sale provided the company with more capital, it did not improve its performance: By 1994, Siemens-Nixdorf Information Systems had lost money for its parent company every year that it had been in existence. In the latter year, the company announced that it expected to eliminate as many as 10,000 jobs.[163]

The small- and medium-sized producers whose existence had been fostered by the Nixdorf company fared better than the larger company, at least for a time. Even though losses at Nixdorf had become chronic by the beginning of the 1990s, Hilpert and Sperling considered the economy of the Paderborn region to be reasonably healthy. Small firms conducted business with Nixdorf but were not dependent on that larger company. The two authors speculated that most of the small- and medium-sized supplier companies in the region could probably continue to survive even without any future orders from Nixdorf.[164] The problem for the region and for the local producers was that Nixdorf had begun the process of creating the kind of extrafirm infrastructure characteristic of the decentralized industrial order, but it fell into crisis before the process was anywhere near being completed. The crisis at Nixdorf affected the company's ability to contribute to (and interest in) the further development of the local infrastructure.

In particular, most producers noted that the region's infrastructure for technology transfer was poorly developed. The *Gesamthochschule* in Paderborn was considered to be underequipped and undernetworked with surrounding producers, while the traditional industrial policy channels within North Rhine Westphalia characteristically overlooked rural east Westphalia and Paderborn.[165] Without the kind of active attention from Nixdorf that had been so successful in the improvement of the vocational education infrastructure, few believed that the political momentum needed for reform at the local university and redirection of *Land*-based technology transfer policies could be generated. Thus when the deep recession descended upon the entire German economy in late 1992, the incipient decentralized industrial practices in the Paderborn region were only weakly institutionalized. It remains an open question whether or not they will have the resilience to survive the downturn.

Conclusion: Crisis in the autarkic industrial order

The above three cases illustrate the range of adjustment strategies that could be found within the autarkic industrial order as it entered the 1990s. With the exception of the BMW AG, all of the adjustment efforts were plagued by self-blocking dynamics generated by the institutions and practices of the autarkic industrial order itself. The tradition of firm-centered radical vertical integration in production, enhanced by the introduction of firm-based systems of codetermination during the postwar period, was tremendously successful during the 1950s and 1960s. But this kind of autarkic producer had great difficulty adjusting to the turbulent and rapidly changing market dynamics of the 1980s and 1990s. The difficulty was that increasingly, successful adjustment involved practices and relations that decentralized production and blurred the boundaries of the firm with the rest of society and the economy. In most cases, even when important levels of management desired change, autarkic firms either did not have the available regional resources or could not construct coalitions of interest internally that would support a strategy of radical reform and extensive decentralization.

7

The national context: 1945–1994

This final chapter returns to the level of analysis that was the preoccupation of Chapter 4. It focuses on the ways in which the individual forms of industrial order were separately accommodated at the national level of the German political economy during the postwar period from 1945 to 1994. As in Chapter 4, successful accommodation of both forms of industrial order within the national political economy will be referred to as coexistence. Throughout this chapter, attention will be paid to the distinctly composite character of governance structures that were constructed to achieve accommodation and coexistence in the national political economy.

The particular story of how each form of regional industrial order was accommodated in the post-World War II period by the institutional structures and political and economic policies of the new West German Federal Republic (FRG) is full of irony.[1] First, the newly erected national state, based upon the third Constitution drawn in Germany in 75 years, had many of the characteristics needed to stably accommodate each form of industrial order within it. The decentralized industrial order was made once again self-governing as local and regional governments were granted significant political and fiscal autonomy in the new legal framework, while the neoliberal, noninterventionist policies of the national government were very accommodating to the autarkic producers. But this achievement of stable coexistence, which ended years of state control and internal divisiveness between the different forms of industrial order, was in many ways completely inadvertent. Allied impatience with German squabbles over the proper relationship between centralization and decentralization was at least as responsible for the composite of structures that emerged as were any clear conceptions on the part of German actors of what was needed to fashion an architecture of governance that would permit the coexistence of autarkic and decentralized forms of industrial order within the political economy.

Secondly, no sooner was the composite of new institutional frameworks in place than did the real underlying relationship between the two forms of industrial order begin to change. By the beginning of the 1960s, the character of the macrolevel problems shifted from the separate accommodation of two forms of industrial order to the management of problems arising from their growing integration. Indeed, the situation in the 1960s created a set of political dilemmas that would have been absolutely inconceivable in the Weimar Republic. Unlike the Weimar situation, the perception during the 1960s was not that the central state intervened too much in the affairs of (both forms of) industry. Rather, it was that the central government did not have the capacity to intervene enough. The institutional levers for the stable governance of an integrated industrial system dominated by large mass-producing firms and their closely linked banks were absent in the Federal Republic and had to be created.

This historically specific constellation in the economy gave rise to a whole series of centralizing reforms in the state and society that ultimately created what we now know, through Alexander Gerschenkron, Andrew Schonfield and their heirs, as the German model of organized capitalism.[2] For example, beginning in the last part of the 1950s, in response to the diffusion of mass production and of the large mass-producing enterprise throughout all regions of the German economy, national-level, coordinated processes of collective bargaining between centralized organizations of employers and trade unions, for the first time in German history, came to control wage setting in the economy as a whole. At the same time, the power of regional institutions of federalism and municipal self-government began to be practically, and then legally, recalibrated so that the central state had more power to influence local policies and coordinate them with its own macroeconomic aims.

These moves toward centralization should not be surprising. As the two previous chapters have shown, large autarkic firms and the universal banks were at this time at the peak of their power, while the continued existence of the decentralized industrial order became invisible behind the belief that the survival of small firms was a technological artifact of the mass-production system. In the ideological mileau of the age, centralization in the polity and in society was understood as a natural expression of the development of industrial society.

The final ironic twist in the postwar story is that before all of the centralizing reforms were even fully in place, the political and economic conditions that had given rise to them completely evaporated. The crisis of the 1970s and the changed economic environment of the 1980s and 1990s, we have seen, resulted initially in a renaissance of small- and medium-sized production in the decentralized regions, and in halting, self-blockage plagued efforts on the part of autarkic firms to mimic decentralized industrial practices. The national political and governance consequences of these developments were very broad in the Federal Republic. The rhetoric of centralization that dominated much of Social Democratic (SPD) rule during the 1970s was supplanted during the 1980s by discourses on the right and left extolling the virtues (and decrying the dangers) of local control, federalism, and decentralization. More concretely, centralized collective bargaining came under pressure by centrifugal forces of local heteronomy in the economy, while regional and local governments both aggressively sought and grudgingly received increased autonomy from the central government.

Such trends toward the recalibration of relations between local and central authorities – much in the manner of conflicts within large corporations themselves – withstood the turmoil engendered by political unification and the onset of deep recession in the 1990s. In the mid-1990s, debate focuses not on whether or not decentralization is necessary, but on what reforms in policy and local and regional governmental structures need to take place to help producers deal with the profound adjustment pressures engendered by the particularly intense pressures for greater decentralization among large and small firms in the economy. These debates are in their beginning stages, and in many respects the self-blockage in industrial firms that the previous chapters described seems to be reproducing itself within the local extrafirm institutions that have traditionally supported them.

With irony stacked upon irony, the ultimate argument of this chapter is that the much vaunted postwar German model of large firms, universal banks, neo-corporatist bargaining and an accommodating central state – in reality a creation of the 1960s and 1970s – was systematically deconstructed during the 1980s and early 1990s. Both its emergence and its deconstruction, moreover, were intimately associated with the efforts to address continuously evolving national-level governance problems generated by each of the forms of industrial order within the German political economy.

By the time that the Federal Republic annexed the bankrupt East German Democratic Republic and reunified Germany in 1990, the institutional framework of Gerschenkronian/organized capitalist Germany, which reflected a particular form of coexistence between the two forms of industrial order, was being replaced with sets of practices and institutional forms of national regulation in the polity and in society that recalled (but did not completely reproduce) much older internally fragmented and regionally diverse German arrangements. Today, as in the Imperial Reich, national debates about industrial adjustment in Germany take for granted the central importance of regionally specific institutional reform as levers in the adjustment process.

This chapter will tell this story in straightforward segments. The initial founding and the institutional accommodation of both forms of industrial order in the polity will be dealt with first, the period of centralization second, and the period of reversal third.

The accommodation of the autarkic and decentralized industrial orders during the economic miracle

Even in the immediate postwar German context of military occupation, political division, and economic reconstruction, the institutional problem of finding a workable framework that could accommodate each of the two forms of industrial order within the national political economy still turned on traditional problems: that is, on regional and local government fiscal and administrative autonomy, and on the constitutional capacity of regional bodies to protect that autonomy. This involved conflicts both over the structure of finance and administration within the new federal state and over the power of the legislative chamber (Bundesrat) representing regional interests.

In both cases, the outcomes were favorable for the reconstitution of the decentralized industrial order and for the continued expansion and growth of autarky. It would be misleading, however, to represent these outcomes as explicit political compromises between these two structural interests. On the one hand, the boundaries of political representation of occupied Germany, drawn for strategic and administrative reasons by the occupying armies, frequently lumped decentralized and autarkic regions together or oddly divided regions with common traditions. As a result, neither form of industrial order was immediately represented in the political discussion, or, if they were, they were distracted by unfamiliar fragmentation.[3] On the other hand, however, it was also the case that political stalemates among the Germans in each case were resolved through the intervention of the Allied governments. These players ultimately produced a stable, liberal solution to a problem that had plagued the German political economy since the fall of the Reich in 1918, without really having any conception of what was actually at stake in that realm.

Reconstructing regional governments: Administration and finance

From the beginning of discussions about the kind of state that should be constructed on occupied German territory, the U.S. and the other occupying powers favored a decentralization of political power in Germany. They wanted to destroy the centralized apparatus of the Nazi regime. By creating a federalist structure, without a large and coherent central bureaucracy, they felt that they would ensure that the new German polity would be governed by a plurality of interests. A federal structure of government and representation, in other words, would guarantee the existence of political opposition. This was seen not only as a way to stave off the return of Nazism, but also as a way to temper the character of a potential socialist electoral victory in the new Republic. A fragmented bureaucracy and strongly autonomous *Länder* (provinces) would make it difficult for a socialist government to institute a comprehensive system of economic planning and thus abandon the market-economy-based system that the allies wanted to construct.[4] Thus, when the allies assembled a parliamentary council of representatives from the various newly created German *Länder* and entrusted it with the task of drawing up a constitution for West Germany, they gave the council three general instructions to guide their process of deliberation: the constitution must protect individual rights, be based on democratic principles, and provide for a federal structure of government.[5]

For their part, German political actors were generally united on the desirability of a federalist structure, but divided on the allocation of fiscal responsibility. The SPD favored the old Weimar model in which the central government retained the sole power to tax and to administer state finances. This, they believed, would enhance the government's capacity to engage in economic planning and redistribution.[6] The Christian Democratic parties, on the other hand, favored a system that gave the regional authorities wide-ranging fiscal autonomy. Part of the rationale for this was consistent with the antisocialist concerns of the

Allies, and stemmed from a desire to prevent the construction of an institutional structure in the new German state that would permit the implementation of economic planning procedures.[7]

Yet, many Christian Democrats argued out of genuine concerns for the stability of regional governance structures, fueled by a deeper historical understanding of their potential vulnerability. They felt that without local fiscal autonomy, regional interests would constantly be subject to the arbitrary good will of the center, and would have no way to protect themselves when the interests of the center led it to neglect or oppose local ends. These concerns harked back not only to the negative experience in the Weimar Republic, but to the basic principles of federalist order that had structured the Second Reich. Konrad Adenauer, who as mayor of Cologne had suffered the fiscal crisis of German cities during the Weimar Republic firsthand, articulated these basic political concerns during a debate on the formulation of the German constitution:

> I take the very materialist position that the autonomy of the *Länder* ... rises and falls with fiscal autonomy. It depends upon whether or not one considers the problem of state finance from a political or a financial perspective. Federal financial administration is correct from a financial point of view, but not from a political point of view. The reason for this can be demonstrated in a single sentence: When the fiscal administration is not in the hands of the *Länder*, then the Federal Government is in the first instance in control of tax revenues. Who wants to be in the position of having to prove to the body that possesses public funds that it should make its allocations after it has claimed it cannot? Who wants to tell another public body when it is supposed to make allocations? Who wants the position of having to force the controller of public monies to act? It is in light of these considerations that the problem of the actual or potential financial autonomy of the *Länder* cannot be separated from the problem of financial administration. The matter must be viewed from a political point of view.[8]

Ultimately, neither Adenauer, the Christian Democratic Union (CDU) nor the SPD got their way in this debate. Instead, the Allies placed pressure on the negotiating parties to adopt a compromise solution. Fiscal responsibilities were divided between the Federal Government and the various *Länder*. All three levels of government were ultimately assigned particular taxes in the *Grundgesetz* (Basic Law) itself, and revenues from the most important taxes (income, corporate, and sales) were to be shared between the different levels of government.[9] Further, at the prodding of the Allies, a system of vertical fiscal equalization (*vertikale Finanzausgleich*) was developed that distributed revenue among the three basic levels of administration according to the governmental responsibilities with which they were entrusted. This result was short of the full local sovereignty over finances that Imperial subgovernments enjoyed and those such as Adenauer desired, but it far exceeded the financial straightjacket that the

Länder and municipalities were forced to endure under the Weimar Republic. The allies, in the end, were persuaded that strong regional interests needed guaranteed access to financial resources.

Bundesrat

Allied intervention also helped to shape the ultimate powers of the Bundesrat, or upper parliamentary house, in the 1949 Basic Law. The parliamentary council was deeply divided between those advocating the creation of a Senate, modeled after that in the U.S., which would provide proportional representation of the various territories within Germany, and those advocating the formation of a Bundesrat, which would represent only the regional governments and have powers equal to those of the Bundestag, or lower house of parliament. The Senate structure was favored by the Social Democrats, who considered it to be more democratic, and by various north German Christian Democrats, including Konrad Adenauer, who had only bad memories of the unequal powers of the regional governments (especially Prussia) in the traditional Imperial Bundesrat. The Bundesrat solution was supported by the southern German states of Bavaria and by the three districts that would eventually become the *Land* of Baden Württemberg, as they felt that the direct representation of the states at the national level would be more likely to insure their integrity as political–economic units.[10] (For location of new *Länder* and zones of occupation, see maps 4 and 5 in Appendix.)

The deadlock between the two positions was broken by a memorandum from the Allied military governors of November 22, 1948, which came out in favor of the Bundesrat solution. Again, worried about the Scilla of Nazism and the Charibdis of socialism, the Allies considered this to be more likely to preserve a decentralization of power in the polity.[11] The new Bundesrat had powers which were both less than those of the Bundesrat in the 1871 Constitution, and more than those of the Reichsrat in the 1919 Weimar constitution.

Unlike the old Imperial Bundesrat, the new West German Bundesrat was not an executive body representing sovereign states, but a chamber within the federal parliament. Unlike the Weimar Reichsrat, however, the West German Bundesrat was invested with the capacity to protect regional and local authorities from undesirable intrusions from the center. Federal officials were prevented from bypassing or overruling state authorities without the express approval of a majority vote of the Bundesrat. All federal legislation was required to be submitted by the government to the Bundesrat before going to the lower house (the Bundestag). Bills affecting the regions directly required the consent of the Bundesrat. Finally, Article 79 III of the Basic Law barred any future amendments to the Constitution that would eliminate the federalist organization of the Federal Republic.[12]

By guaranteeing local autonomy in this way, it is clear that the new structure (whether it intended to or not) created a political and legal environment within which the regions traditionally dominated by the decentralized industrial order could recreate the framework of public and private governance institutions that facilitated the socialization of risk and information that industrial actors in their economies depended on. And, though the particular character of the outcome was not directly the result of their efforts, producers and other actors in the decentralized industrial order seemed more than willing to accept it. Their reasoning, moreover, is not hard to reconstruct: The experience of the Weimar Republic had made clear that the absence of fiscal autonomy at the local and regional level made it difficult for regional governments to perform their crucial roles in the decentralized industrial order.[13] But the solution offered by the Nazis turned out to be no solution at all: Agreeing to have the central state assume the role of the local state (and then, ultimately, of associations) in a regional industrial order not only led to loss of autonomy and self-government, but to defeat and turmoil as well. A nostalgia for self-governing order within the German *industrielle Mittelstand* in the wake of the Nazi defeat was extremely strong.[14]

The peculiarity of the new political structure, however, was that despite its hospitality toward decentralization, it was also found to be extremely congenial by autarkic big business. Certainly, the presence of four occupying armies on German soil, the specter of expansive communism on Germany's borders, and the emergence of a Cold War ideology in which the forces of communism were permitted to be combatted only by the forces of democracy were useful in persuading the politically agnostic autarkic industrialists to support the construction of a parliamentary and federally decentralized regime.

But it was not only that. The economic ideology and policies of the new national government laid great stress on the importance of entrepreneurial autonomy in production and its governance. Ludwig Erhard, the new federal Economics Minister, structured economic policies that emphasized with great ostentation (and with the open and aggressive approval of the Western powers) the virtues of the free market and the importance of limited state intervention in the direct affairs of firms.[15] The new German state involved itself in the "Economic Miracle" of the 1950s in very indirect ways, and always in the interest of creating better conditions for capital formation, technological investment, and growth.[16] Rather than attempt to insert itself into the internal affairs of the autarkic producers, as the Weimar and Nazi states had attempted to do, this new government did everything it could to create an environment in which autonomous industrial actors could prosper.

Indeed, the important thing about the early institutional political economic reality in West Germany was not simply that it allowed both forms of industrial order to reproduce themselves. It was also that it allowed them to change. In particular, the new postwar composite set of national governance frameworks that permitted the coexistence of both forms of industrial order did not prevent producers within the decentralized industrial order from breaking out of the local structures in the order and adopting autarkic strategies of mass production. As we saw, the number of firms, such as Daimler-Benz, doing this increased during the 1950s and 1960s, particularly after the formation of the Common Market. The diffusion of mass production throughout the West German economy ultimately lead to the integration of the two forms of industrial order. Large mass-producing firms organized production and its administration according to the principles of autarkic industrial order, regardless of their regional location, while the producers of capital goods in the decentralized regions continued to organize their activities according to the principles of the decentralized industrial order.

The composite framework of national-level coexistence between the autarkic and decentralized industrial orders during the 1950s did not encourage this integration; it enabled it to occur. The emergence of the larger European market and the presence of American mass producers in Europe were more important causes of the shift into mass production.[17] Once it had occurred, however, integration began to pose governance challenges that could be accommodated by neither of the existing frameworks of accommodation that allowed for the coexistence of the two forms of industrial order in the Federal Republic.

The first sign that new national-level governance structures were needed was the emergence of a particularly German set of neocorporatist arrangements in the area of industrial relations, which, for the first time in German history, established regular rounds of national-level, centralized collective bargaining for the entire national economy. Moreover, unlike the labor–capital corporatism of the ZAG in the Weimar Republic, which was an effort to block the further intrusion of state power into the economy, the industrial partners in the FRG constructed extrapolitical arrangements in an effort to deal with governance problems that the state structure did not, and clearly would not, address. At first it seemed possible that this kind of private centralization would be the only kind of institutional adjustment needed to meet the changing situation in the economy, as people in the state believed that they could easily adapt to the new industrial–economic reality by making adjustments in policy and encouraging change in society. As the decade of the 1960s wore on, however, it became clear that more serious institutional adjustments in the structure of the government itself were necessary to accommodate the governance problems generated by the integration of the autarkic and decentralized industrial orders.

The period of centralization, 1956–1980

Mass production and the macroeconomy

In order to understand the institutional changes that took place in Germany in the late 1950s and 1960s, it is important to understand the very particular macroeconomic dynamics that the integration of the two forms of industrial order had given rise to. An economy dominated by mass producers must be governed in a different way than one that has no mass producers, or that has a mixture of volume and specialty producers without one or the other being dominant. An economy populated primarily by specialty producers (regardless of their association with autarkic or decentralized principles of organization) resembles in its dynamics an economy dominated by competitive markets. The investment calculations of individual producers are extremely sensitive to the

The national context   263

rate of return, i.e., the difference between the revenue earned from the sale of the commodity they sell and the cost of the basic inputs necessary for its production. This is true even though many of the relationships that a producer may have with other producers or even workers that they employ are governed by nonmarket and nonpriced-based factors, such as loyalty, honor, quality, trust, etc. In such cases, the rate of return is not given by the prices in the market but is instead a matter of continual negotiation between the producers and sellers of needed factors.[18]

Such a system is regulated mostly at the microlevel. The major danger to the system is the breakdown of honor-based self-restraint that can come through breakdowns in industrial order: murderous competition, driven by poaching and underpricing among producers, or the sweating of labor and suppliers by playing off their desperation for work and contracts during downturns. We have discussed a broad variety of institutional mechanisms that were created to prevent such practices and maintain the existence of continually negotiated common understandings and self-limitation among actors in industry: finishing associations, term-fixing cartels, *Konzerne*, trade unions that establish minimum prices in the labor market, and so on.

At the macrolevel, the minimum that such a system requires is monetary stability, not so much because stable prices improve calculation, but because inflation makes the process of negotiation between the participating parties difficult. The process is also responsive to fiscal regulation, which shapes the resource boundaries of the environment in which it occurs (e.g., different kinds of taxes or subsidies can change the amount of resources available to, and even the structure of the utility functions of, the parties in negotiation).[19] Historically, in Germany, any more intrusive forms of state intervention at a national level generally produced resistance from the autarkic producers who resented any interference in their affairs and from regional and local governments, who coveted the resources used (or forgone) for their own local ends. Macroeconomic policies roughly coincident with these basic principles of nonintervention were characteristic of the Adenauer governments of the 1950s, not to mention those of Bismarck a half century earlier.[20]

When, however, an economy is dominated by producers engaged in mass production, it is very difficult to govern the macroeconomy in this way. Mass producers make their investment calculations according to completely different criteria than do specialty producers. Their concern is with the level of demand for their product. Because they are so large relative to their total market, mass producers tend to make decisions about investment based upon their estimation of the prospective level of capacity utilization, rather than on their existing rate of return. Moreover, the tremendous costs associated with investment in large, dedicated mass-production processes cause mass producers to be anxious about the capacity of the market to absorb the increased output that their investments would produce.[21]

Now, if the mass producers in an economy are not dominant, or are in rapidly expanding sectors, or, as was the case with the autarkic steel producers in the

Ruhr, are the producers of semifinished products not directly dependent upon the expansion of aggregate demand, macroeconomic policies do not need to differ much from the minimalist ones described in the specialist economy. Regulation can occur instead at the microlevel of the autarkic firm. Individual mass producers can reproduce themselves on the basis of their capacity to judge the movement of demand in their individual business. They can also pursue a variety of market-stabilization strategies, all touched on earlier, such as the formation of cartels that completely control competition and regulate output, or the creation of "variable" capacity through the use of *verlängerte Werkbank* subcontracting, etc. Such strategies enable the individual producer to protect its investments by exerting control over the environment it competes in.

But, if the economy comes to have significant groupings of mass producers, not as isolated cases, but in a broad variety of sectors including finished goods, and especially durable consumer goods markets (automobiles, consumer electronics, etc.) – as increasingly occurred in the West German economy beginning in the latter half of the 1950s – such autarkic forms of microregulation become less adequate as mechanisms for the stabilization of the market environment. As more and more parts of the economy are simultaneously sensitive to the general level of consumer purchasing power, no individual firm or group of firms in an industry can fully control the market environment, and the creation of some kind of framework for the stabilization of aggregate (in this case, national) income levels over time becomes desirable. Producers have an interest both in leveling the business cycle (through the use of fiscal and monetary policy instruments) and in regularizing the setting of wages. In the latter case, the concern is that wages stay in line with the growth of productivity. By staying close to this target, it is possible to ensure that wages do not become so low as to undermine the level of demand (during periods when the labor market is slack), or so high that they threaten the stability of prices or the availability of investible capital in the economy (when the labor market is tight).[22]

Transformation of German industrial relations

It was with background conditions such as these, beginning in the latter half of the 1950s, that German industrialists and trade unions began to engage in regular, centralized, national-level collective bargaining rounds to establish wage rates and general working conditions for all German workers. Beginning in 1956 with the famous Bremen Agreement on working time in the metal industry,[23] collective bargaining in Germany took on a quasicorporatist form. Unlike the highly centralized, fully corporatist bargaining arrangements in countries such as Sweden and Austria, where organized unions representing all industrial workers in all industries bargained directly with an association representing all employers, the changes ushered in through the Bremen accords established a system in which national wage rates were patterned after the rates set in the nation's largest manufacturing branch through a process of centralized national-level bargaining between the metalworkers union (IG Metall) and the Metal Industry Employers Association (Gesamtmetall).[24]

The national context 265

This was a dramatic break from previous tradition in German industrial relations, for two reasons. First, it transformed the character of bargaining from a largely local and regional focus to a national phenomenon. Labor in this way was recognized as a key component of demand in the economy, rather than simply as a factor cost. Second, the new system of centralized national-level patterned bargaining also recalibrated the relative weights of the organizational levels inside the trade unions, essentially reducing the previous de facto sprawling and regionally differentiated structure of relatively autonomous decision-making units to two salient levels of bargaining authority: the central union and the works council. This change effectively recast the trade unions' orientation to the economy from one focused on regional economies to one focused on individual branches and firms, on the one hand, and the macroeconomy, on the other.

Labor as demand

Prior to the Bremen agreements of 1956, national-level agreements (i.e., centrally bargained agreements valid for all workers and firms in an industry) were extremely rare in Germany, and the establishment of a national pattern across industries was virtually unprecedented. Historically, collective bargaining in Germany, with certain exceptions, took place largely on local and regional levels, and, in the Imperial Reich and Weimar Republic, even on firm and plant levels. Prior to 1914, there was only one industry that regularly struck national accords with organized labor: the printing industry. Seventy-seven percent of all collectively bargained contracts in 1913 were struck at the firm level, 11.9% at the local level, and 11% at the regional or district level. Moreover, even these agreements were fairly isolated: almost 90% of the total industrial workforce in prewar Germany had their wages determined by the market and not through collective bargaining.[25]

Most agreements that did exist were struck with or among small- and medium-sized producers, many in decentralized areas. The few agreements that were struck among large autarkic firms took place in the machinery and shipbuilding industries, where high demand for skilled labor existed.[26] As the example of the Solingen cutlery outworkers from Chapter 2 indicated, some collective agreements were integral to the stabilization of decentralized production in that they established minimum wages (subcontract prices) and hence ensured that production strategy in the local industry would be driven by quality and not price-competitive considerations. In other cases, however, collective agreements were simply the outcome of a power struggle between unions seeking to establish a decent level of wages for working people and employers concerned with preventing their labor factor costs from taking too much of their investible earnings. Indeed, most industries and regions saw agreements struck in very erratic patterns with workers winning agreements during upswings in the business cycle and losing them on the downswing.[27] In no case was the Keynesian idea that labor was a decisive component of demand a guiding principle of collective bargaining.

The character of collective bargaining in the Weimar Republic changed significantly in comparison to the pre-World War I period in that many more workers began to be covered by collective agreements. Workers in larger autarkic firms, for example, began for the first time to be extensively covered by collective agreements, including workers in the iron and steel industry. Much of this change in the extent of coverage was the result of a shift in the political balance of power: the Weimar constitution provided for state arbitration, in which the ministry of labor was invested with the power to intervene in collective negotiations and impose a binding award in the event that the negotiating parties could not reach one themselves.[28] By 1927, roughly 70% of all workers had their wages set through collective bargaining. But, for all of that, these agreements were still overwhelmingly struck at the level of the firm and the plant. Ullmann notes that in 1925, 31.1% of all collective agreements were struck with individual firms, 36.2% were struck at a regional or district level, whereas only 1.1% were national in character.[29]

The early years of collective bargaining in the West German Federal Republic were similarly characterized overwhelmingly by regional agreements.[30] It was only after the gradual integration of the different systems of regional industrial order with the diffusion of mass-production strategies and the large autarkic corporation throughout the German economy that the idea of establishing national agreements began to become attractive to employers and seem possible to the trade unions.[31] The emergence of national-level agreements after 1956 was significant because it established, for the first time, a routine "parapublic" national-level procedure for ensuring that the growth of wages in the economy would be explicitly bargained for in light of the health and performance of the national economy.[32] In 1963, employers associations and the trade unions developed a formula for wage setting that pegged wage growth to the growth of productivity in industry, thus ensuring that purchasing power in the economy would stay in line with the growth of capacity.[33]

Thus, in the realm of collective bargaining, trade unions (led by the giant IG Metall) in effect shifted from viewing themselves as exploiters of local market power engaged in a struggle with employers over the pure definition of factor cost to seeing themselves as the bearers of a higher-order (national) responsibility for the larger economic consequences of their wage bargaining.[34] With the establishment of the Konzertierte Aktion in 1967, in which peak organizations of labor and capital were brought together to ensure that wage increases would conform not only to the rate of productivity increase, but to the government's projection for the rate of growth, the transformed bargaining partners were (temporarily) elevated to pillars of state macroeconomic planning.[35]

Streamlining of organization

This movement toward centralized bargaining ultimately had significant consequences for the organizational structure of the unions. The relative weights of the organizational levels inside the unions were recalibrated so that regional levels (district and local offices) were more stringently controlled by the strategic desires of the center. As late as 1954, for example, when IG Metall called a strike in Bavaria, the district and local levels of the union in other regions of Germany still had the freedom to reach independent agreements with organized employers, even as the union was attempting to lead a strike.[36] After the Bremen accord of 1956, districts and locals were not permitted to act so independently.

This change occurred without any formal change in the constitutional structure of the unions themselves. The center always had held considerable formal power in German industrial unions. In the by-laws of IG Metall, for example, the district officers were always appointed by the national union's executive committee.[37] Moreover, it was a cornerstone of the very idea of an industrial union (as opposed to a craft union) that the central office controlled the strike funds and, thereby, held the ultimate authority to sanction local strikes.[38]

Yet, in practice, due to the widely differing regional industrial conditions that had traditionally existed in Germany and the different levels of strength of the unions across regions, in most cases, central unions had always been forced to cede local organizations considerable strategic autonomy. Often, this local independence was reinforced by the fact that a large part of union work at the local level had to do with social policy matters in working class communities that had little to do with wage bargaining.[39] Indeed, it was the significance of this kind of local trade union activity that underlay the decision of the IG Metall to opt for locality-based rather than plant-based locals (*Verwaltungsstellen*) when the formal organization of the union was reconstituted after World War II.[40] Out of similar concerns, the national trade union confederation, the Deutsche Gewerkschaftsbund (DGB), created local organizations, *Ortskartelle*, which facilitated cooperation among union locals from different industries in the same locality to address common problems. With the centralization of bargaining, the informal independence of these local organizations from the central union was dramatically reduced.[41] They increasingly became narrowly administrative, bureaucratic organs delivering information and propaganda from the center to the workers in the plants, and communicating worker interests up to the center.[42]

The paradox of the advent of central bargaining is that at the same time that it undermined the relative autonomy of the local levels of union organization, it enhanced the significance of plant-level organizations within the union. This developed out of the fact that the new centrally struck agreements established only very general guidelines – e.g., minimum wage levels for the various occupational categories – that naturally did not reflect the specific labor market and conjunctural situation in particular plants. Indeed, because the bargained wages were often targeted around averaged indicators of industrial performance and productivity growth, it was invariably the case that the best-performing workers and plants would have been significantly undercompensated if paid the strict collectively bargained wage rate. Without a mechanism to adjust wages upwards to plant-specific performance levels, there was considerable risk that centralized bargaining would create discontent among workers in the most successful plants.

Ultimately, the mechanism the German unions found to do this was the

268   *Industrial constructions*

plant-level works council. As we saw in Chapter 6, Works councils – plant-level representative bodies for employees – have a long and complicated history in Germany, and they have always had a very ambiguous formal relationship to the trade union movement.[43] By the middle of the 1950s, however, this relationship had become stabilized: Works councils were required by law to be separate from the trade union movement, but in practice the fact that most works councilors were also shop stewards in the unions meant that the relationship between union and works councils was de facto a very close one.[44] By the middle of the 1950s, nearly 80% of all works councilors in German metalworking plants were union members.[45]

This strong presence on the shop floor through the works councils was ultimately exploited by the unions as collective bargaining became increasingly centralized. IG Metall systematically incorporated the most important works councilors from the largest and most powerful firms into so-called *Tarifkommissionen*, which collaborated with the central executive bargaining committee in the development of union bargaining strategies.[46] Then, after a general agreement between organized employers and their unions was struck, the individual works councils engaged in a "second round" of wage bargaining with the management of their plants to bring wages up to a level more in line with the plant's performance. This not only effectively institutionalized "wage drift" into the bargaining process, which helped to maintain support for centralized bargaining among the most highly paid workers in the most successful firms,[47] it also elevated the power and significance of the works councils within the power structure and strategic thinking of the trade unions.

It was in this manner that the centralization of bargaining resulted in a kind of streamlined duopoly of authority and discretion within the union movement – the so-called "Dual System" – which reduced the salient categories in postwar West German industrial relations to the national level and the plant. The informal system of internal cooperation and bargaining between the central union and its regional offices that had characterized collective bargaining for most of the history of German industrial trade unionism was in this way simply abandoned. In its place, another informal system of coordination began to emerge, this time between the central union and the works councils of the largest and most successful firms in each respective industry.

The shift to demand management in the 1960s: Macroeconomic policy and constitutional reform

Despite the successful institutionalization of national-level wage setting, by the beginning of the 1960s voices began to be heard within large-scale industry, the business interest associations, government, and the trade unions expressing a desire to achieve some greater predictability about the business cycle and especially about the level of wages in the economy.[48] Indeed, what is particularly interesting about the West German political economy at this time is that, despite a decade of continuous export-lead expansion, the political-economic situation seemed quite fragile to all of the main actors in the economy. The growing integration of the decentralized and autarkic industrial orders, occasioned by the diffusion of mass-production practices throughout the economy, were clearly creating national-level problems of economic governance that, in the eyes of the relevant players, plainly needed to be addressed by national-level mechanisms, if not by the central state itself.

Large industrial producers, for example, worried that the labor movement would use its new labor market strength to wrest unreasonable wage agreements from them (by 1960, there was virtual full employment in the economy as the rate of unemployment fell to 0.6%) and thus began be interested in a role for the state in checking the power of labor. Labor leaders, by this time increasingly influenced by Keynesian ideas of demand management, did indeed want to redistribute wealth to their members, yet they also increasingly believed that the government's refusal to engage in demand-management policies exposed the economy as a whole to unnecessary instability.[49] Government policy makers, for their part, worried that the threat of higher wages, combined with the consistently large trade surpluses, would create inflationary pressures within the economy that would provoke the Bundesbank (central bank) to tighten credit, thus sending the economy inadvertently into recession.

Gradually, a political consensus favoring some form of macroeconomic steering developed among these major groups. Significantly, the plans they ultimately developed involved an important modification in the institutional framework that had accommodated the decentralized industrial order within the national political economy since the end of the 1940s. Increasing the power of the central government entailed some reduction in the autonomy of regional and local governments. The ultimate recalibration in relations that was implemented, however, was a compromise between those interested in preserving local autonomy and those concerned with stabilizing an increasingly integrated political economy.

At first, in the very early part of the 1960s, there were a number of partial attempts at adjusting the existing system of macroeconomic policy making and regulation, but it soon became clear that more dramatic reforms in the political structure were required to be able to accommodate the increasing integration of the different regional economies and to effectively manage the evolution of the macroeconomy.

Two major changes occurred in 1963. In that year, as mentioned, the German unions and employers associations agreed upon the formula that centrally bargained wage rates should be pegged to the rate of productivity growth in the economy. This quite explicitly aimed to establish a self-reinforcing relationship between the growth in productive capacity within mass-producing firms and the level of consumer demand. In the same year, the government established a special panel of macroeconomists, representing five major institutes for independent economic analysis in West Germany,[50] who were mandated to draw up comprehensive analyses and forecasts of the economy's growth. This Sachverständigenrat, or Council of Economic Experts, it was hoped, would provide the government and industrial actors with better long-term information about key economic indicators.[51]

By themselves, however, these changes could not provide the kind of macroeconomic management capacity that many increasingly believed was needed. Pressure for more dramatic reform mounted. In 1964, the first year of Ludwig Erhard's chancellorship, a major proposal for the reform of the economic policy making apparatus within the government was drawn up by a committee composed jointly of representatives of the finance and economics ministries. According to Schonfield, the report "was a plea for a radical reform of the financial machinery of the government designed to enable the state to intervene with great speed and enhanced power in the nations business."[52] The next year, Erhard himself delivered what was to become a very famous speech to the CDU party congress in Düsseldorf. He argued that West Germany needed to make itself into a "formed society" (*Formierte Gesellschaft*) that conquered its problems not through conflict, but through cooperation between classes. The speech was not only important because of its explicit willingness to condone the creation of corporatist bargaining organizations made up of trade unions and employers associations. It was also a clear sign of the government's awareness of the need for more global forms of macroeconomic regulation and of its own limited capacity to accomplish this.[53]

It took a recession and a change in government in 1966/1967, however, to force the government and labor and industry groups into actually making significant reforms.[54] Over the course of the next three years, two new institutional mechanisms for macroeconomic management were created. More importantly, it was found that in order to be able to implement the kind of macroeconomic policies desired, the financial structure of the Federal Republic had to be reformed. In particular, the fiscal authority of the central government, relative to that of the regional and municipal governments, had to be strengthened.

The first major reform was the passage of the "Stability and Growth Act" in 1967, which mandated the implementation of a program of macroeconomic "global guidance."[55] The law enjoined all of the relevant actors to pursue policies that would keep the German economy within the "magic quadrangle" of full employment, steady growth, price stability, and stable value of the mark. To carry out this policy, a structure of cooperation was imposed by the central government upon the policy making process. The different levels of government (federal, regional, and municipal), the Bundesbank, industry associations, and labor met in what was called the Konjunkturrat (or business-cycle council). This council formulated so-called "orientation data," which was to constitute targets for the various actors to keep in mind in the formulation of their own annual strategies. The law also empowered the federal government to use its budget as a policy instrument for regulating the level and growth of aggregate demand. In the case of specific instruments – mostly specific tax rates and depreciation schedules – the government could act without parliamentary approval.[56]

For all of this, however, the central government's capacity to control the economy was still significantly limited. In particular, the fiscal autonomy earlier

The national context 271

accorded to regional and local governments – quite useful when the two forms of industrial order within the West German economy were unintegrated – was now proving to be an obstacle to the development of coherent fiscal policies at a time when the two forms of order were integrated. Said another way, an important piece of the institutional framework of accommodation for the decentralized form of industrial order, embedded in the Basic Law of the land, was obstructing the capacity of actors to construct governance mechanisms to alleviate problems generated by the integration of the two forms of industrial order. By the end of the 1960s, it had become apparent, even to actors within the decentralized regions, that institutional reforms in the structure of the state were needed if the economy were to be effectively managed. The trick was achieving reform without undermining the decentralized industrial order. In 1969, the new Social Democratic/Liberal government instituted a major constitutional reform of the financial structure of Federal Republic that attempted to square this circle. It created greater capacity to intervene on the part of the central state while preserving the relative autonomy of local bodies by attempting to ensure greater cooperation among regional governments for the central government's macroeconomic policies.[57]

This reform had three major features, each of which attempted to enhance the power of the center and circumscribe the autonomous fiscal initiative of the regional and communal authorities. First, it increased the amount of projects that the regional and federal authorities carried out jointly, in particular, areas of public spending, especially concerning the construction of higher educational facilities, hospitals, sports facilities, and the improvement of regional economic structures. Thus, major expenditures on the part of the regional authorities could be influenced by the Federal Government through its financial participation. A further stipulation of the reform (Article 91a of the Basic Law) was that a common system of "framework planing" be developed in which the Federal and regional governments jointly planned common projects in the future.

A second reform measure sought to give the central state the capacity to encourage counter-cyclical outlays in the regions. This was done by giving the central government the right to dispense special investment aid targeted for specific projects. According to the amendment, the outlays should counter disturbances in the economic balance, contribute to an equalization of economic differences, or promote economic growth.[58]

Finally, a joint committee, the Finanzplanungsrat, or Finance Planning Council, was established to impose greater federal influence over the formation of all public budgets in the Federal Republic. Membership in the Finance Council consisted of the finance ministers of all federal and regional governments, plus representatives from the German Diet of Cities (Städtetag), who represented the cities. According to Jack Knott, the council had three purposes: "the creation of a unified system of financial and budgetary statistics; the drawing up of unified economic and budgetary guidelines for financial planning; and the identification of problem areas in fulfilling the macroeconomic function of the public budget."[59] The intention behind the formation of the council, along with the other

272 *Industrial constructions*

reforms, was to bind the budgetary politics of all German governments to the common macroeconomic goals of the state. In so doing, it also explicitly designated fiscal policy measures to be essential instruments of economic steering for the central government.[60]

The transformation of regional interest in this period

There was opposition to the reforms on the part of the various regional governments, but none of the resistance was of a fundamental character. On the one hand, reformers were careful not to threaten the autonomy of the *Länder* in anything like the manner in which the dramatic centralization proposals of the Weimar Republic had done.[61] Regional responsibility for education, police, and social welfare services was considered to be inviolate. Moreover, many of the reforms aimed only at the coordination of regional and federal spending in the interest of a coherent counter-cyclical macroeconomic policy and did not attempt to intervene directly into the construction of local spending priorities.

Nor did the reform affect the autonomous revenue raising capacities of the *Länder*, though in some cases it changed the kind of taxes that could be levied in the interest of enhancing federal control over fiscal mechanisms. Up to 1969, for example, municipalities received 85% of their revenue from business taxes. The 1969 reform, however, transferred 40% of this key fiscal instrument to the federal and regional governments, and replaced the lost revenue by according the cities a greater share of jointly collected income taxes. The federal reforms were concerned, in the end, with the creation of a stable and predictable investment environment for large, mass-producing firms. As a result, investment-sensitive taxes, such as the business tax, were seen as being better held under central government control.

On the other hand, a further reason for the lack of significant opposition to the reforms on the part of the *Länder* had to do with the fact that the integration of the two forms of industrial order meant that in many areas the interests of decentralized and autarkic regions were overlapping. Many large mass-producing companies in decentralized regions, for example, had just as strong an interest in the creation of a stable macroeconomic environment in the country as a whole as mass-producing firms in autarkic regions. As long as there remained sufficient local autonomy for regional authorities to perform the services they had traditionally performed for the small- and medium-sized (now primarily capital-goods) producers within their borders, there was no reason for them to offer fundamental resistance to the reforms in 1967–1969. Similarly, because the reforms aimed at establishing a stable market framework within which independent firms could make confident decisions about investment, and thus did not attempt to make changes in the immediate organization of production and its administration, they found general support throughout both groupings of German business.

The result of this overlapping of regional interest was that partisan, and often class, identities tended to become more salient than regional ones.[62] This became particularly obvious during the struggle over the implementation of extensive domestic reforms during the first Social Democratic government under Willy Brandt. The irony of that time, however, was that the partisan big business and middle class opposition of the CDU to the SPD reforms was exercised primarily through its strong position in the Bundesrat.

Throughout the early 1970s, the new SPD government attempted to implement a broad program of domestic reforms that aimed to improve social welfare, redistribute wealth, and democratize education, among many other agenda items. The Bundesrat emerged as a key source of opposition to these SPD domestic reforms. Since the conservative parties held a majority in the upper house but not in the parliament, they exercised the Bundesrat's constitutional authority to block or redefine legislation until it was acceptable to the governments in the *Länder*. On many issues, such as SPD plans to impose tax increases on wealthy Germans and give tax breaks to lower income ones, the Bundesrat's opposition was clearly a partisan matter: the radical reforms were outright blocked in the federal body.[63] In general, the CDU steadfastly opposed all efforts on the part of the SPD government to intervene in the market economy or interfere with the autonomy of the independent producer (regardless of its size). The Bundesrat was redefined as a tool of parliamentary opposition.

Although the old regional differences took second place to partisan ones during this period, they were not completely eliminated. In many cases of reform, particularly with respect to the educational reforms, it was impossible to separate partisan from federalist sentiments. Proposals to create *Gesamthochschulen*, or comprehensive universities, which eliminated the traditional divisions between *Fachhochschulen* (technical schools/community colleges) and the universities, were rejected by CDU ruled states.[64] In 1970, the Brandt government created a commission, the Bund-Länder Kommission für Bildungsplanung (Joint Commission for Educational Planning), to discuss a government proposal to reform secondary schools (the equivalent of the U.S. high school) by leveling the existing three-way tracked structure (*Realschule*), and creating a single type of *Gesamtschule*, or comprehensive high school. The Commission ultimately came up with a proposal that resembled the SPD's original conception, but most of the CDU *Länder* refused to back it.

In both cases, Baden Württemberg, in particular, was opposed to the reforms of the traditional educational structure because it believed that the creation of such schools would disrupt the intimate ties that existed between its schools and the surrounding decentralized economy.[65] The other regions of decentralized production, located primarily in North Rhine Westphalia and Hesse, were not able to express opposition to the proposed reforms within the federal format because they were located in *Länder* with disadvantageous mixes of autarkic and decentralized interests. In both regions, SPD governments were close to autarkic industry and their unions and tended to vote with the central government on the reforms.[66]

274   *Industrial constructions*

Modell Deutschland *and organized capitalism*

Despite the persistence of political controversy around the institutional features of the decentralized industrial order in areas such as education, the dominant tendency in the German political economy by the end of the 1960s was for regional political identities and institutions to recede from the center of politics. Integration in the industrial economy between the decentralized and autarkic forms of industrial order was the cause of this, and the elevation of partisan and class issues was the consequence. The political economy that emerged is a very familiar one: Large mass-producing firms, close to large universal banks, engaged in cooperative relations with both the state and the trade unions over the best way to manage the West German economy.

As many European and North American countries began to experience difficulties in stabilizing their political economies during the 1970s, the stability and economic power of this historically specific political arrangement in West Germany attracted much attention in international political economic discussion. Schonfield, Peter Katzenstein, Wolfgang Streeck, Claus Offe, and others all became interested analytically in West Germany as a model for the way that cooperative, negotiation based neocorporatist structures could regulate and stabilize an industrial (read mass-production-based) political economy.[67]

At the same time, and with similar analytical interests, historians, most prominent among many perhaps being Gerald Feldman, Charles Maier, and Jürgen Kocka, began to probe back into the German past and investigate the way in which such national-level corporatist arrangements had functioned (and failed) in earlier times.[68] None of these scholars paid much attention to the importance of regional factors in the German political economy, because at the time they were writing such factors had relatively little salience. But the result was that the dominant frameworks for understanding what the German political economy actually was, Social Democratic *Modell Deutschland* ("Model Germany") and "organized capitalism," represented the analytical properties of the political economy as well as its traditions and genealogy, in ways that completely blended out the regional economic traditions and regional institutions that much of this book has been about.

Only in the internal West German policy discussion did the significance of the federalist character of West German politics continue to be salient. But even here, the drift of the discussion underscored the extent to which the integration of the two forms of industrial order within a mass-production economy had shaped public understanding of the West German political system. During the 1970s, a large body of literature arose in SPD circles concerned with the problem of policy making in an interlocking political structure (*Politikverflechtung*). Much of this literature was concerned with how to optimize policy making so that the obstacles of regional resistance to central direction could be overcome. In the view of proponents of active central state policies for technological development and structural adjustment, for example, the interlocking structure of joint central state–regional government projects, combined with a vast array

The national context   275

of autonomous regional government policies, made for a kind of political paralysis in the face of mounting structural crises.[69] The West German state, in their view, was insufficiently centralized to be able to reconnoiter the mounting structural and competitive problems within the mass-production economy.

As the next section will show, however, the incapacity of the central state to get regional cooperation for its policies had little to do with the insufficient centralization of the German state and much to do with a crisis in the underlying integration between the two forms of industrial order in the West German economy. Discussions of insufficient centralization were slowly transformed into discussions about efficient decentralization.

A new period of decentralization

Two sets of general developments during the latter half of the 1970s and the 1980s and 1990s worked together to undermine the viability of the institutional and policy trends toward national-level centralization in state and society outlined in the last section. One development followed from the fact that during the 1970s growing integration of international financial markets occurred at the same time that serious global monetary shocks introduced considerable instability into the international system. The two oil shocks, the international debt crisis, and extremely high interest rates in the United States placed so much pressure on European governments, and in particular the German government, to defend the value of their currencies against overwhelming downward pressures and erratic speculative trends that countries effectively lost the capacity to manage the growth of demand in their macroeconomies in a Keynesian manner.[70] Monetary policy was hostage to the exchange rate and fiscal policies were undermined by the growing size of public debt payments brought on by chronically high interest rates (following the logic of Domar's Law).[71] This imposed austerity caused rates of unemployment to rise significantly throughout Europe and in Germany as well (in the latter case, particularly in the autarkic regions)[72] (see Tables 12 and 13). The high global interest rate environment, however, meant that governments increasingly had little other choice than to address their growing problems by creating better conditions on the supply side in order to get any domestic investment at all.[73]

The other development, of course, was the complete transformation of what constituted the supply side beginning in the late 1970s. As both chapters on postwar industry in Germany have shown, the level of international industrial competition between advanced industrial states intensified considerably during the 1980s and 1990s, undermining the stable mass-production driven trajectory of postwar development. In the face of a continuous and accelerating rhythm of technological and product changes driven by the new competition, firms were no longer capable of stably managing the evolution of technology in their markets, much less of stabilizing their investment and transaction risks through progressive integration.[74] Their resulting efforts to simultaneously reform the in-

Industrial constructions

Table 12 *Percentage unemployment in West Germany, 1976–1986*

	1976	1980	1986
Territorial States			
Baden-Württemberg	3.4	2.3	5.1
Bavaria	5.0	3.5	7.0
Hesse	4.4	2.8	6.8
Lower Saxony	5.4	4.7	11.5
North-Rhine Westphalia	4.9	4.6	10.9
Rhineland-Palatinate	4.8	3.8	8.3
Saarland	6.7	6.5	13.3
Schleswig-Holstein	5.2	4.2	10.9
City-States			
Bremen	5.6	5.3	15.5
Hamburg	3.9	3.4	13.0
West Berlin	3.9	4.3	10.5
Total for Federal Republic of Germany	4.6	3.8	9.0

Taken from Arthur Benz, "Intergovernment Relations in the 1980s," p. 205.

Table 13 *Unemployment and employment in selected OECD nations, 1973–1979 and 1979–1983/1985*

Country	Average annual unemployment rate		Total change in number employed	
	1973–1979	1979–1985	1973–1979	1979–1984
Austria	1.7	3.0*	2.4	−2.0
FRG	2.9	6.0	−3.4	−2.7
GB	4.7	10.3	1.5	−5.6
Sweden	2.0	2.7	7.8	1.8
Belgium	5.8	11.6	0.2	−4.4
Switzerland	0.4†	0.6	−7.5	1.4
France	4.3	8.0	2.2	−1.8
Italy	6.5	9.0	6.3	1.8
Japan	1.8	2.4	4.2	5.2
Norway	1.8	2.4	13.2	5.2
Netherlands	4.5‡	10.3	3.1	3.0
U.S.A.	6.4	7.7	16.2	6.3

*Until 1984.
†From 1975 on.
‡From 1974 on.
Sources: OECD *Economic Outlook* 39; OECD Labour Force Statistics Yearbook, 1963–1983; 1964–1984. Taken from Fritz W. Scharpf, *Crisis and Choice in European Social Democracy*, p. 239.

ternal structure of the firm and decentralize production beyond its boundaries gave rise not only to the different regional experiences within the German economy, as already outlined, but to a variety of new public-good problems at the regional and national level that could only awkwardly be addressed by the national-level state or the central union organizations.

This globally induced prioritization of the supply side, coupled with the redefinition of the strategies and incentives of both groupings of industrial capital in Germany, ultimately resulted in a dramatic recalibration downwards of the allocation of central and local competence and action within two key assemblages of governance structures in the national political economy: The federal structure of the German government and the industrial relations system.[75] In neither case has this recalibration occurred through dramatic formal reform of existing institutional arrangements as occurred in the 1960s. The case of decentralization in the structure of federalism, however, suggests that the formerly decried incompleteness of the previous centralizing reforms may in the end have been a virtue, at least during the boom of the 1980s. Struggles over decentralization in the industrial relations system, on the other hand, suggests that the earlier centralizing and firm-privileging reforms of the 1950s and 1960s may have been overly successful.

Regardless of their success, however, both cases make clear that the broader institutional framework of the German political economy began to be restructured during the 1980s and 1990s in ways that were intended to respond to new governance pressures created by underlying changes in both forms of industrial orders and in their relationship to one another. The trend toward decentralization, finally, seems not to have been disrupted by the experience of German reunification. In the new unified Germany, principles of local self-government and strong federalism – in all public and parapublic institutions governing economic activity – are all valued as essential in the debate surrounding industrial adjustment. No one suggests that the extremely serious economic problems of the German economy today can be resolved through greater centralization. Instead, debates focus on how local and regional institutions can be reformed to be effective in the adjustment process.

The decentralization of the state

Calls for institutional reform of the West German state to allow for greater decentralization and local and regional decision making autonomy could already be heard during the late 1970s, but the real push came after the Christian Democratic government assumed power in 1983.[76] Criticism was articulated initially in the form of frustration with the existing system of joint policy making between the central government and the *Länder*.[77] Neither level of government was satisfied with the existing system for different, though ultimately complimentary reasons.

The central government criticized the joint decision making system because it led to higher levels of spending and disrupted its pursuit of an increasingly restrictive macroeconomic strategy. Since the system required both the *Land* and central government to reach a consensus in order to solve problems, many policies that were intended to be redistributive ultimately became distributive ones.[78] Decisions were oriented toward the status quo and designed to reduce conflict. As a result, they tended to solve disputes by paying both parties off.[79] This system was frustrating to the Social Democratic government in the latter years of the 1970s, as they felt it was a poor form of centralization that inhibited the central state's ability to develop effective central policies to shape industrial adjustment. But, to the Christian Democrats, who were guided by neoliberal beliefs in the virtues of the market, the system was unnecessarily inflationary, bureaucratic and, indeed, too interventionist.[80] It was their view, and the view of much of German business at the time, that the best strategy of adjustment was one that created a stable, noninflationary market environment that enabled producers to restructure themselves without the interference of the central state.

On the other side, many of the richer *Länder*, such as Baden-Württemberg, criticized the system for being too cumbersome in areas of crucial importance, such as industrial policy.[81] The government in Baden-Württemberg was quick to recognize the new dynamism of the decentralized industrial order, and very early on began to construct policies, and even build new institutions (such as the Steinbeis Foundation), that fostered the growth of decentralized industrial production.[82] However, it felt constrained by the bureaucratic process of Federal (*Bund*)–*Land* decision making.

Despite the interest in decentralizing reform on all sides, an actual reform of the constitutional structure of the state never took place. There were three reasons for this. First, a real decentralization of responsibilities within the state would have involved important downward transfers of fiscal resources, which would have been extremely beneficial to rich *Länder*, such as Baden-Württemberg, but extremely disadvantageous to economically distressed regions, such as the autarkic Saarland, North Rhine Westphalia, Lower Saxony, and Bremen. These benefitted from central redistribution of funds from richer regions and from continued Federal government coresponsibility for structural adjustment costs. Such regions therefore tended to defend central mechanisms and commitments that facilitated transfers.

Second, even though the central state favored decentralization (particularly after the Christian Democrats gained power), it did not have the authority to impose reforms on resistant *Länder*. The rules of cooperative federalism, as established in the 1960s, were that the government negotiate with the *Länder* regarding all policies that affected them and especially regarding institutional reforms. The rules governing cooperation gave the disadvantaged *Länder* the leverage to block reform.[83]

The third reason that reform did not occur was that it was ultimately possible to allow for greater flexibility at the lower levels of government without institutional reforms. On the one hand, the central government stopped trying to use the cooperative and interlinked governmental structure as a mechanism for central intervention and direction (as it had in the 1960s and 1970s), and instead

The national context

allowed policy initiatives to come from below. This was especially true in the areas of industrial and social welfare policies, and increasingly as the decade wore on, for technology policies as well.[84] On the other hand, the individual *Länder* were capable of manipulating the complicated system of intergovernmental relations to their own ends, gaining greater autonomy when they desired and insisting on federal participation when it was needed. As Arthur Benz put it in 1989, decentralization in German federalism:

> ... has not been produced by transforming cooperative federalism into a system of separated functions and decision making, but by using the flexibility contained in the complex and entangled institutional structures. The sharing of functions in the federal system makes it possible to shift the focus of policy making from central regulation to decentralized implementation and to use the discretionary powers of lower level governments. When the *Land* and local governments responded to the crisis of centralized policy making, institutional structures of cooperative federalism provided the basis for a de facto decentralization without structural reform.[85]

Quantitative evidence of this kind of decentralization has been particularly marked in the areas of industrial and regional economic policies. Between 1981 and 1984, for example, *Länder* and local governments increased the level of financial subsidies they provided to industrial firms by 7.5% per year, whereas the general level of their annual outlays increased by only 1.5%. By contrast, the federal outlays to industrial producers during the same period only grew at a rate of 3.7% a year, while total annual spending increased at 3.5% a year.[86] Another indication of the growing importance of the regional level was that *Länder* spent more on their own for regional economic development than they did through their obligatory contributions to joint-task regional promotion programs. In 1983, for example, the *Länder* gave out DM 468.4 million in subsidies through their own programs, while contributing a total (not including tax allowances) of DM 334.2 million to joint-task projects.[87]

The importance of such trends toward decentralization in the 1980s, however, was not simply quantitative. From our point of view, the key point is that decentralization effectively reinstated the kind of flexibility at the local and regional level for governments to respond and develop independent policies for the particular regional economic problems they confronted. As the chapters on both of the forms of industrial order in the current period showed, decentralization in industrial production gave rise to an array of regional policies that reflected the needs of the different regional industrial orders in Germany. This involved both the development of an array of technology and innovation policies in Baden-Württemberg, tailored to the needs of the dynamic small- and medium-sized producers in the region's decentralized production system, as well as the development of policies in the Ruhr Valley, the region around Paderborn in North-Rhine Westphalia, Bavaria, and the Saarland to deal with efforts on the part of autarkic producers to achieve greater decentralization in their own operations.⁸⁸ The more that decentralized practices in the economy diffused into the formerly autarkic regions, moreover, the more significant this local and regional flexibility became.

By the beginning of the 1990s, discussion in Germany was not about whether or not decentralization was desirable, but about what form local and regional policies should take. There was tremendous mutual examination and imitation among the *Länder*. The Baden-Württemberg government's local success in providing services to decentralized production was widely copied, even in relatively unindustrialized Schleswig-Holstein.⁸⁹ It was certainly true that in many cases all of this local and regional innovation was not always viewed as a happy event, as cities, especially, found that they were forced to deal with increasing social and economic challenges with less central support.⁹⁰ But in other cases, the withdrawal of the central government was viewed by both the right and the left as an opportunity to enhance community self government.⁹¹

So, just as centralization and integration in the economy during the 1960s fostered centralization and integration in the structure and policy of the state, so decentralization and disintegration in the economy during the 1980s fostered a similar reversal in state structure. Unlike previous periods of significant change in the German economy, however, the changes of the 1980s in the state structure were not driven by formal reforms. Instead, there was an informal recalibration of the weights of the various levels of government. Perhaps the most convincing evidence that the trend toward decentralization in industrial practice nonetheless completely transformed the character of the political economy, however, was the fact that the same formal political structure that during the 1970s was decried as a cumbersome and inefficient form of centralization, was frequently praised by the same analysts during the 1980s as a model of highly adaptable decentralized policy making.⁹²

After the unification of Germany, the complete collapse of the eastern economy, and the onset of crisis in the western economy in the early 1990s, observers have been less sanguine about the capacity of lower-level governments to facilitate industrial adjustment in their regions. Yet, there have been few voices calling for a reversal of the move within the federal structure toward greater responsibility at local and regional levels that transpired during the 1980s. Decentralization within the federalist structure, it appears, continues to be favored over the centralization of economic and industrial policy making at the national level. Its just that in the context of the industrial crisis of the mid-1990s, weaknesses in the structure and practice of service provision to industry at the local and regional level have been revealed.⁹³

Since it was widely imitated during the 1980s, illustration of the current predicament of the regional government in Baden-Württemberg can be taken as paradigmatic of the general situation in regional economic policy. Neither the regional government, nor any of the significant extrafirm institutions in Baden-Württemberg have been able either to stave off the onset of crisis among small, medium-sized, and large firms, or contribute significantly to reorganization within those firms. In large part, the reason for this seems to be that the traditional institutional infrastructure within the region always presupposed an economy of healthy, competitive firms. The activities and services of the supporting institutions in local and regional governments focused on defraying costs and supplying information to firms that were in a position to take advantage of such things (e.g., traditional roles for government involved technology transfer, education, and indirect subsidization). The difference in the current period is that there are very few healthy firms in Baden-Württemberg and the difficulties that firms have, as we saw in Chapter 5, are for the most part internal to the boundaries of the firm. As a result, by the fall of 1994, there was a remarkable paralysis among the key local institutions within the region regarding how to deal with the pervasive crisis within its industrial economy.

The problem is extremely delicate: It is not only not part of the traditional mandate of public and nonfirm institutions, such as the Steinbeis Foundation, or the economic ministries of the *Land* to intervene in the internal restructuring processes of producers. It is also the case that actually engaging in that kind of activity would pose tremendous risks for the public institution: An attempt to get involved in the internal restructuring processes of firms would raise controversial questions of property rights and would place the institution under considerable legitimation pressure if its efforts failed. Given these potential risks, the tendency, at least at this early moment in the mid-1990s, seems to be to avoid taking this kind of action. Instead, the regional government engages in the classic political game of attempting to appear to be acting when in fact one is waiting for others to do so. The formation of the special elite commission by the government in Baden-Württemberg, the Zukunftskommission: Baden-Württemberg 2000 mentioned in Chapter 5, is a classic example of the kind of politics of stalling currently being practiced. Rather than take action, the government fosters discussion and, as it has traditionally done, waits to follow the lead of firms in crisis.

In the end, this situation shows that the self-blockage that Chapters 5 and 6 described within German industrial firms has its correlate within the institutions that support them.[94] Ultimately the current structure of local policy practice will need to be changed, or the experience of self-blockage in the political economy will turn into a more enduring industrial decline. It is too soon to say what such reforms will be. It is possible, however, to say that whatever shape the reform of local institutions and their practice assumes, it will take place through interaction among public and private actors and intimate and local public discussion of their needs and capabilities. State and economy, in other words are likely to restructure together; it is not possible to claim that action on one side will determine the shape and strategy of action on the other.

Decentralization and industrial relations

The changed political and economic situation of the 1970s, 1980s, and 1990s has given rise to very significant changes in the character of German industrial relations. The movement toward centralization in the industrial relations system of the 1950s and 1960s has been entirely checked, and in many areas completely reversed. The trade unions no longer share implicit coresponsibility for the stability of the macroeconomy as they once had. Moreover, though the system of industrial relations received wide attention during the 1980s for its strength and adaptability in dealing with the problem of unemployment,[95] its capacity to deal with the trend toward internal corporate reform and the decentralization of production that began to emerge in the economy during the 1980s and which has intensified during the 1990s has proven to be far more ambiguous. Indeed, its successes in the former realm have in many ways undermined the union movement's capacity to deal with the new trends in the reorganization of production because they reinforced the dualism of power in the industrial relations system between the national level and the plant level that was created in the 1950s and 1960s. Decentralization in production, in particular, poses problems for the trade unions on a regional level, outside the boundaries of the firm: Such decentralization calls for action at a level of organization and policy that has completely atrophied within German industrial relations system.

The dual developments in the macroeconomy and in production outlined above worked together to undermine the central importance of national-level wage bargaining in the German economy. Even though there continued to be central agreements and the patterning of wage bargains, the German central government stopped organizing its macroeconomic policies around Keynesian principles of aggregate-demand management in the mid-1970s.[96] Beginning around the same time, two further developments shifted the focus of the union movement away from wages toward more qualitative issues. First, structural changes in certain industries in autarkic regions, such as steel and shipbuilding, and the significant curtailment in government fiscal stimulation, gave rise to continuously rising rates of unemployment which, though regionally unbalanced, weakened the trade unions' overall position in the national labor market.[97] Second, dramatic changes in production technology and organization, following from the increasing use of microelectronics and the pervasive need for flexibility, created tremendous challenges for the unions at the local level that were only indirectly related to wages.[98] Both of these problems created tremendous centrifugal pressures on central unions.

In the matter of unemployment, localization of bargaining was pressed upon the unions by the employers. Unemployment began to rise in the Federal Republic in the mid-1970s. Between 1978 and 1983, the annual rate of unemployment increased from 4.3% to 9.1%, leaving nearly 2.3 million jobless in the latter year.[99] In 1984, IG Metall launched an offensive against unemployment by demanding the reduction of the work week to 35 hours without any corresponding reduction in pay. Initially, employers completely resisted even engaging in bargaining over work time issues, which they had long regarded as a taboo question that was inappropriately dealt with at the level of central negotiations. Employer resistance was ultimately overcome through a compromise in which employers accepted a reduction in weekly working time (from 40 to 38.5 hours) in exchange for the radical decentralization of subsequent bargaining over the precise way in which the shorter hours would be implemented at the plant level. The key aspect of the accord was that it had an opening clause that explicitly institutionalized a second round of bargaining at the plant level—the central bargain established a set of parameters within which, in the second round of bargaining, works councils and plant management could adopt any particular kind of system they could agree on.[100]

Subsequent agreements (in 1987 and 1990) were both based upon the idea of a second round of bargaining and extended the basic compromise of worktime reductions in exchange for greater local level flexibility in implementation. Many, especially Anglo-American, students of labor movements who have viewed the destruction and decay of central bargaining in their own countries during the 1980s viewed the fact that the German system adapted in this way as a tremendous success for trade unions.[101] Thelen, for example, summed up the 1980s experience as much as a triumph for continued centralization as a shift toward decentralization: "Pressures for decentralization were resolved not through the breakdown of central bargaining, but rather through the flexibilization of central contracts and a shift in the balance within the dual system toward the growing importance of works councils."[102]

Regardless of the validity of such claims regarding the union's experience with the specific issue of work time,[103] there are a variety of reasons to believe that the problem of decentralization has by no means been solved by the trade union movement. Indeed, the institutional consequence of the above agreements was to reinforce the power of precisely those levels of the industrial relations system (the plant works councils and the central union) that are most threatened by the current trends toward internal corporate reform and radical decentralization in production outlined in the previous chapters.[104]

As we saw in the discussions of both regional forms of industrial order, the entire thrust of adjustment pressures during the 1980s and 1990s has been to encourage internal corporate reforms that facilitate cross-departmental collaboration combined with the breakdown of the boundaries of the plant through disintegration and collaborative subcontracting. Large firms tried (with varying degrees of success) to break themselves up and small- and medium-sized firms engaged in relations with larger producers as increasingly equal partners. Ever more sophisticated and flexible production processes, involving team and group organization both in production and development, created demand for completely new types of skilled workers and new forms of organization on the shop floor. All of this transformed (and is transforming) the character of labor markets and their relationship to the institutions that have traditionally governed them, both in and outside the firm.

There are three ways in which the system of industrial relations in Germany, in its current form, is threatened by these changes. First, the new generation of skilled workers being created in contemporary plants has been difficult for the trade unions to recruit in the traditional fashion. This is because the new type of worker is highly skilled, not only with traditional blue collar skills, but with new programming and system-interpretive skills as well.[105] Increasingly, these workers serve a traditional apprenticeship and then go on for further training at a *Fachhochschule* (community college) or even a university. This new trajectory keeps the new workers out of the milieu of the factory and away from acculturating contact with the trade unions and works councils that occurs there for longer periods of time during formative periods of their careers. Moreover, when they come back to the shop floor, they are placed within new production arrangements (teams, U-shaped lines, etc.) in which the traditional skill divisions and hierarchies of status, the defense of which the careers of trade unionists and works councilors have been based upon, no loger exist. On top of all this, such workers tend to view whatever position they have merely as a temporary resting place on the way to more challenging jobs elsewhere. Examples of such workers are technicians, maintenance specialists, highly qualified system regulators, and, increasingly, highly skilled tradesmen (machinists, toolmakers, and so on), all of whom, in the whizbang world of modern production, have become expert in operating multimillion dollar programmable equipment that is extremely important to their employers.[106]

Furthermore, the traditional issues that have been at the heart of trade union policies – a focus on income and job security, protection from speedups, etc. – are not the problems with which these new workers will be concerned if the new production arrangements diffuse more broadly within firms. At the same time, the issues that do resonate with such workers – problems of the opacity of plant decision making and power structures, the absence of any real opportunity for worker influence in product development, concern for their own long-term ability to continue to be able to adapt their hard-won skills to the rapidly changing technological demands of the firm's production – fall outside the traditional bargaining issues of the trade unions. If these workers tend to grow proportionally within the German workforce, then, without an adjustment on the part of the unions, a growing proportion of the German working class could potentially fall outside the union movement.

Secondly, the internal reorganization and the decentralization of production threatens to undermine the unions' traditional strategy of focusing recruiting and bargaining strength on important individual branches of industry (such as the automobile industry) and the largest firms within them. The internal fragmentation of the large firms (and efforts to push such fragmentation even further) makes it difficult for the unions to develop a coherent central bargaining strategy (in the district *Tarifkommissionen*) because it is becoming increasingly difficult for the works council representatives of the largest firms to develop a single firm-wide set of demands. All of the company's operating units – and, hence, the subsidiary works councils in those operating units – are affected by different pressures and pursue very different strategies. This multiplies points of potential conflict and makes consensus difficult to achieve.

The decentralization of production outside of firms complicates this problem still more. In stark contrast to the era in which the different regional industrial orders were integrated, the central union now has increasingly to reconcile the interests of members in a variety of bargaining regions with different sets of concerns and different degrees of leverage. Still more complicating, the enormous growth of subcontracting has often forced two different unions to compete over representation and strategic guidance. In the automobile industry, for example, the IG Metall now has jurisdictional conflicts with the IG Chemie over workers who produce plastic parts in subcontractor firms, as well as with the IG Textil- und Bekleidung over workers that produce car seats.

Finally, much like managers in old functional departments, or policy makers in the traditional industrial policy institutions, the pressures of the moment place pressure on the union and works council to adopt strategies in the face of change that block rather than encourage change. Because in many cases the company they deal with has become so complex, and all dimensions of production are increasingly being thought of by reformers as strategic chips in a larger corporate game, the works council cannot address all the potential problems its members face all at once. Consequently, the works council focuses on the most immediate problem of defending the jobs of both the weakest and lowest qualified members of the workforce as well as of mature workers with traditional skills whose jobs are especially jeopardized by reorganization and outsourcing. Indeed, this strategy is often effective because the works council can find allies within the company itself among particular plant managers or departmental executives who oppose the current changes, or whose particular area of management is threatened by the trend toward decentralization.

Yet, as understandable as this strategy is, it is clear that in light of the changes now occurring in the economy, it places the union, and especially the works council, in an awkward position. In attempting to save traditional jobs, they run the risk of forcing the company to subcontract the kinds of work that would involve the new kinds of higher skilled jobs and alternative production arrangements outside the firm or to parts of the firm located in other countries, where the obstacles to reform are not as high as they are in Germany. Thus, the possibility that the skills and the workers of the second half of the 1990s will all be located outside of areas of union strength – and even outside of Germany – exists in a very real way today within the Federal Republic, at least in part as the direct result of actions the unions themselves have taken to combat it.

An irony in this predicament is that the German labor movement is now weakest in an area that was, for much of its history, its strength: the interfirm and regional level. There have been efforts, many of them initiated by renegade union locals (or groups of them), to respond to the regional labor market pressures – in particular, the greater circulation of skilled workers between local firms – that internal reform and the decentralization of production has begun to create. One local on the Schwäbische Alb in Württemberg attempted to construct a computerized database of local firms, including their products and union members, in an effort to develop the capacity to match members with firm needs through-

286 *Industrial constructions*

out the region. The effort was blocked, however, both by local works councils, which felt threatened by the growing circulation of workers, and by the central union, which felt betrayed by the fact that the local was constructing the database on a network of Macintoshes, rather than on the union's centralized computer system.[107]

These events show that the unions are in important ways experiencing pressures very similar to those alluded to above in the case of local and regional governments, i.e., it is one thing to recognize that the local level is important, and quite another to redraw the internal lines of organizational power in a way that devolves resources and discretion downwards in an effective and appropriate way. The resistance to the alteration of the traditional strategies and structures of the local and regional trade unions and works councils driven by those likely to lose power from the changes is the downside of the consolidation of works council and central union power during the 1980s. It is not unthinkable that the current system of worker representation will be able to reinvent itself in the latter part of the 1990s. As we have seen, the system has done so a number of times in the past.

Transformation of the industrial relations system in Germany must travel a much longer road than was the case with the institutions of German federalism discussed above. Unlike the case of the federalist German state, the German trade union movement very thoroughly centralized itself during the postwar era in a way that completely bypassed the regional level. Thus, whereas the state was able to recalibrate power downwards without significant institutional reform, because when the central state sought to withdraw, local governments eagerly stepped into the breach, this is unlikely to occur without considerable conflict in the union movement. Who knows how such conflicts will be affected by the also inevitable local conflicts regrading precisely how the trade union movement at the local level can or should be involved in the changing structure of the local industrial order. In this context it is very facile, but nonetheless quite safe, to say that the continued resilience of the older characteristics of the German model in the dual system of industrial relations will be the source of tremendous instability as the century comes to an end. If the German economy is able to resolve the problem of self-blockage it is now experiencing and embark on a new course of successful and competitive industrial growth, it seems very likely that it will do so with a radically different industrial relations system.

Conclusion: Constructing governance

This final chapter has traced the way in which the national frameworks of institutions that govern the different regional systems of industrial order in Germany evolved over the course of the postwar period. The aim of the analysis was to analyze how the institutional frameworks were first constituted and then reconfigured as the relationship between the different forms of order changed.

The national context

When the two different forms of industrial order were reconstituted after World War II, a national framework was established (rather inadvertently) that allowed for the independent reproduction of both the decentralized and autarkic industrial orders. This original framework had many of the same virtues contained in the old Imperial structure: It was a composite of national frameworks that reflected considerable regional and local variation.

As the two forms of industrial order began to grow integrated with the diffusion of mass-production practices in the early postwar decades, efforts were made both in the state and in society to alter the national framework of institutions to accommodate the new economic situation. Two developments were critical in this: 1) the creation of a centralized system of collective bargaining capable of governing the process of wage-setting throughout the national economy; 2) the autonomy of regional and local governments was curtailed and governing authority centralized. In both cases, the creation of centralized institutional frameworks was compatible with the interests of producers within both forms of industrial order. Indeed, with the integration of the regional systems through the diffusion of mass production, regional forms of identity began to recede and national partisan and class-based identity claims began to infuse political economic discourse and conflicts.

Finally, with the transformation of production in the 1980s and 1990s, trends toward decentralization and disintegration in the economy have engendered similar pressures within the governing institutions. Though there has been no constitutional redefinition of relations between *Bund* and *Länder* in the context of increasing pressures for decentralization in the economy, there has been a significant informal recalibration of responsibility and initiative downward toward local levels. These trends have intensified, not abated, with the unification of Germany. The industrial relations system has come under pressures to decentralize that are similar to those confronting the institutions of the state. Its capacity to respond, however, has proven to be more limited. A historically specific alliance between the central union and plant-level representative bodies, developed and deeply institutionalized during the initial postwar decades, presents powerful resistance to efforts to respond to the challenge of decentralization by radically transforming the structure of the industrial relations system. The apparent inexorability of the pressures for decentralization combined with the intransigence of the traditional institutional powers promises to give rise to significant conflicts about the future role and purpose of the trade unions in contemporary German society. The way in which labor markets will be governed in Germany in the remainder of the 20th and early 21st centuries, therefore, is completely uncertain.

This uncertainty beclouding the institutional structure of governance in the labor market, naturally, reflects the confused and uncertain state of the recomposition of organization and practice within both the autarkic and decentralized industrial orders, as described in Chapters 5 and 6. It thus appears that in the future, as in the past, the self-definition of economic actors and the constitution of their practices, interests, and institutions of governance at both the local and national levels will evolve simultaneously, through a process of broad political struggle and debate. This should not be surprising. It has been the point of this entire book that such mutually and reciprocally conditioning and defining processes have always shaped the social, political, and economic structure of the division of labor in Germany.

Notes

Notes for Chapter 1

1. The notion of "organized capitalism" has shaped much of the historical literature on the development of the German political economy in the 19th and early 20th centuries. See, for example, Heinrich A. Winkler (ed.), *Organisierte Kapitalismus*; and Hans-Ulrich Wehler, *Das Deutsche Kaiserreich 1871–1918*. "Cooperative managerial capitalism" is the term that Alfred Chandler has recently applied to the German system; see Chandler, *Scale and Scope*. "Coordinated Market Economy" is a term coined by David Soskice with reference to Germany in his "Reinterpreting Corporatism and Explaining Unemployment: Co-ordinated and Non-co-ordinated Market Economies."
2. See especially the essay "Economic Backwardness in Historical Perspective" in Alexander Gerschenkron, *Economic Backwardness in Historical Perspective*, pp. 5–30 and passim. This essay develops the idea of the advantages of backwardness and links institutional forms to the timing of industrialization. See also Gerschenkron, *Continuity in History and Other Essays*, especially pp. 77–256. Gerschenkron's earlier, war-time work on the German agriculture is interesting but less theoretically influential among postWar students of industrial development: Gerschenkron, *Bread and Democracy in Germany*. This book emphasizes the role of agrarian elites, industrial sectors, and producer coalitions as key actors in politics.

    It is extremely important to emphasize that my discussion of Gerschenkron is in no way concerned with the particular causal arguments that Gerschenkron made about the industrialization process (such as the need for a great spurt of growth, the special role of banks, and the production of industrialization ideologies). Nor do I want to claim that the writers that I group together in the "Gerschenkronian tradition" believed in these arguments or that they were Gerschenkronian for these reasons. Even less do I want to suggest that Gerschenkron was the first to come up with all of the observation and arguments that he wove together. Rather, my aim is to construct Gerschenkron as the founder of a very powerful research program that framed the study of German industrialization in the postwar period. In this way, the reader will see, I emphasize two dimensions of Gerschenkron's contribution. First, he provided a clear story to understand the German experience (i.e., that Germany industrialized late and that the institutional structure of the political economy was bound up with that lateness). Second, he applied theoretical categories that were independent of his specific claims (the unitary character of industrialization within national boundaries, the firm as a crucial organizing unit, the pressures of international efficiency standards, and a strict boundary between politics and production) that framed the German experience in a way that highlighted specific actors and organizations. This framing, as the text below will elucidate, has subsequently been built upon and modified throughout the political economy literature in history and the social sciences of the 1960s through the 1980s.

3. Recent writing clearly influenced by Gerschenkron's historical institutionalism ranges well beyond the particular case of Germany. See the following, which are only the most prominent from among many possible examples: Peter Katzenstein, *Small States and World Markets* and *Corporatism and Change*; Chalmers Johnson, *MITI and the Japanese Miracle*; Alice Amsden, *Asia's Next Giant*; Peter Gourevitch, *Politics in Hard Times*; Ronald Rogowski, *Commerce and Coalitions*; and Peter Evans, Dietrich Reuschemeyer, and Theda Skocpol (eds.), *Bringing the State Back In*, especially the contributions in Part One: "States as Promoters of Economic Development and Social Redistribution."

All of these books in one way or another make the narrow Gerschenkronian point that institutions and strategies in the state and economy are called forth at certain points in the industrialization process and that their particular form is shaped by the timing of industrialization relative to international competitors. Moreover, in their focus on industries and sectors as actors, these writers all make the Gerschenkronian assumption that the firm is the primary unit for the organization of production. A fellow traveller and friendly critic of this institutionalism is John Zysman; see *Governments, Markets and Growth* (especially pp. 289 ff). Historical institutionalism is not exhausted by the Gerschenkron approach, but the school's emphasis on the way in which institutional characteristics shape interest formation and action places it solidly in that lineage. A nice survey of the development of historical institutionalism and its relationship to other traditions in the social sciences has recently appeared: see Kathleen Thelen and Sven Steinmo, "Historical Institutionalism in Comparative Politics."

For a recent overview of Gerschenkron's contribution to and influence on the literature on European Industrialization in the 19th century, see the essays in Richard Sylla and Gianni Toniolo (eds.), *Patterns of European Industrialization. The Nineteenth Century*.

4. See Gerschenkron, *Economic Backwardness in Historical Perspective*.

5. It should also be noted that there have been many critiques of Gerschenkron's specific claims about the nature of the development process. His attempt to correlate specific kinds of institutional innovations with specific periods of time in the industrialization process does not work for very many countries. Nor does comparative analysis reveal any need for a great initial spurt of growth or for important industrializing ideologies. For an array of specialist critiques of the particulars of Gerschenkron's theory of industrialization and the advantages of backwardness see, among others: W. A. Ashworth, "Typologies and Evidence: Has Nineteenth Century Europe a Typology of Economic Growth?"; D. Good, "Backwardness and the Role of Banking in the Nineteenth Century European Industrialization"; P. J. Obrien, "Do We Have a Typology for the Study of European Industrialization in the 19th Century?"; and Clive Treblicock, *The Industrialization of the Continental Powers, 1780–1914*. Albert Hirschman provided an early, and sympathetic, critique of Gerschenkron's hypotheses in relation to the problem of industrialization in Latin America. See Hirschman's "The Political Economy of Import-Substituting Indus-

trialization in Latin America," especially pp. 94 ff. Most recently, see Richard Sylla and Gianni Toniolo, *Patterns of European Industrialization*, in particular the careful essay by Tilly on Germany, pp. 175-196.

6. Theories that begin research programs don't have to be right, they just have to generate interesting researchable questions. See the locus classicus of this way of understanding the progress of science, Imre Lakatos, "Falsification and the Methodology of Scientific Research Programmes" as well as the critical discussion by Ian Hacking, "Lakatos' Philosophy of Science."

7. Jürgen Kocka, "The Rise of Modern Industrial Enterprise in Germany"; idem, "Expansion, Integration, Diversifikation"; idem and Hannes Siegrist, "Die hundert größten deutschen Industrieunternehmen in späten 19. und frühen 20. Jahrhundert." The central works by Chandler are *Scale and Scope*, *The Invisible Hand*, *Strategy and Structure*, and (editor, with Herman Daems) *Managerial Hierarchies*.

8. Kocka, "The Rise of Modern Industrial Enterprise in Germany."

9. Ibid.; and Chandler, *Scale and Scope*, pp. 393-592.

10. Jürgen Kocka, "Capitalism and Bureaucracy in German Industrialization Before 1914."

11. The early adoption of diversified bureaucratic structures by Siemens, well before such diversification in American enterprises, is a point that Kocka makes in several places; see the references in note 7 as well as his magisterial *Unternehmensverwaltung und Angestelltenschaft am Beispiel Siemens, 1847-1914*.

12. On the use of the concept "organized capitalism" to describe German industry during the late 19th and first half of the 20th centuries, see the classic essays in Winkler (ed.), *Organisierter Kapitalismus*. Chandler concurs with this characterization of the German economy in his *Scale and Scope* when he refers to German capitalism as "cooperative managerial capitalism." Kocka appreciates Chandler's appreciation in his review of *Scale and Scope* in "German: Cooperation and Competition," especially p. 713.

13. David Landes, *Unbound Prometheus*. Many more specialized studies have been undertaken by German historians: eg. Rainer Fremdling "Foreign Competition and Technological Change"; Ulrich Wengenroth, *Unternehmensstrategien und technischer Forschritt*; Joachim Radkau, *Technik in Deutschland*.

14. Landes, ibid.; Radkau, ibid. pp. 115-221. In general on this topic in this tradition see W. O. Henderson, *The State and the Industrial Revolution in Prussia*; Wolfram Fischer, "The Role of Science and Technology in the Economic Development of Modern Germany"; W. Krieger, "Zur Geschichte von Technologiepolitik und Forschungsförderung in der Bundesrepublik Deutschland"; Peter Lundgreen, B. Horn, W. Krohn, G. Küppers, and R. Paslack, *Staatliche Forschung in Deutschland 1870-1980*; Wilhelm Treue, *Gesellschaft, Wirtschaft und Technik Deutschlands im 19. Jahrhundert*; W. Weber, "Preussische Transferpolitik, 1780-1820." For a relatively recent broad overview of Germany from this point of view, see Otto Keck, "The National System of Technical Innovation in Germany."

15. See especially the initial essays in his *Kapital, Staat und Sozialer Protest*, pp. 15-94.

16. This is the argument given in Richard Tilly, "Germany 1815-1870," and then with greater theoretical, institutional, and sectoral precision in idem., "German Banking, 1850-1914"; idem, "Mergers, External Growth and Finance in the Development of Large-Scale Enterprise in Germany, 1880-1913"; and idem., "Germany." There has been a long ongoing debate on the specific contribution of banks to German industrial growth in the 19th century; see Hugh Neuberger and Houston Stokes,

"German Banks and German Growth, 1883–1913: an Empirical View," which questions the importance of the role of banks and argues that banks benefitted heavy industry at the expense of light industry and that this had negative consequences for growth. Rainer Fremdling and Richard Tilly, "German Banks, German Growth and Econometric History" and the essays by Tilly mentioned above defend the view that banks played a central role in the promotion of growth in the economy, despite the fact that they sponsored large enterprises more than others. See also Wilfried Feldenkirchen, "Banking and Economic Growth," which argues for a more regionally differentiated view of the contribution of banks.

Other, more recent studies of bank–industry relations, in particular that by Volker Wellhöner, have pushed Tilly's modification of Gerschenkron even further by showing that despite their size and importance as sources of capital and their important advisory positions on the boards of large enterprises, large universal banks exercised far less influence over the organizational and strategic development of large German enterprises, even after 1871, than the work of Gerschenkron suggested. The large German banks before 1914, according to Wellhöner's *Grossbanken und Grossindustrie im Kaiserreich*, competed intensely with one another for business among the large concerns. Their chief role in the growth process was as intermediaries between industry and the capital market. Wellhöner's excellent book actually defends much of Gerschenkron's reading of the impact of lateness on the structure of German banking against the more general and total systemic explanation of Rudolf Hilferding's *Finance Capital*. His dispute with Gerschenkron concerns the intensity of the latter's claims regarding bank dominance of industry; see, especially pp., 66–75 and 236–247. Wellhöner's work marks a partial departure from the paradigm, rather than an simple extension of it, by opening up the possibility that the large-firm system of finance operated in a way distinctly different from the way the core postwar literature thought it did. It is a partial departure, however, because, as the argument below will make clear, it continues to privilege large firms and think of industrialization in a unitary way.

17. Pollard's is the seminal contribution to this school of research; see Sidney Pollard, "Industrialization and the European Economy"; idem, *Peaceful Conquest* (Pollard acknowledges his debt to Gerschenkron explicitly in the Preface, p. vii); idem. (ed.), *Region und Industrialisierung*. German research in this area has been superb. See, Hubert Kiesewetter, *Industrielle Revolution in Deutschland 1815–1914*; idem, "Regionale Industrialisierung in Deutschland zur Zeit der Reichsgründung"; Rainer Fremdling and Richard Tilly (eds.), *Industrialisierung und Raum*. A very early, and ultimately flawed, salvo in this direction came from the United States; see Frank Tipton, *Regional Variations in the Economic Development of Germany During the Nineteenth Century*.

18. This is the central focus of some of the major works in Weimar political economy, such as Gerald Feldman, *Iron and Steel in the German Inflation, 1916–1923*; idem. *Vom Weltkrieg zur Weltwirtschaftskrise*; Charles Maier, *Recasting Bourgeois Europe*; Bernd Weisbrod, *Schwerindustrie in der Weimarer Republik*; idem., "Economic Power and Political Stability Reconsidered." See also the many articles focused on industrial politics in the highly influential conference volume, Hans Mommsen, Dietmar Petzina, and Bernd Weisbrod (eds.), *Industrielles System und politische Entwicklung in der Weimarer Republik*.

19. See the stimulating debate between Reinhard Neebe, *Grossindustrie, Staat, und NSDAP 1930–1933;* David Abraham, *The Collapse of the Weimar Republic*; and Henry Ashby Turner, *German Big Business and the Rise of Hitler*.

Notes to pages 7–9

20. This is explicitly the formulation of Feldman in *Iron and Steel in the German Inflation, 1916–1923*, pp. 10–13. Feldman qualifies his claims for the centrality of this industry by pointing out that the chemical and electrotechnical sectors, significant to him also because they had very large firms, vied with iron and steel for the mantel of symbols of Germany's industrial triumph in Europe. Bernd Weisbrod's *Schwerindustrie in der Weimarer Republic* and also his "Economic Power and Political Stability Reconsidered" are explicit arguments for the hegemony of iron and steel in the Weimar economy. Most of the arguments about the political economy of industry in Weimar don't consider alternatives to the large-firm system. Rather they focus on competition within that system, typically between the rising or newer sectors of chemicals, electrotechnical and machinery, against the older sectors of iron, steel, and coal.
21. The earliest and perhaps the most widely influential postwar portrait of the West German political economy is Andrew Schonfield's *Modern Capitalism*, in which the institutions highlighted in the text are given central prominence. Excellent recent historical accounts of the emergence of this system in the postwar Federal Republic are Christian Deubner, "Change and Internationalization in Industry"; Volker Berghahn, *Unternehmer und Politik in der Bundesrepublik* (translated as *The Americanization of West German Industry*); and Simon Reich, *The Fruits of Fascism* (a work on industrial policy toward the automobile industry).
22. For excellent descriptions of the workings of this system, see Kenneth Dyson, "The State, Banks and Industry"; Josef Esser, Wolfgang Fach, and Kenneth Dyson, "Social Market and Modernization Policy"; Josef Esser, Wolfgang Fach, and Werner Väth, *Krisenregulierung*; Frank Vogl, *German Business after the Economic Miracle*; George Küster, "Germany"; Michael Kreile, "The Dynamics of Expansion"; Andrei Markovits (ed.), *Modell Deutschland*.
23. Streeck's most detailed work has focused on the automobile industry, see Streeck, *Industrial Relations in West Germany*; idem, "Industrial Relations and Industrial Change"; idem, "Successful Adjustment in Turbulent Markets"; idem., "On the Institutional Conditions of Diversified Quality Production." Other excellent works in the Streeckian tradition are Lowell Turner, *Democracy at Work*, which focuses on large producers in the automobile industry and in the postal system, and Kathleen Thelen, *Union of Parts*, which focuses on the German metalworkers union, IG Metall, and relies on case studies of large enterprises in the steel, automobile, and consumer-electronics industries.
24. The classic and widely influential economic statement on small firms in the industrialization process is Wolfram Fischer, "Die Rolle des Kleingewerbes im wirtschaftlichen Wachstumsprozess in Deutschland, 1850–1914." Fischer essentially sees the industrialization process not as eliminating small- and medium-sized firms, but as creating dependent and consistently unstable niches for them.
25. See, for example, the characterizations of small business by Ulrich Nocken, *Interindustrial Conflicts and Alliances in the Weimar Republic*; and Heinrich A. Winkler, "Zwischen Panik und Prosperität"; idem, *Zwischen Marx und Monopolen*.
26. On the transformation of the outlook of the German middling classes, see Winkler, *Zwischen Marx und Monopol* and idem, *Liberalismus und Antiliberalismus*. See also the famous argument about the modernizing social revolution of the Nazis given in Ralph Dahrendorf, *Society and Democracy in Germany*
27. For a grand historical discussion of this way of thinking about small- and medium-sized producers, with a good summary of the relevant literature, see Burkhardt Lutz, *Der kurze Traum immerwährende Prosperität*. Another significant work in

the dualist tradition is Werner Sengenberger (ed.), *Der gespaltene Arbeitsmarkt*.
28. On the relative change in small-firm performance in Germany during the 1980s, see Stephanie Weimer, "The Federal Republic Of Germany." It should also be noted that many did not change their views of small firms during the 1980s. A very important literature emerged that attempted to demonstrate how small firms were still very dependent upon large firms. This literature is nicely collected in Bennett Harrison's chapters on Germany in his *Lean and Mean*.
29. See Lutz, *Kurze Traum*....
30. For this kind of argument see Wolfgang Streeck, "The Territorial Organization of Interests and the Logics of Associative Action" (also reprinted in slightly shortened form in *Social Institutions and Economic Performance*, pp. 105–136). Streeck's view is that large firms and the artisanate constitute a mutually dependent, unitary, system. For example, in his "Productive Constraints," Streeck insists that, although the bulk of work on diversified quality production has focused on the experience of large producers, the school is not focused exclusively on large firms and recognizes the crucial role played by the artisanate: He writes: "... work on diversified quality production emphasized the extraordinary potential ... of large firms in Germany for customized quality-competitive production," but he then insists that their capacity to do this " is historically and economically owed to the legally protected presence of a large number of small artisinal firms" (p. 9).
31. The polar emphasis in Wolfgang Streeck's work either on large industry or the artisanate underscores precisely the case I am making: The vast industrial *Mittelstand*, a grouping that can be categorized neither as artisinal nor as large industry, often located in unique regional concentrations notably distinct from many (not all) of the major regional concentrations of large-firm production in Germany, falls entirely through the cracks in his analysis. In the essay "Productive Constraints" Streeck claims that diversified quality production refers only to a specific kind of *product* and leaves open the kind of *process* used to produce it and the kind of *industrial organization* that organizes this production (p. 9). This suggests an uneasiness with his own empirical emphases in the German case and an openness to the incorporation of small- and medium-sized producer forms of organization into his general portrait of the German system. Yet, he never actually does this, nor does he anywhere suggest that small- and medium-sized producers could constitute a competitive system of flexible production alongside of, but not subsumed within, a large-firm-dominated system (or the separate system of artisan *Handwerk*).
32. The tradition of studying the development of the German economy is very long and deep, both in Germany and the United States. Important prewar influences on postwar views are: Thorstein Veblen, *Imperial Germany*; Rudolf Hilferding, *Finance Capital*; Hermann Levy, *Industrial Germany*; Werner Sombart, *Der moderne Kapitalismus, vol. 3*; August F. Sartorius von Waltershausen, *Deutsche Wirtschaftsgeschichte, 1815–1914*; Herbert v. Beckerath, *Modern Industrial Organization*; Robert Brady, *The Rationalization of German Industry*; Otto Jeidels, *Das Verhältnis der deutschen Grossbanken zur Industrie mit besonderer Berücksichtigung der Eisenindustrie*; Jacob Riesser, *Die deutsche Grossbanken und ihre Konzentration*, among others
33. Indeed, this is the title of a book that included one of the most influential synthetic portraits of the German system in the 1960s – Schonfield's *Modern Capitalism*. Schonfield was concerned to show that though cultural and national institutional differences persisted, the advanced industrial nations in the west were all struggling

with similar problems generated by the size of organizations and the scale of production. Schonfield's book is part of a very rich postwar tradition concerned with the development and implications of the large enterprise; see also John Kenneth Galbraith, *The New Industrial State*; Servan Schreiver, *The American Challenge*; Gareth Dyas and Heinz Thanheiser, *The Emerging European Enterprise*; and Michael Porter, *Competitive Strategy*.

34. On the rethinking of Italian industrial economy, for example, see Richard Locke, *Remaking the Italian Economy*. A challenge to the traditional image of Japan was issued by David Friedman's *Misunderstood Miracle* and Toshihiro Nishigushi's *Strategic Industrial Sourcing*.
35. This is the explicit rationale given by Streeck for the significance of studying the various features of the German industrial system. See Streeck "Productive Constraints."
36. A perusal of the index of Gerschenkron's *Economic Backwardness in Historical Perspective*, for example, reveals many references to Smith, Marx, and Schumpeter, and to economists from the German historical school, but none to the postwar neoclassicals.
37. This was true of Gerschenkron and it is true, most recently, of Streeck. See the latter's preface to *Social Institutions and Economic Performance*, where he says: "I maintain that without a full appreciation of the German variant of advanced capitalism, the discourse of political economy will not escape from its present dilemma between the "fake universalism" of neoclassical economics and the particularistic culturalism of popular Japanology" (p. ix).
38. Charles Sabel and Jonathan Zeitlin, "Historical Alternatives to Mass Production" and now their "Stories, Strategies, Structures."
39. For the classical narratives of capitalist economic development, see the historical sections of Adam Smith, *An Inquiry Into the Nature and Causes of The Wealth of Nations*, Book 3, and the sections on absolute and relative surplus value creation in Karl Marx, *Capital*, Vol. 1, parts 3 and 4 (Chapters 7–15).
40. Marx, for example, believed that even though the logic of mechanization and the extension of the division of labor in large-scale factory production tended toward the leveling of skill levels, it would always be the case that skilled workers remained in production – largely as a technical artifact of mechanical machinery itself: "There is a numerically unimportant group whose occupation it is to look after the whole of the machinery and repair it from time to time. . . . This is a superior class of workers, in part scientifically educated, in part trained in a handicraft; they stand outside the realm of factory workers and are added to them only to make up an aggregate. The division of labor is purely technical" (Marx, *Capital*, vol. 1, pp. 545–546). According to a similar logic, Marx also allowed for the continued existence of lower series production because with the growth of a wealthy and concentrated bourgeois class, there would always be an industrial demand for luxury goods (ibid., pp. 572–573).
41. Debates on the implications of increasing returns for industry and market structure within neoclassical economic discussions are very old and notoriously unsettled. In the milieu out of which Schumpeter emerged, the problem was posed in the following way: "How can competitive conditions be reconciled with increasing returns to scale." Or "Do increasing returns produce too much bigness and monopoly?" Defenders of marginalism and early neoclassicism argued no, critics argued yes. The whole controversy was most famously debated in the *Economic Journal* in the 1920s; see Piero Sraffa, "The Laws of Returns under Competitive Conditions"; A.

296   Notes to pages 12–14

C. Pigou, "The Laws of Diminishing and Increasing Costs"; idem, "An Analysis of Supply"; Lionel Robbins, "The Representative Firm"; Allyn Young, "Increasing Returns and Economic Progress"; and D.H. Robertson, Piero Sraffa, and G.F. Shove, "Increasing returns and the representative firm. A Symposium." An important postwar defense is George Stigler, "The Division of Labor is Limited by the Extent of the Market" in his *The Organization of Industry*, pp. 129–141.

42. Many of the most famous early 20th century Marxist classics occupy themselves very explicitly with the large-scale enterprise. See, for example, V. I. Lenin, *Imperialism*; Nicholai Bukharin, *Imperialism and World Economy*; Rudolf Hilferding, *Finance Capital*; Maurice Dobb, *Capitalist Enterprise and Social Progress*; Paul M. Sweezy, *Theory of Capitalist Development*.

43. Joseph Schumpeter, *Theory of Economic Development*, Chapter 2.

44. See ibid, and also idem, *Capitalism, Socialism and Democracy*. A recent book that discusses Schumpeter and also Chandler's contribution to the theory of the modern enterprise and its relationship to industrialization is William Lazonick, *Business Organization and the Myth of the Market Economy*.

45. Marx aficionados will argue about whether or not this reading of Marx is an accurate one. I excuse myself from this debate with the claim that this was probably the reading that would have been given by the institutionalists in the early postwar period. There is in any case ample evidence contained within Marx's writings to support the line of argument advanced in the text. To my mind, the clearest development of the argument from first principles can be found in the first sections of the "German Ideology" in *Collected Works of Marx and Engels*, vol. 3. The best modern reading of Marx along these lines is G. A. Cohen, *Karl Marx's Theory of History. A Defense*.

46. This position was an explicit critique of Rostow's view that all countries industrialized through a series of relatively rigid "stages of growth." See Walt W. Rostow, *The Stages of Economic Growth*. For an interesting overview of contemporary thinking about the role of politics in developing economies during the early postwar period, and some considerations on the influence of Gerschenkron, see Albert O. Hirschman, "The Rise and Decline of Development Economics" in his *Essays in Trespassing*, pp. 1–24. Debate about late industrialization in the Pacific Rim is very much shaped by the categories of debate developed in the text. Neoclassical economists find the success of Asian economies to rest on market forces; those in the Gerschenkronian tradition see the state as playing a crucial role. For an overview of the debate, see for example, Robert Wade, *Governing the Market*, and Alice Amsden, *Asia's Next Giant*. The locus classicus of the Gerschenkronian view in Asia is Chalmers Johnson's *Miti and the Japanese Miracle*. For a critique of these debates in the same spirit of my own book, see David Friedman, *The Misunderstood Miracle*.

47. Schonfield's *Modern Capitalism* is an extensive argument for state economic management and planning that is indicative of views among analysts of advanced industrial states at the time. During the 1980s, many writers, such as John Zysman and his colleagues at the Berkeley Roundtable on International Economics, ultimately pushed the framework to its logical conclusion by arguing that if states played their politics properly and astutely evaluated the evolving standards of efficiency on the world market, they could actually create comparative advantages for their national producers. See for example, Michael Borrus, Laura D'Andrea Tyson, and John Zysman, "Creating Advantage"; John Zysman and Laura Tyson (eds.), *American*

Industry in International Competition; Stephen Cohen and John Zysman, *Manufacturing Matters*.
48. Zysman, placed the broad social categories framing his analysis in the title of his book, *Governments, Markets and Growth*, one of the best books in the entire genre. Zysman's argument is that the way to bridge politics and economics is to see the ways in which institutions in each realm have goals that compel them to pursue both political and economic strategies: "The logic of power (politics) and the logic of money and markets (economics) simply instruct us about different constraints on the same institutions" (p. 299). Missing in this, of course, is the idea that the realm of the economic, understood as where production takes place, can be drawn in a way that integrally involves an institution that simultaneously exists in the political realm. Zysman combines strategies and logics but keeps the realms distinct.
49. Again, this was the central concern to institutionalist writers influenced by Gerschenkron during the 1970s and early 1980s, in particular Zysman, *Governments Markets and Growth*, and Schonfield, *Modern Capitalism*. It was also certainly an indirect concern of Peter Katzenstein; see his "Domestic Structures and the Strategies of Foreign Economic Policies," and *Small States and World Markets*.
50. This kind of coalitional analysis is famously associated with Gerschenkron's *Bread and Democracy in Germany*. Peter Gourevitch is also well known for this style of analysis; see his *Politics in Hard Times*.
51. Even in cases of nationalized industry, it was firms that were made into public bodies.
52. A good overview of these districts is provided in Hans Pohl (ed.), *Gewerbe- und Industrielandschaften vom Spätmittelalter bis ins 20. Jahrhundert*. This excellent volume displays many of the interpretive characteristics being developed in the text.
53. Erhard Lucas, *Zwei Formen von Radikalismus*, on Remscheid; Rudolph Boch, *Handwerker Sozialisten gegen die Fabrikgesellschaft*, and Jochen Putsch, *Vom Ende Qualifizierter Heimarbeit*, on Solingen.
54. The best history of Württemberg is Klaus Megerle, *Württemberg im Industrialisierungsprozess Deutschlands*.
55. Wolfgang Hoth, *Die Industrialisierung einer rheinischen Gewerbestadt*. Elberfeld and Barmen were merged into a single city, called Wuppertal, in the 1920s.
56. Volker Wünderich, *Arbeiterbewegung und Selbstverwaltung*, pp. 205–215.
57. Willy Fraenken, *Die Entwicklung des Gewerbes in den Städten Mönchengladbach und Rheydt im 19 Jahrhundert*; Peter Kreidte, *Ein Stadt am Seiden Faden*.
58. Hubert Kiesewetter, *Industrialisierung und Landwirtschaft*, and Rudolf Forberger, *Industrielle Revolution in Sachsen*.
59. This is true, for example, of the very interesting monographs by Wünderich, *Arbeiterbewegung und Selbstverwaltung*; Hoth, *Die Industrialisierung einer rheinischen Gewerbestadt*; and Forberger, *Industrielle Revolution in Sachsen*.
60. Megerle, *Württemberg*...; Kiesewetter, *Industrielle Revolution*....
61. See Wolfram Fischer, "Die Rolle des Kleingewerbes im wirtschaftlichen Wachstumsprozess in Deutschland, 1850–1914." For a collection of recent reexaminations of Fischer's claims, see Ulrich Wengenroth, *Prekäre Selbständigkeit*. For a recent sweeping reinterpretation of the postwar period that bases itself in the Fischer tradition see Lutz, *Kurze Traum*.
62. This is the argument in Megerle, "Regionale Differenzierung..." (the data in this table has been modified slightly from Megerle's table), and in Megerle, *Württemberg*..., pp. 165–195, especially 172 and 180–195.
63. See Gary Herrigel, "Large Firms, Small firms and the Governance of Flexible Spec-

ialization," and idem, "Industrial Order and the Politics of Industrial Change" for a discussion of this phenomenon and the literature on it. For a comparative European perspective, see Frank Pyke and Werner Sengenberger (eds.), *Industrial Districts and Local Economic Regeneration*.

64. Small- and medium-sized industrial producers in all industrial sectors in Baden Württemberg, for example, all belong to the Chamber of Industry and Commerce, not to the Chamber of Artisans. For an excellent overview of the industrial structure of the industrial *Mittelstand* at the end of the 1980s, see Philip Cooke and Kevin Morgan, "The Future of the Mittelstand." For an interesting historical discussion of the relationship between these alternative industrial forms and the formal institutions of the artisanate, see Rudolf Boch, "Zunfttradition und frühe Gewerkschaftsbewegung." See also the discussion in Chapter 2 below.

65. In addition to the references in notes 52–59, see the essays in Charles Sabel and Jonathan Zeitlin (eds.), *Worlds of Possibility*.

66. For an interesting discussion of the difference between a theory and an explanation in historical sociology, see George Steinmetz, *Regulating the Social*, Chapter 1. Steinmetz, however, is more enthusiastic about theories of critical realism than I am.

67. For more general discussions of the constructivist position that informs my view, see Roberto Mangiabera Unger, *Politics: A Work in Transformative Social Theory*; Charles Sabel and Jonathan Zeitlin, "Stories, Strategies and Structures"; and Charles Sabel, "Learning by Monitoring." Works from parallel theoretical traditions have also been important in the development of the view here: especially Pierre Bourdieu, *Outline of a Theory of Practice*; idem, *Language and Symbolic Power*; and writers from the pragmatic, phenomenological and hermeneutical traditions, in particular: John Dewey, The *Quest for Certainty: A Study on the Relation of Knowledge and Action*; Alfred Schutz, *Collected Papers, vol. 1*; and Paul Ricouer, *Hermeneutics and the Human Sciences*.

68. Sabel and Zeitlin, "Stories, Strategies and Structures."

69. Ibid.

70. Ibid.

71. For deeper elaboration of this conception of agency, see Bourdieu, *Outline*. . . . Sabel and Zeitlin, ibid., contrast this conception of the actor with the way in which the actor is conceived in much of neoclassical theory: .

> [A]djustment proceeds in society and the economy by adaptation rather than natural selection because humans are sentient and more particularly strategic in the sense that using their wits they can find indirect means to their ends. It may seem superfluous to raise this point because it is hard to see how any account of human activity as maximizing behavior of the sort typical of economic history could not at least tacitly assume that the agents are aware enough of the logic of their situation to act purposefully in response to it. But this [neoclassical] idea of sentience and strategy as the virtually automatic response to an unambiguous situation strips self-consciousness of one of its defining features: the ability to consider alternatives, meaning alternative responses to the same situation and speculations about the relative possibilities of creating alternative situations." (page 11)

72. Saying this, naturally, does not imply that adjustment always succeeds. Reflexive and social actors who are capable of learning can also fail to solve problems they encounter. See the examples presented of producers who failed to recast themselves in

Notes to pages 26–34

the decentralized industrial order during the initial decades of the postwar period in Chapter 5. Sabel and Zeitlin, ibid., also present numerous examples of failure. Moreover, by insisting on the analogy of a conversation, there is no need to ignore or discount relative power among the participating actors. For a discussion of this, see Herrigel, "Power in Industrial Districts."

73. Rudolf Boch, "The Rise and Decline of 'Flexible Production.'"
74. Sabel and Zeitlin, "Stories, Strategies and Structures."
75. Indeed, for Schumpeter the very capacity to recognize such vulnerabilities as organizational and technological opportunities was the essence of capitalist development.
76. The logic of the first two options is presented, classically, in Oliver Williamson, *Markets and Hierarchies*. Arguments over the third are instructively outlined in a debate between Oliver Williamson, Alfred Chandler, and Charles Perrow in "Markets and Hierarchies. A Discussion," pp. 432–464. A Schumpeterian framing of these debates is presented in Lazonick, *Business Organization and the Myth of the Market Economy*.
77. See F. A. Hayek, *Law, Legislation and Liberty*, vol. one, pp. 35–54 on spontaneous orders. See the essays by Armen Alchian in his *Economic Forces at Work* for more rigorous attempts to link evolutionary theory to the construction of firms and market institutions within a neoclassical framing.
78. On relational contracts, see Oliver Williamson, *The Economic Institutions of Capitalism*. See also the excellent overview of theories of the firm as an incomplete contract in Jean Tirole, *The Theory of Industrial Organization*, pp. 15–35; and Bengt Holmstrom and Jean Tirole, "The Theory of the Firm."
79. Charles Sabel has recently suggested that the mechanism at work within these decentralized systems is a principle of constitutional ordering. Here decentralized relations of mutual dependence and self-limiting (trusting) behavior are governed by a superintending monitoring institution that adjudicates disputes and fosters self-redefinition, but which does not engage in positive instruction in the manner of a hierarchy. Constitutional orders, moreover, are themselves encased in larger systems of constitutional ordering. See Charles Sabel, "Constitutional Ordering in Historical Context." This view is then further developed and linked to processes of learning in Sabel's "Learning by Monitoring." The account in this book will show considerable sympathy for this characterization of the forces at work in the decentralized industrial order, but at many moments it leaves open the possibility that still something else may be at work. There is simply no consensus view in the literature on how to explain decentralized industrial practice. Because I do not want to make a career of a literature review, I simply mention here that there are many attempts within the growing field of the sociology of the economy (including the new institutionalists in organization theory) to capture the dynamics of decentralized practice theoretically and assert that they have not yet hit upon a solution either. I discuss the sociologists in my, "Industry as a Form of Order."

Notes for Chapter 2

1. Much of the old Herzogtums of Jullich, Berg, and Kleve, the Archibishoprichs of Cologne and Trier, the southwestern Graftschaft Mark.
2. Primarily the areas covered by the old Grossherzogtum, or what was variously known as Hessen-Nassau and Hessen-Darmstadt.
3. So-called Bavarian Pfalz.

4. Specifically the regions of the Vogtland, Erzgebirge, and the area around Chemnitz.
5. These areas differed considerably among themselves along very particular dimensions of the landlord–peasant relationship. Indeed, according to Friedrich Lütge, these regions belonged to three different systems of Agrarian constitutions (*Agrarverfassungen*): the West German (the Rhineland), the Southwest German (Baden and Württemberg), and the Middle German (Thüringen and Saxony). Lütge claims that in addition to these there were two other distinctive constitutions west of the river Elbe in Germany: the Northwest German (lower Saxony, Schleswig Holstein) and the Bavarian. Lütge also identifies a number of hybrid systems: the Hessen system, combining the West and the Middle, without actually being an exact copy of either; the Frankische system, combining the Middle, Western, and Bavarian; and the Friesland, which had a relatively unique system that stretched from Holland to Jutland. All of these systems held in common the system of *Grundherrschaft* in which independent peasant farmers paid rent or taxes to a lord as a traditional tribute for the privilege of being able to use the land. But the rules regarding rent, ownership, the commons, services, local self-government, and inheritance differed among them. *Grundherrschaft* was opposed to the system of *Gutsherrschaft*, or estate farming, which existed in the German lands east of the river Elbe. Here peasant serfs performed direct labor services for aristocratic landlords (Junkers) engaged in large-scale farming.

   In the chapter on autarkic industrial order, we will see that the classic pattern of large-firm-based German industrialization occurred in the Northwest, Bavarian, and Middle German systems, in addition to several *Gutsherrschaft* regions east of the river Elbe. On all of the details regarding these various systems of agrarian relations, see the wonderful book by Friedrich Lütge, *Geschichte der deutschen Agrarverfassung vom frühen Mittelalter bis zum 19. Jahrhundert*, especially Chapter 4, pp. 100–169.
6. See generally, Friedrich Lütge, ibid., and Werner Conze, "The Effects of Nineteenth-Century Liberal Agrarian Reforms on Social Structure in Central Europe."
7. These regions not only differed from those regions, such as Westphalia, Brandenburg, and the Province of Saxony, which play central roles in the traditional firm-centered accounts of German industrialization; they also differed from regions such as Bavaria and lower Saxony, which had significant concentrations of rural industry in the 18th century, but then failed to significantly industrialize in the 19th. For a discussion of these regions, see chapter 3.
8. Intensive agriculture was, of course, possible only where the land was of sufficient quality. In some areas in which partible inheritance was practiced, such as the Schwäbische Alb, the higher elevations of the Black Forest, the Berg Land, and in the partible inheritance regions of Thüringen, the soil was extremely poor and intensive agriculture was not possible. But, for example, in areas along the Rhine in Baden, the Palatinate, and in the Rhineland itself, where the soil was extremely fertile, partible inheritance was associated with the intensification of agriculture and commercial specialization quite early on in early modern period. See B. H. Slicher van Bath, *The Agrarian History of Western Europe, AD 500–1850*, pp. 239 ff, especially 240.
9. On the range of such strategies, and yet further possible variations within given inheritance systems, see David Sabean, "Aspects of Kinship Behavior and Property in Rural Western Europe before 1800."
10. In important areas of both Saxony and Thüringen, for reasons having to do with

the poor quality of the soil, relatively small peasant holdings existed. This was true of the hilly regions north and south of the Thüringen Forest and for the large area south of the line connecting the cities of Plauen, Chemnitz, and Dresden in Saxony (i.e., the Vogtland and the Erzgebirge with its foothills). Both Thüringen and Saxony are difficult cases to categorize because they held within them a number of very different agricultural systems within the same set of property relations. In the northwest and east, in the areas around Leipzig and Dresden in Saxony and the flatland area north of Weimar in so-called Saxon Thüringen, where land was extremely fertile, three-field rotation systems had existed for a long time and showed a steady tendency toward greater intensity and specialization in production. In the areas in the southwest and south in both regions, however, where the soil was poor, the practice of three-field rotation was extremely uncommon and commercialization of grain production – even the subsistence production of potatoes – was difficult to find. In Saxony, holdings sizes in the Leipzig and Dresden regions tended to be larger on the whole than in the Vogtland and Erzgebirge, though even these large holdings were, relative the rest of Germany, only medium-sized. To top it all off, in the Oberlausitz region of Saxony, east of Dresden, estate farming persisted along lines characteristic of East Elbian Junker farming.

Inheritance in Saxony is discussed in Opitz, "Die Vererbung des ländlichen Grundbesitzes in der Nachkriegszeit im Freistaat Sachsen," and in Thüringen in Constantin v. Dietze, "Die Vererbung des ländlichen Grundbesitzes in Mitteldeutschland (Provinz Sachsen, Anhalt, Braunschweig, Thüringen)." Reports on the size of holdings in Saxony and Thüringen in the 18th century can be found in Friedrich-Wilhelm Henning, *Dienste und Abgaben der Bauern im 18. Jahrhundert*, pp. 90–93. See the discussion of holding sizes and agricultural practices in the Kingdom of Saxony in Heinrich Gebauer, *Die Volkswirtschaft im Königreich Sachsen*, pp. 88 ff (where the emphasis is on the relative importance of medium-sized holdings: e.g. in 1887, 57.2% of all arable hectares in Saxony were farmed on middle-sized holdings of between 10–100 hectares) and 115 ff (where the different systems of rotation are outlined). See also Erich Benndorf, *Weltwirtschaftliche Beziehungen der sächsischen Industrie*, pp. 10–18, where the point about the medium-sized character of farms is made. A map showing the distribution of farm size in Saxony (and throughout the Reich) in 1925 is reproduced in Wilhelm Abel, *Geschichte der deutschen Landwirtschaft*, p. 188, which shows small holdings clustered in the south and west of the Saxon Kingdom.

11. The reasons for why Saxony developed such a large class of relatively prosperous cottars are complex. Saxony was a colonized region that was populated by western Germans during the middle ages. The migrant peasants received extremely favorable property conditions, such as predominantly medium-sized holdings held in leasehold, and personal freedom. Unlike all other eastern migrants, the Saxon migrants never lost these property rights. Over time they also developed strong village self-government and law, though villages were still subject to feudal law as well (*Gerichtsherrschaft*). These factors turned out to be decisive after the severe population crisis of the late middle ages, which devastated the Saxon peasantry, wiping out whole villages and vacating many farms. As in many other *Anerbrecht* regions at this time, when population began to grow again in the 17th and 18th centuries, cottars began to emerge by taking over hitherto untilled or abandoned land. But unlike most other German regions, where cottars remained a fairly small class, outnumbered by a larger class of landless and day laborers, the Saxon *Gärtner*

and *Häusler* always remained in the majority. The moderate size of peasant farms, the existence of significant depopulated land and strong village political structures combined to allow the Saxon cottars to continually acquire rights to small amounts of property.

On this unique situation in Saxony, see the excellent monograph by Karlheinz Blaschke, *Bevolkerungsgeschichte von Sachsen bis zur Industriellen Revolution*, especially pp. 159–196, which describes relations between city and countryside and the unique social structure in both. On the uniqueness of peasant rights in Saxony and Thüringen, see the discussion in Lütge, op. cit., p. 159. On cottars elsewhere in Europe and how they fit into rural social structures, see the brief but clear discussion in Slicher van Bath, *Agrarian History*..., pp. 128 ff.

12. This broad swath of the population accounted for over 30% of the population of Saxony by 1750. Slicher van Bath, *Agrarian History*..., p. 190.
13. Josef Mooser's monograph on Minden Ravensburg and Paderborn in Westphalia chronicles how a region dominated by impartible inheritance structures, but with different peasant rights, much larger property holdings, and less unpopulated land, produced only a very small population of rural small holders, *Kötter*, who were analogous to the Saxon *Gärtner* and *Häusler*. Growth in population lead instead to a very large class of propertyless *Heuerlinge* who leased their housing not from the feudal lord, but from peasant farmers or even the *Kötter* and who lived on wage labor. The equivalent class of rural propertyless in Saxony remained insignificant, and indeed declined over time. In 1750, propertyless residents of rural villages accounted for 8.1% of the total Saxon population. In 1843, the same group accounted for only 5.4%. By contrast, *Gärtner* and *Häusler* accounted for 46.8% of the 1843 Saxon population, the largest single group. See Blaschke, *Bevolkerungsgeschichte*... pp. 190 and 191 for the population numbers. On the situation in Westphalia, see Josef Mooser, *Ländliche Klassengesellschaft 1770–1848*, especially pp. 40 ff. The situation in Westphalia will come up again in Chapter 3.
14. Good surveys of the global economic and political context for the emergence and proliferation of proto-industry are: Jan De Vries in *The Economy of Europe in the Age of Crisis, 1600–1750*; Peter Kreidte, "The Origins, the Agrarian Context, and the Conditions in the World Market"; Helga Schultz, "Die Ausweitung des Landhandwerks vor der industriellen Revolution"; and Jerome Blum, *The End of the Old Order in Rural Europe*.
15. All of this is detailed in the article by Karl Heinrich Kaufhold, "Gewerbelandschaften in der frühen Neuzeit, 1650–1800." It is important to note that there were also *Gewerbelandschaften* outside the regions carrying the particular kinds of characteristics I have mentioned: southern lower Saxony around Osnabruck, eastern Westphalia (particularly around Bielefeld-Minden-Ravensburg), Bavarian Schwaben, the Frankisch region around Nuremberg, and Southeast Württemberg (Ulm, Biberach, Ravensburg, Friedrichshafen) in particular were important regions. These regions however, "proto-industrialized" on the basis of very different property relations than the ones mentioned in the text. Peasant holdings tended to be larger in these regions, impartible inheritance dominated, and the soil was for the most part tremendously fertile. These factors, I think, led these *Gewerbelandschaften* to react very differently to the technological and competitive changes in European industry during the 19th century. For the most part, they went into decline. If industrialization occurred in those regions, as we shall see, it did so along lines that I have called autarkic. I will deal with these cases in Chapter 3.

16. See the account in W. O. Henderson, *The Rise of German Industrial Power 1834–1914*, especially pp. 61–70 on linens. The example of Erzgebirge toys is taken from Kaufhold, "Gewerbelandschaften...," p. 128–129.
17. These structures have, of course, received considerable attention in the last two decades in the debate on "proto-industrialization." This literature is very large and growing all of the time. The seminal articles for the current wave of discussion are Franklin F. Mendels, "Agriculture and Peasant Industry in Eighteenth Century Flanders" and Herbert Kisch, "The Textile Industries in Silesia and the Rhineland," both now reprinted in Peter Kreidte, Hans Medick, and Jürgen Schlumbohm (eds.), *Industrialization Before Industrialization*, itself an indispensable source on proto-industry. An older survey of agrarian industry is Hermann Kellenbenz "Rural Industries from the End of the Middle Ages to the Eighteenth Century." More recent surveys can be found in the excellent volume edited by Hans Pohl, *Gewerbe- und Industrielandschaften vom Spätmittelalter bis ins 20. Jahrhundert*, especially the article by Kaufhold, "Gewerbelandschaften...."

    The Göttingen group of Kreidte, Medick, and Schlumbohm argue in a neo-Marxist frame with an emphasis on the shaping role of property and other social relations on the organization and development of industry. A recent critique from a technologically determinist perspective that has received wide attention is Wolfgang Mager, "Proto-industrialisierung und Proto-industrie." Kreidte, Medick, and Schlumbohm have replied in "Sozialgeschichte in der Erweiterung."

    Classic studies of rural industry that have been very influential in the current debate and in my account in the text are Albert Thun, *Die Industrie am Niederrhein und ihre Arbeiter*; F. Furger, *Zum Verlagssystem als Organisationsform des Frühkapitalismus im Textilgewerbe*; Eberhard Gothein, *Wirtschaftsgeschichte des Schwarzwaldes und der angrenzenden Landschaften*; and W. Troeltsch, *Die Calwer Zeughandlunskompagnie und ihre Arbeiter*. Some regions of rural industrial production existed in Germany as far back as the 12th century; see Wolfgang von Stromer, "Gewerbereviere und Protoindustrien in Spätmittelalter und Frühneuzeit."
18. Indeed, smallholders were often very dependent upon outwork in the case of a bad harvest. The cottars in the Erzgebirge and the Vogtland in Saxony, for example, despite extensive industrial engagement, often suffered terribly when the harvest was bad. See Hubert Kiesewetter, *Industrialisierung und Landwirtschaft*, pp. 110–135 and 257 ff.
19. The cameralist writer Johann David Eulner: *Praktische Vorschläge, welcher Gestalt Steuer und Contributionen zum Nutzen eines Landesherren und Ohne Nachteil der Untertanen einzurichten seyn* (1741) wrote:.

    > One may frequently observe how a prince will grant exemption from all imposts to wealthy and endowed persons who establish factories. Why is this so? Assuredly for no other cause but that such persons thus put out much work and with this they help to nourish many hundreds of people, so by that means they come to be of more use to the prince than if all their capital were paid in as taxes. (cited in Bog, "Mercantilism in Germany," p. 167)

    The particular role of the state depended upon the situation locally. Max Barkhausen, "Government Control and Free Enterprise in Western Germany and the Low Countries in the Eighteenth Century," argues that industrial development only first became possible when it was able to escape government controls in the cities. In Saxony, Blaschke claims that the state was neutral vis-à-vis the struggle between the desire of the town to monopolize industrial production and prevent its diffusion into the countryside and the countryside's desire to acquire it because it benefitted from the development of both: the monarch collected rents and taxes from outworkers in the countryside and taxes from the city. See Blaschke, *Bevolkerungsgeschichte...*, p. 161. Finally, Rudolf Boch, shows that in the Duchy of the Berg in the Rhineland, the government and the guilds came together to work out a system of minimum prices in the cutlery trades that limited competition, but enhanced quality and ultimately the exports of the *Gewerbelandschaft*. See Rudolf Boch, *Handwerkersozialisten gegen Fabrikgesellschaft*, pp. 28–35.

20. Cited in Ingomar Bog, "Mercantilism in Germany," p. 181. Mercantilist writers in Germany were known as "cameralists." On the basic structure and evolution of ideas about the economy and about economic policy in German Principalities during the period of Absolutism, see the excellent book by Keith Tribe, *Governing Economy*. On the old European notion of the "Haus" and its importance for structuring relations in the economy see Otto Brunner, "Das 'Ganze Haus' in die alteuropäische 'ökonomie'"; and idem., "Die alteuropäische 'ökonomik'."

21. Heinrich Sieveking, "Geschichte der gewerblichen Betriebsformen und der zünftigen, städtischen und staatlichen Gewerbepolitik." Lorenz von Stein describes this process in the dialectic of society's struggle for self-definition against the state in the introduction to his history of social movements in France, *Der socialismus und communismus des heutigen Frankreichs. Ein beitrag zur Zeitgeschichte*.

22. See the many stories in Wilhelm Soell, *Die staatliche Wirtschaftspolitik in Württemberg im 17 und 18 Jahrhundert*. Soell is in many ways very critical of these policies because they often prevented the more rapid development of the Württemberg economy. He also felt that the main problem was that the Württemberg State was not Absolutist enough, having to deal, as it did, so consistently with the council of estates. The latter often prevented the adoption of policies that would have harmed its members. In Soell's view, this got in the way of progress.

23. This, obviously, is the major drawback of mercantilist systems to the classical and neoclassical traditions. Adam Smith's criticisms of the mercantilists are well known. The liberal Swede, Eli Heckscher, wrote a giant history of mercantilism, decrying the way the system disrupted the beneficial working of the market for over two volumes. See Adam Smith, *The Wealth of Nations*, especially Book IV, Chapters I–VIII; Eli Heckscher, *Mercantilism*. On the other hand, because mercantilist writers and governments tended to think of national economies as integrated wholes, and because they were concerned to maintain both stability and prosperity for the economy as a whole, they were looked at quite favorably by John Maynard Keynes. See his remarks in "Notes on Mercantilism" in *The General Theory*. On the important incomparability between the principles that governed these preindustrial economies and those that govern "modern" ones, see the essay by Brunner, "Die alteuropäische 'Ökonomik'."

24. See Sieveking, "Gewerblichen Betriebsformen...."

25. See Soell, *Staatliche Wirtschaftspolitik...*, p. 118–119, where the story is told in some detail.

26. This story is taken directly from an article by Hans Medick: "Privilegiertes Handelskapital und "kleine Industrie."

27. Monographs displaying this kind are legion. A very good example is Fritz Schulte, *Die Entwicklung der gewerblichen Wirtschaft in Rheinland-Westfalen im 18. Jahrhun-*

dert; Kaufhold, "Gewerbelandschaften...," is also a very detailed and systematic survey. Mager's article "Proto-industrialisierung und Proto-industrie" is very rich, and full of non-German examples as well. Attention to variation in countryside–city relations in particular is given in Rudolf Häpke, "Die ökonomische Landschaft und die Gruppenstadt in der älteren Wirtschaftsgeschichte." For a comparative dimension of town–country relations, see the many essays in Philip Abrams and E. A. Wrigley, *Towns in Society*. For general overview of the early modern period on this precise problem, see Jan de Vries, *European Urbanization 1500–1800*; E.A. Wrigley, "Urban Growth and agricultural change"; and Paul M. Hohenberg and Lynn Hollen Lees, *The Making of Urban Europe, 1000–1500*, pp. 106–178.

28. Good discussions of this can be found in Mager, ibid., and in the very interesting article by Herman Freudenberger and Fritz Redlich, "The Industrial Development of Europe." *Manufakture* are extensively documented in Saxony in the East German book by Rudolf Forberger, *Industrielle Revolution in Sachsen*.

29. Another qualification concerns the designation of merchants, outworkers, and the state as the players in the governance of these systems. Although these actors were typically the ones involved in the administration of the production process, sometimes one or more was absent, or additional players were involved. There were, for example, some cases in which merchants were not involved in governance at all. Iron making in the Siegerland, for example, was coordinated by an ancient rural cooperative. This limited the time that individual furnaces could operate and managed the growth of the surrounding forests so that they would not be depleted through the continuous production of charcoal; see Rainer Fremdling, "Eisen, Stahl und Kohle." In other cases, peasant middlemen intervened between merchant putters-out and the outworkers engaged in direct production. For a good discussion of this type of variety, see Kreidte, Medick, and Schlumbohm, *Industrialization before Industrialization*, pp. 12–38 and 94–125.

30. This is the story that M. Barkhausen tells in "Government Control and Free Enterprise in Western Germany and the Low Countries in the Eighteenth Century."

31. In addition to the Sieveking and Medick articles mentioned above, see also Willi Boelcke, "Wege und Probleme des industriellen Wachstums im Königreich Württemberg." On the beginning of the 19th century in Saxony, see Hubert Kiesewetter, "Staat und Unternehmen Während der Frühindustrialisierung." See also the cases mentioned in note 15.

32. This is an argument that Hans Medick has sought to make into a general characteristic of "proto-industrial" systems. But the evidence seems to show that population increased in some cases, but not in others. It increased in all of the regions I describe here. For Medick's strong claim, see his chapter "The structures and function of population-development under the proto-industrial system" in Kreidte, Medick, and Schlumbohm (eds.), *Industrialization before the Industrialization*. On the mixed evidence, see Kreidte, Medick, and Schlumbohm, "Sozialgeschichte in der Erweiterung."

33. eg. Slicher van Bath, *Agrarian History*..., pp. 239 ff; Abel, *Geschichte der deutschen Landwirtschaft*, pp. 271–303.

34. See the important article by the East German historian, Helga Schultz, "Die Ausweitung des Landhandwerks vor der industriellen Revolution." Hans Medick links the increase in artisans to population increases generated by proto-industrialization "Structures and Function...," pp. 74–93. Kaufhold lists Südwestdeutschland

(66.1 per 1000 inhabitants), Westdeutschland (61.4), Sachsen and Thüringen (60.0), and rechtsrheinisches Bayern (59.4) as having Artisan densities well above the German average (55.9) "Gewerbelandschaften...," pp. 116–117.
35. David Landes, *The Unbound Prometheus*, p. 172.
36. Norman J. G. Pounds, *An Historical Geography of Europe, 1800–1914*, p. 396.
37. See Richard Tilly, "Los von England," p. 203. Tilly suggests that this kind of adjustment was widespread in German industry, not only in textiles.
38. Landes, *Unbound Prometheus*, pp. 173–74. Generally, see Gerhard Egbers, "Innovation, Know-How, Rationalization and Investments in the German Textile Industry During the Period 1871–1935"; Heinz Torkewitz: *Der deutsche Textilmaschinenbau*; Frank Tipton, *Regional Variations in the Economic Development of Germany in the Nineteenth Century* (section on Saxony). Hubert Kiesewetter, in his discussion of the cotton industry in Saxony in *Industrialisierung und Landwirtschaft* tends to become too focused on cottons as a leading sector and misses the level of adaptive detail that I am emphasizing here.
39. See Wolfgang Hoth, *Die Industrialisierung einer rheinischen Gewerbestadt*; Henderson, *The Rise of German Industrial Power 1834–1914*; Landes, *Unbound Prometheus* pp. 166–169.
40. Rainer Fremdling, "Eisen, Stahl und Kohle." See also idem, "Foreign Competition and Technological Change," pp. 50–51: "Except for railway iron, especially rails, most of the new iron products made with pit coal or coke corresponded to traditional indigenous products made with charcoal, in such a way that they were effectively interchangeable."
41. Fremdling, "Eisen, Stahl und Kohle"; Norman J. G. Pounds, *The Ruhr*.
42. See Rudolf Boch, "The Rise and Decline of "Flexible Production"
43. The alternative response open to *Gewerbelandschaften* was to move into lower-quality, high-volume products also aimed at specific markets. In this case the strategy was to avoid the British by selling to markets in underdeveloped regions, primarily in Eastern Europe, where British goods were too expensive. Examples would be the flax-based linen producers in Bielefeld during the first half of the 19th century, or many of the musical instrument, toy, pencil, and luggage makers in the Nuremberg-Furth area of Frankish Bavaria. See Henderson, *German Industrial Power*..., for linen textiles; Walter Egle, "The Progress of Mass Production and the German Small Scale Industries" for toys, shoes, and luggage around Nuremberg; and Justin Michelsohn, *Die bayerische Grossindustrie und ihre Entwicklung seit dm Eintritt Bayerns in das Deutsche Reich*, pp. 133–140, for a discussion of the industrial organization of Bavarian pencil making, and pp. 150–154 for leather products industries. These regions, and the reasons for the prevalence of this kind of low-wage strategy in them, will be dealt with in Chapter 3.
44. Alfred Marshall, *Industry and Trade*, p. 136.
45. On Saxony see Kiesewetter *Industrialisierung und Landwirtschaft*, pp. 441–472, and Forberger, *Industrielle Revolution in Sachsen*; on Elberfeld/Barman, see Wolfgang Hoth, *Die Industrialisierung einer rheinischen Gewerbestadt*; on Württemberg, see Flik, *Die Textilindustrie in Calw und Heidenheim, 1750–1870*.
46. See Tilly, "Los von England," p. 202. He got his statistic from H. Blimberg, *Die deutsche Textilindustrie in der industrielle Revolution*, p. 50.
47. Good descriptions of the technical and organizational developments in these industries, in addition to Hoth, can also be found in Henderson, *German Industrial Power*...; and J.H. Clapham, *Economic Development of France and Germany*

1815-1914, especially pp. 89–96 and 283–303; Rainer Flik, *Die Textilindustrie*.... Schmoller actually makes the point repeatedly that the growth of factory based industry did not compete directly with artisinal production in his *Geschichte der deutschen Kleingewerbe*, especially pp. 159–211.

48. Hoth, *Industrialisierung*..., pp. 158–160, especially notes 1089 and 1094 on the diffusion of the Jacquard loom in Wuppertal; Peter Kreidte, *Ein Stadt am Seiden Faden*, pp. 100–125 for Jacquard looms in the Krefeld silk industry; and Heinrich Gebauer, *Die Volkswirtschaft im Königreich Sachsen*, pp. 549 ff for the same in Saxony.
49. Gebauer *Volkswirtschaft*..., pp. 200–201. Most generally, the rapid adoption of compact sources of power throughout the regions of decentralized production at the end of the 19th century greatly improved the productivity of specialty craftshops. All of the districts in the Rhineland, Saxony, and Württemberg rapidly adopted first gas and then electric motors at the end of the 19th century to drive the different kinds of machines that skilled artisans and homeworkers had in their shops. Hoth, *Die Industrialisierung*...; Eberhard Lucas, *Zwei Formen von Radikalismus*; Charles Sabel and Jonathan Zeitlin, "Historical Alternatives to Mass Production"; Klaus Megerle, *Württemberg im Industrialisierungs Prozess Deutschlands*; Tipton, Regional Variations...; Ernst Barth, *Entwicklungslinien der deutschen Maschinenbauindustrie von 1870 bis 1914*. Each of these sources makes a point of the early introduction of electric motors among small- and medium-sized decentralized producers.
50. Megerle, Württemberg..., p. 98.
51. Ibid., p. 98. In his comparative history of two textile towns in Württemberg in the 19th century, Rainer Flik claims that he uses the terms *Manufacture*, *Fabrik*, and *Verlag* completely interchangeably because it was impossible to determine at any one time where one form left off and the other began; i.e., all were continuously present and intertwined. See Flik, *Die Textileindustrie*..., p. 18.
52. Hoth, *Industrialisierung*..., p. 178.
53. Schmoller, *Geschichte der deutschen Kleingewerbe*, p. 281 table.
54. Hoth, *Industrialisierung*..., pp. 216 ff.
55. Kiesewetter, *Industrialisierung*..., p. 251.
56. On Baden and the Black Forest, see P. F. Walli, *Die dezentralisation der Industrie und der Arbeiterschaft in Grossherzogtum Baden*, and the magisterial work by Eberhard Gothein, *Wirtschaftsgeschichte des Schwarzwaldes und der angrenzenden Landschaften*, especially pp. 673–868. On Thüringen, see Emmanuel Sax, *Das Meininger Oberland, Ruhla und das Eisenacher Oberland* and *Die Korbflechterei in Oberfranken und Coburg*. See also Pounds, *A Historical Geography of Europe*..., p. 396: With reference to textiles in the Saxon-Thüringen-Oberfranken region, Pounds reports: "Much of the weaving, furthermore, remained domestic until the end of the century. Indeed, there were in 1875 no fewer than 12,231 cotton establishments, each with five workers or less, in Oberfranken – the area surrounding Hof. This was described as the last region in Germany where the domestic weaving industry survived, and it was in fact still active there until the 1920s." Generally on the persistence of outwork, see Otto Most, *Der Nebenerwerb in seiner Volkswirtschaftlichen Bedeutung*.
57. Hoth, *Industrialisierung*...; Otto Albert Borman, *Zur Entstehung und Entwicklung der Metallverarbeitenden Industrie im Mönchengladbacher Industriebezirk*; G. I. H. Lloyd, "Labour Organization in the Cutlery Trades of Solingen"; Flik, *Die*

Textilindustrie . . . ; Kreidte, *Eine Stadt am Seiden Faden*; and Emanuel Sax, *Das Meininger Oberland, Ruhla und das Eisenacher Oberland* and *Nebst einer Darstellung*. . . . Sax discusses the woodware and toy industries, pencil and blackboard industries, glass production, metalwares, smoking-pipe head manufacture, cork industries, baskets, and matchmaking.

Other good examples of the variety of ways that mechanization was integrated into traditional forms of production are the iron making regions of the Siegerland and Württemberg. The iron making regions responded to the new British coke-based, puddled steel products by seeking to improve their traditional production methods. (Examples of steel making inventions in charcoal-using regions are given in Fremdling "Eisen, Stahl und Kohle"). The new technologies invented were designed to adapt traditional practices to a new competitive environment. One major consequence was a headlong shift into production for particular market niches, e.g., Siegerland in specialty iron wares and Sauerland in wire, pins, needles, and nails (in addition to Fremdling, see the old, but still good, book by Norman J. G. Pounds, *The Ruhr*) In both areas, foundry production continued to be performed in – relatively small – furnaces, while the finishing work was dispersed throughout many workshops and households in the region. The cause and effect of this orientation to the market was the preservation of traditional regional forms of organization in production and its governance.

58. Benndorf, *Weltwirtschaftliche Beziehungen* . . . , pp. 11–13.
59. Gebauer refers to the same group as Benndorf, though with regard to 1882, the earlier census year; Gebauer, *Volkswirtschaft* . . . , p. 89.
60. Dr. J. Wernicke, *Kapitalismus und Mittelstandspolitik*, p. 802, makes the point that putting-out businesses were not statistically identified in the Imperial Reich in their own category, but were instead classified together with factories – apparently because both were "modern" forms of employment vis à vis traditional *Handwerk*.
61. See tables in Megerle, *Württemberg* . . . , pp. 132–33, which show gradual decline of establishments employing less than 5, but steady increase in still-small (up to 50) and medium-sized (up to 200) workers. This is true of Saxony, Baden, and Württemberg. His figures on the Rhineland are corrupted by inclusion of autarkic Rhineland. Megerle's figures are confirmed by Bormann's study of the metal and machinery industries in Mönchengladbach. He shows that the growth in the larger-sized firms producing entire machines was doubly outpaced by the growth in the size of little shops producing parts. See Otto-Albert Bormann, *Zur Entstehung und Entwicklung der Metallverarbeitenden Industrie im M.-Gladbacher Industriebezirk*, pp. 24–50. See also the description of industrial structure and population development in Saxon industrial districts, which by the end of the 19th century were densely populated by small manufacturing firms, in Georg Lommatzsch, *Die Bewegung des Bevolkerungsstandes im Königreich Sachsen während der Jahre 1871–1890 und deren hauptsächlichste Ursachen*, especially pp. 96–123.
62. David Blackbourn points out that this kind of development is exactly the kind of thing that makes it difficult to precisely identify what the "*Mittelstand*" in the Imperial Reich actually was and what its interests were. See Blackbourn, "The *Mittelstand* in German Society and Politics, 1871–1914," especially pp. 419, 420 ff, and 430 ff. Blackbourn notes that both Robert Bosch and Gottfried Daimler were artisans.
63. Jürgen Kocka notes the emergence of many small- and medium-sized producers at the turn of the century, see his "The Rise of Modern Industrial Enterprise in

Germany." This kind of transformation of outworkers and artisans into small industrial businesses is often missed, or not properly appreciated, in most accounts of the so-called *Mittelstand*. Writers such as Heinrich Winkler, and even David Blackbourn, focus on the categories of who belongs to the *Mittelstand*, such as *Handwerk*, and as a result miss the transformation of the economy that was taking place within and around the groups that the categories focus attention on. *Handwerk* was a static category that was always defined as a realm of social production distinct from industry. Thus, any successful artisan who mechanized production and engaged in industrial pursuits was no longer categorically an artisan. This meant, essentially, that as the process of transformation described in the text increased over the course of the 19th century, artisans, properly categorized, were the least competitive, most rigid producers in a region. If they were very bad at what they did, or proud and poor, or whatever, they were confronted constantly with the threat of losing their autonomy as producers and having to resort to wage labor. But to say that therefore there was a crisis in *Handwerk* at the end of the century overly simplifies the story.
64. Tipton, *Regional Variations* . . . , p. 126.
65. Pounds, *An Historical Geography of Europe*, p. 398; Benndorf, *Weltwirtschaftliche Beziehungen*. . . , p. 70–75.
66. Benndorf, *Weltwirtschaftliche Beziehungen* . . . , (see also the section on machine makers, p. 191 ff); and Megerle *Württemberg*. . . . Even in the large Saxon manufacturing towns, such as Crimmitschau, Plauen, or even Chemnitz, the structure of industry was still dominated by small- and medium-sized firms. For example, there were 80 firms engaged in the notorious 1903 lockout in Crimmitschau's textile industry. According to Tipton, the firms were "considerably above the Saxon average in size," but the average firm size among those 80 firms was only 88 workers. This is, technically, considered to be a "large" firm in the German statistics, which in itself gives an indication of how difficult it is to accurately portray statistically the actual relations that existed in industry; see Tipton, *Regional Variations* . . . , p. 126.
67. See Table 43, p. 486 in Kiesewetter, *Industrialisierung*. . . . Three of the top four regions in terms of firm size, according to this table, were in regions that I call Autarkic: (1) Bavaria, (2) Hannover, (4) Oldenbourg. Baden (3) and Württemberg (5) had 13.3% and 7.7% of total cotton spindles in Germany at that time and 21 and 20 spinning mills, respectively.
68. Benndorf, *Weltwirtschaftliche Beziehungen* . . . , p. 80.
69. Ibid., p. 71, table.
70. Warren goes on to note that much of this industrial life took place in small communities, remarking that

> . . . here, village and country, shop and factory, craft and industry overlapped. There was a fairly extensive flow backward and forward between the land and the mills. Though only one in eight persons worked in the fields and forests, many a household was supported by the "family wage," partly by agriculture, and partly by factory work and home labor. (Donald Warren, *The Red Kingdom of Saxony, Lobbying Grounds for Gustav Stresemann, 1901–1909*, p. 2)

71. An interesting discussion of the self-conceptions and ideologies of the *industriellen Mittelstand* that emphasizes the importance of independence in their thinking can be found in Hans Peter Ullmann, *Der Bund der Industriellen*, pp. 82–99, especially

pp. 104–105. Ullmann's book is incredibly well researched, but suffers from an attachment to the "organized capitalism" framework. See also Tipton, *Regional Variations...*, p. 126; Boelcke, "Wege und Probleme..."; and Alfred Gemming, *Das Handwerkergenossenschaftswesen in Württemberg*. This phenomenon can also be seen clearly in the analysis of Mönchengladbach by Bormann, *Entstehung und Entwicklung*.... It also permeates the ideology of many popular books that glorify the heroes of German small-scale industrialization: see Herbert Helbig (ed.), *Führungskräfte der Wirtschaft in Mittelalter und Neuzeit, 1350–1850*, and *Landeskunde* articles on individual entrepreneurs, including Paul Gehring, "Johannes Bürk und Erhard Junghans"; and Ernst Klein, "Die Hohenheimer Ackergerätefabrik (1819–1904)."

72. It is probably because people's efforts to establish their autonomy were continuously on the edge of failure and success that the people of these regions of decentralized production in Germany have reputations for frugality and pessimism: that is, they are known for being able to make much of dark clouds in otherwise clear skies.

73. Lommatzsch, *Bewegung des Bevolkerungsstandes...*, p. 103. Boch discusses the diversification of the cutlery district, obliquely, in his essay "The Rise and Decline of the Cutlery Industry of Solingen since the 18th Century." Diversification is also the main theme of the book by Bormann, *Zur Entstehung und Entwicklung*....

74. Megerle, *Württemberg...*; and Medick, "Privilegiertes Handelskapital und 'Kleine Industrie'," which makes the latter point

75. Schmoller, *Geschichte der deutschen Kleingewerbe*, pp. 194–95; see table on location of industry.

76. Maurice Dobb has a very interesting discussion of this transformation and of the concept of the undertaker in his *Capitalist Enterprise and Social Progress*.

77. Jürgen Kocka describes this process in "Entrepreneurs and Managers in German Industrialization," especially pp. 501–511.

78. If one follows Blaschke, *Bevolkerungsgeschichte...*, p. 194 ff, factory workers in Saxony seem to have been recruited from a rural non-cottar laborer and servant class, the members of which owned no property, depended already on rural wage labor and generally rented their housing. An analogous class in the cities – servants, propertyless, journeymen – were vulnerable to the lure of the factory. This grew in size with industrialization, but it was, especially at the beginning of the process, a minority within the population. Such landless peoples in Württemberg, Baden, and the Rhineland, where partible inheritance distributed property ownership extremely widely, existed in analogous proportions to the total population.

79. Hermann Schindler, *Die Reutlinger Wirtschaft von der Mitte des 19. Jahrhunderts bis zum Beginn des Ersten Weltkrieges*, especially pp. 13–36; Willy Fränken, *Die Entwicklung des Gewerbes in den Städten Mönchengladbach und Rheydt im 19. Jahrhundert*; Kreidte, *Eine Stadt am seiden Faden*.

80. Heinrich Boecker, *Die deutsche Werkzeugindustrie: Eine Alternative zur Massenproduction?*, Diplomarbeit der Abteilung Wirtschafts- und Sozialwissenschaften an der Universität Dortmund, June 6, 1983.

81. Jürgen Schriewer: "Intermediare Instanzen, Selbstverwaltung und berufliche Ausbildungsstrukturen im historischen Vergleich"; M. E. Taylor, *Education and Work in the Federal Republic of Germany*; Gerhard Adelmann, "Die berufliche Aus- und Weiterbildung in der deutschen Wirtschaft 1871–1918"; and J. J. Lee, "Labor in German Industrialization," especially pp. 453–459: "Training"; and Wolfgang

Streeck, "The Territorial Organization of Interests and the Logics of Associative Action."
82. A helpful overview of the development of these banks in the 19th century – and of their role in the German economy in general today – is presented by Richard Deeg in his dissertation: *Banks and the State in Germany*, especially Chapter 2, pp. 55–111.

Credit banking also grew in importance as regional industries became more robust and their capital needs more sophisticated. Many of the private banks in Württemberg and in the Rhineland grew up by funneling money to the larger establishments, primarily factories, in the district. As the region and the firms grew, so did the banks. Relations between banks and their industrial clients resembled the intimate ties of cooperative banking, yet the sums were considerably larger and the self-conceptions of the actors were more bourgeois than petit-bourgeois. A good case study of banking in Württemberg is Arthur Loewenstein, *Geschichte des württembergischen Kreditbankwesens und seiner Beziehungen zu Handel und Industrie*. See also Richard Tilly's early book on banking in the Rhineland, *Financial Institutions and Industrialization in the Rhineland, 1815–1870* (Madison: University of Wisconsin Press, 1966).
83. Theodore Hamerow, *Restoration, Revolution, and Reaction*, Chapter 2; R.H. Dumke, "Tariffs and Market Structure"; Tipton, *Regional Variation...*, Chapters 2 and 3.
84. Most commercial credit banking prior to 1871 was conducted through private banks, which effectively functioned like venture capital funds. Most of their attention was directed at the autarkic regions and business forms developing in the Ruhr, Berlin, and Silesia. See Richard Tilly, "Germany, 1815–1870."
85. Others were Hermann Wagener and Victor Aime Huber.
86. From "Zuruf an die deutschen Handwerker im Assoziationsbuch für deutsche Handwerker und Arbeiter, 1853," cited in Gemming, *Handwerkergenossenschaftswesen*....
87. Schulze-Delitzsch was also an important figure in the early German labor movement. See Werner Conze, "Möglichkeiten und Grenzen der liberalen Arbeiterbewegung in Deutschland."
88. Deeg, *Banks and the State...*, p. 67–68. See also the article by C. Heiligenstadt, "Die Preussische Centralgenossenschaftskasse"; and Gemming, *Handwerksgenossenschaftswesen*.... According to Deeg

> In the 1860s competing groupings of cooperative banks emerged, separated by varying philosophical principles. Thus there was no single association uniting them, and numerous banks acted as clearing or central banks for different groups of cooperatives. Establishing organizational unity within the cooperative banking sector ... evolved gradually over the following decades." (page 68)

89. The bank, the ancestor of the present day Deutsche Genossenschaftsbank, was a legal personality of its own and in matters of property entirely independent of the Prussian government treasury. But it was under the supervision of the Ministry of Finance. See C. Heiligenstadt, "Die Preussische Centralgenossenschaftskasse."

It should be noted that much writing has been skeptical of the role played by these cooperatives. This is especially the argument of David Blackbourn in his "The Mittelstand...." I disagree with his assessment for two reasons. First, although his work is extremely subtle on the importance of the traditional elements of the

Mittelstand in German society, and I have learned as much from his work as I have from almost anyone else currently writing on the 19th century in this area, it ultimately succumbs to the narrow-track conception of the industrialization process, which understands only the gradual decline of the small in the face of the large. Second, largely for this reason, he himself notes, but dismisses, the fact that the cooperative banks got taken over by small- and medium-sized producers. I am writing about small- and medium-sized producers whose historical, community, and cultural boundaries with the artisans were completely overlapping. Blackbourn takes the division to be much more clear.

90. A good place to begin to get a flavor for these changes is Geoffrey Barraclough, *The Origins of Modern Germany*. A look at a historical atlas is also helpful, e.g., the Bayerishe Schulbuch's *Grosser Historischer Weltatlas, Dritter Teil: Neuzeit*, pp. 22–23, 38, 39, 40, and 48.
91. This transformation in the character of political power was classically analyzed by Otto Hintze in the essays collected together in his, *Staat und Verfassung*. For an excellent case study of this transformation in Württemberg, see Manfred Hettling, *Reform ohne Revolution*.
92. An overview of the various Peasant emancipations in Germany is given in Lütge, *Geschichte der deutschen Agrarverfassung*, pp. 169–237, especially 200–208, and 215–222.
93. In his essay "Economics and Politics in the Age of Modern Capitalism," Otto Hintze refers to this kind of behavior on the part of princes and statesmen as "Political Entrepreneurship" (see especially p. 429).
94. This is discussed in Paul Gehring, "Von List bis Steinbeis"; Boelcke, "Wege und Probleme..."; and Otto Borst, "Staat und Unternehmen in der Frühzeit der Württembergischen Industrie." Kiesewetter, *Industrialisierung...*, Part III, makes the argument that prior to 1833, the Saxon government was primarily concerned with the health of industry because of its effects on employment. After 1833, the government shifted its policies to explicitly encourage industrialization, combining direct subsidies, general support for technological development and technology transfer, and industrial schooling.
95. See the survey in Deeg, *Banks and the State*, pp. 55–110 as well as the case study of Württemberg, Hans Maier's article "Das Modell Baden Württemberg."
96. Kiesewetter, *Industrialisierung...*, Chapter 7 and part III. See also idem, "Staat und Unternehmen während der Frühindustrialisierung"
97. Both citations come from Gehring, "Vom List bis Steinbeis," p. 414.
98. Moritz Mohl, *Aus den gewerbswissenschaftlichen Ergebnissen einer Reise in Frankreich*; see also idem, *Über die württembergische Gewerbs-industrie*.
99. On Steinbeis and the *Centralstelle*, see L. Vischer, *Die industrielle Entwicklung im Königreich Württemberg und das Wirken seiner Centralstelle für Gewerbe und Handel in ersten 25 Jahren*; and Paul Gehring, "Von List bis Steinbeis."
100. Dieter Senghaas, *Vom Europa Lernen*, makes this into a general point. The standard work on the Zollverein, in English, is W. O. Henderson, *The Zollverein*. See also Dumke, "Tariffs and Market Structure...."
101. See Gemming, *Handwerksgennossenschaftswesen...*; Schindler, *Die Reutlinger Wirtschaft*; and Loewenstein, *Geschichte des württembergischen Kreditbankwesens*.
102. In many of these areas of the Western Rhineland, the Catholic church played a very aggressive organizing role. Community and self-government were always central tenets of Rhenish Catholicism – the dominant political force in decentralized

regions on the left bank of the Rhine. The well known social and charitable organization, the *Volksverein für ein Katholisches Deutschland*, was established in Mönchengladbach, by the very political priest Hitz. See Emil Ritter, *Die Katholische-Soziale Bewegung Deutschlands in Neunzehnten Jahrhundert und der Volksverein*; Adolf Birke, *Bischof Ketteler und der deutsche Liberalismus*; and Anton Rausler (ed.), *Entwicklungslinien des deutschen Katholismus*, especially the essays by Rudolf Morsey, Konrad Repgen, Hans Maier, and Hubert Jedin.

103. On the history and development of the IHK's see the old but nevertheless still excellent account by Wolfram Fischer, *Unternehmerschaft, Selbstverwaltung und Staat*.

104. A good overview of the economic experience of the period for Europe in general is W. Arthur Lewis, *Economic Survey, 1919–1939*. An excellent overview of the peculiar economic conditions in the Weimar Republic is Dietmar Petzina and Werner Abelshauser, "Zum Problem der relativen Stagnation der deutschen Wirtschaft in den Zwanziger Jahren."

105. See Mark Granovetter, "Economic Action and Social Structure." The article develops exactly this idea quite well.

106. Herbert von Beckerath's definition is consistent with this:

> The *price-fixing cartel* regulates sales prices by either periodically revised price lists or uniform cost-accounting systems, the cost elements of which, such as the price of raw materials, wages, the proportion of overhead charges, and the profit margin, are uniform for all members and subject to revision by the cartel. (Herbert von Beckerath, *Modern Industrial Organization*, p. 214)

107. Two dissertations on the machinery industry make this point rather strongly: Otto Polysius, *Verbandsstrebungen im deutschen Maschinenbau*; and Elizabeth Harnisch, *Kartellierungsfähigkeit der Maschinenindustrie*. For discussion of cartelization in the textile industry see Enquette Auschuss, *Erste Unterausschuss, dritte Arbeitsgruppe, Zweiter Teil: Entwicklungslinien der industriellen und gewerblichen Kartellierung, Dritter Abschnitt: Textilindustrie A*, and idem, *Textilindustrie B*

108. The Enquette emphasized the rootedness of this industry in a long tradition of artistic artisinal crafts in the textile industry. See "Verband der Deutschen Veredelungsanstalten für baumwollene Gewerbe E.V., Bericht" in *Textilindustrie B*, pp. 1–18.

109. Ibid., p. 7

110. Rudolf Boch, *Handwerkersozialisten gegen Fabrikgesellschaft*; Franz Hendrichs, "Solingen im Ringen mit Sheffield im 19. Jahrhundert"; Franz Hendrichs, "Rationalisierung in der Solinger Industrie"; Lloyd, "Labor Organisation . . ."; and Uta Stolle, *Arbeiterpolitik im Betrieb*. Boch also has an excellent general essay on the way in which the liminal identity of artisan outworkers could result in a variety of different organizational forms to control markets and wages: guilds, cartels, and unions. In some cases artisan guilds became trade unions – as in Solingen – and in other cases they bitterly opposed trade unions. See Boch, "Zunfttradition und frühe Gewerkschaftsbewegung."

111. Beckerath defines a term-fixing cartel in the following way:

> Term-fixing cartels regulate sales terms, i.e., conditions of delivery with regard to terms of payment, including discounts for early payment; charges on arrears; modes of payment (cash three months' acceptance, etc., domestic or foreign

money; determination and guaranty of quality (as a basis for complaints and returns); time and delivery; allowances on returns; delivery of free goods; and packing. This type also concerns itself with options (a buyer's right, within a specified term, to place additional orders for the identical kind and amount of goods at the old price), with conditions applicable to the delivery of goods ordered only by quantity and type, and with reservations as to the execution of the individual pieces, for instance, as to the only or chief task of the cartels in many industries, particularly those producing consumer goods.... (*Modern Industrial Organization*, p. 213)

112. See Paul Steller, "Maschinenindustrie," in Verein für Sozialpolitik, *Störungen im deutschen Wirtschaftsleben während der Jahre 1900 ff*. The Verein für Sozialpolitik volume that contains the Steller article also has a number of other very good industry studies, e.g., on the electro-mechanical industry. On the formation of early term-fixing arrangements and the role of trade associations, see Hermann Edwin Krüger, "Historische und Kritische Untersuchungen über d. freien Interessenvertretung von Industrie, Handel und Gewerbe in Deutschland."
113. See the Enquette Ausschuss volumes on the textile and machinery industries: Enquette Auschuss *Textilindustrie A* and *Textilindustrie B*, and idem, *Erste Unterausschuss, dritte Arbeitsgruppe, zweiter Teil: Entwicklungslinien der industriellen und gewerblichen Kartellierung. Erster Abschnitt: Arbeitsplan, Maschinenbau*. There was a large discussion during the 1920s of term-fixing arrangements, as well as other forms of cartelization, which was fostered by the various industry trade associations: Otto Schulz-Mehrin, *Spezialisierungs- und Verkaufsgemeinschaften im Maschinenbau*; Heinz Muellenseifen, *Kartelle als Produktionsförderer unter besonderer Berücksichtigung der modernen Zusammenschlusstendenzen in der deutschen Maschinenbau-Industrie*; Reichsverbandes der Deutschen Industrie (ed.), *Produktionsförderung durch Kartelle (Auszug aus einer Materialsammlung)*; and "Spezialfabrik oder gemischter Betrieb? Ein Beitrag zur Frage des Gepräges der Spezialfabrik," in *Technik und Wirtschaft*, vol. 29, 1936, pp. 37–42. A good survey in English, written by someone with a good sense of the European and German situation, is Karl Pribram, *Cartel Problems*.
114. See the report on the Association of German Silk Weavers, Krefeld (*Verein deutscher Seidenwebereien, Krefeld*) in Enquette Ausschuss, *Textilindustrie*, A, pp. 1–18.
115. See Hermann Edwin Krueger, "Historische und Kritische Untersuchungen über due freien Interessenvertretung von Industrie, Handel und Gewerbe in Deutschland"; Otto Polysius, *Verbandsstrebungen im deutschen Maschinenbau*; and Elizabeth Harnisch, *Kartellierungsfähigkeit der Maschinenindustrie*; Schulz-Mehrin, *Spezialisierungs . . .* ; Heinz Muellenseifen, *Kartelle. . . .*
116. Though they explain it in a different way, this is the story of the political evolution of the VDMA given in Gerald Feldman and Ulrich Nocken, "Trade Associations and Economic Power."
117. Most of the writers on cartelization in the interwar period prefer to call these arrangements finishing associations rather than specialization cartels because they did not regulate prices. See, for example, Robert Liefmann, *Cartels, Concerns and Trusts* pp. 93–94; and Pribram, *Cartel Problems*, pp. 53–56.
118. See for example Rolf Boehringer, "Spezialisierung, Normung, Typung im deutschen Werkzeugmaschinenbau," which describes the VDF.
119. Schulz-Mehrin, *Spezialisierungs . . .* ; Muellenseifen, *Kartelle . . .* ; Reichsverbandes

der Deutschen Industrie (ed.), *Produktionsförderung*. . . . Karl Lange, the head of the machinery producers trade association, VDMA, makes this argument about codification in his testimony before the Enquette Commission on Cartels: "Karl Lange," Enquette Auschuss, *Erste Unterausschuss, dritte Arbeitsgruppe, Vierter Teil: Kartellpolitik, Zweiterabschnitt, Vernehmungen*, pp. 161–174.

120. See the excellent RDI brochure on cartels, Reichsverbandes der Deutschen Industrie (ed.), *Produktionsförderung*. . . The volume by Max Metzner, *Kartelle als Träger der Rationalisierung* also covers many of the issues relevant to the role of trade associations in the 1920s.

121. This information comes from interviews in the contemporary West German machinery industry, 1985–1994. See also the excellent discussion of the role of the VDMA and the Normenausschuss in Hajo Weber, *Intermediäre Organisation*.

122. Mullenseifen, *Kartelle* . . . ; RDI, *Produktionsförderung*. . . .

123. Heinrich Mengel, *Stukturwandlungen und Konjunkturbewegung in der Werkzeugmaschinen-Industrie*; Friedrich Soltau, *Der Absatz der deutschen Werkzeugmaschinenindustrie*; Werner Schwade, *Untersuchung der vom Binnen- und Weltmarkt abhängigen Produktions- und Absatzbedingungen in der deutschen Maschinenindustrie*; Albert Borsig, "Zur Ausfuhrorganisation der Maschinenindustrie"; Hessenmüller, "Vertriebsgemeinschaften im Maschinenbau"; and F. Isermann, "Wege zur Steigerung der Maschinenausfuhr."

124. Unionmatex is described in the RDI brochure, *Produktionsförderung* . . . , p. 19; see also the history of the Mönchengladbach spinning machinery producer, W. Schlafhorst & Co.: "Schlafhorst-Gute hundert Jahre, 1884–1984," especially pp. 6–7. Schlafhorst was one of the central members of Unionmatex.

125. Others would be the sugar producers, which figure prominently in many accounts of concern formation. See Liefmann, *Cartels* . . . , pp. 246 and 263.

126. A concise summary of these early movements is given in Peter Hayes, *Industry and Ideology. IG Farben in the Nazi Era*.

127. David Noble discusses the role of patents in shaping the character of chemical companies in his *American By Design*, pp. 84–109. Thanks to Charles Sabel for reminding me of this.

128. This figure includes all foreign production facilities owned by the companies in the industry. See generally L. F. Haber, *The Chemical Industry, 1900–1930*.

129. Chemischen Fabrik Griesheim-Elektron and Chemischen Fabrik vormals Weiler ter Meer in Ürdingen.

130. Carl Bosch makes this argument in his testimony to the Enquette Ausschuss: "Ausführungen des Sachverständigen Dr. Bosch über die Produktions- und Absatzverhältnisse der I.G. Farbenindustrie Aktiengesellschaft, Frankfurt/Main," in Enquette Ausschuss, *Die deutsche Chemische Industrie; Verhandlungen und Berichte des Unterausschusses für Gewerbe: Industrie, Handel und Handwerk (III Unterausschuss)*, pp. 111–136.

131. Testimony by Carl Bosch before the Enquette Ausschuss, in *Verhandlungen und Berichte des Unterausschusses für allgemeine Wirtschaftsstruktur; Wandlungen in den wirtschaftlichen Organisationsformen; Wandlungen in den Rechtsformen der Einzelunternehmungen und Konzerne*, p. 437.

132. The importance of keeping process flow continuous was the decisive factor behind the consolidation process. Bosch, the head of IG Farben testified before the Enquette to this effect. In explaining the rationale behind the fusion of the indepen-

dent members of the interest community into a single company – the IG Farben – he explained:

> Changes in the organizational structure of the company were related to the fusion. One main task of the fusion was to get the company to adapt to the conditions on the market. As a result of war we lost a part of our production capacity. This loss, which accounted for 50% of production, had to be compensated for with other production. When a production facility in our industry operates below full capacity, only the last ten percent brings us profit. (Enquette Ausschuss, *Die deutsche Chemische Industrie*, p. 112)

133. See Bosch's testimony in two separate volumes of the Enquette Ausschuss, both cited earlier. There is also an excellent discussion of the formation of the IG Farben and the evolution of organizational thinking in the combine in the article by Wolfram Fischer, "Dezentralisation oder Zentralisation."
134. A good discussion of these changes can be found in Mabel Newcomer, *Central and Local Finance in Germany and England* pp. 42–72; and Arnold Brecht, *Federalism and Regionalism in Germany*, especially pp. 52–73. Harold James also has an excellent, albeit very Thatcherite, discussion of the financial difficulties of cities and regional governments in the Weimar Republic, see James, *The German Slump* especially pp. 39–110 ("Public Finance").
135. An extremely extensive contemporary study on the fiscal crisis of the *Länder* and communes, and the problem of financial equalization (Finanzausgleich) within the Weimar Republic, see Johannes Popitz, *Der Künftige Finanzausgleich zwischen Reich, Ländern und Gemeinden*. More recent histories that deal with Reich *Land* and commune financial relations in Weimar are: Franz Menges, *Reichsreform und Finanzpolitik.*; Waldemar Besson, *Württemberg und die deutsche Staatskrise 1928–1933*, especially pp. 53–59, 83–114, and 159–253; Wolfgang Benz, *Süddeutschland in der Weimar Republik*; and Volker Wünderich, *Arbeiterbewegung und Selbstverwaltung*.
136. James, *The German Slump* p. 76
137. This is all taken directly from James, *The German Slump*, p. 86. James attributes all of this expansion to the megalomaniacal expansion lust of city mayors.
138. James's view is that these projects were all extremely profligate and extravagant. Most of the examples of projects he cites tend to confirm this impression. My view is that he underestimates the significance of local and regional governmental activities in the maintenance of industrial order in decentralized regions. See James, *The German Slump*.
139. Ibid., p. 94.
140. Ibid., p. 101.
141. Ibid., p. 140.
142. See Wünderich, *Arbeiterbewegung und Selbstverwaltung*, especially pp. 246–262. Henry Ashby Turner has a very revealing discussion of the relationship between small industrialists and the Nazis in his *Big Business and the Rise of Hitler*, pp. 191–203 (The section is entitled "Nazis and lesser Businessmen" !). For National Socialist voting patterns, see "Map 5: Regional Strength of the National Socialists, November 1932" in Arnold Brecht, *Regionalism and Federalism in Germany*, p. 40.

If one makes a list of the highest percentages of people voting for the Nazi party in the 1932 elections (July) in the largest German cities, Saxon, Berg Land, and Hessian cities (in boldface) are all on the list:

Notes to pages 70–73

1. Kiel (autarkic) — 46%
2. Königsberg in Prussia (agricultural) — 44%
3. Kassel (autarkic)
   Wuppertal (decentralized)
   Breslau (Autarkic) — 43%
4. **Chemnitz (decentralized)** — 42%
   Stettin (autarkic)
5. Halle (autarkic) — 41%
6. Hannover (autarkic) — 40%
7. **Frankfurt (decentralized)** — 39%
8. **Dresden (decentralized)**
   Nuremberg (autarkic)
   Magdeburg (autarkic) — 38%
9. Hamburg (autarkic) — 33%
10. **Leipzig (decentralized)** — 32%

see Richard F. Hamilton, *Who Voted For Hitler*, p. 485 (Appendix B).
143. Wunderich, *Arbeiterbewegung*...; Turner, *German Big Business*...; and Arthur Schweitzer, *Big Business in the Third Reich*, pp. 60–109. The National Socialists offered them not decentralization, but a centralized state that served their interests rather than those of foreign powers, big capital, or the labor movement.
144. Cologne had 24% of its population vote for the Nazi Party in July 1932; see Hamilton, *Who Voted for Hitler?* Brecht, *Regionalism and Federalism in Germany*, p. 40, marks the Catholic regions on the left bank of the Rhine between Cologne and Aachen as casting less than 20% of their votes for the Nazis in November 1932.
145. See Brecht, *Regionalism and Federalism*..., pp. 41–42 and 161–164.
146. Karl Lange, "Werkzeugmaschinen als Grundlage der Produktionssteigerung"; Otto Nathan, *The Nazi Economic System*, especially pp. 59–83 ("The Use of Cartels as an Agency of Control") and 137–169 ("Control of Production"); Maxine Y. Woolston, *The Structure of the Nazi Economy*, pp. 90–107; Otto Kircheimer, "Changes in the Structure of Political Compromise"; and Sidney Merlin, "Trends in German Economic Control since 1933."
147. Richard J. Overy, "Hitler's War and The German Economy," especially pp. 286 ff.
148. See Gary Herrigel, "Industrial Order in the Machine Tool Industry" and the sources cited there.

Notes for Chapter 3

1. If the reader wants this, he or she can turn most recently to Alfred Chandler's magisterial *Scale and Scope*..., pages 393–592. Good studies of the regions in which autarkic industry developed can be gleaned from Hans Pohl, ed., *Gewerbe- und Industrielandschaften vom Spätmittelalter bis ins 20. Jahrhundert*, especially chapters by Harder-Gersdorff (linen), Fremdling (iron and steel), Hentschel (machinery), Schaefer (electromechanical, paper, glass, and ceramics).
2. The focus on the Ruhr comes at the expense of the much smaller steel regions of the Saar and Silesia. Both of the later regions developed in autarkic ways, that is, primarily based upon the factory form, but they have particularities sufficiently different from the Ruhr that would involve constant narrative digressions in the discussion that, in themselves, would not bring much greater insight into the

autarkic order. Moreover, the Ruhr was overwhelmingly the largest center of steel production. For a region-by-region treatment of the development of steel production in Germany during the 19th century, see Norman J. G. Pounds and William N. Parker, *Coal and Steel in Western Europe*, pp. 210–248. A very nice essay on Silesia is Waclaw Dluboborski, "Wirtschaftliche Region und politische Grenzen." The other German regions of iron and steel production, particularly in the Siegerland, Sauerland, Lahn-Dill, Württemberg, Thüringen and Saxon regions were dealt with in the chapter on the decentralized industrial order.

3. Chandler, op. cit., most recently designates these industries as "great," noting that the label was used by contemporaries. Chandler includes metals – iron and steel, copper, and other nonferrous metals – heavy industrial machinery, both electrical and nonelectrical, and the new chemical industries. He writes: "In these industries German entrepreneurs were first movers in Europe: they succeeded where British entrepreneurs failed. Not surprisingly, these were the industries that attracted the most attention in their day and have continued to interest historians and economists ever since" (p. 429).

4. Two possible objections to this analytic strategy of developing polar types are: 1) it blends out one of the most important industries in these autarkic regions, the electro-mechanical industry, which developed by pursuing both kinds of production strategies at the same time. 2) Unlike the machinery and steel industries, the electro-mechanical industry was one of the so-called "new industries" of the "second" industrial revolution. I don't think either of these objections pose serious problems for my suggested typology. First, as the narrative will show, the steel producers ultimately wound up engaging in both kinds of strategies (scale and scope) and developed organizational structures designed to accommodate them – so the hybrid type ultimately will be dealt with here. Second, the point of "new" industries is that they are based upon technologies (such as electricity or science-based chemicals) that were basically unprecedented, epochal innovations. Neither the steel industry nor the machinery industry can make that kind of claim in general, but the argument that will be made in the text is that in the cases of both steel and machinery, the technologies represented and initiated – unlike those that were implemented in the decentralized regions – complete breaks with the local economic traditions. So, the same effect of a new industry is basically had with the old ones (such as coke-based pig iron making or locomotive and steam engine production).

5. On the existence of impartible inheritance throughout the northwest and middle German regions west of the Elbe, see Friedrich Lütge, *Geschichte der deutschen Agrarverfassung vom frühen Mittelalter bis zum 19. Jahrhundert*, pp. 134–168. On the uniqueness of the size of the cottar class in Saxony, see references in Chapter 2. The excellent case study of two west German regions of impartible inheritance, Minden Ravensburg and Paderborn, by Josef Mooser, *Ländliche Klassengesellschaft 1770–1848*, emphasizes the small size of the independent cottar class relative to the lumpen landless class of day laborers and outworkers in these regions.

6. On this process, see Mooser, *Ländliche Klassengesellschaft*. . . . For overviews of early modern deindustrialization see the essay by Peter Kreidte, "Proto-industrialization between industrialization and deindustrialization" and the excellent collection edited by Hermann Kellenbenz, *Agrarisches Nebengewerbe und Formen der Reagrarisierung im Spätmittelalter und 19/20 Jahrhundert*. Many of the descriptions of misery among homeworkers that are presented in some of the classic early

postwar American histories of 19th century Germany are drawn from these regions, e.g., Theodore Hamerow, *Restoration, Revolution and Reaction*, pp. 21–37.
7. See Gerald Adelmann's case study of post 1850 Bielefeld, "Die Stadt Bielefeld als Zentrum fabrikindustrieller Standortfaktor," in which he points out that factories were introduced quite late and inside the boundaries of the city, not out in the countryside where the traditional industry had been located.
8. Marxist writers such as Maurice Dobb and Robert Brenner place a great deal of emphasis on these conditions being in place for the development of capitalism to root itself in a political economy. See e.g., Maurice Dobb, *Studies in the Development of Capitalism*, and Robert Brenner, "Agrarian Class Structure and Economic Development in Pre-Industrial Europe."
9. I define the Ruhr region as that area roughly bounded by the Ruhr River in the south, the Lippe River in the north, the Rhine River in the West and the city of Unna in the east. Politically, by 1789 parts of this region were incorporated within the Duchy of Mark and the Herzogtums of Kleve and Berg, the Archbishopric of Muenster and the free city of Dortmund. After 1816, the bulk of the region became part of the Prussian province of Westphalia, whereas the southwestern corner belonged to the Rhine province.
10. Karl Heinrich Kaufhold, "Gewerbelandschaften in der frühen Neuzeit, 1650–1800." Kaufhold's survey of *Gewerbelandschaften* in the Graftschaft Mark shows that there was a significant divide between levels of protoindustrial activity, outworking, artisan density, etc. north and south of the Ruhr River. Areas north of the river were much less industrial than those to the south.
11. See Fritz Redlich, "The Leaders of the German Steam Engine Industry During the First Hundred Years."
12. Franz Haniel bought the ailing iron works because he and his friend, business partner, and enthusiast of English technologies Gottlob Jacobi could use the furnaces to supply their new workshop in Sterkrade near the Ruhr to make english machines, especially steam engines. See Hans-Josef Joest, *Pionier im Ruhrrevier*. pp. 1–26. Another early Ruhr steel producer was Alfred Krupp, who came from an old merchant family in Essen. Krupp's father Friedrich started a specialty steel making company in 1810 using traditional charcoal methods. The company never did well and was taken over by his son in 1826. It continued to suffer until the 1840s and the coming of the railroad. There are many works on Krupp. For a short portrait see Ingrid Bauert-Keetman, *Deutsche Industriepioniere*, pp. 31–52.
13. Wilfried Feldenkirchen, *Die Eisen- und Stahlindustrie des Ruhrgebiets, 1879–1914*, p. 19.
14. The Rainer Fremdling essay, "Eisen, Stahl und Kohle," is quite clear on these various processes. N. J. G. Pounds also gives very detailed technical descriptions of the various technologies and their history in Pounds and Parker, *Coal and Steel in Western Europe*, pp. 53–76 and 105–126.
15. Fremdling, "Eisen, Stahl und Kohle," and Pounds and Parker, *Coal and Steel in Western Europe*, pp. 19–104, 105–126, and 210–247; and Gottfried Plumpe, *Die württembergische Eisenindustrie im 19. Jahrhundert*.
16. Harkort came from a prominent family in Westphalia and was a kind of English technology enthusiast. His first workshop was set up in the ancient Castle of Grafen von Altena in Wetter on the Ruhr with the ambition of making a workshop operating in accordance with English methods. He introduced the first puddling

furnace in Germany in 1926. Piepenstock, whose father was a pin manufacturer in the Sauerland, established his puddling operation and rolling mill in Hoerde in 1839. Haniel's firm, the GHH, built its first puddling furnace in 1835. The company was very self-conscious about modeling itself after English producers of the day, so much so that one English visitor remarked that "the order, quiet and businesslike arrangements were quite English." On Harkort, see Fritz Redlich, "The Leaders of the German Steam Engine Industry During the First Hundred Years." On GHH and Piepenstock, see Feldenkirchen, *Eisen, Stahl und Kohle*, pp. 20–21. The English visitor's quote is taken from John Clapham, *The Economic Development of France and Germany*, p. 91.

17. In part due to the challenge of the new nontraditional producers such as Haniel and Piepenstock, the traditional iron producers in the decentralized regions were eventually able to integrate the puddling process into the traditional decentralized system, but it involved considerable renegotiation of traditional policies of fuel management and blast furnace output. None of this negotiation hurt the competitiveness of the industry, but it did slow down the diffusion of the British technology. Fremdling, "Eisen, Stahl und Kohle," and Norman J. G. Pounds, *The Ruhr*.

18. See the good discussion of German iron and steel imports in the first decades of the 19th century by Rainer Fremdling, "Foreign Competition and Technological Change."

19. Horst Wagenblass, *Der Eisenbahnbau und das Wachstum der deutschen Eisen- und Maschinenbauindustrie 1835–1860*. pp. 17–86; Rudolf Boch's Habilitationsschrift also deals with this issue by focusing on the debate between traditional, decentralized producers in the Berg Land and Cologne bankers who wanted to abandon the traditional production methods of the decentralized producers and invest their money in new, potentially much more profitable ventures in the Ruhr. See Rudolf Boch, *Die Entgrenzung der Industrie*.

20. Fremdling, "Eisen Stahl und Kohle," table 1, p. 351, and Feldenkirchen, *Die Eisen und Stahlindustrie des Ruhrgebietes*, p. 27.

21. Feldenkirchen, *Eisen und Stahlindustrie...*, p. 28–32; and Fremdling, "Eisen, Stahl, Kohle," table 2, p. 351.

22. Feldenkirchen, ibid., pp. 22–34. GHH and Krupp also experienced strong growth; Krupp, however, in specialty steels.

23. Ibid, p. 25.

24. The interesting thing about the early Ruhr industrialists is that many of them were inventors or artisans skilled in metallurgy who came from surrounding areas of decentralized production. According to Pounds, "If one considers the place of origin of only the more renowned of the founders of Ruhr industry, its dependence on the older centers of industry is seen to be overwhelming" ("Transformation and Growth in the Nineteenth Century," p. 238–239). In a footnote on p. 239, Pounds goes on to note that "Ruhr industrialists who derived from the Eifel-Aachen area include Hoesch, Thyssen, Poensgen; those from the Sieg-Lahn-Dill include H. D. Piepenstock, Harkort and Roemheid." The speculation seems plausible that the entrepreneurs and investors went to the Ruhr to use new technologies that were incompatible with the traditional practices of their home regions. The Ruhr, finally, was not unique among autarkic regions in this regard. Kocka notes that "the majority of Berlin engineering entrepreneurs – most of whom were artisans – did not originate in Berlin" ("Entrepreneurs and Managers in German Industrialization," footnote 78, p. 716).

25. Feldenkirchen, *Eisen und Stahlindustrie* . . . , pp. 39–42. Information on the founding of the Gewerkschaft Deutsche Kaiser and Thyssen's gradual internal takeover can be found in Wilhelm Treue, *Die Feuer verlöschen nie. August Thyssen-Hütte 1890–1926*, pp. 16–31.
26. An excellent, Chandlerian, analysis of technological dimensions of steel competition and its impact on corporate structure both in Britain and Germany is Ulrich Wengenroth, *Unternehmensstrategien und technischer Fortschritt.* especially pp. 176 ff for a discussion of the Thomas process and 216 ff on the Siemens–Martin open hearth process.
27. For a comparative discussion of the importance of the Ruhr in Europe, see Pounds and Parker, *Coal and Steel* . . . and Norman. J. G. Pounds, *An Historical Geography of Europe 1800–1914*, pp. 508–512.
28. Feldenkirchen, *Eisen und Stahlindustrie* . . . , pp. 140–147. The exception to this were a small number of independent rolling mills that specialized in the production of more complex "secondary" steel products. Even these producers were by and large all swallowed up by World War I.
29. Chandler notes that the Germans were more vertically integrated than even the Americans. (*Scale and Scope*, p. 492). Landes was struck by the degree of Ruhr vertical integration relative to the British:

> In 1902 only twenty-one open hearth firms of seventy two in Britain, with one quarter of the make, had adjacent blast furnaces; whereas integration with smelting was almost universal in the Reich. The same was true of the later stages of manufacture: where the tendency in Westphalia was to build rolling mills on to steel works, British rerollers were relying increasingly on outside sources for their crude metal. (David Landes, *Unbound Prometheus*, p. 263)

30. In this way the argument modifies Juergen Kocka's corrective to the standard Chandlerian account of large-firm organization. Whereas the latter account points to the shaping influence of technologies in the creation of large-scale organizations, Kocka's account points out that the choice of technology and production organization and strategy were shaped by the preexisting character of agrarian Germany. My account, of course, modifies the Kocka argument by claiming that the preexisting infrastructure is regional within Germany and not simply German (or "Central European"). Kocka has made his argument in numerous places, in particular, see: "Expansion, Integration, Diversification; "Die hundert grossten deutschen Industrie Unternehmen im späten 19 und 20 Jahrhundert" with Hannes Siegrist; and "The Rise of the Modern Industrial Enterprise in Germany." Kocka always acknowledges his debt to Alexander Gerschenkron, "Economic Backwardness in Historical Perspective." For Chandler's causal framework and his discussion of German development, see Chandler, *Scale and Scope*, pp. 1–47 and 393–592. For Kocka's continued friendly instruction of Chandler on this point, see Kocka's contribution to "*Scale and Scope*: a Review Colloquium." .
31. The most detailed study of precisely these dynamic processes during the 19th century is now Wengenroth, *Unternehmensstrategien* . . . , especially pp. 73–135.
32. Small wonder that on the basis of examples of this kind Landes concluded that "the trend toward mechanization was inexorable" (*The Unbound Prometheus*, pp. 264–265).
33. The insight is traditionally traced to Karl Marx, *Capital*, vol. 1, Chapters 7–15.
34. Landes, *The Unbound Prometheus*, p. 265.

35. An overview of migration into Germany during this period can be found in Ulrich Herbert, *A History of Foreign Labor in Germany, 1880–1980*, Chapter 1, pp. 9–86.
36. 19.5% of the city's worker population came from abroad: 15.9% from Austria, 1.9% from Holland (the town was close to the Dutch border), 1.4% from Italy, and another 0.3% from many other countries. To that, Lucas notes, should be added 19.5% Deutsch-Poles (ethnic poles with German citizenship). Eberhard Lucas, *Zwei Formen von Radikalismus in der deutschen Arbeiterbewegung*, pp. 40–41.
37. Older autarkic cities, such as Hannover, Kassel, Magdeburg, and Nuremberg, which were already relatively separate from the surrounding countryside prior to industrialization, became increasingly so. See J. J. Lee, "Aspects of Urbanization and Economic Development in Germany 1815-1914"; Medick, Kreidte, and Schlumbohm make a related, yet regionally undifferentiated, argument to this effect in *Industrialization before Industrialization*.
38. Alfred Marshall felt that this kind of autarkic integration in production, which he understood broadly to be a shift from external economies to internal economies, was part and parcel of the industrialization process itself. This is the argument he makes, for example, in the first part of *Industry and Trade*, pp. 1–177; for a summary see pp. 167–170. The title page of Marshall's book bears the inscription: "The many in the one, the one in the many."
39. This story comes from Lucas, *Zwei Formen von Radikalismus . . .* , pp. 21–56. For an account of another autarkic producer's relations with its environs, see Herman Schroeter, "Die Firma Friedrich Krupp und die Stadt Essen."
40. In addition to the various articles by Jürgen Kocka and the book by Chandler mentioned above, see also the article by Hans Pohl "Zur Geschichte von Organization und Leitung deutsche Grossunternehmen seit dem 19 Jahrhundert," pp. 143–178; R. H. Tilly, "Mergers, External Growth and Finance in the Development of Large Scale Enterprise in Germany 1880–1913"; and Jürgen Brockstedt, "Family Enterprise and the Rise of Large-Scale Enterprise in Germany (1871–1914)."
41. Of the 100 firms in 1887 listed in what is now a classic article by Jürgen Kocka and Hannes Siegrist on the largest firms in industrializing Germany, 78% were located in what I classify below as "autarkic regions": The Ruhr accounted for 23% of the top 100 in that year; Central Prussia, including, Berlin, Hannover, and the province of Saxony, accounted for 28%; Silesia 15%; Bavaria 3%; the Saarland 2%; Port Cities 5%; Alsace Lorraine 1%; and Poland 1%. Twenty-two percent of large firms in 1887, by contrast, were located in "decentralized regions" (the Rhineland excluding the Ruhr, the kingdom of Saxony and Thüringen, Baden, Württemberg, and the Rhine–Main region). Of the largest 100 corporations Kocka and Siegrist list in 1907, 81% were located in autarkic regions, and 19% in decentralized regions. See Jürgen Kocka and Hannes Siegrist, "Die hundert grossten deutschen Industrie Unternehmen im späten 19 und 20 Jahrhundert." Again, characteristically, Chandler's three tables of the largest 200 German enterprises in *Scale and Scope* provide no information on location.
42. Wilfried Feldenkirchen, "Concentration in German Industry, 1870–1939," p. 6.
43. Chandler's *Scale and Scope* in many ways confirms the work that Kocka and others have been doing since the early 1970s.
44. The development of functional departments within Ruhr enterprises is chronicled by Feldenkirchen, *Eisen und Stahlindustrie . . .* , Chapter 10, pp. 304–320.
45. Kocka's suggestion for why the Germans were so centralized is persuasive for the autarkic areas (though he refers to Germany in general):

Notes to page 82

The Entrepreneurs of the time do not seem to have spoken much about such functional integration; it was self-evident, obvious and necessary as far as they were concerned. Probably the trend was connected with the relative backwardness of German industry and its consequent relatively rapid development. Industry in Germany had less continuity with the pre-industrial structures than in England. In the industries most important for German development (engineering and the extractive industries), the early industrialists frequently had no established, developed trading structure to utilize. In addition, the producers therefore took over the marketing, when it was a matter of selling technically complicated products and the necessary specialists could only be provided by the manufacturers themselves. Frequently early factory owners seem also to have had a deep distrust of the independent distributer: a frequent motive of the manufacturer seems to have been to make himself "independent" of these people. (Kocka, "Entrepreneurs and Managers in German Industrialization," p. 550–551)

46. Chandler, *Scale and Scope*, pp. 486–496, provides a good overview of the pre-World War I autarkic steel industry. An interesting difference with their counterparts in the United States concerned the durability of family ownership in Germany. In the U.S., when a firm became a joint-stock company, had gone through a considerable period of expansion, and both integrated and diversified its production, it was also typically the case that the actual management of the firm had passed from family run or entrepreneurial management to management by professional managers. Though this was not unheard of in the German industry – professional managers controlled many of the leading steel producers, such as the Gelsenkirchener Bergwerks AG (Emil Kirdorf), the Phoenix AG (Wilhelm Blankenburg), the Deutsch-Luxemburgische Bergwerks-Hütten AG (Albert Voegler) and others – a large percentage of German companies continued to be owned by the original families. And though such firms relied heavily on professional managers and management systems, the owners continued to play very forceful roles in the management and strategic direction of enterprise. Well-known examples in steel making are Krupp, Stinnes, Stumm, Haniel, Klöckner, and Thyssen. See Hannes Siegrist, "Deutsche Grossunternehmen im späten 19 Jh bis zur Weimar Republik." Chandler also notes the prevalence of family enterprises in Germany, but notes that it was, unlike in Britain, in few cases a barrier to the diffusion of professional management practices. Chandler does suggest that a difference between the steel industry and, for example, the large electro-mechanical family enterprises is that in the former control was more personalized and concentrated. At Siemens, he points out, even though the family was still active in management, most decisions were formally required to be made (and in fact were made) by committee (*Scale and Scope*, p. 496).
47. Klaus Harney, "Historische Berufsbildungs- und Qualifikationsforschung am Beispiel der GHH Oberhausen. ".
48. Hermann Schroeter, "Die Firma Krupp und die Stadt Essen," p. 263. It was established in the 1880s; by 1887, 1,267 children had attended the school. Instruction was provided free to Krupp workers, and Krupp absorbed all of the costs of construction, teacher salaries, and materials (for both instruction and recreation).
49. More generally, on the state of vocational education in Germany before the artisinal system was transformed into a national system, see Gerhard Adelmann, "Die

berufliche Aus- und Weiterbilding in der deutschen Wirtschaft 1871–1918," and Albin Gladen, "Die berufliche Aus- und Weiterbildung in der deutschen Wirtschaft 1918–1945" for the actual transformation.

50. David Crew's *Town in Ruhr* is an excellent social historical study of Bochum and the overwhelming role of the Bochumer Verein in shaping the lives of workers there. For a description of the social climate in Krupp works, see Johann Paul, *Alfred Krupp und die Arbeiterbewegung*, pp. 18–121, and Richard Ehrenberg and Hugo Racine, *Krupp'sche Arbeiter-Familien*. On paternalism generally in German firms, see J. J. Lee, "Labor in German Industrialization," especially pp. 453–471; Kocka, "Entrepreneurs and Managers...,"" especially pp. 546–549.

51. See Helmut Croon, "Bürgertum und Verwaltung in den Städten des Ruhrgebiets im 19. Jahrhundert," especially p. 32 and note 14.

52. Ferdinand Graf von Degenfeld-Schonberg, "Die Unternehmerpersöhnlichkeit in der modernen Volkswirtschaft," especially p. 58, as quoted (to the same effect) in Gerald Feldman, *Iron and Steel in the Great Inflation, 1916–1923*, p. 42.

53. See the excellent work by Richard Tilly, especially the essays in Section I "Kapitalmobilisierung, Banken und Staat in der deutschen Industrialisierung," his, *Kapital, Staat und Sozialer Protest in der deutschen Industrialisierung*, pp. 15–94; also see Otto Jeidels, *Das Verhältnis der deutschen Grossbanken zur Industrie mit besonderer Berücksichtigung der Eisenindustrie*. Rudolf Boch points out that many of the initial founders of these banks were merchants from cities in or near decentralized regions, such as Cologne (home of Hansemann and Mevissen), who used their earning from decentralized industrialization to finance autarkic industrialization. See Boch, *Die Entgrenzung der Industrie*. . . .

54. Perhaps the most notable proponents of the view that the German banks were the string pullers of German capitalism are Hilferding and Bukharin. See the classic books: Rudolf Hilferding, *Finance Capitalism*.; Nikolai Ivanovich Bukharin, *Imperialism and World Economy*. Recently, this view has been subject to a careful case-study-based test by Volker Wellhöner, *Grossbanken und Grossindustrie im Kaiserreich*.

55. Kocka, "The Rise of Large Scale Enterprise in Germany," p. 92.

56. The best source on the growth and structure of the German credit banking industry during the industrialization process is Jacob Riesser, *The German Great Banks and Their Concentration in Connection with the Economic Development of Germany*.

57. It is important to emphasize about the decentralized producers that their views of the state were not inconsistent with liberal ideas. Such producers believed in a society distinct from the state, but they also believed that the state had a clear role to play in their economic affairs. An interesting discussion of this concerning the producers in the decentralized ring of regions surrounding the Ruhr for the early 19th century is Helmuth Croon, "Die wirtschaftlichen Führungsschichten im Rheinland und in Westfalen 1790–1850." Rudlof Boch, *Die Entgrenzung der Industrie* . . ., also makes this point about the same producers. In the decentralized regions outside of Prussia, such as Württemberg, Baden, Saxony, etc., the states themselves were more sympathetic to liberalism, constitutionalism, etc. Decentralized industrialization, in other words, was modern; it was simply decentralized.

58. These fears were, moreover, often justified. The Prussian state was suspicious of the emergence of large private organizations and frequently blocked applications for incorporation; see Kocka, "Entrepreneurs and Managers . . . ," p. 539.

59. Kocka again:

Notes to pages 84–87   325

> One should remember that the railways ... were propagated and introduced as an instrument of a long-term development policy (for the benefit of one's own works, town, or country). Thus the most important decisions of the industrial revolution were in one sense political decisions of an increasingly self-confident, organized and forward-looking bourgeoisie. ... Men like Mevissen, Camphausen, Hansemann, Siemens, Harkort, and List saw their entrepreneurial activity not only as a means to personal success, but also as a part of a national civilizing mission. (ibid., p. 529)

60. Cited in Elaine Glovka Spencer, "Rulers of the Ruhr," p. 46, note 14. Businessmen, of course, accepted other honors from the Reich, such as titles as reserve officers in the army or designations as Royal Commercial Councilors (*Kgl. Kommerzienräte*). Nevertheless, as Feldman aptly notes about the Ruhr magnates, "they were still men who had guaranteed entree to the best hotels but not to the best salons" (Gerald Feldman, *Iron and Steel in the German Inflation, 1916–1923*, p. 26). The Feldman book is, in general, a superb modern treatment of the industry and its leaders.
61. Jürgen Kocka, "Family and Bureaucracy in German Industrial Management, 1850–1914" is the modern locus classicus of this argument. Spencer, "Rulers of the Ruhr" applies the argument to the iron and steel industry.
62. Spencer, ibid., p. 47; see also C. Helfer, "Über militärische Einflüsse auf die industrielle Entwicklung in Deutschland."
63. The process of appropriation resembles the kind of development dynamics described as isomorphism by Walter Powell and Paul DiMaggio, "The Iron Cage Revisited," and Niel Fligstein, *The Transformation of Control*.
64. I think that Otto Pflanze's (initial) portrait of the young Bismarck develops this well: see Otto Pflanze, *Bismarck and the Development of Germany*.
65. George Steinmetz has summarized this tension in the state's orientation quite well in Chapter five of his *Regulating the Social* ...
66. Redlich's "Leaders of the German Steam Engine Industry ..." provides a good overview of Prussia's involvement with steam engine building in the 18th and early 19th centuries. W. O. Henderson's chapter "The Role of the State" pp. 71–79 in his *The Rise of German Industrial Power, 1834–1914* provides a good overview of Prussian state activities. Henderson even notes that the giant Prussian holding company, the *Seehandlung*, sponsored the construction of the initial textile factories in Upper Silesia to provide work for the many landless workers left ailing by the decline of the domestic linen industry (p. 74).
67. The top firms are listed in Feldenkirchen, *Eisen und Stahlindustrie* ..., pp. 220–221. For a detailed case study of the battleship building weapons race and its effect on German industry, see Michael Epkenhans, *Die wilhelminische Flottenrüstung, 1908–1914*, pp. 143–312.
68. Feldenkirchen, *Die Eisen und Stahlindustrie*.... Other autarkic producers in other branches profited from government purchases as well: Siemens of Berlin was the leading producer of telegraph technology and then became an equally important producer of telephone equipment and electricity generating equipment. The Allgemeine Elektrizitäts Gesellschaft (AEG), Siemen's large Berlin rival, also was a world leader in the production of electrical generators and power plants.
69. Robert Liefmann outlines these problems in his chapter on the "Origin of Cartels," in *Cartels, Concerns and Trusts*, especially pp. 23 ff.

70. Good discussions of cartelization in general and in the steel industry in particular can be found in Herbert von Beckerath, *Kräfte, Ziele und Gestaltung in der deutschen Industrie*; idem, *Modern Industrial Organization*, pp. 235–280; Hermann Levy, *Industrial Germany*; Robert Liefmann, *Cartels* . . . , pp. 1–224; and Heinrich Mannstädt, *Ursachen und Ziele des Zusammenschlusses im Gewerbe unter besonderer Berücksichtigung der Kartelle und Trusts*.
71. Wengenroth, *Unternehmenstrategien* . . . , p. 139 ff. Feldenkirchen, *Eisen und Stahlindustrie* . . . , pp. 110–128, disagrees with Wengenroth on the significance of this cartel. Wengenroth is impressed by the amount of output the cartel, at least in the 1870s and 1880s, organized. Feldenkirchen is more impressed by the lack of consistent, sustained cartelization throughout the rest of the industry. Wengenroth says that the steel industry was highly cartelized; Feldenkirchen says it was not. Chandler, *Scale and Scope*, pp. 492–493, sides with Feldenkirchen. Nobody disputes that the rail cartel organized such a large portion of industry production, however.
72. A good listing of steel industry cartels and their duration is printed in the appendix of Steven B. Webb, "Tariffs, Cartels, Technology and Growth in the German Steel Industry, 1879 to 1914." Feldenkirchen details the history of the *Stahlschienengemeinschaft* in *Eisen und Stahlindustrie* . . . , pp. 218–219.
73. Feldenkirchen, *Eisen und Stahlindustrie* . . . , pp. 262–268.
74. Ibid, p. 145.
75. Gerald Feldman, *Iron and Steel in the German Inflation, 1916–1923*, p. 33. It is, however, ultimately difficult to actually determine how much each segment of the industry took as part of total sales, see Feldenkirchen, *Eisen und Stahlindustrie* . . . p. 216–217.
76. Lon L. Peters, "Are Cartels Unstable? The German Steel Works Association Before World War One," especially pp. 71–72; Feldenkirchen, *Eisen und Stahlindustrie* . . . , p. 215 writes "The character of products in the iron and steel industry meant that only a few products could be produced for an anonymous market. For most finished products, this was not possible because of the multitude of different specifications that were possible. Sales occurred mainly after the receipt of a specific order."
77. One piece of evidence indicating how the Ruhr steel producers had managed their diversification on the basis of variety of product rather than quantity of product produced is the relative lack of high-volume production capacity they had in these areas, even in the 1920s. Feldman describes the Siemens executive Jastrow's rather deprecating impressions of his trip to the steel works in the Ruhr that had been included in the Siemens–Rhein Elbe Schukert Union in a way that suggests the steel producer's orientation to smaller-volume output: "[Jastrow] was disturbed by the confusion everywhere in evidence because of the overlapping and uncoordinated production programs in the foundries and rolling mills and by the way in which major fabrication and finishing operations had been lodged in inadequate old repair shops converted to new uses. He was surprised at the absence of plants that gave one the "impression of modern mass fabrication" (cited in Feldman, *Iron and Steel* . . . , p. 261).
78. Some clarity on what is meant by specialty and standard is perhaps important. Steel was increasingly produced in integrated and was approaching continuously cast processes that allowed steel and rolling to occur all in one heating. The goal was to minimize the intermediate steps of producing ingots, etc., which then had to be

remelted for rolling. There was a bottom limit beneath which it simply would not be profitable to produce. Specialty producers struggled around this bottom limit, while at the same time expanding the kind of steels and rolling processes that they could run through a complex of furnaces and finishing operations. Mass producers attempted to standardize their output at the expense of variety in order to raise the minimum efficient scale of production.

79. Most postwar studies of the Ruhr have interpreted this situation in the industry in a very different way. The standard view, perhaps now best represented by Feldenkirchen and Chandler, takes for granted that the mass-production strategy would be the inevitable winner. Even Feldman, whose magnificent book in many ways makes the exact opposite conclusion possible, constantly refers to "long term tendencies" pushing toward mass-production (Feldman, *Iron and Steel* . . . , e.g., p. 455). From this point of view, the most rational solution to the problems presented by the process of diversification were not ambiguous at all. Producers were aware of developments taking place in foreign industries, in particular those of the United States, where experience had shown that best practice involved the creation of a large firm that could consolidate existing capacity, eliminate redundant capacity, streamline the product palette, combine marketing and sales forces, and stabilize raw material inputs. This is the US Steel model and something like this did ultimately happen in the German steel industry with the formation of the *Vereinigte Stahlwerke* (Vestag), but only in 1926, nearly 20 years after the problems the combine was to resolve began to appear. Moreover, the Vestag did not include many of the most important prewar producers in the industry – such as Krupp, GHH, Hoechst, Klöckner, and Mannesmann – all of whom had pursued strategies both before and after the war that radically extended their finishing operations, not only in steel products but into machinery building as well. Moreover, they tended to concentrate their steel finishing operations on higher quality products. And, further, unlike the American multidivisional enterprise, these *Konzerne* were run as holding companies with very loose central control. These firms continued to account for half of German steel production throughout the interwar period, despite the formation of the Vestag. Feldenkirchen basically ignores these companies (Wilfried Feldenkirchen, "Concentration in German Industry, 1870–1939," or idem, "Big Business in Interwar Germany"). Chandler interprets these *Konzerne* as products of inflation and is under the impression that they were only short-term solutions that were ultimately to give way in the post-World War II period to the modern multidivisional company (*Scale and Scope*, p. 512). Feldman is aware of the significance of these firms and recognizes that they have continued to exist up to the present day. But he tends to confuse their specialization strategies with the traditional mass-production orientation and as a result ultimately concludes that the industry was without systematic organization (ibid., p. 461). My argument, in contrast, will suggest that the *Konzerne* were attempting to create autarkic industrial districts in order to be able to pursue a specialization strategy on the market. And, it was only after they succeeded in inventing stable organizational strategies for doing this, that the formation of the Vestag was possible in the first place. In order to see this possibility, one has to see the ambiguity in the prewar diversification.

80. See Lon L. Peters, "Are Cartels Unstable?" and Gerald Feldman, "The Collapse of the Steelworks Association, 1912–1919"; Feldenkirchen, *Eisen und Stahlindustrie* . . . , deals with the *Stahlwerksbund* , in a number of places and from a variety

of angles: c.f. pp. 120–124, 144–147, 200–213, and 218–219. Chandler also argues that the cartel was a failure (*Scale and Scope*, p. 492–494). One could make the case that the only reason that the cartel arrangements lasted the three years that they did in the finishing product markets was because they facilitated the integration of the few remaining independent rolling mills into the operations of the larger integrated mills who were seeking to expand their capacity in the new areas by merger. For the logic of this argument, see Mannstädt, *Ursachen und Ziele* . . . , pp. 53–71.

81. August Thyssen was perhaps the greatest advocate of this strategy. See Chandler, *Scale and Scope*, p. 493.
82. Chandler reports that in 1900 Carnegie Steel and Federal Steel accounted for 35% of the steel ingots produced in the United States and 45% of its rails, while the largest German steel producer in 1904, Krupp, accounted for only 9.3% of all German primary steel output. Secondary products were even more fragmented, partially because shifts in demand encouraged broad diversification across the industry and partially because a number of independent rolling mills continued to exist in these markets (Chandler, *Scale and Scope*, p. 492). On the restructuring in the electro-mechanical industry in the early 20th century, see the beginning of Peter Czada's *Die Berliner Elektroindustrie in der Weimarer Zeit*. Chandler also discusses the restructuring (op. cit., pp. 467–474).
83. Feldman suggests that the German steel producers' resistance to American style trusts had cultural and sociopolitical roots (Feldman, *Iron and Steel* . . . , p. 38–39). This kind of argument is confirmed by the following anecdote: When Hugo Stinnes suggested at a meeting of the syndicate that many plants were so inefficient that they had "no right to exist" and that there should be a period without cartels to enable free competition to force consolidation, Emil Kirdorf, the head of a competing firm, referred to Stinnes' remarks as "juvenile." See the story in Peters, "Are Cartels Unstable?" p. 75–76.
84. See discussion in Chapter 2.
85. Feldenkirchen, *Eisen und Stahlindustrie* . . . , pp. 262–268.
86. Feldenkirchen, *Eisen und Stahlindustrie* . . . , pp. 128–149; Webb, "Tariffs . . . ," pp. 318–319, links vertical integration in the industry to cartelization.
87. This information is taken from the extremely competent survey article by Hans Pohl, "Die Konzentration in der deutschen Wirtschaft vom ausgehenden 19. Jahrhundert bis 1945"; Franz Lammert, *Das Verhältnis zwischen der Eisen schaffenden und der Eisen verarbeitenden Industrie seit dem ersten Weltkrieg* also provides a good survey on vertical integration. The number of nonintegrated iron and steel producers, already small before the war, vanished over the course of the 1920s and 1930s. Moreover, nearly all of the steel producers had fully integrated backwards into coal production.
88. Otto Wiskott, *Eisenschaffende und eisenverarbeitende Industrie*, pp. 45–51.
89. On the initial disruption in the steel industry, see Lammert, *Verhältnis* . . . , and Paul Berkenkopf, *Die neuorganisation der deutschen Grosseisenindustrie*. According to Robert Brady, European crude steel capacity increased by 8.3 million tons between 1913 and 1929. (*The Rationalization Movement in Germany*, p. 127.)
90. These factors are all outlined in Karl Lasch, *Entwicklungstendenzen für die Zusammenschlussformen in der deutschen Grossindustrie seit 1914*, pp. 10–68; Arnold Tross, *Der Aufbau der Eisen-und Eisenverarbeitenden Industrie-Konzerne. Deutsch-*

Notes to pages 92–95   329

lands, pp. 127–170; see also Feldman, *Iron and Steel* . . . , especially pp. 110–280.
91. A fifth *Konzern*, the Flick group, was created later in the decade, mainly out of old Silesian holdings. Since the location of the company was mostly outside of the Ruhr, I won't deal with this group in my study.
92. The SRSU was composed of the Siemens & Halske and Siemens Schuckert works and the merged pieces of the Deutsche-Luxemburg company and the Gelsenkirchener Bergwerksgesellschaft.
93. The best sources on the emergence of Konzerne. in the steel industry are Feldman, *Iron and Steel* . . . , pp. 210–279; Arnold Tross, *Der Aufbau der Eisen- und eisenverarbeitenden Industrie-Konzerne. Deutschlands, Ursachen, Formen und Wirkungen des Zusammenschlusses unter besonderer Berücksichtigung der Maschinenindustrie*; Lasch, *Entwicklungstendenzen* . . . ; Otto Wiskott, *Eisenschaffende und eisenverarbeitende Industrie*. More generally, see Liefmann, *Cartels* . . . pp. 225–282; Herbert von Beckerath, *Modern Industrial Organization*, pp. 280–287; and Manfred Nussbaum, "Unternehmenskonzentration und Investitionsstrategie nach dem Ersten Weltkrieg."
94. Tross, *Eisen- und eisenverarbeitenden Industrie* . . . , pp. 48–57.
95. Ibid. pp. 34–43.
96. This is Feldman's characterization. Feldman also calls the general conception "vague"; (*Iron and Steel* . . . , p. 277).
97. These are the words of Otto Heinrich, Siemens director and one of the original masterminds with Hugo Stinnes behind the creation of the SRSU, quoted in Feldman, *Iron and Steel* . . . , p. 222. Chandler also uses the Heinrich quote from Feldman (*Scale and Scope*, p. 509), but he wrongly attributes it to Heinrich Jastrow rather than Otto Heinrich. Feldman claims that the quote comes from an internal Siemens memo written by Heinrich.
98. On the SRSU, see Feldman, *Iron and Steel* . . . pp. 213–244. On Hugo Stinnes, see Peter Wulf, *Wirtschaft und Politik 1918–1924*.
99. Feldman (*Iron and Steel* . . . , p. 215) quotes Stinnes about the rationale for a *Konzern*: "For Stinnes vertical concentration was a matter of principle, because "I do not share the view of the creators of the great American trusts, that every branch of industry must be separate from the others and take care of itself with the single purpose of the greatest possible return." He believed that the return would be greater if they worked in solidarity with one another." Feldman also notes that Stinnes found the expansion into fabrication and other industries more interesting than proposals by some in the industry to rationalize it for more efficient mass production.
100. Krupp didn't do this. Instead it continued to run its old business in the same way and managed its outside businesses though I.G. cooperation.
101. Feldman, *Iron and Steel* . . . , p. 268–269 on GHH; Springorum's testimony to the Enquette Ausschuss on Hoesch, *Die deutsche eisenerzeugendeindustrie, Verhandlungen und Berichte des Unterausschusses für Gewerbe: Industrie, Handel und Handwerk*, pp. 126–127.
102. See Liefmann, *Cartels* . . . , pp. 242–227; von Beckerath, *Modern Industrial Organization*, p. 157–8 and Feldman, *Iron and Steel* . . . , p. 269.
103. Feldman, *Iron and Steel* . . . , p. 268.
104. Testimony of Dr. Ing. Springorum, chief executive officer of Hoesch, January 1, 1928, before the Enquette Ausschuss, reproduced in *Die deutsche eisenerzeugen-*

deindustrie..., p. 127. Springorum's full testimony outlines the postwar development of Hoesch (pp. 125-127); see also Tross, *Eisen-und Eisenverarbeitenden Industrie*..., pp. 98-102.
105. H. Siegrist, "Deutsche Grossunternehmung vom späten 19. Jahrhundert bis zur Weimarer Republik," pp. 87-88.
106. Helmut Maisel, *Diversifikation und Konglomerate Interdependence*, p. 9.
107. Enquette Ausschuss, *Die deutsche eisenerzeugende Industrie*..., p. 31; Paul Berkenkopf, *Die Neuorganisation der deutschen Grosseisenindustrie*, pp. 76-134; von Beckerath, *Modern Industrial Organization*..., pp. 221-222 and 285-287.
108. A blow-by-blow buildup of the considerations and alternatives considered in the formation of the Vereinigte Stahlwerke is given in Berkenkopf, *Neuorganisation*..., pp. 7-86.
109. In addition to the Vestag, horizontal mergers with this kind of aim also took place in the linoleum, gunpowder, textile (especially the Berlin and north Germany based Blumenstein Concern), potash (within the Wintershall-Deutsche-Kaliindustrie A.G.), and cement industries. A further important horizontal merger among volume producers in autarkic regions occurred in the chemical industry when the Berlin company, Rütgerswerk A.G., amalgamated the production capacity and capital of most German producers of roofing paper. Examples galore can be found in Liefmann, *Cartels*..., see, e.g., Chapter 30, "Examples of Concern Formation," pp. 248-259. See also von Beckerath, *Modern Industrial Organization*..., p. 189.
110. Lasch, *Entwicklungstendenzen*..., gives a good outline of the structure of the combine. There is also a graphic display on pp. 89-104; see also the article by Ottfried Dascher, "Probleme der Konzernorganisation"; and the discussion in Feldenkirchen, "Big Business in Interwar Germany," pp. 421-426.
111. Voegler testified that "it was already a clear aim at the founding of the Vereinigte Stahlwerke to cut out or strictly curtail all aspects of finishing that were not immediate aspects of the steel production process. This included all mechanical engineering as well as all specialty steels" (Enquette Ausschuss, *Die deutsche eisenerzeugende Industrie*..., p. 129-130).
112. Enquette Ausschuss, *Die deutsche eisenerzeugende Industrie*..., p. 132.
113. Ibid., pp. 157-158 (Voegler's testimony).
114. As Liefmann notes, this structure was similar to that adopted by the Siemens-Schuckert-Siemens-Halske combine. Liefmann, *Cartels*..., pp. 251-252. Curiously, neither Chandler, *Scale and Scope*, pp. 550-561, nor Feldenkirchen, "Big Business in Interwar Germany," pp. 421-428 make this connection.
115. Liefmann, *Cartels*..., has a good description of these difficulties (pp. 251 ff). Basically, the problem was that the holding company's assets were largely identical to those of the Vestag and it was these, not Vestag's, that were traded on the stock market. Vestag, in other words, was incapable of making an independent move to the capital markets. If it did, then, as Liefmann remarked: "we have a double issue of shares on the same assets, a practice which, if it were to find imitators, deserves unmeasured condemnation." This problem forced the reorganization of the Vestag.
116. Voegler broke his commitment on keeping specialty steels out of the product palette when in the process of rationalizing their facilities the combine discovered that it had enough specialty steel capacity to form an independent company in 1930, the Deutsche Edelstahlwerke, A.G., Krefeld. See Chandler, *Scale and Scope*, p. 552.

117. This story is taken from Levy, *Industrial Germany*, p 167–69, and Waller, "Neuordnung des Stahlvereins." Additional information on the corporate structure of the Vestag can be found in Liefmann, *Cartels* . . . , p. 251–253. Liefmann's account, however, does not describe the second reorganization. A good description of Vestag's journey toward internal decentralization can also be found in Ottfried Dascher, "Problem der Konzernorganization," p. 127 ff. According to Feldenkirchen and Chandler, the reorganization of the Vestag in the 1930s was brought on by the recovery of the international economy (1933?!), which enabled "Vestag executives to complete the administrative reorganizations they had begun in 1926" (Chandler, *Scale and Scope*, p. 556).
118. Chandler, *Scale and Scope*, pp. 552–559.
119. Hans Pohl, "Die Konzentration in der deutschen Wirtschaft vom ausgehenden 19. Jahrhundert bis 1945," pp. 4–44.
120. Kocka, following Sombart, points to an analogous phenomenon at the end of the 19th century on the tail end of the Great Depression; see Jürgen Kocka, "Expansion, Integration, Diversification," p. 216; and Werner Sombart, *Der Moderne Kapitalismus*, Vol. 3, pp. 769 ff.
121. The region around Nuremberg-Furth also exhibited many of the characteristics of the Bielefeld region to be described, especially in the pencil, luggage, and toy industries.
122. See Wilhelm Helmrich, *Wirtschaftskunde des Landes Nordrhein-Westfalen*, chapter on "Ostwestfalen-Lippe," pp. 209–220; Robert Dickenson, *The Regions of Germany*, pp. 62–79.
123. Ludwig Preller, *Sozialpolitik in der Weimarer Republik*, pp. 99–101; Edgar Salin, "Standortverschiebung der deutschen Wirtschaft"; and Goetz Briefs, "Bevolkerungsbewegung und Arbeitsmarktentwicklung."
124. Though at first glance these new clusters of less-efficient producers and home workers may resemble the decentralized systems familiar from the other form of order, it is important to see that they are not the same. Most fundamentally, these new clusters of firms around larger autarkic producers did not enjoy the kinds of infrastructural supports, or the cooperative, decentered features of governance characteristic of the decentralized order. Such institutions were never created in this area. Small supplier firms arose because larger companies were seeking to avoid risk. In the end, they were very dependent upon the larger companies for work, skilled labor, and even outdated technology. The producers in decentralized regions represented an alternative to this form of subordinate, decadent secondary sector. The key difference was the network of institutions that socialized risk in the decentralized industrial order. In the former, small property dominated *Gewerbelandschaft* regions, small- and medium-sized producers absorbed risks that larger companies did not want to bear.
125. See the essays on white-collar workers in Emil Lederer, *Kapitalismus, Klassenstruktur und Probleme der Demokratie in Deutschland, 1910–1940*; Ludwig Preller, *Sozialpolitik in der Weimarer Republik*, pp 133–136 and 191–192; von Beckerath, *Modern Industrial Organization*, and Burkhardt Lutz, *Kurze Traum immerwährender Prosperität*.
126. Kaufhold, after carefully looking at the extent of proto-industrial activity in the Berlin area, concludes that the density of activity in the entire *Kurmark* region was not high enough to warrant designation as a *Gewerbelandschaft*; see Kaufhold, "Gewerbelandschaften in der Frühen Neuzeit," p. 120–124. On the gradual decay

of handicraft in Nuremberg, see ibid., pp. 139 ff, and Ekkard Wiest, *Die Entwicklung des Nürnberger Gewerbes zwischen 1648–1806.*

127. Stein was dispatched to Britain to "inspect English mining and smelting procedures and the iron and metal foundries . . . and to study the application of machinery to these industries." He traveled officially as the Prussian representative Baron vom Stein, but then used the pseudonym "Count Vidi" to engage in illicit efforts to pirate the technology, employing English craftsmen to copy the working engines of Boulton and Watt. He was eventually found out. see the story in Redlich, "The Leaders of the German Steam Engine Industry . . . ," pp. 125–126.

128. Ibid.; and W. O. Henderson, "The Rise of Metal and Armament Industries in Berlin and Brandenburg," pp. 1–17.

129. Redlich, "The Leaders of the German Steam Engine Industry . . . ," pp. 134–135 on Egells – Egell's workshop was sponsored by the Prussian state and received aid in the form of "funds, orders and English machine tools" (p. 135). Kocka uses the term "nursery firm" throughout his essay "Entrepreneurs and Managers . . . ," and with specific reference to Egells, p. 522; Alfred Schroeter, "Die Entstehung der deutschen Maschinenbauindustrie in der ersten Hälfte des 19. Jahrhunderts," p. 69, traces out the main nursery firms and their offspring.

130. A third would be machine tool production, the importation and development of which the state encouraged because of its advantages in weapons production. See W. O. Henderson, "The Rise of Metal and Armament Industries . . ."; Berthold Buxbaum, "Der deutsche Werkzeugmaschinen- und Werkzeugbau im 19 Jahrhundert"; Conrad Matschoss, "Geschichte der Ludw. Loewe & Co. Actiengesellschaft."

131. Redlich, "Leaders of the German Steam Engine Industry . . . ," p. 139. If one lists the steam engine and locomotive producers presented by Redlich, more than half were of merchant or patrician background, the rest were craftsmen educated in state schools and/or "Nursery Firms." General treatments of the industry are also helpful on origins questions: Horst Wagenblass, *Der Eisenbahnbau und das Wachstum der deutschen Eisen- und Maschinenbauindustrie 1835–1860*; Schroeter, "Entstehung der deutschen Maschinenbauindustrie . . . ," pp. 64–74. For more on Maffei, which ultimately became the well known firm Krauss Maffei A.G., see Friedrich Mohl, *Hundert Jahre Krauss Maffei, München 1837–1937.*

132. The one steam engine producing company in the Ruhr that was started by a craftsman, Franz Dinnendahl & Co., ultimately fell into financial collapse. Dinnendahl's company began as a steam engine assembly facility fostered both by coal mines and the iron producers. It held a near monopoly on the production of steam engines in eastern Prussia for nearly twenty years in the beginning of the 19th century. When its major supplier of iron parts, GHH, decided to move into the production of steam engines itself in 1819, Dinnendahl was forced to set up his own foundries and found it extremely difficult to remain profitable. The company sought to stabilize demand by purchasing shares in new coal mines, but this did not prove successful and the company went into decline. See the story in Redlich, op. cit., p. 127–128; Schroeter, "Entstehung der deutschen Maschinenbauindustrie . . ."; Hans Josef Joest, *Pionier im Ruhrrevier.*; Erich Mascke, *Es Entsteht ein Konzern.*

133. On Harkort and GHH, see earlier note in this chapter. The famous Bavarian machinery firms, the A.G. Maschinenfabrik Augsburg and the Maschinenbau A.G. Nuremberg, eventually merged as the M.A.N., were also established by merchants

to produce English and Alsatian technologies. Friedrich Klett, the founder of the Nuremberg company, actually founded his original firm with three English artisans and originally produced steam engines, bridges and rolling stock for the railroad. The Augsburg company had a very complicated beginning in which the ultimate financier of the company, Sander, began the business in 1840 as a partnership with an Alsatian mechanic, Gaspar Dollfuss, who was knowledgeable in steam engine and water turbine construction. This original business venture fell apart because Sander hated managing the business, and also could not get along with Dollfuss. In desperation, Sander ended his association with the Alsatian and transferred managerial control of the business to Carl Buz, a soldier and trained engineer (a specialist in bridge building) from a bourgeois patrician family, and the artisan, Carl August Reichenbach, skilled in the printing press trades. Sander remained in the more comfortable position of owner and financier. Under Dollfuss, the company produced steam engines, water turbines, steam boilers, heating apparatus, and papermaking machinery. Under the new management, the palette concentrated on steam engines and printing presses. Both the Nuremberg and Augsburg companies ultimately built upon their original specialties and became very important producers of diesel motors, bridges, material handling devices, refrigerators, boilers, and many other products. On all of this see Fritz Büchner, *Hundert Jahre Geschichte der Maschinenfabrik Augsburg-Nürnberg*,; Herman-Josef Rupieper, *Arbeiter und Angestellte im Zeitalter der Industrialisierung.* especially pp. 25–36; and Georg Eibert, *Unternehmenspolitik Nürnberger Maschinenbauer (1835–1914).*

134. Wagenblass, *Der Eisenbahnbau* . . .; Becker, "Entwicklung der deutschen Maschinenbau industrie . . . ," especially pp. 171–177.
135. F. Froehlich, *Die Stellung der deutschen Maschinenindustrie im deutschen Wirtschaftsleben und auf dem Weltmarkte,* p. 27, table 13.
136. cf. Eibert, *Unternehmenspolitik* . . .; Kocka/Siegrist, "Hundert grossten deutschen Industrie Unternehmen," pp. 72–74; Georg Stroessner, "Die Fusion der Aktiengesellschaft Maschinenfabrik Augsburg und der Maschinenbau-Actien-Gesellschaft Nürenberg im Jahre 1898"; Wilhelm Treue, "Henschel und Sohn, Ein deutsches Lokomotivbau-Unternehmen, 1860–1912"; Wilfried Feldenkirchen," Zur Kapitalbeschaffung und Kapitalverwendung bei Aktiengesellschaften des deutschen Maschinenbaus im 19. und beginnenden 20. Jh"; Ernst Barth, *Entwicklungslinien der deutschen Maschinenbauindustrie von 1870–1914.* Chandler, *Scale and Scope,* deals with autarkic machinery producers under the Rubric of "Non-Electric Machinery" among the "Great Industries," pp. 456–463.
137. The international race for technological superiority between the British, Americans, and Germans was carried on in the mechanical engineering trades with perhaps more ferocity than anywhere else. The German mechanical engineering firms have created a pantheon of honored inventors and an entire internationally self-conscious literature on the history of technology and firms. Conrad Matschoss, of the VDI was the doyen of these myth makers. See, e.g., the history of Ludwig Leowe cited previously, as well as his other works, e.g., *Die Maschinenfabrik R. Wolf, Magdeburg-Buckau, 1862–1912*; and *Ein Jahrhundert Deutscher Maschinenbau.* The emphasis is always on the inventive and entrepreneurial genius of the proud but modest German technical bourgeois. The obvious American counterpart to Matschoss would be Joseph Wickham Roe, *English and American Tool Builders.*
138. These characteristics of market structure in the machinery industry are a truism in the literature. For an overview of the industry in 1913, see Froehlich, *Stellung der*

deutschen Maschinenindustrie. . . . Many commentators also often noted the remarkable contrast with U.S. machinery producers: see Hermann Levy, *Die Vereinigten Staaten von Amerika als Wirtschaftsmacht*; and idem *Die Weltmarkt 1913 und heute.*

139. Though there was variation, depending upon the particular kind of product. Those that were produced in larger series, such as railroad cars at the Maschinenfabrik Nürnberg, or the American-style machine tools at the Ludwig Leowe company in Berlin, could also use less-skilled workers. See Rupieper, *Arbeiter und Angestellte* . . . , pp. 66–92, and Wolfgang Renzsch, *Handwerker und Lohnarbeiter in der frühen Arbeiterbewegung,* pp. 143–184. Renzsch has a case study of machinery industry workers in Berlin and tends to overemphasize the amount of mass production in the industry.

140. Rupieper (*Arbeiter und Angestellte* . . . , pp. 67–74) discusses the utilization of Nuremberg metalworking artisans by the Cramer Klett company. Such artisans were valued by the company because of their familiarity with metalworking and could be more easily trained in the company workshops.

141. See, for example, the detailed description of the works and the product line of the company in Demag, *Deutsche Maschinenfabrik A.G.: Works at Benrath, Wetter and Duisburg.* Schroeter, "Entstehung der deutschen Maschinenindustrie . . . ," pp. 84–94 has an interesting discussion of the origins of this vertical integration in the technological capacity to separate casting from ironmaking proper, which became possible in Germany in the 1830s. Casting was important for early machinery producers because many key machinery parts, which today would be milled, such as gears, were in the early premilling-machine days cast.

142. See, e.g., the description of the Demag works, ibid. On the early history of the creation of workshops and then of their grouping into specialized product areas, see Becker, "Entwicklung der deutschen Maschinenbauindustrie . . . ," pp. 198–213. For a study of production organization in Berlin machinery factories at the turn of the century, see F. Schulte, *Die Entlohnungsmethoden in der Berliner Maschinenindustrie.*

143. cf. Becker, "Entwicklung . . . ," pp. 228–232; Rupieper, *Arbeiter und Angestellte* . . . , pp. 67–74 and 82–92; E. W. Seyfert, *Der Arbeiternachwuchs in der deutschen Maschinenindustrie.*

144. Kocka/Siegrist, "Hundert grossten deutschen Industrie Unternehmen. . . .".

145. Karl P. Berthold, *Untersuchungen über den Standort der Maschinen-industrie in Deutschland,* p. 94. The location of Berthold's anonymous firm is not explicitly stated to be the Ruhr, but by the description he provides in his text I assume it can be nowhere else. (He describes it as a small city near a large center of iron and steel making, also rich in raw materials and easily accessible to extensive water freight.) The Berthold book is quite good on the degree of diversification that existed within all German machinery producers product palettes.

146. This example is taken from Chandler, *Scale and Scope,* p. 460.

147. For an interesting analysis of the formal and informal systems of shopfloor power in machinery companies, see Lothar Machten, "Zum Innenleben deutscher Fabriken im 19 Jahrhundert."

148. Rupieper, *Arbeiter und Angestellte* . . . , pp. 117–138; see also Ludwig Puppke, *Soziale Politik und soziale Anschauungen Früheninndustrieller Unternehmer in Rheinland Westfalen*; Demag, *Deutsche Maschinenfabrik, AG* . . . , pp. 93 ff.

149. The locus classicus on the evolution of German *Mitbestimmung* or codetermination

Notes to pages 105–109   335

is Hans J. Teuteberg, *Geschichte der industriellen Mitbestimmung in Deutschland.* There is also a shorter, reprise article by Teuteberg, "Ursprünge und Entwicklung der Mitbestimmung in Deutschland."

150. This is Rupieper's conclusion. He chronicles the struggles over the formation of works councils in the MAN companies in *Arbeiter und Angestellte* . . . , pp. 140 ff.

151. See, e.g., Werner Schwade, *Untersuchung der vom Binnen- und Weltmarkt abhaengigen Produktions- und Absatzbedingungen in der deutschen Maschinenindustrie.*

152. cf. Hermann Levy, "Die Enteuropaeisierung der Welthandelsbilanz," and idem, "Die Europaische Verflechtung des Aussenhandels der USA." Eulenberg's article, "Die deutsche Industrie auf dem Weltmarkte" also addresses this problem.

153. This paragraph basically summarizes the arguments from Wilhelm Mengel, *Strukturwandlungen und Konjunkturbewegungen der Werkzeugmaschinen-Industrie*; Friedrich Soltau, *Der Absatz der deutschen Werkzeugmaschinenindustrie*; Ernst Runge, *Die deutsche Maschinenindustrie in den Jahren 1924 bis 1933*; Walter Ostermann, *Marktlage der deutschen Maschinen-Industrie von 1924–1934*; Josef Johannes Pastor, *Die Ausfuhr des deutschen Maschinenbaus und ihre wirtschaftliche Bedeutung.*

154. Froehlich, Stellung der deutsche Maschinenindustrie. . . .

155. "Der Weltmarkt in Maschinen. Seine Verteilung unter die drei Hauptausfuhrländer"; "Die deutsche Maschinenindustrie auf dem europäischen Märkten"; Karl Lange, "Zum Thema: Bilanz der deutschen Handelspolitik 1925–1929"; and Karl Lange, "Die deutsche Ausfuhr in der Weltwirtschaftskrise" (all in *Maschinenbau. Wirtschaftlicher Teil,* 1930 and 1931).

156. Rationalization was coded in many ways during the Weimar Republic. Americans, and many German scholars during the 1960s and 70s tended to interpret it in terms familiar to Americans, i.e., as Taylorism or Fordism or as a way to introduce mass-production techniques into Germany. Brady, *The Rationalization Movement in Germany*, has a detailed section on the machinery industry (pp. 139–168) and takes this kind of view of "rationalization." More recent scholarship has a much more differentiated view. See the very fine recent book by Mary Nolan, *Visions of Modernity. American Business and the Modernization of Germany* (New York: Oxford University Press, 1994).

157. Wilhelm Voegle, "Wirtschaftliche Grenzen der Rationalisierung in der Maschinenindustrie."

158. Friedrich Meyenberg, *Über die Eingliederung der Normungsarbeit in die Organisation einer Maschinenfabrik.*

159. Edgar Hack, *Die Normung und Typisierung Industrieller Erzeugnisse unter besonderer Berücksichtigung der Maschinen- und Kraftfahrzeugindustrie.*

160. Arrangements of this kind were regularly chronicled in the VDMA's monthly economic magazine: *Maschinenbau, Wirtschaftlicher Teil.* Up to circa 1928, Otto Schulz-Mehrin wrote the articles; thereafter it was F. Rohmann, e.g., "Wirtschaftliche Zusammenschlüsse im Maschinenbau und verwandten Industriezweigen im Jahre 1929." There were also 26 *Interessengemeinschaften* formed in the machinery industry in 1927, 29 in 1928 and 37 in 1929.

161. For a variety of examples drawn form producers of foundry equipment, agricultural machinery production, engine production, trucks, and industrial sledgehammers see Otto Schulz-Mehrin, "Ursachen und Zusammenschlusses im Maschinenbau und verwandte Zweigen," especially p. 894; Chandler, *Scale and Scope*, p. 536, gives the example of refrigeration equipment, but for some reason believes

Notes to pages 109–113

that such rationalizations could only be achieved by the *Konzerne*. This wasn't the case.

162. See, e.g., Otto-Schulz Mehrin, "Wie Kann die Rentabilität im deutschen Maschinenbau gebessert werden?"

Notes for Chapter 4

1. For a general discussion of governance mechanisms and an extensive survey of the relevant literature, see J. Rogers Hollingsworth, Phillippe C. Schmitter, and Wolfgang Streeck, eds., *Governing Capitalist Economies*.
2. There are Marxian class-based, Modernization theory group and values-based, and newer structuralist and institutionalist versions of the story, all of which share the general Gerschenkronian/organized capitalism understanding of the German experience of industrialization I am criticizing. For a sampling, see Alexander Gerschenkron, *Bread and Democracy in Germany*; Ralf Dahrendorf, *Society and Democracy in Germany*; Barrington Moore Jr, *Social Origins of Dictatorship and Democracy*, Chapters 7 and 8; Hans Ulrich Wehler, *Das Deutsche Kaiserreich*; Helmut Böhme, *Deutschlands Weg Zur Grossmacht*; Nicos Poulantzas, *Political Power and Social Classes*; Geoff Eley, "The British Model and the German Road." An excellent overview of various views of the Imperial Reich state in relationship to classes is George Steinmetz, "The Central State in Imperial Germany," Chapter 4 of *Regulating the Social*, pp. 73–107.
3. One of the earliest synthetic arguments regarding the governance of the German national political economy is the classic by Rudolf Hilferding, *Finance Capital*. In the postwar period, the paradigmatic work for understanding the emergence of industrial associations and the system of politics that surrounded industrial policy making in developing Germany was Heinrich Winkler, ed., *Organisierte Kapitalismus*. For the Kaiserreich, see S. Mielke, *Der Hansa Bund für Gewerbe, Handel und Industrie 1909–1914*; H. Kälble, *Industrielle Interessenpolitik in der wilhelminischen Gesellschaft*; Wolfgang Fischer, *Unternehmerschaft, Selbstverwaltung und Staat*; Hans-Peter Ullmann, *Bund der Industriellen.*; Helga Nussbaum, *Unternehmern gegen Monopole*. For the Weimar Republic, see Gerald Feldman, *Vom Weltkrieg zur Weltwirtschaftskrise*; Hans Mommsen, Dietmar Petzina, and Bernd Weisbrod, eds., *Industrielles System und Politische Entwicklung in der Weimarer Republik*; Bernd Weisbrod, *Schwerindustrie in der Weimarer Republik*; Charles Maier, *Recasting Bourgeois Europe*; Reinhardt Neebe, *Grossindustrie, Staat und NSDAP 1930–1933*; Henry Turner, *German Big Business and the Rise of Hitler*; Kurt Gossweiler, *Grossbanken Industriemonopole Staat*. On the law and its significance for industry, cf. Jürgen Kocka and Norbert Horn, eds., *Recht und Entwicklung*.
4. Systematic attention to small- and medium-sized producers can be found in Ullman, *Bund der Industriellen*, and Nussbaum, *Unternehmern gegen Monopole*. The former blends the producers into an organized-capitalism perspective and the latter into a state monopoly capitalism one. Neither understands small producers as constituting a viable alternative form of industrialization as is argued here. The work of Heinrich Winkler, which tends to focus on the nonindustrial *Mittelstand*, is the classic analysis of the relationship between declining classes and the rise of fascism; see e.g., H. A. Winkler, *Mittelstand, Demokratie und Nationalsozialismus*. For variations on this theme from the cultural left, see Detlev Peukert, *The Weimar*

Republic, and Rudy Koshar, *Social life, local politics, and Nazism: Marburg, 1880–1935.*

5. The original statement of this argument is Wolfgang Fischer, "Die Rolle des Kleingewerbes im Wirtschaftlichen Wachstumsprozess in Deutschland 1850-1914." The state of this debate has recently been summarized in an excellent volume by Ulrich Wengenroth, *Prekäre Selbständigkeit.* An interesting attempt to interpret the industrialization of Württemberg from this point of view is Klaus Megerle, *Württemberg im Industrialisierungsprozess Deutschlands.*
6. On the competitiveness of German machinery producers prior to World War I, see F. Froehlich, *Stellung der deutsche Maschinenindustrie im deutschen wirtschaft und auf dem Weltmarkt*; Heinrich W. Mengel, *Strukturwandlungen und Konjunkturbewegung in der Werkzeugmaschinen-industrie*; on the competitiveness of textiles, see Enquette Ausschuss: *Entwicklungslinien der industriellen und gewerblichen Kartellierung. Dritter Abschnitt: Textilindustrie A*; and Enquette Ausschuss: *Entwicklungslinien der industriellen und gewerblichen Kartellierung. Dritter Abschnitt: Textilindustrie B.*; for cutlery, see Rudolf Boch, *Handwerkersozialisten gegen der Fabrikgesellschaft*; on Krefeld silk, see Peter Kreidte, *Eine Stadt am seidenen Faden.*
7. For a general overview of the interregional flow of goods and services in Germany in the early 20th century, see the Enquette Ausschuss volume *Die innere Verflechtung der deutschen Wirtschaft.*
8. A very good discussion of the character of the German market before the political unification of Germany is Hubert Kiesewetter, "Economic Preconditions for Germany's Nation-building in the Nineteenth Century." Kiesewetter's point is that although economic unification was achieved, it did not provoke political unification. See also his book, *Industrielle Revolution in Deutschland: 1815–1914*, which makes the argument along the way in the context of his argument about regions and industrialization.
9. Despite the predominant position of the Kingdom of Prussia within the Imperial framework, the German state resembled the United States and Switzerland in this respect far more than it did France, Britain, or Imperial Russia. Extensive discussions of the federalist framework of the Imperial Reich can be found in: Manfred Rauh, *Föderalismus und Parliamentarismus im Wilhelminischen Reich*; and Ernst Deuerlein, *Föderalismus*. A concise outline can be found in Gordon Craig, *Germany 1866–1945*, pp. 39–43. Max Weber has an interesting discussion of German federalism and the nature and limits of Prussian domination in the section "Parlamentarisierung und Föderalismus" (pp. 406–443) in "Parlament und Regierung im neugeordneten Deutschland."
10. The 25 independent states were: the kingdoms of Prussia, Württemberg, and Saxony, the Grand Duchy of Baden, the free cities of Hamburg, Bremen, and Lübeck, and Oldenburg, Brunswick, Saxe-Meiningen, Saxe-Altenburg, Saxe-Weimar, Saxe-Coburg-Gotha, Anhalt, Schwarzburg-Rudolstadt, Schwarzburg-Sondershausen, Waldeck, Reuss older line, Reuss younger line, Schaumburg Lippe, Lippe-Detmold, Hesse, Mecklenburg-Schwerin, and Mecklenburg-Strelitz.
11. This information can be found clearly laid out in Gordon Craig, *Germany 1866–1945*, in the section "The Institutional Structure of the Empire" (pp. 39–43).
12. Weber, "Parlamentarisierung...," p. 418.
13. A reasonable overview of the politics of unification and the negotiations between Bismarck and the various independent, especially southern states can be found in Karl Bosl, "Die Verhandlungen über den Eintritt der süddeutschen Staaten in den

Norddeutschen Bund und die Entstehung der Reichsverfassung." Interesting case studies of Württemberg, in which the desire to protect local autonomy and traditions was very plainly the guiding strategy are: Hans Julius Schoeps, "Preussen und Württemberg 1850–1852"; Eberhard Naujoks, "Württemberg im diplomatischen Kräftespiel der Reichsgründungszeit (1866/70); Folkert Nanninga, "Zur 'deutschen' Politik des Württembergischen Aussenministers von Varnbueler in den Jahren 1864 bis 1870"; Adolf Kapp, "Die öffentliche Meinung in Württemberg 1866."

14. See the overview of this system provided in Alfred Chandler, *Scale and Scope*, pp. 411–415.
15. Michael John, *Politics and the Law in Late Nineteenth Century Germany*, p. 71. See also in particular all of Chapters 3 and 4, pp. 42–103.
16. On the creation of a central bank and of a single currency issuing authority, see Manfred Pohl, *Entstehung und Entwicklung des Universalbankensystems*, especially pp. 23–27; see also Vera C. Smith, *The Rationale of Central Banking*, pp. 49–60 and 100–116.
17. An incredibly good book that clearly outlines the fiscal rights of the German states and localities is Mabel Newcomber, *Central and Local Finance in Germany and England*. See, for the 19th century, especially the chapter "The German post war problem and its historical background," pp. 17–42; another good, concise discussion is in Hans Jaeger, *Geschichte der Wirtschaftsordnung in Deutschland*, pp. 97–107.
18. Debates among German jurists and political philosophers about the constitutional structure and character of the Imperial Reich are very fascinating to read. There are two dimensions to the debates and numerous positions within each of the dimensions. Basically, the two dimensions concern the problem of sovereignty in a federalist state and the character of self-government. The former debate ranges on the one hand between those who think that the German Reich is a Bundestaat, or a sovereign state with member states whose sovereignty is expressed only in the larger whole, and those who think it is a Staatenbund, a unity of sovereign states. On the other hand, there are those, such as Hugo Preuss, who claimed that the whole notion of sovereignty had meaning only in an absolutist context; modern federal states could have no sovereignty.

The other debate, about self-government, has conservative and democratic poles. The conservative self-government position, represented by those such as Rudolf von Gneist, views the local autonomy of cities and regional governments as a dual-edged thing. On the one hand, self-government allows the local population to administer its own affairs; on the other hand, it requires them to do so in the service of the state. The democratic position, represented again by Preuss, and to a certain extent Preuss's teacher Otto Gierke, claimed that local self-government formed the foundation of a democratic order. Local populations in cities could determine their lives. The organizations they constructed, in turn, would enable them to represent their interests at a higher level of territorial representation, and so on up to the state.

Good introductions to this material can be found in Rupert Emerson, *State and Sovereignty in Modern Germany*; and Heinrich Heffter, *Geschichte der deutsche Selbstverwaltung im 19. Jahrhundert*. For the actual participants, see Otto Gierke, *Die Genossenschaftstheorie und die deutsche Rechtsprechung*; Rudolph Gneist, *Die nationale Rechtsidee von den Standen und das preussische Dreiklassenwahlsystem*:

eine social-historische Studi; Hugo Preuss, *Gemeinde, Staat und Reich als Gebeitskörperschaften*.

19. A good description of the way in which this constitutional autonomy allowed local states to defend their interests against actual or feared incursions from the center is given in Donald Warren Jr., *The Red Kingdom of Saxony*, especially Chapter 1: "Lobbying in the Kaiserreich" (pp. 1–25).
20. See the very good and thorough account of what cities could and could not do in W. H. Dawson, *Municipal Life and Government in Germany*. The question of self government of cities in Germany is an extremely interesting one and has been exhaustively treated in Heinrich Heffter, *Die Deutsche Selbstverwaltung im 19. Jahrhundert*. Other good discussions can be found in Hans Herzfeld, *Demokratie und Selbstverwaltung in der Weimarer Epoch*, and Peter Marschalck, "Zur Rolle der Stadt für den Industrialisierungsprozess in Deutschland in der 2. Hälfte des 19. Jahrhunderts." George Steinmetz's recent excellent book, *Regulating the Social*, provides a very learned overview of the position of cities within the Imperial Reich (especially Prussia) in the context of the emergence of the welfare state.
21. The Prussian state government was legally able to influence the affairs of the city through the Mayor. His legal mandate divided his identity between elected representative of the citizens of the town and administrative official of the state. Though this sometimes permitted the central government to root out political tendencies in city government that it did not approve of – social democrats, for example – it resulted in remarkably little practical influence on the economic and social policies of the cities, where considerably local discretion had always been the tradition. On this in particular, see Dawson, *Municipal Life and Government in Germany*, and Steinmetz, *Regulating the Social*. Another good survey of German city politics in the 19th century is James J. Sheehan, "Liberalism and the City in Nineteenth Century Germany."
22. Gerschenkron, *Bread and Democracy*. . . .
23. A good, concise and detailed account of the Centralverband Deutscher Industrieller can be found in the East German Handbook, *Die Bürgerlichen Parteien in Deutschland*. pp. 850–871.
24. For the traditional view on this, see Dirk Stegmann, *Die Erben Bismarks*, Klaus Saul, *Staat, Industrie, Arbeiterbewegung im Kaiserreich*. For more specifically industrial dimensions of autarkic industry-state relations, see Fritz Blaich, *Kartell- und Monopolpolitik im Kaiserlichen Deutschland*.
25. In addition to Blaich, ibid., see the very instructive case study by Charles Medalen, "State Monopoly Capitalism in Germany."
26. Medalen (ibid., p. 106) writes: "Heavy industry was fanatically opposed to government tutelage. Indeed, it expected from the state the same subservience which the Junkers had once taken for granted, and for much the same reasons. Since the nation's power and prosperity now depended upon iron and coal, they demanded that the government adopt their interests and policies as their own. That the (Prussian) administration refused to play handmaiden to industry enraged the magnates of the Ruhr."
27. See the discussion in Ullmann, *Bund der Industriellen*, especially pp. 48–75, and in Warren, *The Red Kingdom of Saxony*.
28. The best studies of the BDI are Helga Nussbaum, *Unternehmer Gegen Monopole*; and Ullmann, *Der Bund der Industriellen*.
29. Ullmann, *Bund der Industriellen*, pp. 99–109.

30. To say that there was institutional continuity in banking is not to say that there were no transition problems in the Weimar banking sector. Some of these problems have already been discussed in Chapter 2. For a more general overview of banking in Weimar, see Pohl, *Entstehung und Entwicklung* . . . , pp. 61–90, and Harold James, *The German Slump*, pp. 39–161. On continuity in the law, see Dieter Grimm, *Recht und Staat der bürgerlichen Gesellschaft*, pp. 165–290, and Franz Wieacker, *Privatrechtsgeschichte der Neuzeit*.
31. Knut Borchardt has attracted a lot of attention recently for making this argument. See the three articles in "Die Strukturschwäche der Weimarer Wirtschaft und die Handlungsmöglichkeit in der Grossen Krise." The debate around these articles is by now extremely extensive. A good survey of the debate, and an intervention in itself, is Charles Maier, "Die Nicht-Determiniertheit ökonomischer Modelle." Most recently, see Theo Balderston, *The Origins and Course of the German Economic Crisis, 1923–1932*, which is very extensive and critical of the Borchardt position.
32. The reasons for the strength of centralization as an institutional strategy among the diverse forces during the revolutionary period in Germany are not entirely clear to me. In part, as the subsequent text will emphasize, it seems clear that there was resentment of the overwhelming power of Prussia within the old Reich. Many forces wanted to break it up and introduce a form of unitary decentralization of the kind that Preuss and others imagined. Yet, it is also clear that there were other influences, both on the right and on the left, which have their roots in the way in which ideological debate and discourse evolved in Germany during the late 19th and early 20th centuries. This is a fascinating field of study, the investigation of which, however, would take us too far away from the matter at hand. I mention this gap in my analysis to let the reader know that I am aware of it, but I find myself forced to leave it for another day.
33. Ebert favored centralization but was willing to make tradeoffs with the member states of the Reich. The two social democrats on the constitutional committee in the national assembly were Max Quarck and Joseph Herzfeld, both of whom were reputed to be zealous centralizers. The best discussion of these different currents can be found in Gerhard Schulz's magisterial *Zwischen Demokratie und Diktatur*, pp. 1–198. The constellation of views around the question of centralization versus federalism is given on pp. 130 ff. Ebert's views on centralization are given on p. 138.
34. Henry Ashby Turner writes: ". . . a number of biases predisposed the men who ran the Economics ministry to look favorably on big business. A product of the war, that ministry continued to bear the marks of its formative years, during which the imperial government chose, in the name of efficiency, to deal predominantly with large firms and the associational organizations they dominated" (*German Big Business and the Rise of Hitler*, p. 35).
35. Gerald Feldman, *Iron and Steel in the German Inflation, 1916–1923*, pp. 100–109 on Möllendorf; Rupert Emerson, *State and Sovereignty in Modern Germany*, pp. 228 ff on Nauman's corporatist ideas; Charles Maier, *Recasting Bourgeois Europe*, pp. 140 ff on Rathenau and ideas of corporatist planning. Maier discusses the differences between left and right corporatist ideas on pp. 140–143.
36. On Preuss's ideas, see Schulz, *Zwischen Demokratie und Diktatur* . . . , pp. 101–174, especially 114–141, and Emerson, *State and Sovereignty in Germany* pp. 126–155 and 209–253. From the horse's mouth, the place to begin is Hugo Preuss, *Gemeinde, Staat, Reich als Gebietskörperschaften*.

37. Preuss proposed the formation of a different set of intermediate-level organizations that would be more organically related to self-governing local-level bodies. Indeed, in the initial constitutional draft of January 1919, he drew up a new map of the German Reich that organized the area of Germany into geographically defined administrative units that had, in many cases, little resemblance to traditional borders among regions. Preuss's main concern was to break up Prussia and thereby rid the new Republic of many of the imbalances of power that the existence of such a large state within a state brought with it. See the map in Arnold Brecht, *Federalism and Regionalism in Germany.* pp. 94–95 and in Robert E. Dickenson, *The Regions of Germany*, p. 6–7. As we will see below, the irony is that Preuss was himself well aware of the needs within decentralized areas for relatively autonomous political bodies. But his focus was on the municipality and not on the regional government – a very Prussian view.
38. Among others, see Franz Menges, *Reichsreform und Finanzpolitik*; Wolfgang Benz, *Süddeutschland in der Weimarer Republik*, pp. 140–163 and 287–298; Karl Schwend, *Bayern zwischen Monarchie und Diktatur*.
39. During the war, Weber wrote a major pamphlet on parliamentary democracy and federalism in which he advocated the formation of a kind of parliamentary federalist republic where the regional governments would be represented in a states senate vaguely modeled after the U.S. senate. See Weber, "Parliament und Regierung...," especially the section "Parlamentarisierung und Föderalismus," pp. 406–443. Weber's style of argument in favor of a federal structure began to increasingly emphasize the practically possible during the revolution itself. See his equally as interesting second pamphlet, "Deutschlands künftige Staatsform." See also the excellent discussion of Preuss and Weber during this period in Schulz, *Zwischen Demokratie und Diktatur*, pp. 114–142.
40. The most important articles of the constitution in this regard were, Article 8, which gave the Reich jurisdiction over all taxes and income, insofar as it could claim them for its own use, and Article 11, which gave the Reich the authority to refuse the regional governments right to levy taxes that might in any way impair the income of the Reich. Article 11 also gave the Reich the sole authority to administer and collect its own taxes, and in this way mandated the creation of the first genuine centralized state bureaucracy in Germany. A further article, Article 84, allowed the central Reich government to control the financial administration of state and local governments "insofar as this is required for the uniform execution of national fiscal laws." See the excellent technical discussion of taxes and Reich, *Land,* and Commune relations in Germany by Newcomber, *Central and Local Finance....* The information in the text, and the quoted passage, are taken from p. 42. Newcomber remarked that "to such an extent were the powers of the Reich increased at the expense of the states, that it has been questioned whether Germany continued to be a Federal state." Finally, the ultimate check on the autonomy of the local governments came from Article 48 of the constitution, which provided, among other things, that if a state failed to carry out the duties imposed upon it by the national constitution or the national laws, the president of the Reich could compel compliance, by force if necessary. As Newcomber pointed out, the provisions concerning the lower levels of government "insure(d) a limited income to state and local governments, but they offer(ed) no real guarantee of adequate income or any independence in adjusting income to needs" (ibid., p. 42–43).
41. Peter Christian Witt, "Finanzpolitik und sozialer Wandel im Krieg und Inflation 1918-1924," p. 412.

42. Bavaria, Württemberg, Baden, and Hesse.
43. See the discussion of the political debates surrounding the composition of the document, as well as an analysis of the document's eight points, in Benz, *Süddeutschland in der Weimarer Republik*, pp. 140–146 ("Das Stuttgarter Program und sein Echo in Weimar").
44. Benz, *Süddeutschland* ... pp. 171–179.
45. See the good discussion in Benz, *Süddeutschland* ... pp. 140–198. Benz quotes one undersecretary in the Württemberg government (Hitzler) as making the following argument: "The larger the distance from Berlin, the less assistance will be made available to affected industries. The Erzberg financial reforms kill all initiatives from the individual states. The reforms are in no sense a simplification of public finances. Rather they represent a dreadful complication of them."
46. See Schulz, *Zwischen Demokratie und Diktatur*, pp. 197–198 and 234 ff.
47. Baden and Württemberg quickly established provisional parliamentary governments in which social democratic, independent social democratic and liberal parties all participated, while the revolutionary government in Bavaria under Kurt Eisner was founded on the basis of revolutionary soldiers and workers councils. After the fall of the revolutionary Eisner government, Bavarian politics shifted rapidly to the right and became the most significant opponent of the republican character of the new Germany. In all the southern cases, the overriding goal was to establish order quickly. See the general discussion in Benz, *Süddeutschland* ... p. 38 ff.
48. A good description of the difference between federalism in Bavaria and Württemberg is given in Waldemar Besson, *Württemberg und die deutsche Staatskrise, 1928–1933*, pp. 92 ff.
49. Wünderich has a very good discussion of Thüringen during the first five years of the Reich in Volker Wünderich, *Arbeiterbewegung und Selbstverwaltung*, pp. 203–214.
50. The external indebtedness of the Reich is often given as the primary reason for the centralization of revenue-raising capacity in the Weimar constitution. Klaus Epstein, the biographer of Matthias Erzberger, the Center Party finance minister who actually pushed through the reforms, makes this argument. See Epstein, *Matthias Erzberger and the Dilemma of German Democracy*, pp. 331–338. Erzberger himself resorted to arguments of this kind during his campaign for reform. See the compilation of his speeches on financial reform, Matthias Erzberger, *Reden zur Neuordnung des deutschen Finanzwesens*. Gerhard Schulz actually maintains that the centralization of the German tax system, given the indebtedness of Germany was inevitable; see Schulz, *Zwischen Demokratie und Diktatur*, p. 216. But there is room to doubt that the centralization was as technocratically inevitable as the traditional argument makes it seem. A recent article by T. Balderston in the *Journal of Economic History* shows that Germany's indebtedness as a result of the war was not significantly greater than highly centralized Great Britain's. The problem in Germany, he argues, was not so much that she incurred debt in the course of the war, but in that her banking system was not capable of creating a secondary market in which the debt could be diffused. See Balderston, "War finance and inflation in Britain and Germany, 1914–1918." A good overview on the financial situation of the Reich, with a good discussion of the reform itself is Witt, "Finanzpolitik ... ," pp. 395–426.
51. Schulz, *Zwischen Demokratie und Diktatur* ... , pp. 174–248 ; Benz, *Süddeutsch-*

land..., pp. 164–197; see also the excellent survey of German Federalism by Ernst Deuerlein, *Föderalismus*, pp. 171–193 (on Weimar).
52. Brecht, *Federalism and Regionalism in Germany*, p. 66.
53. Ibid., pp. 52–70.
54. During the great international economic crisis, the financial needs of the local and regional governments far exceeded the capacity or willingness of the federal government to pay. As a result, the important services that governments provided to workers and producers in the decentralized regions began to deteriorate. Heavy borrowing by government in the local banking system squeezed small- and medium-sized producers out of the market, exacerbating an already difficult adjustment situation. In the end, it is not surprising that this situation would engender disaffection in the decentralized areas for the Weimar structure. See the discussion in Chapter 2.
55. Brecht points out that the administrative problem in the Reich–*Länder* relationship was one of the most vexing during the Weimar Republic (*Federalism*..., pp. 66–70). Harold James has a good discussion of Reich–*Länder*–Commune problems in his book, *The German Slump*, pp. 39–109.
56. Schulz's book, *Zwischen Demokratie und Diktatur*' is the best place to get the details of the many center-periphery government conflicts during the middle years of the Weimar Republic. Brecht's book, *Federalism*..., is a good overview of the main issues (from the slightly biased point of view of one of the main actors). See also Benz, *Süddeutschland*..., for a good discussion of the period up to 1923.
57. From Besson, *Württemberg und die deutsche Staatskrise*..., pp. 99–100. This is excerpted from a formal communique of the Württemberg government to the Reichs Chancellory, November 18, 1927. Composed in the midst of a controversy about the kind of taxes states had access to, it was never sent because the Chancellory issued a public apology and reconfirmation of its commitment to federalism while the document was being composed. Besson makes the point that this kind of struggle was constant during the Weimar Republic. For a view of the Reich–*Länder* relations from the perspective of the Reich, see James, *The German Slump*, p. 46 ff.
58. According to the president of the Association of Central German Industry, which represented small- and medium-sized producers in the decentralized region of Thüringen, a completely centralized state jeopardized regional producers because it would entail the centralization of associational representation and thereby create the preconditions for central planning (Schulz, *Zwischen Demokratie und Diktatur*, p. 480).
59. See Hans Peter Ullmann, *Interessenverbände in Deutschland*, pp. 133–144, and Bernd Weisbrod, *Schwerindustrie in der Weimarer Republik*. See also Bernd Weisbrod, "Economic power and political stability reconsidered," and David Abraham, *The Collapse of the Weimar Republic*, pp. 116–162;.
60. Newcomber, *Central and Local Finance*..., and Johannes Popitz, *Die Kunftige Finanzausgleich zwischen Reich, Ländern und Gemeinden*.
61. See Wünderich, *Arbeiterbewegung und Selbstverwaltung*, especially the section "Städtetag als Interessenverband" (p. 216 ff), as well as "Mülerts Reichsreformprogram" (p. 222 ff).
62. Arnold Köttgen, "Die Krise der Kommunal Selbstverwaltung" (quote on p. 3).
63. Besson, *Württemberg und die deutsche Staatskrise*..., p. 57, and especially Schulz,

Zwischen Demokratie und Diktatur, p. 320 ff. Carl Schmitt actually refers to the existence of regional oppositions emerging within the Weimar structure in his section on federalism in *Hüter der Verfassung*, pp. 94–96. Generally, the section in that book: "Pluralismus, Polykratie und Föderalismus," provides important insight into the way in which the informal (or unintended) cross-cutting dynamics that the structure of the Weimar constitution fostered were perceived at the time.

64. Even at the peak of Weimar stability, between June 1924 and June 1928, David Abraham points out that of the five cabinets in office during this period "only two received an actual vote of confidence upon being presented. Two received a weaker 'acceptance vote,' and the fifth earned a mere 'acknowledgement.' See Abraham, *The Collapse of the Weimar Republic*, p. 46.

Carl Schmitt describes the political dynamic that emerged in the Weimar Republic's marriage of parliamentarism and federalism in the following way:

> The compatibility of federalist organization with parliamentarianism can be explained in reality only in the following way. On the one side there are self-consciously regional parties which represent explicitly regional interests – e.g., the Bavarian Peoples Party – in the national parliament, that is, the German Reichstag. On the other side, and in precisely the opposite sense, there are various social power complexes running throughout all levels of the Reich, giving it in this way a pluralist character, which gain positions of political power at the local and *Länder* levels. Federalist positions and institutions can hence become allies and supports of pluralism at a national level. But, the compatibility of federalism and parliamentarism so defined can only be achieved through a considerable loosening of the coherence and stability of the state as a unit.

Schmitt, who was interested in a strong state that could represent the democratic will of the German *Volk* decisively, viewed this interaction between parliament and federalism as problematic. See Schmitt, *Hüter der Verfassung*, p. 95.

65. The conference was called for in January, 1928. The first meetings took place in October. Schulz, *Zwischen Demokratie und Diktatur*, Chapter 14, and Besson, *Württemberg und der deutsche Staatskrise*, pp. 87–113 both have good accounts of the issues at stake in the conference.

66. See the discussion in Wünderich, *Arbeiterbewegung und Selbstverwaltung*, pp. 216–232.

67. Schulz, *Zwischen Demokratie und Diktatur*, Chapter 14; Besson, *Württemberg und der deutsche Staatskrise*, pp. 87–113.

68. James notes that German industrialists acted very similarly and pursued similar goals under the stabilization governments in the middle years of the Weimar Republic and under the Nazis. See James, *The German Slump*, p. 188. In general, James is fairly explicit in confining the use of the world "industry" to large-sized autarkic producers.

69. See the discussion in Feldman, *Iron and Steel in the German Inflation*, Chapter 1; and Maier, *Recasting Bourgeois Europe*, Chapter 3.

70. Maier, ibid., and Feldman, op cit., are the main sources on this.

71. See the excellent discussion of the factory council movement in Germany in Maier, *Recasting Bourgeois Europe*, pp. 136–153. Franz Neumann quotes the full text of the constitutional article in the introduction to *Behemoth*, p. 12.

72. See Fritz Napthali's *Wirtschaftsdemokratie*. This book was originally published in

1928 and received wide attention. Hans Jaeger's book, *Geschichte der Wirtschaftsordnung in Deutschland*, pp. 161–168, has a good summary of the politics of this issue during the Weimar Republic.
73. See James, *The German Slump*, pp. 210 ff; and Jaeger, *Wirtschaftsordnung*, p. 163–164. Feldman notes that two further laws, passed in 1927, concerning unemployment insurance and work time, similarly aggravated business and piqued their resentment of the political intrusiveness of the Weimar Republic. Gerald Feldman, "Die Sozial- und Wirtschaftspolitik der deutschen Unternehmer 1918–1929," especially p. 187.
74. James, *The German Slump*; Weisbrod, *Schwerindustrie in der Weimarer Republik*; Weisbrod, "Economic Power and Political Stability Reconsidered."
75. See the speeches of Erzberger, which have a very strong populist flavor, *Reden zur Neueordnung* . . . , and the good discussion of the finance reform by Klaus Epstein, *Matthias Erzberger and the Dilemma of German Democracy*, pp. 328–348, especially 336 ff.
76. James, *The German Slump*, pp. 162 ff; Jaeger, *Wirtschaftsordnung*, pp. 158 ff. According to James: "After 1923/24 the Weimar Republic continued to have many of the characteristics of an interventionist welfare state (*Sozialstaat*); and many features of the *Sozialstaat* angered business" (p. 172).
77. Jaeger, *Wirtschaftsordnung*, p. 58. Witt, "Finanzpolitik . . . ," discusses in exhaustive detail the effects of the tax reform.
78. Jaeger, *Wirtschaftsordnung*, p. 158.
79. Turner, *German Big Business* . . . p. 41.
80. Gerald Feldman and Ulrich Nocken, "Trade Associations and Economic Power"; Gerald Feldman, "Das deutsche Unternehmertum zwischen Krieg und Revolution"; Friedrich Zunkel, "Die Gewichtung der Interestgruppen bei der Etablierung des Reichsverbandes der Deutsche Industrie"; Ulrich Nocken, "Interindustrial Conflicts and Alliances as Exemplified by the AVI-Agreement."
81. In addition to the essay cited in the previous note, see the nice summary article by Gerald Feldman, "German Interest Group Alliances in War and Inflation." The ZAG is discussed on pp. 170 ff. Feldman maintains that a major characteristic of the agreement "was the explicit goal of circumventing the bureaucracy and parliament and having demobilization and reconversion dictated by the interests groups" p. 171 Feldman also makes clear that the original business forces behind the formation of ZAG were a handful of industrialists from areas dominated by the autarkic form of industrial order: Hugo Stinnes, Otto Heinrich (Siemens), Carl Friedrich von Siemens (Siemens), Ernst von Borsig (Borsig), Walther Rathenau (AEG), and Anton von Rieppel (MAN) (p. 174).
82. AVI = *Arbeitsgemeinschaft Verarbeitendeindustrie*.
83. Ulrich Nocken is the main historian of the AVI agreement. See Nocken, "Inter-Industrial Conflicts . . . ."
84. See the discussion in Feldman, who in addition to emphasizing the traditional desire for autonomy among autarkic producers also emphasizes their willingness not to reject Moellendorf and Rathenau out of hand in the midst of a highly unstable situation. See Feldman, *Iron and Steel* . . . , Chapters 1 and 2; see also Maier, *Recasting Bourgeois Europe*, Chapter 3.
85. Charles Maier has the best discussion of the coal crisis in *Recasting Bourgeois Europe*, Chapter 3, pp. 194–232; Ulrich Nocken's (highly reductionist) article also has a good survey of corporatist arrangements (both successful and unsuccessful) in

the 1920s. See Ulrich Nocken, "Pluralism and Corporatism in Modern German History."
86. See the discussion in Chapter 3.
87. See Turner's discussion in the section of Chapter 1 entitled "Assets" in *German Big Business . . .*, pp 31–37.
88. See Gerald Feldman, "Die Sozial- und Wirtschaftspolitik der deutschen Unternehmer 1918–1929"; Nocken "Corporatism and Pluralism in Modern German History"; and Weisbrod, "Economic Power and Political Stability Reconsidered."
89. On this, see Abraham, *The Collapse of the Weimar Republic*, pp. 132 ff.
90. Turner is clear about this; see *German Big Business . . .*, pp. 3–46.
91. The initial provisions of the Dawes plan had allowed for Germany to make good her reparations obligations at a rate that corresponded to her ability to pay. An important part of this was the erection of a special transfer bureau within the Reichsbank, headed by the American banker Gilbert, into which reparations monies were paid and then allocated by Gilbert to the various creditors *without endangering the balance of payments*. The fact that this plan had been drawn up by a broad committee of international experts, and then accepted by the Germans, basically made Germany once again creditworthy in the eyes of international, particularly American, bankers. Large autarkic corporations that had been forced to expand through the creation of large holding conglomerates welcomed the infusions of foreign capital that the Dawes plan made possible. So did regional and local governments, who without their own tax base had gone to the foreign credit markets quite aggressively to finance major infrastructural projects. A straightforward description of the Dawes plan can be found in William Carr, *A History of Germany. 1815–1945*, p. 322.
92. Schulz has a very clear discussion of this move on the part of Parker Gilbert in *Zwischen Demokratie und Diktatur*, pp. 568–574. James notes further that Gilbert had prompted the U.S. State department to advise "caution to the American public over loans to German *Länder* and municipalities because article 248 of the Treaty of Versailles provided for a first claim on the Reich and the *Länder* by the allies for reparations damage" (James, *The German Slump*, p. 96). On the relationship between growing public indebtedness at a local and regional level and the weakness of the German banking system, see the discussion in Chapter two, this volume.
93. Schulz, *Zwischen Demokratie und Diktatur*, p. 575.
94. Schulz, *Zwischen Demokratie und Diktatur*. The industrialist who met personally with the Chancellor (at that time it was Marx) were: Kastl and Duisburg (RDI), Reusch (GHH), Borsig (Borsig), Silverberg (Rheinische Kohlensyndikat), Frowein (textiles) and Retzman (affiliation unknown to me).
95. There ought to be a book written on the League for the Renewal of the German Reich, which was also often referred to as the Lutherbund after Hans Luther, its leader. There is an entry on the League written by Kurt Gossweiler in Dieter Fricke (ed.), *Die Bürgerlichen Parteien . . .*, pp. 195–200, which provides information on membership, though the narrative on the significance of the League is a little bizarre. Volker Wünderich has a good discussion of the league in his *Arbeiterbewegung und Selbstverwaltung*, pp. 225–228. Schulz, *Zwischen Demokratie und Diktatur*, also discusses the League on p. 590, but gives it a more pluralistic, less exclusively industry dominated cast. James, however, is very clear on the linkage to autarkic industry; see James, *The German Slump*, p. 74–75.
96. Schulz, *Zwischen Demokratie und Diktatur*, p. 590.

97. Polycratic is a term invented by Johannes Popitz, a bureaucrat in the economics ministry, to describe the Weimar bureaucracy. Popitz's friend, Carl Schmitt, relied heavily on the concept in his discussion of problems in the Weimar Republic in *Hüter der Verfassung*, pp. 71–96.
98. James, *The German Slump*, p. 75.
99. One highly influential argument advocating the superiority of the presidency in a democratic polity – and the inadequacy of parliamentary democracy for stable rule – is given in Schmitt, *Hüter der Verfassung*. The recent biography of Schmitt, by Joseph W. Bendersky, *Carl Schmitt. Theorist for the Reich*, has an excellent discussion of Schmitt's views and the way in which they were taken up in conservative circles in the later Weimar Republic. See also Turner, *German Big Business and the Rise of Hitler*.
100. Schulz, *Zwischen Demokratie und Diktatur*, p. 590 ff; Wünderich, *Arbeiterbewegung und Selbstverwaltung*, 225 ff; and the section on reform in the book by Brecht, *Federalism and Regionalism in German Politics*, pp. 73–93. Brecht was a member of the League for the Renewal of the Reich and a participant in the special *Ländererkonferenz* that negotiated the Reichs reform, representing Prussia.
101. Schulz, *Zwischen Demokratie und Diktatur*, p. 564 ff, especially 585 ff.
102. This fascinating proposal, made by Oskar Muelert, the president of the German Diet of Cities at its seventh congress called for a radical democratization of German politics. He said institutions of democratic self-government should be enhanced at the local level and then systematically constructed at the various higher instances of government. Large cities and territorial districts, in addition to the regional governments, should be represented in the Reichsrat through electoral associations. Cities in this way would be turned into "quasi-statelike district corporations" (*quasi-staatliche Gebietskörperschaften*), and, the influence of the Reichsrat on central state legislation would not be shaped by federal states. Rather, the politics of the center would be shaped by the joint influence of self-governing units of various size. The proposals of Muelert are discussed in Wünderich, *Arbeiterbewegung and Selbstverwaltung*, pp. 222–225. Wünderich rightly points out the debt that these proposals owe to Hugo Preuss' ideas on democratic self-government. Muelert's call for the representation of the cities in the Reichsrat was ultimately dropped because he was purged from the leadership in the German Diet of Cities by a coeterie of mayors sympathetic to the League for the Renewal of the Reich.
103. Brecht, *Federalism and Regionalism in Germany*, p. 77–78; Schulz, *Zwischen Demokratie und Diktatur*, p. 590 ff.
104. Schulz, *Zwischen Demokratie und Diktatur*, pp. 592–606 ("Die "differenzierte Gesamtlosung"). Brecht also has a discussion of the final proposal, but it is colored by his affiliation with the League. He does, however, reprint the report of recommendations of the reform committee as an appendix to his book. See Appendix G, pp. 171–181, in Brecht, *Federalism and Regionalism in Germany*. The official recommendations called for a reevaluation of the system of financial equalization.
105. Besson, *Württemberg und der deutsche Staatskrise*, pp. 105–113.
106. Schulz, *Zwischen Demokratie und Diktatur*, p. 596.
107. Schulz, *Zwischen Demokratie und Diktatur*, p. 592–606; Otto Braun, *Deutscher Einheitsstaat oder Föderativsystem?* Braun was the Minister President of Prussia.
108. Schulz, *Zwischen Demokratie und Diktatur*, section on the *differenzierte Gesamt-*

losung, and Besson, *Württemberg und die deutsche Staatskrise* section on *Reichsreform*, pp. 105-114.
109. Hitler was no federalist, nor was he a proponent of local autonomy. But his rhetoric did aim directly at the resentments of regional interests who felt their autonomy being unreasonably compromised by the incursions of the central Weimar government. Hitler claimed that their resentments were legitimate, but that it was not centralization as such that was to blame, but the fact that the central government was so weak internationally and beholden to hostile, exploitative foreign powers and interests. Central government, he argued in *Mein Kampf* could be a friend of local interests, if it was in control of its own destiny:

> And so today this [Weimar] state, for the sake of its own existence, is obliged to curtail the sovereign rights of the individual provinces more and more, not only out of general material conditions, but from ideal considerations as well. For in draining its citizens of their last drop of blood by its policy of financial extortion, it must inevitably withdraw their last rights if it does not want the general discontent to break out into open rebellion some day.... By inverting the above proposition, the following rule, basic for National Socialists, is derived. A powerful national Reich, which takes into account and protects the outward interests of its citizen to the highest extent, can offer freedom within, without having to fear for the stability of the state. On the other hand, a powerful national government can undertake and accept responsibility for great limitations on the freedom of the individual as well as the provinces, without damage to the Reich idea if in such measures the individual citizens recognizes a means toward the greatness of his nation. (Adolf Hitler, *Mein Kampf* p. 572)

This appeal was not very attractive in the early 1920s, when it was written. But by the beginning of the 1930s, after the failure of all reforms, it appeared to many to be more attractive.
110. Tim Mason, *Sozialpolitik im Dritten Reich*, and idem, *Arbeiterklasse und Volksgemeinschaft*.
111. See James, *The German Slump*, pp. 415-416. (Table on p. 416).
112. Descriptions of the complicated financial mechanisms employed by the Nazis to be able to achieve these effects are given in Karl Hardach, *The Political Economy of Germany in the Twentieth Century*, pp. 53-89; Dietmar Petzina, *Die deutsche Wirtschaft in der Zwischenkriegszeit*, pp. 108-157; Maxine Y. Woolston, *The Structure of the Nazi Economy*, pp. 125-160; Otto Nathan, *The Nazi Economic System. Germany's Mobilization for War*, pp. 107-136. The basic point is that the central state took the capital market for itself (Banking law of 1934), prevented lower-level governments from entering it, and forced private companies to finance out of their own earnings or go to the capital market for short-term funds.
113. The law changing the constitution, known as "The Law for the Reconstruction of the Reich," was passed on January 30, 1934. It read: "The *Land* representative assemblies will be abolished. The sovereign rights of the *Länder* are hereby transferred to the Reich. *Land* governments are subordinate to the governments of the Reich. The Reich governors [regional government heads] are under the administrative supervision of the Reich Minister of the Interior" (cited in Martin Broszat, *The Hitler State*. p. 112).
114. James, *The German Slump*, p. 373.
115. Ibid., pp. 398-413.

116. Woolston, *The Structure of the Nazi Economy*, pp. 63–124; Sidney Merlin, "Trends in German Economic Control Since 1933"; Arthur Schweitzer, *Big Business in the Third Reich*, pp. 197–503; Nathan *The Nazi Economic System*, pp. 59–83 and 137–169; Petzina, *Die deutsche Wirtschaft in der Zwischenkriegszeit*, pp. 117–138; Johann Sebastian Geer, *Der Markt der geschlossenen Nachfrage*.
117. Arthur Schweitzer and others make much of the creation of these cartel laws because they created "monopoly" power in industry and reputedly eliminated smaller producers from the market. As I have been arguing in this book, such cartels saved decentralized production from self-destruction. See Schweitzer, *Big Business and the Third Reich*, especially pp. 239–297. Schweitzer's argument focuses on how artisans lost out to industry in the internal power struggles within the Nazi regime. The analysis here, however, focuses not on the artisanate (*Handwerk*); but on decentralized small- and medium- sized industry (*Industrie*, or *industriellen Mittelstand* or *klein und mittlere Industrie*). The Nazis themselves saw no contradiction between the cartel laws and the continued existence of small- and medium-sized business. They declared that the laws were designed to control ruinous competition and praised the virtues of the small entrepreneur. A recent excellent case study of the rationalization of specialization arrangements among small- and medium-sized producers in the decentralized industrial order during the Nazi period is Franz Henne, *A German Path to Fordism*.

    Dietmar Petzina makes the argument that the Nazi militarization programs accelerated the monopolization process in German industry because it favored production- and investment-goods industries over consumption-goods industries. It is true that much of the consumption-goods industry was composed of small- and medium-sized producers (though not all from decentralized areas; many were located in Augsburg, Bielefeld, Nuremberg, etc). But it is unreasonable to maintain that the investment-goods category of industry is entirely, or even remotely, dominated by autarkic industry. The producer-goods industry contains the autarkic steel producers, but that industry did not become more concentrated as a result of the military expansion. See the unacceptably highly aggregated claim in Petzina, *Die deutsche Wirtschaft in der Zwischenkriegszeit*, p. 138. For counter-evidence, see Gary Herrigel, "Industrial Order in the Machine Tool Industry," and Henne, op cit.
118. Richard J. Overy, "Hitler's War and the German Economy", especially Section 4.
119. Michael Geyer, "Zum Einfluss der Nationalsozialistischen Rüstungspolitik auf das Ruhrgebiet," pp. 201–264. Henne, op. cit.
120. Newcomber, *Central and Local Finance*..., pp. 63 ff.
121. See Richard Overy, "Heavy Industry and the State in Nazi Germany."
122. Fritz Blaich, "Absatzstrategien deutscher Unternehmen im 19. und der ersten hälfte des 20. Jahrhunderts," especially p. 43 ff on the perceptions of large manufacturing exporters on the character of Nazi plans toward industry.
123. Overy, "Hitler's War and the German Economy," p. 286; See also Jonathan Zeitlin's discussion of comparative British, U.S., and German Aircraft manufacture during World War II "Flexibility and Mass Production at War". Zeitlin points out that the Germans made more progress toward mass production than they are often given credit for by people such as Overy. Nonetheless, he agrees that the regime was so bureaucratically contradictory and inefficient that it was difficult for it often to recognize, much less use effectively, some of its accomplishments in industrial restructuring.

124. Overy, "Heavy Industry and the State in Nazi Germany"; Overy, "Hitler's War and the German Economy"; and Alfred Schroeter and Jürgen Bach, "Zur Planung der wirtschaftlichen Mobilmachung durch den deutschen faschistischen Imperialismus vor dem Beginn des zweiten Weltkireges."
125. Woolston, *The Structure of the Nazi Economy*, p. 65.
126. There does seem to be some evidence that the character of military subcontracting led to a process of concentration in certain areas, particularly in Handicraft. See Sidney Merlin, "Trends in German Economic Control Since 1933," p. 183. Petzina also cites a decline in the number of handicraft firms in the mid-1930s, (Petzina, *Die deutsche Wirtschaft* . . . , p. 138). On the other hand, Alan Milward notes that as late as the early 1940s, the armaments components industry was basically composed of "small-scale producers scattered through the countryside. Often they were made in workshops employing no more than 30 men. In such circumstances mass production was unthinkable." Milward, *The German Economy at War*, p. 110. The elimination of firms may have had to do with efforts to create stable sources of supply and moderate competition in supply markets, but it doesn't seem to have led to the emergence of large or dominant firms in these sectors.
127. See Peter Hayes, *Industry and Ideology*; Karl Heinz Roth, "Der Weg zum guten Stern des "Dritten Reichs."

Notes for Chapter 5

1. It is not possible to make the claim I am making here that mass production did not diffuse among German producers until after World War II without admitting blurry boundaries. Some producers succeeded in implementing elements of mass production organization and technology at an earlier time, especially in the 1920s, but the political economic environment had always been too turbulent to allow all of the elements of a general, economy-wide, mass-production system to crystalize and reorient productive resources in that direction. Only when the basic points of political and economic orientation were altered in the 1950s were producers in the automobile industry and parts of the chemical, electromechanical, textile, and machinery industries able to invest in large-scale, capital-intensive volume production in significant scale and numbers. There are some interesting studies of exceptional cases of very early mass production in Germany. See for example Hartmut Petzhold: "Zur Entstehung der Elektronischen Technologie in Deutschland und den USA." As noted in Chapters 2 and 3, there was also a lot of large-series production in various other industries during the 19th century, though always with considerable flexibility, e.g., textiles, steel, and chemicals. Military production also made strides in the direction of modern mass production during World War II. See the article by Zeitlin, "Flexibility and Mass Production at War: Aircraft Manufacture in Britain, The United States and Germany, 1939–1945."
2. See discussion in previous chapters. The classic surveys of this period are W. Arthur Lewis, *Economic Survey, 1919–1939*, and Ingvar Svennilson, *Growth and Stagnation*.
3. Angus Maddison noted the linkage between freer intra-European trade and certainty about investments in 1964:

> Foreign trade has helped to improve the climate in which entrepreneurs operate, not primarily by creating wider area of competition, but by the elimination

of external deflationary shocks, and by the security induced by the feeling that export markets would steadily increase. This new optimism about exports has affected productivity mainly by raising the level of investment and not primarily by improving its allocation. It has been experienced unevenly by different countries, and has had its greatest relative impact in Germany, Italy and the Netherlands. It is curious that most commentators on integration have attached little weight to this, and its impact on investment levels has been discussed largely in connection with the possibility of encouraging a larger inflow of US capital. (Maddison, *Economic Growth in the West*, p. 74).

Good discussions of the growth of European commitments to intracontinental free trade can be found in Alan Milward, *The Reconstruction of Western Europe*. H-J. Küsters, *Die Gründung der Europaische Wirtschaftsgemeinschaft*, is an excellent discussion of the processes surrounding the formation of the original EEC. Benjamin Cohen, "US Foreign Economic Policy" and Robert Gilpin, *US Power and the Multinational Corporation* discuss the quid pro quo character inherent in the common market. See also and more generally, Ernst Mandel, *Die EWG und die Konkurrenz Europa – Amerika* for a Marxian perspective on the international political economic context of the institution.

4. This was certainly the view of German business: see Fritz Hellwig, "The Establishment of a Common Market in Europe"; H Eichner, "Wie steht der deutsche Industrie zum Gemeinsamen Markt?"; "Die Vorbereitung der Unternehmungen auf dem Gemeinsamen Europäischen Markt als betriebswirtschaftliche Aufgabe"; Fritz Baade et al., *Die Wirtschaftsunionen in ihrer Stellung zu den Nationalenwirtschaften und zur Weltwirtschaft*; Rolf Audouard, "Wirkung der Europäischen Wirtschaftsgemeinschaft und der Freihandelszone auf den deutschen Maschinenbau"; "Wettbewerb auf dem Gemeinsamen Markt"; "Kehren die alten Handelsbilanzüberschusse wieder?"; Ernst Otto (ed.), *Die deutsche Industrie im Gemeinsamen Markt*; Karl Albrecht, "Gemeinsamer Markt und Freihandelzone im Urteil deutscher Wirtschaftskreise."

5. This is a standard, and widely accepted, dimension of the various theories of Fordism that are on the market: see e.g., the ambitious overview of the period by Andrew Glyn, Alan Hughes, Alan Lipietz, and Ajit Singh, "The Rise and Fall of the Golden Age."

6. See Wilhelm Hankel, "Germany: Nationalism in the International Economy"; Elmar Altvater, Jürgen Hoffmann, and Willi Semmler, *Vom Wirtschaftswunder zur Wirtschaftskrise*, especially pp. 277–341; and Werner Abelshauser, *Wirtschaftsgeschichte der Bundesrepublik*, 1945–1980, pp. 85–119.

7. A good source on comparative growth rates in the west is Maddison, *Economic Growth in the West*.

8. Ibid., p. 76, table III-1.

9. See Charles Maier, "Between Taylorism and Technocracy." There is also a monograph by Fritz Blaich, *Amerikanische Firmen in Deutschland 1890-1918*, which portrays the United States as a tremendous competitive threat in the first part of the century in mechanical engineering.

10. Blaich's (ibid.) evidence makes this plain: all of his cases are of machinery types that were either themselves mass produced (sewing machines, typewriters) or which were used in mass production (shoe machinery). Americans dominated these markets world-wide because their domestic market was the only one in which mass

production was practiced on a large scale. They competed effectively as niche players with this technology in outside markets. Evidence of the marginality is that even though the Germans effectively ceded the Americans the entire world market for sewing machines, typewriters, cash registers, special agricultural machines, etc., they were nevertheless the world's largest exporters of machinery, when all segments of the branch are taken into consideration, in 1913 and then again, after a period of consolidation in the 1920s, by 1929. See Friedrich Soltau, *Der Absatz der deutschen Maschinenindustrie*; Werner Schwade, *Untersuchung der vom Binnen- und Weltmarkt abhängigen Produktions- und Absatzbedingungen in der deutschen Maschinenindustrie*; J. J. Pastor, *Die Ausfuhr des deutschen Maschinenbaus und ihre Volkswirtschaftliche Bedeutung*.

11. In 1913, the U.S. accounted for 15.9% of total German imports, in 1929, the percentage had fallen to 13.3%, and in 1938 to 7.4%. The largest source of imports for the Germans in 1913 was Western Europe (Great Britain, France, Belgium, Netherlands, Luxemburg, Switzerland) with 21.8%. This same group of countries took 22.1% in 1929. See table 24, "Structure of Foreign Trade by Countries in Percentages, 1913–1970, (A) Reich" in Hardach, *The Political Economy of Germany in the Twentieth Century*, p. 227. On the uneven and mixed character of US export strength in European markets for manufactures in the first part of the 20th century, see Hermann Levy, *Die Vereinigten Staaten von Amerika als Wirtschaftsmacht* and H. Levy *Die Weltmarkt 1913 und heute*. On the general de-Europeanization of U.S. trade during the first part of the century – and especially during the 1920s – see Hermann Levy, "Die Enteuropäisierung der Welthandelsbilanz" and "Die europaische Verflechtung des Amerikanischen Aussenhandels"; Franz Eulenberg, "Die deutsche Industrie auf dem Weltmarkte."

12. John H. Dunning, "Changes in the level and structure of international production: the last one hundred years"; idem, "Capital Movements in the Twentieth Century," and especially idem, "Foreign Capital and Economic Growth in Europe"; Christopher Layton, *Transatlantic Investments*; Bella Belassa, "Tariff Protection in Industrial Countries, An Evaluation"; John H. Dunning, "Technology, United States Investment and European Economic Growth." For foreign direct investment in Germany before the formation of the common market, see Eugene A. Phillipps, "American Direct Investments in West German Manufacturing Industries, 1945 to 1959."

13. J.J. Servan-Schreiber, *The American Challenge*. The book was originally published in 1967.

14. For Bosch, see Ute Stolle, *Arbeiterpolitik im Betrieb*, pp. 146–222; Tilman Fichter, "Betriebspolitik der KPD nach 1945"; and Hans Konradt Herdt, *Bosch 1886–1986*. For Klöckner Humboldt Deutz, see Gustav Goldbeck, *Kraft für die Welt, 1864–1964. Klöckner Humboldt Deutz AG*. On Liebherr, see Martin A Schmitt, "Ein Mann und sein Werk."

15. The year before the two companies had formed an *Interessengemeinschaft* to rationalize the market for luxury cars and heavy trucks that both firms competed in.

16. Both claim to be the first producers of the automobile in the world. This claim is disputed by the French, however. In any case, according to Anita Kugler, the Benz and Co. Gasmotorenfabrik was the largest automobile company in the world in 1900, with 430 workers it produced 572 automobiles in a single year. Anita Kugler, "Von der Werkstatt zum Fliessband."

17. Max Kruk and Gerold Lingnau, *Daimler-Benz. Das Unternehmen*; Daimler-Benz

(ed.), *75 Jahre Motorisierung des Verkehrs*; Karl Heinz Roth, "Der Weg zum guten Stern des 'Dritten Reichs' "; and Rudolf Hoffmann, *Daimler Benz Aktiengesellschaft Stuttgart-Untertürkheim*. All note that both companies produced engines for industrial and seagoing uses. Cars, in the early years, were a sideline. A 1977 SOFI research report (in a section written by Horst Kern) makes the argument that the Automobile industry in the years prior to World War I was for all intents and purposes just like the machinery industry – that is, a subbranch of it, analogous to textile machinery and paper making machinery. See SOFI, "Branchenstrukurmerkmale und grobe Entwicklungslinien des Rationalisierungsprozesses im Fahrzeugbau bis 1960." These observations are basically verified in the recent book on workers at Daimler-Benz: Bernard P. Bellon, *Mercedes in Peace and War*, especially in Chapters 1 and 2.

18. In the very early years, Benz was the leading producer. It established its own independent department in its "Gas Motor Factory" in 1895 and by 1900 it was producing 572 automobiles a year with about 430 workers. The company made only one type of automobile, but the product was anything but standardized. None of the parts of the engines of the automobiles, for example, were interchangeable with one another. All had to be individually cast and filed with every order. According to Anita Kugler, the entire Benz car was constructed in this way out of unique individual parts, though after a general set of designs.

    The Daimler company looked even more like a model specialized producer in the decentralized industrial order. In the 1890s, it produced highly customized automobiles – each car was different from every other. Seeking to expand in the early 20th century, the company adopted a strategy of model production (the first "model" of the Daimler Motor Gesellschaft was the *Mercedes*, named after the daughter of the head engineer of the company). Models made possible the use of interchangeable parts and enabled the company to attain modest scale economies in production. But the production strategy that was followed cannot exactly be described as "mass production." From a total production of 219 motor vehicles (automobiles and trucks) in 1900, Daimler increased its output to 1490 vehicles in 1911. But there were over 14 different models of automobile and four different varieties of truck in that total, so that at the most several dozen of any given type were produced.

    See, Kugler, "Von der Werkstatt...," p. 310.

19. Ibid., p. 316. Kugler is very clear on this point. She argues that the Germans eschewed cheap mass-production methods, even though they had all of the technical ingredients necessary to adopt the assembly line methods developed by Ford:

    > The main argument involved "German quality workmanship," which was placed in programmatic opposition to every form of mass production and above all to the cheap American variety: "here clean and soundly, there slap-dash, finished." Thus the absence of mass production in the pre World War One German automobile industry had little to do with technological backwardness or a lack of awareness on the part of entrepreneurs. Rather it was the consequence of a self conscious business decision. Daimler is from this perspective representative of the broad majority of German automobile producers. (Ibid. p. 315).

20. Direktor Ernst Berge of Daimler remarked that the war was "ein einziger grosser Nimmersatt, dessen Liebspeise Automobile waren" ("an insatiable eater whose

favorite food was automobiles") – classic German metaphor – food and insatiability. Cited in Kugler, "Vom Werkstatt...."

21. These figures are impressive, but one should not be deceived by them. Only the aircraft engines were produced in quantities that resembled the quantities that could be mass-produced in the United States, and these products were relatively homogeneous. Daimler made only the engines. Complicated airplane assembly work was done by other firms. See Kugler, "Von Werkstatt...."

22. See the longitudinal employment tables in Kruk and Lingnau, *Daimler Benz*, p. 324.

23. See Bellon *Mercedes in Peace and War*. Chapter 2, "Work and Workers at Daimler, 1903-1914," pp. 25-60.

24. Both firms underwent fairly dramatic changes that ultimately changed the old system of organization in production. Financial and overcapacity problems that resulted from the transition out of military production ultimately led the two companies to form an *Interessengemeinschaft* in 1924, and then an outright fusion in 1926. See the details around the merger given in Kruk and Lingnau, *Daimler Benz*, pp. 107-118; Rudolf Hoffmann, *Daimler-Benz Aktiengesellschaft*, pp. 7-24; and Karl H. Roth, "Der Weg zum guten Stern...," pp. 28-39.

At the time of the merger, the two companies together employed around 14,000 workers and had combined sales of approximately 100 million RM.

The number of employees in 1925 was 7,855 at Daimler, and 7,250 at Benz. At the end of the year in 1926, the merged company employed only 10,147 workers; the next year, 1927, it increased to 18,124. The last figure mentioned is too high for the 1920s (there was a fairly constant decline of employment at the company until 1932). But the one given for the first year of the merger is too low. In order to give a general sense of the size of the company, I emphasize the approximate number given in the text, which is based upon the employment levels that existed before the merger. See Kruk and Lingnau, *Daimler Benz*, table, p. 324.

Similarly, in sales, 1926 was a below-average year for the company, so to cite that figure would give a misleading sense of the size of the merger. Therefore I give an approximate figure, based upon the 1925 sales of both companies (52 million RM for both). Ibid.

One historical account refers to the two merged companies as "little more than large artisanal shops." Hans Georg Müller, "Liebe war es nicht, was Benz und Daimler zur Fusion trieb."

25. Hoffmann, *Daimler Benz Aktiengesellschaft*, p. 31. According to Kugler, the number of basic model types was even smaller. ("Von Werkstatt...").

26. Hoffmann, *Daimler Benz Aktiengesellschaft*, pp. 31-35.

27. Kugler, "Von Werkstatt..."; Edgar Hack, *Die Normung und Typisierung Industrieller Erzeugnisse unter besonderer Berücksichtigung der Maschinen- und Kraftfahrzeugindustrie*, pp. 96-114, especially 101-106; Hoffmann, *Daimler-Benz Aktiengesellschaft*, pp. 25-31. Bellon also discusses *Gruppenfertigung*, though he claims it was implemented at Daimler during the revolutionary years and not after the fusion of the two companies. In that Daimler almost went bankrupt before the fusion, it seems fairly safe to claim that the consolidation and diffusion of the practice probably had to wait until the years subsequent to the fusion. But, Bellon's description of what *Gruppenfertigung* (he calls it *Gruppenfabrikation*) entailed is quite good (*Mercedes in Peace and War*, Chapter 5, especially pp. 160-164).

28. Kruk and Lingnau, *Daimler Benz*, pp. 109-110; Daimler-Benz, *75 Jahre Motorisierung des Verkehrs, 1886-1961*, pp. 213-218; and Kugler, "Von Werkstatt...."

29. See table, "Produktion, Umsatz und Mitarbeiter 1886–1944," in Kruk and Lingnau *Daimler Benz, Das Unternehmen*, p. 324.
30. Compare the excellent analysis of production at the Ford Motor Company given by David A. Hounshell, *From the American System to Mass Production, 1800–1932*, p. 283 for the 1928 production figure and pp. 217–302 for an extensive discussion of Ford.
31. Kugler, "Von Werkstatt . . ."; and Kruk and Lingnau, *Daimler Benz*, p. 110; but for a discussion of delays in the implementation of truly Fordist production techniques, see pp. 122–125.
32. Kruk and Lingnau, *Daimler Benz*; see graph in the appendix, "Personenwagen-Produktion."
33. Ibid., tables after p. 324 in the appendix. Numbers are current. See also the discussion in Willi Boelke, *Wirtschaftsgeschichte Baden Württembergs*, pp. 481–485.
34. This was generally true for the German economy. The SOFI Report, *Vorstudien zum BMFT-Forschungsprojekt. . .*, underscores this for Daimler and Baden Württemberg.
35. Ibid. and Richard Osswald, *Lebendige Arbeitswelt, Die Sozialgeschichte der Daimler-Benz AG von 1945 bis 1985*, pp. 17–44; "plakate" Gruppe and Helmuth Bauer, "Daimler-Benz von Innen."
36. SOFI, *Vorstudien zum BMFT-Forschungsprojekt . . .*; Marius Hammer, *Vergleichende Morphologie der Arbeit in der Europäischen Automobilindustrie*.
37. "Plakate" Gruppe and Bauer, "Daimler Benz von Innen," pp. 594–589.
38. Transfer lines described in this and the previous paragraphs are taken from H. C. Graf von Scherr-Thoss. *Die deutsche Automobilindustrie*, pp. 397 and 419. See also three articles in the magazine *Der Gewerkschafter* on automation in the automobile industry in which Daimler-Benz is portrayed as one of the most advanced automobile producers in Europe: "Die Automatisierung – Möglichkeiten und gewerkschaftliche Konsequenzen"; "Die Automatisierung in der Bundesrepublik; and Fritz Sternberg, "Die gewerkschaftliche Aufgaben in der Epoche der Automatisierung." Scherr-Thoss claims that by 1956 Daimler-Benz plants were up to 67% automated, but it is not clear what he means by that.
39. See Horst Kern and Michael Schumann, *Industriearbeit und Arbeiterbewusstsein*; Hammer, *Vergleichende Morphologie . . .* , pp. 27–42; and SOFI, *Vorstudien zum BMFT-Forschungsprojekt*.
40. The difference between group production and the mass production made possible by mechanical automation were the investment possibilities that large volumes created. In group production, there were many specialized workshops that produced a narrow range of standardized parts in medium volume. The firm could balance its need for variety and production economies by running a variety of substitutable parts in parallel group workshops. If a specialized workshop lay idle, the costs were still lower than the bottlenecks that the firm incurred in trying to balance volume and flexibility in the old workshop form of organization. But the implementation of mechanical automation systems such as transfer lines implied an abandonment of the attempt to balance volume production and flexibility. Dedicated transfer lines could produce a single product efficiently at high volumes. But it was not feasible for the firm to erect a number of parallel-running transfer lines that could produce substitutable parts, because the costs of erecting such complicated systems of machinery were simply too high. Daimler-Benz was able to

implement these systems by increasingly eliminating part variety and pushing standardization. But it was helped in its ability to do this by a constantly increasing level of demand.

The SOFI report, ibid., underscores the relative uniqueness of Daimler-Benz among German automakers. Its production volumes were lower than the other German producers, and its rates of productivity growth were lower, as were its absolute levels of productivity. Pursuit of specialization strategy coupled with volume production explains the differences. Despite the higher volumes, the company still pursued a strategy of producing relatively expensive luxury automobiles during this period. Mechanical automation did not completely supplant group production in Daimler plants, nor did rationalization completely eliminate afterwork by hand; such innovations only had an impact in some areas of the production process.

41. This was already a topic of conversation in the trade press by the early 1950s. See the articles on Daimler in *Der Volkswirt*, "Der Kapitalschnitt bei Daimler-Benz"; "Älteste Automobilfabrik der Welt"; "Rekordjahr bei Daimler-Benz."
42. This argument is related, though not identical, to the argument about the role of patents among producers within the German chemical industry given in Chapter 2. In general, the producer of fixed models tends to seek ways to reduce its dependence upon suppliers and/or treat its knowledge of how to produce the models as proprietary. Performing production in-house is the easiest way to do both of these things. Another way is to have all of the development and design engineering done in-house and then have subcontractors make parts according to the blueprints. In such situations, firms typically also then make sure that there are a number of suppliers capable of delivering the same part. In the end, many of these remarks about vertical integration are consistent with the standard arguments in transaction-cost economics about small numbers, specialization and uncertainty. See Oliver Williamson, *Markets and Hierarchies*.
43. On Bosch, see H. K. Herdt, *Bosch 1886–1986*; Uta Stölle, *Arbeiterpolitik im Betrieb*, pp. 146–222; Tilman Fichter and Eugen Eberle, *Kampf um Bosch*; and Goetz Küster, *75 Jahre Bosch*.
44. See the discussion of this phenomenon in Michael Piore, "The Technological Foundations of Dualism and Discontinuity"; and Charles Sabel's discussion in *Work and Politics*, pp. 34–59. Under a regime of mass production, both of these latter cases could lead to the creation of a secondary sector of subcontractors. Because their contracts with larger producers are so contingent upon the business cycle, such secondary sector producers tend to be less technologically sophisticated than the companies they supply. The contracting company, or original equipment manufacturer (OEM), retains possession of the design know-how, so such firms are not encouraged to develop their own internal capacities. And further, because the secondary sector firms have work only during particular times of the business cycle, such irregularity tends to inhibit investment in capital equipment. Over an extended period of time, a region full of such relations can turn the secondary sector into a technologically unsophisticated or "backward"-appearing segment of the regional economy.
45. Anita Kugler, "Von Werkstatt zum Fliessband," p. 310.
46. Ibid., p. 312.
47. After the merger in 1926, in which the number of models was reduced to seven and

Notes to pages 155–158

group production methods were adopted, the top management of the company was fairly explicit about the need to imitate the vertical integration strategies of the Ford Motor Co. See Kruk and Lingnau, *Daimler Benz*, p. 110.
48. Daimler-Benz, *Das Verhältnis des Grossbetriebes zu seinen mittelständischen Zulieferern*.
49. Ibid., p. 6; percentages calculated by me.
50. Working Group of Independent Business-people – an association representing the interests of many small- and medium-sized supplier firms.
51. See Daimler-Benz, *Verhältnis*. . . . The company printed a follow-up study in 1962: Daimler-Benz, *Das Grossunternehmen und der industrielle Mittelstand. Eine Untersuchung über die klein- und mittelbetrieblichen Zulieferer der Daimler-Benz AG*.
52. ASU (ed.), *die Ausprache*, November, 11, 1959, p. 397–398.
53. See especially Dieter Kunz, *Die Marktstellung der mittelständischen Zulieferbetriebe*; Jürgen Hützel, *Interdependenzen zwischen Klein und Grossfirmen.*; and idem, *Grosse und kleine Zulieferer*.
54. Kugler, "Von Werkstatt . . . ," and F. Schumann, *Auslese und Anpassung der Arbeiterschaft in der Automobile industrie und einer Wiener Maschinenfabrik*. The automobile industry part of this book, written by Schumann, was a case study of Daimler-Benz. See also Bellon, *Mercedes in War and Peace*, Chapter 2.
55. Kruk and Lingnau, *Daimler Benz*, pp. 107–132; Kugler, "Von Werkstatt . . ."; and Rudolf Hoffmann, *Daimler Benz Aktiengesellschaft*.
56. See the organizational charts on flow of parts between plants in Kruk and Lingnau, *Daimler Benz*, pp. 284–285.
57. Kruk and Lingnau, *Daimler Benz*, Das Unternehmen, p. 107–117; Karl Heinz Roth, "Der Weg zum guten Stern des 'Dritten Reichs'," especially pp. 28–40.
58. It is fascinating to compare the accounts of this process in the house book of Daimler-Benz, Kruk and Lingnau, *Daimler Benz*, pp. 107 ff, to that of Roth's account, "Der Weg zum guten Stern . . . ," pp. 28–40 ("Eine Industriefiliale der Deutschen Bank"). The accounts overlap considerably, but are evaluated very differently. The latter book, in a way that is consistent with traditional notions of finance capitalism or state monopoly capitalism, tries to make much out of the prewar connections between the regional banks and the Deutsche Bank as a way to show the long-time control of the bank over the companies. But the relations strike me as having been far too indirect to have been as shaping as Roth claims.

On the loss of the Middle East markets and its significance for the Deutsche Bank, see Kurt Gossweiler, *Grossbanken – Industriemonopole – Staat*.
59. In fact, initially the Deutsche Bank had contemplated creating a massive south German automobile conglomerate to be modeled after the General Motors corporation in the United States. The new company (which never materialized) would have included not only Daimler and Benz, but Opel in Rüsselsheim and the Bavarian Motor Works in Munich. Again, a comparison of the accounts in the Daimler-Benz in-house book, and that of Roth and the Hamburg group, is fascinating on this incident. The latter gives a particularly good account of struggles between different banking and industrial interests over the formation of a large south German automobile company that could eventually mass-produce along American lines and, in fact, compete with the Americans. The Hamburg line is that the Deutsche Bank was able to foil these interests, which seems to have been true. The Hamburg explanation is that this was because the Deutsche Bank had a risk-averse and militaristic

vision for Daimler-Benz (i.e., safe state contracts for military orders). I find it hard to understand how the military card could have weighed so significantly in the calculations in 1924–1926. It seems rather quite plausible to believe that the Deutsche Bank foiled the efforts of the rival Danat-Bank consortium for control of Daimler-Benz but then discovered that the possibility of moving in an American direction was quite difficult, given the political economy of the market in interwar Germany – Europe. See the account in Roth, ibid., especially the section "Von Sanierungsfusion zur Weltwirtschaftskrise 1924–1932," pp. 71–102.

60. Kruk and Lingnau, *Daimler Benz*; and Roth, "Der Weg zum guten Stern...."
61. See the discussion in Kruk and Lingnau, *Daimler-Benz* ("Zwei neue Grossaktionäre: Neben Abs sitzen Flick und Quandt im Aufsichtsrats-Präsidium"), pp. 194–197. There are also good discussions of Flick and Quandt in Kurt Pritzkoleit's book, *Männer Mächte Monopole*. The entry on Quandt is especially good (pp. 71–99).
62. The larger and more focused on model production the firm became, the larger these separate departments became. Fusion of Daimler and Benz consolidated the design and development resources of both companies, so that by the middle of the interwar period, the company was well known to have significant in-house research and development resources at its disposal. In addition to Kruk and Lingnau, *Daimler Benz*, see Maurice Olley, *The Motor Car Industry in Germany during the period 1939-1945*, pp. 5–13.
63. Naturally, this kind of applied basic research also had significant marketing benefits for the firm. Olley, *The Motor Car Industry in Germany* . . ., pp. 46 ff; Daimler Benz, *75 Jahre Motorisierung des Verkehrs*, pp. 173–204.
64. Piore and Sabel call this the problem of *microregulation* (*The Second Industrial Divide*, pp. 49 ff).
65. See the analysis in Fred Ledermann, *Fehlrationalisierung – der Irrweg der deutschen Automobilindustrie seit der Stabilisierung der Mark*, pp. 102 ff.
66. This combination of specialization and diversification allowed the company to redirect its resources (within limits) to various purposes across the business cycle. The Hamburg people (*Das Daimler-Benz Buch*) argue that this diversification strategy prevented Daimler-Benz from moving into more higher-volume mass-production areas. In their view, this was driven by the interest of the Deutsche Bank to keep the company active in military markets. I tend to think that military markets or not, given the difficulties that all automobile producers had moving in the direction of mass production during the 1920s, the diversification and specialization strategy was fairly prudent.
67. For a lot of information on Daimler-Benz's systematic engagement in military production, see the Hamburg book, *Das Daimler-Benz Buch*, especially the essay by Roth. Bellon's book is also quite good on Daimler-Benz's relationship with the Nazi regime; *Mercedes in War and Peace*, Chapter 7, pp. 215–258.
68. The earliest (1952) percentage is taken from Harald Eichenhofer, "Die Automobilindustrie in der Bundesrepublik,130 p. 288; the 1972 figures are taken from Frank Vogl, *German Business after the Economic Miracle*, p. 236; the figures for the latter part of the 1970s and 1980s come from, Boelke, *Wirtschaftsgeschichte Baden Württembergs*, p. 586.
69. But the company also exported to developing countries. During the 1950s, in fact,

it established truck production facilities in Brazil and Argentina. see Kruk and Lingnau, *Daimler Benz*, pp. 178–188.
70. Kruk and Lingnau, *Daimler Benz*, pp. 211–244.
71. Helmut Storz, *Die relative Krisenfestigkeit der Württembergischen Wirtschaft*, p. 31.
72. The 1950 numbers become even more interesting when one views the percentage of industrial workers employed in metalworking establishments. Sixty percent of the workers employed in metalworking establishments worked in establishments employing more than 200 workers; 31% worked in establishments employing more than 1000. The 1950 numbers can be found in Gerhard Isenberg, "Standortverhaltnisse und Industriestruktur," p. 103.
73. The logic of this argument goes back at least as far as Marx (*Capital*, vol. 1, Chapters 7–15). See the discussion in the introduction to this book.
74. e.g.: Werner Glastetter, *Die wirtschaftliche Entwicklung der Bundesrepublik Deutschland im Zeitraum 1950 bis 1975.*; Altvater, Hoffmann and Semmler, *Vom Wirtschaftswunder zur Wirtschaftskrise*; Wolfram Fischer, "Bergbau, Industrie und Handwerk 1914–1970." In addition to the sectors mentioned, the motor vehicle industry is typically counted as part of the investment-goods branch. This, obviously is not a sector in which the decentralized industrial order was able to reproduce itself to any significant extent. But as a bias in reading the data on the investment-goods sector, the effect that inclusion of the motor vehicle industry has is to exaggerate the role of larger producers. If there were a way to separate out the motor vehicle industry from the category of investment goods, the strength of the small- and medium-sized capital-goods producers, most of whom are located in decentralized areas, would be much more pronounced.
75. If one breaks the categories down into specific branches of industry, the following branches were the fastest growing (in terms of sales) between 1960 and 1974 in the Federal Republic:

Industry	Approximate Increase in Sales, 1960–1974
Platics manufacturing	600%
Electro-technical	400%
Chemicals	400%
Woodworking	350%
Paper	340%
Machinery	330%
Printing	330%
Motor vehicles	320%
Fine mechanical and optical	310%
Steel and light metal construction	305%

Source: *Statistiches Handbuch für den Maschinenbau, 1975*, "Umsatzwachstum der Industriegruppen mit mehr als 100,000 Beschäftigten 1960–1974"

76. This information was taken from a table in Wolfram Fischer, "Bergbau, Industrie und Handwerk 1914–1970," pp. 837. The other sectors besides investment goods are coal mining, basic producers goods (e.g., steel), consumer goods, food and drinks, energy, and construction.

360   Notes to pages 164–165

77. Ibid. In general, on the sectorally differentiated growth experience in the postwar Federal Republic, see Glastetter, *Die wirtschaftliche Entwicklung*. . . . See also Dieter Mertens, "Veränderungen der industriellen Branchenstruktur in der Bundesrepublik 1950–1960"; and Joachim Schmidt, "Veränderungen in der Investitionstätigkeit der deutschen Wirtschaft."

The sector was similarly a leader among West German exporters. By as early as 1957, investment goods accounted for 50.7% of all West German exports (35,968 million DM), whereas the basic production-goods sector accounted for 29.4%. In 1975, investment goods producers took 53.3% of a much greater absolute volume of exports (221,589 million DM). Total exports in the German economy amounted to 35,697 million DM in 1957 and 221,589 million DM in 1975. Data and percentages on exports are calculated from Table 28 in Altvater, Hoffmann, and Semmler, *Vom Wirtschaftswunder zur Wirtschaftskrise*. The table is entitled: "Warenausfuhr und -einfuhr nach Warengruppen in Mio DM," pp. 166.

78. Altvater, Hoffmann, and Semmler, *Vom Wirtschaftswunder zur Wirtschaftskrise*, p. 136.
79. See the Verein Deutscher Maschinenbau Anstalten e.V., *Statistisches Handbuch für den Maschinenbau*, which first appeared in 1949 and catalogues such things.
80. Statistics taken from the *Statistisches Handbuch für den Maschinenbau*, 1952 and 1966.
81. By way of comparative reference, the most concentrated sectors in the West German economy in 1960 were: Oil refining (91.5% of total sales for top 10 firms); tobacco (84.5%); Shipbuilding (69%); motor vehicles (67%). In the machinery industry, this concentration measure showed 13.4% in 1960 (1.2% down from 14.6% in 1954). The least concentrated sector in the West German economy in 1960 was the textile industry, with 7.2% of total sales in the industry taken by the top 10 firms. All of this information has been taken from the table "'Concentration ratios' für die 10 umsatzgrössten Unternehmen in einzelnen Branchen, 1954 und 1960," in Jörg Huffschmid, *Die Politik des Kapitals*. p. 47–48.
82. Calculated from the *Statistisches Handbuch für den Maschinenbau*, 1966, p. 85–87: "Zahl der Betriebe und Beschäftigten im Maschinenbau nach Ländern, Reg. Bezirken und Kreisen. (Stand September 1962)" for the location numbers. Figures on the size of the machinery industry relative to other sectors come from p. 94: "Wichtigste Industriegruppen in den Ländern des Bundesgebietes nach Beschäftigten und Umsatz. 1964 und 1965."

I counted the following as decentralized: KrfSt Krefeld, Mönchengladbach, Rheydt, Solingen, Viersen, Wuppertal; Ldkr. Düsseldorf-Mettmann, Grevenbroich, Mörs, Rees, Rhein-Wupper-Kreis; Reg. Bez Köln; Reg. Bez. Aachen; KrfSt Iserlohn, Siegen, Wanne-Eikel, Wattenscheid; Ldkr. Ennep-Ruhr-Kreis, Iserlohn, Olpe, Söst; . Ldkr. Altena, Arnsberg, Brilon, Lippstadt, Meschede, Siegen, Wittgenstein (87 firms) were not included, even though they are in decentralized areas, because independent employment numbers were not provided by the VDMA handbook. All other areas, notably the Ruhr Valley and the Bielefeld Region are dominated by the autarkic form of industrial order.

In a more general study of the *Mittelstand* in NRW in the mid 1970s, the Prognos AG found that the areas dominated by the decentralized order had more manufacturing firms per 1000 inhabitants than did those regions in NRW that were dominated by the autarkic industrial order. For example, in 1970:

Notes to page 165

	Manufacturing firms per 1000 inhabitants
Köln	6.019
Wuppertal	9.191
Bonn	6.200
Krefeld	6.704
Rehydt	7.424
Remscheid	12.099
Lndkr. Kempen-Krefeld	6.979

These are all in traditionally decentralized areas.

Areas dominated by the autarkic industrial order had fewer manufacturing establishments per 1000 inhabitants. For example:

	Manufacturing firms per 1000 inhabitants
Essen	4.470
Dortmund	4.062
Duisburg	3.580
Bochum	3.599
Oberhausen	3.575
Castrop-Rauxel	3.482
Wanne-Eickel	3.570
Düsseldorf	6.965
Bielefeld	6.694

This data comes from Prognos AG, *Die Entwicklung Kleiner und Mittler Unternehmen in Nordrhein-Westphalia. Ansatzpunkte für eine landesspezifische Mittelstandspolitik* (im Auftrag des Ministers für Wirtschaft, Mittelstand und Verkehr des Landes Nordrhein-Westphalia, Düsseldorf, März 1975) Table 8, p. 201.
83. *Statistisches Handbuch* . . . , various years.
84. Doris Meyer-Haitz, "Struktur und Entwicklung des Maschinenbaus"; see graph on p. 38. Interestingly, of the period between 1955 and 1974, Meyer-Haitz writes: "The machinery producers have in the last twenty years tried to acquire a share of production in a variety of branches by diversifying their production. They seek to specialize on a particular kind of machinery and then look for as many possible different fields of application for their basic model type" (p. 35–36).
85. It is possible, but more complicated, to show that a significant amount of decentralized producers survived in the basic production-goods industries, especially in the nonferrous metal industries and the chemical industry . It was often possible for producers in these sectors to continue producing specialty products in the postwar period by finding market niches that did not require the huge capital-intensive investments that were required in the continuous-process-dominated branches of the iron and steel and chemical industries. Altvater, Hoffmann, and Semmler's table in *Vom Wirtschaftswunder zur Wirtschaftskrise*, p. 136, shows that 47.2% of those

employed in the basic production-goods sector in 1974 were in establishments with less than 1000 workers. Many traditionally decentralized producers of specialty metal wares in the Sauerland and the Siegerland in NRW, for example, were able to reconstitute themselves in the new postwar environment in this way. See Wolfgang Köllman, *Die Strukturelle Entwicklung des südwestfälischen Wirtschaftsraumes, 1945–1967*, pp. 48–101; also see Horst Osterholt, "Die Sauerländische Wirtschaft im Wandel"; and Hermann Stitz, "Die Wirtschaft im Siegerland." The same can be said of specialty chemical producers in the Cologne and Bergisches Land regions of NRW and in the Rhein Main region of Hessen. See Rolf Brune, "Die Köln-Bonner Raum"; Dr. Horst Jordan, "Wirtschaft in Wuppertal und Niederberg"; Günter Oberhoff, "Solingen und Leverkusen." Indeed, despite the giant size of the three firms that were formed out of the breakup of the IG Farben company (Hoechst, Bayer, and BASF), the top 10 firms in the chemical industry accounted for only 40.6% of total sales in the sector in 1960. See Huffschmid, *Die Politik des Kapitals*, p. 47.

86. For the location of the West German textile machinery industry see the dissertations by Rudolf Hillemann, *Die westdeutsche Textilmaschinenindustrie*; and Hanz Emil Selve, *Strukturwandlungen der westdeutschen Maschinenindustrie in der Nachkriegszeit*, appendix on textile machinery. This discussion draws on two previous papers: Charles Sabel, Gary Herrigel, Richard Deeg, and Richard Kazis, "Regional Prosperities Compared"; and Gary Herrigel and Richard Kazis "The Political Economy of Competitiveness."
87. A kind of warp knitting machine invented by a man named Cotton.
88. Hillemann, *Die westdeutsche Textilmaschinenindustrie*, pp. 12–37.
89. Hillemann, *Die westdeutsche Textilmaschinenindustrie*, pp. 53–63 and 107–115. This was true of machinery in general. See VDMA, "Stellungnahme des Finanzausschusses des Wirtschaftsverbändes Maschinenbau zu dem Währungsplan der Gutachter-Kommission des Verwaltungsrates für Wirtschaft in Minden"; idem, "Finanzierung des Wiederaufbaues von Demontagebetrieben"; Alfred Moessner, "Der Maschinenbau und das Exportproblem"; Anon. "Investieren und Exportieren"; Hans Carl Strohmeyer, "Investition, Maschinenexport und Fertigwarenausfuhr"; and "Maschinenexport und Fertigwarenausfuhr."
90. In this case the subsidy programs existed before and after the formation of the Federal Republic, so "government authorities" refers to both the Military Government of the Bizonal area and also the new government of the Federal Republic.
91. Hillemann, *Die westdeutsche Textilmaschinenindustrie*, calls this government program the "*Neubauprogram.*" For the production of looms, cotton gins, and spinning machines, for example, the OMGUS economic administration developed a "Long-Term Program" that made 150 million DM available to willing producers up to the year 1952. See the story on pp. 67 ff.
92. Hillemann, *Die westdeutsche Textilmaschinenindustrie* pp. 68 and 83. In many ways the prewar finishing associations were not only re-established, they were perfected, because the trade associations and banks were given a degree of power to rearrange the structure of the industry that they had never had before nor were they to have again after the *Neubauprogram* expired. For a brief moment, to avert chaos, the association was able to impose a global system of specialization on the industry. This is suggested in the interesting debate that occurred on the condition of the industry in 1951 by a number of leading figures in the branch; see G. Fritzsch, "Förderungen an den deutschen Textilmaschinenbau"; Walter Reiners,

"Lage und Aufgaben des deutschen Textilmaschinenbaues"; Max Paul, "Förderungen an den deutschen Textilmaschinenbau"; and Sieben, "Förderungen an den Textilmaschinenbau."

93. With respect to exports, the Germans had just as quickly gained their preeminent position among the world's leading producers. In 1952, West Germany accounted for 15.3% of world trade in textile machines. Only Britain, with a 34.5% share and the U.S. with a 19% share had more. By 1958, the Germans had become the world's leading exporters with a 26.6% share. See Eduard Strauss, "Westdeutscher Textilmaschinenbau."

94. On the trade associations generally, see Ingo Tornow, "Die deutschen Unternehmerverbände 1945-1950"; and Walther Herrmann, "Der Wiederaufbau der Selbstverwaltung der deutschen Wirtschaft nach 1945." See the general surveys on this process on trade unions, Klaus Schönhoven, *Die deutsche Gewerkschaften*, pp. 198-217; and on the trade associations, Hans-Peter Ullmann, *Interessenverbände in Deutschland*, pp. 228-273.

95. See Richard Deeg, *Banks and the State in Germany*, p. 119.

96. The reconstitution of regional governments and German federalism would be a natural case to deal with here, but since the story concerns the accommodation of decentralization and autarky in the new Federal Republic, it will be dealt with in Chapter 7.

97. The "folding in" of the chambers occurred formally in 1934, but the chambers as organizations in most cases continued to exist alongside the Nazi *Wirtschaftskammern* until the early 1940s. The influence of the Nazi regime on the chambers was nevertheless considerable. The chairman of each chamber and the leading members of the administration were no longer elected by the local members of industry, but instead appointed by the Nazi Ministry of Economics. Moreover, their activities were more closely integrated into the needs of the militarization of German industry, especially after the beginning of the Four Year Plan in 1936. See the competent discussion of the chambers during the Third Reich in Gerda Wülker, *Der Wandel der Aufgaben der Industrie und Handelskammern in der Bundesrepublik*, pp. 69-86. Generally on economic organizations during the Third Reich, see Ingeborg Esenwein-Rothe, *Die Wirtschaftsverbände von 1933-1945*; and Walter Lahme, *Die Wirtschaftsorganisationen in ihrer Bedeutung für das Verhältnis von Staat und Wirtschaft und der berufsständische Gedanke*.

98. See Herrmann, "Wiederaufbau . . . ," pp. 85.

99. Ibid.

100. Wülker, *Wandel der Aufgaben. . .* , has a good discussion of this.

101. Ibid., p. 116.

102. See Winkel, *Geschichte der Württembergischen Industrie. . .*; see also the discussion between E. K. Neumann (Office of Military Government, Hessen) and Prof. Walter Dorn, assistant to OMGUS Head, General Lucius Clay: "Conversation, June 4, 1949," Hauptstaatsarchiv Hessen, Wiesbaden, Bestand 649 (OMGUS, Hessen) OMGH Historical Division, 8/187-2/11, pp. 28-30. I am grateful to Raymond Stokes for providing me with this document.

103. The course of this debate in the Südwestfälischen Industrie und Handelskammer is described in a very detailed and interesting way in Köllmann, *Strukturelle Entwicklung . . .* , p. 23 ff. Harald Winkel's discussion of the negotiations in the U.S. zone of occupation in Württemberg is extremely extensive and interesting. The U.S. was the most dogmatic about the chambers and of the three occupying powers

was the only one to completely disallow the formation of chambers along traditional lines. See Winkel: *Geschichte der Württembergischen Industrie* . . . , pp. 224–262.
104. Wülker, *Wandel der Aufgaben* . . .; Köllmann, *Strukturelle Entwicklung* . . .; Winkel: *Geschichte der Württembergischen Industrie*.
105. Herrmann, "Wiederaufbau der Selbstverwaltung. . . ."
106. The history of this is recounted in Wülker, *Wandel der Aufgaben*. . . .
107. This is clear for example in the way that vocational training was regulated in Württemberg before the 1956 law. Directly after the passage of the military order stripping the chambers of all official duties, the responsibility for vocational training in Württemberg was shifted to the *Landesgewerbeamt*. The chambers were consulted by the government, but were not permitted to be involved in the testing or the issuing of certificates of education. By 1953, the government of Baden Württemberg had shifted all of these activities to the Chamber of Commerce. It continued to provide the official stamp on the programs that the chambers organized until 1956, when the chambers assumed those official duties as well. See the story in Winkel, *Geschichte der Württembergischen Industrie*, pp. 457–461. Similar stories are also related in Herrmann, "Wiederaufbau der Selbstverwaltung . . . ," and Wülker, *Wandel der Aufgaben*. . . .
108. The facts about this are set out clearly in Fritz Voigt, "German Experience with Cartels and their Control during the Pre-War and Post-War Periods," especially pp. 187 ff; a fascinating contemporary account of the decartelization experience, written by one of the members of the OMGUS decartelization commission, is James S. Martin, *All Honorable Men*. A good overview of the period and the early discussion of cartels and deconcentration on the U.S. side is given in Volker Berghahn, *Unternehmer und Politik in der Bundesrepublik*, pp. 85–111; and Walter Damm, *National and International Factors Influencing Cartel Legislation in Post War Germany*.
109. It is interesting to read around in these debates. Paul Hoffmann, the head of the Economic Cooperation Administration, formed after the war, was a clear exponent of this view. In a statement that he gave to the Committee on Foreign Relations of the United States Senate, February 7, 1950, Hoffmann testified that the difficulties for recovery and democratic stability in Germany and Europe had to do with barriers to trade within Europe and to the existence of cartels in their economies. Such constraints on the market prevented the flow of resources and ultimately inhibited economic and political development. The only way to get Europe to the point at which it could be able to make its way through in a "tough modern world," he argued was "to break those barriers down so that you can have a single market, or something close to it, in which you can have large scale manufacturing because you have a large market in which to sell. That is absolutely essential to the development of a kind of Europe we want if Europe is to really be that strong heart that will stand with us and work with us to see that the free world is kept free." (Taken from Hoffmann's testimony in *Executive Sessions of the Senate Foreign Relations Committee (Historical Series) Volume II, Eighty-First Congress, First and Second Sessions, 1949–1950*, p. 184). For evidence that the view presented in the text was not an idiosyncratic one but one that had extremely broad currency during the years of the European Economic miracles, one need only glance at some of the classics of American political science of the period. See, for example, Seymour Martin Lipset, *Political Man*, where the relationship between a moderate middle

class, shorn of traditional attachments and practices and dependent upon mass consumption, is famously established as a cornerstone of stable modern mass democracy.

110. For example, see Wilhelm Röpke, "Klein und Mittelbetriebe in der Volkswirtschaft"; Walter Eucken, "Technik, Konzentration und Ordnung in der Wirtschaft"; Franz Böhm, "Das Reichsgericht und die Kartelle." The neoliberal position is also presented with considerable sympathy in a University of Chicago dissertation from the period: Walter Damm, *National and International Factors Influencing Cartel Legislation in Post-War Germany*, pp. 63–69. The dissertation embodies the affinity between the American and neoliberal positions noted in the text.

111. The firms tend to be grouped within the "Internationalist" camp in studies of the 1950s that care about the political leanings of West German industry. Robert makes reference to a key article in the Frankfürter Allgemeine Zeitung, where many of these firms publicly announced their support of the American version of the cartel law. Rüdiger Robert, *Konzentrationspolitik in der Bundesrepublik*, pp. 251 ff.

112. The key to a successful mass production strategy was control over the evolution of technology. This provided market stability and thereby lowered the risk that firms assumed when they increased their investments in rigid capital equipment in production. Such control could best be achieved within a firm-dominated, highly concentrated industry structure. A cartel could provide market stability, but it made it difficult to control the evolution of technology or produce with adequate scale economies because it kept the number of producers in a market segment high. An oligopolistic structure reduced the number of players in an industry, thereby making the problem of control manageable and allowing adequate economies of scale to be achieved. Moreover, such industrial structures typically had fairly uniform cost structures, elastic demand, and inelastic supply. This induced firms to follow uniform market behavior even in the absence of cartel agreements. Firms following mass-production strategies thus had little incentive to enter into cartels, and were not constrained in their pursuit of other forms of market control; see Voigt, "German Experience with Cartels . . . ," pp. 199 ff.

113. Finally, it is probably fair to assume that the large firms considered it to be politically important to defend the virtues of private property and the market economy against the external threat of communism to the east and the internal threat of socialism within Germany itself. Cartels had become too identified with the planned economy.

114. Erhard's views are nicely laid out in Robert, *Konzentrationspolitik* . . . ; Peter Hüttenberger, "Wirtschaftsordung und Interessenpolitik in der Kartelgesetzgebung der Bundesrepublik, 1949–1957"; and Berghahn, *Unternehmer und Politik*. . . . Erhard himself wrote a number of books extolling the virtues of the market economy and the success of reconstruction in West Germany. The best to read from the point of view of his perspective on cartels, competition, and democracy, is Ludwig Erhard, *Wohlstand Für Alle*, p. 98–117 ("Kartelle – Feinde der Verbraucher").

115. It seems important to note here that the argument that I am developing contradicts almost every other account of the alignment of interests around the cartel law debate that I have read. Typically, Erhard and the Americans are designated the champions of small- and medium-sized producers because they defended the market economy, while the trade associations, especially the BDI, are painted as defenders of the old, cartelized, organized capitalism of Weimar Germany. The

problem with this traditional view is that it has difficulty explaining why the large firms would have publicly come out in support of Erhard. Even more perplexing in the traditional view, is the fact that those spearheading the fight against Erhard within the BDI, such as Fritz Berg, came out of an industrial milieu dominated by the decentralized industrial order. The same was true of Erhard's critics in the Bundesrat, or upper house of parliament, in which the interests of the *Länder* were represented. This contradiction is typically explained away either by saying that Berg was a tool of the large firms, placed at the head of the BDI at a time when large firms had little legitimacy or by claiming that he represented backward and uncompetitive segments of small industry in addition to the large firms. Criticism in the Bundesrat, paradoxically, is explained by heavy lobbying on the part of the BDI. In neither case is any evidence for these claims ever presented. In the end, the problem is that the traditional view cuts up the interests around the cartel law debate on the basis of a view of the economy that systematically mischaracterizes the economic viability or integrity of the decentralized industrial order. The alternative grouping of interest that I suggest fits neither into the traditional conception of the way that industrial politics in advanced industrial societies is supposed to develop, nor does it square with the classic Anglo-liberal assumption that small- and medium-sized firms prosper in free competitive markets.

116. From a speech entitled "Kartellpolitik" given before the Jahresveranstaltung of the BDI on December 4, 1953, contained in Fritz Berg, *Die Westdeutsche Wirtschaft in der Bewährung. Ausgewählte Reden as den Jahren 1950 bis 1965*, pp. 35–49, quote on p. 41.
117. Erhard, the politician, was willing to allow a given number of exceptions underneath a general ban, but even those would be subject to the judgement of the state.
118. The position of the minister of economics in North Rhine Westphalia, Straeter, is interesting in this respect. He argued in the first round of debate on the cartel law, according to Robert,.

> By intimating that the planned cartel office threatened, by virtue of its broadly encompassing powers, to become a mammoth bureaucratic agency of the state, [Straeter] held that it would endanger the freedom of the individual in the economy. In this way he ... raised the problem of the interdependence of sub-orders within society. Like all opponents of the proposal to ban all cartels completely, he believed that the primary danger for the free and democratic political order in the Federal Republic rested not in the concentration of discretionary power in the sphere of production, but rather in the agglomeration of power and dominant authority in the hands of a bloated state apparatus. (*Konzentrationspolitik in der Bundesrepublik*, pp. 206–207)

Curiously, Robert attempts to dismiss the position of Straeter against the form of the law by pointing out that because he came from NRW, he must have been thinking of the interests of the large autarkic producers in the Ruhr. He never demonstrates this, nor does he consider the fact that the economy of NRW is densely populated with regions dominated by the decentralized industrial order with interests in just the kind of self-governing arrangements Straeter is defending. The Hüttenberger article, "Wirtschaftsordnung und Interessenpolitik" is perhaps of all the treatments of the cartel law debate in the 1950s the most sensitive to the deeper political issues at stake.

119. Robert, *Konzentrationspolitik in der Bundesrepublik*,; Hüttenberger, "Wirtschaft-

sordnung und Interessenpolitik"; V.v. Bethusy-Huc, *Demokratie und Interessenpolitik;* T. F. Marburg, "Government and Business in Germany"; Ivo E. Schwartz, "Antitrust Legislation and Policy in Germany"; Damm, *National and International Factors* . . .

120. Hüttenberger, "Wirtschaftsordnung und Interessenpolitik," emphasizes the role of the Bundesrat in blocking the first law. Robert, *Konzentrationspolitik in der Bundesrepublik;* Berghahn, *Unternehmer und Politik in der Bundesrepublik,* and Damm, *National and International Factors* . . . emphasize the key role played by the BDI.

121. At one point, Adenauer encouraged Erhard to bring the BDI directly into negotiations with the bureaucracy of the federal Ministry of Economics. This was ultimately done. The BDI's chief negotiator was Guido Ziersch, a textile manufacturer from Wuppertal and a core member of the left wing of the CDU. Hüttenberg describes Ziersch as the perfect candidate to argue the BDI's case because he made it look like the BDI wasn't representing the interests of big industry. My argument would simply be that he wasn't representing the interests of big industry. See Hüttenberger, "Wirtschaftsordnung und Interessenpolitik," pp. 300–301.

122. Perhaps the ultimate losers in the process were the Ordo-Liberals. They wanted to have a small- and medium-sized firm based economy, governed by the market and protected by a strong state. Most commentators on the cartel law debate point this out. Robert, especially: *Konzentrationspolitik.*

124. Fritz Voigt gives a very concise outline of what the cartel law allowed:

> As far as these exemptions are concerned, a distinction has to be made between *Widerspruchskartelle* (i.e., cartels which will generally come into existence after registration, unless the Federal Cartel office in charge rejects the application, owing to special reasons outlined in par. 12) and *Erlaubniskartelle* (those cartels that are in want of a special approval of the Federal Cartel Office and are not allowed to start their activities before the Federal Cartel Office has made its decision). The former type comprises term-fixing cartels (par. 2), rebate cartels (par.3), cartels which were founded to support specialization and standardization (par. 5.1 and 5.4), and export cartels on conditions that their activities do not encroach upon internal market conditions (par. 6.1). Structural crisis cartels (par. 7), and export cartels (if their activities encroach upon internal market conditions), however, belong to the "Erlaubniskartelle." Furthermore, the law gives the Minister of Economics authority to permit cartels if in exceptional circumstances limitations on competition become necessary in the interest of the economy as a whole or the public welfare (par. 8, sec. 1). Thus the German law allows rationalization cartels and term-fixing cartels, which are not permitted in United States antitrust legislation." (Voigt, "German Experience with Cartels," pp. 191)

124. Hypothetically, such efforts could involve the implementation of better and more efficient production techniques, use of pricing and marketing strategies, as well as merger and acquisition strategies.

125. My characterization of this dynamic is consistent with the view of the mass-production dominated economy outlined by Joseph Schumpeter in his classic *Capitalism, Socialism and Democracy,* especially Chapters 7 and 8. This view is somewhat at odds with more neoclassical accounts which tend to reify both the nature of technology and the market. Thus, Frederic Scherer in his discussion of economies of scale in the determinants of market structure in Chapter 4 of his

useful textbook, *Industrial Market Structure and Economic Performance*, says that the crucial question in evaluating market structure and scale economies concerns the relationship between the size of the minimum optimal scale in relationship to the demand for an industry's output: "Whether there is room for many firms in the market, each large enough to enjoy all scale economies, for only one firm (a natural monopoly situation), or for just a few (natural oligopoly) depends upon two key variables: the relevant technology, and the size of the market" (p. 91). Scherer constructs these two variables as given things, whereas in the analysis in the text, they are taken to be created by the firms in the industry itself.

126. Wolfram Hasselmann and Jürgen Schierholz, *Interregionale Interdependenzen*; Theo Beer et. al., *Die bergische Wirtschaft und ihre Kammer, 1956–1980*, especially pp. 35–62. Many observers of small- and medium-sized producers were aware of the significance of subcontracting for the reproduction of traditional producers. See, for example, Peter Breidenbach, *Die vertikale und horizontale Kooperation von Handwerksbetrieben als Lieferanten industrieller Unternehmungen*. The general significance of subcontracting and the emergence of subcontracting regions will be taken up in greater detail in the chapter that follows.

127. Berg, "Probleme der deutschen Wirtschaft im Zeitalter der Automation," p. 131. This was a speech given to the Sudwestfälisches IHK in October 1956. Other speeches contained in the above volume that are interesting on this point are: "Rationalisierung und Gemeinsamer Markt" (pp. 135 –147) and "Förderung des Mittelstandes" (pp. 347–354).

128. A representative sample of such work is: Hans Rühle von Lilienstein, "Handwerk und Industrie im Gemeinsamen Markt"; W. Wernet, "Wandlungen des Handwerks"; also, anon., "Handwerk-Partner der Industrie"; and Gustav Stein, MdB, "Entwicklungstendenzen der Zulieferertätigkeit." An example of the same argument from the scholarly business literature is K. Klinger, "Zulieferungen und Zulieferer in betriebswirtschaftlicher Sicht." An excellent dissertation on the same topic is Breidenbach, *Vertikale und horizontale Kooperation...*, which summarizes much of the literature from the 1960s.

129. This is generally the way that most of German industrial sociology accounted for the peculiar conditions prevailing in the mechanical engineering sector. See Kern and Schumann, *Industriearbeit und Arbeiterbewusstein*, as well as the new book by the same two authors, *Ende der Arbeitsteilung?*; Karin Benz-Overhage, Eva Brumlop, Thomas von Freyberg, and Zissis Papadimitriou, *Neue Technologien und alternative Arbeitsgestaltung*, especially pp. 226 ff. The view underlay much thinking in social science internationally as well. A sound critique of this way of thinking is developed in Charles Sabel, *Work and Politics*, Chapter 2.

130. This is the trade world described in the seminal article by Raymond Vernon, "International Investment and International Trade in the Product Cycle"; and the studies in Louis T. Wells (ed.), *The Product Life Cycle and International Trade*.

131. See the very important article by Stephen Hymer and Robert Rowthorn, "Multinational Corporations and International Oligopoly." Also, Raymond Vernon's famous autocritical article on the product cycle in 1977 makes the argument that the existence of the United States as the most sophisticated market was the key to the product cycle – and that status could no longer be given to the U.S. ("The Product Cycle Hypothesis in a New International Environment").

132. The essays by Louis T. Wells, Jr., "Automobiles," and J. E. S. Hayward, "Steel,"

provide a good sense of the flavor of these European industrial sectors during the early 1970s.

133. P. E. Rhein, "Europa, Japan und die Internationale Arbeitsteilung"; Loukas Tsoukalis and Maureen White, eds., *Japan and Western Europe. Conflict and Cooperation*; and Masamichi Hanabusa, *Trade Problems between Japan and Western Europe*.

134. Between 1965 and 1974, manufactured exports from developing countries increased from 4.5% to 7.1% of total world manufactured exports. More significantly, these countries grew much faster than the developed countries. Between 1965 and 1974, developing (non-OPEC) countries as a group recorded real growth rates of 16.3%, compared to 10.6% for the world as a whole, 10.8% for the developed countries, and 9.5% for the centrally planned economies (Sanjaya Lall, "Recent Trends in Exports of Manufactures by Newly Industrializing Countries"). According to Lall, "by 1973 manufactures comprised some 22% of the value of all LDC (non-OPEC) exports, and 69% of these were sold to developed countries, 28% to other LDCs (including OPEC), and 3% to the socialist countries."

135. Frank Weiss and Frank Wolter, "Machinery in the United States, Sweden and Germany"; Gerhard Fels, "The Choice of Industry Mix in the Division of Labor between Developed and Developing Countries"; Gerhard Fels and Frank Wolter, "Der Zusammenhang zwischen Produktionsstruktur und Entwicklungsniveau."

136. Folker Fröbel, Jürgen Heinrichs, and Otto Kreye, *Die neue internationale Arbeitsteilung. Strukturelle Arbeitslosigkeit in den Industrieländern und die Industrialisierung der Entwicklungsländer*; and idem, *Umbruch in der Weltwirtschaft. Die globale Strategie: Verbilligung der Arbeitskraft/Flexibilisierung der Arbeit/Neue Technologien*.

137. Rolf Dick, *Die Arbeitsteilung zwischen Industrie und Entwicklungsländern im Maschinenbau*; Frank Dietmar Weiss, *Electrical Engineering in West Germany*; Hugo Dicke, *Strukturwandel im Westdeutschen Strassenfahrzeugbau*; Frank Wolter, *Strukturelle Anpassungsprobleme der westdeutschen Stahlindustrie*.

138. The seeds of this trend were originally described in Piore and Sabel, *The Second Industrial Divide*. For an interesting discussion of the current situation in the mid 1990s, see Michael Storper and Robert Salais, *Worlds of Production*.

139. The importance of microelectronics in the competitive environment of the 1980s was emphasized in Stephen Cohen and John Zysman's *Manufacturing Matters*.

140. For a case study of this dynamic in one industry see Kim B. Clark and Takahiro Fujimoto, *Product Development Performance*.

141. It is important to underscore here what the section on large firms below will make clear: saying that small- and medium-sized producers within the decentralized order performed well during the 1980s does not mean or entail that large producers performed poorly or that they don't somehow matter in the way in which decentralized industrial production in the Germany of the 1980s took place. All I want to do in this section is show that the small- and medium-sized sector performed surprisingly well, given the way that such firms had been understood during the early postwar decades. Others, however, have tried to make the claim that small- and medium-sized firms actually *outperformed* large firms in the late 1970s and 1980s. A summary of the arguments which sides with those who believe that the small- and medium-sized firm sector in Germany grew during the 1980s can be found in Stephanie Weimer, "The Federal Republic of Germany." A central argu-

ment against the idea that small- and medium-sized firms outperformed large ones is Franz-Josef Bade, "The Economic Importance of Small and Medium Sized Firms in the Federal Republic of Germany." From my perspective, the fact that there was even a debate is an indication of the surprising strength of small and medium sized firms. But generally, this debate took place at a level of aggregation that makes it at best tangential to my argument. The evidence, for example, was never broken down by region, much less by the categories I use here, nor within the manufacturing sector, by sectoral performance, etc. Finally, all parties in the debate begin from the assumption that the Germans have for a long time had a very large and strong population of small- and medium-sized firms. An interesting paper that comes close to organizing the regional structure of the Federal Republic according to the regional divisions I have been using concludes that, with some exceptions (Aachen, Karlsruhe) the regions I have designated as being dominated by the decentralized industrial order have been the most prosperous in the Federal Republic, by a wide variety of measures, during the 1980s; see Eleonore Irmen, "Zur Entwicklung der Agglomerationsräume in der Bundesrepublik Deutschland."

142. The experience of capital goods producers dominate discussions of Baden Württemberg's success in the 1980s: see for example Hubert Schmitz, "Industrial Districts"; and the two reports by Philip Cooke and Kevin Morgan, "Industry, Training and Technology Transfer," and "Learning Through Networking." I also have written two articles that emphasize the success of machinery and machine tool producers in decentralized contexts throughout the Federal Republic: "Industrial Order and the Politics of Industrial Change" and "Industry as a Form of Order."

143. Interviews: Traub (Kemper, Smith, Streubel) 9/1985; Index (Borst, Seitz) 1/1986.

144. Interviews: Universal (Schieber) 2/1986; Stoll (Stoll, Hirsch) 7/1986 (with Charles Sabel). Other examples discussed in the business press are: Bizerba, maker of scales and electronic weighing and measuring equipment, *Manager Magazine* 7/1986; and Scharmann, maker of customized flexible manufacturing systems, *Industrie Magazine* 4/1985.

145. See Wayne Nelson, *Maintaining Competitiveness*; also see Interview with Dieter Liekweg, Professor at the Sigmaringen Fachhochschule for Apparel and Apparel Technologies, Sigmaringen, Baden Württemberg, February, 1986. Textile and apparel production is the fourth largest industrial sector in Baden Württemberg behind machinery, motor vehicles, and electronics.

146. On such developments in the furniture industry, see Volker Doehl, "Rationalisierungsstrategien von Abnehmerbetrieben und Anforderungen an die Zulieferer" and Manfred Diess, "Entwicklungen der Arbeitsbedingungen in den Zulieferbetrieben der Möbelindustrie." On the Electro-mechanical industry, see Ulrich Voskamp, Klaus Peter Wittemann, and Volker Wittke, "Perestroika in der Elektroindustrie?" and "Know-How Transfer." See also Harmut Häußermann and Walter Siebel, *Neue Urbanität,* for an argument that places great emphasis on the high-tech industries in southern Germany.

147. This latter point was often lost in academic debates concerning whether or not large series production still existed in the changed environment of the 1980s. The irony in the debate, of course, was that the work that was most often accused of heralding the end of large firms and large-series production, Piore and Sabel's *The Second Industrial Divide*, never actually did that – it argued instead that the rigid system of Fordist mass production would not survive the turbulence of new market conditions and that the paradigmatic forms of flexible organization associated with

craft production would frame adjustment efforts, in large as well as small firms, and even in industries such as steel, chemicals and textiles that were mature mass-production industries (see, e.g., pp. 208–216). For a range of authors who belabored the question of whether or not large-series production would continue to exist in the future, see Cohen and Zysman, *Manufacturing Matters*; Wolfgang Streeck, "On the Social and Political Conditions of Diversified Quality Production"; and Ash Amin and Kevin Robins, "Industrial Districts and Regional Development." On Sabel's view of the relationship between large and small firms in the new environment, see his "Flexible Specialization and the Re-emergence of Regional Economies." On his view of the structure of production processes, see his "Moebius Strip Organizations and Open Labor Markets." As the argument below will make clear, the terms of this debate now look rather dated.

148. For an ideal typical discussion of collaborative manufacturing in the Automobile industry, see my article with Charles Sabel and Horst Kern, "Kooperative Produktion."

149. Both the production of large amounts of value in-house (especially of so-called "core" parts) and the emergence of very specifically circumscribed skills and associated job ladders were soon naturalized in these industries and integrated into the way that people thought about virtue, honor, and status in the industrial society of the decentralized order. One machine tool producer in Reutlingen on the Schwäbische Alb related to me that the German's were shocked in the mid 1950s when American machine tool firms set up production in Germany and subcontracted out for some basic parts. The view then was that such practices were almost *un-virtuous* [interview, Burkhardt & Weber (Andres, Schmieden), January 1986]. In an analogous way, the role of the skilled worker (*Facharbeiter*) assumed dignity and prestige on the one hand, because it became possible to distinguish and evaluate one group of people's special skills from others on the shop floor and in the formal negotiations with employers and, on the other hand, because individual hierarchies of job ladders within skill distinctions gave rise to social status distinctions both in the workplace and outside. On the emergence of skill jurisdictions and the internal rationalization of firms within capital goods industries in the early and mid centuries, see, e.g.,: E. W. Seyfert, *Der Arbeiternachwuchs in der deutschen Maschinenindustrie*; Preller, *Sozialpolitik in der Weimarer Republik*; Thomas von Freyberg, *Industrielle Rationalisierung in der Weimarer Republik*; and Josef Mooser, *Arbeiterleben in Deutschland, 1900–1970*.

150. The way that this system works in Baden Württemberg is described in Sabel, Herrigel, Kazis, and Deeg: "Regional Prosperities Compared."

151. Interviews with Rafi (Pfeffer) 2/1986; Kern & Liebers (Gölgelein) 7/1986.

152. On Dualism, see the above discussion of Daimler Benz, as well as the discussion in chapter six that follows. On the evolution of Japanese subcontracting, see Toshihiro Nishiguchi, *Strategic Industrial Sourcing*.

153. Interview with Rafi (Pfeffer) 2/1986; Kern & Liebers (Gölgelein) 7/1986; Hermann Kolb 2/1986.

154. Interviews at Index-Werke (Borst, Seitz) and Kern & Liebers, op. cit.

155. The equivalent figures for the large commercial banks were 18.2% in 1982 and 28.2% in 1972. Indeed, this strong demand for capital among small- and medium-sized producers continued throughout the 1980s and caused the major commercial banks to completely reorient their strategy of industrial lending. Big commercial banks made up some of the ground that they lost to the savings and cooperative

372   Notes to pages 187–188

banks. Deeg claims that by the end of the decade, well over half of the Deutsche Bank's cash credits went to firms in the *Mittelstand* (Deeg, *Banks and the State in Germany*, pp. 184–85).

156. Ibid., p. 226.
157. Ibid., Chapters 3–8.
158. Ibid., pp. 230 and 194–5.
159. Indirect funding refers to the lack of specifically targeted firms or industries. In effect, the government makes available to any firm below a certain size a partial subsidy for that part of development costs concerned with microelectronic technologies – in any product. Interviews: Vetterman, VDMA, 12/1985; Uwe Thomas, BMFT, 9/1985. For some of the political background on the development of this form of funding, see Hajo Weber, "Technokorporatismus."
160. Nineteen percent of the funds (85.5 million DM) were utilized by machinery firms. VDI/VDE Technologiezentrum, *Wirkungsanalyse zum "Sonderprogram Anwendung der Mikroelektronik*, pp. 18–20 (my calculations). I thank Nick Ziegler for making this material available to me. Ziegler gives extensive treatment to the policies of the BMFT regarding microelectronics and machine tools in his dissertation: *The State and Technological Advance: Political Efforts for Industrial Change in France and the Federal Republic of Germany, 1972–1986.*
161. Hans Horak "Innovationsberatung als Aufgabe der Wirtschaftlicher Selbstverwaltung"; Willi Boelke "Organization und Politik von Industrie, Handwerk und Handel"; Schmitz, "Industrial Districts"; and for a discussion of the IHK's in the Berg Land, see Erich Hoedl et al., *Technik und Arbeitsmarkt*, pp. 37–39.
162. Generally on this, and with clear evidence for the strength of what I call the decentralized regions in the growth of producer services, see Franz Josef Bade, *Regionale Beschäftigungsentwicklung und produktionsorientierte Dienstleistung*, especially pp. 103 ff. The regions that performed best in providing employment between 1976 and 1986 were in the south, and most of those regions were also the leaders in the creation of producer service industries and jobs.
163. Statistische Landesamt Baden-Württemberg: *Verarbeitendes Gewerbe (Umsätze d. Unternehmen), 1975 and 1984*. It should be noted that taxable turnover is a notoriously conservative measure of business activity in West Germany.
164. Taken from Figure 3.15 in Franz Joseph Bade and Klaus Kunzmann, "Deindustrialization and Regional Development in the Federal Republic of Germany," p. 90. The Bavarian cities of Nuremberg and Munich also created a lot of employment in these categories during these years: Nuremberg increased employment in production-related services (R&D, Data processing, strategic planing, etc.) by almost exactly 50% and Munich by much more than that.
165. On the increasing similarity of public and private service offerings, see the interesting and well-argued paper by Klaus Semlinger, "A Marketing Approach for Public Intervention Into Enterprise Decision Making," and Charles Sabel, "Constitutional Ordering in Historical Context."
166. Deeg, *Banks and the State in Germany*, p. 408. On the rationale behind the intensification of consulting services see Johann Löhn, "Technologietransfer in Baden Württemberg."
167. An excellent case study of one such effort among producers of specialized metal parts for the automobile industry in and around the town of Heuberg south of the Schwäbische Alb, see Klaus Semlinger, "Das Steinbeis-Zentrum für Qualitätswesen in Gosheim."

Notes to pages 188–192

168. On Zenit, see *Die Zeit*, 3/10/1985 and 10/18/1985; enthusiasm of the VDMA for Zenit was expressed in interviews with members of the NRW VDMA Board of Directors: Rupert Boekl, 11/1985; Helmut Habig, 11/1985; Dieter Klingelnberg, 11/1985. See also the account in Deeg, *Banks and the State in Germany*, p. 316–18.
169. Deeg, op. cit., p. 318.
170. Ibid., p. 455.
171. The economics minister of NRW, Reimut Jochimson, described the trend in his *Land's* technology policies in the following way:

> These enormous and admirable local efforts are not to be replaced through centralized planning and steering "from above." The NRW Model in technology promotion therefore means decentralization, local consensus and financial support for self-help. In this sense, the *Land* government will promote new forms of cooperation, setting in motion self-steering processes with financial support for a limited time and regressively structured.... (quoted in Deeg, op. cit., p. 317–318.

172. The most characteristic of these voices was perhaps the book by the former premier of Baden Württemberg, Lothar Späth, *Wende in die Zukunft*.
173. For a good summary of the positions of this debate, coupled with an argument that perpetuates it, see Bennett Harrison, *Lean and Mean*.
174. Cooke and Morgan, "Industry, Training and Technology Transfer."
175. For a more detailed description of this process see Sabel, Kern, and Herrigel, "Kooperative Produktion."
176. Good histories of early Bosch are given in Uta Stolle, *Arbeiterpolitik im Betrieb*, pp. 146–222; and Goetz Küster, *75 Jahre Bosch, 1886–1961*.
177. This information on Robert Bosch comes from two interviews that Charles Sabel and I conducted with Horst Sandvoss, Director of Purchasing at the Robert Bosch GmbH, in 7/1986 and 1/1989 (Horst Kern was present at the latter interview as well). A discussion of the "Bosch model" can be found in our paper, Sabel, Herrigel, Deeg, and Kazis, "Regional Prosperities Compared."
178. Interviews at IBM and Hewlett Packard, for example, revealed very similar strategies: IBM, summer 1990 and winter 1989; Hewlett Packard, fall 1987. The single best study of developments in the German electronics industry is that being conducted by Volker Wittke and Ulli Voskamp at the SOFI Institute in Göttingen. See Ulli Voskamp, Klaus Peter Wittemann, and Volker Wittke, "Elektroindustrie im Umbruch"; Volker Wittke, "Elektronisierung und Rationalisierung"; and idem, "Systemische Rationalisierung." Cooke and Morgan discuss similar changes at Daimler-Benz in their "Industry, Training and Technology Transfer."
179. On this phenomenon among large firms in Germany, see my discussion in Herrigel, "Industrial Order and the Politics of Industrial Change"; and the interesting press account in *Manager Magazine*, October 1990: "Vom Diener zum Herrn," pp. 224–233.
180. Interviews at Robert Bosch GmbH (Sandvoss), Shillerhohe, summer 1986 and winter 1989.
181. Semlinger, "Das Steinbeis-Zentrum für Qualitätswesen in Gosheim."
182. A classic treatment of this phenomenon is the earlier work of David Harvey. See his radical classic, *The Limits to Capital*. Further elaborations in the theme appear in his *The Urban Experience*, which also contains an extremely interesting discussion of the transformation of that old model.

183. This was a point frequently overlooked, often because analysts tend to conceive of the activities of the corporation along the lines of the old model rather than that of the new one that actually emerged in the 1980s. A paradigmatic case of work that mixed old principles and new environmental conditions in the analysis of globalization and the corporation was Amin and Robins, "Industrial Districts and Regional Development." I discuss the relationship between large and small firms and regional investment in "Large Firms, Small Firms and the Governance of Flexible Specialization."
184. See, for example, Cooke and Morgan, "Industry, Training and Technology Transfer" and "Learning Through Networking"; Funck and Becher, "Regional Development and Technology Policies"; Klaus Semlinger, "Economic Development and Industrial Policy in Baden Württemberg"; and Robert Hassink, Regional Innovation Policy. I am also implicated in this; see "Large Firms, Small Firms...."
185. Cf. Peter Katzenstein, Industry and Politics in West Germany; Herman Simon, "Lessons from Germany's Mid-Sized Giants."
186. For overviews of the recession in Germany, see Ulrich Heilemann, "Mo' Money?"; Robert Isaak, "Germany: economic powerhouse or stalemate?"; Association of German Economic Research Institutes, "The Economic Situation in Germany"; Rick Atkinson, "Germany Forced To Reexamine Key Elements of Economy."
187. A very good overview of the crisis in Baden Württemberg is Frank Iwer, *Industriestandort Stuttgart 1994*. Iwer points out that average annual rates of job growth fell even more precipitously in the narrower Stuttgart/Böblingen region. Investment-goods industries had 15.5% fewer jobs in 1993 than they did in 1991. Leibinger's pessimism is noted in Frank C. Engelmann, Christian Heyd, Daniel Köstler, and Peter Paustian "The German machine Tool Industry," p. 18. On the crisis in Baden Württemberg, see also Philip Cooke, Kevin Morgan and Adam Price, "The Future of the Mittelstand: Collaboration versus Competition," and Philip Cooke, "The Baden Württemberg Machine Tool Industry." Other decentralized regions, such as the Bergische Land, also performed poorly in this period: see IÖW-Institute für Ökologische Wirtschaftsforschung, Regionalbüro NRW (Wuppertal), *Chance und Risiken einer auf regionale Bedürfnisse ausgerichteten Technologiepolitik*.
188. Taken from the table "Insolvenzen: Schadenhöhe stark steigend," in *Industrie- und Handelskammer Heilbronn: Wirtschaftsdienst*, June 1994, p.14.
189. Commission for the Future.
190. Cf. the Iwer report, ibid., especially pp. 50–59 and 66–82, and the elite *Zukunftskommission* report: Zukunftskommission Wirtschaft 2000, *Aufbruch aus der Krise*. The parties disagreed, predictably, on the relative contribution of wages and work time to high German costs. The unions, persuasively, point out that German wages as well as the total number of hours worked in German factories per week were not actually as out of line with international measures as the employers claimed (Iwer, pp. 30–43). For a very insightful discussion of the structural character of the German crisis that steers a middle course between the two sides see Frieder Naschold, "Jenseits des baden-württembergischen 'Exceptionalism'."
191. A good overview of the general structural and organizational problems in production confronting German industry in the 1990s is Michael Schumann, Volker Baethge-Kinsky, Martin Kuhlmann, Constanze Kurz, and Uwe Neumann, *Trendreport Rationalisierung*.
192. For good descriptions of the new production techniques in Japan, see Shingeo

Shingo, *Non-Stock Production*; idem, *The Shingo Production management System*; Toshihiro Nishigushi, *Strategic Industrial Sourcing*; Masahiko Aoki, *Information, Incentives and Bargaining in the Japanese Economy*; Kazuo Koike and Takenori Inoki (eds.), *Skill Formation in Japan and Southeast Asia*. For a study of new flexible and lean arrangements in the world-wide automobile industry, see James P. Womack, Daniel T. Jones and Daniel Roos, *The Machine That Changed the World*. For an interesting comparison of the progress of U.S. and German producers along various dimensions of this new production system, see Günther Rommel et al., *Simply Superior: Perspectives on German Industrial Competitiveness*. For a critical discussion of the Japanese system, see Christian Berggren, *Alternatives to lean production: work organization in the Swedish auto industry*, and Karel Williams, Collin Haslem, John Williams, Tony Cutler, Andy Adcroft, and Skhdev Johal, "Against Lean Production," in *Economy and Society*, August 1992.

193. There is no intention here to suggest that the alternative system being described in the text exists anywhere in the full form outlined, nor that it must be adopted in the same way in all places. On the contrary! But it is the case that the principles mentioned in the text are at the center of debate world-wide about the reorganization of production, and many have diffused in one form or another, above all in Japan and the United States. For a discussion of the diffusion of these principles, with examples taken from throughout the advanced industrial world, especially Japan and the United States, see Charles F. Sabel, "Bootstrapping Reform." Sabel has also attempted to describe what the alternative system of principles in production are that producers in different countries are striving to achieve – in their own way: see Sabel, "Learning by Monitoring."

194. Womack, Jones and Roos, *The Machine That Changed the World*. This study received tremendous attention in Germany and throughout Europe after it was published. It was also heavily criticized. For one of the most incisive critiques, see Williams, et al., "Against Lean Production. . . ."

195. Ibid., p. 91. Daimler's reaction to this news is discussed in Kevin Morgan, Philip Cooke, and Adam Price "The Challenge of Lean Production in German Industry," pp. 13 ff.

196. Kevin Morgan, "Reversing Attrition? The Auto Cluster in Baden-Württemberg."

197. For a good overview of the current situation in world machine tool markets, see David Finegold, Keith Brendly, Robert Lempert, Donald Henry, and Peter Cannon, *Machines On the Brink*. For a very detailed discussion of struggle over the reorganization of production within German machine tool firms, see Schumann et al., *Trendreport Rationalisierung*, pp. 371–528, especially 406 ff.

198. Schumann et al., *Trendreport Rationalisierung*, pp. 404–405.

199. Ibid. Also see Finegold et al., *Machines on the Brink*, and U.S. Department of Commerce, International Trade Administration, *Industry Outlook 1994; Chapter 16, Metalworking Equipment*. This document is available on the Internet.

200. Cooke, "The Baden Württemberg Machine Tool Industry."

201. The analysis that follows is developed in greater detail in Gary Herrigel and Charles Sabel, "Craft Production in Crisis."

202. It is perhaps obvious, but I think nonetheless important to remind the reader, that rationalization should not be understood as the implementation of mass-production techniques. Rather, rationalization involves the clarification and definition of procedures, norms, and roles in any kind of production process. Werner Abelshauser makes the point that most of the rationalization in the interwar period

occurred in batch-production processes and involved the optimization of the deployment of skilled labor. See Werner Abelshauser, "Two Kinds of Fordism," p. 2.
203. For the development of this argument, see Horst Kern and Charles Sabel, "Verblaßte Tugend." A very detailed summary discussion of German problems with the new work structures can be found in Michael Schumann, et al., *Trendreport Rationalisierung*, "Rationalisierung in Transition: Bestandsaufnahme, Ausblick," pp. 643–664.
204. Interview, June 1994; company and location kept anonymous upon request.
205. Interview, June 1994; company and location kept anonymous upon request.

Notes for Chapter 6

1. See pp. 168–174 in this volume. There was, of course, a proposal to eliminate industrial production entirely from Germany. The so-called "Morganthau Plan," associated with U.S. Treasury Secretary Henry Morganthau, called for the destruction of German industry and the pastoralization of Germany. The rationale for this was that an industrial Germany was, as such, a threat to peace and security in Europe. See the outline by Henry Morganthau Jr., *Germany is Our Problem*. Another critical voice, largely unheeded in the political debate, was that of Eugene Schmalenbach, who argued that the development of modern industry had driven fixed costs so high that they undermined the market economy. His solution was to introduce market-like mechanisms into the internal structure of enterprise and radically decentralize management and operating structures. See Schmalenbach's intriguing arguments in Schmalenbach, *Der Freien Wirtschaft Zum Gedächtnis* and *Pretiale Wirtschaftslenkung*, two volumes.
2. There was some initial hostility toward the universal banks shown by occupying powers, but deconcentration efforts were lacklusterly and inconsequentially carried out. Both the allies and the new German governments feared that the effects of banking deconcentration would be too deleterious to the economy. See Theo Horstmann, *Die Alliierten und die deutsche Grossbanken. Bankenpolitik nach dem Zweiten Weltkrieg in Westdeutschland*, and idem, "The Worst Banking Practice in the World: Inter-Allied Discussion over American Plans to Reform the German Banking System in 1945/46," pp. 93–116.
3. For more on this, see the discussion in Chapter 7 on the National Context. On the construction of neoliberal institutions framing the public regulation of industrial practice, see Hans Jaeger, *Geschichte der Wirtschaftsordnung in Deutschland*.
4. On the advocates of economic democracy in the immediate postwar years in Germany, see, for example, Hans Jürgen Tueteberg, "Ursprünge und Entwicklung der Mitbestimmung in Deutschland," pp. 7–73, especially 45–73; Erich Potthoff, "Zur Geschichte der Mitbestimmung," especially 24 ff; Christoph Klessmann "Betriebsräte und Gewerkschaften in Deutschland 1945-1952," pp. 44–73; Gloria Müller, *Mitbestimmung in der Nachkriegszeit. Britische Besatzungsmacht-Unternehmer-Gewerkschaften*; Franz Josef Stegmann, "Einleitung: Begriff und Formen der Mitbestimmung – Die innerkatholische Mitbestimmungsdiskussion nach 1945," pp. 9–15; Anton Rauscher, *Mitbestimmung: Referate und Diskussion auf der Tagung katholischer Sozialwissenschaftler vom 17. bi 19. Februar 1968 in Mönchengladbach*.
5. Unlike the neoliberals, the belief was that Nazism (and Communism) was not caused by an unruly and monopoly dominated society overwhelming the state, but

by the state overwhelming society. For an insightful American discussion of the political dimension of codetermination at the time, see Clark Kerr, "The Trade Union Movement and the Redistribution of Power in Post War Germany," pp. 535–564.

6. From the concluding declaration by the *Deutsche Gewerkschaftsbund* (DGB) in the British Zone first trade union congress in March 1946. Quoted, more extensively in Gloria Müller, *Mitbestimmung in der Nachkriegszeit. Britische Besatzungmacht-Unternehmer-Gewerkschaften*, p. 71.

7. In many firms immediately after the war, works councils formed to ensure that what little resources firms had could be used productively. Often managers, especially in large firms, recognized the works councils and allied with them in efforts to keep the military government from dismantling their plants for reparations payments. This institution-building occurred mainly at the plant level, and was to a certain extent spontaneous, though workers clearly drew on older workplace-governance structures that had been created during the Imperial and Weimar periods. Müller, *Mitbestimmung in der Nachkriegszeit*, pp. 57–68, provides interesting examples of these spontaneous developments in the iron and steel industry.

8. There was also a 1956 law that extended codetermination to the holding companies of enterprises as well. There are many accounts of the complicated struggles toward legal codetermination in postwar Germany. In addition to the sources already mentioned in note 4, see Gloria Müller, *Strukturwandel und Arbeitnehmerrechte. Die wirtschaftliche Mitbestimmung in der Eisen- und Stahlindustrie, 1945-1975*, pp. 110–183; Herbert J. Spiro, *The Politics of German Codetermination*; Werner Plumpe, "Employers associations and industrial relations in postwar Germany: the case of Ruhr heavy industry", pp. 176–203; Eberhard Schmidt, *Die verhinderte Neuordnung 1945-52. Die Auseinandersetzung um die Demokratisierung der Wirtschaft in den Westzonen und der Bundesrepublik*; Horst Thum, *Mitbestimmung in der Montanindustrie. Der Mythos vom Sieg der Gewerkschaften*. There is also a convenient compendium of important documents from the emergence of Montanmitbestimmung; see Jürgen Peters (ed.), *Montanmitbestimmung. Dokumente ihrer Entstehung*.

These legal victories, moreover, did not come without important compromises for the advocates of economic democracy. Two compromises were most significant. First, although the second law made it mandatory for all industrial enterprises employing more than five persons to allow their workers to elect a works council, the law also insisted that works councils had to be sovereign bodies in no formal way connected to the trade union movement. Moreover, right to participate in works council elections was given to all workers in an enterprise, regardless of whether or not they were members of the union. This was a significant blow to the trade union movement. Second, advocates of codetermination were not able to achieve full parity representation of the work force at all levels of the enterprise, as had been the case in the earlier law for the coal and steel industries. In the second law, workers in all industries outside the coal and steel industries were given the right to only one-third of the seats on the supervisory board of all joint-stock companies, companies with limited partners holding shares and limited liability companies with at least 500 employees. Moreover, unlike the 1951 law, the 1952 law did not provide for a labor-appointed labor director on the management board of enterprises. A very clear and concise outline of the rules of codetermination in Germany is presented by Wolfgang Streeck, "Co-determination: the fourth decade," in *International Yearbook of Organizational Democracy*, pp. 391–422. The article is particularly good at contextualizing the disappointment on the part of trade unions for the losses they felt they received in the final codetermination laws within the general and significant transformation of enterprise governance and industrial relations that the laws actually entailed.

9. Quoted in Müller, *Mitbestimmung in der Nachkriegszeit*, p. 75.
10. The alternative, of course, would be to treat industrial representation as a matter that crossed the boundaries of enterprises into regions or whole industries. This latter conception was, at least initially, very central to the ideology of the councils movement during the revolution that resulted in the Weimar Republic. See, for example, the writing of Hugo Sinzheimer on economic councils, *Arbeitsrecht und Rechtssoziologie*. After World War II, many of the advocates of economic democracy did actually have far broader conceptions of the terrain of economic self-governance that included self-regulating economic committees on the local and national levels. But these extrafirm dimensions of economic democracy seem to have been less central and in any case were whittled away in the battles with the allied governments and the large autarkic enterprises. For a discussion of these early postwar ideas and institutions, see Oskar Negt., Christine Morgenroth, Heiko Geiling, and Edzard Niemeyer. *Emanzipationsinteressen und Organisationsphantasie. Eine ungenutzte Wirklichkeit der Gewerkschaften? Zur Erweiterung sozialkultureller Handlungsfelder am Beispiel der DGB-Ortskartelle*.
11. Andrei Markovits' work, more clearly than many others, draws out this insight about the German left in the postwar period. See especially, *The Politics of West German Trade Unions*.
12. The role that codetermination structures play in fostering cooperation, flexibility, and commitment on the part of both labor and management within individual German enterprises is one of the central themes in Streeck, "Codetermination: The fourth decade." For a nice case study that fleshes out Streeck's arguments in considerable detail, see Kathleen Thelen, *Union of Parts*, on the metalworkers union, IG Metall. Lowell Turner's *Democracy at Work* is also solidly in this tradition. The idea of conflictual solidarity as a way to understand the foundation of German industrial relations was introduced by Friedrich Weltz; see for example his *Introduction of new technologies, employment policies, and industrial relations: a survey carried out for the Anglo-German Foundation for the Study of Industrial Society*.
13. Streeck describes the mechanism that generates information in the following way: "Management in codetermined enterprises is exposed to constant pressures to provide information and to give reasons for its decisions. This has forced it to consider decisions more thoroughly, to take more factors into account, to make underlying assumptions more explicit, and to learn to communicate more freely within the organization in general and with the workforce in particular." In "Codetermination: The fourth decade," p. 413.
14. For discussion and debate of these issues, see the recent volume edited by Hans G. Nutzinger and Jürgen Backhaus, *Codetermination. A Discussion of Different Approaches*.
15. For two discussions from the early post War years of the general belief that German Big Business, especially the steel and chemical industries, helped the Nazis to power and underwrote the war effort, see Gustav Stolper, *German Realities*, pp. 172–196, and Joachim Jösten, *Germany: What Now?*, Part III. Graham D. Taylor discusses

this phenomenon as it affected American anti-trust policies in occupied Germany in his "The Rise and Fall of Anti-Trust in Occupied Germany, 1945–48," especially pp. 27–28. These popular understandings of the implication of German business in Nazism did not, as this and other work has shown, correspond to the actual relationship between the two. Stolper makes this point, in a very impatient way, in the book mentioned above. But on the most recent scholarship, see Henry Turner, *German Big Business and the Rise of Hitler*; Peter Hayes, *Industry and Ideology. IG Farben in the Nazi Era*; Reinhard Neebe, *Grossindustrie, Staat und NSDAP*; and for a general discussion, Dick Geary," The industrial elite and the Nazis," pp. 85–100.

In a more general sense, the idea that there was something intrinsically bad for democratic order and for world peace in German industrial organization is an old chestnut in writing by non-Germans about the German industrial economy, and especially about the chemical and iron and steel industries. Perhaps because both industries were intimately associated with a country's capacity to conduct war in the 20th century, the steel and chemical industries were often singled out as exemplars of Teutonic dysfunctionality. For examples of this kind of sentiment, see William Manchester's *The Arms of Krupp*; Joseph Borkin and Charles Welsh, *Germany's Master Plan: The Story of Industrial Offensive*; Joseph Borkin, *The Crime and Punishment of I.G. Farben*. Simon Reich's recent book, *Fruits of Fascism: Post War Prosperity in Historical Perspective*, reprises these themes but, in a move only comprehensible in postmodern times, applies them to the automobile industry.

All of this said, of course, it remains undeniably true that many large German industrial producers were involved contractually with the Nazi government in a wide variety of areas important to the war effort and the conduct of the holocaust genocide against European Jewry. For discussions of I.G. Farben's involvement with the Nazis and a range of arguments about what to make of that fact see, in addition to Hayes above, Gottfried Plumpe, *Die I.G. Farbenindustrie AG. Wirtschaft, Technik und Politik, 1904–1945*; Peter Wolfram Schreiber, *I.G. Farben. Die unschuldige Kriegsplaner*; and Raymond Stokes, *Divide and Prosper*, chapter 1.

16. The most extreme reform proposal, again, was offered by U.S. Treasury Secretary Henry Morganthau, who called for the complete elimination of German industry. See Henry Morganthau, Jr., *Germany is Our Problem*.
17. From: *Potsdam Agreement. Joint Report on Results of the Anglo-Soviet-American Conference*, Berlin, 1945, released August 2, 1945, excerpts reprinted as Appendix B in Gustav Stolper, *German Realities*, pp. 264–272; quotes in text from p. 267.
18. On the neoliberal position on deconcentration, see Wilhelm Röpke, "Klein und Mittelbetriebe in der Volkswirtschaft," pp. 155–174; Walter Eucken, *Grundsätze der Wirtschaftspolitik*, pp. 225–240; Franz Böhm, "Die Reichsgericht und Kartelle," pp. 197–213; Wilhelm Röpke, *The Social Crisis of Our Time*; and Alexander Rüstow, *Das Versagen des Wirtschaftsliberalismus*. There is a University of Chicago dissertation on the antitrust debate in Germany that provides a very nice overview of the neoliberal sensibility. See Walter Damm, *National and International Factors Influencing Cartel Legislation in Post War Germany*.
19. There was a battle within the American camp between radical progressive trust-busters and more conservative advocates of American-style big business and mass production. Progressive antimonopolists came close to sharing the vision of the competitive market economy held by the Freiburg School, though their ideas of small-scale market competition in the immediate German case were also fused with

significant anti-German feeling. The conservatives were less zealous about the ideal free market – they supported the break up of cartels, but had a more sanguine view of the effect of the size of individual production units on market freedom. As the occupation wore on, the conservatives gradually came to dominate U.S. policy. On the course of U.S. policy, see Volker Berghahn, *Unternehmer und Politik in der Bundesrepublik*, pp. 84–111, and Graham D. Taylor "The Rise and Fall of Anti-Trust in Occupied Germany, 1945–48," pp. 22–39. For an account of the deconcentration and decartelization process by a radical trust-buster, see James D. Martin, *All Honorable Men*.

20. Generally, with these aims in mind, deconcentration efforts were used selectively and aimed at rooting out organizational forms in industry that were thought to be incompatible with the goal of creating a stable, mass-production driven economy. Where there was no intervention, the judgement ultimately was that the organization of the firms and the levels of concentration in the industry were not obstacles to the kind of growth that was desired. Where there was intervention, however, most notably in chemicals and iron and steel, the rationale given was that the organizational framework of the large firms and the levels of concentration in the industry were an obstacle to what was viewed as "healthy" industrial development. For good discussions of the larger designs behind early allied programs, see Taylor, "The Rise and Fall of Anti-Trust in Occupied Germany," and Berghahn, *Unternehmer und Politik*, pp. 69–179. See also notes and discussion in Chapter 5 on the cartel law debate.

21. Tellingly, the only other industry that resembled the iron and steel industry in structure was the chemical industry. Both the Vestag in steel and I.G. Farben in chemicals accounted for roughly half the total output of their respective industries during the 1930s. As we will see in the case below, the largest six firms in the steel industry accounted for over 70% of industry market share. Raymond Stokes reports about I.G. Farben, for example, that "between 1926 and 1938, it possessed between 45 and 48.5% of the total capital invested in all German chemical firms and produced between 25.3 and 31.9 percent of the chemical industry's total turnover." see Raymond G. Stokes, *Divide and Prosper*, p. 13. On sector-crossing vertical integration in both industries, see discussion of the evolution of the steel industry in Chapter 3 and the story of the emergence of I.G. Farben in Chapter 2.

22. For a broad overview of prewar coverage of markets by the steel *Konzerne* and the Vestag, see Stahltreuhändervereinigung, *Die Neuordnung der Eisen und Stahlindustrie im Gebiet der Bundesrepublik Deutschland*, pp. 15–22; see also Enquette Ausschuss, *Die deutsche eisenerzeugende Industrie*, passim, and the discussion of the construction of *Konzerne* and the Vestag in Chapter 3 above.

23. Lucius Clay, ultimately only a moderate enthusiast for deconcentration, was very clear on the unacceptability of the traditional organization of the iron and steel industry. Clay was confident that the breakup of the industry would head in an efficient direction because it would follow a plan drawn up by a committee headed by George Wolf of the United States Steel Corporation, see Clay, *Decision in Germany*, pp. 329–330. On the belief that the traditional German forms of organization blocked the diffusion of American mass-production techniques, see, for example, the testimony of Paul Hoffmann, head of the Economic Cooperation Administration, before the Senate Foreign Relations Committee, *Executive Sessions of the Senate Foreign Relations Committee (Historical Series) Volume II, Eighty*

First Congress, First and Second Sessions, 1949–1950, p. 184 and passim, and more generally, Volker Berghahn, *Unternehmer und Politik*, pp. 20–39.

24. Initially, frustrated by interallied haggling over the precise contours for a unified deconcentration policy, the British military governor unilaterally seized the assets of all of the iron and steel companies in his zone, which included the entire Ruhr Valley, in August 1946. A few months later in 1947, as British power within the Allied occupying Army began to decline, control over assets was shifted to joint American, French, and British control. On these machinations see Isabel Warner, "Allied German Negotiation on the Deconcentration of the West German Steel Industry," in Ian Turner (ed.), *Reconstruction in Post War Germany*, pp. 155–185.

25. Isabel Warner, "Allied German Negotiation...," pp. 155–185, provides a good overview of the negotiations.

26. On the dismantling of the West German steel industry by the occupying powers, see Stahltreuhändervereinigung, *Neuordnung*...; Ernst Schroeder, "Die Westdeutsche Montanindustrie heute"; K.H. Herchenroeder, Johann Schaefer, and Manfred Zapp, *Die Nachfolger der Ruhr Konzerne*; Gerd Baare, *Ausmass und Ursachen der Unternehmungskonzentration der deutschen Stahlindustrie im Rahmen der Montanunion, ein internationaler Vergleich*; Franz Lammert, *Das Verhältnis zwischen der Eisen schaffenden und der Eisen verarbeitenden Industrie seit dem ersten Weltkrieg*, pp. 140–155; and Paul Weil, *Wirtschaftsgeschichte des Ruhrgebietes*. The Stahltreuhandervereinigung, Schroeder article, and Herchenroeder et al. volume all have charts outlining lineages of firms.

27. Cf. Stahltreuhändervereinigung, *Neuordnung*..., pp. 129 ff, 301–304. For complaints about disruptions to rolling mills, see Schroeder, "Westdeutsche Montanindustrie." Schroeder lists nine newly created companies with uneconomic combinations of steel making and rolling capacity. Norman Pounds remarked in 1953: "It is too early to suggest the shape which the future organization of the heavy industry of the Ruhr is likely to take. It is clear, however, that the unwisdom of too great a fragmentation has been realized." In Norman J. G. Pounds, *The Ruhr*, p. 259.

28. Stahltreuhändervereinigung, *Neuordnung*..., pp. 129–131 and 191–193.

29. Ibid., pp. 129–131 and 133–141.

30. Herchenroeder et al., *Nachfolger der Ruhr Konzerne*..., pp. 57–118; Kurt Pritzkoleit, *Männer, Mächte, Monopole*, pp. 131–141.

31. At Hoesch, for example, most of the *Konzern's* prewar coal and all of the larger of its nonsteel manufacturing businesses were grouped into two new and separate companies, the Altenessener Bergwerks AG (coal mining) and the Industriewerte AG (machinery and metalwares). The remaining Hoesch Werke AG was still structured as a holding company, with coal operations run as a subsidiary separate from its steel operations. But, in comparison to the old *Konzern*, company activities were radically centralized and specialized in the manufacture of steel (including both crude and rolled products). Steel capacity at Hoesch was reduced by the loss of the Stahlwerke Hagen. The Westfalenhütte, where all of Hoesch's steel making was concentrated, was one of the largest steel making plants in Germany. See Herchenroeder et al., *Nachfolger der Ruhr Konzerne*, pp. 230–241. Mannesmann's division in to three separate companies is outlined on pp. 199–218 and Klöckner's on pp. 171–194.

32. The company, one of the very oldest steel producers in Germany, went on to

become the largest general machinery producer in Europe and never again reentered the steel business. See the excellent book by the former GHH CEO (*Vorstandsvorsitzender*) Dietrich Wilhelm von Menges, *Unternehmens-Entscheide. Ein Leben für die Wirtschaft*, which describe the *Konzerne's* strategic thinking around the time of decoupling quite well. An overview of the details of decoupling at GHH is presented in Herchenroeder et al., *Nachfolger der Ruhr Konzerne*, pp. 119–140.

33. The steelmaking facilities were never, in fact, sold off. But the family continued to hold the steel interests in a separate holding, apart from the rest of its business, in the manner dictated by the Allied settlement, until the late 1960s, when the firm went bankrupt and had to be completely reorganized. The postwar reforms undermined Krupp as a *Konzern* by essentially dividing it into two: a steel company on the one hand, and a diversified autarkic machinery producer on the other. A good breakdown of the direct holdings of the Krupp Company, which were functionally controlled from the center of the family enterprise, and the daughter companies the company controlled is given in Gert von Klass, *Krupps*, pp. 431–433. See also Herchenroeder et al., *Nachfolger der Ruhr Konzerne*, pp. 145–170. A survey of the company's postwar development is in provided in Dietrich Weder, *Die 200 Grössten deutschen Aktiengesellschaften 1913–1962*, p. 323, and *Wirtschaftswoche*, no. 2, January 14, 1972, pp. 62–63; and *Manager Magazine*, 12/1973, pp. 30–34; and ibid., 11/1975, pp. 27–34.

34. British Zone Law Number 56, American Zone Law Number 78, and French Zone Law Number 96.

35. For clear discussions of the terms of the ECSC treaty with regard to cartelization and price setting, see Duncan Burn, *The Steel Industry 1939–1959*, pp. 407–416 and Lammert, *Das Verhältnis...*, pp. 201–204.

36. An overview of the distribution of rolling mills and their capacity by product is presented in Enquette Auschuss zur Untersuchung der Erzeugungs- und Absatzbedingungen der deutschen Wirtschaft, *Die deutsche eisenerzeugende Industrie*, p. 40, table, "Produktion an einzelnen Walzwerksprodukten nach Grössenklassen im Jahre 1929," and surrounding text pp. 39 and 41–43.

37. See Josef Esser and Werner Väth, "Overcoming the Steel Crisis in the Federal Republic of Germany, 1974–1983." On the expansion of the German steel industry, generally in the 1950s and 1960s, see Lammert, *Das Verhältnis...*, pp. 174–197.

38. Karl Eckart, *Die Eisen-und Stahlindustrie in den beiden deutschen Staaten*, p. 203, offers the 8 million ton figure. Bernd Huffschmid, *Das Stahlzeitalter beginnt erst*, p. 31, provides the 1960 and 1964 figures and breakdowns for rolled products. The remaining percentage in each year is accounted for by "other" rolled products, such as steel pipes.

39. Profile steels (e.g., bar and structural steels) accounted for half of rolled steel output in 1955 but then fell to 45.7% by 1964. Sheet steels, on the other hand, grew from 43 to 48% of total rolled output during the same period (Huffschmid, *Stahlzeitalter...*). For a very good analysis of these changes in steel output with an eye to the changing character of demand, see Lammert, *Das Verhältnis...*, pp. 218–228.

40. Esser and Väth, "Overcoming the Steel Crisis...," p. 633.

41. Figures on rolled steel output taken from UN, *Annual Bulletin of Steel Statistics for Europe*.

42. For a discussion of the development of production in these submarkets for the

Notes to pages 216–219   383

entire postwar period, see Eckart, *Eisen- und Stahlindustrie* ..., pp. 181 ff (crude steel) and 203–216 (rolled products).
43. Another important concentration of integrated works was in the Saarland. Eckart, *Eisen und Stahlindustrie* ..., p. 176.
44. Huffschmid, *Stahlzeitalter* ..., p. 83. Figures taken from his Table 2, p. 81. For a narrative of the decade of investment, see pp. 80–84.
45. Baare, *Ausmass und Ursachen* ..., pp. 108–109.
46. Paul Weil, *Wirtschaftsgeschichte des Ruhrgebiets*, pp. 217–219. Information on blast furnaces is taken from Müller, *Strukturwandel* ..., pp. 365–366. Müller points out that it is usual for a number of blast furnaces to be inoperative and under repair at any given period of time, so the scale of production is even more impressive than its seems. For example, she points out that in 1974 only 76 of the 86 blast furnaces in the industry were actually in operation.
47. Weil, *Wirtschaftsgeschichte* ..., See also Müller, *Strukturwandel* ..., pp. 369–373, and the tables in Eckart, *Eisen- und Stahlindustrie* ..., chronicling the changes in technology and their respective percentages of total output, pp. 161–162 and 186.
48. The shortfall during the 1950s between the level of demand for rolled product and the available domestic supply was so great that producers concentrated their production and investments on a limited number of rolled products in order to be able to achieve better scale economies and get goods to as many German users as they could to prevent them from turning to foreign suppliers. Lammert makes this quite clear, and moreover points out that producers were encouraged to coordinate their production plans by German manufacturers dependent upon rolled steel output (Lammert, *Verhältnis* ..., p. 221).
49. The attentive reader will note that three of these companies – ATH, Phönix, and Rheinstahl – correspond, at least in name, to companies that existed prior to the formation of the Vestag, and were instrumental in its creation. DHHU, as noted above, was a creation of the allies, brought about by the merger of two plants form the old Vestag. Prior to the creation of the Vestag, the Dortmund plant of the DHHU was part of Hugo Stinnes' giant Rhein-Elbe Union, while the Hörder plant belonged to the Phönix group. The two plants were formally linked together by the Vestag during the 1930s, but both continued to operate independently. All of these companies, especially the former three, differed substantially, in holdings and specializations, from these earlier incarnations of themselves.
50. An outline of the two companies is presented in Huffschmid, *Stahlzeitalter* ..., pp. 110–115; on Thyssen family ownership, see Lammert, *Verhältnis* ..., pp. 207–208; Müller, *Strukturwandel* ..., pp. 300–303.
51. Rheinstahl's steel operations were the Eisenwerke Mühlheim-Miederich AG, Eisenwerke Gelsenkirchen AG (grouped together in the Rheinisch-Westfälische Eisen und Stahlwerke Aktiengesellschaft AG) and the Ruhrstahl AG. Throughout the 1950s, these holdings were consolidated within the company, but not expanded. By the early 1960s, Rheinstahl was a broadly diversified mechanical engineering company, active in the steel sector primarily in sheet steels, plates, and specialty castings, but these products accounted for only 6% of company revenues. On Rheinstahl, see Huffschmid, *Stahlzeitalter* ..., pp. 185–191; Müller, *Strukturwandel* ..., pp. 304–305; and Lammert, *Verhältnis* ..., pp. 206–207.
52. Huffschmid, *Stahlzeitalter* ..., pp. 147–155.

53. Hüttenwerk Oberhausen A.G. belonged to GHH until 1945.
54. Krupp's steel interests were grouped in a separate holding that included the Hütten- und Bergwerke Rheinhausen AG.
55. Huffschmid, *Stahlzeitalter*... provides information on the product profile and output of each of these companies, pp. 122–146, 156–184, and 192–197.
56. For discussions of this period see Eckart, *Eisen und Stahlindustrie*..., pp. 254–261; Georg Heinrich Elkmann, *Möglichkeiten und Grenzen der Konzentration in der Eisen- und Stahlindustrie*; and Burkhardt Röper (ed.), *Rationaisierungseffekte der Walzstahlkontore und der Rationalisierungsgruppen*.
57. This was to be done by consolidating existing sales offices and combining large orders to save on freight and to reduce delivery distances.
58. See in particular the various articles in Röper, *Rationalisierungseffekte*....
59. See, e.g., the examples in Erich Schmitz, "Analyse der Wettbewerbseffekte der Kontorverträge von 1967 und der Verträge zur Grundung der vier Rationalisierungsgruppen von 1971."
60. Eckart *Eisen- und Stahlindustrie*..., pp. 254–55.
61. For a complete listing of mergers during the 1970s, see table 52, "Fusionen und Zusammenschlüsse in der Eisen- und Stahlindustrie in der Bundesrepublik Deutschland in den siebziger Jahren," in Eckart, *Eisen und Stahlindustrie*..., p. 257.
62. Mannesmann executives extensively documented their thinking in management journals throughout the 1970s; e.g., Egon Overbeck "Strukturwandel – Neue Chancen für die Unternehmen"; idem, "Strukturwandel Eines Unternehmens"; Franz Josef Weisweiler, "Unternehmensgeschichte in der Produkt-Portfolio-Analyse." On this strategy generally in the German industry, see Manfred Neumann, "Improved Competitiveness of Steel Producing Firms by Means of Diversification."
63. Mannesmann was the first to do so, achieving full reintegration by 1955 of both its separated coal mines and downline manufacturing operations. Hoesch and Klöckner followed soon after, though the latter never reincorporated the largest of its former manufacturing operations, the Klöckner Humboldt Deutz AG. An excellent survey of the process of reintegration is presented in Müller, *Strukturwandel*..., pp. 301 ff.
64. A good systematic overview of the various business operations of the major steel companies in the middle 1960s is provided in Bernd Huffschmid, *Stahlzeitalter*..., pp. 92–228. Thanheiser characterizes most of the major steel producers in 1970 as being either single business firms, or dominant business ones. The only exceptions are predictable: Rheinstahl, GHH (Related Business Diversification) and Krupp (Unrelated Business Diversification). See the concluding table in Thanheiser, "Strategy and Structure in Germany."
65. Krupp was also similarly well endowed with downline manufacturing operations. Indeed, revenues from manufacturing businesses accounted for nearly as much of total revenues as steel production. The difficulty for Krupp, however, was that it was committed to a very awkward internal organization imposed by the allied deconcentration authorities. This commitment kept the various areas of Krupp operations separate from one another and militated against the kind of synergy characteristic of interwar *Konzerne*. On Krupp and Rheinstahl, see the discussions in Huffschmid *Stahlzeitalter*..., pp. 121–146 and 185–191; on GHH, see Hans Josef Jöst, *Pionier im Ruhrrevier*.
66. U.S. based writers on German management during this period confirmed the ex-

istence of centralized management structures, but they interpreted it as an expression of the German character, rather than as a quite new postwar response to the conditions of oligopoly and mass production. See, most prominently, the work of Heinz Hartmann, *Authority and Organization in German Management*, especially pp. 51–78; idem, "Management in Germany." For more popular accounts see the (now fairly widely cited) Fortune Magazine articles from the 1950s: James Bell, "The Comeback of Krupp"; Gilbert Burck, "Can Germany Go Capitalist"; and Gilbert Burck, "The German Business Mind."

67. Alfred Chandler, *Strategy and Structure*, pp. 331–337. Chandler considers the steel industry case to be a comprehensible anomaly to the general trend toward multi-divisionalism. Its high fixed costs and levels of technical integration made decentralization unwieldy.

68. Thanheiser, "Strategy and Structure. . . ."

69. For overviews of the adoption of mass-production techniques in the automobile, elektro-technical, mineral oil, and chemical industries during the 1950s, see the reports in Harry W. Zimmermann (ed.), *Aspekte der Automation*, pp. 3–134.

70. On the role of Nazi planners in the diffusion of mass-production technologies and practices in production, see Reich, *Fruits of Fascism*; Michael Geyer, "Zum Einfluss der Nationalsozialistischen Rüstungspolitik auf das Ruhrgebiet"; and more recently, Franz Henne, *A German Path to Fordism*. Henne does a nice job of showing the influence of Nazi war planning on production organization in automobile supply and consumer electronics.

71. See Reinhard Doleschal, "Zur geschichtlichen Entwicklung des Volkswagenkonzerns"; Walter Henry Nelson, *Small Wonder. The Amazing Story of the Volkswagen*, pp. 117–166; Reich, *Fruits of Fascism*, pp. 147–201.

72. All of this from Walter Henry Nelson, *Small Wonder . . .*, pp. 137–167.

73. The success of the Nuremberg-Furth based Grundig was based on the mass production of radios and other products. There is a short survey of the firm's history in Kurt Pritzkoleit, *Auf Einer Woge von Gold* pp. 287–304.

74. Egon Baumgart, "Die Elektroindustrie der Bundesrepublik im europäischen Markt."

75. Siegfried von Weiher und Herbert Götzeler, *Weg und Wirken der Siemens-Werke im Fortschritt der Elektrotechnik*, 1847–1972 p. 126.

76. On AEG, see Pritzkoleit, *Männer Mächte Monopole*, pp. 281–294, especially pp. 290–291.

77. For a description of Siemens plants, see Siemens-Schuckert (ed.), *Die Entwicklung der Starkstromtechnik*. On the development of Siemens in the 1950s, see the excellent chapter on Siemens in Pritzkoleit, *Männer Mächte Monopole*, pp. 255–265. See also the discussion in Frank Vogl, *German Business after the Economic Miracle*.

78. From Thanheiser's "Strategy and Structure in Germany"; AEG in Pritzkoleit's classic work, *Männer Mächte Monopole*, pp. 281–294.

79. For an interesting contemporary account of the agricultural machinery market right around the time of the formation of the European Economic Community, see Rudolf Geer, *Der Export der deutschen Landmaschinenindustrie*.

80. The general movement into mass production and mechanical automation within areas of light manufacturing gave rise to copious commentary and debate in the contemporary technical and trade press. For a sampling, see; Walter Kurth, "Automation in der Industrie"; Kurt Richebächer, "Einseitige Expansion. Nachholbedarf

an Produktivität"; Manfred Knayer, "Ohne Automation geht es nicht"; "Die Automatisierung. Ein Kennzeichen des 20. Jahrhunderts"; "Die Automatisierung – Möglichkeiten und gewerkschaftspolitische Konsequenzen"; S. B. "Die Automatisierung in der Bundesrepublik"; Fritz Sternberg, "Die gewerkschaftlichen Aufgaben in der Epoche der Automatisierung"; Helmut Goebel, "Neue Entwicklungen im Sondermaschinenbau für die Automobilindustrie"; 8th Aachener Werkzeugmaschinen-Kolloquium 1956, *Entwicklung im Werkzeugmaschinenbau*; K. Pentzlin, "Automatisierung im Lichte der Wirtschafts"; W. Reichel, "Der Stand der Automatisierung auf Grund der Erhebungen des RKW und der OEEC" (see also the additional technical articles in that same issue of *Werkstatttechnik und Maschinenbau*, pp. 62–96); VDI (ed.), *Automatisierung der Fertigung Vorträge der VDI-Tagung, Stuttgart 1961*.

There were also countless speeches by industrialists given on the subject. See Siegfried Balke, "Die technische Entwicklung und der Mensch"; Franz Greiss, "Warum rationalisiert werden muss"; Hanns Meenzen, "Automatisierung – ein Schreckgespenst?"; Karl Kisker, "Die Rationalisierung und der Mensch"; Theodor Litt, "Technischer Fortschritt und menschliche Freiheit"; Carl Neumann, "Technischer Fortschritt als Wirtschaftsprinzip"; Jochen Wistinghausen, "Betriebssoziale Probleme des technischen Fortschritts"; Carl Neumann, "Technischer Fortschritt und Gemeinsamer Markt"; Max Knorr, "Der Mensch und die Automatisierung."

81. For general engineering and business discussion of these issues at the time see Deutsche Gesellschaft für Betriebswirtschaft (ed.), *Zentralprobleme der Vollbeschäftigung*, pp. 57–92; and Zimmermann (ed.), *Aspekte der Automation*. See also from the management-literature discussion Max Pietsch, "Die Auswirkung der "Automation" auf dem Produktionsprozess"; and E. C. Keachie, "Stand der ökonomisch-technischen Betriebsführung (Industrial Engineering) in Deutschland"; Marius Hammer, *Vergleichende Morphologie der Arbeit in der Europäischen Automobilindustrie*; Lutz Moll, Die industrielle Serienfertigung.

82. Nelson, *Small Wonder...*, pp. 147–150.

83. The best book on the evolution of these changes in the organization of work in west Germany is Kern and Schumann, *Industriearbeit und Arbeiterbewusstsein*.

84. Reinhard Döleschal, "Zur geschichtlichen Entwicklung des Volkswagenkonzerns," p. 36.

85. Friedrich Weltz, Gert Schmidt, and Jürgen Sass, *Facharbeiter im Industriebetrieb*, pp. 20–21.

86. This seems to have been true for two reasons. First, the eventual stable structure of the European market was not as clear to producers in the early fifties as it was in the early sixties. Tariffs continued to fragment the flow of intra-European trade, purchasing power in the domestic market was still quite low, and intra-European debates about the eventual role and identity of Germany in Europe all either encouraged producers to maintain some flexibility in their production processes, or discouraged them from making investments in expensive and rigid technologies that would require a large and enduringly stable market environment to adequately amortize. Most of the literature about the demand for machine tools, or about the character of the machine tool park in West German factories confirms this. General purpose, flexible machinery was the rule in German factories until the late 1950s and early 1960s. See W. Erdmann, "Stand der Technik in der Werkzeugmaschinenindustrie Deutschlands"; Kurt Bender, "Sind neue Maschinen unwirtschaftlich?"; Reichel, "Der Stand der Automatisierung..."; H. Goebel, "Einige grund-

sätzliche Überlegungen bei der Auslegung von selbsttätigen Maschinenfliessfertigung"; C. M. Dolezalek, "Ansatzpunkte für die Einführung automatisierter Fertigung"; Alfred Stubenrecht, "Der Einfluss der Automation auf Arbeitsvorbereitung und Arbeitsablauf"; Kurt Biedenkopf, "Massenproduktion, Wettbewerb und europäische Vereinigung"; Tibor Scitovsky, *Economic Theory and Western European Economic Integration*. The Verein deutscher Werkzeugmaschinenfabriken (VDW) also commissioned two extensive rejoinders to a report by Seymour Melman, written in the late 1950s (and unavailable to the author), on the productivity of machine tool production in western Europe. The two pieces were written in 1960 and were apparently circulated only internally within the VDW membership. One paper looks at economic aspects of the problem Melman discusses, the other looks at the technical aspects of the problem. Together the reports give an excellent overview of the trajectory of West German machine tool technology and production at the beginning of the 1960s. See VDW, "Wirtschaftliche Betrachtungen zu dem Bericht von Prof. Melman über die Produktivität der Fertigung in der Werkzeugmaschinenindustrie Westeuropas"; VDW, "Technische Betrachtungen zu dem Bericht von Prof. Melman über die Produktivität der Fertigung in der Werkzeugmaschinenindustrie Westeuropas."

Secondly, the West German labor market was in considerable surplus throughout the early years of the postwar period. Among other things, this was attributable to a stream of over 12 million (often very highly skilled) refugees coming from the east. This, plus labor union willingness to make moderate wage demands, made it profitable to employ skilled labor rather than machinery in production, regardless of the strategy that the firm had in the market. This is a standard argument that everyone makes about the 1950s German economy; see Dietmar Petzina and Werner Abelshauser, "Krise und Rekonstruktion"; Rudi Schmiede, "Das deutsche Wirtschaftswunder 1945–1965"; Elmar Altvater, Jürgen Hoffmann, and Willi Semmler, *Vom Wirtschaftswunder zur Wirtschaftskrise*.

87. The first wave of unskilled foreign workers began to enter West German factories in the last years of the 1950s, beginning a trend in migration that would eventually bring millions of southern Europeans and especially Turks into the Federal Republic; see Altvater, Hoffmann, and Semmler, *Vom Wirtschaftswunder* . . . , pp. 250 ff, and Herbert, *A History of Foreign Labor in Germany*, pp. 193–254.

At the same time, methods used by firms to calibrate incentive systems for wage workers were also altered to accommodate the growth of semi- and unskilled workers working on dedicated machines and automated production lines. The traditional piece-rate system, in which a worker received an amount of money per unit of production, was ill-suited to automated operations, where a worker's capacity to intervene directly in production was limited. Consequently, that system slowly gave way to so-called standard hour plans, in which a worker was credited with an amount of hours for an amount of work accomplished, and then paid at a collectively bargained hourly rate. A clear legal definition of these plans is given by Seyfarth et al., *Labor Relations and the Law in West Germany and the United States* p. 309. The work by Schmiede and Schudlich, *Die Entwicklung der Leistungsentlohnung in Deutschland;* and the classic work by Burkhardt Lutz, *Krise des Lohnanreizes*, chronicle the character and timing of these changes in payment systems and their relationship to changes in technology and work organization.

88. The well-known study by Marc Maurice, Francois Sellier, and J. J. Silvestre, *The Social Foundations of Industrial Power*, shows this to be true in comparison to

France. See also Charles Sabel's discussion of this in *Work and Politics*, Chapter 2.
89. On the beneficial effects of the vocational training system in Germany, see Wolfgang Streeck, *The Role of the Social Partners in Vocational Training and Further Training in the Federal Republic Germany*.
90. See pp. 98–100 this volume.
91. The theoretical underpinnings of this mechanism are outlined by Michael Piore in "The Technological Foundations of Dualism and Discontinuity." For the German reception of these ideas, with applications, see Werner Sengenberger (ed.), *Der gespaltene Arbeitsmarkt*; and Burkhart Lutz, *Der kurze Traum immerwährender Prosperität*, pp. 186–235.
92. Peter Breidenbach, *Die vertikale und horizontale Kooperation von Handwerksbetrieben als Lieferanten industrieller Unternehmungen*, pp. 75–154.
93. Very few small- and medium-sized secondary sector firms ever actually emerged in the Ruhr Valley itself. See the essays by Theo Beckmann, "Das Handwerk im Ruhrgebiet," and "Das Handwerk – heute und morgen." Though these essays focus on the artisanate, they address the problem of small- and medium-sized industrial producers as well.
94. Steel and light metal construction, motor vehicles, and electro-technical.
95. This is taken from the interesting study by Wolfram Hasselmann and Jürgen Schierholz, *Interregionale Interdependenzen*.
96. Theo Beer et al., *Die bergische Wirtschaft und ihre Kammer, 1956–1980*, especially pp. 35–62.
97. Most studies that emphasized the tendencies toward concentration in the German economy during the 1960s pointed to these characteristics of the situation of the small- and medium-sized producer. See, for example, Joerg Huffschmid, *Die Politik des Kapitals*; Erich Hanke, *Mittelstand in der Bundesrepublik*; Helmut Arndt et al., *Konzentration ohne Kontrolle*.
98. See Wolfgang Köllman, *Die strukturelle Entwicklung des südwestfälischen Wirtschaftsraumes 1945–1967*, pp. 122–23 for figures on women, pp. 118–129 for the labor market and workforce structure more generally.
99. Ibid., p. 126–127.
100. On the generally fragmented character of product markets in automobile, electro-technical and other light manufacturing markets – regardless of location in an industrial order – prior to the end of World War II, see, for example, Wilhelm Vershofen, *Die Grenzen der Rationalisierung*; Fred Ledermann, *Fehlrationalisierung*; Gert Magnus, *Untersuchungen über den Wettbewerb zwischen Gross- und Kleinunternehmen der Elektrotechnik und das Maschinenbaues*; Bruno Birnbaum, *Organisierung der Rationalisierung Amerika-Deutschland*. See also Chapters 2 and 3 of this volume.
101. The argument here complements the argument and evidence presented in Chapter 5, pp. 174–177, on postwar losers and the adjustment of decentralized producers into investment goods production.
102. For the numbers presented in the text, see "Kraftfahrzeugindustrie im Wettbewerb" in *Der Volkswirt*, No. 48, 1950, pp. 19–20; and H-O. Lenel, *Ursachen der Konzentration*, pp. 31–32; Harald Eichenhofer, "Die Automobilindustrie in der Bundesrepublik" gives further details on concentration in the early industry. On Nazi and allied efforts, see Reich, *Fruits of Fascism*.
103. Porsche was also a producer of note in the market, but it was clearly a specialty producer with a fairly narrow, high-priced market. And it was very dependent upon

Volkswagen for design business (it operated as one of VW's main designer laboratories) and for distribution. For this reason, it seems reasonable to list only the five major producers in the text. A general study of concentration tendencies in the West German automobile industry during the 1950s and 1960s is Manfred Raisch, *Die Konzentration in der deutschen Automobilindustrie.*

104. For concentration in selected machinery markets, see Kommission der Europäischen Gemeinschaften, *Untersuchungen zur Konzentrationsentwicklung in verschiedenen Untersektoren der Maschinenbauindustrie in Deutschland.* On the electrotechnical industry, see Frank Dietmar Weiss, *Electrical Engineering in West Germany*; and E. Arnst, "75 Jahre Fortschritt in der deutschen Elektroindustrie." The book by Hans-Otto Lenel, *Ursachen der Konzentration unter besonderer Berucksichtigung der deutschen Verhaltnisse,* has a general survey of concentration by sector (pp. 21–41). By all accounts, the degree of concentration within the West German economy increased even more in the 1960s with the diffusion of mass production practices in the economy. See George Küster, "Germany," in Raymond Vernon (ed.), *Big Business and the State;* and Carlos Maya, "Kapitalkonzentration und -zentralisation in der Bundesrepublik Deutschland."
105. Walther Krähe "Die innerbetriebliche Organisation von Konzernen"; Werner Söhngen, "Aktuelle Fragen zur dezentralen Konzernorganisation"; Theodor Wessels, "Wachsende Starrheit der Unternehmungen und ihre Ursachen"; Günther Danert, "Technische Grenzen dezentraler Betriebsorganisation."; E. Potthoff, "Die Leitungsorganisation deutscher Grossunternehmungen im Vergleich zum Westlichen Ausland."
106. Thanheiser, "Strategy and Structure in Germany," p. 141.
107. AEG-Telefunken and Siemens in the electro-mechanical industry reorganized their operations into formal multidivisional structures in 1962 and 1966.
108. The essential similarity between small series investment-good production in the electro-technical and in the machinery industries is noted in SOFI, *Tarifvertragliche Regelungen zur Verbesserung industrieller Arbeitsbedingungen,* pp. 277–305. The idea that the creation of multidivisional structures allows for better centralization of management within divisions is developed in Arthur Stinchcombe, *Information and Organizations,* pp. 100–151.
109. See the report on concentration in the construction machinery and agricultural machinery industries in Kommission der Europäischen Gemeinschaften, *Untersuchungen zur Konzentrationsentwicklung.* . . .
110. For a systematic comparison of the organization of machinery producers in autarkic and decentralized areas during the postwar period in West Germany, see my article "Industrial Order and the Politics of Industrial Change."
111. Peter Steinmüller, *Lage und Entwicklungschancen der deutschen Maschinenindustrie,* especially pp. 41 ff. For the MAN example, see p.194.
112. Hans Baumann, *Maschinenbau* pp. 18–24; see also the article by Justus Fürstenau, "Struktur und Strukturveränderung im Maschinenbau."
113. Ibid.
114. For a general discussion of the mechanics of this business, see Herman Walde and Gerd Berlinghoff, *Das Auslandsgeschäft mit Industrieanlagen.*
115. Dr. Alfred Lukac, "Der Einfluss von Währungsänderungen auf den Export."
116. Rolf Audouard, "Veränderte Exportvorausetzungen"; "Wirkung der Europäischen Wirtschaftsgemeinschaft und der Freihandelszone auf den deutschen Maschinenbau"; "Wettbewerb auf dem Gemeinsamen Markt"; "Kehren die alten Hand-

elsbilanzüberschusse wieder?"; "Warum stagniert Geschäft mit Mexiko?"; Hugo Rupf, "Maschinenfabrikanten sind keine Bankiers."

117. MAN's debt coefficient stood at 415% in the same year, Deutsche Babcock's at 357%. MAN's debt as a percentage of total sales was 66% in 1964, Deutsche Babcock's was 87%. See the interesting article by Dr. Rolf Hofmann, "Neue Probleme der Absatzfinanzierung."

118. See the reference in Dyas and Thanheiser, *The Emerging European Enterprise*, p. 121.

119. This story can be repeated in a variety of different versions. GHH, for example, allowed the Allianz Insurance company to purchase more than 50% of the holding company's stock for similar reasons. In other cases, such as Krupp in the early 1970s, firms sold large chunks of equity to Middle Eastern governments, in Krupp's case, to Iran. On Demag, see the articles by Egon Overbeck "Strukturwandel – Neue Chancen für die Unternehmen"; "Strukturwandel eines Unternehmens"; and Franz Josef Weisweiler, "Unternehmensgeschichte in der Produkt-Portfolio-Analyse."

120. See Bernhard Nagel and Hildegard Kaluza, *Eigentum und Markt im Maschinenbau*, pp. 28–47, for an overview of large-firm, both domestic German and foreign, holdings among large German machinery producers. The numbers reproduced in the text are taken from p. 31.

121. See the discussion in Chapter 5, pp. 178–181. Unfortunately, it is still necessary in this context to point out that the claim in the text is not that mass production no longer exists or is no longer possible. It is simply that it is no longer possible in the same way as it was during the 1950s and 1960s. Ironically, I can think of no better source on precisely this point than Michael Piore and Charles Sabel, *The Second Industrial Divide*.

122. The poor performance of the autarkic industrial order during the post-1974 period was at the root of the problematic north–south divide debate in Germany. The debate was problematic because there were successful regions located in the north (such as the decentralized regions west of the Rhine in North Rhine Westphalia) and economically troubled regions in the south (such as the regions surrounding the autarkic cities of Nuremberg and Augsburg in Bavaria). The kernel of truth in the debate, however, was that autarkic regions, which with the exception of Bavaria were primarily located north of the Main river, disproportionally experienced adjustment problems, while decentralized regions tended to perform better. The one partial exception to this rule is the Munich region, which prospered during the 1980s, largely on the basis of a strong state-sponsored push to develop high-tech military industries. On the north–south divide debate, see Hartmut Häußermann and Walter Siebel, *Neue Urbanität*; Jürgen Friedrichs, Hartmut Häußermann and Walter Siebel (eds.), *Süd–Nord-Gefälle in der Bundesrepublik?*

123. Other similar cases of industrial decline in autarkic areas are the coal industry and shipbuilding. On the latter, see Bo Strath, "Modes of Governance in the Shipbuilding Sector in Germany, Sweden and Japan."

124. Good overviews of the international situation in steel are presented in Walter H. Goldberg (ed.), *Ailing Steel. The Transoceanic Quarrel;* Trevor Bain, *Banking the Furnace*; Ray Hudson and David Sadler, *The International Steel Industry*. Eckart, *Die Eisen und Stahlindustrie*, p. 261, says that German steel producers have not had control of their investment in steel since the mid-1970s (ECSC has).

125. On plant closing in the industry in general, see Hudson and Sadler, *The Interna-*

Notes to pages 236–241   391

tional Steel Industry, pp. 94–101. For a case study of Hoesch in Dortmund, see Lutz Schröter, "Steelworks now!" For a broad quantitative survey of the gradual shrinkage of capacity, producers and employment in the industry, see Eckart, Eisen-und Stahlindustrie. . . .

126. Besides Eckart, the most comprehensive treatment of the crisis in the German steel industry is the book by Josef Esser, Wolfgang Fach, and Werner Väth, Krisenregulierung. On industrial symbolism in the Federal Republic of the 1980s, see Häußermann and Siebel, Neue Urbanität.

127. The following is drawn from a more elaborate theoretical discussion of the reorganization of the corporation with examples drawn from the international automobile industry presented in Charles Sabel, Horst Kern, and Gary Herrigel, "Kooperative Produktion"; and Gary Herrigel and Charles F. Sabel, "Craft Production in Crisis."

128. As noted in the previous chapter, the Japanese have been pioneers of these new techniques; see Aoki, Dore, Shingo, and Nishiguchi. There have also been numerous articles in the Harvard Business Review and the California Management Review over the last several years discussing the implementation of these techniques in western companies; cf., e.g., Robert Hayes and Ramchadran Jaikumar, "Manufacturing's Crisis"; Charles Handy "Balancing Corporate Power"; David A Garvin "Manufacturing Strategic Planning," all of which offer specific conceptions of the general process described in the text. The latter article refers to a more general literature.

129. On this kind of dynamic, in addition to Sabel at al., "Kooperative Produktion . . . , see, for example, Richard Norman and Rafael Ramires, "From Value Chain to Value Constellation."

130. This contextual situation was extensively studied during the 1980s, especially for the Ruhr. See GEWOS, GfAH, and WSI, Strukturwandel und Beschäftigungsperspektiven der Metallindustrie in der Ruhr; Hugo Kämper, "Arbeitslosigkeit im strukturschwachen Ruhrgebiet am Beispiel Essen"; German Bensch, "Auswirkungen kumulierter wirtschaftlicher Benachteiligung auf die Wirtschaftskraft eines Raumes"; Sabine Reichertz, "Verarmung durch Arbeitslosigkeit"; Franz Lehner, Jürgen Nordhause-Janz, and Klaus Schubert, Probleme und Perspektiven des Strukturwandels der Bergbau-Zulieferindustrie; idem, Die Bedeutung der Ruhrkohle AG für die wirtschaftliche Entwicklung des Ruhrgebietes; M. Krummacher, Th. Rommelspacher, and M. Weinemann, "Niedergang einer alten Industrieregion."

131. On this phenomenon in large firms see, Gary Herrigel, "Power in Industrial Districts."

132. Hort Kern and Charles Sabel discuss these dilemmas within large German firms in "Trade Unions and Decentralized Production."

133. There is a two-volume in-house history of the BMW AG by Horst Mönnich, BMW: Eine Jahrhundertgeschichte, which relates in far greater detail the history presented in the text.

134. Sabel et al., "Kooperative Produktion." See also Richard Lamming, "The Causes and Effects of Structural Change in the European Automotive Components Industry." For useful overviews of the European automobile industry in the 1980s, see James M. Laux, The European Automobile Industry, p. 217–252; and Gerald T. Bloomfield, "The world automotive industry in transition." On the German situation, see Reinhard Doeleschal, "Daten und Trends der bundesdeutschen Automobil-Zulieferindustrie."

135. The following paragraphs draw on numerous interviews conducted at BMW in Munich and Regensburg in the winter and spring of 1989.
136. In interviews, members of the purchasing department claimed that this was a complete reversal of the same percentages from a decade before.
137. On this, see *Manager Magazine*, May 1993, "Codewort Pretoria," p. 60–71.
138. The motorcycle group was no slouch either: BMW was the first producer in the world to apply ABS (anti-lock brakes) to motorcycles.
139. *Manager Magazine*, "Codewort Pretoria," p. 68 (graph). See also, Heinz Blüthmann, "Überholt und Abgehängt."
140. For some discussion of internal problems at BMW, see *Industrie-Magazine*, September 1990, "Ende Eines Schönen Traums," pp. 20–28.
141. On the general economic geography of the Munich area and its development since the mid-1970s, see I. Brechnier, E. Ohn, and K. M. Schmals, "Stadtentwicklung, Neu Technologien und Wandel der Arbeit in München."
142. For a short overview of labor agreements at Volkswagen during the late 1970s and 1980s, see Wolfgang Streeck, "Successful Adjustment in Turbulent Markets," pp. 129–134. See also Streeck's *Industrial Relations in West Germany*, which has a great deal of information about Volkswagen up to the early 1980s.
143. In addition to Streeck's work, ibid., see Lowell Turner, *Democracy at Work* and Kathleen Thelen, *Union of Parts*. All do excellent jobs in documenting different dimensions of the negotiations over and the implementation of workplace flexibility at VW. This was also the level of interest of the "New Production Concepts" literature in Germany. See the locus classicus by Horst Kern and Michael Schumann, *Ende der Arbeitsteilung?*
144. See Streeck, ibid., as well as Streeck, "On the Institutional Conditions of Diversified Quality Production."
145. Unless otherwise noted, much of what follows is based upon an extensive series of interviews at VW in Wolfsburg and Emden, which occurred in January and February 1989, and on unpublished protocols and presentations based upon a number of high-level interviews conducted by Horst Kern and Chuck Sabel at VW in Wolfsburg in May 1994.
146. Streeck, "Successful Adjustment...," pp. 132–133.
147. *Spiegel*, 40/1992, pp. 150–154; 31/1993, pp. 82–91; *Manager Magazine*, 4/1992, pp. 35–43; 12/1993, pp. 128–142.
148. *Manger Magazine*, 12/1993, pp. 133–135 – estimate is attributed to Juan Lopez, head of puchasing at VW.
149. *Der Spiegel*, 40/1992, pp. 150–154; 31/1993, pp. 82 ff; *Manager Magazine*, 4/1992, pp. 35 ff; 5/1992, p. 10 (table); *Economist Intelligence Unit. Business Europe*, 12/6/1993, "Can Volkswagen Cut Costs Without Shedding Jobs?" claims that a recent worktime reduction agreement hopes to make it unnecessary for the company to release up to 100,000 workers.
150. The characterization of the developments that follow is based upon a series of interviews at Mannesmann and Krupp, both in the central and at subsidiary companies during the mid-1980s. For published accounts of these developments, see, for example, Egon Overbeck, "Strukturwandel eines Unternehmens (Mannesmann)"; *Wirtschaftswoche*, 11, March 6, 1987, "Anschluss gesucht," pp. 128–134; *Manager Magazine*, 9/86, "Das Auge des Herrn," pp. 46–59; on Krupp, see *Manager Magazine*, 5/1990, "Eins, Zwei, Drei," pp. 64–79.

151. On Mannesmann, see *Wirtschaftswoche*, 11, März 6, 1987, pp. 128–134; *Manager Magazine*, 9/1986, pp. 46–59.
152. Though it occurred in all of the new *Kozerne*, each varied in the extent to which their holdings engaged in intra-*Kozerne* contracting.
153. For a general overview of these trends, see *Manager Magazine*, 10/1990, "Vom Diener zum Herrn," pp. 224–233; *Manager Magazine*, 1/19922, "Weg mit dem Wasserkopf," pp. 127–135.
154. On Mannesmann, see *Wirtschaftswoche*, 11, March 6, 1987, pp. 128–134. This article makes the point that the percentage share of steel pipes in the total sales of the *Kozerne* fell between 1975 and 1986 from 47% to less than 30%; see also *Manager Magazine*, 9/1986, pp. 46–59.
155. *Manager Magazine* article on VDO; *Reuter Textiline Computergram*, December 1990, on sale of Kienzle to DEC; *Reuter Textline Computergram*, August 20, 1993, on continued poor performance throughout the *Konzern* in first half of 1993.
156. On Krupp, in addition to ibid., see *Manager Magazine*, "Das Letzte Aufgebot," 7/1992, pp. 30–41; on Thyssen's troubled mechanical engineering holding, Thyssen Industrie AG of Essen, see *Frankfurter Allgemeine Zeitung*, 1/19/1994 ("Thyssen Industrie Turns Record Profit into Deficit in 1992/1993" – *Reuter Textline Translation*).
157. *Manager Magazine*, 5/1990, p. 76.
158. See the discussion of this in articles on Mannesmann in *Manager Magazine*, 6/1993, 1/1992, and 3/1992; on Krupp, see *Manager Magazine*, 7/1992 and 5/1990. On the competitive difficulties with too many products in the product palette, see Günter Roemmel et al., *Einfach Überlegen*.
159. The character and extent of this self-blockage within autarkic *Kozerne* naturally varied across individual operating units. Some units, such as the Krupp Kautex unit of the Krupp Maschinentechnik AG, located in the decentralized Rheinland, was able to decentralize production considerably more than were other units located in traditional autarkic regions. All Units, however, suffered from the temptation to socialize risk within the *Konzerne* rather than outside.
160. Virtually all of my information on this case comes from the excellent study of the Paderborn region by Josef Hilpert and Hans Joachim Sperling, *Die kleine Fabrik*. I thank Hans Joachim Sperling for numerous discussions of this case with me.
161. Ibid., pp. 50–52 and 80–88.
162. Ibid., pp. 48–50.
163. For an overview of Siemens Nixdorf's performance and an interview with the CEO, see John Riley, "Germany: Interview Hans Dieter Wiedig, Siemens Nixdorf"; for 1994 results, see Mick Elliot, "Germany: Siemens Issues Profit Warning – 1993 Results."
164. Hilpert and Sperling, *Kleine Fabrik*, pp. 50–52.
165. Ibid., pp. 48–50.

Notes for Chapter 7

1. Note that this chapter, like the previous two chapters, deals with the West German Federal Republic and not the East German Democratic Republic (GDR). The two countries were created after the war, when the occupying powers split into hostile

pro- and anticommunist factions. The territories occupied by the anticommunist western forces became postwar West Germany; that occupied by the communist eastern forces postwar East Germany. The GDR included the decentralized regions of Thüringen and Saxony and the autarkic regions of provincial Saxony, Brandenburg, Berlin, and the port city of Rostock. The west got the decentralized areas of Baden, Württemberg, the Rhein Main region, the western Rhineland, the Bergland, Siegerland, and the Sauerland. Western autarkic regions were the Ruhr, Northwest Westphalia, Niedersachsen, the port cities of Hamburg and Bremen, and Bavaria. Both countries also had agricultural regions to which these categories do not apply. Even before the division between the zones became formal, the then allies formally dissolved Prussia in 1947.

2. It was during the 1960s and early 1970s that the organized capitalism model of the German economy was at its most robust as a research program: The central institutions it highlighted were indeed shaping action at many levels of the political economy. Even the small- and medium-sized firms that later were recognized to be anomalies appeared at that time to be following a developmental logic that fit the paradigm. The previous two chapters show how this set of conditions in the economy was a very specific historical constellation. The present chapter will detail the macro-governance changes that occurred during the emergence and subsequent dissolution of this constellation. For references to the organized capitalism model of Germany see Chapter 1.

3. The latter was especially the case in the area that is now Baden Württemberg. These traditionally decentralized regions were divided into three separate political units, divided between two zones of military occupation. Moreover, the criterion used to draw the boundary between the French and American zones in southwest Germany was the location of an autobahn running from northwest to southeast that had strategic value for the American army. See Klaus Jürgen Matz, "Baden und Württemberg." Eventually, the three territories were combined into a single *Land*: Baden Württemberg. On this, see Gebhard Mueller, "Die Entstehung des Bundeslandes Baden Württemberg."

4. This is the entire and reasonably plausible argument made by Volker Schockenhoff, *Wirtschaftsverfassung und Grundgesetz*. It is also an important point about the federalism idea in liberal thought; see the insightful overview and discussion of the American context by Samuel Beer, "Federalism, Nationalism and Democracy in America." For one of the central points of criticism from the left see the antifederalist essay by Franz Neumann, "Zur Theorie des Föderalismus," pp. 207–223. See generally the good overview discussion by Ernst Deuerlein, *Föderalismus*, pp. 223–305.

5. See Neville Johnson, "Territory and Power," especially p. 14; and, most thoroughly, Udo Wengst, *Staatsaufbau und Regierungspraxis, 1948–1953*.

6. Deuerlein, *Föderalismus*; Schockenhoff, *Wirtschaftsverfassung und Grundgesetz*.

7. Again, this is the plausible argument made by Schockenhoff, op. cit. He overemphasizes this dimension of the negotiations, though.

8. Schockenhoff, *Wirtschaftsverfassung...*, pp. 209–210.

9. Section X, article 106a ("Verteilung des Steueraufkommens und des Ertrages der Finanzmonopole") of the *Grundgesetz für die Bundesrepublik Deutschland*, distributes the tax income in the following way:

To the Federal Government go Revenues from: government monopolies for matches and brandy, customs duties, consumer taxes (excluding those reserved for

Notes to pages 260–261

Land and local governments, or to common Federal–Land funds), transport taxes, taxes on stock market transactions, insurance, foreign currency transactions, onetime wealth taxes for postwar burden-sharing payments, special supplementary income and corporation taxes, and taxes raised for the EEC.

To the Länder go Revenues from: taxes on wealth, inheritance, automobiles, land, beer, and gambling casinos. The Länder may also sponsor lotteries.

To Both the Federal and Regional Governments Jointly go Revenues from: income, sales, and corporate taxes. Part of the income taxes collected in a given region are returned by law to the municipalities. Otherwise, income and corporate taxes are divided in half by the Federal Government and the Regional governments. The proportion of sales tax going to the Federal and Regional governments is set by law and is subject to the approval of the Bundesrat (as long as they are not otherwise designated to Land or Common funds).

10. Minister President Ehard of Bavaria presented his position in a letter to a federal minister named Pfeiffer in the following way:

> A satisfying solution would be dependent upon whether or not in the future federal state it will be possible to speak of a contribution of the Länder to the formation of the will of the federation (Bundeswille). An affirmative answer to this question depends both on the authority that this second chamber will have invested in it as well as on the character of its composition. It should have the character of an equally endowed legislative organ alongside the parliament. The Länder should be represented in the chamber by delegates who, for their part, should be the exponents of the democratic will of the Länder. A simple chamber without this arrangement for the representation of the Länder, even if it was given broad authority, such as equal legislative powers, would not provide a sufficient check on unitary and centralizing tendencies. An institution that has the characteristics of the much-touted senate would also be conceivable in a unitary state.

Quoted form Deuerlein, Föderalismus, p. 258. For more general discussions of the controversies surrounding the creation of a Bundesrat see Wengst, Staatsaufbau..., pp. 74–77 and John Ford Golay, The Founding of the Federal Republic of Germany, pp. 44–66.

11. Deuerlein, Föderalismus, p. 258.
12. See the discussion in Deuerlein, Föderalismus, pp. 136–140, for a discussion of the Imperial Bundesrat, pp. 171–177 for a discussion of federalism in Weimar, and pp. 266 ff for a comparison of the West German Bundesrat with its predecessors. A serviceable comparative historical discussion in English is given in Johnson, "Territory and Power," pp. 8–22.
13. For example, of helping small- and medium-sized producers to acquire technology and skills, to market their products in foreign markets and to prepare for longer-term challenges coming from other regions or other nations.
14. This seems fairly clear from a reading of the various postwar histories of chambers of commerce in decentralized regions. See, for example, the remarks of Wolfgang Köllman on the early attitudes and activities of the administrators within the Südwestfälischen Industrie und Handelskammer zu Hagen in his Die strukturelle Entwicklung des südwestfälischen Wirtschaftsraumes, 1945–1967, pp. 23 ff. On the general importance of local self-governance in the period immediately after the war, see Wilhelm Ribhegge, "Die Systemfunktion der Gemeinden," pp. 55 ff, and

Marie Elise Foelz-Schroeter, *Föderalistische Politik und nationale Representation 1945–1947*, who notes on p. 16 that in South Germany and in parts of West Germany "the desire for liberation from centralization imposed by the Nazi regime was dominant already by the time of the collapse. Correspondingly, these areas were very quick to assert their newly acquired independence."

15. Good discussions of the peculiarly German neo-liberal principles behind the new West German states' understanding of their relationship to the economy can be found in Hans Jaeger, *Geschichte der Wirtschaftsordnung in Deutschland*, pp. 223–233. There is also an excellent discussion in Elmar Altvater, Jürgen Hoffmann, and Willi Semmler, *Vom Wirtschaftswunder zur Wirtschaftskrise*, pp. 277–303. Perhaps the classic work of German neoliberalism is Walter Eucken, *Grundsätze der Wirtschaftspolitik*; Erhard's famous statement of his views is *Wohlstand für Alle*.

16. The best source on this is Henry Wallich, *Mainsprings of the German Miracle*. See also the corroborative account, albeit from the left, in Altvater, Hoffmann, and Semmler, *Vom Wirtschaftswunder...*, pp. 289–293.

17. See the discussion in previous chapter and general treatment in Gary Herrigel, *Industrial Organization and the Politics of Industry*, Chapter 3.

18. One reading might suggest that this is all that the Austrian economists thought prices were anyway. See the interesting overview of the views of Hayek and von Mises on this matter presented in a discussion of the famous planning debate by Don Lavoie, *Rivalry and Central Planning: The Socialist Calculation Debate Reconsidered*. For a very interesting discussion of the principles that govern the market world and the interpersonal world at both macro and micro levels of analysis, see Michael Storper and Robert Salais, *Worlds of Production*.

19. The German neoliberal school continually emphasized the need to focus economic policy and the state on the maintenance of an adequate environment within which "competition" could occur stably and in a way that fostered prosperity and growth. This was far preferable to the direct intervention in the decision-making processes of individual producers. For a theoretical explication, see Walter Eucken, *Grundsätze der Wirtschaftspolitik*, Book Four, pp. 241–324.

20. In addition to Chapter 4, see for an overview Jaeger, *Geschichte der Wirtschaftsordnung*.

21. This reasoning is taken from Michael Piore and Charles Sabel, *The Second Industrial Divide*, p. 76 ff. The notion, however, that large mass producing firms are oriented not toward profit but toward market share is a widely held one, or at least was when companies pursued mass-production strategies. The locus classicus is perhaps John Kenneth Galbraith, *The New Industrial State*. For a German view from that time, which believes that this is the case and regrets it, see Hans Otto Lenel, *Ursachen der Konzentration unter besonderer Berücksichtigung der deutschen Verhältnisse*. See also Dieter Grosser, ed., *Konzentration ohne Kontrolle*. Finally, see Storper and Salais, *Worlds of Production*, chapter 2, for an excellent discussion of the different governance problems in a mass-production system (what they call "the industrial world") relative to ones dominated by specialty production.

22. Piore and Sabel, *Second Industrial Divide*, pp. 76–77, and Storper and Salais, *Worlds of Production*, Chapters 2 and 10.

23. The Germans define the "metal industry" as including the following: five production-goods industries (iron and steel, nonferrous metals, foundries, cold rolling mills, and wire and wire products); twelve investment-goods industries (e.g., machinery, electrical equipment, appliances and electronics, motor vehicles, iron and

metalwares, steel construction, aerospace, shipbuilding, precision instruments, and watches), and one consumer-goods industry (musical instruments and recreational equipment). Each one of the sectors belonging to these industries can, naturally, be broken down into additional individual sectors.

24. On the Bremen agreement as the beginning of centralized national-level wage bargaining in postwar West Germany, see Kathleen Thelen, *Union of Parts*, pp. 81 ff. Thelen does a nice job of distinguishing German quasi-corporatism from other more centralized full blown versions. For more detailed standard accounts of this early phase of the postwar labor movement see Theo Pirker, *Die Blinde Macht*, especially Vol 2, Chapter 3 on centralization; Andrei S. Markovits, *The Politics of West German Trade Unions*, pp. 183–194; and a good overview of the development of wage bargaining in Germany is given in Joachim Bergmann, Otto Jacobi, and Walther Mueller-Jentsch, *Gewerkschaften in der Bundesrepublik* pp.175–206. The initial period is discussed on pp. 185–189. Also, a very good, brief, analysis of the development of wage rates in Germany is contained in William Fellner, ed., *The Problem of Rising Prices*, especially pp. 323–355.
25. All of this information is taken from the excellent book by Peter Ullmann, *Tarifverträge und Tarifpolitik in Deutschland bis 1914*, table 9, (p. 231) and p. 100.
26. Notoriously, there were no agreements between the Ruhr steel producers and organized labor. Unions also found it difficult to gain a foothold in the large autarkic electrical-equipment producers. See Elizabeth Domansky-Davidsohn, "Der Grossbetrieb als Organisationsproblem des Deutschen Metallarbeiter-Verbandes vor dem Ersten Weltkrieg." On the geographic distribution of trade union organization in Imperial Germany, see Klaus Schönhoven, *Expansion und Konzentration*, especially part two, pp. 91–149. Lothar Wentzel's study of the DMV provides an overview of the pre-War distribution of representation of the union which shows the two main strengths of the unions to be in small- and medium-sized firms in decentralized areas or in large producers in the machinery and shipbuilding industries: Lothar Wentzel, *Inflation und Arbeitslosigkeit*, pp. 16–33. Markovits points out that the strongholds of the pre–1914 Deutsche Metallarbeiter Verband (DMV) were "in the machinery industries of southern (Baden, Württemberg, northern Bavaria) and central (Saxony, Hesse, Hannover) Germany and Berlin as well as the shipbuilding centers of Hamburg, Bremen, Kiel." see Markovits, *The Politics of the West German Trade Unions*, p. 181.
27. Dick Geary, "Socialism and the German Labor Movement before 1914."
28. On the Weimar system of collective bargaining, see *Deutsche Sozialpolitik 1918–1928*; Hans Hermann Hartwich, *Arbeitsmarkt, Verbände und Staat 1918–1933*, pp. 23–44, 193–230. Hartwich points out that it is difficult to precisely determine how many workers were actually affected by state-imposed binding agreements, but the amount seems in any case to have been high. See also Ludwig Preller, *Sozialpolitik in der Weimarer Republik*, especially pp. 150–164, 180–203.
29. Ullmann, *Tarifverträge...*, p. 101. James notes that "in January 1928 out of a total of 17m employed in Germany, 1.4m workers were covered by Reich contracts and 3.4m by regional agreements," but the source he cites (*Deutsche Sozialpolitik, 1918-1928*, p. 47), actually refers only to contracts subject to Generally Binding Declarations on the part of the Reichsarbeitsministerium. See Harold James, *The German Slump*, p. 210.
30. According to Thelen, "The IG Metall's collective bargaining rounds in the first years of the Federal Republic were organized along industrial lines, but fought on

a regional basis. Regional union officers enjoyed great autonomy in formulating their demands and strategies, and regional bargaining proceeded with little or no coordination by the central union"; *Union of Parts*, p. 81.

31. This line of development is broadly in accord with Peter Swenson's argument that centralized, national-level bargaining becomes possible when product markets and labor markets begin to be national in character. See Peter Swenson, *Fair Shares*, pp. 31–70. Swenson's argument owes a lot to Lloyd Ulman's classic work *The Rise of the National Trade Union*. In the particular case of the Bremen agreement two factors seem to have been important in making that particular agreement the one that initiated national-level negotiations. First, the labor market in Germany was beginning to tighten, with unemployment falling to 4.0% by the end of the year. Second, IG Metall made it clear to the employers that it was willing to negotiate labor-time issues and wage issues together, implicitly indicating that it was willing to take the national macroeconomic situation into account in making an agreement. Compare on this Bergmann, Jacobi, and Mueller-Jentsch, *Gewerkschaften...*, pp. 189 ff.

32. The "para-public" reference is to Peter Katzenstein's view of the importance of such centralized institutions in German society. See his analysis of Germany as a decentralized state and centralized society in *Policy and Politics in West Germany*. Katzenstein discusses the industrial relations system in Chapter 3.

33. Bergmann, Jacobi, and Mueller-Jentsch, *Gewerkschaften...*, pp. 192–197. For a very interesting discussion of the key relationship between productivity and demand under a mass-production regime, see Robert Boyer and Pascal Petit, "The Cumulative Growth Model Revisited."

34. This shift in the self-understanding of the union is noted in Bergmann, Jacobi, and Mueller-Jentsch, *Gewerkschaften...*, pp. 120–154, especially 134 ff.

35. Markovits, *The Politics of West German Trade Unions*, pp. 108–109; Eberhard Schmidt, *Ordnungsfaktor oder Gegenmacht*, pp. 69–80.

36. There are many discussions of the Bavarian metalworkers strike; for one good one see Pirker, *Die Blinde Macht*, vol. II, Chapter 3.

37. For a discussion of the organization of IG Metall, see Projektgruppe Gewerkschaftsforschung, *Rahmenbedingungen der Tarifpolitik. Band 1*, pp. 82–100 and Markovits, *The Politics of the West German Trade Unions*, pp. 174–179.

38. See Rainer Zoll, *Partizipation oder Delegation*, pp. 30–35.

39. This was particularly true in the areas of unemployment, continuing education, workplace health and safety regulations, factory inspections, and accident insurance. Indeed, "[f]or all branches of the trade union movement'," notes Wolfgang Mommsen about the pre-World War I movement, "whatever their political persuasion, direct confrontation at the workshop was subordinate to the general objective of social reform" ("The Free Trade Unions and Social Democracy in Imperial Germany," p. 371). On the educational activities of the trade unions in the Weimar Republic, see W. L. Guttsmann, *Workers Culture in Weimar Germany*, pp. 66 ff, and notes.

40. See the debate on this issue reprinted in Zoll, *Partizipation oder Delegation*, pp. 207–211. This was, moreover, in 1948 when it was still very plausible to think that the unions would have a direct connection with plant-based works councils. The decision to create locality based *Verwaltungsstellen*, therefore, was in this way an explicit recognition by the union of the sovereign importance of the local or "regional" dimension of the union's activities.

41. See Oskar Negt, Christine Morgenroth, Heiko Geiling, and Edzard Niemeyer, *Emanzipationsinteressen und Organisationsphantasie*, which discusses the significance of local cartels of trade unions, *Ortskartelle*, in the early years of the Federal Republic. In the initial years of military occupation and political and economic reconstruction of Germany, the DGB had very ambitious goals for establishing an extrafirm position in local and regional economies. Peter Hubsch details their explicit efforts to create trade union analogues to chambers of commerce at local, regional, and national levels in the British Zone of Occupation. See Hubsch, "DGB Economic Policy with Particular Reference to the British Zone, 1945-1949."
42. On the interest representational role of IG Metall *Verwaltungsstellen* in collective bargaining, see Projektgruppe Gewerkschaftsforschung, *Rahmenbedingungen...*, pp. 89 ff.
43. Most recently on works councils, see Thelen, *Union of Parts*, passim, but on the general history of their postwar reconstitution in particular see pp. 63–83. See also Rainer Zoll, *Partizipation oder Delegation*, pp. 41f.
44. On the considerable maneuvering to achieve and maintain this close relationship, see: Thelen, *Union of Parts*, pp. 74–83; Pirker, *Blinde Macht*, vol. II, Chapters 1–3; Schmidt, *Ordnungsfaktor oder Gegenmacht*, pp. 12–47; Markovits, *The Politics of the West German Trade Unions*, pp. 72–83, 183–194, 288–295, 337–341, 385–400; and Reinhard Krusche and Dagmar Pfeiffer, "Probleme der Gewerkschaftspolitik 1945–1965."
45. Thelen, *Union of Parts*, p. 80.
46. A detailed description of the institutional mechanics of I.G. Metall's bargaining practice is given in Projektgruppe Gewerkschaftsforschung, *Rahmenbedingungen...*, pp. 82–100.
47. Between 1960 and 1970 in the Metalworking industry the collectively bargained wage rate increased at an average annual rate of 7.3%, while the effective wage rate (including wage drift) increased at an annual average rate of 9.4% Thelen, *Union of Parts*, p. 82.
48. See the generally good account of this transformation of political attitudes regarding macroeconomic policy making at the beginning of the 1960s in Volker Berghahn, *Unternehmer und Politik in der Bundesrepublik*, pp. 279–301. Generally, Berghahn's view is that the change became possible 1) because there was a sectoral shift in the weight of finishing-industry sectors versus heavy industry sectors within the economy. The former had more modern, "American" attitudes (although they created a national-level corporatist mechanism known as *Konzertierte Aktion*); and 2) there was a generational change within German industry generally, which brought more westernized characters into power within the corporations. I discount the importance of some sort of shift in cultural attitudes, preferring instead to believe that the Germans were responding to historically unique problems of mass production, which they countered with the institutional, cultural, political, etc. resources that were available to them. They redefined and recomposed their traditional practices and beliefs, and borrowed the same from elsewhere to find workable solutions. I guess, in a word, what I think is most interesting about the postwar German economy is how "un-Americanized" it actually remained.

   Altvater, Hoffmann, and Semmler, *Vom Wirtschaftswunder...*, pp. 303–323, also have an excellent discussion of the transformation of macroeconomic policy making in the 1960s. Another terrific source is the insightful, and tragically unpublished, dissertation by Jeremiah Riemer, *Crisis and Intervention in the West German Economy*.

49. See the discussion of the development of union attitudes about wage bargaining and Keynesianism in Bergman, Jacobi, and Mueller-Jentsch, *Gewerkschaften in der Bundesrepublik*, pp. 132–139. See also the interesting essays by Otto Brenner, head of IG Metall during the 1960s, in Otto Brenner, *Gewerkschaftliche Dynamik in unserer Zeit*, especially pp. 5–43, 147–151, and 161 ff.
50. Institute für Weltwirtschaft, Kiel; Weltwirtschaftliches Institut, Hamburg; Rhein-Westfälisches Institute für Wirtschaftsforschung, Essen; Institute for Economic Research in Berlin; and the IFO-Institute für Wirtschaftsforschung, Munich.
51. Riemer is very good on this council and its theoretical genealogy and predilections. See his article "Alterations in the Design of Model Germany."
52. Schonfield, *Modern Capitalism*, pp. 287–88.
53. See the very thorough discussion of the Formierte Gesellschaft speech in Reinhard Opitz, "Der grosse Plan der CDU"; Berghahn, *Unternehmer und Politik* ..., pp. 286 ff; Altvater, Hoffmann and Semmler, *Vom Wirtschaftswunder* ..., pp. 303–309.
54. See Riemer, "Alterations...," and Berghahn, *Unternehmer und Politic...*, pp. 288 ff for different but overlapping accounts of the crisis.
55. Peter Katzenstein reprints an english translation of this law, formally called "The Law for the Promotion of the Stability and Growth of the Economy" in his, *Policy and Politics in West Germany*, pp. 110–112.
56. Riemer, "Alterations...," and Jack H. Knott, *Managing the German Economy Budgetary Politics in a Federal State*, Chapters 1, 5 and 6.
57. A good discussion of the difficulties involved in coordinating the spending of federal and local governments within federal system in general and pre-1969 Germany in particular is given in Knott, *Managing the German Economy*..., pp. 103–126.
58. The federal rulings on Investionshilfe are in Article 104a IV of the Basic law. Arthur Gunlicks, *Local Government in the German Federal System*, pp. 125 and 184 ff, has a good discussion of the characteristics of the law. See also Hellmut Wollmann, "Investionshilfen."
59. Knott, *Managing the German Economy*, p. 109. There is also an excellent discussion of all of the aspects of these reforms in an article by Ulrich Scheuener, "Kooperation und Konflikt."
60. Scheuner emphasizes this dual aspect of the reforms in "Kooperation und Konflikt."
61. In large part this forbearance on the part of centralizers was grounded in the basic law: Article 79 III bars constitutional amendments affecting the federalist organization of the Federal Republic.
62. Heidenheimer, "Federalism...," pp. 809–828, describes the way in which this process began during the late 1950s.
63. The best discussion of this phenomenon in German politics during the 1970s is Gerhard Lehmbruch, "Party and Federation in Germany." This article is a summary of his book, *Parteienwettbewerb im Bundesstaat*.
64. Radical proposals to democratize the universities and to make them more accessible to working-class youth were not even drafted as a bill, despite widespread support within the Social Democratic Party, because it was clear that the CDU dominated

Bundesrat would veto it. See Gerald Braunthal, *The West German Social Democrats, 1969–82.*
65. See the discussion of the Gesamthochschule in J. Kluver, W. Jost, and K-L Hesse, *Gesamthochschule – Versäumte Chancen?*; and Peter Faultisch and Hartmut Wegener, *Gesamthochschule: Zukunftsmodell oder Reformruine?*. See Gerard Braunthals discussion of the Educational Reforms of the 1970s in his *The West German Social Democrats*, pp. 252–256. Autarkic Saarland and agrarian Schleswig Holstein, Bavaria, and Rheinland Pfalz also refused to back the reforms, also out of federalist resentment of the intrusion of the socialist central state.
66. See Faustich and Wegener, *Gesamthochschule...*, for a case study of the reform in the autarkic region around Kassel in Hesse.
67. Schonfield, *Modern Capitalism*; Peter Katzenstein, ed., *Between Power and Plenty*, conclusion; idem, *Small States in World Markets*, especially in context of remarks on p. 31; idem, *Policy and Politics in West Germany*; Wolfgang Streeck, *Gewerkschaftliche Organisationsprobleme in der sozialstaatlichen Demokratie*; idem, *Industrial Relations in West Germany*; Claus Offe, "The Attribution of Public Status to Interest Groups."
68. See, e.g., Gerald Feldman, *Iron and Steel in the German Inflation*; Charles Maier, *Recasting Bourgeois Europe*; Jürgen Kocka, *Klassengesellschaft im Krieg, 1914–1918*. See also the essays in Heinrich Winkler, ed., *Organisierter Kapitalismus*.
69. See Fritz Scharpf's *Politische Immobilismus und ökonomische Krise*, and idem, *Politische Durchsetzbarkeit innerer Reformen*.
70. The Germans, of course, effectively abandoned the political commitment to manage the economy in the interest of full employment when the central bank (Bundesbank) sacrificed everything to the fight against inflation brought on by the first oil crisis. See John Bispham and Andrea Boltho, "Demand Management," especially pp. 308f.
71. See the very succinct account of these changes, and of their consequences for macroeconomic policy, in Fritz Scharpf, *Crisis and Choice in European Social Democracy*, pp. 238–255. Scharpf writes: "According to 'Domar's Law,' when real interest rates rise above the real growth rate (and thus above the growth of tax income), the escalation of debts service must progressively limit fiscal maneuverability." (p. 245).
72. On the regional distribution of unemployment in the Germany of the 1980s, see the essays in Jürgen Friedrichs, Hartmut Häußermann, and Walter Siebel, eds., *Süd-Nord-Gefälle in der Bundesrepublik?*
73. The rate of return on financial investments in global markets was so high that it discouraged many forms of real (and job-creating) productive investments. If real investment was therefore a policy goal, the government had to create conditions that were attractive to investors. See Scharpf, *Crisis and Choice...*, pp. 246–249.
74. See the account in Chapter 5.
75. These are, moreover, trends that can be found throughout the advanced industrial countries. On the decentralization of industrial policy, see Linda Hesselman, "Trends in European Industrial Intervention"; Bob Jessop, et al., *The Politics of Flexibility*; Peter K. Eisinger, *The Rise of the Entrepreneurial State*. On decentralization in industrial relations, see Richard Locke, "The Resurgence of the Local Union: Industrial Restructuring and Industrial Relations in Italy"; and Wolfgang Streeck, "The Uncertainties of Management in the Management of Uncertainty."

76. Compare Heinz Laufer, *Das föderative System der Bundesrepublik Deutschland*, pp. 216-220; Ernst Bartholome, "Starkung der Eigenstaatlichkeit und Eigenverantwortlichkeit der *Länder* notwendig" pp. 504-508; Hans Uwe Erichsen, "Bund und *Länder* im Bundesstaat des Grundgesetzes."
77. For an exhaustive list of the problems with joint policy making, see Fritz Scharpf, "Die Politikverflechtungs-Falle."
78. This was both in many cases legally required, as in the area of common expenditure projects (*Gemeinschaftsaufgaben*), and politically induced by the demands of party politics.
79. Arthur Benz, "Intergovernmental Relations in the 1980s," p. 206; and Scharpf, Reissert, and Schnabel, *Politikverflechtung*, pp. 218-233.
80. On the austerity of German Social Democrats and the shift to Christian Democratic neoliberalism, see Kenneth Dyson, "Economic Policy."
81. Hartmut Klatt, "Reform und Perspectiven des Föderalismus in der Bundesrepublik Deutschland." See also Lothar Späth, *Die Chancen der Vielfalt: die Föderalismus als moderne Staatsform*.
82. See for example the early report on Baden Württemberg's *Mittelstand*-dominated economy in *Industriemagazine*, December 1976, pp. 83-97 (Sonderteil: Baden Württemberg). In particular see the article "BAWEX: Die Mittelstands-Genossen suchen im Export ihr wirtschaftliches Heil," p. 96 on the young Lothar Späth's new export agency for the industrial *Mittelstand*. This kind of early policy innovation soon resulted in a desire for greater autonomy from the *Bund*.
83. Arthur Benz, *Föderalismus als dynamisches System*.
84. On industrial policies, see, e.g., Karl Reuss, "Die Klassische Gewerbeförderung vor neuen Aufgaben"; and on social policy, Bernd Reissert, "Finanzielle Spielräume für kommunale Beschäftigungspolitik." On the evolution of technology policy, see Edgar Grande, "Die Erosion staatlicher Handlungskapazität?."
85. Benz, "Intergovernmental Relation...," pp. 218-219.
86. Richard Deeg, *Banks and the State in Germany*, p. 251.
87. Ibid., note 30.
88. See references to regional policy in Baden Württemberg in Chapter 5. An excellent study of regional policy problems in the Ruhr is Sybille Stöbe, *Regionalpolitik im Ruhrgebiet und in Nord-Pas de Calais*, pp. 26-100.
89. A good discussion of regional policy debates, especially regarding innovation policies, that pays attention to the influence of Baden Württemberg is the recent dissertation by Robert Hassink, *Regional Innovation Policy*. See also the paper by Philip Cooke and Kevin Morgan, "Industry, Training and Technology Transfer"; and Ulrich Hilpert, ed., *Regional Innovation and Decentralization*. Chuck Sabel is the source of the Schleswig Holstein reference.
90. See Bernhard Blanke, Aldabert Evers, and Hans Wollmann, eds., *Die Zweite Stadt*; and Hartmut Häußermann and Walter Siebel, *Neue Urbanität*.
91. For a range of arguments on the left, see Thomas Schmid, ed., *Entstatlichung*; and Josef Esser and Joachim Hirsch, "Stadtsoziologie und Gesellschaftstheorie." For conservative arguments, see Lothar Späth, *Wende in die Zukunft*; and Thomas Krueder, and Hanno Löwy, eds., *Konservativismus in der Strukturkrise*.
92. Fritz Scharpf, "Der *Bundesrat* und die Kooperation auf der 'dritten Ebene'" pp. 121-162; and idem, "Entwicklungslinien des bundesdeutschen Föderalismus." Scharpf actually argues for even greater decentralization and *Länder* autonomy. See also Renate Mayntz, *Föderalismus und die Gesellschaft der Gegenwart*.

Notes to pages 280–284

93. For excellent overviews of the trends in German Federalism since the unification, see Hartmut Klatt, "German Unification and the Federal System"; Ulrich Exler, "Financing German Federalisms"; Manfred G. Schmidt, "Die politische Verarbeitung der deutschen Vereinigung im Bund-*Länder*-Verhältnis"; and Arthur Benz, "Reformbedarf und Reformchancen des kooperativen Föderalismus nach der Vereinigung."
94. These remarks are based on a round of interviews conducted in Baden Württemberg in June and July of 1994. For an interesting discussion of regional industrial policy in the crisis, see Klaus Semlinger, "Industrial District Politik in Baden Württemberg."
95. See most recently Lowell Turner, *Democracy at Work*; and Thelen, *Union of Parts*. Much of their analyses follow the lead of Wolfgang Streeck, e.g.: "Industrial Relations and Industrial Change"; idem, "Successful Adjustment in Turbulent Markets"; and idem, "Co-determination."
96. Scharpf, *Crisis and Choice*..., pp. 117–157; Gerhard Leithäuser, "Crisis Despite Flexibility," especially pp.181 ff and Altvater, Hoffmann and Semmler, *Vom Wirtschaftswunder*..., Chapter 13, pp. 324–341.
97. The most succinct discussion of the effect of unemployment on collective bargaining in Germany is Wolfgang Streeck, "Neocorporatist Industrial Relations and the Economic Crisis in West Germany." On the general political economic context for German unions in the 1970s and early 80s, see Thelen, *Union of Parts*, pp. 112–121; and Josef Esser, *Gewerkschaften in der Krise*.
98. For a good outline of these challenges, see Charles F. Sabel, "Struktureller Wandel der Produktion und neue gewerkschaftliche Strategien."
99. Thelen, *Union of Parts*, p. 161, and note 6.
100. The best discussion of the work-time issue in the German trade union movement is in Thelen, *Union of Parts*, pp. 155–179. The 1990 agreement committed employers to lower the weekly working time to 35 hours by October 1995.
101. This is Thelen's argument in *Union of Parts*.
102. Thelen, *Union of Parts*, p. 179.
103. One could argue that central bargaining survived during the 1980s because the unions enjoyed a set of favorable conjunctural conditions in the economy. In particular, the IG Metall's bargaining power rested on the existence of virtual full employment in Baden Württemberg at a time when the general economic conditions in Germany were generally good. In this way, the union possessed considerable disruptive power, despite high unemployment nationally. Take this market power away, for whatever reasons, and it is not clear why the employers would continue to be interested in engaging in central bargaining that essentially shoves the bulk of the issues down to the local level. Why not simply deal with them at the local level? Consequences deriving from the evaporation of this market power in the 1990s are addressed below.
104. Much of this argument comes from my discussions with Charles Sabel and Horst Kern, together with whom I conducted in 1989 and 1990 an array of interviews with managers, works councils and unionists in a variety of sectors and regions concerning the problem of subcontracting and decentralized production. For the results of this research see, Charles Sabel, Horst Kern, and Gary Herrigel, "Kooperative Produktion"; and Horst Kern and Charles Sabel, "Trade Unions and Decentralized Production."
105. A fascinating description of these kinds of workers in the electronics industry can

be found in Ulli Voskamp and Volker Wittke, "Junge Facharbeiter in der Produktion – eine Herausforderung für die Gestaltung der betrieblichen Arbeitsorganisation."
106. The most extensive discussion of the new forms of workers in German plants, and the problems generated by efforts to implement new work arrangements, is Michael Schumann, et al., *Trendreport Rationalisierung*.
107. I would like to keep the specific location of this local anonymous. The interview was conducted in July 1990, during the summer deliberations over the reunification of Germany. The head of the IG Metall local, in the course of an extensive discussion of the degree of control the central union attempts to exercise over the activities of the locals, remarked that the "IG Metall was probably the last remaining Stalinist organization in Germany."

Bibliography

Aachener Werkzeugmaschinen-Kolloquium, "Entwicklung im Werkzeugmaschinenbau." Essen: Giradet, 1956.
Abegglen, James C., and George Stalk, Jr., *Kaisha: The Japanese Corporation*. New York: Basic Books, 1985.
Abel, Wilhelm, *Geschichte der deutschen Landwirtschaft*. Stuttgart: Eugen Ulmer, 1963.
Abelshauser, Werner, *Wirtschaftsgeschichte der Bundesrepublik, 1945–1980*. Frankfurt: Suhrkamp, 1983.
Abraham, David, *The Collapse of the Weimar Republic*. Princeton: Princeton University Press, 1981.
Abrams, Philip, and E. A. Wrigley (eds.), *Towns in Society. Essays in History and Historical Sociology*. Cambridge: Cambridge University Press, 1978.
Adelmann, Gerhard, "Die berufliche Aus- und Weiterbildung in der deutschen Wirtschaft 1871–1918." In *Die berufliche Aus- und Weiterbildung in der deutschen Wirtschaft set dem 19. Jahrhundert*. Hans Pohl (ed.). Wiesbaden: Franz Steiner, 1979.
Adelmann, Gerald, "Die Stadt Bielefeld als Zentrum fabrikindustrieller Standortfactor." In *Vom Gewerbe zur Industrie im kontinentalen Nordwesteuropa*. Gerald Adelmann (ed.). Wiesbaden: Steiner, 1986.
Albrecht, Karl, "Gemeinsamer Markt und Freihandelzone im Urteil deutscher Wirtschaftskreise." *Aussenwirtschaft. Zeitschrift für internationale Wirtschaftsbeziehungen* 12(3) (1957): 154–169.
Alchian, Armen, *Economic Forces at Work*. Indianapolis: Liberty Press, 1977.
Almond, Gabriel, and Sidney Verba, *The Civic Culture*. Boston: Little Brown, 1962.
Altvater, Elmar, Jürgen Hoffmann and Willi Semmler, *Vom Wirtschaftswunder zur Wirtschaftskrise. Ökonomie und Politik in der Bundesrepublik*. Berlin: Olle & Wolter, 1980.
Amin, Ash, and Kevin Robins, "Industrial Districts and Regional Development: Limits and Possibilities." In *Industrial Districts and Inter-Firm Cooperation in Italy*. Frank Pyke, G. Beccattini, and W. Sengenberger (eds.). Geneva: International Institute for Labor Studies, 1990, pp. 185–219.
Amsden, Alice, *Asia's Next Giant: South Korea and Late Industrialization*. New York: Oxford University Press, 1989.
Anon., "Die deutsche Maschinenindustrie auf dem europäischen Märkten." *Maschinenbau. Wirtschaftlicher Teil* 9.5 (1930): w53–w55.
Anon., "Der Weltmarkt in Maschinen. Seine Verteilung unter die drei Hauptausfuhrländer." *Maschinenbau. Wirtschaftlicher Teil* 9.2 (1930): w13–w16.

Anon., "Spezialfabrik oder gemischter Betrieb? Ein Beitrage zur Frage des Gespräges der Specialfabrik." *Technik und Wirtschaft* 29 (1936): 37–42.
Anon., "Investieren und Exportieren." *Der Volkswirt* (1949).
Anon., "Kraftfahrzeugindustrie im Wettbewerb." *Der Volksiwrt* 48 (1950): 19–20.
Anon., "Warum stagniert Geschäft mit Mexiko? Ausschlaggebender Einfluss der Vereinigten Staaten." *Aussenhandelsdienst*, January 4 (1952).
Anon., "Die Automatisierung—Möglichkeiten und gewerkschaftspolitische Konsequenzen." *Der Gewerkschafter* 5 (1955): 16–19.
Anon., "Die Automatisierung. Ein Kennzeichen des 20. Jahrhunderts." *VDI-Nachrichten* April 14 (1956): 4 ff.
Anon., "Handwerk-Partner der Industrie. Als Zulieferer heute unentbehrlich. In Spezialitäten ganz gross." *VDI-Nachrichten* 45, November 4 (1964): 22.
Anon., "Das Auge des Herrn." *Manager Magazin*, September (1986): 46–59.
Anon., "Anschluss gesucht." *Wirtschaftswoche*, 11 (March 6) (1987): 128–134.
Anon., "Vom Diener zum Herrn." *Manager Magazin*, October (1990): 224–233.
Anon., "Ende Eines Schönen Traums." *Industrie-Magazine*, September (1990): 20–28.
Anon., "Eins, Zwei, Drei." *Manager Magazin*, May (1990): 64–79.
Anon., "Weg mit dem Wasserkopf." *Manager Magazin*, January (1992): 127–135.
Anon., "Codeword Pretoria." *Manager Magazine*, May (1993): 60–71.
Aoki, Masahiko, *Information, Incentives and Bargaining in the Japanese Economy*. New York: Cambridge University Press, 1988.
Arndt, Helmut et al., *Konzentration ohne Kontrolle Kritik*. Dieter Grosser (ed.). Koln: Westdeutscher Verlag, 1969.
Arnst, E., "75 Jahre Fortschritt in der deutschen Elektroindustrie." *Elektrotechnik*, 48 (1966).
Ashworth, W. A., "Typologies and Evidence: Has Nineteenth Century Europe a Typology of Growth?" *Economic History Review, 2nd Series*, 30 (1977).
Association of German Economic Research Institutes, "The Economic Situation in Germany." *Intereconomics* 27(6) November/December (1992): 301–304.
Atkinson, Rick, "Germany Forced to Reexamine Key Elements of Economy." *Washington Post*, Tuesday, August 9, 1994: A12.
Audouard, Rolf, "Veränderte Exportvorausetzungen." *Der Volkswirt*, "Deutsche Wirtschaft im Querschnitt: Maschinenbau." *Beilage to Number 28*, September 24 (1955).
Audouard, Rolf, "Wirkung der Europäischen Wirtschaftsgemeinschaft und der Freihandelszone auf den deutschen Maschinenbau." *Wirtschaftsdienst*, 9 (1957): 514–518.
Audouard, Rolf, "Wettbewerb auf dem Gemeinsamen Markt. Ein Gespräch zwischen Vertretern verschiedener Wirtschaftszweige." *Wirtschaftsdienst*, 12 (1959): 667–671.
Audouard, Rolf, "Kehren die alten Handelsbilanzüberschusse wieder? Deutschlands Ausfuhrsituation aus der Sicht der Praxis. Interview mit dem stellv. Hauptgeschäftsführer des VDMA, Rolf Audouard." *Wirtschaftsdienst*, 2 (1966).
Ausschuss, Enquette, *Verhandlungen und Berichte des Unterausschusses für allgemeine Wirtschaftsstruktur: Wandlungen in den wirtschaftlichen Organisationsformen: Wandlungen in den Rechtsformen der Einzelunternehmungen und Konzerne*. Berlin: Mittler und Sohn, 1928.
Ausschuss, Enquette, *Die deutsche Chemische Industrie: verhandlungen und Berichte des Unterausschusses für Gewerbe: Industrie, Handel und Handwerk* (III Unterausschuss). Berlin: Mittler und Sohn, 1930a.
Ausschuss, Enquette, *Die deutsche eisenerzeugende Industrie: Verhandlungen und Be-

richte des Unterausschusses für Gewerbe: Industrie, Handel und Handwerk. Berlin: E. S. Mittler und Sohn, 1930b.
Ausschuss, Enquette, *Die innere Verflechtung der deutschen Wirtschaft*. Berlin: E. S. Mittler und Sohn, 1930c.
Ausschuss, Enquette, *Entwicklungslinien der industriellen und gewerblichen Kartellierung. Erster Abschnitt: Arbeitsplan, Maschinenbau*. Berlin: E. S. Mittler und Sohn, 1928.
Ausschuss, Enquette, *Entwicklungslinien der industriellen und gewerblichen Kartellierung. Dritter Abschnitt: Textilindustrie A*. Berlin: E. S. Mittler und Sohn, 1929.
Ausschuss, Enquette, *Entwicklungslinien der industriellen und gewerblichen Kartellierung. Dritter Abschnitt: Textilindustrie B*. Berlin: E. S. Mittler und Sohn, 1930a.
Ausschuss, Enquette, *Kartellpolitik, Zweiter Abschnitt, Vernehmungen*. Berlin: E. S. Mittler und Sohn, 1930b.
Baade, Fritz (ed.), *Die Wirtschaftsunionen in ihrer Stellung zu den Nationalenwirtschaften und zur Weltwirtschaft*. Münster: Edwin Runge, 1951.
Baare, Gerd, "Ausmass und Ursachen der Unternehmungskonzentration der deutschen Stahlindustrie im Rahmen der Montaunion, ein internationaler Vergleich." *Dissertation*, Tübingen, 1965.
Bade, Franz-Josef, "The economic importance of small and medium sized firms in the Federal Republic of Germany." In *New Firms and Regional Development in Europe*. David and Egbert Wever Keeble (eds.). London: Croom Helm, 1986 pp. 256-274.
Bade, Franz-Josef, *Regionale Beschäftigungsentwicklung und produktionsorientierte Dienstleistung*. Berlin: Drucker & Humblot, 1987.
Bade, Franz Josef, and Klaus Kunzmann, "Deindustrialization and Regional Development in the Federal Republic of Germany." In *Industrial Change and Regional Economic Transformation. The Experience of Western Europe*. Lloyd and Hidehiko Suzanami Rodwin (eds.). London: Harper Collins, 1991.
Baden-Württemberg, Statistische Landesamt: *Verarbeitendes Gewerbe, Statistik von Baden Württemberg*. Stuttgart: *Land* Baden Württemberg, various years.
Bain, Trevor, *Banking the Furnace: Restructuring of the Steel Industry in Eight Countries*. Kalamazoo, MI: W. E. Upjohn Institute for Employment Research, 1992.
Baker, Kendall L., Russell J. Dalton, and Kai Hildebrandt, *Germany Transformed. Political Culture and the New Politics*. Cambridge, MA: Harvard University Press, 1981.
Balderston, Theo, "War Finance and Inflation in Britain and Germany, 1914-1918." *Economic History Review (Second Series)* XLII(2) (1989): 222-244.
Balderston, Theo, *The Origins and Course of the German Economic Crisis, 1923-1932*. Berlin: Haude & Spener, 1993.
Balke, Siegfried, "Die technische Entwicklung und der Mensch." *Vortragsreihe des Deutschen Industrieinstituts*, 41 October 11 (1954).
Barkhausen, Max, "Government Control and Free Enterprise in Western Germany and the Low Countries in the Eighteenth Century." In *Essays in European Economic History, 1500-1800*. Peter Earle (ed.). Oxford: Clarendon Press, 1974, pp. 212-273.
Barraclough, Geoffrey, *The Origins of Modern Germany*. New York: Paragon Books, 1979.
Barth, Ernst, *Entwicklungslinien der deutschen Machinenbauindustrie von 1870 bis 1914*. Berlin (East): Akademie-Verlag, 1973.
Bartholome, Ernst, "Starkung der Eigenstaatlichkeit und Eigenverantwortlichkeit der Länder notwendig." *Der Landkreis*, October (1983): 540-508.

Bauer, Helmuth, and "plakate" Gruppe, "Daimler Benz von Innen." *Das Daimler Benz Buch: Ein Rüstungskonzern im 'Tausendjährigen Reich' und Danach.* Hamburger Stiftung fuer Sozialgeschichte des 20. Jahrhunderts (ed.). Nördlingen: GRENO-Verlag, 1988, pp. 594–589.

Bauert-Keetman, Ingrid, *Deutsche Indutriepioniere.* Tübingen: Rainer Wunderlich Verlag, 1966.

Baumenn, Hans, *Maschinenbau. Strukturelle Probleme und Wachstumschancen.* Munich: Duncker & Humblot, 1964.

Baumgart, Egon, "Die Elektroindustrie der Bundesrepublik im europaischen Markt." *Vierteljahresheft zur Wirtschaftsforschung* (1962): 216–231.

Becker, Walter, "Die Entwicklung der deutschen Maschinenbauindustrie von 1850 bis 1870." In *Die deutsche Maschinenindustrie in der Industriellen Revolution.* Alfred Schröter and Walter Becker (eds.). Berlin (East): Akademia, 1962.

Beckmann, Theo, "Das Handwerk im Ruhrgebiet." *Rheinisch-Westfälisches Institut für Wirtschaftsforschung Essen Mitteilungen,* 2 (1967): 169–179.

Beckmann, Theo, "Das Handwerk—heute und morgen." *Rheinisch-Westfälisches Institut für Wirtschaftsforschung Essen Mitteilungen* 2 (1968): 131–146.

Beer, Samual H., "Federalism, Nationalism, and Democracy in America." *American Political Science Review* 72 (1978): 9–21.

Beer, Theo, et al., *Die bergische Wirtschaft und ihre Kammer, 1956–1980.* Wuppertal: Born-Verlag, 1980.

Belassa, Bella, "Tariff Protection in Industrial Countries, An Evaluation." *Journal of Political Economy* 73 (1965): 573–594.

Bell, James, "The Comeback of Krupp." *Fortune,* February (1956).

Bellon, Bernard P., *Mercedes in Peace and War. German Automobile Workers, 1903–1945.* New York: Columbia University Press, 1990.

Bender, Kurt, "Sind neue Maschinen unwirtschaftlich?" *Betriebswirtschaftliche Forschung und Praxis* 6(7/8) (1954): 449–452.

Bendersky, Joseph W., *Carl Schmitt. Theorist for the Reich.* Princeton: Princeton University Press, 1983.

Bendix, Reinhard, *Nation Building and Citizenship.* Berkeley: University of California Press, 1977.

Benndorf, Erich, *Weltwirtschaftilche Beziehungen der Sächsichen Industrie.* Jena: Verlag Gustav Fischer, 1917.

Bensch, German, "Auswirkungen kumulierter wirtschaftlicher Benachteiligung auf die Wirtschaftskraft eines Raumes—dargestellt am Beispiel der Stadt Duisburg." *Informationen zur Raumentwicklung* 9/10 (1987): 561–568.

Benz, Daimler, *Das Verhältnis des Grossbetriebes zu seinen mittelständischen Zulieferern. Eine Untersuchung zur heutigen Situation des industriellen Mittelstandes durchgeführt am Beispiel der Daimler Benz AG.* Stuttgart-Untertürkheim: Daimler-Benz: Volkswirtschaftliche Abteilung, September 1959.

Benz, Daimler (ed.), *75 Jahre Motorisierung des Verkehrs. Jubiläumsbericht der Daimler-Benz Aktiengesellschaft Stuttgart-Untertürkheim, 1886–1961.* Stuttgart: Deutsche Verlags-Anstalt, 1961.

Benz, Daimler, *Das Grossunternehmen und der industrielle Mittelstand. Eine Untersuchung über die klein- und mittelbetrieblichen Zulieferer der Daimler Benz AG,* Stuttgart-Untertürkheim: Daimler-Benz AG, Volkswirtschaftliche Abteilung, December 1962.

Benz, Wolfgang, *Süddeutschland in der Weimar Republik. Ein Beitrag zur deutschen Innenpolitik. 1918–1923.* Berlin: Duncker & Humblot, 1970.
Benz, Arthur, *Föderalismus als dynamisches System.* Opladen: Westdeutscher Verlag, 1985.
Benz, Arthur, "Intergovernmental Relations in the 1980s." *Publius* 19(4) (1989): 206.
Benz, Arthur, "Reformbedarf und Reformchancen des kooperativen Föderalismus nach der Vereinigung." In *Verwaltungsreform und Verwaltungspolitik im Prozeß der deutschen Einigung.* Wolfgang Seibel, Arthur Benz, and Heinrich Mäding (eds.). Baden Baden: Nomos Verlegsgesellschaft, 1993, pp. 454–474.
Benz-Overhage, Karin, Eva Brumlop, Thomas von Freyberg, and Zissis Papadimitrious, *Neue Technologien und alternative Arbeitsgestaltung, Auswirkungen des Computereinsatzes in der industriellen Produktion.* Frankfurt: Campus, 1982.
Berg, Fritz, *Die Westdeutsche Wirtschaft in der Bewährung. Ausgewählte Reden aus den Jahren 1950 bis 1965.* Hagen: Linnepe Verlagsgesellschaft KG, 1966.
Berger, Suzanne and Michael Piore, *Dualism and Discontinuity in Industrial Society.* New York: Cambridge University Press, 1980.
Berggren, Christian, *Alternatives to Lean Production: Work Organization in the Swedish auto industry.* New York: ILR Press, 1992.
Berghahn, Volker, *Unternehmer und Politik in der Bundesrepublik.* Frankfurt: Suhrkamp, 1985.
Bergmann, Joachim, Otto Jacobi, and Walther Müller-Jentsch, *Gewerkschaften in der Bundesrepublik. Gewerkschaftliche Lohnpolitik zwischen Mitgliederinteressen und ökonomischen Systemzwängen.* Frankfurt: Europaische Verlags-Anstalt, 1975.
Berk, Gerald, *Alternative Tracks.* Baltimore: Johns Hopkins Press, 1993.
Berkenkopf, Paul, *Die Neuorganisation der deutschen Grosseisenindustrie.* Essen: G.D. Bädecker, 1928.
Berthold, Karl P., *Untersuchungen über den Standort der Maschinenindustrie in Deutschland.* Jena: Gustav Fischer, 1915.
Besson, Waldemar, *Württemberg und die deutsche Staatkrise 1928–1933.* Stuttgart: Deutsche Verlags Anstalt, 1959.
Bethusy-Huc, V. V., *Demokratie und Interessenpolitik.* Wiesbaden: 1962.
Betriebswirtschaft, Deutsche Gesellschaft für (ed.), *Zentralprobleme der Vollbeschäftigung.* Berlin: Deutscher Betriebswirte-Verlag, 1957.
Biedenkopf, Kurt, "Massenproduktion, Wettbewerb und europaische Vereinigung. Zu einer amerikanischen Betrachtung der wirtschaftlichen Auswirkungen der europäischen Integration." *Europa Archiv,* June 5 (1956): 8915–8918.
Birke, Adolf, *Bischof Ketteler und der deutsche Liberalismus.* Mainz, Grünewald, 1971.
Birnbaum, Bruno, *Organisierung der Rationalisierung Amerika-Deutschland.* Berlin: Reimar-Hobbing, 1927.
Bispham, John, and Andrea Boltho, "Demand Management." In *The European Economy. Growth and Crisis.* Andrea Boltho (ed.). New York: Oxford University Press, 1982, 289–328.
Blackbourn, David, "The Mittelstand in German Society and Politics, 1871–1914." *Social History,* 4 January (1977): 409–433.
Blackbourn, David, and Geoff Eley, *The Peculiarities of German History.* New York: Oxford University Press, 1984.
Blaich, Fritz, *Kartell- und Monopolpolitik im kaiserlichen Deutschland.* Düsseldorf: Droste Verlag, 1973.

Blaich, Fritz, "Absatzstrategien deutscher Unternehmen im 19. und der ersten hälfte des 20. Jahrhunderts." In *Absatzstrategien deutscher Unternehmen: Gestern-Heute-Morgen,* Hans Pohl (ed.). Beiheft 23. *Zeitschrift für Unternehmengeschichte,* Wiesbaden: Franz Steiner Verlag GmbH, 1982, pp. 5–47.

Blaich, Fritz, *Amerikanische Firmen in Deutschland 1890–1918.* Wiesbaden: Steiner, 1984.

Blanke, Bernhard, Aldabert Evers, and Hans Wollmann, "Die Zweite Stadt." *Leviathan,* 7 (1986): Special Issue.

Blaschke, Karlheinz, *Bevolkerungsgeschichte von Schsen bis zur Industriellen Revolution.* Weimar: Hermann Bölhaus Nachfolger, 1967.

Blimberg, H, *Die deutsche Textilindustrie in der Industrielle Revolution.* Berlin (East): Akademie, 1963.

Bloomfield, Gerald T., "The world automotive industry in transition." In *Restructuring the Global Automobile Industry, National and Regional Impacts.* Christopher M. Law (ed.). London: Routledge, 1991, pp. 19–60.

Blum, Jerome, *The End of the Old Order in Rural Europe.* Princeton: Princeton University Press, 1978.

Blüthmann, Heinz, "Überholt und abgehängt. Erstmals baut BMW mehr Autos als Mercedes." *Die Zeit,* 14 April 3 (1993): 9–10.

Boch, Rudolph, *Handwerker Sozialisten gegen die Fabrikgesellschaft.* Göttingen: Vandenhoeck & Ruprecht, 1985.

Boch, Rudolf, "Zunfttradition und frühe Gewerkschaftsbewegung. Ein Beitrag zu einer beginnenden Diskussion mit besonderer Berücksichtigung des Handwerks im Verlagssystem." In *Prekäre Selbständigkeit, Zur Standortbestimmung vom Handwerk, Hausindustrie und Kleingewerbe im Industrialisierungsprozess.* Ulrich Wegenroth (ed.). Stuttgart: Franz Steiner, 1989.

Boch, Rudolf, "Die Entgrenzung der Industrie. Zur Industrialisierungsdebatte im rheinischen Wirtschaftsbürgertum, 1814–1857." *Habilitationsschrift.* Universität Bielefeld, 1990.

Boch, Rudolf, "The Rise and Decline of "Flexible Production": The Cutlery Industry of Solingen Since the 18th Century." In *Worlds of Possibility: Alternatives to Mass Production During the Period of Industrialization.* Charles F. Sabel and Jonathan Zeitlin (eds.). Paris: Maison des Sciences de L'Homme, forthcoming.

Boecker, Heinrich, "Die deutsche Werkzeugindustrie: Eine Alternative zur Massenproduktion?" *Diplomarbeit der Abteilung Wirtschafts-und Sozialwissenschaften.* Universität Dortmund, 1983.

Boelcke, Willi, "Wege und Probleme des industriellen Wachstums in Königreich Württemberg." *Zeitschrift für Württembergische Landesgeschichte* 32(2) (1973): 436–520.

Boelcke, Willi, *Wirtschaftsgeschichte Baden Württembergs.* Stuttgart: Konrad Theiss, 1987.

Boelcke, Willi, "Organization und Politik von Industrie, Handwerk und Handel." In *Verbände in Baden Württemberg.* H. Schneider (ed.). Stuttgart, Kohlhammer, 1987.

Bog, Ingomar, "Mercantilism in Germany." In *Revisions in Mercantilism.* D. C. Coleman (ed.). London: Metheun, 1969.

Borchardt, Knut, "Die Strukturwäche der Weimarer Wirtschft und die Handlungsmöglichkeit in der grossen Krise." In *Wachstum, Krisen, Handlugsspielräume der Wirtschaftspolitik. Studien zur Wirtschaftsgeschichte des 19. und 20. Jahrhunderts.* Knut Borchardt (ed.). Göttingen: Vandenhoeck & Ruprecht, 1982, pp. 165–224.

Borkin, Joseph and Charles Welsh, *Germany's Master Plan: The Story of Industrial Offensive*. New York: Duell, Sloane and Pearce, 1943.
Borkin, Joseph, *The Crime and Punishment of I.G. Farben*. New York: Free Press, 1978.
Bormann, Otto-Albert, "Zur Entstehung und Entwicklung der Metallverarbeitenden Industrie im Monchengaldbacher Industriebezirk." *Dissertation*, Köln, 1924.
Borrus, Michael, Laura D'Andrea Tyson, and John Zyzsman, "Creating Advantage: How Government Policies Shape International Trade in the Semiconductor Industry." In *Strategic Trade Policy and the New International Economics*. Paul Krugman (ed.). Cambridge, MA: MIT Press, 1987.
Borsig, Albert, "Zur Ausfuhrorganisation der Maschinenindustrie." *Technik und Wirtschaft* 21(10) (1928): 265–269.
Borst, Otto, "Staat und Unternehmen in der Frühzeit der Württembergischen Industrie." *Tradition. Zeitschrift Für Firmen Geschichte und Unternehmebiographie* 11(3–4) (1966): 105–127, 153–174.
Bosch, Karl, "Ausführungen des Sachsverständigen Dr. Bosch über die Produktions- und Absatzverhältnisse der I.G. Farbenindustrie Aktiengesellschaft, Frankfurt/Maine." In *Die deutsche Chemische Industrie: verhandlungen und Berichte des Unterausschusses für Gewerbe: Industrie, Handel und Handwerk (III Unterausschuss)*. Enquette Ausschuss (ed.). Berlin: Mittler und Sohn, 1930, pp. 111–136.
Bosl, Karl, "Die Verhandlungen über den Eintritt der süddeutschen Staaten in den norddeutschen Bund und die Entstehung der Reichsverfassung." In *Reichsgründung 1870/71. Tatsachen, Kontroversen, Interpretationen*. Theodor Schneider und Ernst Deuerlein (eds.). Stuttgart: Seewald, 1970.
Boyer, Robert, and Pascal Petit, "The Cumulative Growth Model Revisited." *CEPREMAP/CNRS*, Paris, 1987.
Böcker, Heinrich, "Die Deutsche Werkzeugindustrie: Eine Alternative zur Massenproduction?" *Diplomarbeit der Abteilung Wirtschafts- und Sozialwissenschaften*, Universität Dortmund, 1983.
Böhm, Franz, "Die Reichsgericht und die Kartelle." *Ordo. Jahrbuch für die Ordnung von Wirtschaft und Gesellschaft* 1 (1948): 197–213.
Böhme, Helmut, *Deutschlands Weg zur Grossmacht, Studien zum Verhältnis von Wirtschaft und Staat während der Reichsgründungszeit, 1848–1881*. Cologne: Kiepenheuer & Witsch, 1966.
Böhringer, Rolf, "Spezialisierung, Normung, Typung im deutschen Werkzügmaschinenbau." *Vierjahresplan*, 1939.
Brady, Robert, *The Rationalization Movement in Germany*. Berkeley: University of California Press, 1933.
Braun, Otto, *Deutscher Einheitsstaat oder Föderativsystem?* Berlin: Carl Henmanns, 1927.
Braunthal, Gerald, *The West German Social Democrats, 1969–82. Profile of a Party in Power*. Boulder, CO: Westview Press, 1982.
Brecht, Arnold, *Federalism and Regionalism in Germany. The Division of Prussia*. New York: Oxford University Press, 1945.
Breckner, I., E. Ohn, and K. M. Schmals, "Stadtentwicklung, Neu Technologien und Wandel der Arbeit in München—Formen der Betroffenheit und Versuche ihre Bewältigung." In *Regionalentwicklung zwischen Technologieboom und Restvewertung. Die Beispiele Ruhr und Mühcnen*. Arbeitsgruppen Ruhrgebiet und München (ed.). Bochum: Germinal Verlag, 1985, pp. 115–233.
Breidenbach, Peter, "Die vertikale und horizontale Kooperation von Handwerksbetrieb-

en als Lieferanten industrieller Unternehmungen." *Dissertation,* Wirtschafts- und Sozialwissenschaftlichen Fakultät. Köln, 1968.

Brenner, Otto, *Gewerkschaftliche Dynamik in unserer Zeit.* Frankfurt: Europäische Verlags-anstalt, 1966.

Brenner, Robert, "Agrarian Class Structure and Economic Development in Pre-Industrial Europe." In *The Brenner Debate.* T. H. Aston and C. H. E. Philpin (eds.). New York: Cambridge University Press, 1987.

Briefs, G., "Bevolkerungsbewegung und Arbeitsmarktentwicklung." In *Strukturwandlungen der deutschen Wolkwirtschaft.* Bernard Harms (ed.). Berlin: Reimar-Hobbing, 1929.

Brockstedt, Jürgen, "Family Enterprise and the Rise of Large Scale Enterprise in Germany [1871-1914]—Ownership And Management." In *Family Business in the Era of Industrial Growth: Its Ownership and Management,* Akio Okochi and Shigeaki Yasuoka Okochi (eds.). International conference on Business History 10, Tokyo: University of Tokyo Press, 1984.

Broszat, Martin, *The Hitler State. The Foundation and Development of the Internal Structure of the Third Reich.* London: Longmann Group, 1981.

Brubaker, Rogers, *Citizenship and Nationhood in France and Germany.* Cambridge, MA: Harvard University Press, 1992.

Brune, Rolf, "Die Köln-Bonner Raum: Eine Problemregion?" *Mitteilungen des Rheinisch-Westfälischen Instituts für Wirtschaftsforschung Essen* 30(3) (1979): 151–171.

Brunner, Otto, "Die alteuropäische 'Oekonomik'." *Zeitschrift für Nationaloekonomie* 13 (1952): 114–139.

Brunner, Otto, "Das 'Ganze Haus' in die alteuropäische 'Oekonomie'." In *Neue Wege der Verfassungs- und Sozialgeschichte.* Otto Brunner (ed.). Göttingen: Vandenhoek & Ruprecht, 1980.

Bukharin, Nikolai Ivanovich, *Imperialism and World Economy.* New York: International Publishers, 1929.

Burck, Gilbert, "Can Germany Go Capitalist?" *Fortune,* 1954a: 114–256.

Burck, Gilbert, "The German Business Mind." *Fortune,* May (1954b): 112f.

Burn, Duncan, *The Steel Industry 1939–1959. A Study in Competition and Planning.* Cambridge: Cambridge University Press, 1961.

Buxbaum, Berthold, "Der deutsche Werkzeugmaschinen- und Werkzeugbau im 19. Jahrhundert." *Betreige zur Geschichte der technik und Industrie* 9 (1919): 97–129.

Büchner, Fritz, *Hundert Jahre Geschichte der Maschinenfabrik Augsburg-Nürnberg.* Nuremberg: MAN, 1940.

Carr, William, *A History of Germany. 1815–1945.* New York: St. Martin's Press, 1969.

Castoriadis, Cornelius, *The Imaginary Institution of Society.* Cambridge, MA: MIT Press, 1987.

Chandler, Alfred D. Jr., *Strategy and Structure.* Cambridge, MA: MIT Press, 1962.

Chandler, Alfred D., *The Visible Hand. The Managerial Revolution in American Business.* Cambridge, MA: Harvard University Press, 1977.

Chandler, Alfred D., *Scale and Scope. The Dynamics of Industrial Capitalism.* Cambridge, MA: Harvard University Press, 1990.

Chandler, Alfred, Roy Church, Albert Fishlow, Neil Fligstein, Thomas Hughes, Jürgen Kocka, Hidemasa Morikawa, and Frederic M. Scherer, "Scale and Scope:

Bibliography 413

A Review of Colloquium." *Business History Review* 64 Winter (1990): 690–758.
Clapham, J. H., *Economic Development of France and Germany 1815–1914*. New York: Cambridge University Press, 1961.
Clark, Kim B., and Takahiro Fujimoto, *Product Development Performance. Strategy, Organization and Management in the World Auto Industry*. Cambridge, MA: Harvard Business School Press, 1991.
Clay, Lucius D., *Decision in Germany*. Melbourne: William Heinemann Ltd., 1950.
Coase, Ronald H., *The Firm, the Market, and the Law*. Chicago: University of Chicago Press, 1988.
Cohen, Benjamin, "US Foreign Economic Policy." *Orbis* 15(1) (1971): 232–247.
Cohen, G. A., *Karl Marx's Theory of History. A Defense*. Princeton: Princeton University Press, 1978.
Cohen, Stephen, and John Zysman, *Manufacturing Matters*. New York: Basic Books, 1987.
Committee, Senate Foreign Relations, Executive Sessions of the Senate Foreign Relations Committee (Historical Series) Volume II, Eighty First Congress, First and Second Sessions, 1949–1950. Washington, DC: 1951.
Conradt, David, *The German Polity, Fifth ed*. New York: Longman, 1992.
Conze, Werner, "The Effects of Nineteenth-Century Liberal Agrarian Reforms on Social Structure in Central Europe." In *Essays in European Economic History 1789–1914*. F. Crouzet, W. H. Chaloner and W. M. Stern (eds.). London: Edward Arnold, 1969, pp. 53–81.
Conze, Werner, "Möglichkeiten und Grenzen der liberalen Arbeiterbewegung in Deutschland: das Bespiel Schultze-Delitzsch." In *Interessenverbände in Deutschland*. Heinz J. Varian (ed.). Köln: Kiepenheuer & Witsch, 1973.
Cooke, Philip, and Kevin Morgan, "Learning Through Networking: Regional Innovation and the Lessons of Baden Württemberg." British Council, Cardiff City Council, Welsh Development Agency, Welsh Office, 1990.
Cooke, Philip, and Kevin Morgan, "Industry, Training and Technology Transfer: The Baden Württemberg System in Perspective." British Council, Cardiff City Council, Welsh Development Agency, Welsh Office, 1990.
Cooke, Philip, "The Baden Wuerttemberg Machine Tool Industry: Regional Responses to Global Threats." Center for Advanced Studies, University of Wales, Cardiff, 1994.
Craig, Gordon, *The Politics of the Prussian Army, 1640–1945*. New York: Oxford University Press, 1964.
Craig, Gordon, *Germany 1866–1945*. New York: Oxford University Press, 1978.
Crew, David, *Town in Ruhr*. New York: Columbia University Press, 1979.
Croon, Helmut, "Bürgertum und Verwaltung in den Städten des Ruhrgebiets im 19. Jahrhunderts." *Tradition: Zeitschrift für Firmengeschichte und Unternehmerbiographie* 9(1) (1964): 23–41.
Croon, Helmuth, "Die wirtschaftlichen Führungsschichten im Rheinland und in Westfalen 1790–1850." In *Führungskräfte der Wirtschaft in Mittelalter und Neuzeit. 1350–1850*. Herbert Helbig (ed.). Limburg/Lahn: C. A. Starke Verlag, 1973, pp. 311–338.
Czada, Peter, *Die Berliner Elektroindustrie in der Weimarer Zeit*. Berlin: Colloquium, 1969.
Dahrendorf, Ralf, *Society and Democracy in Germany*. New York: Norton, 1967.

Dalton, George (ed.), *Tribal and Peasant Economies: Readings in Economic Anthropology.* Garden City, NY: The Natural History Press, 1967.
Damm, Walter, "National and International Factors Influencing Cartel Legislation in Post War Germany." *Dissertation,* Committee on International Relations. University of Chicago, 1958.
Danert, Günther, "Technische Grenzen dezentraler Betriebsorganisation. Ein Beitrag zum Problem pretialer und bürokratischer Betriebslenkung." *Zeitschrift für Handelswissenschaftliche Forschung* 4(9) (1952): 407–412.
Dascher, Ottfried, "Probleme der Konzernorganisation." In *Industrielles System und Politische Entwicklung in der Weimarer Republik.* H. Mommsen, Dietmar Petzina, and Bernd Weisbrod (eds.). Konigstein/Ts: Athenaeum, 1977), 127-137.
Dawson, W. H., *Municipal Life and Government in Germany.* London: Longmans, 1916.
de Vries, Jan, *The Economy of Europe in the Age of Crisis, 1600–1750.* Cambridge: Cambridge University Press, 1976.
de Vries, Jan, *European Urbanization 1500–1800.* London: Metheun, 1984.
Deeg, Richard, "Banks and the State in Germany: The Critical Role of Subnational Institutions in Economic Governance." *Ph.D. Dissertation,* Department of Political Science. MIT, 1992.
Demag, Deutsche Maschinenfabrik A. G.: *Works at Benrath, Wetter and Duisburg* Duisburg: Demag, 1913.
Deubner, Christian, "Change and Internationalization in Industry: Toward a Sectoral Interpretation of West German Politics." *Industrial Organization* 38(3): 501–535.
Deuerlein, Ernst, *Föderalismus. Die historischen und philosophischen Grundlagen des Föderativen Prinzips.* Munich: Paul List, 1972.
Dewey, John, *The Quest for Certainty, John Dewey, The Later Works.* Jo Ann Boydston (ed.). Carbondale, IL: Southern Illinois University Press, 1988, Volume 4: 1929.
Dick, Rolf, *Die Arbeitseilung zwischen Industrie und Entwicklungsländern im Maschinenbau.* Tübingen: JCB Mohr, 1981.
Dicke, Hugo, *Strukturwandel im Westdeutschen Strassenfahrzeugbau.* Tübingen: JCB Mohr, 1978.
Dickenson, Robert, *The Regions of Germany.* London: Kegan Paul, Trench, Trubner and Co., 1945.
Diess, Manfred, "Entwicklungen der Arbeitsbedingungen in den Zulieferbetrieben der Möbelindustrie." In *Systemische Rationalisieruung und Zulieferindustrie. Sozialwissenschaftliche Aspekte zwischenbetrieblicher Arbeitsteilung.* Norbert Altman and Dieter Suaer (eds.). Frankfurt: Campus, 1989, pp. 29–88.
Dietze, Constantin V., "Die Vererbung des Ländlichen Grundbesitzes in Mitteldeutschland (Provinz Sachsen, Anhalt, Braunschweig, Thüringen)." In *Die Vererbung des Ländlichen Grundbesitzes in der Nachkriegszeit, Band 1: Deutsches Reich.* Max Sering and Constantin V. Dietze (eds.). Munich/Liepzig: Dinker & Humblot, 1930, pp. 216-255.
DiMaggio, Paul, and Sharon Zukin (eds.), *Structures of Capital.* New York: Cambridge University Press, 1989.
DiMaggio, Paul, and Walter Powell (eds.), *The New Institutionalism in Organizational Analysis.* Chicago: University of Chicago Press, 1991.
Dluboborski, Waclaw, "Wirtschaftliche Region und politische Grenzen: die Industrialisierung des oberschlesischen Kohlenbeckens." In *Region und Industrialisierung.* Sidney Pollard (ed.). Göttingen: Vandenhoeck & Ruprecht, 1980.

Dobb, Maurice, *Capitalist Enterprise and Social Progress*. London: G. Routledge and Sons, 1925.
Dobb, Maurice, *Studies in the Development of Capitalism*. New York: International Publishers, 1963.
Dolezalek, C. M., "Ansatzpunkte für die Einführung automatisierter Fertigung." *Werkstattstechnik 50*(3) (1960): 107–111.
Domansky-Davidsohn, Elizabeth, "Der Grossbetrieb als Organizationsproblem des Deutschen Metallarbeiter-Verbandes vor dem Ersten Weltkrieg." In *Arbeiterbewegung und industrieller Wandel. Studien zu gewerkschaftlichen Organisationsproblemen im Reich und an der Ruhr*. Hans Mommsen (ed.). Wuppertal: Peter Hammer, 1980, pp. 95–116.
Dore, Ronald, *Flexible Rigidities: Industrial Policy and Structural Adjustment in the Japanese Economy, 1970–1980*. London: Athlone Press, 1986.
Döhl, Volker, "Rationalisierungsstrategien von Abnehmerbetrieben und Anforderungen an die Zulieferer—Das Beispiel Möbelindustrie." In *Systemische Rationalisieruung und Zulieferindustrie. Sozialwissenschaftliche Aspekte zwischenbetrieblicher Arbeitsteilung*. Norbert Altmann and Dieter Sauer (eds.). Frankfurt: Campus, 1989, pp. 29–88.
Döleschal, Reinhard, "Zur geschichtlichen Entwicklung des Volkswagenkonzerns." In *Wohin läuft VW. Die Automobilproduktion in der Wirtschaftskrise*. Reinhard Doleschal and Rainer Dombois (eds.). Hamburg: Rowohlt Taschenbuch Verlag, 1982, pp. 18–54.
Döleschal, Reinhard, "Daten und Trends der bundesdeutschen Automobil-Zulieferindustrie." In *Zulieferer im Netz. Neustrukturierung der Logistik am Beispiel der Automobilzulieferung*. Hans Gerhard Mendius and Ulrike Wendeling-Schroeder (eds.). Cologne: Bund Verlag, 1991.
Dumke, R. H., "Tarrifs and Market Structure: The German Zollverein as a Model for Economic Integration." In *German Industry and German Industrialisation*. W. R. Lee (ed.). London: Routledge, 1991.
Dunning, John H., *Studies in International Investment*. London: George Allen and Unwin, 1970.
Dunning, John H., "Technology, United States Investment and European Economic Growth." In *The International Corporation. A Symposium*. Charles P. Kindleberger (ed.). Cambridge, MA: MIT Press, 1970, pp. 141–178.
Dunning, John H., "Changes in the Level and Structure of International Production: the Last One Hundred Years." In *The Growth of International Business*. Mark Casson (ed.). London: George Allen and Unwin, 1983, pp. 84–139.
Dyson, Kenneth, "The State, Banks, and Industry: The West German Case." In *State, Finance, and Industry: A Comparative Analysis of Post War Trends in Six Advanced Industrial Economies*. Andrew Cox (ed.). New York: St. Martin's Press, 1984.
Dyson, Kenneth, "Economic Policy." In *Developments in West German Politics*. Gordon Smith, William E. Patterson and Peter H. Merkl (eds.). Durham: Duke University Press, 1989, pp. 148–167.
Eckart, Karl, *Die Eisen-und Stahlindustrie in den beiden deutschen Staaten*. Stuttgart: Franz Steiner Verlag Wiesbaden GmbH, 1988.
Edinger, Lewis, *Politics in West Germany*. Boston: Little Brown, 1977.
Egbers, Gerhard, "Innovation, Know-How, Rationalization and Investments in the German Textile Industry During the Period 1871–1935." manuscript, 1993.

Egle, Walter, "The Progress of Mass Production and the German Small Scale Industries." *Journal of Political Economy* 46 February-December (1938): 376–395.

Ehrenberg, Richard and Hugo Racine, *Krupp'sche Arbeiter-Familien. Entwicklung und Entwicklungs-faktoren von drei generationen deutscher Arbeiter*. Jena: Gustav Fischer, 1912.

Eibert, Georg, *Unternehmenspolitik Nürnberger Maschinenbauer*. Stuttgart: Klett-Cotta, 1979.

Eichenhofer, Harald, "Die Automobilindustrie in der Bundesrepublik." *Wirtschaftsdienst*, 5 (1954): 288.

Eichner, H., "Wie steht der deutsche Industrie zum Gemeinsamen Markt?" *Der Gemeinsamer Markt: Grundgedanken, Problemen und Tatsachen zu Europäische Wirtschaftsgemeinschaft*, Europa Union Deutschlands (ed.). Bonn: Europa Union Deutschlands, 1957.

Eichner, H., "Die Vorbereitung der Unternehmungen auf dem Gemeinsamen Europäischen Markt als betriebswirtschaftliche Aufgabe." *Zeitschrift für Handelswissenschaftliche Forschung* 11(7) (1959): 350–411.

Eisinger, Peter K., *The Rise of the Entrepreneurial State. State and Local Economic Development Policy in the United States*. Madison: University of Wisconsin Press, 1988.

Eley, Geoff, "The British Model and the German Road: Rethinking the Course of German History Before 1914." In *The Peculiarities of German History*. David Blackbourn and Geoff Eley (eds.). New York: Oxford University Press, 1984.

Elkmann, Georg Heinrich, *Möglichkeiten und Grenzen der Konzentration in der Eisen- und Stahlindustrie*. Düsseldorf: Verlag Stahleisen mbH, 1970.

Elliot, J. H., "A Europe of Composite Monarchies." *Past and Present* 137 (November) (1992): 48–71.

Elliott, Mick, "Germany: Siemens Issues Profit Warming—1993 Result." *Electronics Weekly* 19 January (1994).

Emerson, Rupert, *State and Sovereignty in Modern Germany*. New Haven: Yale University Press, 1928.

Engel, Josef and Ernst Walter Zeeden, *Großer Historischer Weltatlas: Neuzeit*, 4 ed. Munich: Bayrische Schulbuch Verlag, 1981.

Engelmann, Frank C.; Christian Heyd, Daniel Koestler, and Peter Paustian, "The German Machine Tool Industry." Appendix 2 of David Finegold, et al.: *Machines On The Brink. The Decline of the US Machine Tool Industry and Prospects For Its Recovery*. Santa Monica, CA: RAND, 1994 DSR-496-OSTP: 51.

Epkenhans, Michael, *Die wilhelminische Flottenrüstung, 1908-1914. Weltmachtstreben, industrielle Fortschritt, sozialer Integration*. München: R. Oldenberg Verlag, 1991.

Epstein, Klaus, *Matthias Erzberger and the Dilemma of German Democracy*. New York: Howard Fertig, 1971.

Erdmann, W., "Stand der Technik in der Werkzeugmaschinenindustrie Deutschlands." *Das Industrieblatt. Fachzeitschrift für die Metallverarbeitende Industrie* 56(1) (1956): 1–6.

Erhard, Ludwig, *Wohlstand Für Alle*. Düsseldorf: Econ Verlag, 1957.

Erichsen, Hans Uwe, "Bund und Länder im Bundesstaat des Grundgesetztes." *Jura* July (1986): 337–344.

Erzberger, Matthias, *Reden zur Neueordnung des deutschen Finanzwesens*. Berlin: Hobbing, 1919.

Esenwein-Rothe, Ingeborg, *Die Wirtschaftsverbände von 1933–1945*, Schriften des Vereins für Sozialpolitik N.F. 37. Berlin: Duncker & Humblot, 1965.
Esser, Josef, *Gewerkschaften in der Krise*. Frankfurt: Suhrkamp, 1982.
Esser, Josef, Wolfgang Fach, and Werner Väth, *Krisenregulierung. Zur politischen Durchsetzung ökonomischer Zwänge*. Frankfurt: Suhrkamp, 1983.
Esser, Joseph, Wolfgang Fach, and Kenneth Dyson, "Social Market and Modernization Policy: West Germany." In *Industrial Crisis: A Comparative Study of State and Industry*. Kenneth Dyson and Stephen Wilkes (eds.). New York: St. Martin's Press, 1984.
Esser, Josef, and Werner Väth, "Overcoming the Steel Crisis in the Federal Republic of Germany, 1974–1983." In *The Politics of Steel: Western Europe and the Steel Industry in the Crisis Years, 1974–1984*. Yves Meny and Vincent Wright (eds.). Berlin: Walter de Gruyter, 1986, pp. 632–633.
Esser, Josef and Joachim Hirsch, "Stadtsoziologie und Gesellschaftstheorie. Von der Fordismus-Krise zur "post-fordistischen" Regional- und Stadtstruktur." In *Die Materialität des Städtischen*. W. Prigge (ed.). Basel: Birkhäuser, 1987.
Eucken, Walter, "Technik, Konzentration und Ordnung in der Wirtschaft." *Ordo* 3 (1950): 3–19.
Eucken, Walter, *Grundsätze der Wirtschaftspolitik*. Tübingen: JCB Mohr (Paul Siebeck), 1990 (1952).
Eulenberg, Franz, "Die deutsche Industrie auf dem Weltmarkte." In *Strukturwandlungen der Deutschen Volkswirtschaft*. Bernhard Harms (ed.). Berlin: Reimar Hobbing, 1929, pp. 389–421.
Evans, Richard (ed.), *Society and Politics in Wilhelmine Germany*. London: Croom Helm, 1978.
Evans, Peter, Dietrich Reuschemeyer, and Theda Skocpol (eds.), *Bringing the State Back In*. New York: Cambridge University Press, 1985.
Exler, Ulrich, "Financing German Federalism: Problems of Financial Equalization in the Unification Process." In *Federalism, Unification and European Integration*. Charlie Jeffre and Roland Sturm (eds.). London: Frank Cass, 1993, pp. 22–37.
Faultisch, Peter, and Hartmut Wegener, *Gesamthochschule: Zukuntfsmodell oder Reformruine? Beispiel Gesamthochschule Kassel*. Bad Honnef: Bock & Herchen, 1981.
Feldenkirchen, Wilfried, *Die Eisen- und Stahlindustrie des Ruhrgebiets, 1879–1914*. Stuttgart: Franz Steiner Wiesbaden, 1982.
Feldenkirchen, Wilfried, "Zur Kapitalbeschaffung und Kapitalverwendung bei Aktiengesellschaften des deutschen Maschinenbaus im 19. and beginnenden 20. Jahrhundert." *Vierteljahrschrift für Sozial-und Witschaftsgeschichte* 69(1) (1982): 38–74.
Feldenkirchen, Wilfried, "Big Business in Interwar Germany: Organizational Innovation at Vereinigte Stahlwerke, IG Farben and Siemens." *Business History Review* 61 (1987): 417–451.
Feldenkirchen, Wilfried, "Concentration in German Industry, 1870–1939." In *The Concentration Process in the Enterpreneurial Economy Since the Late 19th Century*. Hans Pohl (ed.). Stuttgart: Franz Steiner Verlag Wiesbaden, 1988.
Feldenkirchen, Wilfried, "Banking and Economic Growth: Banks and Industry in the Nineteenth Century and Their Changing Relationship During Industrialization." In *German Industry and German Industrialisation*. W. R. Lee (ed.). London: Routledge, 1991, pp 116–147.
Feldman, Gerald, "The Collapse of the Steelworks Association, 1912–1919." In *Sozialge-*

schichte Heuete. Hans-Ulrich Wehler (ed.). Göttingen: Vandenhoeck & Ruprecht, 1974.

Feldman, Gerald, and Ulrich Nocken, "Trade Associations And Economic Power: Interest Group Development in the German Iron and Steel and Machine Building Industries 1900–1933." *Business History Review* 49 (1975): 1–47.

Feldman, Gerald, *Iron and Steel in the German Inflation, 1916–1923.* Princeton: Princeton University Press, 1977.

Feldman, Gerald, "German Interest Group Alliances in War and Inflation." *Organizing Interests in Western Europe.* Suzanne Berger (ed.). New York: Cambridge University Press, 1981.

Feldman, Gerald, *Vom Weltkrieg zur Weltwirtschaftskrise.* Göttingen: Vandenhoek & Ruprecht, 1984.

Fellner, William (ed.), *The Problem of Rising Prices.* Paris: OECD, 1961.

Fels, Gerhard, and Frank Wolter, "Der Zusammenhang zwischen Produktionsstruktur und Entwicklungsniveau." *Weltwirtschaftliches Archiv* 106 (1971): 240–278.

Fels, Gerhard, "The Choice of Industry Mix in the Division of Labor between Developed and Developing Countries." *Weltwirtschaftliches Archiv* 108 (1972): 71–121.

Fichter, Tilman, "Betriebspolitik der KPD nach 1945: Am Beispiel der Firma Bosch." *Kampf um Bosch.* Tilman Fichter and Eugen Eberle (eds.). Berlin: Wagenbach, 1974, pp. 46–82.

Finegold, David, and Keith Brendly, Robert Lempert, Donald Henry, and Peter Cannon, *Machines On the Brink: The Decline of The US Machine Tool Industry and Prospects For Its Recovery.* RAND DRR-496-OSTP, Prepared for the Office of Science and Technology Policy, 1994.

Fischer, Wolfram, *Unternehmerschaft, Selbstverwaltung und Staat. Die Handelskammern in der deutschen Wirtschafts und Staatsverfassung des 19. Jh.* Berlin: Dunker & Humblot, 1964.

Fischer, Wolfram, "Die Rolle des Kleingewerbes im wirtschaftlichen Wachstumsprozess in Deutschland, 1850–1914." In *Wirtschaftliche und soziale Probleme der gewerblichen Entwicklung im 15/16. und 19. Jahrhundert.* Friedrich Lütge (ed.). Stuttgart: Fischer, 1968.

Fischer, Wolfam, "Bergbau, Industrie und Handwerk 1914–1970." In *Handbuch der deutschen Wirtschafts- und Sozialgeschichte, Band 2.* Herman Aubin and Wolfgang Zorn (eds.). Stuttgart: Ernst Klett, 1976.

Fischer, Wolfram, "The Role of Science and Technology in the Economic Development of Modern Germany." In *Science Technology and Economic Development.* W. Beranek and G. Ranis (eds.). New York: Praeger, 1978, pp. 71–113.

Fischer, Wolfram, "Dezentralisation oder Zentralisation—kollegiale oder autoritäre Führung? Die Auseinandersetzung um die Leitungstruktur bei der Entstehung des I. G. Farben-Konzerns." In *Recht und Entwicklungen der Grossunternehmen im 19. und frühen 20. Jahrhundert.* Norbert Horn and Jürgen Kocka (eds.). Göttingen: Vandenhoeck & Ruprecht, 1979.

Flik, Rainer, *Die Textilindustrie in Calw und Heidenheim, 1750–1870.* Wiesbaden: Franz Steiner, 1990.

Forberberger, Rudolf, *Industrielle Revolution in Sachsen.* Berlin (Ost): Akademie, 1982.

Foucault, Michel, *Language, Counter-Memory and Practice.* Ithaca: Cornell University Press, 1977.

Foucault, Michel, *Power/Knowledge.* New York: Vintage, 1980.

Fölz-Schröter, Marie Elise, *Föderalistische Politik und nationale Representation 1945–*

1947. *Westdeutsche Länderregierungen, zonale Bürokratien und politische Partien im Widerstreit.* Stuttgart: Deutsche Verlags-Anstalt, 1974.
Fränken, Willy, *Die Entwicklung des Gewerbes in den Städten Mönchengladbach und Rheydt in 19 Jahrhundert.* Köln: Rheinisch-Westfälischen Wirtschaftsarchiv, 1969.
Fremdling, Rainer, and Richard Tilly, "German Banks, German Growth, and Econometric History." *Journal of Economic History* 36 (1976): 416–424.
Fremdling, Rainer, and Richard Tilly (eds.), *Industrialisierung und Raum. Studien zur regionalen Differenzierung im Deutschland des 19. Jahrhunderts.* Stuttgart: Klett Cotta, 1979.
Fremdling, Rainer, "Eisen, Stahl und Kohle." In *Gewerbe- und Industrielandschaften vom Spätmittelalter bis ins 20. Jahrhundert.* Hans Pohl (ed.). Vierteljahreschrift Für Sozial- und Wirtschaftsgeschichte. Beiheft Nr. 78. Stuttgart: Franz Steiner Verlag Wiesbaden GmbH, 1986.
Fremdling, Rainer, "Foreign Competition and Technological Change: British Exports and the Modernization of the German Iron Industry From the 1820s to the 1860s." In *German Industry and German Indistrualisation.* W. R. Lee (ed.). London: Routledge, 1991.
Freudenberger, Herman, and Fritz Redlich, "The Industrial Development of Europe: Reality, Symbols, Images." *Kyklos* 17 (1964): 372–403.
Fricke, Dieter (ed.), *Die bürgerlichen Parteien in Deutschland, 1830–1945.* Band 1. Leipzig: VEB Bibliographisches Institut, 1968; Band 2, 1970.
Friedland, Roger, and A. F. Robertson (eds.), *Beyond the Marketplace.* New York: Aldine de Gruyter, 1990.
Friedman, David, *The Misunderstood Miracle: Industrial Development and Political Change in Japan.* Ithaca: Cornell University Press, 1988.
Friedrichs, Jürgen, Hartmut Häusermann, and Walter Siebel (eds.), *Süd-Nord-Gefälle in der Bundesrepublik?* Opladen: Westdeutscher Verlag, 1986.
Fritzsch, G., "Forderungen an den deutschen Textilmaschinenbau." *Melliand Textilberichte* 32 May (1951): 352–356.
Fröbel, Folker, Jürgen Heinrichs, and Otto Kreye, *Die neue internationale Arbeitsteilung. Strukturelle Arbeitslosigkeit in den Industrieländern und die Industrieaalisierung der Entwicklungsländer.* Hamburg: Rowohlt Taschenbuch Verlage GmbH, 1977.
Fröbel, Folker, Jürgen Heinrichs, and Otto Kreye, *Umbruch in der Weltwirtschaft. Die glabale Strategie: Verbilligung der Arbeitskraft/Flexibilisierung der Arbeit/Neue Technologien.* Hamburg: Rowohlt Taschenbuch Verlag, GmbH, 1986.
Fröhlich, Fr., *Die Stellung der deutschen Maschinenindustrie im deutschen Wirtschaftsleben und auf dem Weltmarkt.* Berlin: Julius Springer, 1914.
Funck, R., and Gerhard Becher, "Regional Development and Technology Policies: Some Lessons From the German Experience." *European Planning Studies* 2 (1994): 81–96.
Furger, Fridolin, *Zum Verlagssystem als Organisationsform des Frühkapitalismus im Textilgewerbe,* Beiheft zur Vierteljahreschrift für Sozial- und Wirtschaftsgeschichte, 11 ed. Stuttgart: w. Kohlhammer, 1927.
Fürstenau, Justus, "Struktur und Strukturveränderung im Maschinenbau." *Die Maschinenbau-Industrie in der Bundesrepublik Deutschland,* ed. Institut für Bilanzanlyze. Schriftenreihe Branchenanalysen No. 23. Frankfurt: Institut für Bilanzanalysen, 1974, pp. 4–8.
Galbraith, John Kenneth, *The New Industrial State.* New York: Mentor, 1978.

Garvin, David A., "Manufacturing Strategic Planning." *California Management Review* Summer (1993): 85–106.

Geary, Dick, "The industrial elite and the Nazis." *The Nazi Machtergreifung*. Peter D. Stachura (ed.). London: 1983, pp. 85–100.

Geary, Dick, "Socialism and the German Labor Movement before 1914." *Labour and Socialist Movements in Europe before 1914*. Dick Geary (ed.). London: Berg, 1989, pp. 101–136.

Gebauer, Heinrich, *Die Volkwirtschaft im Königreich Sachsen, historisch, geographisch und statstisch dargestellt. Band 1*. Dresden: Wilhelm Bänsch, 1893.

Geer, Rudolf, "Der Export der Deutschen Landmaschinenindustrie. Eine Untersuchung der Entwicklung set 1945 und der ökonomischen Bestimmungsgrössen für den Wettbewerb im Rahmen der Europäischen Wirtschafts-Unionen." *Dissertation*, Nuremberg, 1960.

Geer, Johann Sebastian, *Der Markt der geschlossenen Nachfrage. Eine morphologische Studie über die Eisenkontingentierung in Deutschland. 1937–1945*. Berlin: Duncker & Humblot, 1961.

Geertz, Clifford, *Peddlers and Princes*. Chicago: University of Chicago Press, 1963.

Gehring, Paul, "Von List bis Steinbeis. Aus der Frühzeit der Württembergischen Landesgeschichte." *Zeitung Für Württembergischen Landesgeschichte* 7 (1943): pp. 405–444..

Gehring, Paul, "Joannes Bürk und Erhard Junghans. Ein Betrag zur Frügeschichte der Schwäbischen Uhrenindustrie." *Zeitschrift für Württembergische Landesgeschichte* 14 (1955): 145–161.

Gemming, Alfred, *Das Handwerkergenossenschaftswesen in Württemberg*. Stuttgart: Verlag von Ferdinand Enke, 1911.

Gerschenkron, Alexander, *Economic Backwardness in Historical Perspective*. Cambridge, MA: Harvard University Press, 1962.

Gerschenkron, Alexander, *Bread and Democracy in Germany*. New York: Howard Fertig, 1966.

Gerschenkron, Alexander, *Continuity in History and Other Essays*. Cambridge, MA: Harvard University Press, 1968.

GEWOS, GfAH, and WSI, *Strukturwandel und Beschäftigungsperspektiven der Metallindustrie in der Ruhr*. Düsseldorf: IG Metall Vorstand, Frankfurt and Hans Böckler Stiftung, 1988.

Geyer, Michael, "Zum Einfluss der Nationalsozialistischen Rüstungspolitik auf das Ruhrgebiet." *Rheinische Vierteljahresblätter* (1981): 201–264.

Giddens, Anthony, *The Constitution of Society*. Berkeley: University of California Press, 1984.

Giddens, Anthony, *The Nation State and Violence*. Berkeley: University of California Press, 1985.

Gierke, Otto, *Die Genossenschaftstheorie und die deutsche Rechtsprechung*. Berlin: Weidmannsche Buchhandlung, 1887.

Gilpin, Robert, *US Power and the Multinational Corporation*. New York: Basic Books, 1975.

Gladen, Albin, "Die berufliche Aus- und Weiterbildung in der deutschen Wirtschaft 1918–1945." In *Die berufliche Aus- und Weiterbildung in der deutschen Wirtschaft set dem 19. Jahrhundert*. Hans Pohl (ed.). Wiesbaden: Franz Steiner, 1979.

Glastetter, Werner, *Die wirtschaftliche Entwicklung der Bundesrepublik Deutschland im Zeitraum 1950 bis 1975. Befunde und Aspekte*. Berlin: Springer, 1977.

Bibliography

Glouchevitch, Philip, *Juggernaut: The German Way of Business. Why It is Transforming Europe—and the World*. New York: Simon & Schuster, 1992, p. 239.

Glyn, Andrew, Alan Hughes, Alan Lipietz, and Ajit Singh, "The Rise and Fall of the Golden Age." In *The Golden Age of Capitalism. Reinterpreting the Postwar Experience*. Stephen A. Marglin and Juliet B. Schor (eds.). New York: Oxford University Press, 1990, pp. 39–125.

Gneist, Rudolph, *Die nationale Rechtsidee von den Standen und das preussische Dreiklassenwahlsystem : eine sozial-historische Studie*. Hildesheim: G. Olms, 1962.

Golay, John Ford, *The Founding of the Federal Republic of Germany*. Chicago: University of Chicago Press, 1958.

Goldbeck, Gustav, *Kraft für die Welt, 1864–1964. Klöckner Humbold Deutz AG*. Düsseldorf: Econ Verlag, 1964.

Goldberg, Walter H (ed.), *Ailing Steel. The Transoceanic Quarrel*. New York: St. Martin's Press, 1986.

Good, D., "Backwardness and the Role of Banking in Nineteenth Century European Industrialization." *Journal of Economic History* 33 (1973).

Gossweiler, Kurt, "Bund zur Erneuerung des Reiches." in *Die bürgerlichen Parteien in Deutschland, 1830–1945*. Dieter Fricke (ed.). Leipzig: VEB Bibliographisches Institut, 1968. Band 1: pp 195–200.

Gossweiler, Kurt, *Grossbanken Industriemonopole Saat. Okonomie und Politik des staatsmonopolistischen Kapitalismus in Deutschland 1914–1932*. Berlin (East): VEB Deutscher Verlag der Wissenschaften, 1971.

Gothein, Eberhard, *Wirtschaftsgeschichte des Schwartzwaldes und der angrenzenden Landschaften*. Strassburg: Karl J. Trübner, 1892.

Gourevitch, Peter, *Politics in Hard Times. Comparative Responses to International Economic Crises*. Ithaca: Cornell University Press, 1986.

Göbel, Helmut, "Neue Entwicklungen im Sondermaschinenbau für die Automobilindustrie." *Werkstatt und Betrieb. Zeitschrift für Maschinenbau und Fertigung* 86(3) (1953): 93–102.

Göbel, H., "Einige grundsätzliche Ueberlegungen bei der Auslegung von selbsttätigen Maschinenfliessfertigung." *Werkstattstechnik und Maschinenbau* 48(3) (1958).

Graf von Scherr-Thoss, H. C., *Die deutsche Automobilindustrie. Eine Dokumentation von 1886 bis heute*. Stuttgart: Deutsche-Verlags Anstalt, 1974.

Grande, Edgar, "Die Erosion staatlicher Handlungskapazität? Einige Arbeitshypothesen zu neueren forschungs- und technologiepolitischen Entwicklungen in der BRD." unpublished manuscript, Cologne: Max Planck Institut für Gesellschaftsforschung, 1990.

Granovetter, Mark, "Economic Action and Social Structure: The Problem of Embeddedness." *American Journal of Sociology* 91(3) (1985): 481–510.

Greiss, Franz, "Warum rationalisiert werden muss." *Vortragsreihe des Deutschen Industrieienstituts* 44 November 1 (1954).

Grimm, Dieter, *Recht und Staat der bürglichen Gesellschaft*. Frankfurt: Suhrkamp, 1987.

Grosser, Dieter (ed.), *Konzentration ohne Kontrolle*. Cologne/Opladen: Westdeutscher Verlag, 1969.

Gunlicks, Arthur, *Local Government in the German Federal System*. Durham: Duke University Press, 1986.

Guttsmann, W. L., *Workers Culture in Weimar Germany Between Tradition and Commitment*. Oxford: Berg, 1989.

Haber, F. L., *The Chemical Industry, 1900–1939.* Oxford: Oxford University Press, 1971.
Hack, Edgar, "Die Normung und Typisierung Industrieller Erzeugnisse unter besonderer Berücksichtigung der Maschinen- und Kraftfahrzeugindustrie." dissertation, Fakultät für Wirtschafts- und Sozialwissenschaften. Friedrich Alexander Universität Erlangen-Nürnberg, 1962.
Hamerow, Theodor, *Restoration, Revolution, and Reaction. Economics and Politics in Germany, 1815–1848.* Princeton: Princeton University Press, 1958.
Hamilton, Richard F., *Who Voted for Hitler.* Princeton: Princeton University Press, 1982.
Hammer, Marius, *Vergleichende Morphologie der Arbeit in der Europäischen Automobilindustrie: Die Entwicklung zur Automation.* Tübingen: J.C.B. Mohr (Paul Siebeck), 1959.
Hanabusa, Masamichi, *Trade Problems Between Japan and Western Europe.* Farnborough: Saxon House, for the Royal Institute of International Affairs, 1979.
Handy, Charles, "Balancing Corporate Power: A New Federalist Paper." *Harvard Business Review* November-December (1992): 59–72.
Hanke, Erich, *Mittelstand in der Bundesrepublik. Ein Beitrag zu Problemen der Bundnispolitik im antimonopolitistischen Kampf.* Frankfurt: Verlag Marxistische Blätter, 1973.
Hankel, Wilhelm, "Germany: Nationalism in the International Economy." In, *West Germany: A European and Global Power.* Wilfred Kohl and Giorgio Basevi (eds.). Lexington, MA: D.C. Heath and Company, 1980, pp. 21–43.
Hardach, Karl, *The Political Economy of Germany in the Twentieth Century.* Berkeley: University of California Press, 1976.
Harney, Klaus, "Historische Berufsbildungs- und Qualifikationsforschung am Bespiel der GHH Oberhausen. Arbeitskräftebeschaffung, Wanderung, Belegschaftsorganisation und der Ausbildung im Hinblick auf die Enstehung Schulischen Angebots." *Zeitschrift für Unternehmengeschichte* 28 (1983): 1–38.
Harnisch, Elisabeth, "Kartellierungsfähigkeit der Maschinenindustrie." Heidelberg, 1917.
Harrison, Bennett, *Lean and Mean: The Changing Landscape of Corporate Power in the Age of Flexibility.* New York: Basic Books, 1994.
Hartmann, Heinz, *Authority and Organization in German Management.* Princeton: Princeton University Press, 1959.
Hartmann, Heinz, "Management in Germany." In *Management in the Industrial World. An International Analysis.* Frederick Harbison and Charles A. Myers (eds.). New York: McGraw Hill, 1959, pp. 265–284.
Hartwich, Hans Hermann, *Arbeitsmarkt, Verbände und Staat 1918–1933: Die öffentliche Bindung unternehmerischer Funktionen in der Weimarer Republik.* Berlin: Walter de Gruyter, 1967.
Harvey, David, *The Limits to Capital.* New York: Oxford University Press, 1982.
Harvey, David, *The Urban Experience.* Baltimore: Johns Hopkins Press, 1989.
Hasselmann, Wolfram, and Jürgen Schierholz, *Interregionale Interdependenzen. Das Ruhrgebiet als Absatzmarkt für die Wirtschaft der Randzonen dargestellt am Beispiel Westmünsterland und Remscheid.* Münster: Institut für Siedlungs- und Wohnungswesen der Westfälische Wilhelms-Universität Münster, 1971.
Hassink, Robert, "Regional Innovation Policy: Case Studies from the Ruhr Area, Baden

Württemberg and the North East of England." *Ph.D. Dissertation.* Faculteit Ruimtelijke Wetenschappen Rijksuniversiteit Utrecht, Netherlands, 1992.

Hayek, Friedrich, A., *Law, Legislation and Liberty: A New Statement of the Liberal Principles of Justice and Political Economy, Volume 1: Rule and Order.* Chicago: University of Chicago Press, 1973.

Hayes, Peter, *Industry and Ideology. IG Farben in the Nazi Era.* Cambridge: Cambridge University Press, 1987.

Hayes, Robert, and Ramchadran Jaikumar, "Manufacturing's Crisis: New Technologies, Obsolete Organizations. Getting beyond functional divisions, top down decision making, piecemeal investment and bottom line accounting." *Harvard Business Review* September–October (1988): 77–85.

Hayward, J. E. S., "Steel." In *Big Business and the State. Changing Relations in Western Europe.* Raymond Vernon (ed.). Cambridge, MA: Harvard University Press, 1974, pp. 255–274.

Häpke, Rudolf, "Die ökonomische Landschaft und die Gruppenstadt in der älteren Wirtschaftsgeschichte." In *Aus Sozial- und Wirtschaftsgeschichte: Gedächtnisschrift Für Georg Von Below.* Stuttgart: W. Kohlhammer, 1928, pp. 82–105.

Häußermann, Hartmut, and Walter Siebel, *Neue Urbanität.* Frankfurt: Suhrkamp, 1987).

Heckscher, Eli, *Mercantilism.* London: Allen and Unwin, 1935.

Heffter, Heinrich, *Geschichte der deutsche Selbstverwaltung im 19. Jahrhundert.* Stuttgart: Köhler, 1950.

Heidenheimer, Arnold J., "Federalism and the Party System: The Case of West Germany." *American Political Science Review* 12(3) (1958): 809–828.

Heilemann, Ulrich, "Mo' Money? Medium Term Perspectives of the West German Economy." *Economie Appliquée* 46(1) (1993): 63–82.

Heiligenstadt, C., "Die Preussische Centralgenossenschaftskasse." In *Conrad's Handwörterbuch,* 3rd ed. 1910.

Helbig, Herbert (ed.), *Führungskräfte der Wirtschaft in Mittelalter und Neuzeit, 1350–1850.* Limburg/Lahn: C. A. Starke Verlag, 1973.

Helfer, C., "Über militärische Einflüsse auf die industrielle Entwicklung in Deutschland." *Schmollers Jahrbuch* 133 (1963): 597–609.

Hellwig, Fritz, "The Establishment of a Common Market in Europe. The attitude of German business and management towards Integration." *Erweiterte Niederschrift eines Vortrages in Rahmen einer Vortragsrheie über Probleme der Integration, veranstaltet von Johns Hopkins University Center in Bologna am 18 Februar 1957,* (Schnittarchiv der Deutsche Gesellschaft für Auswärtige Politik. Ordner Europa, 501: 12.1.12.1953 bis 22.1.1957: 1957).

Helmrich, Wilhelm, *Wirtschaftskunde des Landes Nordrhein-Westfalen.* Düsseldorf: August Bagel, 1960.

Henderson, W. O., *The Zollverein.* Cambridge: Cambridge University Press, 1939.

Henderson, W. O., *The State and the Industrial Revolution in Prussia.* Liverpool: Liverpool University Press, 1958.

Henderson, W. O., "The Rise of Metal and Armaments Industries in Berlin and Brandenburg." In *Studies in the Economic Policies of Frederick the Great.* W. O. Henderson (ed.). London: Frank Cass and Co., 1963.

Henderson, W. O., *The Rise of German Industrial Power. 1834–1914.* Berkeley: Campus, 1975.

Hendrichs, Franz, "Rationalisierung in der Solinger Industrie." *Technik und Wirtschaft* 22(3) (1929): 66–70.

Hendrichs, Franz, "Solingen im Ringen mit Sheffield im 19. Jahrhundert Im Gütegedanken zum Erfolg." *VDI-Nachrichten* 16 August 7 (1954): 4.

Henne, Franz, "A German Path to Fordism. The Socio-Economic Transformation of a Region: The Bergische Land and Märkische Sauerland. 1930–1960." *Ph.D. dissertation*, Department of History. University of Chicago, 1993.

Henning, Friedrich-Wilhelm, *Dienste und Abgaben der bauern im 18. Jahrhundert*. Stuttgart: Gustav Fischer, 1969.

Herbert, Ulrich, *A History of Foreign Labor in Germany 1880–1980*. Ann Arbor: University of Michigan Press, 1990.

Herchenröder, K. H., Johan Schäfer, and Manfred Zapp. *Die Nachfolger der Ruhrkonzerne. Die Neuordnung der Montanindistrie*. Düsseldorf: Econ Verlag, 1953.

Herdt, Hans Konradt, *Bosch 1886–1986. Porträt eines Unternehmens*. Stuttgart: Deutsches Verlags-Anstalt, 1986.

Herrigel, Gary, and Richard Kazis, "The Political Economy of Competitiveness: The Case of Textile Machinery in the United States and West Germany." unpublished paper, 1987.

Herrigel, Gary, "Industrial Order and the Politics of Industrial Change." In *Industry and Politics in West Germany*. Peter Katzenstein (ed.). Ithaca: Cornell University Press, 1989, pp. 185–220.

Herrigel, Gary, "Industrial Organization and the Politics of Industry. Centralized and Decentralized Production in Germany." *Dissertation*, Department of Political Science. MIT, 1990.

Herrigel, Gary, "Industrial Order in the Machine Tool Industry. A Comparison of Germany and the United States." In *Betriebliche Sozialeverfassungen unter Veränderungsdruck. Konzepte, Variante, Entwicklungstendenzen*. Eckhardt Hildebrandt (ed.). Berlin: edition sigma, 1991.

Herrigel, Gary, "Industry as a Form of Order. A Comparison of the Historical Development of the Machine Tool Industries in Germany and the United States." In *Governing Capitalist Economies*. Wolfgang Streeck, Phillipe Schmitter, and J. Rogers Hollingsworth (eds.). New York: Oxford University Press, 1992.

Herrigel, Gary, "Power in Industrial Districts." In *The Embedded Firm*. Gernot Grabher (ed.). London: Routledge, 1992, pp. 227–251.

Herrigel, Gary, "Large Firms, Small Firms and the Governance of Flexible Specialization: Baden Württemberg and the Socialization of Risk." In *Country Competitiveness: Technology and the Organizing of Work*. Bruce Kogut (ed.). New York: Oxford University Press, 1993.

Herrigel, Gary, and Sabel, Charles, "Craft Production in Crisis: Industrial Restructuring in Germany during the 1990s." In *Conference Proceedings Globalization and Regionalization: Implications and Options for the Asian NIEs. Honolulu, Hawaii, 15–17 August*. Hawaii: Imin International Conference Center: 1994.

Herrmann, Walther, "Der Wiederaufbau der Selbstverwaltung der deutschen Wirtschaft nach 1945." *Zeitschrift für Unternehmensgeschichte* 23(2) (1978): 81–96.

Herzfeld, Hans, *Demokratie und Selbstverwalltung in der Weimarer Epoch* (Schriftenreihe des Vereins zur Pflege Kommunalwissenschaftlicher Aufgaben e.V.). Berlin: Kohlhammer, 1957.

Hesselmann, Linda, "Trends in European Industrial Intervention." *Cambridge Journal of Economics* 7 (1983): 197–208.

Hessenmüller, Dipl. Ing, "Vertriebsgemeinschaften im Maschinenbau." *Technik und Wirtschaft* 23(9) (1930): 256–257.

Hettling, Manfred, *Reform Ohne Revolution: Bürgertum, Bürokratie und kommunale Selbstverwaltung in Württemberg von 1800 bis 1850.* Göttingen: Vandenhoeck & Ruprecht, 1990.

Hilferding, Rudolf, *Finance Capital. A Study of the Latest Phase of Capitalist Development.* London: Routledge, Kegan Paul, 1985.

Hillemann, Rudolf, "Die westdeutsche Textilmaschinenindustrie. Ihre Entwicklung seit 1945 und ihre Marktprobleme." *Dissertation,* Münster, 1951.

Hilpert, Josef, and Hans Joachim Sperling, *Die kleine Fabrik. Beschäftigung, Technik und Arbeitsbeziehung.* Munich and Mering: Rainer Hampp Verlag, 1990.

Hilpert, Ulrich (ed.), *Regional Innovation and Decentralization. High Tech Industry and Government Policy.* London: Routledge, 1991.

Hintze, Otto, *Staat und Verfassung. Gesammelte Abhandlungen zur allgemeinen Verfassungsgeschichte.* Göttingen: Vandenhoeck & Ruprecht, 1967a.

Hintze, Otto, *Regierung und Verwaltung. Gesammelte Abhandlungen zur Staats- Rechts- und Sozialgeschichte Preussens.* Göttingen: Vandenhoeck & Ruprecht, 1967b.

Hintze, Otto, "Economics and Politics in the Age of Modern Capitalism." In *The Historical Essays of Otto Hintz.* Felix Gilbert (ed.). New York: Oxford University Press, 1975.

Hirsch, Joachim, *Kapitalismus ohne Alternative?* Frankfurt: Campus, 1988.

Hirschman, Albert O., *A Bias for Hope. Essays on Development and Latin America.* New Haven: Yale University Press, 1971.

Hirschman, Albert O., *Essays in Trespassing.* New York: Cambridge University Press, 1981.

Hitler, Adolf, *Mein Kampf.* Boston: Houghton Mifflin, 1971.

Hoffmann, Rudolf, *Daimler Benz Aktiengesellschaft Stuttgart-Untertürkheim, Musterbetriebe Deutscher Wirtschaft Band 12: Die Automobilindustrie.* Berlin: Organisation Verlegsgesellschaft, 1930.

Hofmann, Dr. Rolf, "Neue Probleme der Absatzfinanzierung." *Der Volkswirt* 17 April 4 (1966): 644–646.

Hohenberg, Paul M., and Lynn Hollen Lees, *The Making of Urban Europe, 1000–1500.* Cambridge, MA: Harvard University Press, 1985.

Holborn, Hajo, *A History of Modern Germany.* Princeton: Princeton University Press, 1959.

Hollingsworth, J. Rogers, Phillippe C. Schmitter, and Wolfgang Streeck (eds.), *Governing Capitalist Economies. Performance and Control of Economic Sectors.* New York: oxford University Press, 1994.

Holmström, Bengt, and Jean Tirole, "The Theory of the Firm." In *Handbook of Industrial Organization.* R. Schmalensee and R. Willig (eds.). Amsterdam: North Holland, 199.

Horak, Hans, "Innovationsberatung als Aufgabe der Wirtschaftlicher Selbstverwaltung." *Mittlerer Neckar* 5 (1978): 11–13.

Horn, Norbert, and Jürgen Kocka (eds.), *Recht und Entwicklung der Grossunternehmen in 19. und frühen 20. Jahrhundert.* Göttingen: Vandenhoeck & Ruprecht, 1979.

Horstmann, Theo, "The Worst Banking Practice in the World." Inter-Allied Discussion over American Plans to Reform the German Banking System in 1945/1946." In *German Yearbook on Business History 1986.* Hans Pohl (ed.). Berlin: Springer-Verlag, 1987, pp. 93–116.

Horstmann, Theo, *Die Alliierten und die deutsche Grossbanken. Bankenpolitik nach dem Zweiten Weltkrieg in Westdeutschland.* Bonn: Bouvier Verlag, 1991.
Hoselitz, Bert F., and Wilbert E. Moore (eds.), *Industrialization and Society.* Mouton: UNESCO, 1966.
Hoth, Wolfgang, *Die Industrialisierung einer rheinischen Gewerbestadt—dargstellt am Beispiel Wuppertal.* Köln: Rheinisch-Westfälischen Wirtschaftsarchiv zu Köln, 1975.
Hounshell, David A., *From the American System to Mass Production, 1800–1932.* Baltimore: Johns Hopkins Press, 1984.
Hödl, Erich, and Hella Groth, Rainer Mönig, Bernd Seidler, "Technik und Arbeitsmarkt. Grundzüge eines Politikmodelles zur sozialverträglichen Technikgestaltung in der Stadt Wuppertal." Bergische Universität-Gesamthochschule Wuppertal, 1989.
Hödl, Erich, and Bernd Seidler, "Industriestruktur und Innovationstätigkeit in Wuppertal." *Fachbereichs Wirtschaftswissenschaft der Bergischen Universität—Gesamthochschule Wuppertal,* 1989.
Hubsch, Peter, "DBG Economic Policy with Particular Reference to the British Zone, 1945–1949." In *Reconstruction in Post War Germany. British Occupation Policy and the Western Zones, 1945–1955.* Ian D. Turner (ed.). Oxford: Berg, 1989, pp. 271–300.
Hudson, Ray, and David Sadler, *The International Steel Industry. Restructuring, State Policies and Localities.* London: Routledge, 1989.
Huffschmid, Bernd, *Das Stahlzeitalter beginnt erst.* Munich: Verlag Moderne Industrie, 1965.
Huffschmid, Jörg, *Die Politik des Kapitals. Konzentration und Wirtschaftspolitik in der Bundesrepublik.* Frankfurt: Suhrkamp, 1970.
Hüttenberger, Peter, "Wirtschaftsordung und Interessenpolitik in der Kartelgesetzgebung der Bundesrepublik, 1949–1957." *Vierteljahreshefte für Zeitgeschichte* 24(3) (1976): 287–307.
Hützel, Jürgen, *Interdependenzen zwischen Klein und Grossfirmen. Eine empirische Untersuchung am Beispiel der Metallindustrie Baden-Württembergs.* Tübingen: Institut für Angewandte Wirtschaftsforschung, 1981a.
Hützel, Jürgen, *Grosse und kleine Zulieferer. Eine Untersuchung zur Nachfragemacht industrieller Abnehmer.* Tübingen: Institut für Angewandte Wirtschaftsforschung, 1981b.
Hymer, Stephen, and Robert Rowthorn, "Multinational Corporations and International Oligopoly: The Non-American Challenge." In *The International Corporation. A Symposium.* Charles Kindleberger (ed.). Cambridge, MA: MIT Press, 1970, pp. 57–95.
Inglehart, Ronald, *The Silent Revolution. Changing Values and Political Styles Among Western Publics.* Princeton: Princeton University Press, 1977.
Inglehart, Ronald, *Culture Shift in Advanced Industrial Society.* Princeton: Princeton University Press, 1990.
IÖW-Institute Für Ökologische Wirtschaftsforschung, Regionalbüro NRW (Wuppertal), *Chance und Risiken einer auf regionale Bedürfnisse ausgerichteten Technologiepolitik: Zusammenfassung: Theoretischer Ansatz und Beispiele für die Entwicklungsperspektiven der Region Bergisches Land,* Düsseldorf: Ministerium für Arbeit, Gesundheit und Soziales des Landes Nordrhein Westfalen, 1990.
Irmen, Eleonore, "Zur Entwicklung der Agglomerationsräume in der Bundesrepublik Deutschland." *Informationen zur Raumentwicklung* 11/12 (1989): 811–822.

Isaak, Robert, "Germany: economic powerhouse or stalemate?" *Challenge* 35(5) September (1992): 41ff.
Isenberg, Gerhard, "Standortverhaltnisse und Industriestruktur: Ein vergleich zwischen Nordrhein-Westfalen und Baden Württemberg." *Raum und Verkehr* 1 (1956): 103.
Iserman, F., "Wege zur Steigerung der Maschinenasufuhr." *Technik und Wirtschaft* 24(2) (1931): 29–33.
Iwer, Frank, "Industriestandort Stuttgart 1994. Entwicklung und Perspektiven der Metallindustrie." *Regionale Branchenanalyse im Auftrag der IG Metall Verwaltungsstelle Stuttgart.* IMU-Institut fuer Medienforschung und Urbanistik, 1994.
Jaeger, Hans, *Geschichte der Wirtschaftsordnung in Deutschland.* Frankfurt am Main: Suhrkamp, 1988.
James, Harold, *The German Slump. Politics and Economics 1924–1936.* Oxford: Clarendon Press, 1986.
Jeidels, Otto, *Das Verhältnis der deutschen Grossbanken zur Industrie mit besonderer Berücksichtigung der Eisenindustrie.* Leipzig: Duncker & Humblot, 1905.
Jessop, Bob (ed.), *The Politics of Flexibility. Restructuring State and Industry in Britain, Germany and Scandinavia.* Aldershot: Edward Elgar, 1991.
John, Michael, *Politics and Law in Late Nineteenth Century Germany.* Oxford: Clarendon, 1989.
Johnson, Chalmers, *MITI and the Japanese Miracle: The Growth of Industrial Policy, 1925–1975.* Stanford: Stanford University Press, 1981.
Johnson, Neville, "Territory and Power: Some Historical Determinants of the Constitutional Structure of the Federal Republic of Germany." In *German Federalism Today.* Charlie Jeffrey and Peter Savigear (eds.). New York: St. Martin's Press, 1991, pp. 8–22.
Jordan, Horst, "Wirtschaft in Wuppertal und Niederberg." In *Die westdeutsche Wirtschaft und ihre führenden Männer. Lesebuch der deutschen Industrie. Land Nordrhein Westfalen. Teil III: Bergisches Land.* Julius Keil (ed.). Oberursel: Wirtschaftslesebuch-Verlag Dr. Julius Keil GmbH, 1975, pp. 18–28.
Jöst, Hans-Josef, *Pionier im Ruhrrevier. Gutehoffnungshütte-Vom ältesten Montan-Unternehmen Deutschlands zum größten Maschinenbau-Konzern Europas.* Stuttgart: Seewald, 1982.
Jösten, Joachim, *Germany: What Now?* Chicago: Ziff-Davis Publishing Co., 1948.
Kapp, Adolf, "Die öffentliche Meinung in Württemberg 1866." *Württembergische Vierteljahreshefte für Landesgeschichte* 16 (1907): 157–236.
Katzenstein, Peter (ed.), *Between Power and Plenty. Foreign Economic Policies of Advanced Industrial States.* Madison: University of Wisconsin Press, 1978.
Katzenstein, Peter, *Small States and World Markets.* Ithaca: Cornell University Press, 1985a.
Katzenstein, Peter, *Corporatism and Change.* Ithaca: Cornell University Press, 1985b.
Katzenstein, Peter, *Policy and Politics in West Germany. The Growth of a Semi-Sovereign State.* Philadelphia: Temple, 1987.
Katzenstein, Peter (ed.), *Industry and Politics in West Germany. Toward a Third Republic.* Ithaca: Cornell University Press, 1989.
Kaufhold, Karl Heinrich, "Gewerbelandschaften in der frühen Neuzeit, 1650–1800." In *Gewerbe-und Industrielandschaften vom Spätmittelalter bis ins 20 Jahrhundert.* Heinrich Pohl (ed.). Stuttgart: Franz Steiner Verlag Wiesbaden GmbH, 1986.
Kälble, H., *Industrielle Interessenpolitik in der wilhelminischen Gesellschaft. Centralverband deutscher Industrie.* Berlin: Walter de Gruyter, 1967.

Kämper, Hugo, "Arbeitslosigkeit im strukturschwachen Ruhrgebiet am Beispiel Essen." *Informationen zur Raumentwicklung* 9/10 (1987): 557–560.
Keachie, E. C., "Stand der ökonomisch-technischen Betriebsführung (Industrial Engineering) in Deutschland." *Zeitschrift für Handelswissenschaftliche Forschung* 10(12) (1958): 672–678.
Keck, Otto, "The National System for Technical Innovation in Germany." In *National Innovation Systems: A Comparative Analysis*. Richard R. Nelson (ed.). New York: Oxford University Press, 1993, pp. 115–157.
Kellenbenz, Hermann, "Rural Industries in the End of the Middle Ages to the Eighteenth Century." In *Essays in European Economic History 1500–1800*. Peter Earle (ed.). Oxford: Clarendon Press, 1974.
Kellenbenz, Hermann (ed.), *Agrarisches Nebengewerbe und Formen der Reagrarisierung im Spätmittelater und 19./20. Jahrhundert*. Stuttgart: G. Fischer (1975).
Kern, Horst, and Michael Schumann, *Industriearbeit und Arbeiterbewusstsein*. Frankfurt: Europaische Verlagsanstalt, 1970.
Kern, Horst, and Michael Schumann, *Ende der Arbeitsteilung?* Munich: Beck, 1984.
Kern, Horst, and Charles F. Sabel, "Trade Unions and Decentralized Production. A Sketch of Strategic Problems in the West German Labor Movement." *Politics and Society* 19(4) (1992): 373–402.
Kern, Horst, and Sabel, Charles, "Verblaß te Tugend. Die Krise des deutschen Produktionsmodells." In *Soziale Welt Sonderband: Umbrüche gesellschaftlicher Arbeit* (1993).
Kerr, Clark, "The Trade Union Movement and the Redistribution of Power in Post War Germany." *Quarterly Journal of Economics* 68(4) (1954): 535–564.
Keynes, John Maynard, *The General Theory of Employment, Interest and Money*. New York: Harcourt, Brace Jovanovich, 1936.
Kiesewetter, Hubert, "Staat und Unternehmen Während der Frühindustrialisierung: Das Königreich Sachsen als Paradigma." *Zeitschrift für Unternehmengeschichte* 29 (1984).
Kiesewetter, Hubert, "Economic Preconditions for Germany's Nation-Building in the Nineteenth Century." In *Nation-Building in Central Europe*. Hagen Schultze (ed.). Leamington Spa: Berg, 1987).
Kiesewetter, Hubert, *Industrialisierung und Landwirtschaft*. Köln: Böhlau Verlag, 1988.
Kiesewetter, Hubert, *Industrielle Revolution in Deutschland, 1815–1914*. Frankfurt: Suhrkamp, 1989.
Kircheimer, Otto, "Changes in the Structure of Political Compromise." In *Politics, Law and Social Change. Selected Essays*. Otto Kircheimer (ed.). New York: Columbia University Press, 1969.
Kisker, Karl, "Die Rationalisierung und der Mensch." *Vortragsreihe des Deutschen Industrieinstituts* 5 January 30 (1956).
Klatt, Hartmut, "Reform und Perspectiven des Föderalismus in der Bundesrepublik Deutschland." *Aus Politik und Zeitgeschichte* 28(12) July (1986): 16–21.
Klatt, Harmut, "German unification and the Federal System." In *Federalism, Unification and European Integration*. Charlie Jeffrey and Roland Sturm (eds.). London: Frank Cass, 1993, pp. 1–21.
Klein, Ernst, "Die Hohenheimer Ackergeräterfabrik (1819–1904)." *Zeitschrift für Württembergische Landesgeschichte* 22 (1963): 302–367.
Klessmann, Christoff, "Betriebsträte und Gewerkschaften in Deutschland 1945–1952."

In *Politische Weichenstelluingen im Nachkriegsdeutschland, 1945–1953*. Heinrich A. Winkler (ed.). Göttingen: Vandenhoeck & Ruprecht, 1979, pp. 44–73.

Klinger, K., "Zulieferungen und Zulieferer in betriebswirtschaftlicher Sicht." *der Betrieb* 12(45) November 11 (1959).

Kluver, J., W. Jost, and K-L Heese (eds.), *Gesamthochschule – Versaeumte Chancen? Zehn Jahre Gesamthochschulen in Nordrhein Westfalen*. Opladen: Leske & Budrich, 1983.

Knayer, Manfred, "Ohne Automation geht es nicht." *Der Volkswirt* 51–52 (1955): 50–52.

Knight, Jack, *Institutions and Social Conflict*. New York: Cambridge University Press, 1992.

Knorr, Max, "Der Mensch und die Automatisierung." *Vortragsreihe des Deutschen Industrieinstituts* 22 June 1 (1958).

Knott, Jack H., *Managing the German Economy Budgetary Politics in a Federal State*. Lexington, MA: Lexington Books, 1981.

Kocka, Jürgen, *Unternehmensverwaltung und Angestelltenschaft am Beispiel Siemens, 1847–1914*. Stuttgart: Klett, 1969.

Kocka, Jürgen, "Family and Bureaucracy in German Industrial Management, 1850–1914." *Business History Review* 45(2) Summer (1971): 133–156.

Kocka, Jürgen, *Klassengesellscahft im Krieg, 1914–1918*. Göttingen: Vandenhoeck & Ruprecht, 1973.

Kocka, Jürgen, "Expansion, Integration, Diversifikation. Wachstumstrategien industrielle Grossunternehmen in Deutschland vor 1914." In *Von Kleingewerbe zur Großindustrie*. Harald Winkler (ed.). Berlin: Dunker & Humblot, 1975.

Kocka, Jürgen, "Entrepreneurs and Managers in German Industrialisation." In *The Cambridge Economic History of Europe, Volume 7, The Industrial Economies: Capital, Labor and Enterprise. Part One: Britain, France, Germany and Scandinavia*. Peter Mathias and M. M. Postan (eds.). Cambridge: Cambridge University Press, 1978.

Kocka, Jürgen, and Hannes Siegrist, "Die hundert grössten deutschen Industrieunternehmen in späten 19. und freuhen 20. Jahrhundert. Expansion. In Diversification und Integration im internationalen Vergleich." In *Recht und Entwicklung der Grossunternehmen, 1860–1920*. Nörbert and Jürgen Kocka Horn (eds.). Göttingen: Vandenhoeck & Ruprecht, 1979.

Kocka, Jürgen, "The Rise of Modern Industrial Enterprise in Germany." In *Managerial Hierarchies: Comparative Perspectives on the Rise of the Modern Industrial Enterprise*. Alfred D. and Herman Daems Chandler (eds.). Cambridge, MA: Harvard University Press, 1980.

Kocka, Jürgen, "Capitalism and Bureaucracy in German Industrialization Before 1914." *Economic History Review* 34(3) (1981a): 453–468.

Kocka, Jürgen, "Class Formation, Interest Articulation, and Public Policy: The Origins of the German White Collar Class in the Late Nineteenth and Early Twentieth Centuries." In *Organizing Interests in Western Europe*. Suzanne Berger (ed.). New York: Cambridge University Press, 1981b.

Kocka, Jürgen, "Germany: Cooperation and Competition." *Business History Review* 64 Winter (1990): 711–716.

Koenigsberger, H. G., "Diminum Regale or Diminum Politicum: Monarchies and Parliaments in Early Modern Europe." In *Politicians and Virtuosi. Essays in Early Modern History*. H. G. Koenigsberger (ed.). London: Hambledon, 1986.

Koike, Kazuo, and Takenori Inoki (eds.), *Skill Formation in Japan and Southeast Asia.* Tokyo: Tokyo University Press, 1987.

Köllman, Wolfgang, *Die Strukturelle Entwicklung des südwestfälischen Wirtschaftsraumes. 1945-1967.* Hagen: Linnepe Verlagsgesellschaft KG, 1969.

Kommission der Europäischen Gemeinschaften, *Untersuchungen zur Konzentrationsentwicklung in verschiedenen Untersektoren der Maschinenbauindustrie in Deutschland: Landwirtschaftliche Maschinen und Ackerschleppern, Büromaschinen, Textilmaschinen und Zubehör, Bau-und Baustoffmaschinen and Hebzeug und Fördermittel,* Brussels, EEC, 1975.

Koshar, Rudy, *Social life, local politics, and Nazism: Marburg, 1880-1935.* Chapel Hill: University of North Carolina Press, 1986.

Köttgen, Arnold, "Die Krise der Kommunal Selbstverwaltung." In *Kommunale Selbstverwaltung zwischen Krise und Reform. Ausgewählte Schriften.* Arnold Köttgen (ed.). Stuttgart: Kohlhammer, 1968.

Krähe, Walther, "Die innerbetriebliche Organisation von Konzernen." *Zeitschrift fur handelswissenschaftliche Forschung. "Organisation der Konzerne." Bericht über eine Arbeitstagung der Schmalenbach-Gesellschaft am 23 Januar 1953 in Essen* (1953): 153-168.

Kreidte, Peter, "The Origins, the Agrarian Context, and the Conditions of the World Market." In *Industrialization Before Industrialization.* Peter Kreidte, H. Medick and J. Schlumbohm (eds.). New York: Cambridge University Press, 1981, pp. 12-37.

Kreidte, Peter, Hans Medick, and Jürgen Schlumbohn (eds.), *Industrialization Before Industrialization.* New York: Cambridge University Press, 1981.

Kreidte, Peter, *Ein Stadt am Seiden Faden, Haushalt, Hausindustrie, und soziale Bewegung in Krefeld in der Mitte des 19 Jahrhunderts.* Göttingen: Vandenhoeck & Ruprecht, 1991.

Kreidte, Peter, Hans Medick, and Jürgen Schlumbohn, "Sozialgeschichte in der Erweiterung—Proto-industrialisierung in der Verengung? Demographie, Sozialstruktur, Moderne Hausindustrie: eine Zwischenbilanz der Protoindustrialisierungs-Forschung (Teil 1)." *Geschichte und Gesellschaft* 18 (1991): 70-87.

Kreile, Michael, "The Dynamics of Expansion." In *Between Power and Plenty: Foreign Economic Policies of Advanced Industrial States.* Peter Katzenstein (ed.). Madison: University of Wisconsin Press, 1978.

Krieger, W., "Zur Geschichte von Technologiepolitik und Forschungsförderung in der Bundesrepublic Deutschland." *Vierteljahreshefte für Zeitgeschichte* 35 (1987): 247-271.

Kruk, Max, and Gerold Lingnau, *Daimler-Benz. Das Unternehmen.* Mainz: Hase & Köhler, 1986.

Krummacher, M., Th. Rommelspacher and M.Weinemann, "Niedergang einer alten Industrieregion. Analysen zur Perspektive des Ruhrgebiets." In *Regionalentwicklung zwischen Technologieboom und Restvewertung. Die Beispiele Ruhrgebiet und München* Arbeitsgruppe Ruhrgebiet/Arbetisgruppe München (ed.). Bochum: Germinal Verlag, 1985, pp. 17-114.

Krusche, Reinhard, and Dagmar Pfeiffer, "Probleme der Gewerkschaftspolitik 1945-1965." In *Die Linke im Rechtstaat, Band 1: Bedingungen sozialistischer Politik 1945-1965.* Bernhard Blanke (ed.). Berlin: Rotbuch Verlag, 1976, pp. 139-158.

Krüder, Thomas, and Hanno Löwy (eds.), *Konservativismus in der Strukturkrise.* Frankfurt: Suhrkamp, 1987.

Krüger, Hermann Edwin, "Historische und Kritische Untersuchungen über die freien

Interessungvertretung von Industrie, Handel und Gewerbe in Deutschland." *Schmollers Jahrbuch* 33 (1909).
Kugler, Anita, "Von der Werkstatt zum Fliessband." *Geschichte und Gesellschaft* 13(3) (1987).
Kunz, Dieter, *Die Marktstellung der mittelständischen Zulieferbetriebe. Eine Untersuchuung der Zuliefererverhältnisse in der gewerblichen Wirtschaft Baden-Württembergs*. Stuttgart: Institut für Südwestdeutsche Wirtschaftsforschung, 1972.
Kurth, Walter, "Automation in der Industrie." *Der Volkswirt* (1954).
Küster, Goetz, *75 Jahre Bosch. 1886–1961 Ein geschichtlicher Rückblick*. Stuttgart: Deutsche Verlagsanstalt, 1961.
Küster, George, "Germany." In *Big Business and the State*. Raymond Vernon (ed.). Cambridge, MA: Harvard/Belknap, 1974, pp. 64–86.
Küsters, H-J, *Die Gründung der Europaische Wirtschaftsgemeinschaft*. Baden-Baden: Nomos Verlag, 1982.
Läpple, Dieter, "Sud-Nord-Gefälle' Metapher für raümlichen Folgen einer Transformationsphase: Auf dem Weg zu einem post-taylorischen Entwicklungsmodell?" In *Süd-Nord-Gefälle in der Bundesrepublik?* Jürgen Friedrichs Hartmut Haüsermann, and Walter Siebel (eds.). Opladen: Westdeutscher Verlag, 1986, pp. 97–114.
Lahme, Walter, "Die Wirtschaftsorganisationen in ihrer Bedeutung fuer das Verhältnis von Staat und Wirtschaft und der berufsständische Gedanke." *Dissertation*, Rechts- und Staatswissenschaftlichen Fakultät, Phillipps-Universität zu Marburg, 1941.
Lall, Sanjaya, "Recent Trends in Exports of Manufactures by Newly Industrializing Countries." In *Developing Countries in the International Economy. Selected Papers*. Sanjaya Lall (ed.). London: Macmillan, 1981.
Lammert, Franz, "Das Verhältnis zwischen der Eisen schaffenden und der Eisen verarbeitenden Industrie seit dem ersten Weltkrieg." *Dissertation*, Wirtschafts- und Sozialwissenschaftlichen Fakultät. Universität zu Köln, 1960.
Lamming, Richard, "The Causes and Effects of Structural Change in the European Automotive Components Industry." *Center for Technology Policy and Industrial Development*. MIT, 1989.
Landes, David, *The Unbound Prometheus. Technological Change and Industrial Development in Western Europe from 1750 to the Present*. New York: Cambridge University Press, 1969.
Lange, Karl, "Zum Thema: Bilanz der deutschen Handelspolitik 1925–1929." *Maschinenbau. Wirtschaftischer Teil* 9(3) (1930): W25–W28.
Lange, Karl, "Die deutsche Ausfuhr in der Weltwirtschaftskrise." *Maschinenbau. Wirtschaftlicher Teil* 10(1) (1931): W1–W2.
Lange, Karl, "Werkzeugmaschinen als Grundlage der Produktionssteigerung." *Vierjahresplan*, 1939.
Lasch, Karl, *Entwicklungstendenzen für die Zusammenschlussformen in der deutschen Grossindustrie seit 1914*. Düsseldorf: Industrie-Verlag u. Druckerei A. G., 1930.
Laufer, Heinz, *Das föderative System der Bundesrepublik Deutschland*. Munich: Bayerische andeszentrale für politische Bildungsarbeit, 1985.
Laux, James M., *The European Automobile Industry*. New York: Twayne Publishers, 1992.
Lavoie, Don, *Rivalry and Central Planning: The Socialist Calculation Debate Reconsidered*. New York: Cambridge University Press, 1985.
Layton, Christopher, *Transatlantic Investments*. Paris: The Atlantic Institute, 1970.

Lazonick, William, *Business Organization and the Myth of the Market Economy*. New York: Cambridge University Press, 1991.
Lederer, Emil (ed.), *Kapitalismus, Klassenstruktur und Probleme der Demokratie in Deutschland. 1910–1940*. Göttingen: Vandenhoeck & Ruprecht, 1979.
Ledermann, Fred, *Fehlrationalisierung—der Irrweg der deutschen Automobilindustrie seit der Stabilisierung der Mark*. Stuttgart: C. E. Pöschel, 1933.
Lee, J. J., "Labour in German Industrialisation." In *The Cambridge Economic History of Europe, Volume 7, The Industrial Economies: Capital, Labor and Enterprise. Part One: Britain, France, Germany and Scandinavia*. Peter Mathias and M. M. Postan (eds.). Cambridge: Cambridge University Press, 1978, pp. 442–491.
Lee, W. R. (ed.), *German Industry and German Industrialisation*. London: Routledge, 1991.
Lehmbruch, Gerhard, *Parteienwettbewerb im Bundesstaat*. Stuttgart: Kohlhammer, 1976.
Lehmbruch, Gerhard, "Party and Federation in Germany: A Developmental Dilemma." *Government and Opposition* 13 (1978): 151–177.
Lehner, Franz, Jürgen Nordhause-Janz, and Klaus Schubert, *Die Bedeutung der Ruhrkohle AG fuer die wirtschaftliche Entwicklung des Ruhrgebietes* (Abschlussbericht einer Studie im Auftrag der Ruhrkohle Bergbau und Umwelt GmbH, Bochum). Bochum: Ruhrkohle AG, 1988.
Lehner, Franz, Jürgen Nordhause-Janz, and Klaus Schubert, "Probleme und Perspektiven des Strukturwandels der Bergbau-Zulieferindustrie." In Bochum: Ruhrkohle AG, 1989.
Leibinger, Berthold, "Entwicklungstendenzen in Werkzeugmaschinenbau." Manuscript of public lecture delivered at Friedrich-Alexander Universität, Erlangen/Nuremberg, 1986.
Leithäuser, Gerhard, "Crisis Despite Flexibility: The Case of West Germany." In *The Search for Labour Market Flexibility. The European Economies in Transition*. Robert Boyer (ed.). Oxford: Clarendon Press, 1988, pp. 171–188.
Lenel, Hans-Otto, *Ursachen der Konzentration unter besonderer Berucksichtigung der deutschen Verhaltnisse*. Tübingen: JCB Mohr, 1962.
Lenin, V. I., *Imperialism. The Highest Stage of Capitalism*. New York: International Publishers, 1933.
Levy, Hermann, *Die Vereinigten Staaten von Amerika als Wirtschaftsmacht*. Leipzig: Gustasv Fischer, 1923.
Levy, Hermann, *Die Weltmarkt 1913 und Heute*. Leipzig: Gustav Fischer, 1926a.
Levy, Hermann, "Die Enteuropäisierung der Welthandelsbilanz. *Weltwirtschaftliches Archiv* 23 (1926b): 338–.
Levy, Hermann, "Die europaische Verflechtung des Amerikanischen Aussenhandels." *Weltwirtschaftliches Archiv* 37(1) (1993): 164–192.
Levy, Hermann, *Industrial Germany. A Study of its Monopoly Organizations and their Control by the State*. London: Frank Cass, 1966.
Lewis, W. Arthur, *Economic Survey, 1919–1939*. London: George Allen and Unwin, 1949.
Liefmann, Robert, *Cartels, Concerns and Trusts*. New York: E. P. Dutton, 1932.
Lipset, Seymour Martin, *Political Man: The Social Bases of Politics*. New York: Anchor/Doubleday, 1963.
Litt, Theodor, "Technischer Fortschritt und menschliche Freiheit." *Vortragsreihe des Deutschen Industrieinstituts* 7 February 13 (1956).

Lloyd, G. I. H., "Labour Organisation in the Cutlery Trades of Solingen." *Economic Journal* 18 (1908).
Locke, Richard, "The Resurgence of the Local Union: Industrial Restructuring and Industrial Relations in Italy." *Politics & Society* 18(3) (1991): 347–379.
Locke, Richard, *Remaking the Italian Economy*. Ithaca: Cornell University Press, 1995.
Lommatzsch, Georg, *Die Bewegung des Bevolkerungsstandes in Königreich Sachsen während der Jahre 1871–1890 und deren hauptsächlichste Ursachen*. Dresden: Wilhelm Bänsch, 1894.
Löhn, Johann, "Technologietransfer in Baden Württemberg." *Feinwerktechnik & Messtechnik* 1 (1985): Sonderdruck.
Lösch, August, *Raumliche Ordnung der Wirtschaft*, 1944.
Löwenstein, *Geschichte des Württembergischen Kreditbankwesens und seiner Beziehungen zu Handel und Industrie*. Tübingen: Mohr, 1912.
Lucas, Erhard, *Zwei Formen von Radikalismus in der deutschen Arbeiterbewegung*. Frankfurt/Main: Roter Stern Verlag, 1976.
Lukac, Dr. Alfred, "Der Einfluss von Währungsänderungen auf den Export." In *Die Maschinenbau-Industrie in der Bundesrepublik Deutschland*, ed. Thomas Eyermüller. Schriftenreihe Branchenanalysen, No. 23, Frankfurt Institut für Bilanzanalysen, 1974.
Lundgreen, Peter, B. Horn, W. Krohn, G. Küppers, and R. Paslack, *Staatliche Forschung in Deutschland 1870–1980*. Frankfurt: Campus, 1986.
Lutz, Burkhardt, *Krise des Lohnanreizes. Ein empirisch-historischer Beitrag zum Wandel der Formen betrieblicher Herrschaft am Beispiel der deutschen Stahlindustrie*. Frankfurt: Europäische Verlagsanstalt, 1975.
Lutz, Burkhardt, *Der kurze Traum immerwährende Prosperität. Eine neuinterpretation der industriellkapitalistischen Entwicklung um Europa des 20 Jahrhunderts*. Frankfurt: Campus, 1984.
Lütge, Friedrich, *Geschichte der deutschen Agrarverfassung vom frühen Mittelalter bis zum 19. Jahrhundert*. Stuttgart: Eugen Ulmer, 1963.
Machten, Lothar, "Zum Innenleben deutsche Fabriken im 19. Jahrhundert. Die formelle und die informelle Verfassung von Industriebetrieben, anhand von Beispielen aus dem Bereich der Textil- und Maschinenbauproduktion (1869–1891)." *Archiv für Sozialgeschichte* 21 (1981): 179–236.
Maddison, Angus, *Economic Growth in the West. Comparative Experience in Europe and North America*. New York: Twentieth Century Fund, 1964.
Mager, Wolfgang, "Proto-indistrialisierung und Proto-industrie. Vom Nutzen und Nachteil zweier Konzepte." *Geschichte und Gesellschaft* 14 (1988): 275–303.
Magnus, Gert, "Untersuchungen über den Wettbewerb zwischen Gross- und Kleinunternehmen der Elektrotechnik und das Maschinenbaues." *Dissertation*, Technische Hochschule Fredericana zu Karlsruhe, 1936.
Maier, Charles, "Between Taylorism and Techanocracy. European Ideologies and the Vision of Industrial Productivity in the 1920's." *Journal of Contemporary History* 2 (1970): 27–61.
Maier, Charles, *Recasting Bourgeois Europe. Stabilization in France, Germany and Italy in the Decade After World War One*. Princeton: Princeton University Press, 1975.
Maier, Charles, "Die Nicht-Determiniertheit ökonomischer Modelle Überlegungen zu Knut Borchardts These von der 'kranken Wirtschaft' der Weimarer Republik." *Geschichte und Gesellschaft* 11 (1985): 275–294.
Maier, Hans, "Das Modell Baden Württemberg. Über institutionelle Vorausetzungen

differenzierter Qualitätsproduktion—Eine Skizze." *Wissenschaftszentrum Berlin Für Sozialforschung*, 1987.
Maisel, Helmut, *Diversifikation und Konglomerate Interdependence: Ein Beitrag zu den Wettbewerbswirkungen diagonaler Konzentration*. Frankfurt: R. G. Fischer, 1984.
Manchester, William, *The Arms of Krupp*. Boston: Little Brown, 1968.
Mandel, Ernest, *Die EWG und die Konkurrenz Europa—Amerika*. Frankfurt: Europäische Verlagsanstalt, 1968.
Mannstädt, Heinrich, *Ursachen und Ziele des Zusammenschlusses im Gewerbe unter besonderer Berücksichtigung der Kartelle und Trusts*. Jena: Gustav Fischer, 1916.
Marburg, Theodore F., "Government and Business in Germany: Public Policy toward Cartels." *Business History Review* 38(1) (1964): 78–101.
Markovits, Andrei (ed.), *The Political Economy of West Germany: Modell Deutschland*. New York: Praeger, 1982.
Markovits, Andrei, *The Politics of West German Trade Unions*. New York: Cambridge University Press, 1986.
Marschalck, Peter, "Zur Rolle der Stadt für den Industrialisierungsprozess in Deutschland in der 2. Hälfte des 19. Jahrhunderts." In *Die deutsche Stadt im Industriezeitalter: Beiträge zur modernen deutschen Stadtgeschichte*. Jürgen Reulecke (ed.). Wuppertal: Peter Hammer, 1978, pp. 57–66.
Marshall, Alfred, *Industry and Trade. A Study of Industrial Technique and Business Organization, and of Their Influences on the Conditions of Various Classes and Nations*. London: Macmillan, 1919.
Martin, James S., *All Honorable Men*. Boston: Little Brown, 1950.
Marx, Karl, *Capital. A Critique of Political Economy*. New York: Vintage Books, 1977.
Marx, Karl, and Friederich Engels, "The German Ideology." In Karl Marx and Friederich Engels, *Collected Works of Marx and Engels*, Vol. 5. Moscow: Progress Publishers, 1975, pp. 19–539.
Maschke, Erich, *Es Entseht ein Konzern. Paul Reusch und die GHH*. Tubingen: Wunderlich, 1969.
Mason, Tim, *Arbeiterklasse und Volksgemeinschaft*. Opladen: Westdeutscher Verlag, 1975.
Mason, Tim, *Sozialpolitik im Dritten Reich*. Opladen: Westdeutscher Verlag, 1977.
Matschoss, Conrad, *Die Maschinenfabrik R. Wolf, Magdeburg-Buckau. 1862–1912*. Berlin: J. Springer, 1912.
Matschoss, Conrad, *Die Bedeutung der Personlichkeite für die industrielle Entwicklung*. Berlin: E. S. Mittler, 1917.
Matschoss, Conrad, *Ein Jahrhundert deutscher Maschinenbau. Von der mechanischen Werkstätte bis zur deutschen Maschinefabrik 1819–1919*. Berlin: 1922.
Matschoss, Conrad, *Die Geschichte der Ludwig Leowe & Co. Aktiengesellschaft. Berlin. 60 Jahre Edelarbeit, 1860 bis 1929*. Ludwid Leowe & Co. A. G. Berlin: VDI-Verlag, GmbH, 1930, pp. 1–59.
Matz, Klaus Jürgen, "Baden und Württemberg." In *Die Länder und der Bund. Beiträge zur Entstehung der Bundesrepublik Deutschland*. Walter Forst (ed.). Essen: Reimar Hobbing GmbH Verlag, 1989, pp. 33–62.
Maurice, Mark, Francois Sellier and J. J. Silvestre, *The Social Foundations of Industrial Power: A Comparison of France and Germany*. Cambridge, MA: MIT Press, 1986.
Maya, Carlos, "Kapitalkonzentration und -zentralisation in historischer Sicht." In *Monopoletheorie Kontrovers. Zur neueren Theorie und Empire des Monopols*. Otwald Demele and Willi Semmler (eds.). Berlin: Olle & Wolter, 1980, pp. 65–88.

Mayntz, Renate, "Föderalismus und die Gesellschaft der Gegenwart." *Max Planck Institut für Gesellscahftsforschung, Köln*, 1989.

Medalen, Charles, "State Monopoly Capitalism in Germany: The Hibernia Affair." *Past and Present* 78 (1978): 82–112.

Medick, Hans, "Priviligiertes Handelskapital und 'kleine industrie'. Production und Productionsverhaltnisse im Leinengewerbe des altwürttembergischen Oberamts Urach im 18. Jahrhundert." *Archiv für Sozialgeschichte* 23 (1983): 267–310.

Meenzen, Hanns, "Automatisierung -ein Schreckgespenst?" *Vortragsreihe des Deutschen Industrieinstituts* 34 August 22 (1955).

Megerle, Klaus, "Regionale Differenzierung des Industrialisierungsprozesses: Überlegungen am Beispiel Württembergs." In *Industrialisierung und Raum. Studien zur regionalen Differenzierung im Deutschland des 19 Jahrhunderts*. Rainer Fremdling and Richard Tilly (eds.). Stuttgart: Klett-Cotta, 1979, pp. 105–131.

Megerle, Klaus, *Württemberg im Industrialisierungsprozess Deutschlands*. Stuttgart: Klett-Cotta, 1982.

Mehrin, Otto Schulz, "Ursachen und Zusammenschlusses im Maschinenbau und verwandte Zweigen." *Maschinenbau. Wirtschaftlicher Teil* 6(18) (1927): 891–896.

Mehrin, Otto Schulz, "Wie Kann die Rentabilität im deutschen Maschinenbau gebessert werden?" *Maschinenbau. Wirtschaftlicher Teil* 6(3) (1927): 115–117.

Mengel, Heinrich, "Strukturwandlungen und Konjunkturbewegung in der Werkzeugmaschinen-Industrie." *Dissertation*, Halle-Wittenberg, 1931.

Menges, Franz, *Reichsreform und Finanzpolitik. Die Aushölung der Eigenstaatlichkeit Bayerns auf Finanzpolitischen Wege in der Weimare Republik, Beiträge zu einer historischen Strukturanalyse Bayerns im Industriezeitalter*, Band 7. Berlin: Duncker & Humblodt, 1971.

Merlin, Sidney, "Trends in German Economic Control Since 1933." *Quarterly Journal of Economics* February (1943): 169–207.

Mertens, Dieter, "Veränderungen der industriellen Branchenstruktur in der Bundesrepublik 1950-1960." In *Wandlungen der Wirtschaftsstruktur der BRD*, Hans Köning (ed.). Berlin: Verein für Sozialpolitik, 1962: 439ff.

Metzner, Max, *Kartelle als Träger der Rationalisierung. Einer Materialsammlung*. Berlin: Drucker & Humblot, 1955.

Meyenberg, Friedrich, *Über die Eingleiderung der Normungsarbeit in die Organisation einer Maschinenfabrik*. Berlin: Julius Springer, 1924.

Meyer-Haitz, Doris, "Struktur und Entwicklung des Maschinenbaus." *Baden Württemberg in Wort and Zahl Statistische Monatshefte* 22(1) (1974): 34–40.

Michelsohn, Justin, "Die bayerische Grossindustrie und ihre Entwicklung seit dem Eintritt Bayerns in das Deutsche Reich." *Dissertation*, Friedrich Alexanders Universität Erlangen, 1907.

Mielke, S., *Der Hansa Bund Für Gewerbe, Handel und Industrie 1909-1914*. Göttingen: Vandenhoeck & Ruprecht, 1976.

Milward, Alan, *The Germany Economy at War*. London: Athlone Press, 1965.

Milward, Alan, *The Reconstruction of Western Europe*. Berkeley: University of California Press, 1984.

Moessner, Alfred, "Maschinenbau und das Exportproblem." *Der Volkswirt* 1949: 13–14.

Mohl, Moritz, *Über die württembergische Gewerbs-industrie*. Stuttgart/Tübingen: J. G. Cottschen Buchhandlung, 1828.

Mohl, Moritz, *Aus den Gewerbswissenschaftlichen Ergebnissen einer Reise in Frankreich*. Stuttgart/Tübingen: J. G. Cottschen Buchhandlung, 1845.

Mohl, Friedrich, *Hundert Jahre Krauss Maffei, München 1837–1937*. Munich: Krauss Maffei, 1937.
Moll, Lutz, "Die industrielle Serienfertigung. Begriffliche Abgrenzung und Erscheinungsformen." *Dissertation*. Erlangen-Nuremberg, 1972.
Mommsen, Hans, Dietmer Petzina and Bernd Weisbrod (eds.), *Industrielles System und politische Entwicklung in der Weimarer Republik*. Kronberg/Ts: Athenaeum, 1977.
Mommsen, Wolfgang, "The Free Trade Unions and Social Democracy in Imperial Germany." In *The Development of Trade Unionism in Great Britain and Germany, 1880–1914*. Wolfgang and Hans-Gerhard Husung Mommsen (eds.). London: George, Allen and Unwin, 1985, pp. 371–389.
Moore, Barrington, *The Social Origins of Dictatorship and Democracy*. Boston: Beacon Press, 1966.
Mooser, Josef, *Ländliche Klassengesellschaft 1770–1848*. Göttingen: Vandenhoeck & Ruprecht, 1984.
Mooser, Josef, *Arbeiterleben in Deutschland, 1900–1970*, Neue Historische Bibliothek. Hans Ulrich Wehler (ed.). Frankfurt: Suhrkamp, 1984.
Morgan, Kevin, Philip Cooke, and Adam Price, "The Challenge of Lean Production in German Industry." Regional Industrial Research, Department of City and Regional Planning, University of Wales, College of Cardiff, 1992.
Morgan, Kevin, "Reversing Attrition? The Auto Cluster in Baden-Württemberg" Stuttgart: 1994.
Morganthau, Henry, Jr., *Germany is Our Problem*. New York: Harper, 1945.
Most, Otto, *Der Nebenerwerb in seiner Wolkswirtschaftlichen Bedeutung*. Jena: Gustav Fischer, 1903.
Mönnich, Horst, *BMW Eine Jahrhundertgeschichte*, Band 1: *Vor der Schallmauer 1916–1945*; and Band 2: *Der Turm 1945–1972*, Düsseldorf: Econ Verlag, 1986.
Mössner, Alfred, "Investieren und Exportieren" *Der Volkswirt*, 1949.
Mössner, Alfred, "Der Maschinenbau und das Exportproblem." *Der Volkswirt* 31 (1949): 13–14.
Müllenseifen, Heinz, *Kartelle als Produktionsförderer unter besonderer Berüksichtigung der modernen Zusammenschlusstendenzen in der deutschen Maschinenbau-Industrie*. Berlin: Julius Springer, 1926.
Müller, Gebhard, "Die Entstehung des Bundeslandes Baden Württemberg." *Zeitschrift für Württembergische Landesgeschichte* 36 (1977): 236–261.
Müller, Georg, "Liebe war es nicht, was Benz und Daimler zur Fusion trieb." *Handelsblatt* 19 January 28 (1986): 19.
Müller, Gloria, *Mitbestimmung in der Nachkriegszeit. Britische Besatzungsmacht-Unternehmer-Gewerkschaften*. Düsseldorf: Schwann, 1987.
Müller, Gloria, *Strukturwandel und Arbeitnehmerrechte. Die wirtschaftliche Mitbestimmung in der Eisen- und Stahlindustrie, 1945–1975*. Essen: Klartext Verlag, 1991.
Nagel, Bernhard, and Hildegard Kaluza, *Eigentum und Markt im Maschinenbau*. Baden-Baden: Nomos Verlagsgesellschaft, 1988.
Nanninga, Folkert, "Zur 'deutschen' Politik des Württembergischen Aussenministers von Varnbüler in den Jahren 1864 bis 1870." *Zeitschrift für Württembergische Landesgeschichte* 32 (1973): 113–149.
Napthali, Fritz, *Wirtschaftsdemokratie. Ihr Wesen, Weg and Zeil*. Frankfurt: Europäische Verlagsanstalt, 1966.
Naschold, Frieder, "Jeneseits des baden-württembergischen 'Exceptionalism': Struktur-

problem der deutschen Industrie." Arbeitsbericht Nr. 38, Akademie Für Technikfolgenabschätzung in Baden Wurttemberg, Stuttgart, November, 1994.
Nathan, Otto, *The Nazi Economic System. Germany's Mobilization for War*. Durham, NC: Duke University Press, 1944.
Nations, United, *Annual Bulletin of Steel Statistics for Europe*. New York: United Nations, 1973–1978.
Naujoks, Eberhard, "Württemberg im diplomatischen Kräftespiel der Reichsgründungszeit (1866/70). Zur Problematik der deutschen Politik des Freiherrn von Varnbüler." *Zeitschrift für Württembergische Landesgeschichte* 30 (1971): 201–240.
Neebe, Reinhardt, *Grossindustrie, Staat, und NSDAP 1930–1933*. Göttingen: Vandenhoeck & Ruprecht, 1981.
Negt, Oskar, Christine Morgenroth, Heiko Geiling, and Edzard Niemeyer, *Emanzipationsinteressen und Organisationsphantasie. Eine ungenutzte Wirklichkeit der Gewerkschaften? Zur Erweiterung sozialkultureller Handlungsfelder am Beispiel der DGB-Ortskartelle*. Cologne: Bund-Verlag, 1989.
Nelson, Walter Henry, *Small Wonder. The Amazing Story of the Volkswagen*. Boston: Little Brown, 1970.
Nelson, Wayne, "Maintaining Competitiveness: Lessons from the West German Textile Industry." *Masters Thesis*, Department of Political Science. MIT, 1987.
Neuberger, Hugh and Houston Stokes, "German Banks and German Growth, 1883–1913: An Empirical View." *Journal of Economic History* 34 (1974): 710–731.
Neumann, E. K., and Walter Dorn, "Conversation, June 4, 1949." Haupstaatsarchiv Hessen, Wiesbaden, Bestand 649 (OMGUS, Hessen) OMGH Historical Division, 8/187-2/11, 1949, pp. 28–30.
Neumann, Karl, "Technischer Fortschritt als Wirtschaftsprinzip." *Vortragsreihe des Deutschen Industrieinstituts* 8 February 20 (1956).
Neumann, Karl, "Technischer Fortschritt und Gemeinsamer Markt." *Vortragsreihe des Deutschen Industrieinstituts* 25 June 24 (1957).
Neumann, Manfred, "Improved Competitiveness of Steel Producing Firms by Means of Diversification." In *Ailing Steel*. Walter Goldberg (ed.). New York: St. Martin's Press, 1986, pp. 439–444.
Neumann, Franz, "Zur Theorie des Förderalismus." In *Demokratischer und autoritärer Staat*. Franz Neumann (ed.). Frankfurt: Fischer Taschenbuch Verlag, 1986, pp. 207–223.
Newcomber, Mabel, *Central and Local Finance in Germany and England*. New York: Columbia University Press, 1937.
Nishigushi, Toshihiro, *Strategic Industrial Sourcing*. New York: Oxford University Press, 1992.
Noble, David, *America by Design*. New York: Oxford University Press, 1977.
Nocken, Ulrich, "Interindustrial Conflicts and Alliances as Exemplified by the AVI-Agreement." In *Industrielles System und politische Entwicklung in der Weimarer Republik*. Hans Mommsen Dietmer Petzina and Bernd Weisbrod (eds.). Kronberg/Ts: Athenaeum, 1977, pp. 693–704.
Nocken, Ulrich, "Interindustrial Conflicts and Alliances in the Weimar Republic: Experiments in Societal Corporatism." *Ph.D. dissertation*, University of California, Berkeley, 1977.
Nocken, Ulrich, "Pluralism and Corporatism in Modern German History." In *Industrielle Gesellschaft und politisches System. Beiträge zur politischen Sozialgeschichte*.

Dirk Stegmann Bernd Jürgen Wend and Peter Christian Witt (eds.). Bonn: Verlag Neu Gesellschaft, 1978, pp. 37–58.

Nolan, Mary, *Visions of Modernity. American Business and the Modernization of Germany.* New York: Oxford University Press, 1994.

Norman, Richard, and Rafael Ramirez, "From Value Chain to Value Constellation: Designing Interactive Strategy." *Harvard Business Review* July-August (1993): 65–77.

Nussbaum, Helga, *Unternehmern gegen Monopole. Über Struktur und Aktionen antimonopolistischer bürgerlicher Gruppen zu Beginn des 20. Jahrhunderts.* Berlin: Akademia, 1966.

Nussbaum, Manfred, "Unternehmenskonzentration und Investstrategie nach dem ersten Weltkrieg. Zur Entwicklung des deutschen Grosskapitals während und nach der grossen Inflation unter besonderer Berücksichtigung." *Jahrbuch für Wirtschaftsgeschichte* 2 (1974): 51–75.

Nutzinger, Hans G., and Jürgen Backhaus (eds.), *Codetermination. A Discussion of Different Approaches.* Berlin: Julius Springer, 1989.

O'Brien, P. J., "Do We Have a Typology for the Study of European Industrialization in the Nineteenth Century?" *Journal of Economic History* 15(2) (1986): 291–333.

Oberhoff, Günter, "Solingen und Leverkusen. Zwei Weltbegriffe—Zwei Schwerpunkte in einem alten Wirtschaftsraum." In *Die westdeutsche Wirtschaft und ihre führenden Männer. Lesebuch der deutschen Industrie. Land Nordrhein Westfalen. Teil III: Bergisches Land,* Julius Keil (ed.). Oberursel: Wirtschaftslesebuch-Verlag Dr. Julius Keil GmbH, 1975.

Offe, Claus, "The Attribution of Public Status to Interest Groups." *Organizing Interests in Western Europe.* S. Berger (ed.). New York: Cambridge University Press, 1981, pp. 123–158.

Offe, Claus, *Contradictions in the Welfare State.* Cambridge, MA: MIT Press, 1984.

Offe, Claus and Helmut Wiesenthal, "Two Logics of Collective Action." In *Disorganized Capitalism. Contemporary Transformations of Work and Politics.* Claus Offe (ed.). Cambridge, MA: MIT Press, 1985, pp. 170–220.

Olley, Maurice, *The Motor Car Industry in Germany during the period 1939–1945.* London: British Intelligence Objectives Sub-Committee, HMSO, 1949.

Opitz, Dr., "Die Vererbung des Ländlichen Grundbesitzes in der Nachkriegzeit im Freistaat Sachsen." In *Die Vererbung des Ländlichen Grundbesitzes in der Nachkriegszeit, Band 1: Deutsches Reich,* Max Sering and Constantin V. Dietze (eds.). Munich/Liepzig: Dunker & Humblot, 1930, pp. 189–216.

Opitz, Reinhard, "Der grosse Plan der CDU: die 'Formierte Gesellschaft'." *Blätter für deutsche und internationale Politik* 10(9) (1965): 750–777.

Osswald, Richard, *Lebendige Arbeitswelt, Die Sozialgeschichte der Daimler-Benz AG von 1945 bis 1985.* Stuttgart: Deutsche Verlags-Anstalt, 1986.

Osterhold, Horst, "Die Sauerländische Wirtschaft im Wandel. Industrielle Entwicklung zwischen Hellweg und oberem Ruhrtal." In *Die westdeutsche Wirtschaft und ihre führenden Männer. Lesebuch der deutschen Industrie. Land Nordrhein-Westfalen. Teil II: Sauerland und Siegerland,* Julius Keil (ed.). Oberursel: Wirtschaftslesebuch-Verlag Dr. Julius Keil GmbH, 1974, pp. 19–29.

Ostermann, Walter, "Marktlage der deutschen Maschinenindustrie von 1924–1934." *Dissertation,* Freiburg i. Br., 1936.

Otto, Ernst (ed.), *Die deutsche Industrie im Gemeinsamen Markt.* Baden-Baden: August Lutzeyer, 1957.

Overbeck, Egon, "Strukturwandel—Neue Chancen für die Unternehmen." *Schmalenbachs Zeitschrift fuer betriebswirtschaftliche Forschung* 29(4) (1977): 179–189.
Overbeck, Egon, "Strukturwandel Eines Unternehmens (Mannesmann)." *Zeitschrift für Betriebswirtschaft* 2 (19820: 127–139.
Overy, Richard J., "Hitler's War and the German Economy: A Reinterpretation." *Economic History Review* 35 (1982): 272–291.
Overy, Richard, "Heavy Industry and the State in Nazi Germany: The Reichswerke Crisis." *European History Quarterly* 15 (1985): 313–340.
Panzar, J., and R. Willig, "Economies of Scope." *American Economic Review* 71(2): 268–272.
Parsons, Talcott, *Essays in Sociological Theory*, Revised Edition. New York: Free Press, 1954.
Pastor, Josef Johannes, "Die Ausfuhr des deutschen Maschinenbaus und ihre Volkswirtschaftliche Bedeutung." *Dissertation*, Köln, 1937.
Paul, Max, "Forderungen an den deutschen Textilmaschinenbau." *Melliand Textilberichte 32* September (1951): 674.
Paul, Johann, *Alfred Krupp und die Arebeiterbewegung*. Dusseldorf: Schwann, 1987.
Pentzlin, K., "Automatisierung im Lichte der Wirtschafts- und Bevolkerungsentwicklung." *Werkstattstechnik und Maschinenbau* 48(2) (1958): 58–59.
Peters, Jürgen (ed.), *Montanmitbestimmung. Dokumente ihrer Entstehung*. Cologne: Bund-Verlag, 1979.
Peters, Lon L., "Are Cartels Unstable? The German Steel Works Association Before World War One." In *Technique, Spirit and Form in the Making of Modern Economies: Essays in Honor of William N. Parker*, Gary Saxonhouse and Gavin Wright (eds.). Supplement 3 ed. Research in Economic History. Greenwich, CT: JAI Press, 1984, pp. 61–86.
Petzhold, Hartmut, "Zur Entstehung der Elektronischen Technologie in Deutschland und den USA. Der Beginn der Massenproduction von Elektronenroehren 1912–1918." In *Geschichte und Gesellschaft*, 13 Jg, 1987/Heft 3.
Petzina, Dietmar, and Werner Abelshauer, "Zum Problem der relativen Stagnation der deutschen Wirtschaft in den Zwanziger Jahren." In *Industrielles System und Politische Entwicklung in der Weimarer Republik*, Hans Mommsen, Dietmar Petzina, and Bernd Weisbrod (eds.). Kronberg/Ts: Athenaeum, 1977a.
Petzina, Dietmar, *Die deutsche Wirtschaft in der Zwischenkriegszeit*. Wiesbaden: Steiner, 1977b.
Petzina, Dietmar, and Werner Abelshauser, "Krise und Rekonstruktion. Zur Interpretation der gesamtwirtschaftlichen Entwicklung im 20. Jahrhundert." In *Deutsche Wirtschaftsgeschichte im Industriezeitalter. Konjunktur, Krise, Wachstum*. Dietmar Petzina and Werner Abelshauser (eds.). Königstein/Ts: Athenaeum, 1981, pp. 47–93.
Peukert, Detlev, *The Weimar Republic*. London: Penguin Press, 1991.
Pflanze, Otto, *Bismarck and the Development of Germany. The Period of Unification. 1815–1871*. Princeton: Princeton University Press, 1963.
Phillips, Eugene A., "American Direct Investments in West German Manufacturing Industries, 1945 to 1959." *Current Economic Comment* 22(2) (1960): 29–44.
Pietsch, Max, "Die Auswirkung der "Automation" auf dem Produktionsprozess." *Zeitschrift für Handelswissenschaftliche Forschung* 8.8/9 (1956): 449–458.
Pigou, A. C., "The Laws of Diminishing and Increasing Costs." *Economic Journal* June (1927), Vol. 27, pp. 188ff.

Pigou, A. C., "An Analysis of Supply." *Economic Journal* June (1928), Vol. 38, pp. 238ff.
Piore, Michael, "The Technological Foundations of Dualism and Discontinuity." *Dualism and Discontinuity in Industrial Societies*, Suzanne Berger and Michael Piore (eds.). Cambridge: Cambridge University Press, 1980.
Piore, Michael and Charles F. Sabel, *The Second Industrial Divide: Possibilities for Prosperity*. New York: Basic Books, 1984.
Pirker, Theo, *Die Blinde Macht: Die Gewerkschaftsbewegung in der Bundesrepublik*. Berlin: Olle & Wolter, 1979.
Plumpe, Gottfried, *Die württembergische Eisenindustrie im 19. Jahrhundert*. Wiesbaden: Franz Steiner, 1982.
Plumpe, Gottfried, *Die I.G. Farbenindustrie AG. Wirtschaft, Technik und Politik, 1904–1945*. Berlin: Duncker & Humblodt, 1990.
Plumpe, Werner, "Employers associations and industrial relations in postwar Germany: The Case of Ruhr Heavy Industry." In *The Power to Manage? Employers and Industrial Relations in Comparative-historical Perspective*, Steven Tolliday and Jonathan Zeitlin (eds.). London: Routledge, 1991, pp. 176–203.
Pohl, Hans, "Die Konzentration in der deutschen Wirtschaft vom ausgehenden 19. Jahrhundert bis 1945." In *Die Konzentration in der deutschen Wirtschaft seit dem 19. Jahrhundert*, Hans Pohl and Wilhelm Treue (eds.). Beiheft 11 ed. *Zeitschrift für Unternehmensgeschichte*. Wiesbaden: Franz Steiner, 1978, pp. 4–44.
Pohl, Hans, "Zur Geschichte von Organization und Leitung deutsche Grossunternehmen seit dem 19 Jahrhundert." *Zeitschrift für Unternehmensgeschichte* 26(3) (1981): 143–178.
Pohl, Hans (ed.), *Gewerbe- und Industrielandschaften vom Spätmittelalter bis ins 20. Jahrhundert*. Zeitschrift für Unternehmensgeschichte, Beiheft Nr. 78. Stuttgart: Franz Steiner Verlag Wiesbaden GmbH, 1986.
Pohl, Manfred, *Entstehung und Entwicklung des Universalbankensystems*. Frankfurt: Fritz Knapp, 1986.
Polanyi, Karl, *The Great Transformation*. Boston: Beacon Press, 1944.
Polanyi, Karl, Conrad Arensberg, and Harry Pearson (eds.), *Trade and Market in Early Empires*. New York: Free Press, 1957.
Pollard, Sidney, "Industrialization and the European Economy." *The Economic History Review* 26(4) (1973).
Pollard, Sidney (ed.), *Regionen und Industrialisierung*. Göttingen: Vandenhoeck & Ruprecht, 1979.
Pollard, Sidney, *Peaceful Conquest: The Industrialization of Europe, 1760–1970*. New York: Oxford University Press, 1981.
Polysius, Otto, "Verbandsstrebungen im deutschen Maschinenbau." *Dissertation*, Würzburg, 1921.
Popitz, Johannes, *Der Künftige Finanzausgleich zwischen Reich, Ländern und Gemeinden. Gutachten, erstattet der Studiengesellschaft für den Finanzausgleich*. Berlin: Otto Liebmann, 1932.
Potthoff, E., "Die Leitungsorganisation deutscher Grossunternehmungen im Vergleich zum Westlichen Ausland." *Zeitschrift für Handelswissenschaftliche Forschung* 8(7) (1956): 407–422.
Potthoff, Erich, "Zur Geschichte der Mitbestimmung." In *Zwischenbilanz der Mitbestimmung*, Erich Potthopff, Otto Blume, and Helmut Duvernell (eds.). Tübingen: JCB Mohr (Paul Siebeck), 1962, pp. 1–54.
Poulantzas, Nicos, *Political Power and Social Classes*. New York: Verso, 1978.

Pounds, Norman J. G., *The Ruhr. A Study in Historical and Economic Geography*. Bloomington: Indiana University Press, 1952.
Pounds, Norman J. G., and William N. Parker, *Coal and Steel in Western Europe*. London: Faber and Faber, 1957.
Pounds, Norman J. G., *An Historical Geography of Europe, 1800–1914*. New York: Cambridge University Press, 1985.
Powell, Walter, and Paul DiMaggio, "The Iron Cage Revisited: Institutional Isomorphism and Collective Rationality in Organizational Fields." In *The New Institutionalism in Organizational Analysis*, Walter Powell and Paul DiMaggio (eds.). Chicago: University of Chicago Press, 1991.
Preller, Ludwig, *Sozialpolitik in der Weimarer Republik*. Stuttgart: Franz Mittelbach Verlag, 1949.
Preuss, Hugo, *Gemeinde, Staat und Reich als Gebeitskörperschaften*. Berlin: Julius Springer, 1889.
Pribram, Karl, *Cartel Problems. An Analysis of Collective Monopolies in Europe with American Application*. Washington, DC: Brookings Institution, 1935.
Pritzkoleit, Kurt, *Männer, Mächte, Monopole. Hinter den Türen der westdeutschen Wirtschaft*. Düsseldorf: Karl Rauch, 1956.
Pritzkoleit, Kurt, *Männer, Mächte, Monopole. Hinter den Türen der westdeutschen Wirtschaft*, Second Edition. Düsseldorf: Karl Rauch, 1960.
Pritzkoleit, Kurt, *Auf Einer Woge von Gold, Der Triumph der Wirtschaft*. Munich: Drömer, Knauer, 1964.
Prognos, AG, "Die Entwicklung Kleiner und Mittler Unternehmen in Nordrhein-Westfalen. Ansatzpunkte für eine landesspezifische Mittelstandspolitik." Düsseldorf: Auftrag des Ministers für Wirtschaft, Mittelstand und Verkehr des Landes Nordrhein-Westfalen, 1975.
Projectgruppe Gewerkschaftsforschung, IG Metall, *Rahmenbedingungen der Tarifpolitik. Band 1: Gesamtwirtschaftliche Entwicklung und Organisationen der Tarifparteien*. Frankfurt: Campus, 1979.
Puppke, Ludwig, *Soziale Politik und soziale Anschauungen Frühenindustrieller Unternehmer in Rheinland Westfalen*. Köln: Rheinische-Westfälischen Wirtschaftsarchiv zu Köln, 1966.
Putsch, Jochen, *Vom Ende Qualifizierter Heimarbeit. Entwicklung und Strukturwandel der Solinger Schneidewarenindustrie von 1914–1960*. Köln: Rheinland Verlag, 1989.
Pyke, Grank, G. Becattini, and Werner Sengenberger (eds.), *Industrial Districts and Inter-firm Co-operation in Italy*. Geneva: International Institute for Labour Studies, 1990.
Pyke, Frank, and Werner Sengenberger (eds.), *Industrial Districts and Local Economic Regeneration*. Geneva: International Institute for Labour Studies, 1991.
Radkau, Joachim, *Technik in Deutschland. Vom 18. Jahrhundert bis zur Gegenwart*. Neue Historische Bibliothek. Frankfurt: Suhrkamp, 1989.
Raisch, Manfred, *Die Konzentration in der deutschen Automobilindustrie*. Berlin: Duncker & Humblot, 1973.
Rauh, Manfred, *Förderalismus und Parlamentarismus im wilhelminischen Reich*. Düsseldorf: Drost Verlag, 1973.
Rauscher, Anton, *Mitbestimmung: Referate und Diskussion auf der Tagung katholischer Sozialwissenschaftler vom 17. bi 19. Februar 1968 in Mönchengladbach*. Cologne: J. P. Bachem, 1968.

Rauscher, Anton (ed.), *Entwicklungslinien des deutschen Katholismus*. Munich: Ferdinand Schöninngh, 1973.

Redlich, Fritz, "The Leaders of the German Steam Engine Industry During the First Hundred Years." *Journal of Economic History* 4(2) (1944): 121–148.

Reich, Simon, *Fruits of Fascism. Post War Prosperity in Historical Perspective*. Ithaca: Cornell University Press, 1990.

Reichel, W., "Der Stand der Automatisierung auf Grund der Erhebungen des RKW und der OEEC." *Werkstattstechnik und Maschinenbau* 48(2) (1958): 60–62.

Reichertz, Sabine, "Verarmung durch Arbeitslosigkeit—dargestellet am Beispiel Essen." *Informationen zur Raumentwicklung* 9/10 (1987): 551–555.

Reichsarbeitsministerium, *Deutsche Sozialpolitik 1918–1928. Erinnerungsschrift des Reichsarbeitsministerium*. Berlin: Mittler & Sohn, 1929.

Reichsverbandes der Deutschen Industrie (ed.), *Produktionsförderung durch Kartelle* (Auszug aus einer Materialsammlung). Berlin, 1929.

Reiners, Walter, "Lage und Aufgaben des deutschen Textilmaschinenbaues." *Melliand Textilberichte* 32 August (1951): 577–578.

Reissert, Bernd, "Finazielle Spielräume für kommunale Beschäftigungspolitik." In *Lokale Beschaftigungspolitik*, Hans E. Maier and Hellmut Wollmann (eds.). Basel: Birkhäuser Verlag, 1986, pp. 35–64.

Renzsch, Wolfgang, *Handwerker und Lohnarbeiter in der frühen Arbeiterbewegung*. Göttingen: Vandenhoeck & Ruprecht, 1980.

Reuss, Karl, "Die Klassiche Gewerbeförderung vor neuen Aufgaben. Gewerbeförderung in Baden Württemberg und ihre lokale Verankerung." In *Lokale Beschaftigungspolitik*, Hans E. Maier and Hellmut Wollmann (eds.). Basel: Birkhäuser Verlag, 1986, pp. 148–178.

Rhein, P. E., "Europa. Japan und die Internationale Arbeitsteilung." *Europa Archiv* 7 (1981): 209–216.

Ribhegge, Wilhelm, "Die Systemfunktion der Gemeinden. Zur deutschen Kommunalgeschichte seit 1918." In *Kommunale Demokratie. Beiträge für die Praxis der kommunalen Selbstverwaltung*, Rainer Frey (ed.). Bonn: Verlag Neue Gesellschaft GmbH, nd, 55ff.

Richenbächer, Kurt, "Einseitige Expansion. Nachholbedarf an Produktivität—Eine innerbetriebliche und wirtschaftspolitische Aufgabe." *Der Volkswirt* 19 (1955): 11–12.

Ricoeur, Paul, *Hermeneutics and the Human Sciences*, John B. Thompson (ed.). New York: Cambridge University Press, 1981.

Ricoeur, Paul, *Time and Narrative*. Chicago: University of Chicago Press, 1984.

Riemer, Jeremiah, "Alterations in the Design of Model Germany: Critical Innovations in the Policy Machinery for Economic Steering." In *The Political Economy of West Germany: Modell Deutschland*, Andrei S. Markovits (ed.). New York: Praeger, 1982, pp. 53–89.

Riemer, Jeremiah, "Crisis and Intervention in the West German Economy: A Political Analysis of Changes in the Policy Machinery During the 1960s and 1970s." *Ph.D. Dissertation*, Cornell University, 1983.

Riesser, Jacob, *Die deutsche Grossbanken und ihre Konzentration*. Jena, 1910.

Riesser, Jacob, *The German Great Banks and their Concentration in Connection with the Economic Development of Germany*. Washington, DC: Government Printing Office, 1911.

Riley, John, "Germany: Interview Hans Dieter Wiedig, Siemens Nixdorf." *Computer Weekly* November 11 (1993).
Ritter, Emil, *Die KatholischeSoziale Bewegung Deutschlands in Neunzehnten Jahrhundert und der Volksverein.* Köln: J. P. Bachem, 1965.
Robbins, Lionel, "The Representative Firm." *Economic Journal* September (1928), Vol. 38, pp. 387ff.
Robert, Rüdiger, *Konzentrationspolitik in der Bundesrepublik—Das Beispiel der Entstehung des Gesetzes gegen Wettbewerbsbeschränkungen.* Berlin: Duncker & Humblodt, 1976.
Robertson, D. H., Piero Sraffa and G. V. Shove, "Increasing Returns and the Representative Firm. A Symposium." *Economic Journal* March (1930).
Roe, Joseph Wickham, *English and American Toolbuilders.* New Haven: Yale University Press, 1916.
Rogowski, Ronald, *Commerce and Coalitions.* Princeton: Princeton University Press, 1989.
Rohmann, F., "Wirtschaftliche Zusammenschlüsse im Maschinenbau und verwandten Industriezweigen im Jahre 1929." *Maschinenbau. Wirtschaftlicher Teil* 9(18) (1930): W67–W70.
Rommel, Günther, and Felix Brück, Raimund Diedrichs, Rolf-Dieter Kempis, Jürgen Kluge, *Einfach überlegen: das Unternehmenskonzept, das die Schlanken schlank und die Schnellen schnell macht.* Stuttgart: J. B. Metzlersche Verlagsbuchhandlung und Carl Ernst Poeschel Verlag, GmbH, 1993.
Rommel, Günther, and Felix Brück, Raimund Diedrichs, Rolf-Dieter Kempis, Jürgen Kluge, *Simply Superior: Perspectives on German Industrial Competitiveness.* Boston: Harvard Business School Press, 1995.
Rorty, Richard, *The Consequences of Pragmatism.* Minneapolis: University of Minnesota Press, 1982.
Rorty, Richard, *Contingency, Irony and Solidarity.* New York: Cambridge University Press, 1988.
Rorty, Richard, *Objectivity, Relativism and Truth.* New York: Cambridge University Press, 1990.
Rosenberg, Hans, *Bureaucracy, Aristocracy, and Autocracy. The Prussian Experience 1660–1815.* Boston: Beacon Press, 1958.
Rostow, Walt Whitman, *The Stages of Economic Growth.* New York: Cambridge University Press, 1960.
Roth, Karl Heinz, "Der Weg zum guten Stern des "Dritten Reichs": Schlaglichter auf die Geschichte der Daimler Benz AG und ihrer Vorläufer, 1890–1945." In *Das Daimler Benz Buch. Ein Rüstungskonzern im 'Tausendjährigen Reich' und Danach,* ed. Hamburger Stiftung für sozial Geschichte. Nördlingen: GRENO-Verlag, 1988, pp. 28–391.
Röper, Burkhardt (ed.), *Rationaisierungseffekte der Walzstahlkontore und der Rationalisierungsgruppen.* Berlin: Duncker & Humblot, 1974.
Röpke, Wilhelm, "Klein und Mittelbetriebe in der Volkswirtschaft." *Ordo 1* (1948): 155–175.
Röpke, Wilhelm, *The Social Crisis of our Time.* New Brunswick, NJ: Transaction Publishers, 1992 (1944).
Röstow, Alexander, *Das Versagen des Wirtschaftsliberalismus.* Bad Godesberg: Helmut Küpper Vormals Georg Bondi, 1950.

Runge, Ernst, "Die deutsche Maschinenindustrie in den Jahren 1924 bis 1933, ein Beitrag zur Diskussion über die Zukunft der deutschen Handelspolitik und des deutschen Industrieexports." *Dissertation*, Giessen, 1936.

Rupf, Hugo, "Maschinenfabrikanten sind keine Bankiers." In *Deutsche Wirtschaft im Querschnitt: Maschinenbau, Beilage to Number 28 Der Volkswirt* (September 24) (1955).

Rupieper, Herman-Josef, *Arbeiter und Angestellte im Zeitalter der Industrialisierung. Eine sozialgeschichtliche Studie am Bespiel der Maschinefabriken Augsburg und Nürnberg (MAN), 1837–1914*. Frankfurt: Campus, 1982.

S.B., "Die Automatisierung in der Bundesrepublik. Bemerkungen zu einem Bericht des rationalisierungs-Kuratoriums der Deutschen Wirtschaft (RKW)." *Der Gewerkschafter* 7 (1957): 15–18.

Sabean, David, "Aspects of Kinship Behavior and Property in Rural Western Europe Before 1800." In *Family and Inheritance. Rural Society in Western Europe 1200–1800*, Jack Goody, Joan Thirsk and E. P. Thompson (eds.). Cambridge: Cambridge University Press, 1976, pp. 96–111.

Sabel, Charles F., *Work and Politics*. New York: Cambridge University Press, 1982.

Sabel, Charles, and Jonathan Zeitlin, "Historical Alternatives to Mass Production: Politics, Markets and Technology in Nineteenth Century Industrialization." *Past and Present* 108 (1985): 134–176.

Sabel, Charles F., "Struktureller Wandel der Produktion und neue gewerkschaftliche Strategien." *Prokla* 62 March (1986): 41–60.

Sabel, Charles, Gary Herrigel, Richard Deeg, and Richard Kazis, "Regional Prosperities Compared: Baden Württemberg and Massachusetts in the 1980s." *Wissenschaftszentrum Berlin für Sozialforschung*, 1987.

Sabel, Charles F., "Flexible Specialization and the Re-emergence of Regional Economies." In *Reversing Industrial Decline?* Paul and Jonathan Zeitlin Hirst (eds.). London: Berg, 1989, pp. 17–70.

Sabel, Charles F., "Moebius Strip Organizations and Open Labor Markets: Some Consequences of the Reintegration of Conception and Execution in a Volatile Economy." In *Social Theory for a Changing Society*, James S. Coleman and Pierre Bourdieu (eds). New York: Russell Sage Foundation/Westview Press, 1991, pp. 23–62.

Sabel, Charles, Horst Kern, and Gary Herrigel, "Kooperative Produktion. Neue Formen der Zusammenarbeit zwischen Endfertigern und Zulieferern in der Automobilindustrie und die Neuordnung der Firma." In *Zulieferer im Netz. Neustrukturierung der Logistik am Beispiel der Automobilzulieferung*, Hans Gerhard Mendius and Ulrike Wendeling-Schroeder (eds.). Köln: Bund Verlag, 1991, pp. 203–227.

Sabel, Charles F., "Constitutional Ordering in Historical Context." In *Games in Hierarchies and Networks*, Fritz Scharpf (ed.). Baden Baden: Nomos Verlag, 1991.

Sabel, Charles, "Learning by Monitoring." In *Handbook of Economic Sociology*, Niel Smelser and Richard Swedberg (eds.). Princeton, NJ: Russell Sage and Princeton University Press, 1993.

Sabel, Charles, "Boostrapping Reform: Rebuilding Firms, the Welfare State and Unions." *Politics & Society* 34, 1 (1995): 5–48.

Sabel, Charles F., and Jonathan Zeitlin, "Stories, Strategies, Structures: Rethinking Historical Alternatives to Mass Production." In *Worlds of Possibility: Flexibility and Mass Production in Western Industrialization*, C. F. Sabel and J. Zeitlin (eds). Paris: Maison Des Sciences de L'Homme, forthcoming.

Sabel, Charles F., and Jonathan Zeitlin (eds.), Worlds of Possibility: Flexibility and Mass Production in Western Industrialization. Maison Des Sciences de L'Homme, forthcoming.
Sahlins, Marshall, *Stone Age Economics*. Chicago: Aldine, 1972.
Salin, Edgar, "Standortverschiebung der deutschen Wirtschaft." In *Strukturwandlungen der deutschen Wolkwirtschaft*, Bernard Harms (ed.). Berlin: Reimar-Hobbing, 1929.
Samuel, Raphael, "The Workshop of the World: Hand Power and Steam Technology in Mid-Victorian Britain." *History Workshop Journal 3* (1977).
Saul, Klaus, *Staat, Industrie, Arbeiterbewegung im Kaiserreich*. Düsseldorf: Bertelsmann Universitätsverlag, 1974.
Sax, Emmanuel, *Das Meininger Oberland, Die Hausindustrie in Thüringen. Wirtschaftliche Studien*. Jena: Gustav Fischer, 1884, 1: .
Sax, Emmanuel, *Ruhla und das Eisenacher Oberland, Die Hausindustrie in Thüringen. Wirtschaftliche Studien*. Jena: Gustav Fischer, 1885, 2: .
Sax, Emmanuel, *Die Korbflechterei in Oberfranken und Coburg. Hausindustrien in Neustadt A. R. und Bürgel, Die Hausindustrie in Thüringen. Wirtschaftliche Studien*. Jena: Gustav Fischer, 1888.
Scharpf, Fritz, *Politische Durchsetzbarkeit innerer Reformen*. Göttingen: Verlag Otto Schwartz, 1974.
Scharpf, Fritz, *Politische Immobilismus und ökonomische Krise. Aufsätze zu den politischen Restriktionen der Wirtschaftspolitik in der Bundesrepublik*. Königstein/Ts: Athenaeum, 1977.
Scharpf, Fritz W., Bernd Reissert and Fritz Schnabel (eds.), *Politikverflechtung II. Kritik und Berichte aus der Praxis. Beiträge zu einer Arbeitstagung des Wissenschaftszentrums* Berlin. Frankfurt: Athenaeum, 1977.
Scharpf, Fritz, "Economic and Institutional Growth of Full Employment Strategies: Sweden, Austria and West Germany." In *Order and Conflict in Contemporary Capitalism*, John H. Goldthorpe (ed.). Oxford: Clarendon Press, 1984.
Scharpf, Fritz, "Die Politikverflechtungs-Falle: Europäische Integration und deutscher Föderalismus im Vergleich." In *Politische Vierteljahresschrift* 26 December (1985): 323–356.
Scharpf, Fritz, "Der Bundesrat und die Kooperation auf der 'dritten Ebene'." In *Vierzig Jahre Bundesrat, ed. Bundesrat*. Baden-Baden: Nomos Vrelegsgesellschaft, 1989, pp. 121–162.
Scharpf, Fritz, "Entwicklungslinien des bundesdeutschen Föderalismus." Unpublished manuscript, Max Planck Institut für Gesellschaftsforschung, Köln, 1990.
Scharpf, Fritz, *Crisis and Choice in European Social Democracy*. Ithaca: Cornell University Press, 1991.
Scherer, Frederic, *Industrial Market Structure and Economic Performance (Second Edition)*. Boston: Houghton-Mifflin, 1980.
Scheuener, Ulrich, "Kooperation und Konflikt. Das Verhältnis von Bund und Länder im Wandel." In *Staatstheorie und Staatsrecht. Gesammelte Schriften*. Ulrich Scheuener (ed.). Berlin: Duncker & Humblodt, 1978, pp. 399–414.
Schiele, Otto, "Nur Noch Sieger. Wettbewerbsfähiger durch Fertigungsautomation," *Blick durch die Wirtschaft* 2/3 (1986): 3.
Schindler, Hermann, *Die Reutlinger Wirtschaft von der Mitte des 19. Jahrhunderts bis zum Beginn des Ersten Weltkrieges*. Tübingen: Mohr, 1969.
Schlafhorst, W. & Co., "Schlafhorst Gute hundert Jahre, 1884–1984." *Rundmagazin Sonderausgabe* 12 (1984).

Schmalenbach, Eugene, *Pretiale Wirtschaftslenkung*. Bremen-Horn: Industrie und Handelsverlag Walter Dorn, 1948.
Schmalenbach, Eugene, *Der Freien Wirtschaft Zum Gedächtnis*. Cologne: Westdeutscher Verlag, 1949.
Schmid, Thomas (ed.), *Entstaatlichung. Neue Perspecktiven auf das Gemeinwesen*. Berlin: Wagenbach, 1988.
Schmidt, Eberhard, *Die verhinderte Neuordnung 1945–52. Die Auseinandersetzung um die Demokratisierung der Wirtschaft in den Westzonen und der Bundesrepublik*. Frankfurt: Europäische Verlagsanstalt, 1970.
Schmidt, Eberhard, *Ordnungsfaktor oder Gegenmacht. Die politische Rolle der Gewerkschaften*. Frankfurt: Suhrkamp, 1987.
Schmidt, Joachim, "Veränderungen in der Investitionstätigkeit der deutschen Wirtschaft—Zur Entwicklung der Investitionsgüterstruktur 1960 bis 1968." *Mitteilungen des Rheinisch-Westfälischen Instituts für Wirtschaftsforschung* 34 (1983): 271–292.
Schmidt, Manfred, G., "Die Politische Verarbeitung der deutschen Vereinigung im Bund-Länder Verhältnis." In *Verwaltungsreform und Verwaltungspolitik im Prozeß der deutschen Einigung*, Wolfgang Seibel, Arthur Benz, and Heinrich Mäding (eds.). Baden Baden: Nomos Verlagsgesellschaft, 1993, pp. 448–453.
Schmiede, Rudi, "Das deutsche Wirtschaftswunder 1945–1965." In *Die Linke im Rechtsstaat. Band 1, Bedingungen sozialistischer Politik 1945–1965*, Bernhard Blanke (ed.). Berlin: Rotbuch Verlag, 1976, pp. 107–138.
Schmiede, Rudi, and Edwin Schudlich, *Die Entwicklung der Leistungsentlohnung in Deutschland. Eine historisch-theoretische Untersuchung zum Verhältnis von Lohn und Leistung unter kapitalistischen Produktionsbedingungen* (Forschungsberichte des Institutes für Sozialforschung, Frankfurt am Main). Frankfurt: Campus Verlag, 1977.
Schmitt, Martin A., *Ein Mann und sein Werk: Liebherr*. Immenstadt/Allgäu: Liebherr-Holding GmbH, Eberl, 1980.
Schmitt, Carl, *Hüter der Verfassung*. Berlin: Duncker & Humblodt, 1985.
Schmitz, Erich, "Analyse der Wettbewerbseffekte der Kontorvertraege von 1967 und der Verträge zur Grundung der vier Rationalisierungsgruppen von 1971" In *Rationalisierungseffekte der Walzstahlkontore und der Rationalisierungsgruppen*, Burkhardt Röper (ed.). Berlin: Duncker & Humblot, 1974, pp. 21–22.
Schmitz, Hubert, "Industrial Districts: Model and Reality in Baden Württemberg." In *Industrial Districts and Local Economic Regeneration*, Frank Pyke and Werner Sengenberger (eds.). Geneva: International Institute for Labor Studies, 1991.
Schmoller, Gustav, *Zur Geschichte der deutschen Kleingewerbe im 19. Jahrhundert*. Halle: Verlag und Buchhandlung des Waisenhauses, 1870.
Schmoller, Gustav, *Grundriss der Allgemeinen Volkswirtschaftslehre. Erster, grösserer Teil*. Leipzig: Duncker & Humblot, 1900.
Schockenkoff, Volker, *Wirtschaftsverfassung und Grundgesetz. Die Auseinandersetzungen in den Verfassungsberatungen 1945–1949*. Frankfurt: Campus, 1986.
Schonfield, Andrew, *Modern Capitalism. The Changing Balance of Public and Private Power*. New York: Oxford University Press, 1965.
Schönhoven, Klaus, *Expansion und Konzentration. Studien zur Entwicklung der Freien Gewerkschaften in Wilhelminischen Deutschland 1890–1914*. Stuttgart: Klett-Cotta, 1980.

Schönhöven, Klaus, *Die deutsche Gewerkschaften*. Frankfurt: Suhrkamp, 1987.
Schöps, Hans Julius, "Preussen und Württemberg 1850–1852." *Zeitschrift für Württembergische Landesgeschichte* 30 (1971): 382–403.
Schreiber, Peter Wolfgang, *I.G. Farben. Die unschuldige Kriegsplaner*. Stuttgart: Neuer Weg, 1978.
Schriewer, Jürgen, "Intermediare Instanzen, Selbstverwaltung und berufliche Ausbildungsstrukturen im historischen Vergleich." *Zeitscrift Für Pädegogik* 32(1) (1986): 69–113.
Schröder, Ernst, "Die Westdeutsche Montanindustrie heute." *Der Volkswirt* 44 (1952): 27–32.
Schröter, Herman, "Die Firma Friedrich Krupp und die Stadt Essen." *Tradition: Zeitschrift für Firmengeschichte und Unternehmerbiographie* 6 December(1961).
Schröter, Alfred, "Die Entstehung der deutschen Maschinenbauindustrie in der ersten Hälfte des 19. Jahrhunderts." In *Die deutsche Maschinenindustrie in der Industriellen Revolution*. Alfred and Walter Becker Schröter (eds.). Berlin (Ost): Akademia, 1962.
Schröter, Alfred and Jürgen Bach, "Zur Planung der wirtschaftlichen Mobilmachung durch den deutschen faschistischen Imperialismus vor dem Beginn des zweitnWeltkrieges." *Jahrbuch für Wirtschaftsgeschichte* 1 (1978): 31–47.
Schulte, Fritz, *Die Entwicklung der gewerblichen Wirtschaft in Rheinland-Westfahlen im 18. Jahrhundert*. Schriften Zur Rheinisch-Westfälischen Wirtschaftsgeschichte (Köln: Rheinisch-Westfälischen Wirtschaftsarchiv Zu Köln, 1959).
Schultz, Helga, "Die Ausweitung des Landhandwerks vor der industriellen Revolution. Begunstigende Faktoren und Bedeutung Für die "Protoindustrialisierung"." *Jahrbuch Für Wirtschaftsgeschichte* III (1982): 79–90.
Schultz-Mehrin, Otto, *Spezialisierungs- und Verkaufsgemeinschaften im Maschinenbau*. Charlottenburg (Berlin): VDMA, 1926.
Schulz, Gerhard, *Zwischen Demokratie und Diktatur. Verfassungspolitik und Reichsreform in der Weimarer Republik. Band 1: Die Periods der Konsolidierung und der Revision des Bismarckschen Reichsaufbaus 1919–1930*. Berlin: Walter de Gruyter, 1963.
Schumann, F., *Auslese und Anpassung der Arbeiterschaft in der Automobile industrie und einer Wiener Maschinenfabrik*. Leipzig: Duncker & Humblodt, 1911.
Schumann, Michael, Volker Baethge-Kinsky, Martin Kuhlmann, Constanze Kurz, and Uwe Neumann, *Trendreport Rationalisierung. Automobile Industrie. Werkzeugmaschinenbau, Chemische Industrie*. Berlin: Edition Sigma, 1994, p. 670.
Schumpeter, Joseph, *The Theory of Economic Development: An Inquiry into Profits, Capital, Credit, Interest, and the Business Cycle*. New York: Oxford University Press, 1949.
Schumpeter, Joseph, *Capitalism, Socialism and Democracy*. New York: Harper Torchbooks, 1976.
Schutz, Alfred, *The Problem of Social Reality. Collected Works, Volume 1*. Maurice Natanson (ed.). The Hague: Martinus Nijhoff, 1962.
Schwade, Werner, "Untersuchung der vom Binnen- und Weltmarkt abhängigen Produktions- und Absatzbedingungen in der deutschen Maschinenindustrie." *Dissertation*, Erlangen, 1934.
Schwartz, Ivo E., "Antitrust Legislation and Policy in Germany—A Comparative Study," *University of Pennsylvania Law Review* 105.5 (1957): 617–690.

Schweitzer, Arthur, *Big Business and the Third Reich*. Bloomington, IN: Indiana University Press, 1964.

Schwend, Karl, *Bayern zwischen Monarchie und Diktatur. Beiträge zur bayerischen Frage in der Zeit von 1918 bis 1933*. Munich: 1954.

Scitovsky, Tibor, *Economic Theory and Western European Economic Integration*. London: Allen and Unwin, 1962.

Selve, Hanz Emil, "Strukturwandlungen der westdeutschen Maschinenindustrie in der Nachkriegszeit." *Dissertation*, Köln, 1957.

Semlinger, Klaus, "A Marketing Approach for Public Invervention Into Enterprise Decision Making." Paper delivered at the 10th European Group for Organizational Studies Colloquium on "Societal Change between Market and Organization," Vienna, July 15–17: 1991.

Semlinger, Klaus, "Das Steinbeis-Zentrum fuer Qualitätswesen in Gosheim. Eine kleinbetriebliche Kooperationsinitiative auf dem Weg zum Erfolg." Unpublished manuscript, Institut Für Sozialwissenschaftliche Forschung e.V (München), 1991.

Semlinger, Klaus, "Industrial District Politik in Baden Württemberg—Zwischen Neubesinnung und Neuanfang." Paper delivered at the conference: "Explaining Regional Competitiveness and the Capability to Innovate. The Case of Baden Württemberg. Stuttgart, July 1994.

Semlinger, Klaus, "Economic Development and Indistrual Policy in Baden Wuerttemberg: Small Firms in a Benevolent Environment." *European Planning Studies* 1 (1993): 435–463.

Sengenberger, Werner (ed.), *Der gespaltene Arbeitsmarkt. Probleme der Arbeitsmarktsegmentation*. Frankfurt: Campus Verlag, 1978.

Senghass, Dieter, *Vom Europa Lernen*. Frankfurt: Suhrkamp, 1982.

Servan-Schreiber, J. J., *The American Challenge*. New York: Athenaeum, 1979.

Seyfarth, Shaw, Fairweather, and Geraldson, *Labor Relations and the Law in West Germany and the United States*. Ann Arbor, MI: University of Michigan Press, 1969.

Seyfert, E. W., *Der Arbeiternachwuchs in der deutschen Maschinenindustrie*. Berlin: Julius Springer, 1920.

Sheehan, James J., "Liberalism and the City in Nineteenth Century Germany." *Past and Present* 51 (1971): 117–137.

Shingo, Shingeo, *Non-Stock Production: The Shingo System for Continuous Improvement*. Cambridge, MA: Productivity Press, 1987.

Shingo, Shigeo, *The Shingo Production Management System. Improving Process Functions*. Cambridge, MA: Productivity Press, 1992.

Sieben, "Forderungen an den Textilmaschinenbau." *Melliand Textilberichte* 32 October (1951): 746ff.

Siegrist, Hannes, "Deutsche Grossunternehmen im späten 19. Jahrhundert bis zur Weimar Republik." *Geschichte und Gesellschaft* 6 (1980): 66–102.

Siemens-Schuckert (ed.), *Die Entwicklung der Starkstromtechnik bei den Siemens-Schukertwerken*. Munich: Graphische Kunstanstalten F. Bruckmann, 1953.

Sieveking, Heinrich, "Geschichte der gewerblichen Betriebsformen und der zünftigen, städtischen und staatlicht Gewerbepolitik." In *Grundriss der Sozialökonomik. VI. Abetilungen: Industrie, Bergwesen, Bauwesen*. E. Gothein (ed.). Tübingen: JCB Mohr (Paul Siebeck), 1914,

Simon, Herman, "Lessons from Germany's Mid-Sized Giants." *Harvard Business Review* March–April (1992).

Sinzheimer, Hugo, *Arbeitsrecht und Rechtssoziologie: gesammelte Aufsatze und Reden, Schriftenreihe der Otto Brenner Stiftung.* Otto Kahn-Freund and Thilo Ramm (eds.). Frankfurt: Europaische Verlagsanstalt, 1976, 4.
Slicher van Bath, B. H., *The Agrarian History of Western Europe, AD 500–1850.* London: Edward Arnold, 1963.
Smith, Adam, *An Inquiry Into the Nature and Causes of the Wealth of Nations.* New York: The Modern Library, 1937.
SOFI, *Branchenstrukurmerkmale und grobe Entwicklungslinien des Rationalisierungsprozesses im Fahrzeugbau bis 1960." Vorstudium zum BMFT-Forschungsprojekt "Tarifvertragliche Regelungen zur Verbesserung industrieller Arbeitsbedingungen."* Göttingen: SOFI, 1977, pp. 323–254.
Soltau, Friedrich, "Der Absatz der deutschen Werkzeugmaschinenindustrie." *Dissertation,* Halle-Württemberg, 1930.
Sombart, Werner, *Der Moderne Kapitalismus Vol. 3: Das Wirtschaftsleben im Zeitalter des Hochkapitalismus.* Munich: Duncker & Humblot, 1927.
Söhngen, Werner, "Aktuelle Fragen zur dezentralen Konzernorganisation." *Zeitschrift für Handelswissenschaftliche Forschung* 13 (1961): 520–528.
Söll, Wilhelm, "Die staatliche Wirtschaftspolitik in Württemberg im 17. und 18. Jahrhundert." *Dissertation,* Tübingen, 1934.
Soskice, David, "Reinterpreting Corporatism and Explaining Unemployment: Co-ordinated and Non-co-ordinated Market Economies." In *Labor Relations and Economic Performance,* Renato Brunetta and Carlo Dell'aringa (eds.). London: Macmillan, 1990.
Späth, Lothar, *Die Chancen der Vielfalt: d. Foderalismus als moderne Staatsform.* Stuttgart: Verlag Bonn aktuell, 1979.
Späth, Lothar, *Wende in die Zukunft. Die Bundesrepublik auf dem Weg in die Informationsgesellschaft.* Hamburg: Rowohlt, 1985.
Spencer, Elaine Glovka, "Rulers of the Ruhr: Leadership and Authority in German Big Business before 1914." *Business History Review* 53.1 Spring (1979): 40–64.
Spiro, Herbert J., *The Politics of German Codetermination.* Cambridge, MA: Harvard University Press, 1958.
Sraffa, Piero, "The Laws of Returns Under Competitive Conditions." *Economic Journal* December (1926).
Stahltreuhändervereinigung, *Die Neuordnung der Eisen und Stahlindustrie im Gebiet der Bundesrepublik Deutschland.* Munich: C. H. Beck'sche Verlagsbuchhandlung, 1954.
Stegmann, Dirk, *Die Erben Bismarcks. Parteinen und Verbände in der Spätphase des wilhelminischen Deutschlands. Sammlungspolitik 1897–1918.* Köln: Kiepenauer & Witsch, 1970.
Stegmann, Franz Josef, "Einleitung: Begriff und Formen der Mitbestimmung—Die innerkatholische Mitbestimmungsdiskussion nach 1945." In *Die soziale Katholzismus und die Mitbestimmung in Deutschland.* Franz Josef Stegmann (ed.). Munich: Verlag Ferdinand Schöningh, 1978, pp. 9–15.
Stein, Gustav, "Entwicklungstendenzen der Zulieferertätigkeit. Die grosse Chance der Klein und Mittelbetriebe." *Industriekurier* 192 December 9 (1965): 6.
Stein, Lorenz von, *Der socialismus und communismus des heutigen Frankreichs. Ein beitrag zur zeitgeschichte.* Leipzig: Otto Wigand, 1842.
Steinkühler, Franz, "Gewerkschaftliche Position zur sozialen Beherrschbarkeit der Technik," *Gewerkschaftliche Monatshefte* 9 (1985).

Steinmetz, George, *Regulating the Social. The Welfare State and Local Politics in Imperial Germany*. Princeton: Princeton University Press, 1993.
Steinmüller, Peter, *Lage und Entwicklungschancen der deutschen Maschinenindustrie*. Frankfurt: Gewiplan, 1977.
Steller, Paul, "Die Maschinenindustrie." In *Störungen im deutschen Wirtschaftsleben während der Jahre 1900ff.* Verein für Sozialpolitik (ed.), Leipzig: Dunker & Humblot, 1903.
Stern, Fritz, *The Politics of Cultural Despair*. Berkeley: University of California Press, 1961.
Stern, Fritz, *The Failure of Illiberalism: Essays on the Political Culture of Modern Germany*. New York: Columbia University Press, 1972.
Sternberg, Fritz, "Die gewerkschaftlichen Aufgaben in der Epoche der Automatisierung," *Der Gewerkschafter* 11 (1957): 10–12.
Stigler, George, *The Organization of Industry*. Chicago: University of Chicago Press, 1968.
Stinchcombe, Arthur, *Information and Organizations*. Berkeley: University of California Press, 1990.
Stitz, Hermann, "Die Wirtschaft im Siegerland. Industrielle Entwicklung und Strukturwandel." In *Die westdeutsche Wirtschaft und ihre führenden Männer. Lesebuch der deutschen Industrie. Land Nordrhein-Westfalen. Teil II: Sauerland und Siegerland*. Julius Keil (ed.). Oberursel: Wirtschaftslesebuch-Verlag Dr. Julius Keil GmbH, 1972, pp. 19–29.
Stokes, Raymond, *Divide and Prosper: The Heirs of I. G. Farben under Allied Authority*. Berkeley: University of California Press, 1988.
Stolle, Uta, *Arbeiterpolitik im Betrieb, Frauen und Männer, Reformisten und Radikale, Fach und Massenarbeiter bei Bayer, BASF, Bosch und in Solingen (1900–1933)*. Frankfurt: Campus, 1980.
Stolper, Gustav, *German Realities*. New York: Reynal and Hitchcock, 1948.
Storper, Michael, and Robert Salais, *Worlds of Possibility: Collective Action and the Economic Identities of Nations and Regions*. Cambridge, MA: Harvard University Press, forthcoming 1996.
Storz, Helmut, "Die relative Krisenfestigkeit der württembergischen Wirtschaft." *Dissertation,* Munich, 1933.
Stöbe, Sybille, "Regionalpolitik im Ruhrgebiet und in Nord-Pas de Calais. Ein deutschfranzösicher Vergleich." *Diplomarbeit*, Universität Gesamthochschule-Duisburg, 1987.
Strath, Bo, "Modes of Governance in the Shipbuilding Sector in Germany, Sweden and Japan." In *Governing Capitalist Economies. Performance and Control of Economic Sectors*. J. Rogers Hollingsworth, Phillippe C. Schmitter and Wolfgang Streeck (eds.). New York: Oxford University Press, 1994.
Strauss, Eduard, "Westdeutscher Textilmaschinenbau." *Wirtschaftsdienst* 8 (1952): 508–511.
Streeck, Wolfgang, *Gewerkschaftliche Organisationsprobleme in der sozialstaatlichen Demokratie*. Königstein/Ts: Athenaeum, 1981.
Streeck, Wolfgang, "Co-determination: the fourth decade." In *International Perspectives on Organizational Democracy*. B. Wilpert and A. Sorge (eds.). London: John Wiley and Sons, 1984a, pp. 391–422.
Streeck, Wolfgang, *Industrial Relations in West Germany: A Case Study of the Car Industry*. New York: St. Martin's Press, 1984b.

Streeck, Wolfgang, "Neocorporatist Industrial Relations and the Economic Crisis in West Germany." In *Order and Conflict in Contemporary Capitalism*. John Goldthorpe (ed.). New York: Oxford University Press, 1984c, pp. 291–314.

Streeck, Wolfgang, "Industrial Relations and Industrial Change: the Restructuring of the World Automobile Industry in the 1970s and 1980s." *Economic and Industrial Democracy* 8 (1987a): 437–462.

Streeck, Wolfgang, "The Uncertainties of Management in the Management of Uncertainty: Employers, Labor Relations and Industrial Adjustment in the 1980s." *Work, Employment and Society* 1.2 (1987b): 281–308.

Streeck, Wolfgang, *The Role of the Social Partners in Vocational Training and Further Training in the Federal Republic Germany*. Berlin: CEDEFOP, 1987c.

Streeck, Wolfgang, "Successful Adjustment in Turbulent Markets: The Automobile Industry." In *Industry and Politics in West Germany. Toward the Third Republic*. Peter Katzenstein (ed.). Ithaca: Cornell University Press, 1989, pp. 113–156.

Streeck, Wolfgang, "On the Social and Political Conditions of Diversified Quality Production." In *No Way to Full Employment?* Frieder Naschold (ed.). Berlin: Sigma, 1990.

Streeck, Wolfgang, "On the Institutional Conditions of Diversified Quality Production." In *Beyond Keynsianism: The Socio-Economics of Production and Employment*. Egon Matzner and Wolfgang Streeck (eds.). London: Edward Elgar, 1991, pp. 21–61.

Streeck, Wolfgang, *Social Institutions and Economic Performance. Studies of Industrial Relations in Advanced Capitalist Economies*. London: Sage, 1992a.

Streeck, Wolfgang, "Productive Constraints: on the Institutional Conditions of Diversified Quality Production." In *Social Institutions and Economic Performance: Studies of Industrial Relations in Advanced Capitalist Economies*. Wolfgang Streeck (ed.). London: Sage, 1992b, pp. 1–40.

Streeck, Wolfgang, "The Territorial Organization of Interests and the Logics of Associative Action: The Case of Handwerk organization in West Germany." In *Regionalism, Business Interests, and Public Policy*. William D. Coleman and Henry J. Lacek (eds.). London: Sage, 1989.

Strohmeyer, Hans Carl, "Investition, Maschinenexport und Fertigwarenausfuhr." *Der Volkswirt* (1949a): 12.

Strohmeyer, Hans Carl, "Maschinenexport und Fertigwarenausfuhr." *Der Volkswirt* (1949b): 10.

Strössner, Georg, "Die Fusion der Aktiengesellschaft Maschinenfabrik Augsburg und der Maschinenbau-Actien-Gesellschaft Nürnberg im Jahre 1898." *Tradition: Zeitschrift für Firmengeschichte und Unternehmerbiographie* 5.3 (1960): 97–115.

Stubenrecht, Alfred, "Der Einfluss der Automation auf Arbeitsvorbereitung und Arbeitsablauf." In *Zentralproblem der Vollbeschäftigung*. Deutsche Gesellschaft für Betriebswirtschaft (ed.). Berlin: Deutscher Betriebswirte-Verlag, 1957, pp. 65–80.

Svennilson, Ingvar, *Growth and Stagnation in the European Economy*. Geneva: United Nations, 1954.

Sweezy, Paul M., *The Theory of Capitalist Development*. New York: Monthly Review Press, 1942/1970.

Swenson, Peter, *Fair Shares. Unions, Pay and Politics in Sweden and West Germany*. Ithaca: Cornell University Press, 1989.

Sylla, Richard, and Gianni Toniolo (eds.), *Patterns of European Industrialization: The Nineteenth Century*. London: Routledge, 1991.

Taylor, Graham D., "The Rise and Fall of Anti-Trust in Occupied Germany, 1945–1948." *Prologue* 11.1 (1979): 22–39.
Taylor, M. E., *Education and Work in the Federal Republic of Germany*. London: Anglo-German Foundation for the Study of Industrial Society, 1981.
Technologiezentrum, VDI/VDE, *Wirkungsanalyse zum Sonderprogram Anwendung der Mikroelektronik: Forschungsbericht.* Berlin: Markt & Technik Verlag A.G., 1986.
Thanheiser, Heinz, "Strategy and Structure in Germany." In *The Emerging European Enterprise*. Heinz Thanheiser and Gareth Dyas (eds.). London: MacMillan, 1976, pp. 139–151.
Thanheiser, Heinz, and Gareth Dyas, *The Emerging European Enterprise*. London: Macmillan, 1976.
Thelen, Kathleen, and Sven Steinmo, "Historical Institutionalism in Comparative Politics." In *Structuring Politics. Historical Institutionalism in Comparative Analysis*. Sven Steinmo, Kathleen Thelen and Frank Longstreth (eds.). New York: Cambridge University Press, 1992, pp. 1–33.
Thelen, Kathleen, *Union of Parts. Labor Politics in Post War West Germany*. Ithaca: Cornell University Press, 1992.
Thompson, E. P., *The Poverty of Theory and Other Essays*. New York: Monthly Review Press, 1978.
Thum, Horst, *Mitbestimmung in der Montanindustrie. Der Mythos vom Sieg der Gewerkschaften*. Stuttgart: Deutsche Verlags-Anstalt, 1982.
Thun, Albert, *Die Industrie am Niederrhein und ihre Arbeiter*, Vols. 1 & 2. Leipzig: 1879.
Tilly, Richard, "Germany, 1815–1870." In *Banking in the Early Stages of Industrialization: A Study in Comparative Economic History*. Rondo Cameron (ed.). New York: Oxford University Press, 1967.
Tilly, Richard, *Kapital, Staat, und sozialer Protest in der deutschen Industrialisierung*. Göttingen: Vandenhoeck & Ruprecht, 1980.
Tilly, Richard, "Mergers, External Growth and Finance in the Development of Large-Scale Enterprise in Germany, 1880–1913." *Journal of Economic History* 42.3 (1982): 629–658.
Tilly, Richard, "German Banking, 1850–1914: Development Assistance for the Strong," *Journal of European Economic History* 15.1 (1986): 113–152.
Tipton, Frank, *Regional Variations in the Economic Development of Germany in the Nineteenth Century*. Middletown: Wesleyan University Press, 1976.
Tirole, Jean, *The Theory of Industrial Organization*. Cambridge, MA: MIT Press, 1989.
Torkewitz, Heinz, "Der deutsche Textilmaschinenbau: ein Beitrag zur deutschen Wirtschaftgeschichte." *Dissertation*, München, 1934.
Tornow, Ingo, "Die deutschen Unternehmerverbände 1945–1950. Kontinuität oder Diskontinuität?." In *Vorgeschichte der Bundesrepublik Deutschland. Zwischen Kapitulation und Grundgesetz*. Josef Becker, Theo Stammen, and Peter Waldmann (eds.). Munich: Wilhelm Fink, 1979, pp. 235–260.
Treblicock, Clive, *The Industrialization of the Continental Powers, 1780–1914*. London: 1981.
Treue, Wilhelm, *Die Feuer verlöschen nie. August Thyssen-Huette 1890–1926*. Dusseldorf: Econ Verlag, 1966.
Treue, Wilhelm, "Henschel und Sohn, Ein deutsches Lokomotivbau-Unternehmen, 1860–1912." *Tradition: Zeitschrift für Firmengeschichte und Unternehmerbiographie* 19 (1974): 3–23.

Treue, Wilhelm, *Gesellschaft, Wirtschaft und Technik Deutschlands im 19. Jahrhundert.* Munich: Deutschetaschenbuch Verlag, 1975.
Tribe, Keith, *Governing Economy: The Reformation of German Economic Discourse 1750–1840.* Cambridge: Cambridge University Press, 1988.
Troeltsch, W., *Die Calwer Zeughandlungskompanie und ihre arbeiter. Studien zur Gewerbe- und Sozialgeschichte Altwürttembergs.* Jena: Gustav Fischer, 1897.
Tross, Arnold, *Der Aufbau der Eisen- und Eisenverarbeitenden Industrie-Konzerene Deutschlands. Ursachen, Formen und Wirkungen des Zusammenschlusses unter besonderer Berücksichtigung der Maschinenindustrie.* Berlin: Julius Springer, 1923.
Tsoukalis, Loukas, and Maureen White (eds.), *Japan and Western Europe. Conflict and Cooperation.* London: Butterworth, 1981.
Tueteberg, Hans Jürgen, *Geschichte der industriellen Mitbestimmung in Deutschland. Ursprung und Entwicklung ihrer Vorläufer im Denken und in der Wirklichkeit des 19. Jahrhundert.* Tübingen: J.C.B. Mohr (Paul Siebeck), 1961.
Tueteberg, Hans J., "Ursprünge und Entwicklung der Mitbestimmung in Deutschland" In *Mitbestimmung. Ursprünge und Entwicklung.* Hans Pohl (ed.). ed. *Zeitschrift für Unternehmensgeschichte*, Beiheft 19. Wiesbaden: Franz Steiner, 1981, pp. 7–73.
Turner, Henry Ashby Jr., *German Big Business and the Rise of Hitler.* New York: Oxford University Press, 1985.
Turner, Ian (ed.), *Reconstruction in Post War Germany: British Occupation Policy and the Western Zones, 1945–1955.* London: Berg Publishers, 1989.
Turner, Lowell, *Democracy at Work. Changing World Markets and the Future of Labor Unions.* Ithaca: Cornell University Press, 1992.
Ullmann, Hans-Peter, *Der Bund der Industriellen, Organization, Einfluss und Politik klein- und mittelbetrieblicher Industrieller im Deutschen Kaiserreich 1895–1914.* Göttingen: Vandenhoeck & Ruprecht, 1976.
Ullmann, Hans-Peter, *Interessenverbände in Deutschland.* Frankfurt: Suhrkamp, 1988.
Ullmann, Peter, *Tarifverträge und Tarifpolitik in Deutschland bis 1914.* Frankfurt: Peter Lang, 1977.
Ulman, Lloyd, *The Rise of the National Trade Union. The Development and Significance of its Structure, Governing Institutions and Economic Policies.* Cambridge, MA: Harvard University Press, 1955.
Unger, Roberto Mangabiera, *Politics: A Work in Transformative Social Theory.* New York: Cambridge University Press, 1988.
Unger, Roberto Mangabeira, *Social Theory: Its Situation and its Task. Volume One of Politics, a Work in Constructive Social Theory.* New York: Cambridge University Press, 1988.
United States Senate, *Executive Sessions of the Senate Foreign Relations Committee (Historical Series) Volume II, Eighty-First Congress, First and Second Sessions, 1949–1950.* Washington DC: United States Senate, 1950.
VDI (ed.), *Automatisierung der Fertigung Vorträge der VDI-Tagung, Stuttgart 1961.* Düsseldorf: VDI Verlag, 1962.
VDMA, Verein Deutscher Maschinenbau-Anstalten e.V:, *Statistisches Handbuch für den Maschinenbau.* Frankfurt: Maschinenbau-Verlag GmbH, various years.
VDW, Verein deutscher Werzeugmaschinenbaus:, "Wirtschaftliche Betrachtungen zu dem Bericht von Prof. Melman über die Produktivität der Fertigung in der Werkzeugmaschinenindustrie Westeuropas." (Unpublished Manuscript in VDW Archives, Frankfurt: 1960).

VDW, Verein deutscher Werzeugmaschinenbaus:, "Technische Betrachtungen zu dem Bericht von Prof. Melman über die Produktivität der Fertigung in der Werkzeugmaschinenindustrie Westeuropas." (Unpublished manuscript in the VDW archives, Frankfurt: 1960).

Veblen, Thorstein, *Imperial Germany*. Ann Arbor, MI: University of Michigan Press, n.d.

Vernon, Raymond, "International Investment and International Trade in the Product Cycle." *The Quarterly Journal of Economics* 80.2 (1966): 190–207.

Vernon, Raymond (ed.), *Big Business and the State*. Cambridge, MA: Harvard University Press, 1974.

Vernon, Raymond, "The Product Cycle Hypothesis in a New International Environment." *Oxford Bulletin of Economics and Statistics* 41.4 (1979): 255–267.

Vershofen, Wilhelm, *Die Grenzen der Rationalisierung*. Nurnberg: Verlag Hochschulbuchhandlung Krische & Co., 1927.

Vischer, L., *Die Industrielle Entwicklung im Königreich Württemberg und das Wirken Seiner Centralstelle Für Gewerbe und Handel in ersten 25 Jahren*. Stuttgart: Verlag von Carl Grüninger, 1875.

Vogl, Frank, *German Business After the Economic Miracle*. New York: John Wiley and Sons, 1973.

Voigt, Fritz, "German Experience with Cartels and their Control during the Pre-War and Post-War Periods." In *Competition, Cartels and their Regulation*. John Perry Miller (ed.). Amsterdam: North Holland, 1962, pp. 168–213.

von Beckerath, Herbert, *Kräfte, Ziele und Gestaltung in der deutschen Industrie*. Jena: Georg Fischer, 1923.

von Beckerath, Herbert, *Modern Industrial Organization: An Economic Interpretation*. New York: McGraw Hill, 1933.

von Degenfeld-Schonberg, Ferdinand Graf, "Die Unternehmerpersöhnlichkeit in der modernen Volkswirtschaft." *Schmollers Jahrbuch* 55 (1929): 55–75.

von Freyberg, Thomas, *Industrielle Rationalisierung in der Weimarer Republik*. Frankfurt: Campus Verlag, 1989.

von Klass, Gert, *Krupps. The Story of an Industrial Empire*. London: Sidgewick and Jackson, 1954.

von Lilienstein, Hans Rühle, "Handwerk und Industrie im Gemeinsamen Markt. Aus Konkurrenten werden Partner. Neue Funktionenen fuer den Kleinbetrieb." *VDI-Nachrichten* 41, October 7 (1964): 19.

von Menges, Dietrich Wilhelm, *Unternehmens-Entscheide. Ein Leben für die Wirtschaft*. Düsseldorf: Econ Verlag, 1976.

von Stromer, Wolfgang, "Gewerbereviere und Protoindustrien in Spätmittelalter und Fruehneuzeit." In *Gewerbe- und Industrielandschaften vom Spätmittelalter bis ins 20. Jahrhundert*. Hans Pohl (ed.). Vierteljahreschrift Für Sozial-und Wirtschaftsgeschichte. Stuttgart: Franz Steiner Verlag Wiesbaden GmbH, 1986, Beiheft Nr. 78: 39–112.

von Weiher, Siegfried and Herbert Götzeler, *Weg und Wirken der Siemens-Werke im Fortschritt der Elektrotechnik, 1847–1972. Ein Beitrag zur Geschichte der Elektroindustrie*. (Tradition" Zeitschrift für Firmengeschichte und Unternehmensbiographie Beiheft Nr. 8) Wiesbaden: Franz Steiner, 1972.

Voskamp, Ulrich, Klaus Peter Wittemann, and Volker Wittke, "Know-How Transfer." *IBM Nachrichten* 33.267 (1983): 64–70.

Voskamp, Ulrich, Klaus Peter Wittemann, and Volker Wittke, "Perestroika in der Elektroindustrie? Produktionsarbeit zwischen Umbruch und Strukturkonservatismus."

Unpublished manuscript, SOFI Soziologisches Forschungsinstitut Göttingen, 1989.
Voskamp, Ulli, Klaus Peter Wittemann, and Volker Wittke, *Elektroindustrie im Umbruch. Zur Veränderungsdynamik von Produktionsstrukturen, Rationalisierungskonzepten und Arbeit. Zwischenbericht.* Göttingen: SOFI, 1989.
Voskamp, Ulrich, and Volker Wittke, "Junge Facharbeiter in der Produktion—eine Herausforderung für die Gestaltung der betrieblichen Arbeitsorganisation." *Siemens: Informationen zur Gestaltung der Arbeit* 9 (1991): offprint.
Vögle, Wilhelm, "Wirtschaftliche Grenzen der Rationalisierung in der Maschinenindustrie." *Maschinenbau. Wirtschaftlicher Teil* 8.2 (1929): W13–W14.
Wade, Robert, *Governing the Market. Economic Theory and the Role of Government in East Asian Industrialization.* Princeton: Princeton University Press, 1990.
Wagenblass, Horst, *Der Eisenbahnbau und das Wachstum der deutschen Eisen- und Maschinenbauindustrie 1835–1860. Ein Beitrag zur Geschichte der Industrialisierung Deutschlands.* Stuttgart: Gustav Fischer Verlag, 1973.
Walde, Herman, and Gerd Berlinghoff, *Das Auslandsgeschaeft mit Industrieanlagen.* Munich: Verlag Moderne Industrie, 1967.
Waller, Peter, "Neuordnung des Stahlvereins." *Deutsche Volkswirt* November 3, 1933 1933: 213–216.
Walli, P. F., *Die dezentralisation der Industrie und der Arbeiterschaft in Grossherzogtum Baden.* Karlsruhe: Braunschen, 1906.
Wallich, Henry, *Mainsprings of the German Miracle.* New Haven: Yale University Press, 1955.
Warner, Isabel, "Allied German Negotiation on the Deconcentration of the West German Steel Industry." In *Reconstruction in Post War Germany: British Occupation Policy and the Western Zones, 1945–1955.* Ian Turner (ed.). London: Berg Publishers, 1989, pp. 155–185.
Warren, Donald, *The Red Kingdom of Saxony, Lobbying grounds for Gustav Streseman, 1901–1909.* Hague: Martinus Nijhoff, 1964.
Webb, Steven B., "Tariffs, Cartels, Technology and Growth in the German Steel Industry, 1879–1914." *Journal of Economic History* 40.2 (1980): 302–329.
Weber, Hajo, "Intermediäre Organisation, Zur Organization von Wirtschaftsinteressen zwischen Markt, Staat und Gewerkschaften. Eine Eimpirisch Komparitiv Untersuchung der Wirtschaftsverbände des Maschinenbaus und der Arbeitgeberverbände der Metallindustrie." *Ph.D. dissertation,* Department of Sociology. Bielefeld, 1984.
Weber, Hajo, "Technokorporatismus. Die Steuerung des Technologischen Wandels durch Staat, Wirtschaftsverbaende und Gewerkschaften." Unpublished manuscript, Bielefeld, 1986.
Weber, Max, *The Agrarian Sociology of Ancient Civilizations.* London: Verso, 1988.
Weber, Max, "Parliament und Regierung im neugeordneten Deutschland." In *Gesammelt Politische Schriften.* Johannes Wincklemann (ed.). Tübingen: JCB Mohr (Paul Siebeck), 1988a, pp. 306–443.
Weber, Max, "Deutschlands künftige Staatsform." In *Max Weber, Gesammelt Politische Schriften.* Johannes Wincklemann (ed.). Tübingen: JCB Mohr (Paul Siebeck), 1988b.
Weber, Max, *Wirtschaft und Gesellschaft.* Johannes Winkelmann (ed.). Tübingen: JCB Mohr (Paul Siebeck), 1972.
Weber, W., "Preussische Transferpolitik 1780–1820." *Technikgeschichte* 42 (1983): 181–196.

Weder, Dietrich, "Die 200 Grössten deutschen Aktiengesellschaften 1913–1962. Beziehungen zwischen Grösse, Lebensdauer und Wettbewerbschancen von Unternehmen." *Dissertation,* Frankfurt, 1968.
Wehler, Hans-Ulrich, *Das Deutsche Kaiserreich 1871–1918.* Göttingen: Vandenhoeck & Ruprecht, 1973.
Wehler, Hans-Ulrich, "Der Aufsteig des Organisierten Kapitalismus und Interventionsstaates in Deutschland." In *Organisierter Kapitalismus. Voraussetzungen und Anfänge.* Heinrich August Winkler (ed.). Göttingen: Vandenhoeck & Ruprecht, 1974, pp. 18–35.
Weil, Paul, *Wirtschaftsgeschichte des Ruhrgebietes.* Essen: Siedlungsverband Ruhrkohlenbezirk Essen, 1970.
Weimer, Stephanie, "The Federal Republic of Germany." In *The Reemergence of Small enterprises. Industrial Restructuring in Industrialized Countries.* Werner Sengenberger, Gary Loveman, and Michael Piore (eds.). Geneva: International Institute for Labor Studies, 1990, pp. 98–143.
Weisbrod, Bernd, *Schwerindustrie in der Weimarer Republik. Interessenpolitik zwischen Stabilisierung und Krise.* Wuppertal: Peter Hammer, 1978.
Weisbrod, Bernd, "Economic Power and Political Stability Reconsidered: Heavy Industry in Weimar Germany." *Social History* 4.2 (1979): 241–263.
Weiss, Frank, and Frank Wolter, "Machinery in the United States, Sweden and Germany—An Assessment of Changes in Comparative Advantage." *Weltwirtschaftliches Archiv* 111.2 (1975): 282–309.
Weiss, Frank Dietmar, *Electrical Engineering in West Germany: Adjusting to Imports from Less Developed Countries.* Tübingen: JCB Mohr, 1978.
Weisweiler, Franz Josef, "Unternehmensgeschichte in der Produkt-Portfolio-Analyse—dargestellt am Beispiel des Hauses Mannesmann." *Schmalenbachs Zeitschrift für betriebswirtschaftliche Forschung* 34.3 (1982): 281–289.
Wellhöner, Volker, *Grossbanken und Grossindustrie im Kaiserreich.* Göttingen: Vandenhoeck & Ruprecht, 1989.
Wells, Louis T. (ed.), *The Product Life Cycle and International Trade.* Boston: Harvard University Press, 1972.
Wells, Louis T., "Automobiles." In *Big Business and the State. Changing Relations in Western Europe.* Raymond Vernon (ed.). Cambridge, MA: Harvard University Press, 1974, pp. 229–254.
Weltz, Friedrich, Gert Schmidt, and Jürgen Sass, *Facharbeiter im Industriebetrieb. Eine Untersuchung in Metalverarbeitenden Betrieben.* Frankfurt: Athenaeum Verlag, 1974.
Weltz, Friedrich, *Introduction of new technologies, employment policies, and industrial relations: a survey carried out for the Anglo-German Foundation for the Study of Industrial Society.* London: Anglo-German Foundation for the Study of Industrial Society, 1978.
Wengenroth, Ulrich, *Unternehmensstrategien und technischer Forschritt. Die deutsche und die britische Stahlindustrie, 1865–1895.* Göttingen: Vandenhoeck & Ruprecht, 1986.
Wengenroth, Ulrich (ed.), *Prekäre Selbständigkeit. Zur Standortbestimmung von Handwerk, Hausindustrie und Kleingewerbe im Industrialisierunsprozess.* Stuttgart: Franz Steiner, 1989.
Wengst, Udo, *Staatsaufbau und Regierungspraxis, 1948–1953.* Düsseldorf: Droste Verlag, 1984.

Wentzel, Lothar, *Inflation und Arbeitslosigkeit. Gewerkschaftlichekämpfe und ihre Grenzen am Beispiel des Deutschen Metallarbeiter-Verbandes, 1919–1924*. Hanover: SOAK-Verlag, 1981.
Wernet, W., "Wandlungen des Handwerks. Deutliche expansion seit dem Vorigen Jahrhundert." 4(1]4): 9.
Wernicke, Dr. J., *Kapitalismus und Mittelstandspolitik*. Jena: Gustav Fischer, 1907.
Wessels, Theodor, "Wachsende Starrheit der Unternehmungen und ihre Ursachen." *Zeitschrift für Handelswissenschaftliche Forschung* 10.2 (1958): 66–75.
Wieacker, Franz, *Privatrechtsgeschichte der Neuzeit. Unter besonderer Berucksichtigung der deutschen Entwicklung*. Göttingen: Vandenhoeck & Ruprecht, 1967.
Wiest, Ekkard, *Die Entwicklung des Nürnberger Gewerbes zwischen 1648–1806*. Stuttgart: Gustav Fischer, 1968.
Williams, Karel, Colin Haslam, Andy Adcroft, Sukhdev Johal, and John Williams, "Against Lean Production." *Economy and Society 1992*. August (1992).
Williamson, Oliver O., *Markets and Hierarchies*. New York: Free Press, 1975.
Williamson, Oliver O., *The Economic Institutions of Capitalism. Firms, Markets and Relational Contracting*. New York: Free Press, 1985.
Williamson, Oliver, Alfred Chandler, and Charles Perrow, "Markets and Hierarchies: A Discussion." In *The Essential Alfred Chandler. Essays Toward a Historical Theory of Big Business*. Thomas K. McCraw (ed.). Boston: Harvard Business School Press, 1988, pp. 432–464.
Winkel, Harald, *Geschichte der württembergischen Industrie-und Handelskammern Heilbronn, Reutlingen, Stuttgart/Mittlerer Neckar und Ulm, 1933–1980; zum 125 jahrigen Bestehen*. Stuttgart: Undustrie und Handelskammern Heilbronn, Muttlerer Neckar (Sitz Stuttgart), Reutlingen und Ulm, 1980, p. 739.
Winkler, Heinrich A., *Mittelstand, Demokratie und Nationalsozialismus. Die politische. Entwicklung v. Handwerk u. Kleinhandel in d. Weimarer Republik*. Köln: Kiepenheuer & Witsch, 1972, p. 307.
Winkler, H. A., *Organisierter Kapitalismus. Voraussetzungen und Anfänge*. Göttingen: Vandenhoeck & Ruprecht, 1974.
Winkler, Heinrich A., *Liberalismus und Antiliberalismus: Studien zur politische und Sozialgeschichte der 19. und 20. Jh*. Göttingen: Vandenhoeck & Ruprecht, 1979, 38.
Winkler, Heinrich A., *Zwischen Marx und Monopolen: der deutsche Mittelstand vom Kaiserreich zur Bundesrepublik Deutschland*. Frankfurt: Fischer Taschenbuch Verlag, 1991.
Wiskott, Otto, *Eisenschaffende und eisenverarbeitende Industrie*. Bonn/Leipzig: Kurt Schroeder, 1929.
Wistinghausen, Jochen, "Betriebssoziale Probleme des technischen Fortschritts." *Vortragsreihe des Deutschen Industrieinstituts* 19, May 13 (1957).
Witt, Peter Christian, "Finanzpolitik und sozialer Wandel im Krieg und Inflation 1918–1924." In *Industrielles System und politische Entwicklung in der Weimarer Republik*. Hans Mommsen, Dietmar Petzina, and Bernd Weisbrod (eds.). Kronberg/Ts: Athenaeum, 1977.
Wittke, Volker, "Elektronisierung und Rationalisierung. Zur Veränderungsdynamik von Produktionsarbeit in der Elektroindustrie." In *Trends betrieblicher Produktionsmodernisierung*. L. Preis, R. Schmidt, and R. Trinczek (eds.). Opladen: West Deutscher Verlag, 1989, pp. 130–136.
Wittke, Volker, "Systemischer Rationalisierung. Zur Analyse aktueller Umbruchspro-

zesse in der industriellen Produktion." *SOFI Mitteilungen* 17, December (1989): 53–68.

Wollmann, Hellmut, "Investionshilfen." In *Politikverflechtung II. Kritik und Berichte aus der Praxis. Beiträge zu einer Arbeitstagung des Wissenschaftszentrums Berlin*. Fritz W. Scharpf, Bernd Reissert, and Fritz Schnabel (eds.). Frankfurt: Athenaeum, 1977, pp. 18–29.

Wolter, Frank, "Strukturelle Anpassungsprobleme der westdeutschen Stahlindustrie: Zur Standortfrage der Stahlindustrie in hochindustrialisierten Ländern." *Kieler Studien*. Tübingen: JCB Mohr, 1974.

Womack, James P., Daniel T. Jones, and Daniel Roos, *The Machine That Changed the World*. New York: Rawson Associates, 1990.

Woolston, Maxine Y., *The Structure of the Nazi Economy*. New York: Russell and Russell, 1941.

Wrigley, E. A., "Urban Growth and Agricultural Change: England and the Continent in the Early Modern Period." In *People, Cities and Wealth*. E. A. Wrigley (ed.). London: Basil Blackwell, 1987, pp. 157–196.

Wulf, Peter, *Wirtschaft und Politik 1918–1924*. Stuttgart: Ernst Klett, 1979.

Wülker, Gerda, *Der Wandel der Aufgaben der Industrie und Handelskammern in der Bundesrepublik*. Hagen: Linnepe Verlagsgesellschaft KG, 1972.

Wünderich, Volker, *Arbeiterbewegung und Selbstverwaltung*. Wuppertal: Peter Hammer, 1980.

Young, Allyn, "Increasing Returns and Economic Progress." *Economic Journal* 38 (December) (1928): 527ff.

Zeitlin, Jonathan, "Flexibility and Mass Production at War: Aircraft Manufacture in Britain, The United States and Germany, 1939–1945." *Technology and Culture* 36, 1 (January) (1995): 46–79.

Ziegler, J. Nicholas, "The State and Technological Advance: Political Efforts for Industrial Change in France and the Federal Republic of Germany, 1972–1986." *Ph.D. Dissertation*, Harvard University, 1989.

Zimmermann, Hary W. (ed.), *Aspekte der Automation*. Basel: Kyklos Verlag, 1960.

Zoll, Rainer, *Partizipation oder Delegation. Gewerkschaftliche Betriebspolitik in Italien und in der Bundesrepublik Deutschland*. Frankfurt: Campus, 1981.

Zukunftskommission 2000, *Aufbruch aus der Krise*. Stuttgart: Staatsministerium Baden Württemberg.

Zunkel, Friedrich, "Die Gewichtung der Interestgruppen bei der Etablierung des Reichsverbandes der deutsche Industrie." In *Industrielles System und politische Entwicklung in der Weimarer Republik*. Hans Mommsen, Dietmar Petzina, and Bernd Weisbrod (eds.). Kronberg/Ts: Athenaeum, 1977, pp. 637–647.

Zysman, John, *Governments, Markets, and Growth*. Ithaca: Cornell University Press, 1983.

Zysman, John, and Laura Tyson, *American Industry in International Competition: Government Policies and Corporate Strategies*. Ithaca: Cornell University Press, 1983.

Interview list

Hans-Joachim Andres. Burkhardt & Weber GmbH & Co. KG, Werkzeugmaschinenfabrik. Oberingenieur, Abteilungsleiter, Technische Normung, Basisentwicklung, Versuch, Patentwesen. January 1986
Rolf Auduoard. VDMA, Ehemalige Hauptgeshäftsführer (1966–1974). September 1985
Michael Auer. Steinbeis Foundation Economic Promotion, Project Manager. June 1994
Werner Babel. Maho Werkzeugmaschinenbau Babel & Co., Owner. September 1985
Dr. Wolfgang Baronius. Chemie AG Bitterfeld-Wolfen, Zentrallbereich, Unternehmensverwaltung, Direktor. August 1991
Anton Bay. BMW AG, Regensburg, Leiter Fertigung, Werk Regensburg. February 1989
Lorenz Becker. Sulzer Morat GmbH, Managing Director. July 1986
Wilheim Becker. BMW AG, Munich, Chief of Purchasing. January 1989
Hans-Jachen Beilke. Trumpf GmbH & Co., Maschinenfabrik, Assistant to the President. January 1986
Helmut Belz. Ingersoll Maschinen und Werkzeuge GmbH, President. September 1985
Dieter W. Bertsch. Daimler-Benz AG, Stuttgart, Abteilungsdirektor, Leiter Materialwessen, Planung und Controlling. January 1989
Dr. Erhard Bieger. Geschäftsführer, Des Verbandes Der Automobilindustrie E.V. January 1989
Rolf Blaettner. MMI (Employers Association Metal Industry Baden-Württemberg), Assessor. June 1994
Herr Manfred Borst. Index-Werke, Hahn & Tessky, Esslingen, Kaufmannische Geschäftsleiter. November 1985
Jürgen Braus. Kolbenschmidt AG, Executive Vice President. June 1994
Friedrich Buehre. E.A.H. Naue GmbH & Co. KG, Sales. February 1989
Hans-Jörg Bullinger. IAT, IAO: Frauenhof Institute, Director of Institute for Industrial Engineering. June 1994

460 Interview List 1985–1994

Wolf Dieter Burkart. ZF Friedrichshafen AG, Central Production Management. June 1994

Jürgen Burmeister. Landes Kreditbank Baden Württemberg, stv. Direktor. July 1986

Dr. Volker Charbonnier. Treuhandanstalt, Direktor. October 1989

Peter Christ, Die Zeit, Wirtschaftsredaktion. Fall 1988

Gerlinde De Backer. Gbr. Scheller GmbH, Marketing & P.R.. July 1986

Jürgen Dechamps. W. Schlafhorst & Co., Legal Assistant to Dr. Klaus V. Der Pahlen. January 1986

Dr. Klaus V. Der Pahlen. W. Schlafhorst & Co., Mitglied Der Geschäftsleitung. January 1986

Walter Deschler. Steiger & Deschler GmbH, Interglas-Textil GmbH, President. November 1986

Prof.Dipl.Ing. Dieter Diemel. Liebherr-Werk Biberach GmbH, Konstruktionsleiter Kranbau, Prokurist. February 1986

Ulrich Diller. ZF Friedrichshafen AG, Director. June 1994

Dr. Jur. Karl Engelhardt. Daimler-Benz AG, Sindelfingen, Abteilungsdirektor, Zentral-Einkauf Produktiv 5. January 1989

Dr. Werner G. Faix. IBM Deutschland GmbH, Leiter Schulung und Personalentwicklung. September 1989

Wilfried Flister. Memminger GmbH, General Sales Manager. July 1986

Dr. Franke, Heinz Friedrich. Magistrat der Stadt Halle, Amtsleiter Wirtschaftsförderung. August 1991

Peter Früauf. Verband, Deutscher Maschinen- und Anlagenbau e.V. (VDMA), Fachgemeinschaft Buro und Informationstechnik. February 1986

Kurt Gabler. Robert Bosch GmbH, Abteilungsleiter, Zentraleinkauf/Einkaufkoordination. January 1989

Dr. Peter Gadow. Rathaus Schöneberg, Mitglied Des Abgeordnetenhauses von Berlin, F.D.P.- Fraktion. October 1991

Prof. Dr. Wolf Gaebe. Universität Stuttgart. June 1994

Richard Gaul. BMW AG, Munich, Leiter, der Presseabteilung. January 1989

Dr. Alexander Gerybadze. Arthur D. Little International, Inc., Associate Director. October 1988

Herman Geywitz. Reinecker Maschinenbau GmbH & Co., Geschäftsführer. January 1986

Ulrich Gölgelein. Hugo Kern und Liebers GmbH &Co., Textilingenieur, Technische Beratung, Qualitätssteuerung und -planung. July 1986

Reinhard Gruber. Müller Weingarten, Abteilungsleiter Gesamtmechanik. June 1994

Bernd Haase. Haase & Kühn Nadelfabrik, Owner. July 1986

Dr. Helmut Habig. Westfalia Separartor AG, Mitglied des Vorstandes. November 1985

Willi Haller. Baden-Württemberg, Family owned cleaning equipment firm. September 1986

Gerd Hammerschmidt. ABB-Asea Brown Boveri AG, Leiter. June 1994

Hubert Handeik. Gildemeister Unternehmensleitung, Leiter Zentrale Absatzförderung, Handlungsbevollmächtiger. February 1986
Thomas Handtmann. Albert Handtmann Mashinenfabrik GmbH & Co., Technische Director, Technische Leiter. February 1986
Uwe Haug. Steinbeis Foundation Economic Promotion, System Marketing Coordinator. June 1994
Wilfried Heger. Landes Kreditbank- Baden Württemberg, Direktor. July 1986
Eberhard Herrmann. Fachhochschule für Druck Stuttgart. February 1986
Herr Hettfleisch. Zinzer Textilmashinenfabrik. July 1986
Christian Heyd. Universität Stuttgart. June 1994
Walter Hiller. Volkswagen AG, Wolfsburg, Gesamtbetriebsrat VW. January 1986
Horst Hinz. Vorstand IG Metal, Abteilung Wirtschaft. November 1985
Peter Hirsch. Stoll, Prokurist Vertriebsleiter. July 1986
Hans-Georg Hoch. Stadt Remscheid Der Obersdirektor, Verkehrsförderung. November 1985
Gisbert Hoffmann. ZF Friedrichshafen AG, Konzernbeauftragter TQM (VVQ). June 1994
Otto Hoffman. Rathaus Schöneberg, Mitglied Des Abgeordnetenhauses Von Berlin, Stellv. Fraktionsvorsitzender F.D.P.-Fraktion. October 1991
Helmut Holtappels. VDMA (German Machinery and Plant Manufacturers Association), Textile Machinary Branch of VDMA. July 1986
Werner Iske. General Electric-Deutschland, Manager, Application Engineer – Operator Interfaces & Training. September 1985
Lothar Janiak. Carl-Zeiss-Jena, Presse und Öffentlichkeitsarbeit. October 1991
Uwe C. Jenssen. Treuhandanstalt, Division 1, Machine Tool Industry. September 1991
Dieter Jungmann. Fried. Krupp GmbH, Hauptabteilungsleiter. January 1986
Peter Kadetschka. AUDI AG, Leiter Personalwesen. June 1994
Dr.-Ing. Hermann Kaiser. IHK, Technologie-Fabrik Karlsruhe, Unternehmens und Technologie Beratung. July 1990
Siegfried Kappel. Volkswagen AG, Wolfsburg, Zentralplanung Produktion, Leiter Technologieplanung Fahrzeuge. January 1989
Gerhard Kaufhold. Staatsministerium Baden-Württemberg, Regierungsdirektor. July 1986
Dr. Bernd Kastler. Degussa AG, Counsel. May 1988
Simon V. Kemper. Traub GmbH Maschinenfabrik, Owner. September 1985
Dr.-Ing. Günter Kessler. Hahn & Kolb, Prokurist, Technische Produkt-Leitung. January 1986
Diether Klingelnberg. Geschäftsführender Gesellschafter, Klingelnberg Söhne, Remschied. November 1985
Dieter Klumpp. Industrie- und Handelskammer (IHK), Geschäftsführer, Leiter der Abteilung, Volkswirtschaft und Statistik. July 1986
Volkhard Köhler. Volkswagen AG, Wolfsburg, Prokurist, Leiter des Bereiches, Planung u. Systemanalyse E & L, u. RGW-Projekte. January 1989

Dieter Kolb. ABB Management Services GmbH, Personalmarketing. June 1994

Hermann Kolb. Werner & Kolb Werkzeugsmachinen GmbH, Owner. September 1985

Herr Koppel. Volkswagen AG, Wolfsburg, Produktionsplanung. January 1989

Herbert Korradi Jr.. Fr. Korradi K.G. Werkzeugmaschinenfabrik, Son of Owner. Kempton, January 1986

Helmut Krcmar. Universität Hohenheim, June 1994

Helmut Kritzler. Albrecht Bäumer KG Spezzialmaschinenfabrik, Prokurist. February 1986

H.-J. Kummert. Volkswagen AG, Einkauf und Logistik Koordination Ausland. January 1989

Prof. Dr.-Ing Walter Kunerth. Siemens AG, Executive Director, Head of the Automative Systems Division. January 1989

Herr Dr. Kurt Lauk. Zinser Textilmaschinenfabrik, Ebersach/Fils. July 1986

Wigbert Graf v. Ledebur. BMW AG, Regensburg, Leiter, Physische Logistik, Werk Regensburg. February 1989

Berthold Leibinger. Trumpf GmbH & Co., Geschäftsführender Gesellschafter. January 1986

Hans Leitner. Former Presse Chef of the VDMA (active in VDMA from 1949 to 1983), Speech Writer. Frankfurt, March 1986

Prof. Dieter Liekweg VDI. Steinbeiss Stiftung: Technischer Beratungsdienst an der Fachhochschule, Sigmaringen, Leiter des Technisches Beratungsdienstes. January 1986

Ulrich Lochmann. State Government of Baden Württemberg, Deputy Director, Press and Government Office. May 1986

Prof. Dr. Johann Löhn. Commissioner for Technology Transfer of the State of Baden-Württemberg, Chairman of the Executive Board Steinbeis Foundation for Economic Promotion. July 1986

Herr Lucy. Daimler-Benz, Representative of the Gesamtbetriebsratsvorsitzender. January 1989

Ulrich Mack. Staatsministerium Baden-Württemberg. July 1990

Dr. Johannes Marcy. Chemie AG Bitterfeld-Wolfen, Leiter des Vorstandsbüros. September 1991

Dr. Detlef Marquardt. Norddeutsche Landesbank Girozentrale, Bankdirector, Leiter des Bereiches Kommunikation und Marketing, Pressersprecher. May 1986

Helmut Maschke. Scharmann GmbH & Co., Sales Director. September 1985

Herbert Masing. ESAB-Masing GmbH, Gesch-Führender Gesellschafter. September 1985

Eberhard Maurer. Landeshauptsadt Stuttgart Bürgermeisteramt, Wirtschaftreferant. July 1986

Anton May. Self-employed, Makes large sun umbrellas for Outdoor Cafes. February 1986

Gerhard Meier-Röhn. Süddeutscher Rundfunk-Fernsehen, Landespolitik, "Bericht aus Stuttgart." May 1986
Horst Menzel. Zahnradwerk Neunstein Gmbh & Co., Bereichsleiter Produktion. June 1994
Franz-Josef Meuer. Krupp Kautex Maschinenbau GmbH, Einkauf. February 1986.
Arno Mock. A. Friedr. Flender GmbH & Co. K.G., Managing Director and German Machinery and Plant Manufacturers Association (VDMA), Chairman of Foreign Trade Committee. November 1985
Wolfgang Möller. Stihl, Abteilungsreferent Arbeitsplanung. June 1994
Bruno Neubig. Werner und Kolb Werkzeugmaschinen GmbH, Vetriebsleiter, Prokurist. February 1986
Ernst Neuffer. Industrie- und Handelskammer Grossraum Neckar, Geschäftsführer, Leiter der Abteilung Industrie. July 1986
Evelyn Neusius. Staatsministerium Baden-Württemberg. July 1986
Martin Oelgemöller. Keiper Recaro GmbH & Co., Leiter Fertigungsplanung. February 1989
Karin Benz Overhange. I.G. Metall, Automation Specialist. January 1986
Dr.rer.pol. Detlef Perner. Wirtschafts- Und Sozialwissenschaftliches Institut Des Deutschen, Gewerkschaftsbundes (WSI). May 1986
Josef Pfeffer. Rafi, Geschäftsführer, Entwicklung, Marketing, Vertrieb. February 1986
Dipl.-Ing. Hermann Pfiz. EX-CELL-O GmbH, Assistant General Manager. January 1986
Bernd Pischetsrieder. BMW AG, Leiter Technische, Zentralplanung. February 1989
Peter Popp. Jena Glaswerk GmbH, Geschäftsführer. October 1991
Heinz J. Preissler. BMW AG, Munich, München, General Manager, International Purchases. January 1989
Ulrich Rackwitz. E.A.H. Naue GmbH & Co. KG, Director For Law, Finance and Personell. February 1989
Dr. Karl Reuss. Agency for the Promotion of Trade and Industry, State of Baden-Wuerttemberg, President. July 1986
Eberhard Romberg. Robert Bosch GmbH, Zentraleinkauf, Investitionsgüter und Betriebsmittel. January 1989
Rolf W. Rütten. KLOPP Werkzeugmaschinefabrik GmbH, Geschäftsführer, Solingen, January 1986.
Dr. Georg Sandberger. Eberhard-Karls-Universität Tübingen, Kanzler. October 1986
Horst Sandvoss. Robert Bosch GmbH, Purchasing Director. July 1986/January 1989
Heinz Schaab. Alfred Teves GmbH, Geschäftsführer Vetrieb/ Marketing. February 1989
Prof. Wolfgang Schaech. Textiltechnikabteilung, FH Reutlingen. January 1986

Wolfgang Schaefer. SPD (Fraktion im Landtag von Sachsen-Anhalt), Ausschussvorsitzender Finanzen. September 1991

Bernhard Schanze. Landratsamt Rudolstadt, Thuringen, Amtsleiter für Wirtschaftsörderung. October 1991

Dr. Ingeborg Scharf. UGZ (Unternehmensservice-Zentrum GmbH Jena-Linz). Jena, Thuringen, September 1991

Herward Scharnberg. A. Friedr. Flender GmbH & Co. K.G., Vertrieb Europa. November 1985

Dipl. -Ing Schieber. Universal Maschinenfabrik, Manufacturer of Flachstrickmaschinen. Westhausen, February 1986

Theo Schirmer, AUDI AG, Vorsitzender Des Betriebsrats, Werk Neckars Ulm. June 1994

Dieter Schlenkermann. GETRAG, Geschäftsführer. June 1994

Ludwig E. Schmieden. Burkhardt + Weber GmbH & Co. KG, Werkzeugmaschinenfabrik, Prokurist Kaufm. Verkauf. January 1986

Gunther Schmigalle. Deutsche Bank AG, London Branch, Corporate Finance. May 1986.

Adolf Schmitt. ABB - Asea Brown Boveri, Stellv. Konzernbetriebsrat, Mannheim. June 1994

Jürgen Schmitz. Ingersoll, Vice President, Marketing. September 1985

Alfred Schneider. LIBA, Area-Manager. July 1986

Manfred G. Schneider-Rothaar. Deutsche Länderbank, Frankfurt, Managing Director. July 1985

Manfred Schoch. BMW AG, München, Vorsitzender des Gesamtbetriebsrates. January 1989

Dr. Wolfgang Schreck. Daimler-Benz, Bremen, Direktor. February 1989

Dr. Christian Schulz. ABB-Asea Brown Boveri AG, Assistent Des Direktors. June 1994

Hans Gunther Schuster-Bäumer. Bäumer Maschinenfabrik, Prokurist. February 1986

Dr.-Ing. Karl-Eugen Schwartz. Alfred Schütte Vertriebs-Gesselschaft GmbH, Cologne, February 1986

Peter Seitz. Index-Werke KG Hahn & Tessky, Handlungsbevollmächtigter und Abteilungsleiter. January 1986

Alfred Siegel. Alber & Bitzer KG, ALBI-Maschinenfabrik, Albstadt, July 1986

Gert Silbermann. Daimler-Benz AG, Bremen, Leiter der Hauptabteilung Materialwirtschaft. February 1989

David H. R. Smith. Traub Machine Tools Limited, Managing Director. September 1985

Dr. Marlies Stadelmeier. Steinbeis Foundation For Economic Promotion, Division Manager International Technology Transfer. November 1993

Volker Steinwascher. Volkswagen AG, Wolfsburg, Einkauf u. Logistik, Leiter RGW-Projekte. January 1989

Heinz-Peter Stoll. Stoll Textilmaschinenfabrik GmbH, Diplomkaufmann. Reutlingen, July 1986

Frank Stroh. Bevollmächtigter, Industriegewerkschaft Metall Verwaltungsstelle. Heilbronn/Neckarsulum, November 1993/June 1994

Heinz H. Struebel. Traub Machine Tools Limited, Technical Director. September 1985

Rolf Tappe . Volkswagen AG, Emden, Leitung Allgemeine Planung. January 1989.

Herbert Thoma. Bullmerwek G.O. Stumpf GmbH, Leiter der Entwicklung und Konstruktion. February 1986

Herr Uwe Thomas. Bundesministerium für Forschung und Technologie, Bonn, Head of the microelectronics section of BMFT. October 1985

Prof. Dr.-Ing. Hans Tränkle. FH Reutlingen, Maschinenbauingenieur. February 1986

Dr. Armin Tshermak von Seysenegg. Ministerium Für Wirtschaft, Mittelstand und Technologie Baden-Württemberg, Regierungsdirektor, Leiter des Referats Grundsatzfragen der Technologiepolitik. October 1988

Herr Ulrich. Volkswagen AG, Wolfsburg, Abteilungsleiter Produktionsplanung. January 1989

Norbert Umlauf. Westfalia Separator AG, Sales Department. November 1985

Günther Vetterman. VDMA, Geschäftführer, Forschungskuratorium Maschinenbau in the VDMA, Head of the Fachgemeinschaft Kraftmaschinen, Member of the General Management of the VDMA. February 1986

Norbert Vogel. Mannesmann Demag, Duisburg, Prokurist, Hüttentechnik. January 1986

Peter Wagener. Stihl, Andreas Stihl, Exec. Vice-Pres. Hum. Resources. June 1994

Hans-Georg Weber. Homag (Hornberger Maschinenbaugesellschaft mbH+Co.KG), Prokurist, Leiter Marketing und Vertrieb. February 1986

Dr. Jürgen Weiskman. Tridelta AG, Vorstand, Finanzen/Controlling

Frau Welcker. Alfred Schütte Vertriebs-Gesellschaft GmbH, Assistant to Dr. Ing. Schwartz. February 1986

Dr. Peter Wilfert. MMI (Employers Association Metal Industry Baden-Württemberg), Director. June 1994.

Dr.-Ing. Hans-Henning Winkler. Chiron-Werke GmbH, Geschäftführer. January 1986

F. Stefan Winter. BDI (Federation of German Industries Bundesverband der Deutschen Industrie, e.V), Head of Department, Trade Promotion and International Market Policy. May 1986

Hans Wolters. Daimler-Benz AG, Stuttgart, Direktor. January 1989

Prof. Frank F. Wurm. STW (Steinbeis-Stiftung Für Wirtschaftsförderung). Biberach, February 1986

Peter Zeilinger. BMW AG, Leiter Materialbedarfssplanung und Versorgungssteuerung. January 1989

Gerhard Zimmermann. Steinbeis-Stiftung Für Wirtschaftsförderung, Regieeerungsbeauftragter Für Technologietransfer Baden-Württemberg. January 1986

Appendix: Maps

Map 1. Economic regions in the German Imperial Reich.

Map 2. Selected geographical regions of the German Imperial Reich.

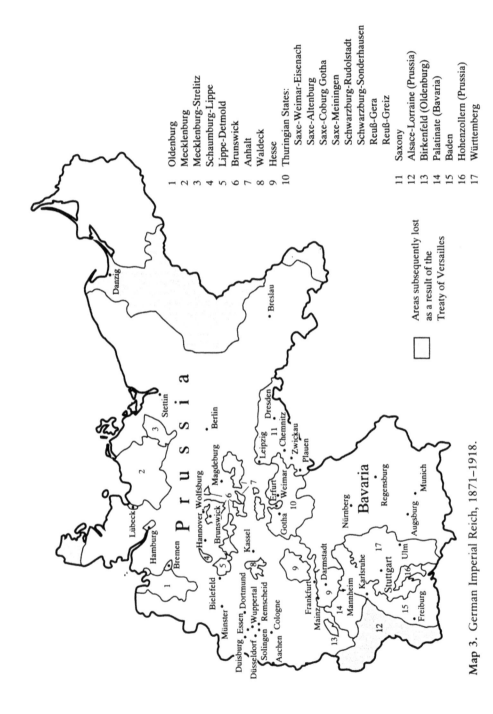

Map 3. German Imperial Reich, 1871–1918.

Map 4. Allied Zones of Occupation in Germany, 1945.

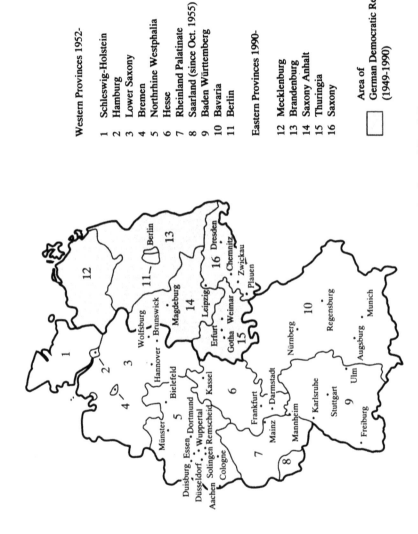

Map 5. Political boundaries in the Federal Republic of Germany.

Index

accommodation of industrial orders at national level: defined, 112f, 255
Adenauer, Konrad, 259, 260, 263
Agfa, 65
aircraft industry, 241, 244
Allgemeine Elektrizitätsgesellschaft (AEG), 21, 172, 224, 225, 229
Arbeitsgemeinschaft Selbständiger Unternehmern (ASU), 155–156
Arbeitsgemeinschaft Verarbeitende Industrie (AVI) (Working Group of Finishing Industries): agreement, 134
ASEA-Brown-Boveri (ABB), 201
Association of Railway Administrations, 117f
Association of Saxon Industrialists (Verein Sachsiche Industriellen), 122
Association of Württemberg Industrialists (Verein Württembergische Industiellen), 122
Attlee, Clement, 211
Audi AG, 229
August Thyssen-Hütte AG, 21, 78–79, 81, 92, 95, 96, 217, 218, 219, 220, 221, 222, 248, 249, 250
autarkic enterprises: and universal credit banks, 83–84, 207; logic of internal reform and decentralization after 1970s within, 237, 238–239, 244–253; ambivalent relationship to state, 84–86, 207; attempt by Nixdorf to create an industrial district, 251–253
autarkic industrial order: defined, 20, 72, 206; regional preconditions for, 73–75; production in (see Ruhr steel industry, machinery industry, automobiles, light manufacturing, *Gewerbelandschaften*), governance in (see Ruhr steel industry, machinery industry, automobiles, light manufacturing, *Gewerbelandschaften*), national level governance of, 115–121, 131–136, 257–286; crisis and transformation since 1970, 235–253; absolute decline since 1970s, 236; halting adjustment plagued by self-blockage since the 1970s, 236–253
automobile industry, 99, 149–163, 176, 185, 194ff, 223ff, 231, 235, 238–239, 240–247, 264, 285; concentration within, 231
automobile parts supply industry, 153–156, 172, 176, 180, 182, 185, 190f, 240–247, 249

Bade, Franz-Josef, 188
banking, 292n, 311n; composite architecture of national system, 118–119, 123
BASF (Badische Analin und Sodafabrik AG), 65, 67
Bauknecht GmbH, 232
Baumann, Hans, 233
Bayer AG, 65
Beckerath, Herbert, 313n–314n
Benndorf, Erich, 46, 47
Benz, Arthur, 279
Berg, Fritz, 172–173, 176
Berge, Ernst, 149, 353n
Berghahn, Volker, 399n
Berliner Maschinenbau AG vormals L Schwartzkopff, 101
Besson, Waldemar, 130, 138
Betriebsvervassungsgesetz (Works Constitution Act), 132, 208–209
biotechnology, 188
Bismarck, Otto, 263
Blackbourn, David, 308n–309n, 311n–312n
Blankenburg, Wilhelm, 323n
BMW AG (Bayerische Motoren Werke), 231, 232, 240–244, 251; BMW aircraft engine production, 241; ZS Motorsport GmbH,

473

474 Index

BMW AG (cont.) 242; ZT Technik GmbH, 242, 243; ZX Motorfahräder GmbH, 242, 243; Bezugsartenkreis, 242; and Nazis, 241; as systems integrator, 241ff
Boch, Rudolf, 324n
Bochumer Verein für Bergbau u. Gustahlfabrikation, 78, 85; Gußtahlwerk Bochumer Verein AG, (post Vestag), 213
Borsig Machinery, 101
Borsig, Ernst von, 345n
Bosch, Dr. Carl, 67, 315n–316n
Bosch, Robert, 46
Brandt, Willy, 273
Bruening, Heinrich, 139
Bund der deutsche Industrie (Federation of German Industry) (BDI—post-1945), 172f, 176
Bund der Industriellen (Federation of German industrialists) (BDI—pre-1914), 122ff, 129
Bund zur Erneuerung des Reiches (League for Renewal of the Reich), 136–139, 346n
Bund-Länder Kommission für Bildungsplanung (Joint Commission for Educational Planning), 273
Bundesbank (Central Bank), 269, 270

cardboard industry, 229
cartels: price fixing, 61–62; term fixing, 62–63; specialization cartels/finishing associations, 63–65, 167–168, 263; legislation within Nazi regime, 140; in steel industry, 87–89, 98; Stahlschienengemeinschaft (Rail Cartel), 87; Stahlwerkbund (Steel Works Asociation), 89; cartel-law conflict in 1950s, 170–174; Fritz Berg on cartels and small firms, 172–173
Casella, 65
Cecigram, 243
CentralVerband für deutsche Industrie (CVDI)—(Central Association of German Industry), 121ff, 129
Centralstelle für Gewerbe und Industrie, 57
ceramics industry, 241
Chandler, Alfred, 5, 12, 13, 27, 82, 97, 222, 318n, 321n, 323n, 327n, 329n
Charlottenhütte AG, 95
chemical industry, 42, 58, 65f, 164, 229, 235
clock and watch making industry, 36, 52
clothing and apparel industry, 180, 182
CNC machine tools, 181, 198, 252
coal mining, 122, 236; 1920 coal crisis, 134
Codetermination, 208–209; limits of after initial postwar laws, 377n

coexistence of industrial orders at national level: defined, 112, 255
collaborative manufacturing, 182–193, 239, 240–244
Communities of Interest (Interessengemeinschaften—IG's), 65ff
constructivist political economy, 22ff
Continental-Gummi AG, 156
coordinated specialization, 63–65, 161, 166–168, 175–176, 183; encourages creation of specialized jurisdiction and internal value creation, 183, 199f
corporatism: labor-capital corporatism, 133–134, 262, 264–268; inter-industry coporatism, 134; Konzertierte Aktion, 266; corporatist Gemeinwirtschaft, 134
cottar class: in Saxony, 35–36, 301n–302n, 303n; in Westphalia, 74–75, 302n
Cramer Klett Co., 103
Cromme, Gerhard, 250
cutlery industry, 15, 18, 42, 45, 62, 114

Daimler-Benz AG, 142, 149–163, 172, 190, 192, 194, 196, 210, 223, 231, 241, 261; production at, 149–156, 353n, 354n; group production (Gruppenfertigung) at, 150–151, 355n; dualist subcontracting by, 153–156; governance at, 156–162; ownership structure of, 159; research and development at, 159–160; vocational training at, 159–160; and Nazi regime, 161
Daimler, Gottlieb, 46
Dawes Plan, 135, 346n
decentralized industrial order: defined, 20; origins, 34–41, 300n–301n; initial industrialization within, 41–58; periods of recomposition, 58–71, 166–174, 177–193; crisis in, 193–204; market context for, 41–43, 58, 59–60, 163–166, 178–181; production in, 37–40, 43–49, 58–60, 166–168, 182–186; governance of, 37–40, 49–58, 60–71, 168–174, 186–189; role of regional governments within, 53–58, 68–71, 166–168, 169, 173, 188, 192–193; national level governance of, 115–123, 136–139, 257–286; large firms in, 149–163, 189–192, 261; post-World War II survival of capital goods producers within, 163–193, 262
Deckel AG, 244
Deeg, Richard, 311n
Deutsch-Lux (Deutsch-Luxemburgische Bergwerks-Hütten AG), 92, 96, 323n
Deutsche Bank, 156, 157–159, 357n

Deutsche Gewerkschaftsbund (DGB), 208–209, 267; Ortskartelle, 267
Dortmund-Hörde Hüttenunion (DHHU) (post-1945), 213, 218, 219
Deutsche Maschinenfabrik AG (Demag) (see also Mannesmann-Demag), 21, 101, 105, 221, 234–235
Deutsche Städtetag (German Diet of Cities), 137, 271
dezentralisierte Manufaktur (decentralized manufactory), 39
differenzierte Gesamtlosung (Weimar Republic reform proposal), 137
Digital Electronics Corp., 249
diversified quality production, 244–247
Domar's Law, 275, 401n
Dortmunder Union, 78
Dürrkoppwerke AG, 99

Ebert, Friedrich, 125
Eisenwerk-Gesellschaft Maximilianshütte AG, 213
electrical engineering/electro-mechanical industry, 58, 163–166, 201–202, 235, 318n; consumer electronics, 162, 176, 180, 223ff, 231, 249, 264; toasters, 232; microelectronics, 180, 182, 185, 201, 241, 249; computers, 249, 251–253
environmental technology, 188
Erhard, Ludwig, 172, 173, 261, 270
Erzberger, Matthias, 132, 342n
Eulner, Johann David, 303n
European Coal and Steel Community (ECSC), 146, 214, 215; decartelization and, 214
European Economic Community (EEC)/Common Market, 146, 148, 261
European Free Trade Area (EFTA), 146

F.A.J. Egells Machinery, 100, 101, 332n
Fachhochschulen (Community Colleges), 51, 188, 191, 273, 284
Fachschule für Kleineisenindustrie, 51
Federal Ministry for Research and Technology (BMFT), 187
Federal Republic of Germany: constitution of, 255, 259, 260, 271; federalism in, 255, 256, 258–262, 268–273, 275–281, 394n; Bundesrat, 173, 174, 257, 260–262, 273; Bundestag, 174, 260; composite national architecture of industrial governance mechanisms during 1950s within, 257–262; convergence of national industrial governance mechanisms during 1960s and 1970s, 262–275; decentralization in national industrial governance in 1980s–1990s, 275–286; collective bargaining within, 266–268, 281–286; transformation of regional interests in 1960s within, 272–273
Feldenkirchen, Wilfried, 81, 326n, 327n
Feldman, Gerald, 88, 95, 274, 326n, 327n, 329n, 345n
Finanzplanungsrat (Finance Planning Council), 271
fine mechanical and optical industry, 58, 163–166, 182, 185
Flick, Friedrich, 159
Ford Motor Co., 151, 231, 241
Formierte Gesellschaft (Formed Society), 270
Franz Dinnendahl and Co., 332n
Freiburg (Ordo-Liberal) School, 171, 172, 211, 379n
Fremdling, Rainer, 6
Friedrich Flender GmbH & Co. KG, 233
Friedrich Krupp AG, 21, 78, 81, 85–86, 92–93, 212, 219, 234, 236, 248, 249, 319n, 323n, 382n, 384n; and Wilhelmine navy buildup, 85–86; Hüttenwerk Rheinhausen AG, (Krupp), 213, 236; Westfälische Drahtindustrie, 93; Germania Shipyards, 93; Grusenwerk Magdeburg-Buckau, 93; Blechwalzwerk Capito und Klein, 93; intra-*Konzern* subcontracting within, 250
Funke, Carl, 84
furniture industry, 182

Gebauer, Heinrich, 46
Gebrüder Stoll Strickmaschinenfabrik, 182
Gelsenkirchener Bergwerksgesellschaft, 92, 323n
General Motors—Opel AG, 231, 241
Genossenschaftsbanken (Cooperative Banks), 52–53, 187
German Democratic Republic, 257, 393n
Gerschenkron, Alexander, 3ff, 27f, 121, 256, 289n–290n
Gesamthochschulen, 273
Gesamtmetall (Metal Industry Employers Association), 264
geteilte Betriebe, 44, 45
Gewerbelandschaften: impartible-inheritance-based, 73–75, 98–100, 107, 228, 229, 302n, 306n; impartible-inheritance-based distinguished from basic features of decentralized industrial order, 331n; partible-inheritance-based, 34–36
Geyer, Michael, 140
Gierke, Otto, 338n
Gilbert, Parker, 135

Gildemeister AG, 99
glass industry, 229
Grundgesetz (Basic Law), 259, 260, 271
Grundherrschaft: defined, 300n
Grundig AG, 224, 229, 232
Gutehoffnungshütte (GHH), 21, 75–77, 78, 85, 92–93, 94, 95, 101, 212, 214, 222, 320n; J. Tafel Eisenwerk, 92; Maschinenfabrik Esslingen, 92; Maschinenfabrik Fritz Neuemeyer AG, 92; Zahnradfabrik Renk AG, 92; Hapag, 93; Deutsche Werft, 93, 96; Hüttenwerk Oberhausen AG, (HOAG) (until 1947 GHH), 213, 214, 219
Gutsherrschaft: defined, 300n

Handwerk (artisans): relative underpopulation of in autarkic industrial order, 80
Handwerkerbildungszentrum, Paderborn, 252
Haniel, Franz, 77, 81, 319n, 320n, 323n
Hanoversiche Maschinenbau AG (Hanomag), 101
Hansemann, David, 83, 324n
Harkort and Kamp, 101
Harkort, Friedrich, 77, 319n–320n
hatmaking industry, 15, 42
Heinrich, Otto, 345n
Henschel & Söhne AG, 21, 101, 234
Herman Kolb Werkzeugmaschinen, 185
Hilpert, Josef, 251, 252, 253
Hitler, Adolf, 223, 348n
Hoechst AG (Farbwerk Hoechst AG), 65, 67
Hoerder Verein, 77, 78, 85, 96
Hoesch Werke AG (Eisen-und Stahlwerk "Hoesch" AG), 78–79, 92, 94, 95, 212, 214, 219, 222, 232, 248, 381n
Hoffmann, Paul, 364n
Hugo Boss, 182
Hüttenwerke Phönix AG, 213

IBM, 190
IG Chemie (Chemical Workers Union), 285
IG Farben (IG Farbenindustrie AG), 67, 68, 142
IG Metall (Metalworkers Union), 194, 202, 245, 264–268, 281–286, 403n
IG Textil- und Bekleidung (textile and apparell workers), 285
Ilseder Hütte AG, 213
immigrant workers, 152, 230, 387n
Imperial Reich, 115–123; constitution of, 116, 117, 128; Bundesrat (Federal Council), 117, 260; legal position of cities within, 119–120; composite national architechture of industrial governance within, 115–121; industrial politics within, 121–123; collective bargaining in, 265f
IMU Institute, 194
Index-Werke AG, 181, 186, 197
industrial concentration, 234; in investment goods after World War II, 165; barriers to in pre-World War I steel industry, 87–91; high levels in mass production branches, 174–177, 230–231; growth of in post-World War II steel industry, 220f, 360n
industrial relations system, 8, 262, 264–268, 281–286
Industrie und Handelskammer (IHK) (Chambers of Commerce), 57–58, 166–168, 169–170, 187, 193, 363n–364n; and Nazis, 363n
industrielle Mittelstand, 20, 53, 80, 114, 122f, 187, 261
information technology, 188
International Motor Vehicle Project (MIT) (x, 196
iron and steel industry, 164, 165, 210–222, 229, 236, 248; Ruhr Iron and Steel Industry, 75–98, 210–222, 236, 263, 317n–318n; emergence of Ruhr industry, 75–78; production in Ruhr, 78–81, 216–217; governance in Ruhr, 81–86, 217–222; deconcentration and decartelization, 211–216; adjustment periods in, 86–98, 210–222; problems of order in individual product markets, 86–87; problems of order in the industry as a whole, 87–91, 217–221; oligopoly-creating strategy in, 214f; *Konzern*-creating strategy in, 214f; mergers in post-World War II industry, 220; internal structure of steel enterprises during post-World War II economic miracle, 221–222; in decentralized industrial order, 42, 58, 305n, 308n

Jacquard loom, 26, 44
James, Harold, 140, 316n, 346n, 397n
Jastrow, Heinrich, 326n, 329n
Jil Sander, 182
Jochimson, Reimut, 373n

Kalle, 65
Kapital- und Unternehmungsbeteiligungsgesellschaften (KBG), 187
Katzenstein, Peter, 13, 274
Keiper Recaro GmbH & Co., 246
Kern-Liebers GmbH & Co., 185, 186

Index

Keynesian demand management policies, 146, 268–272; crisis in, 275f, 282
Kiesewetter, Hubert, 6, 16, 47
Kirdorf, Emil, 84, 323n
Klöckner Werke AG, 92, 94, 212, 214, 219, 248, 323n; Nordwestdeutscher Hütten- und Bergwerksverien, (Klöckner-post Vestag), 213
Klöckner-Humboldt-Deutz AG, 149, 162
Knott, Jack, 271
Kocka, Jürgen, 5, 12, 13,27, 81, 83, 100, 274, 308n–309n, 321n, 322n–323n, 324n–325n
Köllmann, Wolfgang, 230
Konjunkturrat (business-cycle council), 270
Kontoren (steel product sales offices), 220f
Konzerne: formation of in steel industry, 92–95, 327n; *Technologie-Konzerne*, 249; post-World War II breakup of, 211ff; Konzerne creating strategy in steel industry, 214ff; return to *Konzerne* structures during 1980s, 248–251
Köttgen, Arnold, 129
Krauss-Maffei AG, 244; Maffei Machinery Company, 101
Krupp, Friedrich, 84
Krupp, Alfred, 82
Kugler, Anita, 155, 353n
Kunzmann, Klaus, 188

Länderkonferenz, 130, 131, 136ff
Landes, David, 5, 13, 41, 79, 80, 321n
lasers industry, 180
Leibinger, Berthold, 194
Liebherr Holding GmbH, 149, 162
Liegen, Carl, 133
Liefmann, Robert, 330n
light manufacturing (automobiles, consumer electronics, etc.), 223–232; organization of mass production in, 225–230; relatively high number of skilled workers within, 227; diffusion of dualism within, 227–230; governance in, 230–232
List, Friedrich, 57
Loewe Opta, 243
Ludwig Loewe AG, 101
Luitpoldhütte AG, 213

machinery industry, 58, 63–65, 100–109, 113, 163–166, 185, 231, 232–235, 248–251, 265; agricultural equipment and tractors, 162, 225, 233; armatures, 225, 233; ball bearings, 180; bicycles, 172; boilers, 101, 104; bridges, 101; central heating systems, 101; construction machinery, 101, 162, 225, 233; diesel engines, 162, 233; gear units and power drives, 104, 233; locomotives, 100–101, 232; machine tools, 48–49, 63–65, 99, 185, 194ff, 201, 202–203, 228; motors/engines, 101, 104; office machinery, 185, 225, 228; printing machinery, 101, 104, 233; pumps, 101, 225; sewing machines, 99, 225, 228; shipbuilding, 236, 265; steam engines, 100, 104; steel making equipment, 101, 104; textile machinery, 49, 65, 101, 166–168; valves, 101, 180, 233
Maddison, Angus, 350n–351n
Maffei, Josef Anton von, 101
Magirus, 229
Maier, Charles, 274
MAN (Maschinenfabrik-Augsburg-Nuremberg AG), 21, 101, 104, 105, 107, 141, 229, 233, 234, 332n–333n
Mannesmann AG, 92, 172, 212, 214, 219, 221, 222, 248–249; Hartmut and Braun AG, 249; Kienzle, 249; ANT Nachrichtentechnik GmbH, 249; PCS Peripherie Computer Systeme GmbH, 249; Alfa Systeme Partner GmbH, 249; Fichtel and Sachs AG, 249; VDO Adolph Schindling, 249; Hansche Werke AG, (Mannesmanröhren-Werke—post-Vestag decomposition), 213
Mannesmann-Demag AG, 221, 235, 249
Mannesmann-Rexroth AG, 249
Marshall Plan, 146
Marshall, Alfred, 42–43, 48, 322n
Marx, Karl, 11, 13, 295n
Maschinenbau Buckau R. Wolf AG, 101
Maschinenfabrik Fahr, 93
mass production: creation of political economic preconditions for at mid-century in Europe, 146–149; adoption at Daimler-Benz, 149–163, 355n–356n; diffusion of within autarkic industrial order after World War II, 209–232; diffusion defined, 210, 350n; principle of dedication, 226f; principle of automation, 226f; connection to democracy in world view of American Occupying Powers, 171–174; assembly lines, 149–156; mechanical automation, 152–153, 225ff; produces integration between autarkic and decentralized industrial orders, 149–166, 261–262, 266, 269; and macroeconomic governance, 262–264; and control over the evolution of technology, 365n
Medalen, Charles, 339n
Megerle, Klaus, 6, 16, 17, 47
mergers, 109, 161–162, 220, 234
Messerschmidt Bolkow Blohm (MBB), 244

Index

metalwares industry, 15, 26, 42, 45, 51, 114, 229
Mevissen, Gustav, 83, 324n
Meyer-Haitz, Doris, 361n
Miele, 232
Mietfabriken (rented factories), 44
Milward, Alan, 350n
Modell Deutschland, 274
Moellendorf, Wickert, 125, 134
Mohl, Moritz, 57
Mommsen, Wolfgang, 398n
Montanmitbestimmungsgesetz (Codetermination Law in the coal and steel industry), 208
Morganthau Plan, 376n
Müller Weingarten (Maschinenfabrik Müller-Weingarten AG, 201
Muelert, Oskar, 347n
musical instruments industry, 36; violins, 36

National Diet of Chambers of Commerce (DIHT), 172f, 347n
Newcomber, Mabel, 341n
Nissan Motors, 195–196
Nixdorf Computer, 251–253
Nixdorf, Heinz, 253

Offe, Claus, 274
Orenstein and Koppel AG, 101, 233
organized capitalism, 1–3, 5ff, 256, 257, 274–275, 289n, 290n, 393n–394n
Osram, 232
Overy, Richard, 140, 141

Phoenix AG für Bergbau u. Hüttenbetrieb, 77, 85, 95, 96, 323n
Phoenix-Rheinrohr AG, 218–219
photo-voltaics industry, 180
Piepenstock, Hermann, 77, 81, 320n
plastics/injection molding industry, 180, 186, 229, 241
PM-Putzmeister Werke, 182
Politikverflechtung, 274
Pollard, Sidney, 6
Popitz, Johannes, 138
Porsche, 244
Porsche, Ferdinand, 223
Pounds, Norman J. G., 307n, 320n, 381n
Preuss, Hugo, 125, 129, 338n–339n, 341n, 347n
printing industry: collective bargaining in, 265

Quandt, Harald, 159

Quandt, Herbert, 159

Rafi, 185
railroads, 77
Rathenau, Walter, 125, 134, 345n
rationalization: in the machinery industry, 108f; multiple meanings of, 335n
Redlich, Fritz, 101, 332n
Reichsverband Deutscher Industrie (RDI) (National Association of German Industry), 129, 135, 136
Reichswerke Herman Goering, 141
Rhein-Elbe Union, 92f, 95
Rheinische Creditbank, 158
Rheinische Stahlwerke AG (Rheinstahl), 78–79, 95, 96, 214, 217, 218, 219, 222; Gussstahlwerk Witten (steel works of), 217; Hanomag-Henschel (heavy truck subsidiary of), 161; purchased by August Thyssen Hütte, 221
Rheinwestfälische Hüttenschule, 85
Rieppel, Anton von, 345n
Robert, Rüdiger, 366n
Robert Bosch GmbH, 142, 149, 154, 155, 162, 190f, 192, 201), development of collaborative subcontracting at, 190; reform of internal hiearchies within, 190–191; joint venture with Siemens in consumer electrical goods, 224
Rombacher Hüttenwerke, 95
Rostow, Walt Whitman, 10

Sabel, Charles, 11, 24, 25, 26, 298n, 299n
Sachverständigenrat (Council of Economic Experts), 269–270
Sass, Jürgen, 227
Schaffhausen'scher Bankverein, 83
Scharpf, Fritz, 401n
Scherer, Frederic, 367n–368n
Schmidt, Gerd, 227
Schmitt, Carl, 344n
Schmoller, Gustav, 45
Schonfield, Andrew, 13, 256, 274, 294n–295n
Schulz, Gerhard, 136
Schulze-Delitzsche, Hermann, 53
Schumpeter, Joseph, 10, 12–13, 27f, 367n
Selbstverwaltung (self-government), 173–174, 258–262, 280, 338n; in cities in Rhineland, 120, 339n; Muelert proposal during Reich reform debate, 347
Semlinger, Klaus, 191
Siegrist, Hannes, 322n, 323n
Siemens AG, 21, 172, 224, 225, 227, 229, 232, 244, 251–253, 323n; Siemens Rhein

Index

Elbe Schuckert Union (SRSU), 92f, 326n; joint venture with Robert Bosch in consumer electrical goods, 224; Siemens-Nixdorf Information Systems, 251, 253
Silverberg, Paul, 135
Smith, Adam, 11, 13
Solow, Robert, 10
Sparkassen (savings banks), 55, 69–70, 168, 187; Girozentrale, 168
Sperling, Hans Joachim, 251, 252, 253
Stability and Growth Act, 270
Stahl- und Walzwerke Rasselstein/Andernach AG, 213
Stahlschienengemeinschaft, 87
Stahltreuhändervereinigung (Deconcentration Authority for the Steel Industry), 212
Stahlwerkbund, 89
Stahlwerke Bochum, AG, 213
Stalin, Josef, 211
Standard Elektrik Lorenz (SEL), 149, 162, 190
steel making technology: charcoal based versus coke based, 76, 77; puddling, 75, 76, 77, 79; Siemens-Martin "open hearth," 78, 79, 83, 217; Bessemer, 78, 79, 83; Basic Oxygen Furnace, 217; Thomas Converter, 78, 79, 83, 217; Rolling Mills, 101, 103, 211–213, 216, 217, 221; Blast Furnaces, 101, 103, 211–213, 216, 217, 221; steel mills, 211–213, 216, 217, 221
Stein, Freiherr von, 100, 332n
Steinbeis Foundation, 31, 188, 278, 281
Steinbeis, Ferdinand, 57
Stinnes, Hugo, 84, 93–94, 323n, 345n
Streeck, Wolfgang, 8, 13, 244–247, 274, 294n, 378n
Stumm Konzern, 92, 95, 323n
Stuttgarter Programm, 126
surgical instruments industry, 18

Technische Hochschule Berlin-Charlottenburg, 85
telecommunications industry, 249
textile industry, 15, 18, 36, 41, 42, 43, 44, 45, 49, 51, 58, 61–62, 114, 167, 180, 182; lace, 15, 36, 41, 44, 114; woolen, 36, 41, 43; linen, 36, 41; silk, 18, 36, 43, 45–46, 51; cotton, 36, 41, 43, 45, 49
Thanheiser, Heinz, 222, 225, 232
Thelen, Kathleen, 283, 397n
Third Reich, 70–71, 139–142, 161, 166, 207, 208–209, 258, 260, 261, 348n; composite national architechture of industrial governance within, 139–142; abolition of regional parliaments within, 140; restrictions on spending by regional and city governments within, 140, 141; American post–World War II conceptions of, 170, 171, 211; Nazi efforts to encourage mass production in automobiles and consumer electronics, 223, 231; Nazis and cartels, 349n
Thyssen, August, 81
Tilly, Richard, 6, 13, 291n–292n
Tipton, Frank, 309n
toy-making industry, 15, 18, 58
Toyota Motor Company, 195–196
TPZ, 188
transfer lines, 225, 226; diffusion within Daimler-Benz, 152–153
Traub Maschinenfabrik, 181, 197
Treaty of Versailles, 92
Truman, Harry S., 211
Turner, Henry Ashby, 133, 340n
typification, 108f, 150, 153–154

Ullmann, Peter, 266
Uniform Civil Code, 117f, 123
Universal Maschinenfabrik (Westhausen) GmbH & Co. KG, 182

Verband der Mitteldeutschen Industrie (Association of Central German Industry), 129, 343n
Verband Westdeutscher Stoff-Druckereien und Stück-Färbereien (Association of West German Fabric Printers and Parcel-Dyers), 62
Verein deutscher Maschinenbau-Anstalten/Verein deutscher Maschinen und Anlagenbauer (Association of German Machinery and Plant-Builders) (VDMA), 63, 64, 187, 188; Normenausschuss (Norm Committee of the VDMA), 64
Vereinigte Drehbank Fabriken (VDF), 63
Vereinigte Stahlwerke AG (Vestag), 91, 95–98, 211, 212, 218, 219, 327n; production at, 96; governance at, 96–98; Handelsunion AG (post-Vestag new creation trading company), 214; Deutsche Edelstahlwerke AG, (post-Vestag new creation), 213; Rheinisch-Westfälische Eisen- und Stahlwerke AG, (Vestag new creation), 213; Bergbau- und Industriewerte GmbH, (post-Vestag new creation), 213; Hüttenwerke Siegerland AG, (post Vestag new creation), 213; Gußtahlwerk Witten AG, (post-Vestag new creation), 213; Rheinische Röhrenwerke AG, (post-Vestag new creation), 213; Niederrheinische Hütte AG, (post-Vestag new creation), 213; Stahlwerke Südwestfalen

Vereinigte Stahlwerke AG (*cont.*)
  AG, (post-Vestag new creation), 213; Ruhrstahl AG, (post-Vestag new creation), 213
Verlag system, 37–40
verlängerte Werkbank (dualist subcontracting), 98–100, 153–156, 228–230, 233, 240, 264
vertikale Finanzausgleich (vertical fiscal equalization), 259
Vocational Training: development of, 52; within autarkic order, 82, 103–104, 227, 252; within decentralized order, 52, 199, 365n–366n; at Daimler-Benz, 159–160
Voegler, Albert, 96, 323n
Voight, Fritz, 367n
Volkswagen AG (VW), 172, 223–224, 225, 229, 231, 232, 241, 244–247; creation by Nazis, 223f; Beetle, 223, 226; Karman Ghia, 226; committment to American mass-production technologies at, 223–224; specialization of plants at, 225f; gradual decline in numbers of skilled laborers at, 226–227; diversified quality production at, 244–247; VW-Audi, 231; example of self-blockage at Emden plant, 246; Passat, 246; Golf, 247
Vulkan Werke Hamburg and Stettin AG, 101

Wandel & Goltermann GmbH & Co., 201
Warren, Donald, 48, 309n
weapons industry, 141, 185
Weber, Max, 117, 126
Wecherlin, Ferdinand, 56
Weimar Coalition, 127
Weimar Republic, 123–139, 259, 260, 261, 262, 272; constitution of, 123, 124, 125, 128, 139, 266, 341n–342n; federalism in, 125–131, 136–139; relative powers of Reichstag and Reichsrat within, 128, 129, 260; legal position of cities within, 129, 131, 135, 137, 347n; industrial politics within, 130, 134–135; divisions between autarkic and decentralized industrial order within, 136–139; collective bargaining in, 265f
Weltz, Frieder, 227
Wilhelm Karman Co., 226
Winkler, Heinrich August, 309n
Wirtschaftsgruppen, 70, 140
Witt, Peter-Christian, 126
wood industry, 229
Woolston, Maxine Y., 141–142
Works Councils, 131–132, 202, 208–209, 244–247, 248, 263, 268, 283, 285f, 376n; central role postwar industrial relations system, 266–268; role in crisis of industrial relations system in 1990s, 281–286
Wülker, Gerda, 169
Württembergische Vereinsbank, 158

Xaver Fendt & Co., 233

Zeiss Optik, 156
Zeitlin, Jonathan, 11, 24,25, 26, 298n
ZENIT, 188
Zentral Verband Elektrischer Industrie (ZVEI)—(electrical producers trade association), 187, 188
Zentralarbeitsgeimeinschaft der industriellen und gewerblichen Arbeitgeber und Arbeitnehmer Deutschlands (ZAG), 133f, 262, 345n
ZIN, 188
Zollverein, 116
Zukunftskommission: Baden-Württemburg 2000, 194, 281
Zysman, John, 296n–297n

For EU product safety concerns, contact us at Calle de José Abascal, 56–1°,
28003 Madrid, Spain or eugpsr@cambridge.org.